AF855804

Dear Colleague,

As instructors, we like to help students learn to deal knowledgeably and proficiently with the ethical issues that they will face in their professional lives. And, as we (the authors) know from experience, it can be difficult to find tools that can help us do this job effectively. Therefore, it is extremely gratifying that over the years so many professors have chosen to use our textbook, Issues and Ethics in the Helping Professions, *with their students. We are indebted to the many students, professors, and expert reviewers who have provided us with valuable feedback that has helped us create the current edition.*

We hope you will take just a few moments to look through the following pages to learn about the ways that we have updated Issues and Ethics in the Helping Professions *to meet the needs of today's helping environments. Up-to-date coverage of technology and privacy issues, as well as increased exploration of multicultural perspectives, are just the beginning of the refinements you will find in the new edition.*

As always, a number of helpful tools are available to enhance your use of this book. We are especially enthusiastic about the new Ethics in Action CD-ROM. *This unique multimedia learning tool allows students to view role-plays dealing with common ethical dilemmas in a variety of settings and gives them the opportunity to review and expand their knowledge in a hands-on way with interactive exercises and activities. In addition, a new, inexpensive booklet,* Codes of Ethics for the Helping Professions, *offers codes of ethics for the major helping professional organizations, including ACA, NASW, NOHSE, APA, ASCA, AAMFT and others, all in one compact resource. We also continue to offer, for institutional purchase, the* Ethics in Action *video, which features role-plays, discussions, and more. This video, along with other useful instructors' materials, is available for your use in preparing for and presenting your lectures.*

We hope that you'll try this new edition and its accompanying materials in your classroom and that you will find that they offer innovative and effective ways to prepare students for the challenges they will face as professionals. We look forward to hearing your feedback!

Sincerely,

Gerald Corey *Marianne Schneider Corey* *Patrick Callanan*

P.S. After you've read through the Preview on the following pages, please join us online at **http://www.wadsworthtours.com**, *where you can experience a demonstration of the new* Ethics in Action CD-ROM *and view a clip of the Institutional Video!*

Preview

List of Reviewers for Corey, Corey, and Callanan's *Issues and Ethics in the Helping Professions, Sixth Edition*

The authors give their sincerest thanks to those who contributed thoughtful insight to the revision of this text.

Reviewers:

Dr. Richard Boettcher, Ohio State University
Dr. Gerhard Carrier, Alvin Community College
Robin Carter, California State University, Sacramento
Dr. John Geisler, Western Michigan University
Dr. Andrew Getzfeld, New Jersey City University
Dr. Mary Hermann, Mississippi State University
Dr. Brandon Hunt, Penn State University
Dr. James Malley, Central Connecticut State University
Dr. Twinet Parmer, Central Michigan University
Dr. Sarah Shaw, University of Northern Colorado
Dr. Eileen Stenzel, Calumet College
Dr. Valorie Thomas, Stetson University
Dr. John Tweten, San Jose State University
Toni Wallace, Student Reviewer
Dr. Susan B. Wilkie, University of New Orleans

These individuals have reviewed portions of the text based upon their areas of expertise:

Honie Abramowicz, MSW
Dr. Robert Haynes, Atascadero State Hospital, Borderline Productions
Dr. Laura Urbanski Forrest, California State University, Long Beach
Dr. Rose Marie Hoffman, California State University, Long Beach
Dr. Allen Ivey, University of Massachusetts
Dr. Mary Bradford Ivey, Microtraining Associates
Dr. Mikel Hogan-Garcia, California State University, Fullerton
Dr. Mary Moline, Loma Linda University
Dr. Patrice Moulton, Northwestern State University
Dr. Paul Pederson, University of Hawaii
Dr. Robert Wubbolding, Center for Reality Therapy
Dr. John Doyle, California State University Fullerton
Dr. Jose Cervantes, California State University Fullerton

The right choice *at the right time...*

If you want a text that offers:

- Up-to-date coverage of the major Helping Professions Codes of Ethics integrated into every chapter, including ACA, APA, AAMFT, and NASW
- Content reviewed by a panel of experts for currency and student friendliness
- Up to the minute accuracy
- Interactive and personal activities
- Timely new technology tools

...choose *Issues and Ethics in the Helping Professions!*

Features that get students to *actively* think through issues...

The chapter-opening self-inventory features help students focus on the key topics that will be discussed in that chapter.

4

Pre-Chapter Self-Inventory

Directions: For each statement, indicate the response that most closely identifies your beliefs and attitudes. Use the following code:

5 = I *strongly agree* with this statement.
4 = I *agree* with this statement.
3 = I am *undecided* about this statement.
2 = I *disagree* with this statement.
1 = I *strongly disagree* with this statement.

_____1. Well-trained, sensitive, and self-aware therapists who do not impose their own values on clients are better qualified to be multicultural counselors.
_____2. To counsel effectively, I must be of the same ethnic background as my client.
_____3. Basically, all counseling interventions are multicultural.
_____4. I must challenge cultural stereotypes when they become obvious in counseling situations.
_____5. Contemporary counseling theories can be applied to people from all cultures.
_____6. As with any attempt to correct a problem, there exists a possibility of overcorrection in the multicultural movement.
_____7. I will be able to examine my behavior and attitudes to determine the degree to which cultural bias might influence the interventions I make with clients.
...re needed for counseling members of ethnic or racial minor-...
...essionals need to take into account the ethnic and cultural ...h themselves and their clients.
...n of majority-group counselors is to alert their clients to the ... them.
... health practitioner facilitates assimilation of the minority

and he makes no further mention of suicide. After five more sessions, he calls in to cancel an appointment and does not schedule another appointment. Dottie does not pursue the case further.

- What are the ethical and legal implications of the therapist's practice? Explain your position.
- If you had been in Dottie's shoes, what might you have done?
- Would you have contacted this client after he canceled? What are your thoughts about Dottie not doing that?

◆ **The case of Alejandro.** During the initial interview, Simone asks the counselor, Alejandro, how long she might need to be in therapy. Alejandro tells Simone that the process will take a minimum of 2 years of weekly sessions. She expresses dismay at such a lengthy process. Alejandro says that this is the way he works and explains that in his experience significant change is a slow process that demands a great deal of work. He tells Simone that if she cannot commit to this time period he would be willing to give her a referral.

- Did Alejandro take care of the need for informed consent?
- Did Alejandro have an ethical and a professional obligation to explain his rationale for the 2 years of therapy?
- Should Alejandro have been willing to explore alternatives to his approach to therapy, such as the possible values of short-term counseling?
- Given Alejandro's statement of minimum length of therapy, would it have been ethical for him to offer short-term counseling to Simone?

Open-ended case examples and situations stimulate thought and assist readers in formulating their own ethical stances.

Interactive exercises

that challenge and motivate students

Your value system influences every facet of your counseling practice, including your assessment strategies, your views of goals of treatment, the interventions used, the topics explored during the sessions, and evaluations of therapy outcomes. Indeed, no therapy is value free. You must avoid indoctrinating clients with a particular set of spiritual or religious values (or lack of such values, as the case may be). You have an ethical responsibility to be aware of how your beliefs affect your work and to make sure you do not unduly influence your clients.

Your Personal Stance

As you formulate your own position on the place of spiritual and religious values in the practice of counseling, reflect on these questions:

- What connection, if any, do you see between spirituality and religion?
- What are your views concerning established and organized religion?
- Has religion been a positive, negative, or neutral force in your life?
- Is it appropriate to deal with religious issues in an open and forthright manner as clients' needs arise in the counseling process?
- Do clients have the right to explore their religious concerns in their therapy?
- Are therapists forcing their values on their clients when they decide what topics can be discussed?
- If you have no religious or spiritual commitment, how might this hinder or help you in working with clients who hold strong religious convictions?
- Are you willing to refer a client to a rabbi, minister, or priest if it appears that clients have questions that you are not qualified to answer?
- How does a counselor in a public school deal with spiritual or religious issues that students may bring up? Do parents need to be informed that spiritual

Discussion questions involve readers in the learning process.

Opportunities for students to make the most of multimedia!

13. Do this exercise in pairs, with one student acting as the counselor and the other acting as the client. The counselor actively tries to convert the client to some value or point of view that the counselor holds. The job of the counselor is to try to persuade the client to do what the counselor thinks would be best for the client. This exercise can give you a feeling for what it is like to persuade a person to adopt your point of view and what it is like to be subjected to persuasion. Then switch roles.

Ethics in Action CD-ROM Exercises

14. In the *Ethics in Action* CD-ROM, complete the self-in
24–25 and bring this to class for discussion.

15. In video role play #4, The Divorce, it is clear that the
agenda for the client, who has decided to leave her husband
The counselor's line of inquiry is about who will look after
children. The client feels misunderstood and does not think
help to her. Have one student role-play Gary (the counselor in
another student role-plays his supervisor. As the supervisor,
you see being played out.

16. In video role play #5, Doing It My Way, Sally (the cou
ing to influence her client to think about the effect of her beh
ents. Charlae is seeking increased independence and wants to
her parents and be "free." Her father wants her to stay at hor
to live at college in the dorms. Sally suggests that Charlae talk
about this, but she just wants to move out, without any dis
parents. Sally is concerned about what Charlae's parents' re
she moves out without involving her parents in this decision
could really care less what they think." Sally wants Charlae
consequences and the effect on her parents and the fact that
sacrifices for her. Have one student role-play the counselor, while another student becomes Sally's supervisor. Through role-playing, demonstrate how you might approach the counselor as her supervisor. What would you most want Sally to consider?

17. In video role play #6, The Promiscuous One, the client (Suzanne) is having indiscriminate sexual encounters and her counselor, Richard, expresses concern for her. Suzanne reports meeting a guy in a bar and having sex with him, which she says is the best she has had in a week. He asks if she is protecting herself from pregnancy and/or HIV. She claims she has the greatest life as it is. Suzanne says, "I am not going to get HIV. People are blowing it totally out of proportion." She says she doesn't know why he is so worried about it, for after all, it is her life. Richard then focuses on how Suzanne's behavior plays out the recurring theme of abandonment by her father. She thinks there is no connec-

InfoTrac® College Edition Resources

For additional readings, explore InfoTrac College Edition, our online library. Go to *http://www.infotrac.college.com/wadsworth* and select these key word searches:

informed W1 consent
informed consent couns*
informed consent therap*
record* couns*
record* therap*
mental health managed care
malpractice liability in psychotherapy
malpractice AND psych*
involuntary commitment
repressed W1 memory W1 syndrome
false memory
online W1 couns*

Key words are listed in a form that enables the search engine to locate a wider range of articles in the online university library. Key words should be entered exactly as shown, including asterisks, "Wl," "W2," "AND," and other search engine tools.

Activities for the *Ethics in Action CD-ROM* have been added to each chapter.

Every chapter now contains *InfoTrac College Edition* keywords that direct students to online articles that can expand their knowledge of subjects relevant to that chapter.

New, timely discussion

of the latest issues surrounding technology and its uses and abuses

Chapter 5, **Client Rights and Counselor Responsibilities**, now includes updated and expanded information on record keeping and documentation, ethical and clinical issues for online counseling, and the role of technology in the counseling process.

Client Rights and Counselor Responsibilities 163

recordings because they can benefit from listening to them or by having colleagues listen to their interactions with clients and give them feedback. It is essential for trainees or counselors to secure the permission of clients before making any kind of electronic recording.

The Counselor's Responsibilities in Record Keeping

From an ethical, legal, and clinical perspective, an important responsibility of mental health practitioners is to keep adequate records on their clients. Maintaining thorough clinical notes has a dual purpose: (a) to provide the best service possible for clients, and (b) to provide a basis for safeguarding practitioners in the event of a lawsuit by documenting their decisions and the actions they have taken. At times, therapists may operate on the assumption that keeping clinical records is not an effective use of the limited time they have. Some therapists would rather devote their time in delivering service to clients instead of recording process and progress notes. Remley and Herlihy (2001) assert that it is possible to keep adequate records *and* provide quality treatment. It is a wise policy for counselors to document their actions in crisis situations such as cases involving potential danger of harm to oneself, others, or physical property. At the same time, it is not in the best interests of clients when counselors are more concerned about record keeping as a self-protective strategy rather than devoting their energy to providing quality services to clients. Although keeping records is a basic part of a counselor's practice, Remley and Herlihy suggest that it is critical to balance the need to maintain adequate records with the obligation to provide quality counseling services: "Counselors who find themselves devoting inordinate or excessive amounts of time creating and maintaining records probably need to reevaluate how they are spending their professional time and energy" (p. 109).

Many practitioners believe that accurate and detailed clinical records can provide an excellent defense against malpractice claims, and entire books and monographs are devoted to the subject. Rivas-Vazquez, Blais, Rey, and Rivas-Vazquez (2001) contend that the documentation of clinical services has taken on unprecedented importance for mental health professionals. From their perspective, the main objectives of documentation practices are (a) to structure quality care, (b) to decrease liability exposure, and (c) to fulfill requirements for reimbursement. According to Rivas-Vazquez and his colleagues, the adage, "if it is not documented, it did not happen" has never been more relevant than in today's climate of heightened awareness of potential liability exposure. These authors outline the specific domains required for comprehensive documentation practices. Professional ethics codes also outline the requirements of good record keeping (see the box titled Ethics Codes on Record Keeping). A useful book on this subject is *Documenting Psychotherapy: Essentials for Mental Health Practitioners* (Moline, Williams, & Austin, 1998). Moline and colleagues suggest that the practice of keeping adequate records is more than a way to lessen the

200 Chapter 6

- Do people have a right to waive their privacy, even when their b
might be threatened?

Practitioners should exercise caution with regard to the priv
clients. It is easy to invade a client's privacy unintentionally. Exam
of the most pressing situations in which privacy is an issue
employer's access to an applicant's or an employee's psychologic
ents' access to their child's school and health records, and a third-p
access to information about a client's diagnosis and prognosis. I
mount importance to respect the privacy of your clients and to alw
caution in discussing your work publicly. Nagy (2000) states that y
reveal identifying information about clients, orally or in writing,
fact that they consult you, without their formal consent. He adds th
to understand state and federal laws pertaining to privacy and the rules of your employment setting as well, and how they might affect your work in therapy, research, consulting, and supervision.

Most professional codes of ethics contain guidelines to safeguard a client's right to privacy. An example of such a standard is the APA (1992) ethics code: "In order to minimize intrusions on privacy, psychologists include in written and oral reports, consultations, and the like, only information germane to the purpose for which the communication is made."

One other area where privacy is an issue involves practitioners who also teach courses, offer workshops, write books and journal articles, and give lectures. If these practitioners use examples from their clinical practice, it is of the utmost importance that they take measures to adequately disguise their clients' identities. Additionally, those who teach counseling courses need to explain to their students that they should adequately disguise identities of their clients in any reports they give in class. Of course, students' personal comments in class are also to be kept confidential.

We think it is a good practice to inform clients if you are likely to use your clinical experience in writing or in lectures. One relevant guideline on this issue of privacy is given by the NASW (1999): "Social workers should respect clients' right to privacy. Social workers should not solicit private information from clients unless it is essential to providing service or conducting social work evaluation or research. Once private information is shared, standards of confidentiality apply."

Privacy Issues With Telecommunication Devices

The use of the telephone, answering machines, voice mail, pagers, faxes, cellular phones, and e-mail can pose a number of potential ethical problems regarding the protection of privacy of clients. Mental health practitioners need to exercise caution in discussing confidential or privileged information with anyone over the telephone. Remley and Herlihy (2001, pp. 124–125) offer these guidelines for counselors using the telephone:

Chapter 6, **Confidentiality**, now discusses privacy issues related to telephones, answering machines, voicemail, pagers, faxes, cellular phones, and e-mail.

A current and comprehensive look *at diversity issues*

116 Chapter 4

society and embrace a cross-cultural approach in support of the worth, dignity, potential, and uniqueness of each individual." The ACA's nondiscrimination standard states:

> Counselors do not condone or engage in discrimination based on age, color, culture, disability, ethnic group, gender, race, religion, sexual orientation, marital status, or socioeconomic status. (A.2.a.)

The ACA also calls upon counselors to respect differences:

> Counselors will actively attempt to understand the diverse cultural backgrounds of the clients with whom they work. This includes, but is not limited to, learning how the counselor's own cultural/ethnic/racial identity impacts her or his values and beliefs about the counseling process. (A.2.b.)

In addition, specific ACA standards deal with diversity in most areas of theory, practice, training, and research.

In the most recent revision of the NASW *Code of Ethics* (1999), cultural competence and recognition of social diversity are clearly linked to ethical practice. Here are two relevant guidelines:

> Social workers should have a knowledge base of their clients' cultures and be able to demonstrate competence in the provision of services that are sensitive to clients' cultures and to differences among people and cultural groups. (1.05.b.)

> Social workers should obtain education about and seek to understand the nature of social diversity and oppression with respect to race, ethnicity, national origin, color, sex, sexual orientation, age, marital status, political belief, religion and mental or physical disability. (1.05.c.)

The APA ethics code (1992) indicates that part of competence implies understanding diversity:

> Where differences of age, gender, race, ethnicity, national origin, religion, sexual orientation, disability, language, or socioeconomic status significantly affect psychologists' work concerning particular individuals or groups, psychologists obtain the training, experience, consultation, or supervision necessary to ensure the competence of their services, or they make appropriate referrals. (1.08.)

Pedersen (2000) contends that the code of ethics of both the APA and the ACA are culturally biased and culturally encapsulated. For example, both contain an unstated bias toward an individualistic perspective, which is not necessarily appropriate for collectivistic cultures. Ethical guidelines appropriate in one cultural context may not be appropriate in contrasting cultural settings. Most ethics codes caution practitioners about establishing dual relationships, which can cloud judgment and result in client exploitation. However, working with clients from a more collectivistic culture or those in a rural community might well require counselors to relate to their clients through many different roles and relationships. Another example is a counselor who might be sanctioned by an ethics committee for promoting dependency for continuing to see a client in therapy for no fee until this client was in a position to pay for the services. The assumption underlying most ethics codes is that there is an absolute

The section on **multicultural perspectives and diversity** now appears in Chapter 4. It includes more comprehensive coverage for counseling gay, lesbian, and bisexual clients, as well as more information on topics such as the limitations of ethics codes from a cultural diversity perspective.

The new CD-ROM lets students see *Ethics in Action*—right on their desktop!

New! The ***Ethics in Action* CD-ROM** creates a helpful multimedia learning environment for your students. They'll find insightful video clips and workbook exercises that help test their knowledge and skill for various ethical dilemmas from the *Ethics in Action: Student Video and Workbook*, as well as links to various ethics Web sites. *(Available for packaging with the text;* *see page 7 for details.)*

Tools
that foster interactive learning

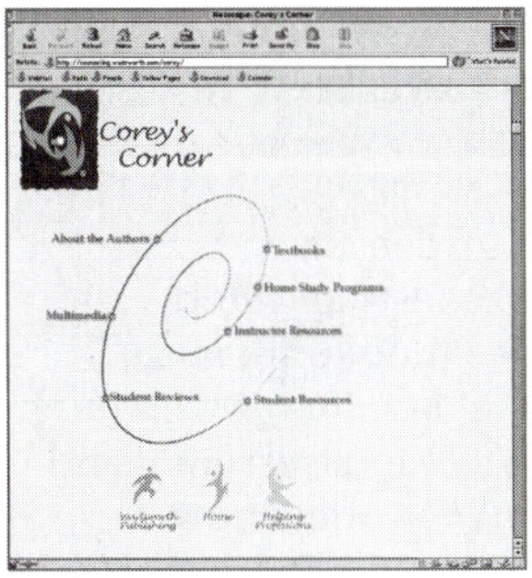

Coreys' Corner
Inside your home for the Helping Professions on the Web!

Accessible through
http://counseling.wadsworth.com

Coreys' Corner is filled with indispensable teaching aids, including Microsoft® *PowerPoint®* slides, sample video clips, Web links, *InfoTrac College Edition* keywords, and a resource integration guide. You'll also find a link to an easy-to-navigate product tour, which lets you explore the text and its resources inside a lively "virtual classroom."

Students will find online quizzes for every chapter, Web links, links to the various helping professional associations' codes of ethics, *InfoTrac College Edition* keywords and career information, all helpful as they plan for success in your course and in their future occupations.

New!
Ethics in Action CD-ROM
Package the CD-ROM with the text for half price!

ISBN: 0-534-59895-1; Bundled with the text: ISBN: 0-534-95804-4

On this interactive CD-ROM, Jerry and Marianne Corey demonstrate an integrative approach to common ethical dilemmas in a variety of settings. The CD-ROM includes 60 minutes of video, vignettes demonstrating ethical situations and responses, commentary from the Coreys, and group interaction and discussion. Each video segment is accompanied by activities and exercises that link the CD-ROM to the text, as well as written explorations of the material presented.

InfoTrac® College Edition
Four months of FREE access packaged with every new student copy of this text!

This world-class, online university library offers the full text of articles from hundreds of scholarly and popular publications. Updated daily and going back as much as four years, *InfoTrac College Edition* is a great way to expand your course beyond the pages of a text...from putting together reading assignments to using articles to launch your lectures, ignite discussions, or open whole new worlds of information and research for students. Contact your Brooks/Cole Thomson Learning sales representative for more information. Available to colleges and universities only.

InfoTrac® College Edition Student Guide for Counseling

ISBN: 0-534-24718-0;
Bundled with the text: ISBN: 0-534-95822-2

This 24-page booklet provides a detailed user's guide for students on how to use the *InfoTrac College Edition* database, including log in help, complete search tips, and a topic list of suggested keyword search terms for Counseling. Available FREE when packaged with the text. Contact your Brooks/Cole Thomson Learning representative for ordering information.

Codes of Ethics for the Helping Professions

ISBN: 0-534-55700-7
Bundled with the text, please use ISBN 0-534-95813-3

This brief, inexpensive supplement gives students quick and easy access to the codes of ethics for the major helping professions organizations, including ACA, NASW, NOHSE, APA, ASCA, AAMFT and others.

Chapter Quizzes

ISBN: 0-534-51443-X

Package the text with Chapter Quizzes for FREE!

ISBN: 0-534-98747-8

This FREE booklet enables your students to quiz themselves on the book's chapter content. Available only when packaged with the text.

Solutions *for Presentation, Course Management, and Testing*

Ethics in Action: Institutional Video

ISBN: 0-534-35620-6

This video shows the Coreys co-leading a group of counseling students who are attending a weekend workshop. By watching the role-plays, challenging questions, students' comments, and lively discussion presented on this video, students will gain a clearer picture and a better understanding of the topics and issues raised in your course. The Institutional Video is directly linked to Chapters 1 – 9 and 11 of *Issues and Ethics in the Helping Professions, Sixth Edition.* A complimentary *Facilitator's Resource Manual* accompanies the video.

This video is available for department purchase through Thomson Learning Customer Service. To receive a Preview Video and Workbook, please use ISBN 0-534-57638-9.

Instructor's Resource Manual

ISBN: 0-534-51438-3

The *Instructor's Manual* contains perspectives on the teaching of ethics, a *Resource Integration Guide,* listings of useful Web sites, *InfoTrac College Edition* key words, updated transparency masters (available in Microsoft® *PowerPoint®* as well), a course outline, study guide focus questions to provoke thought, chapter quizzes for each chapter, a practice exam, online quiz items, a student evaluation of the course, and a final exam.

Microsoft® PowerPoint® Slides

Add a multimedia element to your lectures!

These slides, for your classroom use, are available at an instructors-only, password-protected section of Coreys' Corner.

ExamView® Computerized Testing

Cross-Platform Windows and Macintosh. ISBN: 0-534-51439-1

Create, deliver, and customize tests and study guides (both print and online) in minutes with this easy-to-use assessment and tutorial system. *ExamView* offers both a *Quick Test Wizard* and an *Online Test Wizard* that guide you step-by-step through the process of creating tests, while its "WYSIWYG" capability allows you to see the test you are creating on the screen exactly as it will print or display online. You can build tests of up to 250 questions using up to 12 question types. Using *ExamView's* complete word-processing capabilities, you can enter an unlimited number of new questions or edit existing questions. *ExamView* also includes an electronic test bank of text-specific questions for this edition of the text.

ExamView® and ExamView Pro® are trademarks of FSCreations, Inc.

Take your course beyond the classroom!

WebTUTOR™ WebTutor® on WebCT and Blackboard

WebTutor WebCT ISBN: 0-534-51864-8
Text and WebTutor on WebCT ISBN: 0-534-98774-5
WebTutor Blackboard ISBN: 0-534-51863-X
Text and WebTutor on Blackboard ISBN: 0-534-98783-4

This Web-based teaching and learning tool is rich with study and mastery tools, communication tools, and course content. Use *WebTutor* to provide virtual office hours, post syllabi, set up threaded discussions, track student progress with the quizzing material, and more. For students, *WebTutor* offers real-time access to a full array of study tools, including chapter outlines, chapter summaries, suggested activities, chapter inventories, chapter quizzes, InfoTrac keywords and Web links. *WebTutor* also provides rich communication tools including a course calendar, asynchronous discussion, "real time" chat, and an integrated e-mail system.

6 *th edition*

Issues and Ethics in the Helping Professions

Gerald Corey

California State University, Fullerton
Diplomate in Counseling Psychology,
American Board of Professional Psychology

Marianne Schneider Corey

Private Practice/Consulting

Patrick Callanan

Private Practice

BROOKS/COLE
THOMSON LEARNING™

Australia • Canada • Mexico • Singapore • Spain • United Kingdom • United States

BROOKS/COLE
THOMSON LEARNING™

Sponsoring Editor: *Julie Martinez*
Editorial Assistant: *Catherine Broz*
Assistant Editor: *Shelley Gesicki*
Marketing: *Caroline Concilla / Megan Hansen / Tami Strang*
Production Editor: *Tessa Avila*
Production Service: *The Cooper Company*
Manuscript Editor: *Kay Mikel*
Cover Design: *Lisa Henry*
Cover Image: *Judith Harkness*
Indexer: *Mimi Lawson*
Print Buyer: *Vena Dyer*
Typesetting: *TBH Typecast, Inc.*
Printing and Binding: *Phoenix Color Corp*

For more information about this or any other Brooks/Cole product, contact:
BROOKS/COLE
511 Forest Lodge Road
Pacific Grove, CA 93950 USA
www.brookscole.com
1-800-423-0563 (Thomson Learning Academic Resource Center)

Printed in the United States of America

10 9 8 7 6 5 4 3 2 1

Library of Congress Cataloging-in-Publication Data
Corey, Gerald.
Issues and ethics in the helping professions / Gerald Corey, Marianne Schneider Corey, Patrick Callanan.
p. cm.
Includes bibliographical references and index.
ISBN 0-534-35615-X
1. Psychotherapists—Professional ethics. 2. Counselors—Professional ethics. I. Corey, Marianne Schneider. II. Callanan, Patrick. III. Title.

RC455.2.E8 C66 2002
174'.2—dc21

Dedicated to
the friends, colleagues, clients, and
students who helped us to see and appreciate the complexities
and subtleties of ethical thinking and practice.

Photography by Dawn Harman

Gerald Corey is Professor Emeritus of Human Services at California State University at Fullerton. He received his doctorate in counseling from the University of Southern California. He is a Diplomate in Counseling Psychology, American Board of Professional Psychology; a licensed psychologist; a National Certified Counselor; a Fellow of the American Psychological Association (Counseling Psychology); and a Fellow of the Association for Specialists in Group Work.

Jerry received the Outstanding Professor of the Year Award from California State University at Fullerton in 1991, and was the recipient of the Association for Specialists in Group Work's Eminent Career Award in 2001. He teaches both undergraduate and graduate courses in group counseling, as well as courses in experiential groups, the theory and practice of counseling, and ethics in counseling practice. With his colleagues he has conducted workshops in the United States, Canada, Germany, Ireland, Belgium, Scotland, Mexico, and China, with a special focus on training in group counseling. He often presents workshops for professional organizations, special intensive courses at various universities, and residential training and supervision workshops for group leaders. In his leisure time, Jerry likes to travel, hike and bicycle in the mountains, and drive his 1931 Model A Ford.

Recent publications by Jerry Corey, all with Brooks/Cole/Thomson Learning, include:

- *Issues and Ethics in the Helping Professions,* Sixth Edition (2003, with Marianne Schneider Corey and Patrick Callanan)
- *Becoming a Helper,* Fourth Edition (2003, with Marianne Schneider Corey)

- *Groups: Process and Practice,* Sixth Edition (2002, with Marianne Schneider Corey)
- *I Never Knew I Had a Choice,* Seventh Edition (2002, with Marianne Schneider Corey)
- *Theory and Practice of Counseling and Psychotherapy,* Sixth Edition (and *Manual*) (2001)
- *Case Approach to Counseling and Psychotherapy,* Fifth Edition (2001)
- *The Art of Integrative Counseling* (2001)
- *Theory and Practice of Group Counseling,* Fifth Edition (and *Manual*) (2000)
- *Group Techniques,* Second Edition (1992, with Marianne Schneider Corey, Patrick Callanan, and J. Michael Russell)

Jerry is co-author, with his daughters Cindy Corey and Heidi Jo Corey, of an orientation-to-college book entitled *Living and Learning* (1997), published by Wadsworth. He is also co-author (with Barbara Herlihy) of *Boundary Issues in Counseling: Multiple Roles and Responsibilities* (1997) and *ACA Ethical Standards Casebook,* Fifth Edition (1996), both published by the American Counseling Association.

He has also made three videos on various aspects of counseling practice: (1) *Student Video and Workbook for the Art of Integrative Counseling* (2001, with Robert Haynes); (2) *The Evolution of a Group: Student Video and Workbook* (2000, with Marianne Schneider Corey and Robert Haynes); and (3) *Ethics in Action* CD-ROM (2003, with Marianne Schneider Corey and Robert Haynes). All of these student videos and workbooks are available through Brooks/Cole/Thomson Learning.

Photography by Dawn Harman

Marianne Schneider Corey is a licensed marriage and family therapist in California and is a National Certified Counselor. She received her master's degree in marriage, family, and child counseling from Chapman College. She is a Fellow of the Association for Specialists in Group Work and was the recipient of this organization's Eminent Career Award in 2001. She also holds memberships in the American Counseling Association; the Association for Spiritual, Ethical, and Religious Values in Counseling; the Association for Counselor Education and Supervision (both national and regional); the Western Psychological Association; and the Association for Specialists in Group Work.

Marianne has been actively involved in leading groups for different populations, providing training and supervision workshops in group process, facilitating a self-exploration group for graduate students in counseling, and co-facilitating training groups for group counselors and weeklong residential workshops in personal growth. She sees groups as the most effective format in which to work with clients and finds it the most rewarding for her personally. With her husband, Jerry, Marianne has conducted training workshops, continuing-education seminars, and personal-growth groups in Germany, Ireland, Belgium, Mexico, and China, as well as regularly doing these workshops in the United States. In her free time Marianne enjoys traveling, reading, visiting with friends, and hiking.

Marianne has co-authored several articles in group work, as well as the following books (published by Brooks/Cole/Thomson Learning):

- *Issues and Ethics in the Helping Professions,* Sixth Edition (2003, with Gerald Corey and Patrick Callanan)
- *Becoming a Helper,* Fourth Edition (2003, with Gerald Corey)
- *Groups: Process and Practice,* Sixth Edition (2002, with Gerald Corey)
- *I Never Knew I Had a Choice,* Seventh Edition (2002, with Gerald Corey)
- *Group Techniques,* Second Edition (1992, with Gerald Corey, Patrick Callanan, and J. Michael Russell)

Marianne has made several videos (with accompanying student workbooks) for Brooks/Cole/Thomson Learning: *Ethics in Action* CD-ROM (Student Version); *Ethics in Action* (Institutional Version); and *The Evolution of a Group.*

Marianne and Jerry have been married since 1964. They have two adult daughters, Heidi and Cindy. Marianne grew up in Germany and has kept in close contact with her family there.

Photo courtesy of Patrick Callanan

Patrick Callanan is a licensed marriage and family therapist in private practice in Santa Ana, California. In 1973 he graduated with a bachelor's degree in Human Services from California State University at Fullerton, and then received his master's degree in professional psychology from United States International University in 1976. In his private practice he works with individuals, couples, families, and groups.

Patrick is on the part-time faculty of the Human Services Program at California State University at Fullerton, where he regularly teaches an internship course. He also offers his time each year to the university to assist in training and supervising group leaders and co-teaches an undergraduate course in ethical and professional issues. Along with Marianne Schneider Corey and Gerald Corey, he received an Award for Contributions to the Field of Professional Ethics by the Association for Spiritual, Ethical, and Religious Values in Counseling in 1986.

Patrick co-authored *Group Techniques*, Second Edition (1992). In his free time, Patrick enjoys reading, antique hunting, cycling, walking fast, and playing racquetball, tennis, and golf.

Contents

10 Issues in Theory, Practice, and Research 354

11 Ethical Issues in Couples and Family Therapy 394

12 Ethical Issues in Group Work 420

Preface

Issues and Ethics in the Helping Professions is written for both graduate and undergraduate students in the helping professions. This book is suitable for courses in counseling, human services, couples and family therapy, counseling and clinical psychology, and social work. It can be used as a core textbook in courses such as practicum, fieldwork, internship, and ethical and professional issues or as a supplementary text in courses dealing with skills or theory. Because the issues we discuss are likely to be encountered throughout one's professional career, we have tried to use language and concepts that will be meaningful both to students doing their fieldwork and to professionals interested in improving their skills through continuing-education seminars or independent reading.

In this book, we involve readers in learning to deal with the professional and ethical issues that most affect the actual practice of counseling and related helping professions. We raise the following questions: How do therapists' values and life experiences affect the therapeutic process? What are the rights and responsibilities of both the client and the counselor? As professionals, how can we determine our level of competence? How can we provide quality services for culturally diverse populations? What major ethical issues face practitioners in couples and family therapy? in group work? in community agencies? in private practice?

Our goal is both to provide a body of information and to teach readers a process of thinking about and resolving the basic issues they will face throughout their careers. For most of the issues we raise, we present various viewpoints to stimulate discussion and reflection. We also present our views and personal commentaries, when appropriate, to challenge readers to formulate their own positions.

The ethics codes of various professional organizations offer some guidance for practice. However, these guidelines leave many questions unanswered. We believe students and professionals alike must ultimately struggle with the issues of responsible practice, deciding how accepted ethical principles apply in the specific cases they encounter.

We have tried to make this book a personal one that will involve our readers in an active and meaningful way. To this end we have provided many opportunities to respond to our discussions and to draw on personal experiences. Each chapter begins with a self-inventory designed to help readers focus on the key topics to be discussed in the chapter. Within the chapters we frequently ask readers to think about how the issues apply to them. Open-ended cases and situations are presented to stimulate thought and to assist readers in formulating their own positions. We also cite related literature when exploring ethical and professional issues. This book combines the advantages of both the textbook and a student manual. Instructors will find an abundance of material and suggested activities, surely more than can be covered in a single course.

An *Instructor's Resource Manual* is available that contains chapter outlines, suggestions for teaching an ethics course, test items, additional exercises and activities, InfoTrac® College Edition online resources, transparency masters, and study guide questions. An electronic version of the *Instructor's Resource Manual* is available for all platforms.

The professional codes of ethics discussed in Chapter 1, including those for ACA, NASW, NOHSE, APA, ASCA, and AAMFT, are available in a booklet *Codes of Ethics for the Helping Professions,* which can be packaged with the text.

A new integrated learning package entitled *Ethics in Action* CD-ROM has been developed to enhance the sixth edition of *Issues and Ethics in the Helping Professions. Ethics in Action* CD-ROM is designed to bring to life the ethical issues and dilemmas counselors often encounter and to provide ample opportunity for discussion, self-exploration, and problem solving of these issues and dilemmas. Videos on the CD-ROM are based on a weekend workshop co-led by Marianne Schneider Corey and Gerald Corey for a group of counseling students, which included challenging questions and lively discussion, role plays to bring the issues to life, and comments from the students and the Coreys. Additional material on the CD-ROM is designed to provide a self-study guide for students who are also reading this book. The video portion is divided into three segments: ethical decision making, values and the helping relationship, and boundary issues and multiple relationships in counseling. At the end of several chapters in this book are suggested activities and guidelines for integrating the CD-ROM with this textbook.

ACKNOWLEDGMENTS

We would like to thank the book's reviewers for their helpful suggestions: Richard Boettcher, Ohio State University; Gerhard Carrier, Alvin Community College; Robin Carter, California State University at Sacramento; John Geisler, Western Michigan University; Andrew Getzfeld, New Jersey City University; Mary Hermann, Mississippi State University; Brandon Hunt, Penn State University; James Malley, Central Connecticut State University; Twinet Parmer, Central Michigan University; Sally Shaw, University of Northern Colorado; Eileen Stenzel, Calumet College; Valorie Thomas, Stetson University; John

Tweten, San Jose State University; Toni Wallace, student reviewer, California State University at Fullerton; and Susan Wilkie, University of New Orleans.

We received specialized assistance on selected chapters from the following people. For Chapter 9 on supervision, we would like to thank Laura Urbanski Forrest, California State University, Long Beach; Rose Marie Hoffman, California State University, Long Beach; Robert Haynes, Borderline Productions; and Patrice Moulton, Northwestern State University.

For Chapter 4 on multiculturalism, we thank Paul Pedersen, University of Hawaii; Allen E. Ivey, University of Massachusetts, Amherst; Mary Bradford Ivey, Microtraining Associates; and Robert Wubbolding, Center for Reality Therapy in Cincinnati.

For Chapter 13 on community work, our thanks to Paul Pedersen, University of Hawaii; Allen E. Ivey, University of Massachusetts, Amherst; Mary Bradford Ivey, Microtraining Associates; Mikel Hogan-Garcia, California State University at Fullerton; John Doyle, California State University at Fullerton; Jose Cervantes, California State University at Fullerton; and Honie Abramowicz, Orange County Bar Foundation.

For Chapter 10 on theory and practice, our thanks to Allen E. Ivey, University of Massachusetts, Amherst, and Mary Bradford Ivey, Microtraining Associates.

Finally, for Chapter 11 on couples and family therapy we thank Mary Moline, Loma Linda University.

The members of the Brooks/Cole team continue to offer support for all our projects. It is a delight to work with a dedicated staff of professionals who go out of their way to give their best. These people include Julie Martinez, the editor of counseling and human services; Cat Broz, who coordinated the reviewing process; Tessa Avila, the production manager on the project; Cecile Joyner, the production editor; and Kay Mikel, the manuscript editor of this edition, whose fine editorial assistance kept this book reader friendly. We appreciate Mimi Lawson's work in compiling the index.

Gerald Corey
Marianne Schneider Corey
Patrick Callanan

1

The Focus of This Book

Working both independently and together, the three of us have, over the years, confronted a variety of professional and ethical issues that do not have clear-cut solutions. Exchanging ideas has helped us clarify our positions on these difficult issues, and conversations with students and colleagues have shown us that others wrestle with similar questions. We have become convinced that students in the helping professions need to think seriously about these problems before they begin practicing.

We have discovered that many of the issues relevant to beginning professionals resurface later and take on different meanings at various stages of professional development. Therefore, this book will be useful both to experienced practitioners and to students about to embark on their professional careers. We have tried to avoid the trap of dispensing prescriptions or providing simple solutions to complex problems. Our main purpose is to give you the basis for formulating your own ethical guidelines within the broad limits of professional codes and divergent theoretical positions. We raise what we consider to be central issues, present a range of views on these issues, discuss our position, and provide you with many opportunities to refine your own thinking and actively develop your position.

As you read this book, you will realize that we have certain biases and viewpoints about ethical behavior. We hope you will see these stances as our points of view rather than the correct points of view. We try to keep our viewpoints open to revision. We state our position on issues not to sway you to adopt our view but to challenge you to devise your own position. In the end, you are responsible for your own ethical practice; however, do not think you are free to choose any set of ethical views merely because it "feels right."

The various mental health professions have developed codes of ethics that are binding on their members. As a professional, you are expected to know the ethics code of your specialty and be aware of the consequences of practicing in ways that are not sanctioned by the organization. In addition, responsible prac-

Introduction to Professional Ethics

tice requires that you use informed, sound, and responsible judgment. It is essential that you demonstrate a willingness to consult with colleagues, to keep yourself up to date through reading and continuing education, and to continually examine your behavior.

Codes of ethics provide general standards, but these guidelines are not sufficiently explicit to deal with every situation. It is often difficult to interpret ethics codes, and opinions differ over how to apply them in specific cases. Consequently, in your professional work you will retain a significant degree of freedom and will encounter many situations that demand the exercise of sound judgment to further the best interests of your clients.

Be prepared to reexamine many of the issues discussed here throughout your professional life. Even if you resolve some of these issues at the initial stage of your development as a counselor, these topics are likely to take on new dimensions as you gain experience. Minor questions may become major concerns as you progress in your profession. Many students burden themselves with the expectation that they should resolve all possible issues before they begin to practice. However, the definition and refinement of such concerns is an ongoing evolutionary process that requires an open and self-critical attitude. Our goal is to give you a flexible framework and a direction for working through ethical dilemmas. Your challenge is to find your own answers to the questions we raise here.

Some Suggestions for Using This Book

In this book we deal with the central professional and ethical issues you are likely to encounter in your work with clients. Our aim is to stimulate you to form your own opinions on these issues and to be able to justify them.

In writing this book we frequently imagined ourselves in conversations with our students. Whenever it seems appropriate, we state our own thinking and offer a commentary on how we arrived at the positions we hold. We think it is important to reveal our biases, convictions, and attitudes; then you can critically evaluate our stance. On many issues we present a range of viewpoints. Our hope is that you will give constant attention to ways of integrating your own thoughts and experiences with the positions we explore. In this way you will not only absorb information but also deepen your understanding.

The format of this book is different from that of most traditional textbooks. This is a personal manual that can be useful to you at various stages in your professional development. The many questions and exercises interspersed in the text are intended to stimulate you to become an active participant. If you take the time to do the exercises and complete the surveys and inventories, you will have met the challenge to reflect personally on these issues, and you will have a record of your reactions to them.

We have intentionally provided an abundance of exercises in each chapter, more than can be integrated in one semester or in one course. We invite you to decide which questions and exercises have the most meaning for you now. At a later reading of the book, you may want to consider questions or activities that you omitted on your initial reading.

We would like to make several specific suggestions for getting the most from this book and from your course. Many of these ideas come from students who have been in our classes. In general, you will get from this book and course whatever you are willing to invest of yourself, so it is important to clarify your goals and to think about ways of becoming actively involved. Here are some suggestions that can help you become an active learner.

- *Be prepared.* You can best prepare yourself to become active in your class by spending time reading and thinking about the questions we pose. Completing the exercises and responding to the questions and open-ended cases will help you focus on where you stand on controversial issues.
- *Examine your expectations.* Students often have unrealistic expectations of themselves. You may think you should have all the right answers worked out before you begin to work with people. If you have not had much experience in counseling clients, you can begin to become involved in the issues we discuss by thinking about situations in which friends have sought you out when they were in need of help. You can also reflect on the times when you were experiencing conflicts and needed someone to help you gain clarity. In this way you may be able to relate the material to events in your own life even if your counseling experience is limited.
- *Complete the self-assessment survey.* The multiple-choice survey at the end of this chapter is designed to help you discover your attitudes concerning most of the issues we deal with in this book. We encourage you to take this inventory before you read the book to see where you stand on these issues at this time. We also suggest that you take the inventory again after you complete the book. You can then compare your responses to see what changes have occurred in your attitudes as a result of the course and your reading of the book.
- *Identify your viewpoint by reviewing the self-inventories.* Each chapter begins with an inventory designed to stimulate your thinking about the issues that

will be explored in the chapter. You may want to bring your responses to class and compare your views with those of fellow students. You may also find it useful to retake the inventory after you finish reading the chapter to see whether your views have changed.

- *Think about the examples, cases, and questions.* Many examples in this book are drawn from actual counseling practice in various settings with different types of clients. We frequently ask you to consider how you might have worked with a given client or what you might have done in a particular counseling situation. We hope you will take the time to think about these questions and briefly respond to them as you read each chapter.
- *Do the end-of-chapter suggested activities.* Each chapter ends with suggested activities intended to help you integrate and apply what you have learned. These exercises involve doing things both in class and on your own. The purpose of these aids is to make the issues come alive and to help you apply your ideas to practical situations.
- *Explore the InfoTrac® College Edition resources.* This vast online library of current articles enables you to expand your reading in areas of particular interest to you. We encourage you to make frequent use of this valuable resource as questions arise throughout the course.

As you read and think about the cases and end-of-chapter exercises and activities, formulate your own personal ethical perspective on the issues they raise. We encourage you to use this book in any way that involves you personally in thinking about the issues raised. Focus selectively on the questions and activities that have the most meaning for you at this time, and remain open to new issues as they assume importance for you. As you read this book and get actively involved in your ethics course, we hope you will discover additional ways to work through the process of making ethical decisions.

Professional Codes of Ethics

Various professional organizations have established codes of ethics that provide broad guidelines for mental health practitioners. Some of the professional mental health organizations that have formulated codes are the American Counseling Association (ACA, 1995), the American Psychological Association (APA, 1992), the National Association of Social Workers (NASW, 1999), the National Organization for Human Service Education (NOHSE, 2000), and the American Association for Marriage and Family Therapy (AAMFT, 2001). Many of all of these codes of ethics are excerpted throughout this book as we address special areas of ethical concern (see the box titled Codes of Ethics).

Each national professional organization has a different, but similar, set of codes, emphasizing different themes. Also, national certification boards, other professional associations, specialty areas within the counseling profession, and state regulatory boards all have their own ethics documents. Herlihy and Remley (1995) have written about the problems associated with this proliferation of codes, indicating that multiple codes are counterproductive. They conclude:

Codes of Ethics

Each major mental health professional organization has its own code of ethics, and we strongly recommend that you obtain a copy of the ethics code of at least one mental health profession and familiarize yourself with the basic standards for ethical practice. Ethics codes do not provide specific answers to the ethical dilemmas you will encounter, but they do offer general guidance. It is essential that you know the basic content of the codes of your profession.

The ethics codes listed here can be purchased as an accompanying supplement to this textbook. Alternatively, you may obtain particular codes of ethics by contacting the organizations directly.

1. *Code of Ethics and Standards of Practice,* American Counseling Association (ACA, 1995)
2. *Ethical Principles of Psychologists and Code of Conduct,* American Psychological Association (APA, 1992)
3. *Code of Ethics,* National Association of Social Workers (NASW, 1999)
4. *AAMFT Code of Ethics,* American Association for Marriage and Family Therapy (AAMFT, 2001)
5. *Ethical Standards of the National Organization for Human Service Education* (NOHSE, 2000)
6. *Ethical Standards for School Counselors,* American School Counselor Association (ASCA, 1998)
7. "Ethical Code for the International Association for Marriage and Family Counselors" (1993)
8. "Ethical Guidelines for Counseling Supervisors," Association for Counselor Education and Supervision (1993)
9. *Ethical Standards for Internet On-line Counseling* (ACA, 1999)
10. "Standards for the Ethical Practice of Web Counseling," National Board for Certified Counselors (1997)

"When a single, unified code of ethics is universally accepted by the counseling profession, future revisions will be a much more manageable task, and the public and counselors themselves will be clearer regarding the ethical obligations of professional counselors" (p. 133).

Using Codes of Ethics

Become familiar with the ethics codes of your specialization, but know that you will be challenged in the application of these codes in your practice. The ethics codes offered by most professional organizations are broad and general rather than precise and specific. Your own ethical awareness and problem-solving skills will determine how you translate these general guidelines into professional day-to-day behavior. As Welfel (2002) indicates, codes of ethics are not cookbooks for responsible professional behavior. Indeed, they offer unmistakably clear guidance for only a few problems. Ethics codes are necessary, but not sufficient, for exercising ethical responsibility. It is essential that you be aware of the limitations of such codes (Bersoff, 1994; Herlihy & Corey, 1996a; Herlihy & Remley, 1995; Ibrahim & Arredondo, 1990; Lanning, 1997; Mabe & Rollin, 1986; Mappes, Robb, & Engels, 1985; Pope & Vasquez, 1998). Here are some of the problems you may encounter when you strive toward an ethically responsible practice:

- Some issues cannot be handled solely by relying on ethics codes.
- Some codes lack clarity and precision, which makes enforcement difficult.

- Simply learning the ethics codes and casebooks will not prepare counselors for ethical practice.
- Consumers of counseling services may not have the knowledge or experience to determine whether a therapist is practicing ethically.
- Ethics codes are designed more to protect professionals than to protect clients.
- Conflicts sometimes emerge within ethics codes as well as among various organizations' codes.
- Practitioners who belong to multiple professional associations, are licensed by their state, and hold national certifications may be responsible to practice within the framework of numerous codes of ethics, yet these codes may not be uniform.
- Ethics codes tend to be reactive rather than proactive.
- A practitioner's personal values may conflict with a specific standard within an ethics code.
- Codes may conflict with institutional policies and practices.
- Ethics codes need to be understood within a cultural framework; therefore, they must be adapted to specific cultures.
- Because of the diverse viewpoints within any professional organization, not all members will agree with all proposed standards.

In the *Code of Ethics* of the National Association of Social Workers (NASW, 1999) the limits of the code are succinctly described:

> A code of ethics cannot guarantee ethical behavior. Moreover, a code of ethics cannot resolve all ethical issues or disputes, or capture the richness and complexity involved in striving to make responsible choices within a moral community. Rather a code of ethics sets forth values, ethical principals and ethical standards to which professionals aspire and by which their actions can be judged.

It is clear that codes are not intended to be a blueprint that removes all need for the use of judgment and ethical reasoning. Pope and Vasquez (1998) maintain that formal ethical principles can never be substituted for an active, deliberative, and creative approach to meeting ethical responsibilities. They remind us that ethics codes cannot be applied in a rote manner, mainly because each client's situation is unique and calls for a different solution. Final authority rests with the helper. The most difficult part of being an ethical counselor is having to make decisions and then assuming personal responsibility for the consequences (Lanning, 1997). This process needs time to be done well, and it should include consultation.

Herlihy and Corey (1996a) suggest that codes of ethics fulfill three objectives. First, the basic purpose of ethics codes is to educate professionals about sound ethical conduct. Reading and reflecting on the standards can help practitioners expand their awareness, clarify their values, and find a direction in dealing with the challenges of their work. Second, ethical standards provide a mechanism for professional accountability. Practitioners are obliged not only to monitor their own behavior but also to encourage ethical conduct in their colleagues. One of the best ways for practitioners to protect themselves from malpractice suits is to practice within the spirit of the ethics codes. Third, codes of ethics serve as catalysts for improving practice. When practitioners must interpret and apply the codes in their own practices, the questions raised often help to clarify their positions on dilemmas that do not have simple or absolute answers.

We should always keep in mind that the primary purpose of codes of ethics is to safeguard the welfare of clients by providing what is in their best interest. Ethics codes are also designed to safeguard the public and to guide professionals in their work so that they can provide the best service possible. The community standard (what professionals *actually* do) is generally less rigorous than the ethical standard (what professionals *should* do). It is important to keep informed of what others in your local area and subspecialties are doing in their practices. If, for any reason, you decide not to follow a specific ethical guideline, be sure you have a reasonable rationale for your course of action. Realize also that there are consequences for violating the codes of your profession.

If you agree with and follow all the codes of your profession, does this necessarily mean that you are an ethical professional? What else might you need to do to be an ethical person and practitioner? This is a complex question, and you may find that you answer it differently in different situations.

Ethics Codes and the Law

Ethical issues in the mental health professions are regulated by both laws and professional codes. Laws and ethics codes provide guidelines, yet neither offers clear-cut answers to situational problems. *Laws* define the minimum standards society will tolerate; these standards are enforced by government. An example of a minimum standard is safety on the road and maximum miles per hour in certain zones. All of the codes of ethics state that practitioners must act in accordance with relevant federal and state statutes and governmental regulations. It is essential that practitioners be able to identify legal problems as they arise in their work because many of the situations they encounter that involve ethical and professional judgment will also have legal implications.

Counselors often have difficulty determining when they have a legal problem, or what to do with this legal issue once it has been identified (Remley & Herlihy, 2001). Crawford (1999) points out that counselors do not have to be lawyers to practice with a lawful perspective. As is the case with ethical dilemmas, Crawford tells us not to expect to find simple solutions to every legal problem. One of the reviewers of this book, Mary Hermann, an attorney and counselor educator, teaches a course on school law. She finds that her students get frustrated because they want concrete answers to legal problems. She tells us that most of the time even legal scholars can only speculate about the answers to these legal problems. Stating this reality immediately helps to get students thinking about their options and making the best choices they can make under the circumstances rather than searching for some mythical "right answer" to a legal issue (personal communication, February 25, 2001).

Lacking a definitive answer of what is legal or illegal, some professionals increasingly limit their options of ways to work with clients out of fear of a possible lawsuit. This raises a potential ethical issue of delivering less than effective services, especially if this narrowing of available options to clients is not clearly expressed during the initial interview.

Laws and ethics codes, by their very nature, tend to be reactive, emerging from what has occurred rather than anticipating what may occur. We hope you will not limit your behavior to obeying statutes and following ethical standards but will develop a sensitivity to doing what is best for your clients by working toward the best standards of practice. It is very important that you acquire this ethical sense at the beginning of your professional program. Remember that the basic purpose of practicing ethically is to further the welfare of your clients.

At times there may be conflicts between the law and ethical principles, and in these cases the values of the counselor come into play. Conflict between professional codes and the law may arise in areas such as advertising, confidentiality, and clients' rights of access to their own files. On this point, the National Association of Social Workers (1999) guideline is clear: "When such conflicts occur, social workers must make a responsible effort to resolve the conflict in a manner that is consistent with the values, principles, and standards expressed in this *Code*. If a reasonable resolution of this conflict does not appear possible, social workers should seek proper consultation before making a decision."

One example of a potential conflict between legal and ethical standards involves counseling minors. This is especially true as it pertains to counseling children or adolescents in school settings. Counselors may be committed to following ethical standards in maintaining the confidentiality of the sessions with a minor, yet at times parents may have a legal right to information that is disclosed in these sessions. Counselors often struggle between doing what they believe to be ethically appropriate for their client and their legal responsibilities to parents.

Another example of a potential conflict between legal and ethical standards pertains to breaking confidentiality of a client who is HIV-positive by informing a third party of his or her condition. A new standard has been added to the American Counseling Association's *Code of Ethics* (1995) regarding contagious fatal diseases, which suggests that practitioners may be justified in reporting to an identifiable third party, under certain circumstances. Generally, there is no legal imperative to do so at this time, but Utah's state statute seems to extend counselors' duty to warn to include a client's possible transmission of communicable diseases (Glosoff, Herlihy, & Spence, 2000). Practitioners may act in ways they deem to be ethical only to find that they have broken a legal standard. This topic is explored in more detail in Chapter 6.

In cases of conflict between ethics and the law, the American Psychological Association's ethics code (APA, 1992) indicates that psychologists should seek to resolve the conflict in a way that complies with the law and at the same time most nearly conforms to the code. The American Counseling Association's

Code of Ethics and Standards of Practice (1995) defers to the law, which means that counselors must practice within the requirements of the law. In ethical dilemmas involving legal issues, seek legal advice from colleagues familiar with the law and from legal counsel (Remley, 1996). In those cases where neither the law nor an ethics code resolves an issue, therapists are advised to consider other professional and community standards and their own conscience as well.

Evolution of Ethics Codes

Ethics codes for professional organizations are not static; they must be revised as new concerns arise. The codes of ethics of most of the professional organizations have undergone several revisions. Codes are established by a group of professionals for the purpose of protecting consumers, providing guidelines for practitioners, and clarifying the professional stance of the organizations. As such, these codes do not convey ultimate truth, nor do they provide ready-made answers for the ethical dilemmas practitioners must face. Casebooks can never replace the informed judgment and goodwill of the individual counselor. They are tools that must be used wisely in making difficult decisions in complex situations. We want to emphasize again the need for a level of ethical functioning higher than merely following the letter of the law or the code. For instance, you might avoid a lawsuit or professional censure by ignoring cultural diversity, but many of your ethnically diverse clients could suffer from your insensitive professional behavior.

Professional Monitoring of Practice

Most professional organizations have ethics committees, elected or delegated bodies that oversee the conduct of members of the organization. The main purposes of these ethics committees are to educate the association's membership about ethics codes and to protect the public from unethical practices. As a rule, these committees meet regularly to process formal complaints against individual members of the professional organization.

When a complaint is lodged against a member, the committee launches an investigation and deliberates on the case. Eventually, a disposition is reached. The complaint may be dismissed, specific charges within the complaint may be dismissed, or the committee may find that ethical standards have been violated and impose sanctions. Generally, possible sanctions include a reprimand; probation or suspension for a specified period of time; a recommendation that the member be allowed to resign from the organization; a recommendation that the member be expelled; or a recommendation that a specific course of remedial action be taken, such as obtaining ongoing supervision or personal therapy. Expulsion or suspension of a member is a major sanction. Members have the right to appeal the committee's decision, and once the appeals process has been completed or the deadline for appeal has passed, the sanctions of suspension and expulsion are published in writing in the journal of the professional organization. Practitioners who are expelled from the association may also face the loss of their license or certificate to practice, but only if the state board conducts an independent investigation. National and state certification boards may revoke a counselor's certification, and state licensure boards have the power to prohibit practice or issue reprimands to professionals (Chauvin & Remley, 1996). Cases that result in expulsion are often serious enough to involve law enforcement and criminal charges. Many cases also result in civil court proceedings, which are usually published in the local press.

Ethical Decision Making

Some Key Terms

Although values and ethics are frequently used interchangeably, the two terms are not identical. *Values* pertain to beliefs and attitudes that provide direction to everyday living, whereas *ethics* pertain to the beliefs we hold about what constitutes right conduct. Ethics are moral principles adopted by an individual or group to provide rules for right conduct. *Morality* is concerned with perspectives of right and proper conduct and involves an evaluation of actions on the basis of some broader cultural context or religious standard.

Ethics represents aspirational goals, or the maximum or ideal standards set by the profession, and they are enforced by professional associations, national certification boards, and government boards that regulate professions (Remley, 1996). Codes of ethics are conceptually broad in nature and generally subject to interpretation by practitioners. Although these minimum and maximum standards may differ, they are not necessarily in conflict.

Bersoff (1996) describes *ethical conduct* as the result of a combination of knowledge and a clear conception of the philosophical principles that underlie an ethics code. Ethical conduct grows out of sound character that leads you to respond with maturity, judgment, discretion, wisdom, and prudence.

Community standards (or *mores*) vary on an interdisciplinary, theoretical, and geographical basis. The standard for a counselor's social contact with clients may be different in a large urban area than in a rural area or between practitioners employing an analytic versus a behavioral approach. Community standards often become the ultimate *legal* criteria for determining whether practitioners are liable for damages because these standards often define what is considered reasonable behavior when a case involving malpractice is litigated. Courts have consistently found that mental health care providers have a duty to exercise a reasonable degree of skill, knowledge, and care. Reasonableness is usually defined as the care that is ordinarily exercised by others practicing within that specialty in the professional community.

Professionalism has some relationship to ethical behavior, yet it is possible to act unprofessionally and still not act unethically. For instance, not returning a client's telephone calls promptly might be viewed as unprofessional, but it would probably not be considered unethical unless the client were in crisis.

Some situations cut across these concepts. For instance, sexual intimacy between counselors and clients is considered unethical, unprofessional, immoral, and illegal. Keep the differences in the meanings of these various concepts in mind as you read.

Levels of Ethical Practice

One way of conceptualizing professional ethics is to contrast lower level ethical functioning with higher level functioning. *Mandatory ethics* describes a level of ethical functioning wherein counselors merely act in compliance with minimal standards, acknowledging the basic "musts" and "must nots." *Aspirational ethics* describes the highest standards of conduct to which professional counselors can aspire and requires that counselors do more than simply meet the letter of the ethics code. It entails an understanding of the spirit behind the code and the principles on which the code rests. Practitioners who comply at the first level, mandatory ethics, are generally safe from legal action or professional censure. At the higher level of ethical functioning, aspirational ethics, practitioners go further and reflect on the effects their interventions may have on the welfare of their clients. The ethics codes of both the ACA (1995) and the APA (1992) include a *mandatory* section (a set of enforceable standards intended to be specific enough to use as compelling rules and resulting in sanctions if they are broken) and an *aspirational* section (a higher set of standards reflecting ideal principles). For example, the 1995 ACA *Code of Ethics and Standards of Practice* addresses both mandatory and aspirational ethics. Courts of law and state licensure boards now require the counseling profession to define minimal standards to which all counselors may be held accountable. The *Standards of Practice* does this; it is comparatively brief and specifies minimal behaviors required of professional counselors (mandatory ethics) that can be understood and evaluated by individuals outside the counseling profession. The *Code of Ethics* is lengthier, gives more detailed guidance regarding the standards of practice, and includes statements describing the best practice (aspirational ethics) that represents the ideals of the profession (Herlihy & Corey, 1996a).

When the word *unethical* is used, people too often think of gross violations of established codes. In reality, most violations of ethics probably happen quite inadvertently in counseling practice. If practitioners are not aware of the subtle ways their behavior can adversely affect their clients, such behavior can go unnoticed, and the clients will suffer. For instance, a private practitioner whose practice is not flourishing may prolong the therapy of his clients and justify his actions on theoretical grounds. He is likely to ignore the fact that the prolongation of therapy is influenced by his financial situation. Or school counselors may be so focused on academic and scheduling issues that they do not reach out to the community and develop the network with other helping professionals that is needed to make productive referrals of families and students in crises. In school systems teachers and others often label students and families as dysfunctional or unmotivated. The counselor needs to advocate and help others look for strengths and reframe limitations if progress is to be made. The counselor can be an ethical model in a system where ethics is not given priority consideration. Practitioners can easily find themselves in an ethical quagmire based on competing role expectations. The best way to maintain a clear ethical position is to focus on your clients' best interests.

Many ethical violations are hard to detect. Clients' needs are best met when practitioners monitor their own ethics. Ethical violations may go undetected because only the individual who committed the violation knows about it. Rather than just looking at others and proclaiming "That's unethical!" we encourage you to challenge your own thinking and apply guidelines to your behavior by asking yourself, "Is what I am doing in the best interests of my clients?"

Principle Ethics and Virtue Ethics

Several writers have developed models for ethical decision making (Cottone, 2001; Forester-Miller & Davis, 1995; Hill, Glaser, & Harden, 1995; Jordan & Meara, 1990; Keith-Spiegel & Koocher, 1985; Kitchener, 1984; Lanning, 1997; Loewenberg & Dolgoff, 1992; Meara, Schmidt, & Day, 1996; Paradise & Siegelwaks, 1982; T. S. Smith, McGuire, Abbott, & Blau, 1991; Stadler, 1986a; Tymchuk, 1981). This section is an amalgamation of elements from these various models.

In a major article entitled "Principles and Virtues: A Foundation for Ethical Decisions, Policies, and Character," Meara, Schmidt, and Day (1996) differentiate between principle ethics and virtue ethics. *Principle ethics* is a set of obligations and a method that focuses on moral issues with the goals of (a) solving a particular dilemma or set of dilemmas and (b) establishing a framework to guide future ethical thinking and behavior. Principles typically focus on acts and choices, and they are used to facilitate the selection of socially and historically acceptable answers to the question "What shall I do?"

A thorough grounding in principle ethics opens the way for another important perspective, virtue ethics. *Virtue ethics* focuses on the character traits of the counselor and nonobligatory ideals to which professionals aspire rather than on solving specific ethical dilemmas. Simply stated, principle ethics asks "Is this situation unethical?" whereas virtue ethics asks "Am I doing what is best for my client?" Even in the absence of an ethical dilemma, virtue ethics compels the professional to be conscious of ethical behavior. Meara and her colleagues (1996) maintain that it is not a question of subscribing to one or the other form of ethics. Rather, professional counselors should strive to integrate virtue ethics and principle ethics, which they believe results in better ethical decisions and policies.

Some counselors concern themselves primarily with avoiding malpractice suits rather than with thinking of what is best for their clients. Their practices are influenced by following the law and ethics codes so that they will stay out of trouble. Other counselors, although also concerned with avoiding litigation, are first and foremost interested in doing what is best for their clients. Such counselors would consider it unethical to use techniques that might not result in the greatest benefit to their clients or to use techniques in which they were not thoroughly trained, even though these techniques might not lead to a lawsuit. For example, a Gestalt therapist might refer a client to a cognitive-behavioral therapist because, in her opinion, the client is more suited to the latter approach. Although this therapist could legally and ethically justify seeing this client, it may be more "virtuous" to refer the client in this instance. As Jordan and Meara (1990) write, "The ideals of professional psychology must include conscientious decision making, but they also must include virtuous deciders, who emphasize not so much what is permitted as what is preferred" (p. 112).

Meara et al. (1996) identify four core virtues—prudence, integrity, respectfulness, and benevolence—that are appropriate for professionals to adhere to in making ethical decisions. They also describe five characteristics of virtuous professionals, which they see as being at the heart of virtue ethics.

- Virtuous agents are motivated to do what is right for the right reasons. They are positively motivated to do what is right because they judge it to be right, not simply because they feel obligated or fear the consequences.
- Virtuous agents possess vision and discernment, which involve sensitivity, judgment, and understanding and leads to decisive action. They know which principles to apply to a situation and how to apply them.
- Virtuous agents possess compassion that involves a regard for the welfare of others and a sensitivity to the suffering of others. They are able to take actions to reduce their clients' pain.
- Virtuous agents possess self-awareness. They have a capacity for self-observation; they know how their assumptions, convictions, and biases are likely to affect their interactions with others.
- Virtuous agents are connected with and understand the mores of their community and the importance of community in moral decision making, policy setting, and character development. They understand the ideals and expectations of their community.

Virtue ethics focuses on ideals rather than obligations and on the character of the professional rather than on the action itself. To meet the goals, ideals, and needs of the community being served, both principles and virtues need to be considered because both are important elements in thinking through ethical concerns.

◆ **A case illustrating virtue ethics.** Your client, Kevin, is progressing well; then he informs you that he has lost his job and will not be able to continue seeing you because of his inability to pay your fees. Here is how four different therapists handled a similar situation:

Therapist A: I'm sorry but I can't continue seeing you without payment. I'm giving you the name of a local community clinic that provides low-cost treatment.

Therapist B: It's not my policy to see people without payment, but I appreciate the difficulty you find yourself in through no fault of your own. I'll continue to see you, and you pay whatever portion of my fee you can afford. In addition I want you to seek out a community agency and do volunteer work in lieu of the full payment.

Therapist C: I suggest that you put therapy on hold until you can financially afford it.

Therapist D: I can't afford to see you without payment, but I am willing to suggest an alternative plan. Continue writing in your journal, and once a month I will see you for half an hour to discuss your journal. You pay what you can afford for these sessions. When your financial situation has been corrected, we can continue therapy as usual.

What are your reactions to the various therapists' responses? Which position appeals to you the most? Why? Can you think of any other responses? Would you be willing to see a client without payment? Why or why not? Do you have any questions about the ethics of any of these therapists?

In considering what you might do if you were the therapist in this case, reflect on the provisions pertaining to *pro bono* (or free) services in these ethics codes:

> Social workers elevate service to others above self-interest. Social workers draw on their knowledge, values, and skills to help people in need and to address social problems. Social workers are encouraged to volunteer some portion of their professional skills with no expectation of significant financial return (pro bono service). (NASW, 1999)

> Counselors contribute to society by devoting a portion of their professional activity to services for which there is little or no financial return (pro bono). (ACA, 1995)

Commentary. If you did not want to abandon your client, you could refer Kevin to an agency that would see him without a fee, assuming such a facility exists in your area. You could also see him as part of your pro bono services. Ethically you are obliged to provide the best quality of care; however, you may be part of a managed care system that limits the number of sessions and has a very limited focus of goals and treatment. Even though you want to do what is best for your client, you may be unable to provide pro bono care without creating other problems for yourself.

Moral Principles to Guide Decision Making

Building upon the work of others, especially Kitchener (1984), Meara et al. (1996) describe six basic moral principles that form the foundation of functioning at the highest ethical level as a professional: autonomy, nonmaleficence, beneficence, justice, fidelity, and veracity. Applying these ethical principles and the related ethical standards is not as simple as it may seem, especially when dealing with culturally diverse populations. (See Chapters 4 and 13 for more on this issue.) These moral principles involve a process of striving that is never fully complete. We have illustrated each of these six basic moral principles by citing a specific ethical guideline from the ACA *Code of Ethics* (1995) and by providing a brief discussion of the cultural implications of using each principle.

- *Autonomy* refers to the promotion of self-determination, or the freedom of clients to choose their own direction. Respect for autonomy entails acknowledging the right of another to choose and act in accordance with his or her wishes, and the professional behaves in a way that enables this right of another person. This is the ACA guideline: "Counselors encourage client growth and development in ways that foster the clients' interest and welfare; counselors avoid fostering dependent counseling relationships" (A.1.b.).

The helping services are based on traditional Western values of individualism, independence, interdependence, self-determination, and making choices for oneself. It often appears as though Western cultures promote individualism above any other cultural value. However, many cultures might follow a different path, stressing decisions with the welfare of the family and the community as a priority. We cannot apply a rigid yardstick of what is a value priority in any culture without exploring how a particular client views priorities. To not do so with a client from any culture is to stereotype the client's culture. For instance, what are the implications of the principle of autonomy when it is applied to clients who do not place a high priority on the value of being autonomous? Does it constitute an imposition of values for counselors to steer clients toward autonomous behavior when such behavior could lead to problems with others in their family, community, or culture? What about promoting autonomy for those incapable of it (for example, dependent youths)?

- *Nonmaleficence* means avoiding doing harm, which includes refraining from actions that risk hurting clients. Professionals have a responsibility to avoid engaging in practices that cause harm or have the potential to result in harm. The ACA code states that "In the counseling relationship, counselors are aware of the intimacy and responsibilities inherent in the counseling relationship, maintain respect for clients, and avoid actions that seek to meet their personal needs at the expense of clients" (A.5.a.).

What are the cultural implications of the principle of nonmaleficence? Traditional diagnostic practices can be inappropriate for certain cultural groups. For instance, a therapist may assign a diagnostic label to a client based on a pattern of behavior the therapist judges to be abnormal, such as inhibition of emotional expression, hesitation to confront, being cautious about self-disclosing, or not making direct eye contact while speaking. Yet these behaviors may be considered to be normal in certain cultures. Another example may be a school counselor who inappropriately labels a boy as hyperactive or ADHD, which may color the perceptions of other staff members in a negative way so they pressure the parents to get the boy on medication. Practitioners need to develop cultural awareness and sensitivity in using assessment, diagnostic, and treatment procedures.

- *Beneficence* refers to promoting good for others. Ideally, counseling contributes to the growth and development of clients within their cultural context. Whatever counselors do can be judged against this criterion. The following ACA guideline illustrates beneficence: "The primary responsibility of counselors is to respect the dignity and to promote the welfare of clients" (A.1.a.).

Consider the possible consequences if a counselor encourages a Vietnamese client to behave more assertively toward his father. The reality of this situation may be that the father would refuse to speak again to a son who confronted him. Even though counselors may be operating with good intentions and may think they are being beneficent, they may not always be doing what is in the best interest of the client. Is it possible for counselors to harm clients unintentionally by encouraging a course of action that has negative consequences? How can counselors know what is in the best interest of their clients? How can counselors determine whether their interventions will lead to growth and development in their clients?

• *Justice,* or fairness, means providing equal treatment to all people. Everyone, regardless of age, sex, race, ethnicity, disability, socioeconomic status, cultural background, religion, or sexual orientation, is entitled to equal access to mental health services. An example might be the school counselor making a home visit to a parent who cannot come to the school because of transportation or child care issues and poverty. To ensure that client populations have equal access to professional services, the ACA code encourages counselors to offer pro bono services: "Counselors contribute to society by devoting a portion of their professional activity to services for which there is little or no financial return (pro bono)" (A.10.d.).

Traditional mental health services may not be just and fair to everyone in a culturally diverse society. If intervention strategies are not relevant to some segments of the population, justice is being violated. How can practitioners adapt the techniques they use to fit the needs of diverse populations? How can new helping strategies be developed that are consistent with the worldview of culturally different clients?

• *Fidelity* means that professionals make honest promises and honor their commitments to those they serve. This entails fulfilling one's responsibilities of trust in a relationship. ACA's code encourages counselors to inform clients about counseling and to be faithful in keeping commitments made to clients: "When counseling is initiated, and throughout the counseling process as necessary, counselors inform clients of the purposes, goals, techniques, procedures, limitations, potential risks, and benefits of services to be performed, and other pertinent information" (A.3.a.).

Fidelity involves creating a trusting and therapeutic relationship whereby people can search for their own solutions. However, what about clients whose culture teaches them that counselors are experts who have the function of providing answers for clients' specific problem situations? What if a client expects the counselor to provide a solution to a particular problem? If the counselor does not meet the client's expectations, is trust being established?

• *Veracity* means truthfulness. Unless practitioners are truthful with their clients, the trust required to form a good working relationship will not develop. The principle of veracity is found in this ACA guideline: "Counselors take steps to insure that clients understand the implications of diagnosis, the intended use of tests and reports, fees, and billing arrangements. Clients have the right to expect confidentiality and to be provided with an explanation of its limitations, including supervision and/or treatment team professionals; to obtain clear information about their case records; to participate in the ongoing counseling plans; and to refuse any recommended services and be advised of the consequences of such refusal" (A.3.a.).

Informed consent is a part of being truthful with clients. What would you do to ensure that your clients understand the informed consent process? How can underserved populations be taught to be active consumers of social services?

Therapists often need to function in the role of advocate, community organizer, consultant, or agent for change in the communities they serve. These roles are quite different from traditional psychotherapy, and practitioners should reexamine ethical issues in light of these unfamiliar roles. The six principles discussed here are a good place to start in determining the degree to which your practice is consistent with promoting the welfare of the clients you serve.

Finally, Meara et al. (1996) raise some cautions and caveats with regard to virtue ethics. First of all, "Who decides what is virtuous?" As ethical professionals, you must regularly reassess your concept of virtue. Avoid rationalizations and attempts to justify your actions under the guise of following the right path. Meara et al. suggest that "We need to reassess systematically our motives and perspectives and the virtues we encourage. We need, as well, to be open to exploring and even adopting virtues different from our own" (p. 47).

Steps in Making Ethical Decisions

When making ethical decisions, ask yourself these questions: "Which values should I rely on? What values do I hold? How do my values affect my work with clients? Why do I hold certain values?" The National Association of Social Workers (1999) cautions that you must be aware of your clients' as well as your own personal values, cultural and religious beliefs, and practices when making ethical decisions. Acting responsibly implies recognizing any conflicts between personal and professional values and dealing with them effectively.

Ethical decision making is not a purely cognitive and linear process that follows neatly step by step. Indeed, it is crucial to acknowledge that emotions play a part in how we make ethical decisions. As a practitioner, your feelings will likely influence how you interpret both your client's behavior and your own behavior. Furthermore, if you are uncomfortable with an ethical decision and do not adequately deal with this discomfort, it will certainly influence your future behavior with your client. An integral part of recognizing and working through an ethical concern is discussing your beliefs and values, motivations, feelings, and actions with a supervisor or a colleague.

In the process of making the best ethical decisions, it is also wise to involve your clients as fully as possible. Because you are making decisions about what is best for the welfare of your clients, you should discuss with them the nature of the ethical dilemma that pertains to them. The feminist model for ethical decision making calls for maximum involvement of the client at every stage of the ethical decision-making process (Hill et al., 1995): Consultation with the client "as fully as is possible and appropriate" is an essential step in ethical decision making (p. 27). Hill, Glaser, and Harden (1995) suggest that the client should be included throughout the process whenever possible, as can be seen in their seven-step model:

1. Recognizing a problem
2. Defining the problem (collaboration with client is essential at this stage)
3. Developing solutions (with client)
4. Choosing a solution
5. Reviewing the process (with client) and rechoosing
6. Implementing and evaluating (with client)
7. Continuing reflection

Walden (1997) suggests that important therapeutic benefits can result from inclusion of the client in the ethical decision-making process, and she offers some strategies for accomplishing this goal at both the organizational and individual levels. When we make decisions about a client *for* the client rather than *with* the client, Walden maintains that we rob the client of power in the relationship. When we create a collaborative therapeutic relationship, the client is empowered. By soliciting the client's perspective, we stand a good chance of achieving better counseling results and the best resolution for any ethical questions that arise. Not only are there potential therapeutic benefits to be gained by including clients in dealing with ethical concerns, but such practices also imply functioning at the aspirational level. In fact, Walden questions whether it is truly possible to attain the aspirational level of ethical functioning *without* including the client's voice in ethical concerns. By adding the voice and the unique perspective of the consumers of professional services, we indicate to the public that we as a profession are genuinely interested in protecting the rights and welfare of those who make use of our services. Walden sees few risks in bringing the client into ethical matters, and there are many benefits to both the client and the professional.

The social constructivism model of ethical decision making shares some aspects of the feminist model but focuses primarily on the social aspects of decision making in counseling (Cottone 2001). This model redefines the ethical decision-making process as an interactive rather than an individual or intrapsychic process and places the decision in the social context itself, not in the mind of the person making the decision. This approach involves negotiating, consensualizing, and when necessary, arbitrating. In dealing with an ethical dilemma or concern, Cottone states that

> the ethically sensitive professional operating from a social contructivism mode would take several steps: (a) obtain information from those involved, (b) assess the nature of the relationships operating at that moment in time, (c) consult valued colleagues and professional expert opinion (including ethics codes and literature), (d) negotiate when there is a disagreement, and (e) respond in a way that allows for a reasonable consensus as to what should happen or what really occurred. Every

> relationship involved must be examined for potential linkage to another (possibly adversarial) system of thought. In addition, every relationship must be assessed for a potential conflict of opinion over what should or did happen. If consensus is not possible, further negotiation, interactive reflection, or arbitration may be necessary. (p. 43)

Keeping in mind the feminist model of ethical decision making, Walden's views on including the client's voice in ethical concerns, and a social constructivism model of ethical decision making, we present our approach to thinking through ethical dilemmas. Following these steps may help you think through ethical problems.

1. *Identify the problem or dilemma.* Gather as much information as possible that sheds light on the situation. Clarify whether the conflict is ethical, legal, clinical, professional, or moral—or a combination of any or all of these. The first step toward resolving an ethical dilemma is recognizing that a problem exists and identifying its specific nature. Because most ethical dilemmas are complex, it is useful to look at the problem from many perspectives and to avoid simplistic solutions. Ethical dilemmas do not have "right" or "wrong" answers, so you will be challenged to deal with ambiguity. Consultation with your client begins at this initial stage and continues throughout the process of working through an ethical problem, as does the process of documenting your decisions and actions.
2. *Identify the potential issues involved.* After the information is collected, list and describe the critical issues and discard the irrelevant ones. Evaluate the rights, responsibilities, and welfare of all those who are affected by the situation. Part of the process of making ethical decisions involves identifying competing moral principles. Consider the basic moral principles of autonomy, nonmaleficence, beneficence, justice, fidelity, and veracity and apply them to the situation. It may help to prioritize these principles and think through ways in which they can support a resolution to the dilemma. Good reasons can be presented that support various sides of a given issue, and different ethical principles may sometimes imply contradictory courses of action.
3. *Review the relevant ethics codes.* Ask yourself whether the standards or principles of your professional organization offer a possible solution to the problem. Consider whether your own values and ethics are consistent with, or in conflict with, the relevant codes. If you are in disagreement with a particular standard, do you have a rationale to support your position? You can also call your professional organization and seek guidance on any specific concern relating to the interpretation of an ethical standard.
4. *Know the applicable laws and regulations.* It is essential for you to keep up to date on relevant state and federal laws that apply to ethical dilemmas. This is especially critical in matters of keeping or breaching confidentiality, reporting child or elder abuse, dealing with issues pertaining to danger to self or others, parental rights, record keeping, testing and assessment, diagnosis, licensing statutes, and the grounds for malpractice. In addition, be sure you understand

the current rules and regulations of the agency or organization where you work.

5. *Obtain consultation.* At this point, it is generally helpful to consult with a colleague or colleagues to obtain a different perspective on the problem. Consider consulting with more than one professional, and do not limit the individuals with whom you will consult to those who share your viewpoint. If there is a legal question, seek legal counsel. After you present your assessment of the situation and your ideas of how you might proceed, ask the person for feedback on your analysis. Are there any factors you are not considering? Are you considering all of the ethical, clinical, and legal issues involved in the case? It is wise to document the nature of your consultation, including the suggestions provided by those with whom you consulted. Consultation is important in court cases because consultation illustrates the attempt to adhere to community standards by finding out what your colleagues in the community would do in the same situation. Because of your involvement in the situation, you may have trouble seeing the forest for the trees. Consultation can help you think about information or circumstances that you may have overlooked. In making ethical decisions, you must justify a course of action based on sound reasoning. Consultation with colleagues, whether it is formal or informal, provides an opportunity to test your justification. Remember to document the nature of your discussions with those whom you consult.

6. *Consider possible and probable courses of action.* Brainstorming is useful at this stage of ethical decision making. By listing a wide variety of courses of action, you may identify a possibility that is unorthodox but useful. Of course, one alternative is that no action is required. As you think about the many possibilities for action, discuss these options with your client as well as with other professionals.

7. *Enumerate the consequences of various decisions.* Ponder the implications of each course of action for the client, for others who are related to the client, and for you as the counselor. Again, a discussion with your client about consequences for him or her is most important. Consider using the six fundamental moral principles (autonomy, nonmaleficence, beneficence, justice, fidelity, and veracity) as a framework for evaluating the consequences of a given course of action.

8. *Decide on what appears to be the best course of action.* In making the best decision, carefully consider the information you have received from various sources. The more obvious the dilemma, the clearer is the course of action; the more subtle the dilemma, the more difficult the decision will be. After deciding, try not to second-guess your course of action. You may wonder if you have made the best decision in a given situation, or you may realize later that another action might have been more beneficial. Hindsight does not invalidate the decision you made based on the information you had at the time. Once you have made what you consider to be the best decision, do what you can to evaluate your course of action. Reflecting on your assessment of the situation and the actions you took are essential if you are to learn from your experience. This is where reviewing your notes can be particularly helpful in assessing the

process. Follow up to determine the outcomes and see if any further action is needed. To obtain the most accurate picture, involve your client in this process.

The procedural steps we have listed here should not be thought of as a simplified and linear way to reach a resolution on ethical matters. However, we have found that these steps stimulate self-reflection and encourage discussion with clients and colleagues. Using this process, we are confident that you will find your own best solution.

Self-Assessment: An Inventory of Your Attitudes and Beliefs About Professional and Ethical Issues

This inventory surveys your thoughts on various professional and ethical issues in the helping professions. The inventory is designed to introduce you to issues and topics presented in this book and to stimulate your thoughts and interest. You may want to complete the inventory in more than one sitting, giving each question your full concentration.

This is not a traditional multiple-choice test in which you must select the "one right answer." Rather, it is a survey of your basic beliefs, attitudes, and values on specific topics related to the practice of therapy. For each question, write in the letter of the response that most clearly reflects your viewpoint at this time. In many cases the answers are not mutually exclusive, and you may choose more than one response if you wish. In addition, a blank line is included for each item so you can provide a response more suited to your thinking or qualify a chosen response.

Notice that there are two spaces before each item. Use the space on the left for your answer at the beginning of the course. At the end of the course, take this inventory again, placing your answer in the space on the right. Cover your initial answers so you won't be influenced by how you originally responded. Then you can see how your attitudes have changed as a result of your experience in this course.

You may want to bring the completed inventory to your beginning class session to compare your views with those of others in the class. Such a comparison might stimulate some debate and help get the class involved in the topics to be discussed. In choosing the issues you want to discuss in class, circle the numbers of those items that you felt most strongly about as you were responding. You may find it instructive to ask others how they responded to these items in particular.

___ ___ 1. If I were working with a client who could no longer continue because of his or her inability to pay my fees, I would most likely
   a. be willing to see this person at no fee until his or her financial position changed.
   b. give my client the name of a local community clinic that provides low-cost treatment.

c. suggest some form of bartering of goods or services for therapy services.
d. lower my fee to whatever the client could afford.
e. ______________________________

___ ___ 2. For those who wish to become therapists, I believe personal psychotherapy
a. should be required for licensure.
b. is not an important factor in developing the capacity to work with others.
c. should be encouraged but not required.
d. is needed only when the therapist has some form of psychological impairment.
e. ______________________________

___ ___ 3. To be an effective helper, I believe a therapist
a. must like the client personally.
b. must be free of any personal conflicts in the area in which the client is working.
c. needs to have experienced the same problem as the client.
d. needs to have experienced feelings similar to those being experienced by the client.
e. ______________________________

___ ___ 4. If I were faced with an ethical dilemma, the first step I would take would be to
a. review the relevant ethical codes.
b. consult with an attorney.
c. identify the problem or dilemma.
d. quickly decide on what appears to be the best course of action.
e. ______________________________

___ ___ 5. For me, being an ethical practitioner *mainly* entails
a. acting in compliance with minimal ethical standards.
b. reflecting on the effects that my interventions are likely to have on the welfare of my clients.
c. avoiding obvious violations of my profession's ethical codes.
d. thinking about the legal implications of everything I do.
e. ______________________________

___ ___ 6. If I were an intern and was convinced that my supervisor was encouraging trainees to participate in unethical behavior in an agency setting, I would
a. first discuss the matter with the supervisor.
b. report the supervisor to the director of the agency.
c. ignore the situation for fear of negative consequences.
d. report the situation to the ethics committee of the state professional association.
e. ______________________________

___ ___ 7. Practitioners who work with culturally diverse groups without having cross-cultural knowledge and skills

a. are violating the civil rights of their clients.
b. are probably guilty of unethical behavior.
c. should realize the need for specialized training.
d. can be said to be practicing ethically.
e. ________________________________

___ ___ 8. If I had strong feelings, positive or negative, toward a client, I think I would most likely
a. discuss my feelings with my client.
b. keep my feelings to myself and hope they would eventually disappear.
c. discuss my feelings with a supervisor or colleague.
d. accept my feelings as natural unless they began to interfere with the counseling relationship.
e. ________________________________

___ ___ 9. I won't feel ready to counsel others until
a. my own life is free of problems.
b. I have experienced counseling as a client.
c. I feel very confident and know that I will be effective.
d. I have become a self-aware person and developed the ability to continually reexamine my own life and relationships.
e. ________________________________

___ ___ 10. If a client evidenced strong feelings of attraction or dislike for me, I think I would
a. help the client work through these feelings and understand them.
b. enjoy these feelings if they were positive.
c. refer my client to another counselor.
d. direct the sessions into less emotional areas.
e. ________________________________

___ ___ 11. Practitioners who counsel clients whose sex, race, age, social class, or sexual orientation is different from their own
a. will most likely not understand these clients fully.
b. need to understand the differences between their clients and themselves.
c. can practice unethically if they do not consider cross-cultural factors.
d. are probably not going to be effective with such clients because of these differences.
e. ________________________________

___ ___ 12. If I were faced with a counseling situation where it appeared that there was a conflict between an ethical and legal course to follow, I would
a. immediately consult with an attorney.
b. always choose the legal path first and foremost.
c. strive to do what I believed to be ethical, even if it meant challenging a law.

d. refer my client to another therapist.
e. ______________________________

___ ___ 13. In terms of appreciating and understanding the value systems of clients who are culturally different from me,
a. I see it as my responsibility to learn about their values and not impose mine on them.
b. I would encourage them to accept the values of the dominant culture for survival purposes.
c. I would attempt to modify my counseling procedures to fit their cultural values.
d. I think it is imperative that I learn about the specific cultural values my clients hold.
e. ______________________________

___ ___ 14. If a client came to me with a problem and I could see that I would not be objective because of my values, I would
a. accept the client because of the challenge to become more tolerant of diversity.
b. tell the client at the outset about my fears concerning our conflicting values.
c. refer the client to someone else.
d. attempt to influence the client to adopt my way of thinking.
e. ______________________________

___ ___ 15. With respect to a client's right to make his or her own end-of-life decisions, I would
a. always use the principle of a client's self-determination as the key in any dilemma of this sort.
b. tell my client what I thought was the right course to follow.
c. suggest that my client see a clergy person or a physician.
d. encourage my client to find meaning in life, regardless of his or her psychological and physical condition.
e. ______________________________

___ ___ 16. I would tend to refer a client to another therapist
a. if I had a strong dislike for the client.
b. if I did not have much experience working with the kind of problem the client presented.
c. if I saw my own needs and problems getting in the way of helping the client.
d. if the client seemed to distrust me.
e. ______________________________

___ ___ 17. My ethical position regarding the role of values in therapy is that, as a therapist, I should
a. never impose my values on a client.
b. expose my values, without imposing them on the client.
c. teach my clients what I consider to be proper values.
d. keep my values out of the counseling relationship.
e. ______________________________

_____ 18. If I were to counsel lesbian and gay clients, a major concern of mine would be
a. maintaining objectivity.
b. not knowing and understanding enough about this lifestyle.
c. establishing a positive therapeutic relationship.
d. pushing my own values.
e. ______________________________

_____ 19. Of the following, I consider the most unethical form of therapist behavior to be
a. promoting dependence in the client.
b. becoming sexually involved with a client.
c. breaking confidentiality without a good reason to do so.
d. accepting a client who has a problem that goes beyond my competence.
e. ______________________________

_____ 20. Regarding the issue of counseling friends, I think that
a. it is seldom wise to accept a friend as a client.
b. it should be done rarely, and only if it is clear that the friendship will not interfere with the therapeutic relationship.
c. friendship and therapy should not be mixed.
d. it should be done only if it seems appropriate to both the client and the counselor.
e. ______________________________

_____ 21. Regarding confidentiality, I believe it is ethical to
a. break confidence when there is reason to believe clients may do serious harm to themselves.
b. break confidence when there is reason to believe that a client will do harm to someone else.
c. break confidence when the parents of a client ask for certain information.
d. inform the authorities when a client is breaking the law.
e. ______________________________

_____ 22. A therapist should terminate therapy with a client when
a. the client decides to do so and not before.
b. the therapist judges that it is time to terminate.
c. it is clear that the client is not benefiting from the therapy.
d. the client reaches an impasse.
e. ______________________________

_____ 23. A sexual relationship between a *former* client and a therapist is
a. ethical if the client initiates it.
b. ethical only 2 years after termination of therapy.
c. ethical only when client and therapist discuss the issue and agree to the relationship.
d. never ethical, regardless of the time that has elapsed.
e. ______________________________

___ ___ 24. Concerning the issue of physically touching a client, I think that touching
- a. is unwise, because it could be misinterpreted by the client.
- b. should be done only when the therapist genuinely thinks it would be appropriate.
- c. is an important part of the therapeutic process.
- d. is ethical when the client requests it.
- e. ________________________________

___ ___ 25. A clinical supervisor has initiated sexual relationships with former trainees (students). He maintains that because he no longer has any professional responsibility to them this practice is acceptable. In my view, this behavior is
- a. clearly unethical, because he is using his position to initiate contacts with former students.
- b. not unethical, because the professional relationship has ended.
- c. not unethical but is unwise and inappropriate.
- d. somewhat unethical, because the supervisory relationship is similar to the therapeutic relationship.
- e. ________________________________

___ ___ 26. Regarding the role of spiritual and religious values, as a counselor I would be inclined to
- a. ignore such values for fear that I would impose my own beliefs on my clients.
- b. actively strive to get my clients to think about how spirituality or religion could enhance their lives.
- c. avoid bringing up the topic unless my client initiated such a discussion.
- d. conduct an assessment of my client's spiritual and religious beliefs during the intake session.
- e. ________________________________

___ ___ 27. In the practice of couples and family therapy, I think the
- a. therapist's primary responsibility is to the welfare of the family as a unit.
- b. therapist should focus primarily on the needs of individual members of the family.
- c. therapist should attend to the family's needs and try to hold the amount of sacrifice by any one member to a minimum.
- d. therapist has an ethical obligation to state his or her bias and approach at the outset.
- e. ________________________________

___ ___ 28. The practice of limiting the number of therapy sessions a client is entitled to under a managed care plan is
- a. unethical as it can work against a client's best interests.
- b. a reality that I expect I will have to accept.
- c. an example of exploitation of a client's rights.

d. wrong because it takes away the professional's judgment in many cases.
e. ________________________________

______ 29. If a client were to offer me a gift, I would
a. accept it cheerfully.
b. never accept it under any circumstances.
c. discuss the matter with my client.
d. attempt to figure out the motivations for my client's offer.
e. ________________________________

______ 30. Regarding bartering with a client in exchange for therapy services, my position is that
a. it all depends on the circumstances of the individual case.
b. I would consider this practice if the client had no way to pay for my services.
c. the practice is unethical.
d. before agreeing to bartering I would always seek consultation.
e. ________________________________

______ 31. Concerning the role of diagnosis in counseling, I believe
a. diagnosis is essential for planning a treatment program.
b. diagnosis is counterproductive for therapy, because it is based on an external view of the client.
c. diagnosis is dangerous in that it tends to label people, who then are limited by the label.
d. the usefulness of diagnosis depends on the theoretical orientation and the kind of counseling a therapist does.
e. ________________________________

______ 32. Concerning the place of testing in counseling, I think that tests
a. generally interfere with the counseling process.
b. can be valuable tools if they are used as adjuncts to counseling.
c. are essential for people who are seriously disturbed.
d. can be either used or abused in counseling.
e. ________________________________

______ 33. Regarding the issue of psychological risks associated with participation in group therapy, my position is that
a. clients should be informed at the outset of possible risks.
b. these risks should be minimized by careful screening.
c. this issue is exaggerated because there are no real risks.
d. careful supervision will offset some of these risks.
e. ________________________________

______ 34. Regarding the practice of counseling via the Internet, I believe
a. the practice is fraught with ethical and legal problems.
b. this is a form of technology with real promise for many clients who would not seek out face-to-face counseling.
c. anything but dealing with simple problems would not be appropriate with this form of technology.

d. I would never provide Internet counseling without also having some personal contact with the client.
e. ______________________________

___ ___ 35. As an intern, if I thought my supervisor was inadequate, I would
a. talk to my supervisor about it.
b. continue to work without complaining.
c. seek supervision elsewhere.
d. feel let down by the agency I worked for.
e. ______________________________

___ ___ 36. My view of supervision is that it is
a. a place to get answers to difficult situations.
b. an opportunity to work on my personal problems.
c. valuable to have when I reach an impasse with a client.
d. a way for me to learn about myself and to get insights into how I work with clients.
e. ______________________________

___ ___ 37. In working with clients from different ethnic groups, it is most important to
a. be aware of the sociopolitical forces that have affected these clients.
b. understand how language can act as a barrier to effective cross-cultural counseling.
c. refer these clients to some professional who shares their ethnic and cultural background.
d. help these clients modify their views so that they will be accepted and not have to suffer rejection.
e. ______________________________

___ ___ 38. To be effective in counseling clients from a different culture, a counselor must
a. possess specific knowledge about the particular group he or she is counseling.
b. be able to accurately "read" nonverbal messages.
c. have had direct contact with this group.
d. treat these clients no differently from clients from his or her own cultural background.
e. ______________________________

___ ___ 39. Concerning the counselor's responsibility to the community, I believe
a. counselors should educate the community concerning the nature of psychological services.
b. counselors should attempt to change patterns that need changing.
c. community involvement falls outside the proper scope of counseling.
d. counselors should become involved in helping clients use the resources available in the community.
e. ______________________________

__ __ 40. If I were working as a counselor in the community, the major role I would expect to play would be that of
a. a change agent.
b. an adviser.
c. an educator or a consultant.
d. an advocate.
e. ____________________

Chapter Summary

This introductory chapter has focused on the foundations of creating an ethical sense and has explored various perspectives on teaching the process of making ethical decisions. Professional codes of ethics are indeed essential for ethical practice, but merely knowing these codes is not enough. The challenge comes with learning how to think critically and knowing ways to apply general ethical principles to particular situations. We encourage you to become active in your education and training (see box titled Internet Resources for information on joining a professional association). We also suggest that you try to keep an open mind about the issues you encounter during this time and throughout your professional career. An important part of this openness is a willingness to focus on yourself as a person and as a professional as well as on the questions that are more obviously related to your clients.

Suggested Activities

Note to the student. At the end of each chapter we have deliberately provided a range of activities for instructors and students to choose from. Our purpose is to invite you to personalize the material and develop your own positions on the issues we raise. We suggest that you choose those activities that you find the most challenging and meaningful.

1. As a practitioner, how will you determine what is ethical and what is unethical? How will you develop your guidelines for ethical practice? Make a list of behaviors that you judge to be unethical. After you have thought through this issue by yourself, you may want to explore your approach with fellow students.

2. Take the self-assessment survey of your attitudes and beliefs about ethics in this chapter. Now circle the five items that you had the strongest reactions to or that you had the hardest time answering. Bring these items to class for discussion.

3. Look over the professional codes of ethics of one or more of the professional organizations. What are your impressions of each of these codes? To what degree are they complete? To what degree do they provide you with the needed guidelines for ethical practice? What are the values of such

Internet Resources

American Counseling Association (ACA)

Student memberships are available to both undergraduate and graduate students enrolled at least half-time or more at the college level.

ACA membership provides many benefits, including a subscription to the *Journal of Counseling and Development* and also a monthly newspaper entitled *Counseling Today,* eligibility for professional liability insurance programs, legal defense services, and professional development through workshops and conventions. ACA puts out a resource catalog that provides information on the various aspects of the counseling profession, as well as detailed information about membership, journals, books, home-study programs, videotapes, audiotapes, and liability insurance. For further information, contact:

American Counseling Association
5999 Stevenson Avenue
Alexandria, VA 22304-3300
Telephone: (703) 823-9800 or (800) 347-6647)
Fax: (703) 823-0252
Web site: *http://www.counseling.org*

American Psychological Association (APA)

The APA has a Student Affiliates category rather than student membership. Journals and subscriptions are extra. Each year in mid-August or late August the APA holds a national convention. Membership includes a monthly subscription to a journal, *American Psychologist,* and a magazine, *Monitor on Psychology,* 11 times a year. For further information, contact:

American Psychological Association
750 First Street, NE
Washington, DC 20002-4242
Telephone: (202) 336-5500 or (800) 374-2721
Fax: (202) 336-5568
Web site: *http://www.apa.org*

National Association of Social Workers (NASW)

NASW membership is open to all professional social workers, and there is a student membership category. The NASW Press, which produces *Social Work* and the *NASW News* as membership benefits, is a major service in professional development. NASW has a number of pamphlets available. For information, contact:

National Association of Social Workers
750 First Street, NE, Suite 700
Washington, DC 20002-4241
Telephone: (202) 408-8600 or (800) 638-8799
Fax: (202) 336-8311
Website: *http://www.socialworkers.org*

American Association for Marriage and Family Therapy (AAMFT)

The AAMFT has a student membership category. Members receive the *Journal of Marital and Family Therapy,* which is published four times a year, and a subscription to six issues yearly of *Family Therapy News.* For membership applications and further information, contact:

(continued)

(continued)

American Association for Marriage and Family Therapy
1133 15th Street, NW, Suite 300
Washington, DC 20005-2710
Telephone: (202) 452-0109
Fax: (202) 223-2329
Web site: *http://www.aamft.org*

National Organization for Human Service Education (NOHSE)

The National Organization for Human Service Education (NOHSE) is made up of members from diverse disciplines—mental health, child care, social services, gerontology, recreation, corrections, and developmental disabilities. Membership is open to human-service educators, students, field-work supervisors, and direct-care professionals. Student membership is $25 per year, which includes a subscription to the newsletter (the *Link*), the yearly journal, *Human Services Education;* and discount prices for the yearly conference (held in October). For further information about membership in the National Organization for Human Service Education, contact:

Naomi Wipert
5326 Avery Road
New Port Richey, FL 34652
Telephone: (813) 929-2363
Fax: (813) 929-2915
Web site: *http:www.nohse.com*

codes? What limitations do you see in them? What do the various codes have in common?

Ethics in Action CD-ROM Exercises

The *Ethics in Action* CD-ROM and this text deal with the topic of ethical decision making—with emphasis on the eight steps in making ethical decisions. Other topics explored in the first part of the CD-ROM include the role of codes of ethics in making decisions and basic moral principles as they apply to resolving ethical dilemmas.

In Part 1 of the CD-ROM program, three role plays provide concrete examples of applying the steps in making ethical decisions described in this chapter. The role plays illustrate ethical dilemmas pertaining to teen pregnancy, interracial dating, and culture clash between client and counselor. After viewing each of these three vignettes, we strongly encourage you to complete the exercises that are a part of each role-play situation.

To make the fullest use of this integrated learning package, conduct small group discussions in class and engage in role-playing activities. Students can assume the role of counselor for the vignette and demonstrate how they would deal with the dilemma presented by the client. For those not using the CD-ROM, descriptive summaries of the vignettes are provided with these exercises to facilitate role plays and class discussions. We hope that the material in the CD-ROM, and this text as well, will be a catalyst for students to try out alternative approaches to dealing with each ethical challenge presented.

InfoTrac® College Edition Resources

For additional readings, explore InfoTrac College Edition, our online library. Go to *http://www.infotrac.college.com/wadsworth* and select these key word searches:

ethical decision making model*
ethical community standard*
standard* practice psych*
aspirational ethic*
mandatory ethic*

Key words are listed in a form that enables the search engine to locate a wider range of articles in the online university library. Key words should be entered exactly as shown, including asterisks, "Wl," "W2," "AND," and other search engine tools.

2

Pre-Chapter Self-Inventory

The pre-chapter self-inventories can help you identify and clarify your attitudes and beliefs about the issues to be explored in the chapter. Keep in mind that the "right" answer is the one that best expresses your thoughts at the time. We suggest that you complete the inventory before reading the chapter; then, after reading the chapter and discussing the material in class, complete the inventory again to see whether your positions have changed in any way.

Directions: For each statement, indicate the response that most closely identifies your beliefs and attitudes. Use the following code:

5 = I *strongly agree* with this statement.
4 = I *agree* with this statement.
3 = I am *undecided* about this statement.
2 = I *disagree* with this statement.
1 = I *strongly disagree* with this statement.

_____1. Unless therapists have a high degree of self-awareness, there is a real danger that they will use their clients to satisfy their own needs.

_____2. Before therapists begin to practice, it is essential that they be free of personal problems and conflicts.

_____3. Counselors or therapists should be required to undergo their own therapy before they are licensed to practice.

The Counselor as a Person and as a Professional

_____4. Counselors who satisfy personal needs through their work are behaving unethically.

_____5. Many professionals in the counseling field face a high risk of burnout because of the demands of their job.

_____6. Counselors who know themselves can avoid experiencing overidentification with their clients.

_____7. Strong feelings about a client are a sign that the counselor needs further therapy.

_____8. Feelings of anxiety in a beginning counselor indicate unsuitability for the counseling profession.

_____9. A competent counselor can work with any client.

_____10. I fear that I will have difficulty challenging my clients.

_____11. A professional counselor avoids getting involved socially with clients or counseling friends.

_____12. A major fear of mine is that I will make mistakes and seriously hurt a client.

_____13. Real therapy does not occur unless a transference relationship is developed.

_____14. When therapists are not aware of their own needs, they may misuse the power they have in the therapeutic situation.

_____15. An experienced and competent counselor should not need either periodic or ongoing personal psychotherapy.

Introduction

A primary issue in the helping professions is the role of the counselor *as a person* in the therapeutic relationship. Because counselors are asking clients to look honestly at themselves and to choose how they want to change, counselors must open their own lives to the same scrutiny. Counselors repeatedly ask themselves these questions: "What makes me think I am capable of helping anyone? What do I personally have to offer others who are struggling to find their way? Am I doing in my own life what I urge others to do?"

Counselors and psychotherapists usually acquire an extensive theoretical and practical knowledge as a basis for their practice. But they also bring their human qualities and their life experiences to every therapeutic session. Professionals can be well versed in psychological theory and can learn diagnostic and interviewing skills and still be ineffective helpers. If counselors are to promote growth and change in their clients, they must be willing to promote growth in their own lives. This willingness to live in accordance with what they teach is what makes counselors "therapeutic persons." If mental health professionals are stagnant themselves, it is doubtful that they can inspire clients to make life-affirming choices. Ethical problems can arise when therapists are unable to carry out this modeling role, which is critical in encouraging clients to change.

In this chapter we deal with some of the ways therapists' personal needs and problems can present ethical issues for the client-therapist relationship. It is difficult to talk about the counselor *as a professional* without considering personal qualities. A clinician's beliefs, personal attributes, level of personal functioning, and ways of living inevitably influence the way he or she carries out a professional role, which to us is central to ethical practice. Some of the issues we address, however, are specifically related to the counselor's professional identity. Although these professional issues are dealt with throughout this book, in this chapter we take up problems that are closely linked to the counselor's personal life: self-awareness, influence of counselor's personality traits, goals, needs, transference, countertransference, personal dynamics, job stress, and the challenge to balance life roles.

Self-Awareness and the Influence of the Therapist's Personality and Needs

Professionals who work intimately with others have a personal responsibility to be committed to awareness of their own life issues. Moreover, without a high level of self-awareness, counselors will most likely obstruct the progress of their clients as the focus of therapy shifts from meeting the client's needs to meeting the needs of the therapist. Consequently, practitioners must be aware of their own needs, areas of "unfinished business," personal conflicts, defenses, and vulnerabilities and how these may interfere in their professional relationships. In this section we consider two specific areas that we think you need to examine if you are going into one of the helping professions: personal needs and unresolved conflicts.

Motivations for Becoming a Counselor

Ask yourself these two critical questions: "What are my motivations for becoming a counselor?" and "What are my rewards for counseling others?" There are many answers to these questions. Therapists often experience excitement and a deep sense of satisfaction from being with people who are struggling to achieve self-understanding and who are willing to experience pain as they seek a better life. Some counselors appreciate the feeling of being instrumental in others' life changes. Still others value the opportunity to question their own lives as they work with their clients. In many ways therapeutic encounters serve as mirrors in which therapists can see their own lives reflected. As a result, therapy can become a catalyst for change in the therapist as well as in the client.

Of course, therapists *do* have their own personal needs, but these needs do not have to assume priority or get in the way of a client's growth. Most people who enter the helping professions want to nurture others, and they need to know that they are being instrumental in helping others to change. In this sense, they need to have a sense from clients that they are a significant force in their lives. But to keep these needs from interfering with the progress of their clients, therapists need to be aware of the possibility of working primarily to be appreciated by others instead of working toward the best interests of their clients.

The rewards of practicing psychotherapy are many, but one of the most significant is the joy of seeing clients move from being victims to assuming control over their lives. Therapeutic progress can be blocked, however, when therapists use their clients, perhaps unconsciously, to fulfill their own needs. Out of an exaggerated need to nurture others or to feel powerful, for example, people sometimes feel that they know how others should live. The tendency to give advice and to direct another's life can be especially harmful in a therapist because it leads to excessive dependence on the part of clients and perpetuates their tendency to look outside themselves for answers. Therapists who need to feel powerful or important may begin to think that they are indispensable to their clients or, worse still, try to *make* themselves so.

The goals of therapy can also suffer when therapists with a strong need for approval focus on trying to win the acceptance, admiration, and even awe of their clients. Guy (2000) reminds us of the danger of depending on our clients as the main source for meeting our needs of admiration or belonging. To the degree to which we are unaware of our needs and personal dynamics, we will probably use our work primarily to satisfy our own unmet needs or will steer clients away from exploring conflicts that we ourselves are unwilling to acknowledge. Some therapists may be primarily motivated by a need to get confirmation from their clients of their self-worth, both personally and professionally. Because clients often feel a need to please their therapist, clients are easily drawn into taking care of their therapist's psychological needs.

When therapists are not sufficiently aware of their own needs, they may misuse the power they have in the therapeutic situation. For example, a quick approach of prescribing solutions to problems may spring from the therapist's need to feel a sense of achievement and accomplishment. Some therapists feel ill at ease if their clients fail to make instant progress; consequently, they may push their clients to make decisions prematurely or even make decisions for them.

As you consider your own needs and their influence on your work as a therapist, ask yourself these questions:

- How can I know when I'm working for the client's benefit and when I'm working for my own benefit?
- How much might I depend on clients to tell me how good I am as a person or as a therapist? Am I able to appreciate myself, or do I depend primarily on others to validate my worth and the value of my work?
- Am I getting my needs for nurturance, recognition, and support met from those who are significant in my life? Do I look to my clients to meet my needs to be appreciated?
- Do I feel inadequate when clients don't make progress? If so, how could my attitude and feelings of inadequacy adversely affect my work with these clients?

Therapists who tell clients what to do with their lives or use the sessions to buttress their own sense of self-worth diminish the autonomy of their clients and invite increased dependence in the future. Monitor your behavior to be sure you are not depending on your clients to fulfill your need for self-worth.

Unresolved Personal Conflicts

Despite the pitfalls awaiting the unaware, therapists need not resolve all their personal difficulties before they begin to counsel others. Indeed, such a requirement would eliminate almost everybody from the field. In fact, a counselor who rarely struggles or experiences anxiety may have real difficulty relating to a client who feels desperate or caught in a hopeless conflict. Moreover, if therapists flee from anxiety-provoking questions in their own lives, they probably will not be able to effectively encourage clients to face such questions. The important point is that counselors can and should be *aware* of their biases, their areas of denial, and the issues they find particularly difficult to deal with in their own lives, especially as they influence their ability to effectively render services. Most ethics codes address this issue, including this APA (1992) guideline on the importance of recognizing personal problems and conflicts:

> Psychologists recognize that their personal problems and conflicts may interfere with their effectiveness. Accordingly, they refrain from undertaking an activity when they know or should know that their personal problems are likely to lead to harm to a patient, client, colleague, student, research participant, or other person to whom they may owe a professional or scientific obligation. (1.13)

To illustrate, suppose that you are experiencing a rough time in your life. You feel unresolved anger and frustration. Your home life is tense, and you are wrestling with some pivotal decisions about what you want to do with the rest of your life. Perhaps you are having problems with your clients or your spouse. You may be caught between fears of loneliness and a desire to be on your own, or between your fear of and need for close relationships. Can you counsel others effectively while you are struggling with your own uncertainty?

The critical point is not *whether* you happen to be struggling with personal questions but *how* you are struggling with them. Do you see your part in creating your own problems? Are you aware of your alternatives for action? Do you recognize and try to deal with your problems, or do you invest a lot of energy in denying their existence? Do you find yourself generally blaming others for your problems? Are you willing to consult with a therapist, or do you tell yourself that you can handle it, even when it becomes obvious that you are not doing so? In short, are you willing to do in your own life what you expect your clients to do?

If you are unaware of your own conflicts, you will be in a poor position to pay attention to the ways in which your personal life influences your work with your clients, especially if some of their problem areas are also problem areas for you. For example, suppose a client is trying to deal with feelings of hopelessness and despair. How can you intensively explore these feelings if, in your own life, you are busily engaged in cheering everybody up? If hopelessness is an issue you do not want to face personally, you will probably steer the client away from exploring it. Or consider a client who wants to explore her feelings about homosexuality. Can you facilitate this exploration if you are very uncomfortable in this area? If you feel discomfort in talking about homosexual issues and do not want to deal with your discomfort, can you stay with your client emotionally when she brings up this topic?

Because you will have difficulty staying with a client in an area that you are reluctant or fearful to deal with, consider what present unfinished business in your own life might affect you as a counselor. What unresolved conflicts are you aware of, and how might these conflicts influence the way you counsel others?

◆ **The case of Rollo.** Rollo is an intern completing his clinical hours for licensure. He came from a family where both parents abused alcohol. The clinic specializes in the treatment of children from abusive homes. Rollo finds himself easily moved to tears as he works with the children. At times he becomes angry with the parents of these children, and he agonizes over the plight of the children. He typically devotes extra time beyond the scheduled activities, he finds it difficult to say "no" to his clients, and his personal life, as a result, suffers. It comes to the attention of his supervisor that he frequently seems stressed and short-tempered with other staff members. In their supervision hour, Rollo retorts that the agency is not doing enough for the children. He proceeds to tell his supervisor how much he is affected by them and how he is continually trying to come up with ways to help them. After listening to Rollo, his supervisor suggests that Rollo consider personal therapy to further explore the way in which he is affected by these children.

- Do you see anything unethical in Rollo's behavior? Is there a point where personal involvement can be counterproductive? How would you determine that?
- Do you agree with the supervisor's suggestion of personal therapy? Why or why not?
- What possible conflicts are you aware of in your life that might get in your way of helping certain clients through their difficulties? If you are moved to tears by your clients, does that imply that you have unresolved conflicts? Does anger directed toward abusive parents mean that you have unresolved conflicts with your parents?

Personal Therapy for Counselors

Throughout this chapter we stress the importance of counselors' self-awareness. A closely related issue is whether those who wish to become counselors should themselves undergo psychotherapy and whether continuing or periodic personal therapy is valuable for practicing therapists. We are not speaking of therapy for remediation of deep conflicts but of therapeutic experiences aimed at increasing awareness of yourself in the world. There are many ways to accomplish this goal: individual therapy, group counseling, consultation with colleagues, continuing education (especially of an experiential nature), and reading. Other less formal avenues to personal growth are reflecting on and evaluating the meaning of your work and life, remaining open to the reactions of significant people in your life, enjoying music and the arts, traveling, experiencing different cultures, being outdoors, meditating, engaging in spiritual activities, enjoying physical exercise, and spending time with friends and family.

Personal Therapy During Training

In a study conducted by Coster and Schwebel (1997), psychologists favored recommending personal therapy in general to all students but not requiring it unless it appeared to be professionally necessary. There are several reasons why potential counselors should be encouraged to experience their own therapy. First, those who expect to counsel others do well to know what the experience of being a client is really like. We do not assume that most potential therapists are "sick" and in need of being "cured," but then we do not make that assumption about most clients either. Therapy can help you take an honest look at your motivations in becoming a counselor. Through therapy you can explore how your needs influence your actions, how you use power in your life, what your values are, and whether you have a need to persuade others to be like you.

When students are engaged in practicum, fieldwork, and internship experiences and the accompanying individual and group supervision sessions, the following issues tend to surface:

- A need to tell people what to do
- A desire to take away all pain from clients
- A need to have all the answers and to be perfect
- A need to be recognized and appreciated
- A tendency to assume too much responsibility for the changes of clients
- A fear of doing harm, however inadvertently
- A tendency to deny or not recognize client issues that may relate to their own

As students begin to practice counseling, they sometimes become aware that they are taking on a professional role that resembles the role they played in their family. They may recognize a need to preserve peace by becoming the caretaker of others. During their childhood they may have assumed adult roles with their own parents by trying to take care of them. Now, as adults, they may continue to take on most of the responsibility for the changes their clients make. When students become aware of concerns such as these, individual and group therapy can provide a safe place to explore and talk about the painful memories that are often associated with these personal issues. In the process, students experience firsthand what their clients experience in therapy. If counseling students do not experience this process of internal searching, it is unlikely that they will be able to facilitate an in-depth exploration by their clients. If they have not traveled the path, how can they serve as a guide for others?

Another reason for undergoing therapy is that most of us have blind spots and unfinished business that may interfere with our effectiveness as therapists. Most of us have areas in our lives that are not developed and that limit our effectiveness, both as persons and as counselors. Although it is not necessary for counselors to have fully resolved all of their personal problems, you at least need to be aware of the nature of such problems and the ways in which those problems may affect your professional work. Personal therapy is one way of coming to grips with your dynamics as well as working through unresolved conflicts, which to us is an example of practicing aspirational ethics.

Ideally, potential counselors might participate in a combination of individual and group therapy, because the two therapy types complement each other. Individual therapy provides an opportunity to look at yourself in some depth. Many counselors will experience a reopening of old emotional wounds as they engage in intensive work with their clients. For example, their therapeutic work may bring to the surface guilt feelings that need to be resolved. If students are in private therapy while they are doing their internship, they can productively bring such problems to their sessions.

Group therapy, in contrast, provides members with the opportunity to give and get feedback from others. It enables participants to become increasingly aware of their interpersonal style and gives them a chance to experiment with new behaviors in the group setting. It also provides an avenue to generalize experiences and to realize that they are not alone in what they think and feel. The reactions you receive from others can help you learn about personal attributes that could be either strengths or limitations in your work as a counselor.

Many training programs in counselor education recognize the value of having students participate in personal-awareness groups with their peers. A group can be set up specifically for the exploration of personal concerns, or such exploration can be made an integral part of training and supervision groups. Whatever the format, students will benefit most if they are willing to focus on themselves personally and not merely on their "cases." Unfortunately, some beginning counselors tend to focus primarily on client dynamics, as do many supervisors and counselor educators. What trainees are learning by being in a group would be more meaningful if they were open to exploring questions such as these: "How am I feeling about my own value as a counselor? Do I like my relationship with my client? What reactions are being evoked in me as I work with this client?" By becoming personally invested in the therapeutic process, students can use their training program as a real opportunity for expanding their own awareness.

It is important for teachers and supervisors to clarify the fine line between training and therapy in the same way that fieldwork agencies must maintain the distinction between training and service. Although these areas overlap, it is clear that the emphasis for students should be on training in both academic and clinical settings, and it is the educator's and supervisor's responsibility to maintain that emphasis. The informed consent process is especially important in cases where the instructor also functions in the role of the facilitator of a group experience. We discuss this topic at greater length in Chapters 7, 8, and 9.

Holzman, Searight, and Hughes (1996) conducted a survey to investigate the experience of personal therapy among clinical psychology graduate students. Nearly 75% of the respondents reported receiving personal therapy at some point in their lives, most during graduate school. Of those who had been in therapy prior to or during graduate school, 99% reported that they were still in therapy or would consider getting involved in therapy again. Among those receiving therapy, the average length of treatment was 1.5 years. Generally, they saw their experience in personal therapy as being positive, and they viewed this experience as important for practicing as a therapist. The students in this study entered personal therapy for a variety of reasons. Personal growth was endorsed by more than 70% of respondents as one reason for seeking therapy. Other reasons included desiring to improve as a therapist (65%), adjusting to a life transition or a developmental issue (56%), and dealing with depression (38%). The vast majority of the sample entered treatment voluntarily rather than meeting a requirement of their graduate program. These graduate students viewed therapy as something more than a way to deal with distress in their lives. They perceived their therapy as providing them with valuable experiential learning that complemented their education and supervision as clinical psychologists.

This study sheds a positive light on the degree to which many graduate students want therapy for personal enrichment and as a source of training. It challenges counselor education programs to work with therapy providers outside the program to offer psychological services to graduate students in their programs. Because of the ethical problems of counselor educators and supervisors providing therapy for their students and supervisees, faculty members have an obligation to become advocates for their students by identifying therapeutic resources students can afford. There are both practical and ethical reasons to prefer professionals external to a program (who are not part of a program and who do not have any evaluative role in the program) when providing psychological services for students. Practitioners from the community could be hired by a counselor-training program to conduct therapeutic groups, or students might take advantage of either individual or group counseling from a community agency, a college counseling center, or a private practitioner.

One of the reviewers of this book commented on this issue as it pertains to school counselors, estimating that fewer than 50% of the students in his program have experienced personal therapy. At the same time, he asserts that many school counselors are faced with the stresses of providing services to students, families, and staff in numbers that would burden a mental health clinic.

We think counselor educators go too far in the direction of protecting the rights of counselor trainees in those instances where they refuse to require any form of self-exploratory experience as part of their program lest it invade the privacy of students. It is important to protect students' rights to privacy, but we are also very concerned about protecting the public. One way to ensure that the consumer will get the best help available is to prepare students both academically and personally for the challenges they will face when they become practitioners.

If graduate training programs require some form of personal therapy, there should be a focus to this endeavor. Exploring potential areas of countertransference is an excellent focus, yet it is still the student's task to identify aspects of his or her life for discussion in therapeutic sessions. A follow-up paper could be most useful to students in conceptualizing the meaning of their therapeutic experience and providing them with an avenue to integrate what they learned about themselves and how they can more effectively use themselves in their professional work. This process could lead to a reduction of potential unethical behavior in a student's professional life. It is essential, however, that the contents of this personal paper not be used as part of the basis to retain or dismiss students from a training program.

The ethics codes of some professional organizations caution against requiring personal therapy for trainees or converting supervision sessions into therapy sessions for supervisees. The codes emphasize the right of students and trainees to make informed decisions about disclosing personal matters. For example, both the ACA and the APA state that mixing personal counseling with education, training, and supervision constitutes what is known as a dual or multiple relationship. This may raise ethical issues if the counselor educator is required to evaluate the student. In the section dealing with teaching, training, and supervision, the ACA (1995) provides this guideline:

> If students or supervisees request counseling, supervisors or counselor educators provide them with acceptable referrals. Supervisors or counselor educators do not serve as counselors to students or supervisees over whom they hold administrative, teaching, or evaluative roles unless this is a brief role associated with a training experience. (F.3.c.)

Although it is not appropriate for supervisors to function as therapists for their supervisees, good supervision is therapeutic in the sense that the supervisory process involves dealing with the supervisee's personal limitations, blind spots, and impairments so that clients are not harmed. Working with difficult clients or dealing with resistance tends to affect trainees in personal ways. Certainly, it is a challenge for both trainees and experienced therapists to recognize and deal with transference in effective therapeutic ways. Countertransference issues can work either in favor of or against the establishment of effective client-therapist relationships. A study by Sumerel and Borders (1996) indicates that supervisors who are open to discussing personal issues with supervisees in an appropriate manner do not necessarily affect the supervisor-supervisee relationship negatively.

We believe it is appropriate for supervisors to encourage their supervisees to consider personal therapy with another professional as a route to becoming more effective both personally and professionally. Therapists need training that opens them up to themselves and teaches them about vulnerability, discipline, and freedom in their professional training.

A more detailed exploration of the multiple roles and responsibilities of supervisors, along with ethical issues in combining therapy with supervision, is included in Chapter 9. At this point, ask yourself these questions:

- What kind of self-exploration have I engaged in prior to or during my training?
- How open am I to looking at personal characteristics that could be either strengths or limitations as a counselor?
- What am I willing to do to work through personal problems I have at this time?

◆ **The case of a required personal-growth group.** Miranda is a psychologist in private practice who is hired by the director of a graduate program in counseling psychology. She assumes that the students have been informed that they will be required to attend her personal-growth class, and she is given the impression that the students are eagerly looking forward to it. When she encounters the students at the first class, however, she meets with resistance. They express resentment that they were not told that they would be expected to participate in a personal-growth group, and they say they have not really given their consent. They are attending out of fear that there will be negative consequences if they do not.

- If you were a student in this program, what might your reactions have been?
- Is it ever ethical to mandate self-exploration experiences?
- If you were the director of the program, how might you handle the situation?

- The students knew from their orientation and the university's literature that this graduate program included some form of self-exploration. Was this disclosure sufficient for ethical purposes?
- If you were Miranda, what would you do in this situation? How would you deal with the students' objections?

Ongoing Therapy for Practitioners

Experienced practitioners can profit from a program that will challenge them to reexamine their beliefs and behaviors, especially as these pertain to their effectiveness in working clients. Truly committed professionals engage in a lifelong self-examination as a means of remaining self-aware and genuine.

In a national survey of therapists as patients, Pope and Tabachnick (1994) found that of the 84% who had been in personal therapy only two individuals described it as unhelpful. Respondents mentioned three outcomes as the most beneficial aspects of therapy: self-awareness or self-understanding, self-esteem or self-confidence, and improved skills as a therapist. The problem areas most often mentioned as being addressed in personal therapy were depression or general unhappiness, marriage or divorce, relationship concerns, self-esteem and self-confidence, anxiety, career, academics, and family of origin. Of those who had terminated, 63% reported that they would consider resuming therapy. Although only 13% of the respondents had been required by their graduate programs to participate in personal therapy, a substantial majority (70%) believed that graduate programs in psychology should "probably" or "absolutely" require therapy for therapists in training. A smaller majority (54%) believed that state licensing boards "probably" should make personal therapy a requirement for licensure.

Some licensing boards require therapy as a way for practitioners to recognize and monitor their countertransference. We think this provides a rationale for psychotherapy for both trainees and practitioners. Guy and Liaboe (1986a) suggest that a periodic course of psychotherapy may improve therapists' personal relationships and general well-being. The negative consequences that conducting therapy can have on therapists' interpersonal functioning include decreased emotional investment in their families, a reduction in their circle of friends, a tendency to socialize less with friends, and a tendency to become aloof and emotionally distant with friends and family. Guy and Liaboe maintain that both professional organizations and licensing and certification boards are ethically obligated to take an active role in monitoring professionals in the field. Such bodies could encourage periodic supervision, consultation, or psychotherapy for practitioners. These measures can be instrumental in reducing or eliminating the potential negative consequences of practicing psychotherapy. Mahrer (2000) makes the case for mental health professionals to use psychotherapy "on oneself, for oneself, and by oneself":

> I find that there is almost always a huge hiatus between what most psychotherapists rely on and trust in their own personal lives and what they rely on and trust in their professional work with clients. It seems sensible that if therapists truly have

> faith in some of the methods they use in their professional work, they would use these methods on and for themselves in their personal lives. (p. 228)

◆ **The case of Daniel.** Daniel has a busy private practice. He is observed by a colleague sipping from a vodka bottle kept in his desk drawer. The colleague expresses her concern for him and the potential risks involved in his behavior. He reassures her that he never gets inebriated but that it helps him get through the day.

- Would you have a problem with Daniel's behavior?
- Does his assertion that "I never get inebriated" suffice to render the situation harmless?
- Is his method of stress reduction acceptable and ethical? Would you personally challenge Daniel to seek personal therapy to deal with his stress and his use of alcohol?
- As his colleague, what ethical obligation, if any, do you have to report the matter?

Therapists must be prepared to recognize and deal with their unresolved personal issues and their reactions to their clients. A high degree of self-awareness and a deep respect and concern for clients are safeguards. In the next section we explore ways in which transference and countertransference can facilitate or interfere with therapy.

Transference and Countertransference

Although the terms *transference* and *countertransference* are derived from psychoanalytic theory, they are universally applicable to counseling and psychotherapy and refer to the client's general reactions and orientation to the therapist and to the therapist's reactions in response (Gelso & Carter, 1985). Conceptualizing transference and countertransference broadly, Gelso and Carter assume that these processes are universal and that they occur, to varying degrees, in most relationships. The therapeutic relationship can intensify the natural reactions of both client and therapist, and how practitioners handle both their feelings and their clients' feelings will have a direct bearing on therapeutic outcomes. If these issues are not attended to, clients' progress will most likely be impeded. Therefore, this matter has implications from both an ethical and a clinical perspective.

Transference: The "Unreal" Relationship in Therapy

Transference is the process whereby clients project onto their therapists past feelings or attitudes they had toward significant people in their lives. Transference typically has its origins in early childhood and constitutes a repetition of past repressed material. Through this process, clients' unfinished business produces a distortion in the way they perceive and react to the therapist. The feelings clients experience in transference may include love, hate, anger, ambivalence, and dependency. The essential point is that these feelings are rooted in past relationships but are now directed toward the therapist. The potential effects of transference demonstrate why counselors must be aware of their personal reactions. If therapists are unaware of their own dynamics, they may miss important therapeutic issues instead of challenging their clients to understand and resolve the feelings they are bringing into the present from their past.

Transference is not a catch-all concept intended to explain every feeling clients express toward their therapists. If a client expresses anger toward you, it may be justified. If you have not been truly present for the client and have responded in a mechanical fashion, your client may be expressing legitimate disappointment. Similarly, if a client expresses affection toward you, these feelings may be genuine; dismissing them as infantile fantasies can be a way of putting distance between yourself and your client. Of course, most of us would be less likely to interpret positive feelings as distortions aimed at us in a symbolic fashion than we would negative feelings. But it is possible for therapists to err in either direction—being too quick to explain away negative feelings or too willing to accept whatever clients tell them, particularly when they are hearing how loving, wise, perceptive, or attractive they are. To understand the real import of clients' expressions of feelings, therapists will have to actively work at being open, vulnerable, and honest with themselves. Although ethical practice implies that therapists are aware of the possibility of transference, they also need to be aware of the danger of discounting the genuine reactions their clients have toward them.

We will now present a series of brief, open-ended cases in which we ask you to imagine yourself as the therapist. How do you think you would respond to each client? What are your own reactions?

◆ **The case of Shirley.** Your client, Shirley, seems extremely dependent on you for advice in making even minor decisions. It is clear that she does not trust herself and that she often tries to figure out what you might do in her place. She asks you personal questions about your marriage and your family life. Evidently, she has elevated you to the position of someone who always makes wise choices, and she is trying to emulate you in every way. At other times she tells you that her decisions typically turn out to be poor ones. Consequently, when faced with a decision, she vacillates and becomes filled with self-doubt. Although she says she realizes that you cannot give her the answers, she keeps asking you what you think about her decisions.

- How would you deal with Shirley's dependent behavior?
- How would you respond to her questions about your private life?
- If many of your clients expressed the same thoughts as Shirley, is there anything in your counseling style that you may need to examine?

◆ **The case of Marisa.** Marisa is disappointed in her counseling. She doesn't know if you really care about her. She wants to be more special to you, rather than "just another student on your caseload."

- How would you deal with Marisa's expectations?
- Is there a potential ethical issue in the manner in which you would respond to her?
- Would you be inclined to tell her how she affected you? Why or why not?

◆ **The case of Binh.** Binh treats you as an authority figure. He once said that you seem to judge him and that he is reluctant to say very much because you would consider much of what he said to be foolish. Although he has not confronted you directly since then, you sense some signs of hostility. On the surface, however, Binh seems to be trying very hard to please you by telling you what he thinks you want to hear. He seems convinced that you will react negatively and aggressively if he tells you what he really thinks.

- How would you respond to Binh?
- How might you deal with his indirect expressions of hostility?
- How might you encourage Binh to express his feelings and work through them?

Countertransference: Clinical Implications

So far we have focused on the transference feelings of clients toward their counselors, but counselors also have emotional reactions to their clients, some of which may involve their own projections. It is not possible to deal fully here with all the possible nuances of transference and countertransference. Instead, we will focus on improperly handling these reactions in the therapeutic relationship, a situation that directly pertains to ethical practice.

Countertransference can be considered, in the broad sense, as any projections by a therapist that can potentially get in the way of helping a client. For instance, counselor anxiety, the need to be perfect, the need to be a "parent" to a student, or the need to solve a client's problems might all be manifestations of countertransference. Ethically, therapists are expected to deal with these reactions in some form of supervision or consultation so that "their problem" does not become the client's problem. There are also deeper issues, some of which may be unconscious, that evoke strong reactions to the client. It may be helpful to consider the countertransference material being stirred up as a way of interpreting subtle messages from the client. The client might actually want an "aloof therapist" because of a fear that more difficult material would surface if the therapist were more approachable. If a therapist becomes frustrated with a client, it could be that this client, because of anxiety, wants progress to stop.

Countertransference can be either a constructive or a destructive element in the therapeutic relationship. A therapist's countertransference can illuminate some significant dynamics of a client. A client may actually be stimulating reactions in a therapist by the ways in which he or she makes the therapist into a key figure from the past. The fact that the client may have stimulated the countertransference in the therapist does not make this the client's problem. The key here is how the therapist responds. The therapist who recognizes these patterns can eventually help the client change old dysfunctional themes. Destructive countertransference occurs when a counselor's own needs or unresolved personal conflicts become entangled in the therapeutic relationship, obstructing or destroying a sense of objectivity. In this way, countertransference becomes an ethical issue, as is illustrated in the case that follows.

◆ **The case of Lucia.** Lucia is a Latina counselor who has been seeing Thelma, who is also a Latina. Thelma's presenting problem was her depression related to an unhappy marriage. Her husband, an alcoholic, refuses to come to counseling with Thelma. She works full time in addition to caring for their three children and her husband. Lucia is aware that she is becoming increasingly irritated and impatient with her client's "passivity" and lack of willingness to take a strong stand with her husband. During one of the sessions, Lucia says to Thelma: "You are obviously depressed, yet you are not willing to take action to change your situation. You have been talking about your miserable marriage for several months and blaming your husband for how you feel. You keep saying the same things, and nothing changes. Your husband refuses to seek treatment for himself or to cooperate with your therapy, yet you are not doing anything to change your life for the better." Lucia says this in an annoyed and critical way. Thelma seems to be listening but does not respond. When Lucia reflects on this session she becomes aware that she has a tendency to be more impatient and harsh with female clients from her own culture, especially over the issue of passivity. She realizes that she has not invited Thelma to explore ways that her cultural background and socialization have influenced her decisions. In talking about this case with a supervisor, Lucia explores why she seems to be triggered by women like Thelma. She recognizes that she has a good deal of unfinished business with her mother, whom she experienced as extremely passive. She also admits to her supervisor that she stayed in an oppressive marriage for many years out of fear of taking action.

- If you were Lucia's supervisor, what would you most want to say to her?
- Both the therapist and the client share a similar cultural background; to what extent should that have been examined?
- If you were Lucia's supervisor, would you suggest self-disclosure as a way to help her client? What kind of therapist disclosure might be useful? Can you see any drawbacks to therapist self-disclosure in this situation?
- Because of Lucia's recognition of her countertransference with passive women, would you suggest that she refer Thelma to another professional? Why or why not?
- What reactions do you have to the manner in which Lucia dealt with Thelma? Could any of Lucia's confrontation be viewed as therapeutic? What would make her confrontation nontherapeutic?
- Are there any ways that Lucia's recognition of her own struggles with her mother and with her former husband could actually facilitate her work with women like Thelma?
- What are the main ethical dimensions in this case?

If you found yourself in a situation where your unresolved personal problems and countertransference reactions were interfering with your ability to work effectively with a particular client, what actions do you think you would take?

Commentary. Regardless of how self-aware and insightful counselors are, the demands of practicing therapy are great. The emotionally intense relationships therapists develop with a client can be expected to tap into their own unresolved conflicts. Because countertransference may be a form of identification with the client, the counselor can easily get lost in the client's world and be of little therapeutic value. In the case of Lucia, the ethical course of action would be for Lucia to involve herself in personal therapy to work through some of her unresolved issues. Supervision would enable her to monitor her reactions to certain behaviors of clients that remind her of aspects in herself that she despises. When counselors become overly concerned with meeting their own needs or pushing their own personal agendas, their behavior becomes unethical.

If countertransference is recognized by counselors, they can seek supervision and perhaps their own therapy if their countertransference is pervasive. Ethical practice requires that practitioners remain alert to their emotional reactions to their clients, that they attempt to understand such reactions, and that they do not meet their own needs at the expense of their clients' needs.

Countertransference: Ethical Implications

Countertransference can show itself in many ways. Each example in the following list presents an ethical issue because the therapist's effective work is obstructed by countertransference reactions:

1. *Being overprotective with a client* can reflect a therapist's deep fears. A counselor's unresolved conflicts can lead him or her to steer a client away from those areas that open up the therapist's painful material. Such counselors may treat some clients as fragile and infantile, softening their remarks and protecting these clients from experiencing pain and anxiety. This may thwart clients in their struggle. If clients are not challenged to deal with their conflicts, they are likely to avoid them.

- Are you aware of reacting to certain types of people in overprotective ways? If so, what might this behavior reveal about you?
- Do you find that you are able to allow others to experience their pain, or do you have a tendency to want to take their pain away quickly?

2. *Treating clients in benign ways* may stem from a counselor's fear of their anger. To guard against this anger, the counselor creates a bland counseling atmosphere. This tactic results in exchanges that are superficial. Watkins (1985) mentions the danger of losing therapeutic distance, with the result that the client-counselor interchange degenerates into either a friendly conversation or a general "rap session."

- Do you ever find yourself saying things to guard against another's anger?
- What might you say or do if you became aware that your exchanges with a client were primarily superficial?

3. *Rejecting a client* may be based on the therapist's perception of the client as needy and dependent. Instead of moving toward the client to protect him or her, the counselor may move away from the client. The counselor remains cool and aloof, stays distant and unknown, and does not let the client get too close (Watkins, 1985).

- Do you find yourself labeling a client as unmotivated?
- Do you find yourself wanting to create distance from certain types of people?
- What can you learn about yourself by looking at those people whom you are likely to reject?

4. *Needing constant reinforcement and approval* can be a reflection of countertransference. Just as clients may develop an excessive need to please their therapists to feel liked and valued, therapists may have an inordinate need to be reassured of their effectiveness. Many beginning practitioners expect instant results with their clients. When they do not see immediate positive results, they become discouraged and anxious. If a client is not getting better, they fear that the client will not like them. They engage in self-doubt and wonder about their therapeutic effectiveness.

- Do you need to have the approval of your clients? How willing are you to confront them even at the risk of being disliked?
- What is your style of confronting a client? Do you tend to confront certain kinds of clients more than others? What does this behavior tell you about yourself as a therapist?

5. *Seeing yourself in your clients* is another form of countertransference. This is not to say that feeling close to a client and identifying with that person's struggle is necessarily countertransference. However, beginning therapists often identify with a client's problems to the point that they lose their objectivity. They become so lost in a client's world that they are unable to distinguish their own feelings. Or they may tend to see traits in their clients that they dislike in themselves. Sometimes the particularly "difficult" client can function as a mirror for the counselor. There are many "difficult" clients, a few of whom exhibit extreme resistance, silence, lack of motivation, and annoying mannerisms. The behaviors counselors react to most strongly in these clients are often the very traits that they dislike in themselves. Thus, an overly demanding client who never seems satisfied with what his or her therapist is doing can be a reminder of the therapist's own demanding nature.

- Have you ever found yourself so much in sympathy with others that you could no longer be of help to them? What would you do if you felt this way about a client?
- From an awareness of your own dynamics, list some personal traits of clients that would be most likely to elicit overidentification on your part.

6. *Developing sexual or romantic feelings* toward a client exploits the vulnerable position of the client. Seductive behavior on the part of a client can easily lead to the adoption of a seductive style by the therapist, particularly if the therapist is unaware of his or her own dynamics and motivations. However, it is natural for therapists to be more attracted to some clients than to others, and these feelings do not necessarily mean that they cannot counsel these clients effectively. More important than the mere existence of such feelings is the manner in which therapists deal with them. Feelings of attraction can be recognized and even acknowledged without becoming the focus of the therapeutic relationship. The possibility that therapists' sexual feelings and needs might interfere with their work is one important reason therapists should experience their own therapy when starting to practice and should consult other professionals when they encounter difficulty due to their feelings toward certain clients. Besides being unethical and countertherapeutic, it is also illegal in many states to sexually act out with clients, a topic that we will discuss in detail in Chapter 7.

- What would you do if you experienced intense sexual feelings toward a client?
- How would you know whether your sexual attraction to a client was countertransference?

7. *Giving advice compulsively* can easily be encouraged by clients who seek immediate answers to ease their suffering. The opportunity to give advice places therapists in a superior, all-knowing position, and they may delude themselves into thinking that they do have answers for their clients. Some therapists experience impatience with their clients' struggles toward autonomous decision making. Such counselors may engage in excessive self-disclosure, especially by telling their clients how they have solved a particular problem for themselves. In doing so, the focus of therapy shifts from the client's struggle to the needs of the counselor. Even if a client has asked for advice, there is every reason to question whose needs are being served when a therapist falls into advice giving.

- Do you ever find yourself giving advice? What do you think you gain from it? In what ways might the advice you give to clients represent advice that you could give yourself?
- Are there any times when advice is warranted? If so, when?

8. *Desiring a social relationship with clients* may stem from countertransference, especially if it is acted on while therapy is taking place. Clients occasionally let their therapist know that they would like to develop a closer relationship than is possible in the limited environment of the office. They may, for instance, express a desire to get to know their therapist as "a regular person." Mixing personal and professional relationships often ends up souring the relationship and could lead to a lawsuit. This is a topic we will examine in Chapter 7. Ask yourself these questions:

- If I establish social relationships with certain clients, will I be as inclined to confront them in therapy as I would be otherwise?
- Will my own needs for preserving these friendships interfere with my therapeutic activities and defeat the purpose of therapy?
- Am I sensitive to being called a "cold professional," even though I may strive to be real and straightforward in the therapeutic situation?
- Why am I inclined to form friendships with clients? Does this practice serve my own or my clients' best interests?

Client Dependence

Clients have a right to expect that counseling will enable them to move toward increased change, autonomy, and interdependence. Certainly, a counselor who fosters clients' dependence rather than autonomy is thwarting their progress. Clients frequently experience a period of dependence on counseling or on their counselor. This temporary dependence is not necessarily a bad thing, nor does it take away from clients' autonomy. Some clients exaggerate the importance of being independent. They see the need to consult a professional as a sign of weakness. When these people do allow themselves to need others, their dependence does not necessarily mean that the therapist is unethical.

An ethical issue does arise, however, when counselors *encourage* dependence on the part of their clients. They may do so for any number of reasons. Counselor interns need clients, and sometimes they may keep clients coming to counseling longer than is necessary because they will look bad if they "lose" a client. Some therapists in private practice might fail to challenge clients who show up and pay regularly, even though they appear to be getting nowhere. Some therapists foster dependence in their clients in subtle ways out of a need to feel important. When clients insist on answers, these counselors may readily tell them what to do. Dependent clients can begin to view their therapists as all-knowing and all-wise; therapists who have a need to be perceived in this way may act in ways that will keep their clients immature and dependent.

DiVerde-Nushawg and Walls (1998) conducted a study of the use of pagers by clinicians and noted countertransference aspects of this practice related to promoting client dependence. Some clinicians believe they should be available to take all messages from their clients, and they have every voice mail or answering machine message paged to them, whether they are at home or in session with another client. This behavior may be based on a need to appear competent, to have solutions to every problem, and to be perceived as being in great demand. These therapists may be using their professional role as a way to avoid facing their own problems. DiVerde-Nushawg and Walls recommend that therapists develop a generalized pager policy that is consistent with their clinical theory so that they avoid acting out their countertransference. Misuse or overuse of pagers might reflect therapists' grandiosity of how essential they are to their clients' lives and to their cures:

> When clinicians consider themselves indispensable to their patients outside of sessions and communicate that indirectly through their pager protocols, not only does their self-importance become inflated, but they also become an emotional burden to the patients they are supposed to be helping. (p. 370)

In essence, practitioners who think they must be available 24 hours a day for any reason are probably communicating to their clients that they are not able to function on their own without therapist direction. There are ethical implications involved for therapists who implicitly or explicitly promote between-session phone calls even when clients are not in a crisis. This practice may be meeting the therapist's needs for self-importance more than the autonomy of the client.

Client dependence can be fostered in other ways as well. If therapists are inclined to offer quick solutions to a client's problems, they could be preventing his or her empowerment. With the growth of managed care in the United States as an alternative to traditional fee-for-service delivery systems, the client-counselor relationship is changing in many ways. In the relatively brief treatment and the restricted number of sessions allowed in most managed care plans, client dependence is often less of an issue than it might be with longer term therapy. However, even using short-term, problem-oriented therapy aimed at solutions, clients can still develop an unhealthy dependence on therapists.

Like many other ethical issues discussed here, encouraging dependence in clients is often not clear-cut in practice. To stimulate you to think of possible ways that you might foster dependence or independence in your clients, consider these illustrative cases.

◆ **The case of Marcia.** Marcia is single and ready to graduate from college. She tells you that she has ambivalent feelings about graduating because she feels that now she is expected to get a job and live on her own. This prospect frightens her, and she doesn't want to leave the security she has found as a college student. As she puts it, she doubts that she can "make it in the real world." Marcia doesn't trust her own decisions. When she does make choices, the results, in her eyes, are often disastrous. Her style is to plead with you to advise her whether she should date, apply for a job, leave home, go on to graduate school, and so forth. Typically, Marcia gets angry with you because you are not being directive enough. She feels that you have more knowledge than she does and should therefore give her more guidance. She says: "Why am I coming here if you won't tell me what to do? If I could make decent decisions on my own, I wouldn't need to come here in the first place!"

- How do you imagine you would feel if Marcia were your client?
- How might you respond to her continual prodding for answers?
- How do you imagine you would feel about her statements that you weren't doing your job and that you weren't being directive enough?
- What steps would you take to challenge her?

- In what ways do you think it would be possible for you to tie into her dependency needs and foster her dependence on you for direction instead of freeing her from you?
- If Marcia were covered under managed care, how might this affect how you would work with her?

◆ **The case of Eduardo.** Eduardo, a young counselor, encourages his clients to call him at home when they need to. He has a pager that often alerts him to messages when he is in sessions with clients. Eduardo expects himself to be on call at all times. He frequently lets sessions run overtime, lends money to clients when they are "down and out," devotes many more hours to his job than he is expected to, and is willing to take on a large caseload. He says that he lives for his work and that it gives him a sense of being a valuable person. The more he can do for people, the better he feels.

- How might his style of counseling either help or hinder a client?
- Do you see any potential ethical issues in the way Eduardo treats his clients?
- What are the potential consequences to clients who are interrupted during a session with Eduardo's pager beeping?
- In what ways could Eduardo's style be keeping his clients dependent on him?
- Can you identify with him in any ways? Do you see yourself as potentially needing your clients more than they need you?

Delaying Termination as a Form of Client Dependence

Most professional codes have guidelines that call for termination whenever further therapy will not bring significant gains, but some therapists have difficulty letting go of their clients. They run the risk of unethical practice because of either financial or emotional needs. Obviously, termination cannot be mandated by ethics codes alone; it rests on the honesty and the goodwill of the therapist. We agree with Kramer (1990) that, more than at any other phase of therapy, the ending demands that therapists examine and understand their own needs and feelings. Therapists are challenged to confront their own dependence and anxieties honestly. Kramer emphasizes the therapist's role in enabling clients to understand and accept the termination process: "A general philosophy that is respectful of patients and sees them as autonomous, proactive, and self-directive is essential if the therapist is to facilitate healthy, productive endings" (p. 3). In our view, the ultimate sign of an effective therapist is his or her ability to help clients reach a stage of autonomy, wherein they no longer need a therapist.

Most of the ethics codes of the various professions state that practitioners should terminate services to clients when such services are no longer required, when it becomes reasonably clear that clients are not benefiting from therapy, or when the agency or institution limits do not allow provision of further counseling services. Apply the general spirit of these codes to these questions:

- How would you determine when services are no longer required?
- What criteria would you use to determine whether your client is benefiting from the therapeutic relationship?
- What would you do if your client feels he or she is benefiting from therapy but you don't see any signs of progress?
- What would you do if you are convinced that your client is coming to you seeking friendship and not really for the purpose of changing?
- What are the ethical issues involved if your agency limits the number of sessions yet your client is clearly benefiting from counseling? What if termination is likely to result in harm to the client?

As a therapist, put yourself in each of the following two situations. Ask yourself what you would do, and why, if you were confronted with the problem described.

◆ **The case of Jesse.** After five sessions your client, Jesse, asks: "Do you think I'm making any progress toward solving my problems? Do I seem any different to you now than I did 5 weeks ago?" Before you give him your impressions, you ask him to answer his own questions. He replies: "Well, I'm not sure whether coming here is doing that much good or not. I suppose I expected resolutions to my problems before now, but I still feel anxious and depressed much of the time. It feels good to come here, and I usually continue thinking about what we discussed after our sessions, but I'm not coming any closer to decisions. Sometimes I feel certain this is helping me, and at other times I wonder whether I'm just fooling myself."

- What criteria can you employ to help you and your client assess the value of counseling for him?
- Does the fact that Jesse continues to think about his session during the rest of the week show that he is probably getting something from counseling? Why or why not?

◆ **The case of Enjolie.** Enjolie has been coming regularly to counseling for some time. When you ask her what she thinks she is getting from the counseling, she answers: "This is really helping. I like to talk and have somebody listen to me. I often feel like you are the only friend I have and the only one who really cares about me. I suppose I really don't do that much outside, and I know I'm not changing that much, but I feel good when I'm here."

- Is it ethical to continue the counseling if Enjolie's main goal is the "purchase of friendship"? Why or why not?
- Would it be ethical to terminate Enjolie's therapy without exploring her need to see you?
- If you thought Enjolie was using her relationship with you to remain secure and dependent but that she believed that she was benefiting from the relationship, what might you do? How do you imagine you would feel if you continued to see Enjolie even though you were convinced that she wasn't changing?

Manipulation Versus Collaboration

Psychotherapy is a process that teaches people how to be honest with themselves; therefore it is of the utmost importance for therapists to be honest with their clients. Unfortunately, there are many ways for therapists to deceive or manipulate clients, often under the guise of being helpful and concerned. Therapists who have plans for what they want their clients to do or be and who keep these plans hidden can be considered manipulative. Other therapists may attempt to control their relationships with their clients by keeping therapy a mysterious process and maintaining a "therapist as expert" stance that excludes the client as a partner.

To offset the danger of manipulating clients toward ends that they have not chosen, clients can be given an active role in deciding what happens to them in the therapeutic relationship. Some therapists use a contract containing specific goals and the criteria for evaluating when these goals have been met. Proponents say that a contract emphasizes the partnership of client and therapist.

Sidney Jourard (1968) contrasts manipulation with dialogue. He sees psychotherapy as "an invitation to authenticity" in which the therapist's role is to be an exemplar. Therapists can foster their clients' honesty and invite them to drop their pretenses only by dropping their own defenses and meeting their clients in an honest manner. According to Jourard, "the psychotherapist is the teacher in the therapeutic dance, and the patient follows the leader" (pp. 64–65). One of the best ways for therapists to demonstrate their goodwill is by avoiding manipulation and being open, trusting, and vulnerable to their clients. If counselors manipulate their clients, they can expect manipulation in return; if they are open, however, their clients may be open as well. As Jourard says:

> If I want [a client] to be maximally open, but I keep myself fully closed off, peeking at him through chinks in my own armor, trying to manipulate him from a distance, then in due time he will discover that I am not in that same mode; and he will then put his armor back on and peer at me through chinks in it, and he will try to manipulate me. (p. 641)

Manipulation can work in subtle ways. Consider the degree to which you think the behavior of the therapist in the following example is manipulative and unethical.

◆ **The case of Gwendolyn.** Among Clyde's patients is Gwendolyn, a middle-aged widow. She has been seeing him for one year on a regular basis because of her loneliness and depression. Much of the dialogue of the sessions is now social in nature. Gwendolyn continually tells Clyde how much she enjoys the sessions and how meaningful they are to her. She has connections with a professional sports franchise and has been able to obtain choice tickets for him. At times he lets it be known when he needs tickets for specific events.

- Is it unethical for Clyde to continue to see Gwendolyn when the sessions are primarily social?

- Is it ethical to ask for and to accept the tickets? Why or why not?
- Could this arrangement be construed as a manipulation of the therapeutic relationship? Explain.
- Would mere enjoyment of the sessions on Gwendolyn's part warrant the continuation of therapy?

Stress in the Counseling Profession

Warning: Bumpy Road

Counseling can be a hazardous profession, and its stresses stem from the nature of the work, from the professional role expectations of counselors, and from the individual dynamics of the practitioner. Mental health practitioners are typically not given enough warning about the hazards of the profession they are about to enter. Radeke and Mahoney (2000) offer some sound advice: "Persons considering a career in psychotherapy should be informed that it will be likely to result in changes in their personal lives. Their development may be accelerated, their emotional life may be amplified, and they are likely to feel both stressed and satisfied by their work" (p. 82).

Many counselors in training look forward to a profession in which they can help others and, in return, feel a deep sense of self-satisfaction. They are not told that the commitment to self-exploration and to inspiring this search in clients is fraught with difficulties. Effective practitioners use their own life experiences and personal reactions to help them understand their clients and as a method of working with them. As you will recall, the process of working therapeutically with people opens up personal themes in the therapist's life. The counselor, as a partner in the therapeutic journey, can be deeply affected by a client's pain. The activation of painful memories resonates with the practitioner's own life experiences. Unfinished business is stirred up, and old wounds are opened. In short, pain connects with pain. If these countertransference issues are not recognized, they can have ethical and painful implications for the therapist. Clinicians overburdened with stress cannot work effectively.

Many of the stressful client behaviors we will discuss in this section could easily be understood as countertransference issues of the therapist. When therapists assume full responsibility for their clients' lack of progress, for instance, they are not helping clients to be responsible for their own therapy. Therapists should explore this situation with their clients. In this exploration they may discover together how assuming too much responsibility actually is a barrier to client empowerment.

Practitioners who have a tendency to readily accept full responsibility for their clients often experience their clients' stress as their own. It is important to recognize when this is happening. Some signs to look for are irritability and emotional exhaustion, feelings of isolation, abuse of alcohol or drugs, reduced personal effectiveness, indecisiveness, compulsive work patterns, and drastic changes in behavior. To assess the impact of stress on you both personally and

Most Stressful Client Behaviors for Therapists

Deutsch's Findings

1. Suicidal statements
2. Anger toward the therapist
3. Severely depressed clients
4. Apathy or lack of motivation
5. Client's premature termination

Farber's Findings

1. Suicidal statements
2. Aggression and hostility
3. Premature termination
4. Agitated anxiety
5. Apathy and depression

professionally, answer these questions posed by Bennett, Bryant, VandenBos, and Greenwood (1990):

- Do you ignore your problems out of fear?
- Have you learned techniques for managing stress, such as meditation, time management, and relaxation training?
- Are you able to take care of your personal needs?
- Are you aware of the signs and symptoms warning you that you are in trouble?
- Do you listen to your family, friends, and colleagues when they tell you that stress is getting the better of you?
- Do you consider seeking help when you notice you are exhibiting signs of stress?

Although it is not realistic to expect to eliminate the strains of daily life, you can develop practical strategies to recognize and cope with stress that is having adverse effects on you.

Sources of Stress

Deutsch (1984) and Farber (1983b) found surprisingly similar results in their surveys of therapists' perceptions of stressful client behavior (see the box titled Most Stressful Client Behaviors for Therapists). In both studies therapists reported that clients' suicidal statements were the most stressful. Other sources of stress that therapists reported in the Deutsch (1984) study included these:

- Being unable to help distressed clients feel better
- Seeing more than the usual number of clients
- Not liking clients
- Having self-doubts about the value of therapy
- Having professional conflicts with colleagues
- Feeling isolated from other professionals
- Overidentifying with clients and failing to balance empathy with appropriate professional behavior
- Being unable to leave client concerns behind when away from work
- Feeling sexual attraction to a client
- Not receiving expressions of gratitude from clients

Other writers have identified major sources of stress that frequently result in burnout. Kramen-Kahn and Hansen (1998) identify business aspects, economic uncertainty, professional conflicts, time pressures, sense of enormous responsibility, excessive workload, and caseload uncertainties as the most frequently endorsed occupational hazards of psychotherapists. According to Brown and O'Brien (1998), crisis intervention and other frontline mental health workers experience these sources of stress that often lead to burnout: lacking full involvement in the decision-making process related to work; feeling that their abilities are not being fully utilized on the job; being taxed by regulations, procedures, and paperwork; and being exposed to discomfort and dangers in their work setting. Sapienza and Bugental (2000) believe one of the main causes of burnout is the pressure of assuming the responsibility of solving the problems that clients bring to therapy. Lazarus (2000) views avarice and greed as the major stressors in a therapist's life. Striving to make more and more money often increases work-related pressures and emotional strain. Lazarus emphasizes how essential it is for professionals to replenish themselves. The challenge is to create a style of life that enables professionals to nourish themselves so that they can prevent distress and burnout.

Beside these sources of stress, we add the stresses associated with working in managed care and educational systems. For mental health professionals who deal with managed care, pressures revolve around getting a client's treatment approved, justifying needed treatment, quickly alleviating a client's problem, dealing with paperwork, and the anxiety of being put in an ethical dilemma when clients are denied clinically necessary further treatment. For school counselors, there are the expectations of "fixing the kid's behavioral problem," as well as being available to support teachers and administrators in dealing with their frustrations.

A growing body of research suggests that many therapists experience negative effects with respect to their ability to relate meaningfully with family and friends (Guy & Liaboe, 1986a). More than half of the therapists in Farber's study (1983a, 1983b) reported that conducting therapy had decreased their emotional investment in their own families. In the area of friendships, some therapists reported that their work had hindered their ability to be genuine, spontaneous, and comfortable with friends (Farber, 1983b). Farber notes a trend for therapists to reduce their circle of friends and to socialize less during their career. One interpretation of these findings is that many therapists experience stress and negative consequences from their work.

Practitioners who set exceptionally high personal goals and those with perfectionistic strivings related to helping others often report a high level of stress. Skovholt (2001) writes about the hazards of practice and points out that people tend to seek out helpers only when they are unable to solve their own problems or when their problems become too large to handle. Those in the helping professions may experience demoralizing hopelessness when confronted with what may appear to be unsolvable problems.

Deutsch (1984) describes the three most stressful beliefs of helpers, all of which pertain to doing perfect work with clients:

- "I should always work at my peak level of enthusiasm and competence."
- "I must be able to cope with any client emergency that arises."
- "I have to help every client."

Here are some other irrational beliefs that may lead to stress:

- "When a client does not make progress, it is my fault."
- "I should not take time off from work when I know a particular client needs me."
- "My job is my life."
- "I am expected to be a model of mental health."
- "I need to be 'on call' at all times."
- "A client's needs always come before my own."
- "I am the most important person in my client's life."
- "I am responsible for my client's behavior."
- "I have the power to control my client's life."

It is interesting to note that these stress-inducing beliefs are all related to the basic reasons many people choose the helping professions. Therapists need to be needed, to feel important, to have an impact on the lives of others, to have the power to influence others, and to be significant. When practitioners are able to do these things successfully, they are likely to feel that they are making a significant difference in the lives of their clients. When they feel that they are not making a difference and are not reaching clients, the effects can be negative in a dramatic fashion.

Deutsch (1984) makes the point that therapists' cognitions provide clues to the experience of stress. Beliefs that create stress are those that goad the counselor to constantly produce at maximum levels, a pace that eventually leads to burnout. When therapists do not live up to unrealistically high levels of performance, they often experience frustration. When they fall short of their own idealized expectations, they view the slow progress in their clients as evidence of their failure and lack of competence. The underlying assumption that creates stress is this: "If I do not live up to my high expectations, I am personally incompetent and inadequate." From this vantage point, the crucial factor in therapists' experience of stress is not difficult client behaviors but the beliefs therapists hold about their own role in helping others. If therapists assume that they are completely responsible for the success or failure of therapy, they are burdening themselves needlessly and creating their own stress. They are showing strong co-dependent behavior, and, as we have said previously, depriving their clients of their rightful share of responsibility for what they choose to do with their lives. The ethical question is, "To what degree does a therapist's behavior resulting from stress have negative implications for a client's progress?"

Counselor Impairment

Burnout and impairment are related in that burnout, unless it is recognized and effectively dealt with, often results in impairment. Maslach and Leiter (1997) define burnout thusly: "Burnout is the index of the dislocation between what people are and what they have to do. It represents an erosion in values, dignity, spirit, and will—an erosion of the human soul" (p. 17). Impairment is the presence of an illness or severe psychological depletion that is likely to block a professional from being able to deliver effective services and results in consistently functioning below acceptable practice standards. A number of factors can negatively influence a counselor's effectiveness, both personally and professionally, including substance abuse, physical illness, and burnout. Impaired counselors are unable to effectively cope with stressful events, and they are also unable to adequately carry out their professional duties. Those therapists whose inner conflicts are consistently activated by client material may respond by trying to stabilize themselves rather than facilitating the growth of their clients.

Clearly, impaired counselors are not helping their clients. For example, the sexually exploitive behavior of counselors is often a manifestation of impairment (Emerson & Markos, 1996). Counselors who become sexually involved with clients often show these personality characteristics:

- Fragile self-esteem
- Difficulty establishing intimacy in their personal life
- Professional isolation
- A need to rescue clients
- A need for reassurance about one's attractiveness
- Substance abuse of some kind

Benningfield (1994) identifies other personal characteristics associated with impaired functioning. These signs include lack of empathy, loneliness, poor social skills, social isolation, discounting the possibility of harm to others, preoccupation with personal needs, justification of behavior, and denial of professional responsibility to clients and students. Because a common characteristic of impairment is denial, Herlihy (1996) points out that professional colleagues may need to confront the irresponsible behavior of an impaired counselor. Herlihy suggests confronting the impaired counselor with sensitivity and respect. Benningfield maintains that the responsibility for addressing the assessment, remediation, and prevention of professional impairment lies not just with the impaired practitioner, ethics committees, or licensing boards but also with colleagues. Although most therapists know that supervision, consultation, and therapy are useful resources for dealing with personal problems, they may be hesitant to actually make use of these resources without the challenge from and encouragement of colleagues.

Colleagues can play a critical role in helping impaired practitioners recognize their condition and take remedial action. However, as Benningfield (1994) points out, all therapists have an ethical responsibility to themselves, to their

Ethics Codes on Professional Impairment

The codes of ethics for marriage and family therapists, social workers, psychologists, and counselors address practitioner impairment and provide guidance for practitioners whose unresolved personal problems intrude into their professional work. Here are four examples:

> Marriage and family therapists seek appropriate professional assistance for their personal problems or conflicts that may impair work performance or clinical judgment. (AAMFT, 2001, 3.3)
>
> Social workers whose personal problems, psychosocial distress, legal problems, substance abuse, or mental health difficulties interfere with their professional judgment and performance should immediately seek consultation and take appropriate remedial action by seeking professional help, making adjustments in workload, terminating practice, or taking any other steps necessary to protect clients and others. (NASW, 1999, 4.05.b.)
>
> When psychologists become aware of personal problems that may interfere with their performing work-related duties adequately, they take appropriate measures, such as obtaining professional consultation or assistance, and determine whether they should limit, suspend, or terminate their work-related duties. (APA, 1992, 1.13.c.)
>
> Counselors refrain from offering or accepting professional services when their physical, mental, or emotional problems are likely to harm a client or others. They are alert to the signs of impairment, seek assistance for problems, and, if necessary, limit, suspend, or terminate their professional responsibilities. (ACA, 1995, C.2.g.)

clients and students, and to their colleagues to monitor their own professional practice (see box titled Ethics Codes on Professional Impairment). She suggests that therapists should engage in an ongoing process of self-assessment as a way to increase their awareness of problematic attitudinal and behavioral patterns that may lead to serious impairment. Here are some of the questions Benningfield offers for this self-assessment:

- Is my personal life satisfying and rewarding? Are my relationships what I want them to be?
- To what degree am I taking care of myself, both physically and emotionally?
- Would I be willing for other therapists I respect to know about my professional conduct and decisions? Am I willing to express my vulnerabilities through consultation or peer supervision?
- Can I acknowledge and disclose my mistakes? Am I willing to acknowledge my limitations in my professional roles?
- Am I generally consistent in my practice?
- Do I think or fantasize about a relationship that goes beyond being a professional with some clients or students? Do I talk about subjects in therapy that are not related to clients' concerns?

In their investigation of psychologists' ethical beliefs about burnout and continued professional practice, Skorupa and Agresti (1993) found that psychologists perceive burnout to be a form of impairment. They also found that psychologists who believe it is unethical to practice while impaired tend to see fewer clients per week and have greater knowledge about burnout prevention strategies than those who do not hold this belief as strongly. The investigators suggested several implications for practitioners. First, graduate training programs should include a course on burnout and prevention strategies. Second, practitioners need to monitor their professional practices, especially the number of client contact hours per week, as these may be related to burnout. Continuing education can be especially useful in learning self-monitoring. Third, counselors who work in mental health agencies and schools may be at greater risk for burnout than are private practitioners, and they may need to take special precautions to avoid burnout and impairment.

One of our reviewers observed that stress and burnout are occupational hazards in the school counseling context, which is focused on academics and teacher needs. Although school counselors have a multiplicity of demands on them, they often must function alone with little opportunity for their own supervision or for talking about how their work is affecting them personally. Time for a counselor's supervision is not built into the educational day.

According to Guy (1987), although there is a need for better identification of impaired therapists and more effective remedial programs, there is an even greater need to prevent emotional distress and impairment *before* it results in professional incompetence:

> A proactive stance that attempts to address the causes of impairment would be far more effective and efficient than a reactive stance that focuses on the results of distress. Furthermore, such measures could prevent unnecessary patient harm and therapist suffering. (p. 232)

Some of the preventive steps Guy cites include continued education, personal therapy, periodic supervision, and peer interaction.

What is the profession doing to address the difficulties of distressed and impaired practitioners? Barnett and Hillard (2001) conducted a survey of all 59 state and provincial psychological associations (SPPAs) to examine the programs and resources available for impaired psychologists. Between 1998 and 1999, the findings of their survey indicated that 69% of all SPPAs (41 out of 59) reported that a colleague assistance program did not exist for distressed or impaired psychologists. Of these 41 SPPAs, 24% reported that they had a formal colleague assistance program available in the past. Some of the most common reasons given for discontinuing such a program included lack of use (70%), risk of liability too great (10%), and lack of volunteer support (10%). Furthermore, 61% of these 41 SPPAs reported that there were no plans to develop a program in the future, and 54% stated that a need for such resources was not perceived by the SPPA leadership. The authors of this survey indicate that the field of psychology has been slow to address issues of professional impairment, and they suggest that the profession of psychology may wish to emulate the lead of other healing professions that have effective means of preventing, identifying, and treating professional impairment. Barnett and Hillard write: "Having an established and effective assistance program model from which to conceptualize would help the field of psychology to develop effective colleague assistance programs, as well as refine those programs that are already in existence" (p. 209).

We encourage you to reflect on the sources of stress in your life. What patterns do you see? How effectively are you managing stress? Do you see ways that this stress could lead to burnout or impairment? What steps can you take to recognize danger signals before you become an impaired practitioner? What preventive measures are you willing to take? Are you open to periodic supervision? Would you ask for help from peers or colleagues? Would you seek personal therapy if you recognized you were not doing well? What kind of life do you have apart from your practice? Do you have a passion in your life for anything other than your work? By developing a method of self-assessment for danger signs leading to impairment, you are taking important steps toward preventing problems for both yourself and your clients.

Maintaining Vitality

Although burnout and the professional impairment associated with it have received much publicity from professional groups, many mental health practitioners are not adequately prepared to deal with the challenge of maintaining their vitality. Graduate training programs in the helping professions should prepare students for the disappointments they will encounter in the course of their training and in the jobs they eventually secure. Students can be prepared for both the joys and the pains of the profession they are choosing. Students need to learn about the rewards and frustrations of helping others. Also, it is good that they be informed about the hazards of this profession. If students are not adequately prepared, they may be especially vulnerable to early disenchantment and high rates of burnout due to unrealistic expectations. There is an ethical mandate for training programs to design strategies to prevent burnout and to teach students the importance of developing healthy attitudes.

We fully agree with Skovholt (2001), who develops the notion that sustaining the personal self is a serious ethical obligation: "Maintaining oneself personally is necessary to function effectively in a professional role. By itself, this idea can help those in the caring fields feel less selfish when meeting the needs of the self" (p. 146). For Skovholt, self-care involves searching for positive life experiences that lead to zest, peace, excitement, and happiness. The demands of professional work cannot be met if practitioners are not engaged in self-care.

It is useful to conceptualize counselor vitality from the perspective of wellness, and several models of wellness can be applied to counseling practitioners. In a study on well-functioning, Coster and Schwebel (1997) surveyed experienced professional psychologists who identified factors that contributed to their ability to function well. The dimensions that were most often mentioned included self-awareness and monitoring; support from peers, spouses, friends, mentors, and colleagues; values; and a balanced life that allowed time for family and friends, not just work.

Myers, Sweeney, and Witmer (2000) define wellness as "a way of life oriented toward optimal health and well-being in which body, mind, and spirit are integrated by the individual to live more fully within the human and natural community" (p. 252). Myers and colleagues borrow from the Adlerian perspective and identify five life tasks on their wheel of wellness that are a basic part of healthy functioning. As we look briefly at each of these components, consider how you might benefit from balancing these life tasks more effectively.

- *Spirituality* is an awareness of a being or force that goes beyond the material dimension and gives a deep sense of wholeness or connectedness to the universe. Do you have a definition of spirituality? How do you find it reflected in the way you live and work?
- *Self-direction* involves a sense of mindfulness and intentionality in meeting major life tasks. A sense of worth, a healthy sense of control, realistic beliefs, emotional awareness and coping, problem solving and creativity, a sense of humor, good nutrition, exercise, self-care, gender identity, and cultural identity are all part of self-direction. How do each of these components play out in your life? Is self-direction important to you? Identify some ways you feel in control of your life and some ways that you do not.
- *Work and leisure* provide a sense of accomplishment. List your weekly activities. Do you have a balance between work and leisure? When you consider your family of origin, what did you learn about the role of work and leisure in life?
- *Friendship* incorporates all of one's social relationships that involve a connection with others. Do you have the kind of friends that you want? Are your friendships nourishing to you? Do you have time in your life to reach out to others without remuneration? Are you ever not a therapist?
- *Love* involves long-term, intimate, trusting, compassionate, and mutually committed relationships. Do you have a love relationship in your life? To what degree does that relationship refurbish you emotionally?

Preventing yourself from becoming an impaired professional requires that you become committed to promoting your own wellness from a holistic perspective. Perhaps the most basic way to retain your vitality as a person and as a professional is to realize that you are not a bottomless pit and cannot give and give without replenishing yourself. How are you replenished? What life do you have away from your work? How much time do you devote to it? What are you passionate about in your life? Is it just your work? And finally, do you have a good support system?

Counselors, in practice as well as in training, often ignore the signs that they are becoming depleted. They may view themselves as having unlimited capacities to give, and at the same time they may not pay attention to taking care of their own needs for nurturing, recognition, and support. However, simply recognizing that you cannot be a universal giver without getting something in return is not enough to keep you alive as a person and a professional. In writing about self-care, Lazarus (2000) points to the importance of nourishing ourselves both physically and emotionally. He suggests asking yourself these fundamental questions:

- What fun things can I do?
- What positive emotions can I generate?
- What sensory experiences can I enjoy?
- What empowering and pleasant mental images can I conjure up?
- What positive self-talk can I employ?
- Which amiable people can I associate with?
- What specific health-related activities can I engage in?

Self-care is not a luxury, but an ethical mandate. You cannot provide nourishment to your clients if you don't nourish yourself. But Skovholt (2001) notes that those in the helping professions are experts at one-way caring, and he warns of the dangers involved in this practice. Those who spend most of their professional time in caring for others need to acquire the art of caring for self by nurturing the emotional self, the financial self, the humorous self, the loving self, the nutritious self, the physical self, the playful self, the priority-setting self, the recreational self, the relaxation–stress reduction self, the solitary self, and the spiritual or religious self.

It is essential to create an action plan and make a commitment to carry out this plan. Learning to cope with personal and professional sources of stress generally involves making some fundamental changes in your lifestyle. Unfortunately, counselors in training are often in a rush to obtain their degree or credential. They struggle to support a family financially and emotionally as well as take more classes than they can manage in a quality or responsible way. When wellness is not promoted during training, it is unlikely to occur in one's professional practice.

At this point, take some time to ask yourself what basic changes, if any, you are willing to make in your behavior to promote your own wellness. Remember, this is routinely the question you ask your clients.

Chapter Summary

One basic component in therapeutic practice is our own personality as an instrument of change. We may possess knowledge and technical skills yet still be ineffective in significantly reaching our clients if we do not keep our instruments finely tuned. The life experiences, attitudes, and caring that we bring to our practice are crucial factors in establishing an effective therapeutic relationship. If we are unwilling to engage in self-exploration, it is likely that our fears, resistances, personal conflicts, and personal needs will interfere with our ability to be present for our clients.

Personal therapy during training and throughout therapists' professional careers can increase the chances that counselors will be better able to focus on the welfare of their clients. Therapists are unable to take clients on any journey that they have not been on; therefore ongoing self-exploration is critical. By focusing on your own personal development, you will be better equipped to deal with the range of transference reactions your clients are bound to have toward you. You will also be better able to detect potential countertransference on your part and have a basis for dealing with such reactions in a therapeutic manner. There is a potential for unethical behavior in mismanaging countertransference, and you may find that you need to review your personal concerns periodically throughout your career. This honest self-appraisal is an essential quality of effective helpers.

Stress and the inevitable burnout that typically results from inadequately dealing with chronic sources of stress also raise ethical questions. Therapists who are psychologically and physically exhausted cannot be of real help to their clients. Counselors who have numbed themselves to their own pain are ill-equipped to deal with the pain of their clients. Impaired practitioners may do more harm than good for those who seek their assistance. There is no simple answer to the question of how to maintain your vitality, but you are challenged to find your own path to achieving wellness and to preventing burnout.

Suggested Activities

These activities and questions are designed to help you apply your learning. Many of them can profitably be done alone or with another person; others are designed for discussion either with the whole class or in small groups. We suggest that you select those that seem most significant to you and write on these issues in your journal.

1. In small groups in your class, explore your reasons for going into a helping profession. This is a basic issue, and it is one that many students have trouble putting into concrete words. What motivated you to seek this type of work? What do you think you can get for yourself? What do you see yourself as being able to do for others?
2. In your journal or in small groups, explore these questions: What personal needs of yours will be met by counseling others? To what degree might your personal needs get in the way of your work with clients? How can you recognize and meet your needs—which are a real part of you—without having them interfere with your work with others?
3. In small groups share your own concerns over becoming a counselor. What major problems do you expect to face as a beginning counselor? What can you learn about yourself from a discussion of your concerns?
4. This exercise deals with the fundamental question, "Who has a right to counsel anybody?" Form small groups of perhaps three persons, and take turns briefly stating the personal and professional qualities that you can offer people. Afterward, explore any self-doubts you have concerning your ethical right to counsel others.
5. What results would you look for when working with clients? How would you answer these questions: Is the counseling doing any good? Is my intervention helping my client make the changes he or she wants to make? How effective are my techniques?
6. Think of the type of client you might have the most difficulty working with. Then become this client in a role-playing fantasy with one other student.

Have your partner attempt to counsel you. After you have had a chance to be the client, change roles and become the counselor. Your partner then becomes the type of client you just role-played.

7. In small groups explore the issue of how willing you are to disclose yourself to your clients. Discuss the guidelines you would use to determine the appropriateness of self-disclosure. What are some areas you would feel hesitant about sharing? How valuable do you think it is to share yourself in a personal way with your clients? What are some of your fears or resistances about making yourself known to your clients?

8. In small groups discuss some possible causes of professional burnout and examine specific ways you would deal with this problem. After you have explored this issue in small groups, reconvene as a class and make a list of the causes and solutions that your groups have come up with.

Ethics in Action CD-ROM Exercises

9. In video role play #2, Big Brother, the client (Richard) reports that his sister is dating an Asian man. Richard is "pissed off" and says that he is not going to let that happen. He adds that his sister is not going to mess with his family like that. The counselor (Nadine) asks Richard if he thinks his sister should live to make him happy. He says, "My sister is going to do what I say and that's just it!"

This vignette shows how a counselor's own unfinished personal issues can get in the way of counseling an upset client. Explore the potential countertransference issues on the part of the counselor in this situation. What ethical issues involved in countertransference are not dealt with in an effective manner? How does this vignette illustrate the importance of counselor self-awareness? In class, reenact the role play by having several students take the role of counselor to show alternative perspectives.

InfoTrac® College Edition Resources

For additional readings, explore InfoTrac College Edition, our online library. Go to *http://www.infotrac.college.com/wadsworth* and make these key word searches:

countertransference
transference
counselor stress
counselor impairment
therap* impairment
mental AND health AND burnout

Key words are listed in a form that enables the search engine to locate a wider range of articles in the online university library. Key words should be entered exactly as shown, including asterisks, "Wl," "W2," "AND," and other search engine tools.

3

Pre-Chapter Self Inventory

Directions: For each statement, indicate the response that most closely identifies your beliefs and attitudes. Use the following code:

5 = I *strongly agree* with this statement.
4 = I *agree* with this statement.
3 = I am *undecided* about this statement.
2 = I *disagree* with this statement.
1 = I *strongly disagree* with this statement.

_____1. It is both possible and desirable for counselors to remain neutral and keep their values from influencing clients.

_____2. Counselors should influence clients to adopt values that in their opinion seem to be in the clients' best interests.

_____3. It is appropriate for counselors to express their values as long as they do not try to impose them on clients.

_____4. Counselors should challenge clients to make value judgments regarding their own behavior.

_____5. Before I can effectively counsel a person, I have to decide whether our life experiences and values are similar enough that I will be able to understand that person.

Values and the Helping Relationship

_____6. Clarifying values is a major part of the counseling process.
_____7. I would never try to influence my clients to consider my values.
_____8. I have a clear idea of what I value and where I acquired my values.
_____9. I tend to have difficulty with people who think differently from the way I do.
_____10. Ultimately, the choice of living or dying rests with my clients, and therefore I do not have the right to persuade them to make a different choice.
_____11. I have an ethical obligation to ask myself when I would have to refer a client because of a conflict in our values.
_____12. Sometimes it is ethical to impose my values on my clients, especially if I have their best interests at heart.
_____13. To be helpful to a client, a counselor must accept and approve of the client's values.
_____14. There are no fundamental conflicts between counseling and religion or spirituality; therefore it is possible to consider religious or spiritual concerns in a therapeutic relationship.
_____15. If a client complained of having no meaning in life, I would be inclined to introduce a discussion of spirituality or religion as one way to find purpose.

Introduction

The question of values permeates the therapeutic process. In this chapter we want to stimulate your thinking about your values and life experiences and the influence they will have on your counseling. We ask you to consider the possible impact of your values on your clients, the effect your clients' values will have on you, and the conflicts that may arise if you and your clients have different values.

Can therapists keep their values out of their counseling sessions? Richards, Rector, and Tjeltveit (1999) address this fundamental question by summarizing theoretical and research literature that discredits the notion that therapists can and should keep their values out of therapy. Research has shown that counselors' values influence every phase of the therapeutic process, including the theories of personality and therapeutic change, assessment strategies, therapy goals, identifying what client problems will be treated, choice of techniques, and evaluations of therapeutic outcomes. Clients are influenced by therapists' values and often adopt some of these values.

In our view it is neither possible nor desirable for counselors to be completely neutral in this respect. Although it is not the counselor's function to persuade clients to accept a certain value system, we do think it is crucial for counselors to be clear about their own values and how they influence their work with clients, perhaps even unconsciously.

Clarifying Your Values and Their Role in Your Work

When therapists expose their values, it is important that they clearly label them as their own. Then values can be discussed in an open and noncoercive way, which can assist clients in their exploration of their own values and the behavior that stems from these values. Clinicians may not agree with the values of their clients, but it is essential that they respect the rights of their clients to hold a different set of values. The way therapists deal with clients' values can raise ethical issues. Richards, Rector, and Tjeltveit (1999) do not think therapists should attempt to teach their clients specific moral rules and values because doing so violates clients' diversity and prevents clients from growing by making their own choices based on their values. Bergin (1991) writes, "It is vital to be open about values but not coercive, to be a competent professional and not a missionary for a particular belief, and at the same time to be honest enough to recognize how one's value commitments may not promote health" (p. 399). Bergin sees the core challenge as being able to use values to enhance the therapeutic process without abusing the therapist's power and exploiting the client's vulnerability:

> During treatment, therapists must make important decisions about how to enhance clients' functioning on the basis of professional values that are frequently implicit. At these decision points, therapist, client, and concerned others should collaborate in arriving at the goals toward which change is directed. (p. 396)

Not everyone who practices counseling or psychotherapy would agree with these views. At one extreme are counselors who have definite, absolute value systems. They believe their job is to exert influence on their clients to adopt the *proper* values. Such counselors would tend to direct their clients toward the attitudes and behaviors that *they* judge to be in their clients' best interests. At the other extreme are counselors who are so anxious to avoid influencing their clients that they make themselves invisible. They keep themselves and their values hidden so they will not contaminate their clients' process.

As a therapist you certainly have your own personal values, but the therapeutic environment imposes an equally strong value of avoiding a judgmental attitude. Holmes (1996) and Edwards and Bess (1998) clarify this concept of *therapeutic neutrality* in their writings. If you cannot accomplish this neutrality (objectivity), it is essential that you own this as your problem, rather than the client's. Inform your client of the areas in which you think you cannot be neutral. We hope that there would be very few instances in which you would tell clients you could not work with them because you do not agree with their value system. Your job is not to approve or disapprove of your clients' values but to help them explore and clarify their beliefs and apply their values to solving their own problems. The only exception to this would be values and behavior that violate the law.

We do not view counseling as a form of indoctrination, nor do we believe the therapist's function is to teach clients "proper" behavior. It is unfortunate that some well-intentioned mental health professionals believe their job is to help people conform to socially acceptable standards. It seems presumptuous to suppose that counselors know what is best for others. We agree with Holmes (1996) in his contention that "when psychotherapy becomes certain of itself or its values, it ceases to be psychotherapy and becomes something akin to a proselytizing religion" (p. 272). We question the implication that counselors have a greater wisdom than their clients and can prescribe ways of being happier. No doubt, teaching is a part of counseling, and clients do learn in both direct and indirect ways from the opinions and examples of their counselors, but counseling is not synonymous with preaching, persuasion, or instruction.

However, neither do we favor the opposite extreme of trying so hard to be "objective" that counselors keep their personal reactions and values hidden from clients. Counselors who adopt this style are not likely to do more than mechanical therapy. In our opinion, clients demand a lot more involvement from therapists than mere reflection and clarification. Clients want and need to know where their therapists stand so they can test their own thinking. We believe clients are helped by this kind of honest involvement.

Practitioners will inevitably incorporate certain value orientations into their therapeutic approaches and methods. Goals are usually based on values and beliefs, and clients may adopt goals that the therapist thinks are beneficial. But if clients change the direction of their values without being aware of what they are doing, they are being deprived of self-determination (Brace, 1997). It may be appropriate at times for the therapist to do more than merely watch clients make "bad decisions" without interference. Bergin (1991) asserts that it is irresponsible for a therapist to fail to inform clients about alternatives: "We need to be honest and open about our views, collaborate with the client in setting goals that fit his or her needs, then step aside and allow the person to exercise autonomy and face consequences" (p. 397).

Brace (1997) enumerates ten rules or ethical guidelines for counselors assisting clients in developing their own counseling goals: (1) examine goals before they are adopted to be sure these goals are in the best interest of the client; (2) ensure that goals are mutually consistent; (3) justify the pursuit of end goals and the means to attain these goals; (4) assess all causal and contributory factors that pertain to the goals; (5) inform the client of their values, especially if such values are likely to influence the client's choice of goals; (6) avoid or correct errors in clinical judgment; (7) assess the risks that the client's goals might pose to the client or to others; (8) consider how the client's goals may affect others; (9) avoid deceiving clients; (10) and honor any promises made to the client.

The following questions may help you to begin thinking about the role of your values in your work with clients:

- Some professionals consider it unethical to influence clients in specific value directions. An example is a counselor who would influence a client to stay married for the sake of the children. Do you think it is ever justified to influence a client's choice of values? If so, when and in what circumstances?
- Do you worry that openly discussing your values with certain clients might unduly influence their decision-making process?
- Is it possible for therapists to interact honestly with their clients without making value judgments? Is it desirable for therapists to avoid making such judgments?
- If you were convinced that your client was making a "self-destructive decision," would you express your concerns?
- Do you think the therapist is responsible for informing clients about a variety of value options?
- Are you impressed when your clients adopt your beliefs and values?
- Can you remain true to yourself and at the same time allow your clients the freedom to select their own values, even if they differ sharply from yours?
- How do you determine whether a conflict between your values and those of your client necessitates a referral to another professional?
- What specific values do you consider to be essential to the therapeutic process?
- How does honestly exposing your clients to your viewpoint differ from subtly "guiding" them to accept your values?
- To what degree do you need to have had life experiences that are similar to those of your clients? Is it possible that too much similarity in values and life experiences might result in therapy that is not challenging for the client? Might you think that you already know the client and therefore need to explore less?

Because your values will significantly affect your work with clients, it is incumbent on you to clarify your assumptions, core beliefs, and values and the ways in which they enter the therapeutic process. For example, counselors who have "liberal" values may find themselves working with clients who have more traditional values. If these clinicians privately scoff at conventional values, can they truly respect clients who do not think as they do? Or if counselors have a strong commitment to values that they rarely question, whether these values are conventional or unconventional, will they be inclined to promote these values at the expense of their clients' free exploration of attitudes and beliefs? If counselors rarely reexamine their own values, it is unlikely that they will provide a climate in which clients can reexamine their values.

From time to time your values may present some difficulty for you in your work with clients. In the following sections we examine some sample cases and issues that can help you clarify what you value and how your values might influence the goals of counseling and the interventions you make with your clients. As you read these examples, keep the following questions in mind:

- What is my position on this issue?
- Where did I develop my views?
- Are my values open to modification?
- Am I open to being challenged by others?
- Do I insist that things remain the same?
- Do I feel so deeply committed to any of my values that I am likely to want my clients to accept them? Am I closed to clients with a different set of values?
- When would I feel the need to disclose my values to my clients? Why?
- How can I communicate my values without imposing those values on clients?
- Do my actions reveal that I respect the principle of clients' self-determination that is consistent with their culture?
- How are my own values and beliefs reflected in the manner in which I help my clients set their goals?

The Ethics of Imposing Your Values on Clients

Counselors are cautioned to become aware of how their personal values influence their professional work. ACA's (1995) guideline reads, "Counselors are aware of their own values, attitudes, beliefs, and behaviors and how these apply in a diverse society, and avoid imposing their values on clients" (A.5.b.).

A national survey found a consensus among a representative group of mental health practitioners that basic values such as self-determination are important for clients to become mentally healthy and to guide and evaluate the course of psychotherapy (Jensen & Bergin, 1988). Other basic values include developing effective strategies for coping with stress; developing the ability to give and receive affection; increasing one's ability to be sensitive to the feelings of others; becoming able to practice self-control; having a sense of purpose for living; being open, honest, and genuine; finding satisfaction in one's work; having a sense of identity and self-worth; being skilled in interpersonal relationships; having deepened self-awareness and motivation for growth; and practicing good habits of physical health. These values were considered to be universal, and practitioners surveyed based their therapy on them.

It is now generally recognized that the therapeutic endeavor is a value-laden process and that all therapists, to some degree, communicate their values to clients (Richards & Bergin, 1997). There is an abundance of evidence that shows that therapy is not only value laden but that counselors and clients often have different value systems (Zinnbauer & Pargament, 2000). Some researchers have found evidence that clients tend to change in ways that are consistent with the values of their therapists, and clients often adopt the values of their counselors (Zinnbauer & Pargament, 2000). It will be difficult to avoid communicating your values to your clients, even if you do not explicitly share them. What you pay attention to during counseling sessions will direct what your clients choose to explore. The methods you use will provide them with clues to what you value.

Your nonverbal behavior and body language also give clients indications of how you are being affected. If clients feel a need to have your approval, they may respond to these cues by acting in ways that they imagine will meet with your favor. Suppose, for example, that an unhappily married man knew or surmised that you really thought he was wasting good years of his life in the marriage and he proceeded with a divorce mostly because of his perceptions of your beliefs. Although you may have decided not to coerce clients to believe and act in ways that agree with your own values, the subtle messages you project can be powerful influences on clients' behavior. For example, a school counselor may communicate her disapproval of a teacher who has frequent classroom management issues. A student who is referred to this counselor may believe that his or her version of classroom conflict is being supported by the counselor.

Value Conflicts: To Refer or Not to Refer

Some counselors believe they can work with any client or with any problem. They may be convinced that being professional means being able to assist anyone. Others are so unsure of their abilities that they are quick to refer anyone who makes them feel uncomfortable. Somewhere between these extremes are the cases in which your values and those of your client clash to such an extent that you question your ability to function in a helping way.

Yarhouse and VanOrman (1999) assert that value conflicts between clients and therapists are inevitable. The challenge for therapists is to recognize when their values clash with a client's values to the extent that they are not able to function effectively. Merely having a conflict of values does not necessarily require a referral; it is possible to work through such conflicts successfully. In fact, we think of a referral as the last resort. Before making a referral, explore your part of the difficulty through consultation. What barriers within you would prevent you from working with a client who has a different value system? Merely disagreeing with a client or not particularly liking what a client is proposing to do is not ethical grounds for a referral. We would hope that you recognize instances of such value conflicts and think about this question: "Why is it necessary that there be congruence between my value system and that of my client?"

If you have sought consultation and still feel that you are "stuck," you need to consider a referral. It is our belief that *how* the referral is done is crucial. Be sure the referral is explained in such a way that it is made clear to the client that it is your problem and not the client's. It can be very burdensome to clients to be saddled with your disclosure of not being able to get beyond value differences. Clients may interpret this as a personal rejection and suffer harm as a result. Consider the descriptive list of potential clients that follows and indicate whether you feel you could work with the client or would refer the client to someone else because of a conflict of value systems. Use the following code:

A = I *could* work with this person.
B = I *would have difficulty* working with this person.
C = I *could not* work with this person.

____ 1. A person with fundamentalist religious beliefs
____ 2. A woman who says that if she could only turn her life to Christ she would find peace
____ 3. A person who shows little development of a conscience, who is strictly interested in his or her own advancement, and who uses others to achieve personal aims
____ 4. A gay or lesbian couple hoping to work on conflicts in their relationship
____ 5. A man who wants to leave his wife and children for the sake of sexual adventures with other women to bring excitement to his life
____ 6. A woman who has decided to leave her husband and children to gain her independence but who wants to explore her fears of doing so
____ 7. A woman who wants an abortion but wants help in confirming her decision
____ 8 A teenager who is having unsafe sex and sees no problem with this behavior
____ 9. A high school student who is sent to you by his parents because they suspect he is abusing drugs
____ 10. A person who is very cerebral and is convinced that feelings are confusing and should be avoided
____ 11. A man who believes the only way to discipline his children is through corporal punishment
____ 12. An interracial couple coming for premarital counseling
____ 13. A high school student who seeks counseling to discuss conflicts she is having with her adopted parent from a different culture

___14. A high school student who thinks she may be lesbian and wants to explore this gender identification
___15. A single parent wanting to adopt a child
___16. A man who has found a way of cheating the system and getting more than his legal share of public assistance
___17. A woman who comes with her husband for couples counseling while maintaining an extramarital affair
___18. An interracial couple wanting to adopt a child and being faced with their respective parents' opposition to the adoption
___19. A client from another culture who has values very different from your own
___20. A mother who is intent on blaming the school for her son's behavior problems and constantly makes excuses for the child

Go back over the list, and pay particular attention to the items you marked "C." Why do you think you would have difficulty working with these people? In assessing the ethical ramifications of declining to work with certain clients, what are the potential risks and benefits of making a referral? If you decide not to make a referral, what are the possible risks and benefits to the client if you work with this person?

Case Studies of Possible Value Conflicts

In this section we present some case studies of possible value conflicts. Try to imagine yourself working with each of these clients. How do you think your values would affect your work with them?

◆ **The case of Candy.** Candy is a 14-year-old student who is sent to you because of her problematic behavior in the classroom. Her parents have recently divorced, and Candy is having difficulty coping with the breakup. Eventually, she tells you that she is having sexual relations with her boyfriend without using any form of birth control.

- What are your thoughts about Candy's sexual activity?
- If you sense that her behavior is an attempt to overcome her feelings of isolation, how might you deal with it?
- Would you try to persuade her to use birth control? Why or why not?
- Do you see any ethical and/or legal implications in the ways you responded to these questions?

You have been working with Candy for several sessions now, and she discovers that she is pregnant. Her boyfriend is 15 and declares that he is in no position to support her and a child. She has decided to have an abortion but feels anxious about following through with it. How would you respond? In the blanks put an "A" if you agree more than disagree with the statement, and put a "D" if you mainly disagree.

___ I would encourage Candy to follow her own judgment.

___ I would encourage Candy to consider other options, such as adoption, keeping the child as a single parent, marrying, and so on.

___ I would reassure Candy about having an abortion, telling her that thousands of women make this choice.

___ I would consult with a supervisor or a colleague about the possible legal implications in this case.

___ I would attempt to arrange for a family session, or at least a session with Candy and her parents, as a way to open communication on this issue.

___ I would encourage Candy to explore all the options and consequences of each of her choices.

___ I would inform Candy's parents, because I believe they have a right to be part of this decision-making process.

___ I would refer Candy to an outside agency or practitioner because her problems are too complex for counseling in a school setting.

___ I would pay particular attention to helping Candy clarify her value system; I would be sensitive to her religious and moral values and the possible implications of specific choices she might make.

___ I would refer Candy to another professional because of my opposition to abortion.

___ I would tell Candy that I am personally opposed to (or in favor of) abortion, that I want to remain her counselor during this difficult time, and that I will support whatever decision she makes for herself.

Commentary. Candy's case illustrates several complex problems. What do you do if you feel that you cannot be objective because of your views on abortion? Do you refer Candy to someone else? If you do, might she feel that you think less of her because of her decision? If you are firmly opposed to abortion, could you support Candy in her decision to go ahead with it? Would you try to persuade her to have the baby because of your views on abortion? Ask yourself what your goals in working with her would be. What are your values in a case such as hers?

One possible course of action would be to tell Candy about your values and how you feel they would influence your work with her. If you feel that you could not work effectively with her, explore your reasons for making this decision. Why is it crucial that her decision be compatible with your values? Do you necessarily have to approve of the decisions your clients make? Do you see a distinction between a counselor suggesting having or not having an abortion as opposed to helping a client make her decision on the matter?

When the subject of abortion arises, some women may be reluctant to consider this option, either because of their value system or because of feelings of guilt, shame, and fear. Other women may feel ambivalent and may want to explore all of their options. How would you react to not being allowed to explore abortion as one option for your client? Do you think it is unethical to fail to discuss all of a client's options if this is her desire?

◆ **The case of Paul.** Paul comes to an agency with many difficulties and anxieties, one of which is his antipathy toward interracial marriage. He expresses disappointment in his daughter and in himself as a father because of her engagement to a man of another race. Paul has gone as far as threatening to disinherit her if she marries this man. What this client does not know is that the social worker herself is in an interracial marriage. The therapist discloses this fact and lets him know of her difficulties with what she perceives as his prejudices.

- How do you react to her self-disclosure?
- Would a referral be in order? Why or why not?
- What are your values in this situation, and what might you do or say if you were the counselor?

Commentary. To Paul, the therapist might say, "I am willing to work with you on this problem. I have some personal insights and experience in this situation because I myself am in an interracial marriage. Knowing this, how would it be for you to work with me?"

Your views on racial issues can have an impact on your manner of counseling in certain situations. Think about what your responses to the following statements tell you about how your values might operate in cases pertaining to racial concerns. In the space, put an "A" if you agree more than you disagree with the statement, and put a "D" if you disagree more than you agree.

___ I could effectively counsel a person of a different race.
___ I would be inclined to refer a person of a different race to a counselor of that race because the client is bound to have more trust in a therapist of the same race.
___ My approach to counseling would entail modifying my practices and techniques in working with clients who are racially and culturally different.
___ Interracial marriages in this society are almost doomed to failure because of the extra pressures on them.
___ Interracial marriages pose no greater strain on a relationship than do interfaith marriages.
___ I have certain racial (cultural) prejudices that would affect my objectivity in working with clients of a different race (culture) from mine.

◆ **The case of Lupe.** Lupe is a social worker in a community mental health agency, which is sponsoring workshops aimed at preventing the spread of AIDS. The agency has attempted to involve the local churches in these workshops. One church withdrew its support because the workshops encouraged "safer" sexual practices, including the use of condoms, as a way of preventing AIDS. A church official contended that the use of condoms is contrary to church teachings. Being a member of this church, Lupe finds herself struggling with value conflicts. She believes the teachings of her church and thinks the official had a right to withdraw his support of these workshops. But she is also aware that many people in the community she serves are at high risk for contracting AIDS because of both drug usage and sexual practices. In an attempt to resolve this value conflict, Lupe seeks out several of her colleagues, each of whom responds differently:

Colleague A: I would encourage you to tell your clients and others in the community that you have value conflicts between agency practice and your religious beliefs and, for that reason, you are voluntarily resigning from the agency.

Colleague B: I hope you will be up front with the people you come in contact with by telling them of your values and providing them with adequate referrals so they can get information about prevention of this disease. But you do owe it to them not to steer them in the direction you think they should move.

Colleague C: I think it is best that you not disclose your values or let them know that you agree with the church's views. Instead, work toward changing their behavior and modifying their values directly. After all, in this case the end justifies the means.

Colleague D: More harm can come by your failure to provide necessary information. Even though your values are in sympathy with the church's position, ethically you owe it to the community to teach them methods of safe sex.

If Lupe were to seek you out and ask for your advice, consider what you might say to her. In formulating your position, answer these questions:

- Which of her colleagues comes closest to your thinking, and why?
- With which colleague do you find yourself disagreeing the most, and why?
- Would Lupe be ethical if she did not disclose her values to her clients? Why or why not?
- Given the gravity of this situation and the possibility of the spread of disease, is Lupe ethically bound to provide people who are at high risk with facts and information about prevention?
- What advice would you be inclined to give Lupe, and what does this response tell you about your values?

Shared Life Experiences and Values

To what degree do you share the view that you must have had life experiences similar to those of your clients? You can help people whose experiences, values, and problems are different from yours by tuning in to their feelings and relating them to your own. Counselors need not have experienced each of the struggles of their clients to be effective in working with them. When the counselor and the client connect at a certain level, cultural and age differences can be transcended. Consider for a moment whether you can communicate effectively with

- an elderly person.
- a person of a different racial, ethnic, or cultural group.
- a person with a disability.
- a delinquent or a criminal.
- a person who is abusing alcohol or drugs.

It is possible for a relatively young counselor to work effectively with an elderly client. For example, the client may be experiencing feelings of loss, guilt, sadness, and hopelessness. The young counselor can empathize with these feelings even though the counselor's experiences that resulted in some of these same feelings were quite different. It is essential, however, that the counselor be sensitive to the differences in their backgrounds, a subject we examine in Chapter 4.

To facilitate your reflection on whether you need to have life experiences or a value system similar to that of your client, assess what factors in your life would either help or hinder you in establishing a good working relationship with the client described in each of the following cases.

◆ **The case of Imelda.** Imelda is a 60-year-old teacher who is thinking about going to law school because it is something she has wanted to do for a long time. She has taught government and history in community colleges for 30 years, and now she wants to retire early to take up a new profession. Imelda wonders whether she has the stamina to endure long hours of study, and she is asking herself whether leaving teaching at this stage in life would be a wise move.

- What experiences have you had that could help you understand Imelda's desires and conflict?
- How do you respond to a person beginning law school at the age of 60?
- Would you be inclined to encourage Imelda to take a risk, or would you favor her staying with a secure job in her situation?
- How might your answers to the preceding questions affect the way you would counsel her, or how might they indicate your bias?

◆ **The case of Alberto.** Alberto, a Latino client, comes to a community college counseling center on the recommendation of one of his friends. His presenting problem is depression, chronic sleep disturbance, and the imminent threat of failing his classes. During the initial session you are aware that he is extremely guarded. As a counselor, you may assume that self-disclosure and openness to feelings enhance life. Alberto discloses little about himself or how he is feeling. Although he will answer your questions briefly, you sense that he is withholding much information from you.

- How sensitive are you to your client's sense of privacy? Have you considered that keeping one's thoughts and feelings to oneself might be valued in certain cultures?
- Assume that over time Alberto becomes more self-disclosing and expressive, not only with you but also within his environment. What are the pros and cons of that?
- Is it ethical to encourage Alberto to be more self-disclosing without first understanding the cultural context? Explain.
- How might your intervention reflect your lack of understanding of the importance of the extended family in certain cultures?

- Can you think of some reasons why Alberto's cautiousness may be more adaptive than maladaptive?

◆ **The case of Sylvia.** At a community clinic Sylvia, who is 38, tells you that she is an alcoholic. During the intake interview she says, "I feel so much remorse because I've tried to stop my drinking and haven't succeeded. I am fine for a while, and then I begin to think that I have to be a 'perfect' wife and mother. I see all the ways in which I do not measure up—how I let my kids down, the many mistakes I've made with them, the embarrassment I've caused my husband—and then I get so down I feel compelled to drink. I know that what I am doing is self-destructive, but I haven't been able to stop."

- What experiences have you had with alcoholism or its treatment?
- Do you see Sylvia as having a disease? as suffering from a lack of willpower? as an irresponsible, indulgent person?
- Does the fact that Sylvia is a woman affect your view of her problem?
- Would you encourage Sylvia to attend Alcoholics Anonymous?
- Is it ethical to treat Sylvia's psychological problems without first attending to her addiction problem?

◆ **The case of Jan.** Jan is a physicist, born and educated in northern Europe. Jan's lifestyle and interests center on intellectual pursuits, and he tends to show very little affect in most situations. His wife is having an affair, and he seeks your counsel, not so much on his own initiative but because of the encouragement of colleagues who think he can use some guidance. He talks calmly about the potential breakup of his family and indicates that he has discussed the matter with his wife. In essence, he has asked her to decide the outcome. Jan is in your office to find a logical explanation for why the affair occurred. He does not display any strong emotional reactions to the situation. He gives no clues to how he is feeling about it.

- Would you consider Jan's cultural and educational background in dealing with his reaction to his situation?
- Would you immediately pursue the expression of feeling? Can you see yourself challenging Jan for intellectualizing? Why or why not?

Commentary. This example illustrates another type of cultural difference. Although we do not deny the value of expressing emotional reactions to a situation such as Jan's, we would be especially sensitive to his cultural background and his conditioning. In certain cultures openly admitting having been affected by a situation such as this is equivalent to a loss of face or pride. Jan might never show the degree of emotionality that we assume to be appropriate, but that does not mean that he cannot express an emotional reaction. To push for the norm of expressing feelings could be counterproductive and potentially unethical. Although this example could apply to many American men as well, it is even more representative of Jan's cultural conditioning not to share his feelings.

◆ **The case of Mathew.** You are the counselor for Mathew, who has a history of being expelled from school. He has spent much of his life in and out of juvenile court. The rules of the gang he belongs to dictate how he lives. He is silent during most of your first session, but he does let you know that he doesn't really trust you, that he is only there because the court sent him, and that you cannot possibly understand what his life is about.

- Have you had any life experiences that would qualify you to counsel Mathew?
- What are your immediate reactions to him?
- Would you want to change some of his values? For example, would you want to see him finish school? stop being involved in gang fights? take counseling seriously?
- If you have not had the kinds of experiences growing up that Mathew has had, could you still communicate effectively with him and understand his view of the world?

◆ **The case of Luigi.** Luigi is a middle-aged parent who says that he is not seeking personal counseling but wants advice on how to manage his teenage daughter. According to Luigi, his daughter is immature and unruly. She isn't learning self-discipline, socializes too much, and works too little. She doesn't respect her parents, or any other adults, and in other ways she is a disappointment and a worry to him. In Luigi's eyes, the full responsibility for the conflict in his family rests with his daughter. You surmise that he doesn't see any need to examine his own behavior or how the family may be involved in the problem.

- How do you imagine you might relate to Luigi?
- Would your own values get in the way of understanding his values?
- Do you think you might want to get him to look at his own part in the family disturbances?
- Would you be able to help him understand the larger picture of family systems issues?
- Would you accept him as a client, even if he wanted to focus on how he could change his daughter?
- Would family therapy be indicated?

When you experience discomfort due to a client's very different values or life experiences, try to extend yourself and develop ways to work with this client. Let us again emphasize that we question the ethics of resorting to a referral in all cases where the therapist experiences discomfort. If you have difficulty relating to people who think differently from the way you do, you can work on being more open to diverse viewpoints. This openness does not entail accepting other people's values as your own. Instead, it implies being secure enough in your own values that you are not threatened by really listening to, and deeply understanding, people who think about life differently. Listen to your clients with the intent of understanding what their values are, how they arrived at them, and the meaning these values have for them and then communicate this acceptance. This acceptance of your clients can significantly broaden you as a person and as a professional. It does not require that you change your values.

Religious and spiritual values, parental rights, and end-of-life decisions are particularly sensitive and complex issues. As you read the following sections, attempt to clarify your values in these areas and think about how your views might either enhance or interfere with your ability to establish contact with certain clients.

The Role of Spiritual and Religious Values in Counseling

The field of counseling and psychotherapy has been slow to recognize the need to address spiritual and religious concerns, but these issues have been the subject of increasing debate in recent years. There is now widespread interest in the spiritual and religious beliefs of both counselors and clients and how such beliefs might be incorporated in therapeutic relationships (see W. R. Miller, 1999). There is a growing awareness and willingness to explore spiritual and religious matters within the context of counseling and counselor education programs (Burke & colleagues, 1999), and the major professional organizations are increasingly recognizing the importance of spiritual issues in counseling practice. Survey data of both practicing counselors and counselor educators indicate that spiritual and religious matters are therapeutically relevant, ethically appropriate, and potentially significant topics for the practice of counseling in secular settings (Burke & colleagues, 1999).

Counselors ask just about every imaginable question about a client's life, yet many are reluctant to inquire about the influence and meaning of spirituality and religion in an individual's life. If a counselor does not raise the issue of how spirituality influences clients, then clients might well assume that such matters ought to be excluded from counseling. Because spiritual and religious values play a major part in human life and in an individual's search for meaning, clients' spiritual values should be viewed as a potential resource in therapy rather than as something to be ignored.

Spirituality and religion are critical sources of strength for many clients, are the bedrock for finding meaning in life, and can be instrumental in promoting healing and well-being. Some clients cannot be understood without appreciating the central role of religious or spiritual beliefs and practices. There is growing empirical evidence that our spiritual values and behaviors can promote physical and psychological well-being (Benson & Stark, 1996; Richards & Bergin, 1997; Richards, Rector, & Tjeltveit, 1999). Exploring these values with clients can be integrated with other therapeutic tools to enhance the therapy process.

For some clients, spirituality entails embracing a religion. Other clients value spirituality yet do not have any ties to a formal religion (see the box titled Some Thoughts on Spirituality). There are many paths toward fulfilling spiritual needs, and it is not your role as a helper to prescribe any particular pathway. Instead, your job is to assist your clients in exploring their values to determine the degree to which they are living within the framework of this

Some Thoughts on Spirituality

Some individuals claim to be deeply spiritual, yet they are not affiliated with any formal religion. Here are some viewpoints on the nature of spirituality and how it relates to religion.

- "*Spirituality* refers to a personal inclination or desire for a relationship with the transcendent or God; *religion* refers to the social or organized means by which persons express spirituality" (Grimm, 1994, p. 154).
- "Spirituality refers to a general sensitivity to moral, ethical, humanitarian, and existential issues without reference to any particular religious doctrine. Spiritually oriented individuals may or may not be affiliated with organized religion" (Genia, 1994, p. 395).
- "Spirituality from my perspective is larger than religion, although one's religious practices may be an expression of one's spirituality. For me, spirituality refers to a way of being in the world that acknowledges the existence of a transcendent dimension. It includes an awareness of the connectedness of all that is, and accepts that all of life has meaning and purpose and is thus sacred" (Becvar, 1994, p. 13).
- "Spirituality may be defined as: the animating force in life, represented by such images as breath, wind, vigor, and courage. Spirituality is the infusion and drawing out of spirit in one's life. It is experienced as an active and passive process" (Summit on Spirituality, 1995, p. 30).
- "Spirituality is also described as a capacity and tendency that is innate and unique to all persons. This spiritual tendency moves the individual toward knowledge, love, meaning, hope, transcendence, connectedness, and compassion. Spirituality includes one's capacity for creativity, growth, and the development of a values system. Spirituality encompasses the religious, spiritual, and transpersonal" (Summit on Spirituality, 1995, p. 30).

value system. We suggest that you monitor yourself for subtle ways that you might be inclined to push certain values in your counseling practice. For instance, you could influence clients to embrace a spiritual perspective, or you could influence them to give up certain beliefs that you think are no longer functional for them. It is critical to keep in mind that it is the client's place to determine what specific values to retain or modify.

In their discussion of spirituality and religion, Faiver, Ingersoll, O'Brien, and McNally (2001) comment on the fundamental qualities of spirituality:

> We believe spirituality is an innate human quality. Not only is it our vital life force, but at the same time it is also our experience of that vital life force. Although this life force is deeply part of us, it also transcends us. It is what connects us to other people, nature, and the source of life. The experience of spirituality is greater than ourselves and helps us transcend and embrace life situations. (p. 2)

Spirituality is generally seen to be less formal than religion, which entails a set of codified beliefs that connect us to a God or gods and that influence our daily life. Kelly (1995b) suggests that religion is the way people express their devotion to a deity or to an ultimate reality. In this sense, religion is expressed through major faiths such as Judaism, Christianity, Islam, Hinduism, Buddhism, Confucianism, and Taoism, as well as the many institutionalized variations within each of these world religions. According to Faiver, Ingersoll,

O'Brien, and McNally (2001), across the world's diverse cultures are many who find their answers through religion, which is the means by which they express their spirituality.

Religious Teachings Versus Counseling

Religious beliefs and practices affect many dimensions of human experience, including how to handle guilt feelings, authority, and moral questions, to name a few. Both religion and counseling help people ponder questions of "Who am I?" and "What is the meaning of my life?" At their best, both counseling and religion are able to foster healing through an exploration of self: by learning to accept oneself; forgiving others and oneself; admitting one's shortcomings; accepting personal responsibility; letting go of hurts and resentments; dealing with guilt; and learning to let go of self-destructive patterns of thinking, feeling, and acting.

Although religion and counseling are comparable in a number of respects, some key differences exist. For example, counseling does not involve the imposition of counselors' values on clients, whereas religion often involves teaching doctrines and beliefs to which individuals are expected to conform. Some therapists, from Sigmund Freud to Albert Ellis, have been antagonistic toward religion, and some religious leaders have viewed therapy with suspicion. There are religious leaders who have reacted negatively to counseling as a secular force, and psychotherapists who have reacted negatively to religion, describing it as a defense mechanism or as a form of denial.

Although religion, and spirituality in general, is consistently reported as integral to American's lives, counselors often leave an exploration of religious/spiritual concerns out of the therapeutic process (Faiver, O'Brien, & Ingersoll, 2000). This decision may limit the effectiveness of therapy for some clients. If, during the assessment process or later in counseling, clients indicate that they are concerned about any of their religious beliefs or practices, this is a useful focal point for exploration. In your counseling practice it is essential that you be sensitive to the needs of your clients, listen to them and let them lead the way, and demonstrate a willingness to talk about areas they indicate they want or need to explore.

Personal Beliefs and Values of Counselors

Approximately 96% of Americans believe in God, and 75% of the U.S. population view religious faith as being a very important part of their lives. However, only 33% of psychologists believe religious faith is important in their own lives (Plante, 1999). If mental health practitioners are to effectively serve diverse clients, it is essential that these helpers pay attention to their preparedness to be helpful to their clients. Counselors must understand their own spiritual/religious beliefs if they hope to gain an in-depth appreciation of the beliefs of their clients (Faiver et al., 2001).

Your value system influences every facet of your counseling practice, including your assessment strategies, your views of goals of treatment, the interventions used, the topics explored during the sessions, and evaluations of therapy outcomes. Indeed, no therapy is value free. You must avoid indoctrinating clients with a particular set of spiritual or religious values (or lack of such values, as the case may be). You have an ethical responsibility to be aware of how your beliefs affect your work and to make sure you do not unduly influence your clients.

Your Personal Stance

As you formulate your own position on the place of spiritual and religious values in the practice of counseling, reflect on these questions:

- What connection, if any, do you see between spirituality and religion?
- What are your views concerning established and organized religion?
- Has religion been a positive, negative, or neutral force in your life?
- Is it appropriate to deal with religious issues in an open and forthright manner as clients' needs arise in the counseling process?
- Do clients have the right to explore their religious concerns in their therapy?
- Are therapists forcing their values on their clients when they decide what topics can be discussed?
- If you have no religious or spiritual commitment, how might this hinder or help you in working with clients who hold strong religious convictions?
- Are you willing to refer a client to a rabbi, minister, or priest if it appears that clients have questions that you are not qualified to answer?
- How does a counselor in a public school deal with spiritual or religious issues that students may bring up? Do parents need to be informed that spiritual issues may be discussed in counseling?

You may think that a client has accepted an unnecessarily strict and authoritarian moral code, but you need to understand what these beliefs mean to your client, whatever your own evaluation of them for yourself might be. Consider these examples as you think about your personal stance on the role of spiritual and religious values in counseling.

◆ **The case of Holly.** Holly, your client, has a major internal conflict. She is living with her boyfriend, whom she loves very much. But Holly knows her church would disapprove of the way she is living, and she is experiencing a great deal of guilt over what she sees as a moral transgression.

- How might your views on the above situation affect your counseling?
- Would you consider her guilt as pathological? If so, how would you deal with it?

◆ **The case of Yolanda.** Yolanda is a devout Catholic. After a marriage of 25 years, her husband left her. She has now fallen in love with another man and very much wants a relationship with him. But because her religion does not recognize divorce, Yolanda feels guilty about her involvement with another man. She sees her situation as hopeless, and she cannot find a satisfactory solution. Living alone for the rest of her life scares her. But if she marries the man, she fears that her guilt feelings will eventually ruin the relationship.

- How would your values influence your interventions in this case?
- Would you recommend that Yolanda talk to a priest?
- If Yolanda asked you what she should do or what you think about her dilemma, how would you respond?

◆ **The case of Jeremiah.** Jeremiah is in a student support group that you are leading in a high school. He calls himself a "born-again Christian," and he feels that he has found peace and strength in his own life. In a sincere and caring way, Jeremiah wants to pass on to other group members what has become very meaningful to him. Several members respond negatively, asserting that he is pushing his values.

- As a group leader, how would you intervene?
- What reactions do you think you would have toward Jeremiah, and how might your reactions either inhibit or enhance your ability to work with him?
- If your views were very similar to those of Jeremiah, what interventions might you make and what are the ethical implications?

◆ **The case of Kieran.** Kieran is a counselor in private practice who has strong religious beliefs. He is open about this in his professional disclosure statement, explaining that his religious beliefs play a major part in his personal and professional life. Carmel comes to Kieran for counseling regarding what she considers to be a disintegrating marriage. Kieran has strong convictions that favor preserving the family unit. After going through an explanation of the informed consent document, Kieran asks Carmel if she is willing to join him in a prayer for the successful outcome of the therapy and for the preservation of the family. Kieran then takes a history and assures Carmel that everything can be worked out. He adds that he would like to include Carmel's husband in the sessions. Carmel leaves and does not return.

- Do you see any potential ethical violations on Kieran's part?
- If Kieran came to you for consultation, what might you say to him?

Commentary. Although we applaud Kieran's frankness in presenting his values, we question his approach to Carmel. He does not assess the client's state of mind, her religious convictions, if any, the strength of her convictions, or her degree of comfort with his approach. Carmel may have felt pressured to agree with him in this first session, or she may not have had the strength to disagree openly. The ethical issue is captured in this question: Did Kieran take care of the client's needs, or did he take care of his own needs at Carmel's expense?

Including Spiritual and Religious Values in Counseling

Counseling can help clients gain insight into the ways their core beliefs and values are reflected in their behavior. Clients may discover that what they are doing is based on beliefs that are no longer functional, which implies that they will need to reexamine their values. Miranti and Burke (1995) maintain that helpers must be prepared to deal with spiritual issues that lie at the very core of the client's being. The spiritual domain may offer clients in crisis solace and comfort. For many people, it is a major sustaining power that keeps them going when all else fails. The guilt, anger, and sadness that clients experience often results from a misinterpretation of the spiritual and religious realm, which can lead to depression and a sense of worthlessness. Clinicians must remain open and nonjudgmental, for the spiritual beliefs clients hold can be a major source of strength as they make crucial life decisions.

Ethical practice sometimes demands that mental health professionals be willing and able to refer a client to a minister, priest, or rabbi. In addition, some gang-involved teenagers respond well to strict ministries such as Victory Outreach or Breakout Ministries, and referrals can be made to these resources or to church-based youth groups for positive role model experiences. It is well for practitioners to become knowledgeable about members of the religious community that they can collaborate with and refer clients to when it is appropriate. McMinn and colleagues (1998) outline the therapists' role in collaborating with clergy, but little by way of continuing education is available on the topic of collaboration between counselors and clergy. If a client adheres to religious values and practices, should the therapist get input from a clergy person? When is there an ethical responsibility to refer a client for clarification of an issue pertaining to their problem and their faith? McMinn and colleagues write: "Because of the prominence of religious communities in American life, some have referred to organized religion as the 'sleeping giant' when it comes to delivering mental health services" (pp. 564–565).

Spirituality and religion receive only modest attention in mental health training programs and almost none in school counseling programs. Much remains to be done in providing education and training dealing with religious and spiritual issues. If counselors are to meet the challenge of addressing the role of spirituality in the lives of their clients, they need training in both coursework and fieldwork as well as inspiration and leadership from their teachers. At the Summit on Spirituality (1995), at the Association for Counselor Education and Supervision convention, participants generated a list of proposed competencies that all counselors should acquire as part of their training.

Counselors should be able to

- explain the relationship between religious, spiritual, and transpersonal phenomena.
- describe religious, spiritual, and transpersonal beliefs and practices from the perspective of diversity.
- describe their religious, spiritual, or transpersonal beliefs.

- identify key events in their lives that contributed to the development of their belief system and explain how those events contributed.
- engage in self-exploration of their religious, spiritual, and transpersonal beliefs that support or hinder respect and valuing of different belief systems.
- demonstrate empathy for and understanding of a variety of religious, spiritual, and transpersonal phenomena.
- acquire knowledge needed to better understand a client's religious and spiritual worldview by requesting information from the clients themselves or from outside resources.
- assess the relevance of the religious, spiritual, and transpersonal domains in the client's therapeutic issues.
- use a client's religious, spiritual, or transpersonal phenomena in pursuit of the client's therapeutic goals as befits the client's expressed preferences.
- identify when their understanding or tolerance of religious, spiritual, or transpersonal worldview is insufficient to adequately serve the client.
- seek consultation, seek further training or education, and demonstrate appropriate referral skills when their own limits of tolerance or competence are reached.

These counselor competencies in spirituality were proposed by the Association for Spiritual, Ethical, and Religious Values in Counseling (ASERVIC) for inclusion in the Standards of the Council for Accreditation of Counseling and Related Educational Programs (CACREP). A more detailed list of the spiritual competencies developed by ASERVIC can be found in Faiver, Ingersoll, O'Brien, and McNally (2001, pp. 178–180).

How might these spirituality competencies best be attained? Spirituality and religious frameworks could be included in cultural diversity training for counselors. Burke and colleagues (1999) maintain that when educators present a balanced approach to including spirituality/religious issues in training programs they are modeling openness to these concerns and to their relevance in counseling. They contend that when this openness is not modeled the chances for the unconscious imposition of values and beliefs is increased. We agree with this position. Programs need to challenge students to look at what they believe and how their beliefs and values might influence their work.

Some cautions. Spirituality is an existential issue. Although it is important to be open to dealing with spiritual and religious issues in counseling, counselors should be cautious about introducing religious themes and be aware of the potential for countertransference. For example, a therapist who has a hostile attitude toward religion because of his or her own strict religious upbringing or a therapist with a strong religious faith could have intense reactions toward a client who portrays judgmental and critical attitudes of people who hold to a religion. Therapists must guard against making decisions for their clients. Some counselors may push their religious beliefs, and others may impose their nonreligious or antireligious attitudes.

◆ **The case of Sheila.** Sheila is a rational emotive behavior therapist who claims to be an atheist. She has a strong bias against any kind of spiritual or religious influences, considering these beliefs to be irrational. Her client Brendan describes an unhappy marriage as one of the issues he struggles with. When she suggests to him that perhaps he should consider leaving his marriage, he replies that this is out of the question. He informs her that he has a deep spiritual conviction that this is his destiny. If he were to go against his destiny, he would suffer on some other level. Sheila replies: "Have you ever considered that your convictions may be unhealthy, not only for you but also for your children? Are you willing to look at this?" Brendan seems taken aback. He tells the counselor, "I think that what you just said was insensitive to the way I believe. I am not sure that you can help me." Brendan leaves abruptly.

- What do you think about Sheila's approach?
- Are any ethical issues raised in the way Sheila dealt with Brendan? If so, what are the issues?
- Would you be comfortable responding as Sheila did? Why or why not?
- Did Sheila take care of her needs or of Brendan's needs?
- Would Sheila necessarily have to agree with Brendan's spiritual beliefs to work with him? Explain.
- How would you work with this client?

Commentary. We have concerns about Sheila describing Brendan's spiritual beliefs as "unhealthy." Brendan's reasons for staying in his marriage (his spiritual values) could have been explored rather than being quickly judged. This kind of approach demonstrates the imposition of the therapist's values, not an exploration of the client's concerns.

◆ **The case of Rory.** Rory, who has been in counseling for some time with Teresa, sees himself as a failure and cannot move past his guilt. He insists that he cannot forgive himself for his past. He is in great turmoil and berates himself for his aberrant ways. Teresa knows that Rory is a profoundly religious man and asks during one of the sessions: "How would you view and react to a person with a similar struggle as yours? What kind of God do you believe in? Is your God a punitive or loving God? What does your religion teach you about the forgiveness of sin?" Teresa is attempting to utilize Rory's convictions to reframe his thinking. Once he begins to look at his behavior through the eyes of his religious beliefs, his attitudes toward his own behavior change dramatically. Because Rory believes in a loving God, he finally learns to be more forgiving of himself.

- How do you react to how Teresa worked with Rory?
- Do you agree or disagree with using Rory's religious beliefs as an intervention?
- By doing this, was Teresa imposing her values? Explain.

Commentary. If Teresa had used her own religious beliefs to reframe Rory's thinking, we would have concerns. If she were his minister, rabbi, or priest, it would be acceptable for her to teach these values. But that is not the role of a counselor. However, Teresa noticed a discrepancy between Rory's religious beliefs and his assessment of his behaviors. By using the client's own belief system, she assisted him in reframing his self-assessment and in the process helped him to be true to his own belief system.

Spiritual and Religious Values in Assessment and Treatment

Traditionally, when a client comes to a therapist with a problem, the therapist explores all the factors that contributed to the development of the problem. Even though a client may no longer consider himself or herself to be religious or spiritual, a background of involvement in religion should be explored as part of the client's history. These beliefs may have been factors in the development of the problem, and thus could be part of the problem.

Faiver and O'Brien (1993) and Kelly (1995b) believe it is essential to understand and respect the client's religious beliefs and to include such beliefs in their assessment and treatment practice. The first step is to include spiritual and religious dimensions as a regular part of the intake procedure and the early phase of the counseling process. Faiver and O'Brien devised a form to assess the religious beliefs of clients, which they use to glean relevant information on the client's belief system for diagnostic, treatment, and referral purposes. They suggest that the assessment process can include questions pertaining to spiritual and religious issues as they are relevant to a client's presenting problems, questions about the roles religion and spirituality have played or currently play in a client's life, and questions about how religious and spiritual beliefs might be related to the client's cognitive, affective, and behavioral processes. For example, is guilt an issue? What is the source of guilt, and does it serve any functional purpose?

In assessing a client, Faiver and O'Brien (1993) think it is essential to consider the client's problems from a holistic perspective. Kelly (1995b) endorses the notion of including items pertaining to general information about the client's spirituality and religion that serve the purposes of (a) obtaining a preliminary indication about the relevance of spirituality and religion for each client, (b) gathering information that the helper might refer to at a later point in the helping process, and (c) indicating to the client that it is acceptable to talk about religious and spiritual concerns.

Spirituality is a significant force for many clients, and it is especially important for practitioners to pursue spiritual concerns if clients initiate them. Assessment is a process of looking at all the potential influences on a client's problem. The exploration of spirituality/religious influences is just as significant as exploring family-of-origin influences. Practitioners should remain finely tuned to their clients' stories and to the reasons clients sought professional assistance.

◆ **The case of Anami.** Anami is a counselor in a university counseling center. A first-generation Asian American, Tai, is caught between the religion of his parents, who are Buddhist, and his emerging beliefs. Since entering the university environment, Tai has begun to question his Buddhist upbringing, yet he has not found anything to replace his parents' values. He feels lost and does not know what to believe.

Anami considers herself to be a holistic counselor, and she assesses clients from a holistic perspective, which includes asking questions about family history, personal history, religious and spiritual upbringing, life turning points, physical health, nutrition, and social relationships. In the process of the assessment, she discovers that many of the issues Tai is struggling with pertain to Buddhism. Anami tells Tai: "I think I can assist you in the things you struggle with, but I have limited knowledge of the Buddhist religion. With your permission I would like to consult on specific matters with a colleague who is a Buddhist. I may also recommend a Buddhist teacher to you to help you clarify some specific beliefs you mentioned in the assessment. Is this acceptable to you?" Tai nods in agreement.

- What do you think of the way Anami handled this case?
- Would you have done anything differently, and if so, what?
- Do you think Anami should have referred Tai because of her lack of familiarity with Buddhism?

Commentary. We find little to disagree with in the way Anami handled the case. We like the way she recognized and acknowledged her limitations, for being willing to educate herself on these matters, and also for being willing to consult with someone who has greater expertise than she does.

End-of-Life Decisions

In March 1990 Bruno Bettelheim, a well-known psychoanalyst and author, stunned the psychological community when he took his own life. In an interview with Celeste Fremon (Fremon, 1991), Bettelheim had shared some of his views on the right to take one's own life. He told Fremon that although he was not afraid of dying he did fear suffering. As people grow older, he contended, there is a greater likelihood that they will be kept alive without a purpose. At age 86, Bettelheim was no longer able to do most of the things that brought him enjoyment and meaning, such as hiking, reading, and writing. He made a decision to end his life. His situation highlights the issue of a person's right to choose the manner and time of death, especially in the event of terminal illness.

Studies of attitudes toward suicide reveal sharp divisions of opinion regarding the meaning of the decision to end one's life. Some regard this a basic personal right, whereas others consider it a sign of moral evil or personal pathology (Neimeyer, 2000). In their article on the need for ethical reasoning regarding physician-assisted suicide, Kiser and Korpi (1996) suggest that mental health professionals may need to reconsider their views of suicide and how to treat suicidal clients. Instead of considering all individuals who are contemplating suicide as being "mentally ill" persons who should be prevented from ending their lives, certain individuals should be viewed as being capable of making autonomous and rational decisions about ending their life. When this view is taken, therapists are free to explore alternatives to suicide while at the same time respecting the client's autonomy and freedom of choice.

End-of-life decisions have become an increasingly controversial issue since the Death with Dignity Act became law in Oregon in 1997. Werth and Holdwick (2000) provide definitions for some key concepts related to this issue. *Rational suicide* means that a person has decided—after going through a decision-making process and without coercion from others—to end his or her life because of extreme suffering involved with a terminal illness. *Aid-in-dying* consists of providing a person with the means to die; the person self-administers the death-causing agent, which is usually medication. *Hastened death* involves speeding up the dying process, which can entail withholding or withdrawing life support.

There are arguments both in favor of and in opposition to rational suicide. Most of the arguments favoring rational suicide center on the premise that individuals should have the right to make appropriate decisions about their lives when they are terminally ill. Those who favor rational suicide also provide guidelines for determining whether a suicide is rational (Abeles & Barlev, 1999; Farberman, 1997). Based on a survey of ethicists, suicidologists, and forensic psychologists, Werth (1996) provides a set of criteria to evaluate whether a person's suicide or hastened death is rational:

- The person considering suicide has an unremitting and hopeless condition.
- The person is acting under his or her own free will—is under no outside pressure to make the choice.
- The person has engaged in a sound decision-making process that includes consultation with a mental health professional who can make an assessment of mental competence; exploration of the person's values regarding suicide; consideration of the impact on significant others; and discussions with objective others (medical and religious professionals) and with significant others.

When these steps are followed, Werth concludes that an informed and rational choice can be made.

Suicide: A Free and Rational Choice?

As a counselor, you need to be willing to discuss end-of-life decisions when clients bring such concerns to you. If you are closed to any personal examination of this issue, you may interrupt these dialogues, cut off your clients' exploration of their feelings, or attempt to provide clients with your own solutions based on your values and beliefs. Kiser (1996) has argued that counselors need to examine their own personal, moral, and ethical beliefs regarding rational suicide and, in particular, physician-assisted suicide. He contends that for those counselors whose belief systems do not condone rational suicide or physician-assisted suicide, the ethical course for them to follow is to disqualify themselves from such cases and refer the client to another competent professional qualified to assist the client.

Although there are no easy answers to right-to-die questions, Albright and Hazler (1995) remind us that counselors *do* face these situations *with* their clients. Counselors must clarify their own beliefs and values pertaining to end-of-life decisions so they can assist their clients in making decisions within the framework of their own belief and value systems. What is your position on an individual's right to decide about matters pertaining to living and dying? What religious, ethical, and moral beliefs do you hold that might enable you to support a client's decision about ending his or her life under certain circumstances? How might your beliefs get in the way of assisting your client in making his or her own decision? Your role as a counselor is to assist clients in making the best decision in the context of their own values, but be aware of the laws of your state and the ethical guidelines of your professional organization concerning an individual's freedom to make end-of-life decisions.

Once counselors understand their own perspective on right-to-die issues, they can focus on the needs of their clients. Albright and Hazler (1995) point out some of the areas counselors need to explore from the worldview of their clients:

- Within what personal, religious, and moral framework does the client exist?
- What are the client's religious and philosophical beliefs that are the source of meaning in life?
- What type of support system does the client have, and how do relatives view the client's decision?
- How hopeless is the client's illness?
- To what degree have alternatives and decisions been explored?
- What kind of decision-making skills does the client have, and can the counselor help improve those skills?
- What kind of referral resources are available if the counselor is unable or unwilling to handle the situation?

Albright and Hazler (1995) acknowledge that counselors will be faced with difficult decisions on what actions to take with clients who are doing their best to make decisions. Some of the following interventions aimed at providing direction for clients struggling with end-of-life situation may be helpful:

- Learn as much as possible about the course of clients' illnesses, prognoses, and available treatments.
- Know the clients' family support systems and what their views are regarding end-of-life decisions.
- Realize that clients who are near death often need help coping with their psychological pain as well as their physical suffering. Explore clients' fears about dying, the impact of their religious beliefs on their decision or how religion provides them with meaning, and assist them in achieving closure on any unfinished business with others.
- Assume the role of a resource person for these clients.
- Help clients understand the importance of various personal and formal documents associated with the end of life.

- Regardless of the decisions clients make, offer compassion, acceptance, and understanding related to the difficulties in dealing with life and death issues.
- Realize the role of offering comfort to loved ones and friends after the death.

Werth and Holdwick (2000) suggest some additional steps therapists can take when dealing with end-of-life issues. These include giving prospective clients information about the limitations of confidentiality as it applies to assisted death, if applicable; making full use of consultation throughout the process; keeping risk management–oriented notes; and assessing the impact of external coercion on clients' decision making.

Policy Statement on End-of-Life Decisions

The National Association of Social Workers developed a policy statement pertaining to client self-determination in end-of-life decisions (NASW, 1994a). This statement is based on the principle of client self-determination, the premise that choice should be intrinsic to all aspects of life and death. According to the NASW document, end-of-life decisions are the choices individuals make about terminal conditions regarding their continuing care or treatment options. These options include aggressive treatment of the medical condition, life-sustaining treatment, medical intervention intended to alleviate suffering (but not to cure), withholding or withdrawing life-sustaining treatment, voluntary active euthanasia, and physician-assisted suicide. A terminal condition is one where there is no reasonable chance of recovery and where the application of life-sustaining procedures would serve only to postpone the end of life. Here are some excerpts from the NASW report:

> Social workers have an important role in helping individuals identify the end-of-life options available to them. This role must be performed with full knowledge of and compliance with the law and in accordance with the *NASW Code of Ethics.* Social workers should be well informed about living wills, durable power of attorney for health care, and legislation related to advance health care directives.
>
> A key value for social workers is client self-determination. Competent individuals should have the opportunity to make their own choices but only after being informed about all options and consequences. Choices should be made without coercion. Therefore, the appropriate role for social workers is to help patients express their thoughts and feelings, to facilitate exploration of alternatives, to provide information to make an informed choice, and to deal with grief and loss issues.
>
> Social workers should be free to participate or not participate in assisted-suicide matters or other discussions concerning end-of-life decisions depending on their own beliefs, attitudes, and value systems. If a social worker is unable to help with decisions about assisted suicide or other end-of-life choices, he or she has a professional obligation to refer patients and their families to competent professionals who are available to address end-of-life issues.
>
> It is inappropriate for social workers to deliver, supply, or personally participate in the commission of an act of assisted suicide when acting in their professional role. Doing so may subject the social worker to criminal charges. If legally permissible, it

> is not inappropriate for a social worker to be present during an assisted suicide if the client requests the social worker's presence. The involvement of social workers in assisted suicide cases should not depend on race or ethnicity, religion, age, gender, economic factors, sexual orientation, or disability.

This policy statement provides social workers with some general guidelines by which they can examine the ethical and legal issues pertaining to end-of-life decisions. The literature reveals an increase of professional interest in issues related to death and dying, yet despite this trend there do not seem to be any standard guidelines for counselors or psychologists when working with terminally ill individuals regarding the right to refuse treatment or to exercise choice in deciding to end their lives (Farrugia, 1993; Kiser, 1996). Kiser (1996) points out that the American Counseling Association has yet to establish guidelines for addressing a counselor's role and responsibility in relation to physician-assisted suicide for terminally ill individuals. In the Netherlands physician-assisted suicide is a legal means of ending one's life (Kiser, 1996), but in the United States physician-assisted suicide is a highly controversial issue. Although Oregon's Death with Dignity Act was first passed in 1994, it did not go into effect until 1997. Subsequently, both Washington and California placed measures legalizing assisted suicide on their ballots—both initiatives failed.

A Counselor's Responsibilities

What is the role of mental health professionals in counseling people who are considering some form of hastened dying process? Werth and Holdwick (2000) suggest that if a therapist is working with a client who brings up hastened death—and the therapist's values do not allow for the possibility of a hastened death as the best option for an individual—then this therapist should not be obligated to provide professional services in this case. We question this viewpoint. Why should a therapist's views pertaining to right-to-die issues be treated differently from any other divergent set of values clients might hold? We agree with Farberman (1997) that "The role of the psychologist working with a terminally ill patient who wishes to end his or her life is not to control the patient's decision but to attempt to ensure that the patient's decision-making process is rational, well-reasoned, and free of coercion" (p. 545).

A related matter to the role of the therapist is who should be trained to provide assistance for people contemplating rational suicide and hastened death decisions? Silverman (2000) is not convinced that all students and professionals should be trained for situations and careers that they probably will not encounter in their practices. He states: "I would contend that rational suicide and hastened death decisions may well be the exception rather than the day-to-day experience of most mental health professionals" (p. 543). We disagree with Silverman's contention and believe training programs should include instruction in how to address these critical issues. Although some practitioners may not regularly encounter clients who are considering rational suicide, how can they ethically function when a long-term client eventually brings up an end-of-life decision? If the request for assistance in hastening the end of life came from a new client, perhaps a therapist could refer this client. But if a long-term client brings up ending his or her life, this client might feel abandoned if the therapist makes a referral to another professional. We believe all mental health professionals need to have at least minimal exposure in a number of critical areas: HIV and AIDS, domestic violence, multicultural concerns, chemical dependency—and end-of-life decisions.

The counseling profession faces the challenge of formulating ethical and procedural guidelines on right-to-die issues, especially in light of advances in medical technology, the aging of the population, and the AIDS epidemic. Counselors will increasingly be expected to assist clients in end-of-life decisions. It is essential for counselors to be both proactive and reactive to the needs of individual clients, families, and other professionals (Farrugia, 1993). Now let's examine some specific cases involving end-of-life decisions.

◆ **The case of Festus.** A counselor has been seeing a client named Festus who has been diagnosed with an aggressive and painful cancer. After a series of chemotherapy and pain medication, Festus tells the counselor that nothing seems to work and that he has decided to end his life. They discuss his decision for several sessions, examining all aspects, and Festus becomes even clearer about his decision to end his life. Here are four counselors' responses to the decision Festus has made.

Counselor A: Both the law and my code of ethics require that I report this matter.

Festus: Do what you have to do. If you report me, I will simply say that I was not seriously considering it, and I won't see you any more.

Counselor B: I have a great deal of difficulty accepting your decision. I would like to explore with you some possible ways to find meaning in your life in spite of your suffering. I am asking you not to take any action for at least 3 weeks to give us time to talk about ways you might find meaning in this situation.

Counselor C: Although the law requires that I report you, it does not seem like the right or effective thing to do. Our relationship has come to mean a lot to both of us, especially at a time like this. You could always stop seeing me and kill yourself anyhow. I will continue to see you as long as you choose to come, and I will help you deal with your pain in any way that I can.

Counselor D: Write a letter to me terminating therapy. Once I receive the letter, our relationship is over.

Consider each of these approaches, and then clarify what you would do in this situation.

- What are your thoughts about each counselor's response? Which one comes closest to your thinking?
- What would you want to say to Festus?
- Is it ethical to impose your values on Festus in this case? Why or why not?
- Do you think the state has the right to decide how individuals with terminal illnesses will die?

Commentary. Many therapists are likely to struggle with what they see as a conflict between choosing the ethical as opposed to the legal path. Following a strictly legal course, the therapist would be free from any lawsuit, and the counselor could exercise his or her duty to protect. If the counselor does report this situation, we think the counselor's value to Festus is ended. Festus might be put on a required 72-hour hold for psychiatric evaluation and then released. Free to do whatever he intended to do, it would be very difficult to prevent him from carrying out his plan.

We do not suggest that you ignore the law, but when you encounter this kind of case, the proper course is not always clear. If you do not report, you may be thinking of the client's autonomy, self-determination, and welfare. You could reason that your client is of sound mind and that he has a right to decide not to live in extreme pain. You could also think about providing him with the maximum degree of support as long as he wants this. However, if you do not report him and he does end his life, the family could sue you for breach of your professional duty. If you do report, and he terminates his therapy, you will not be in a position to offer support or to help him in other ways. If you follow the letter of the law, your therapeutic relationship with this client is most probably ended.

◆ **The case of Buford.** Buford, age 15, cannot get along with his new stepfather, so he moves into his grandmother's apartment where she lives alone. Shortly thereafter, Buford develops an illness that attacks his nervous system, causing him to be too weak to attend school. The school assigns a home teacher who tells the school counselor that Buford is saying he does not want to live with this illness. The counselor visits Buford and is able to develop a relationship. Buford's mood seems to lift, but within 3 weeks he speaks again of suicide, indicating that he does intend to die with this disease. He tells the counselor that he plans to take his grandmother's pills. Buford also states that if the counselor tells his grandmother or his parents he will kill himself for sure. The counselor feels confused and powerless.

- How would you deal with this situation?
- Does the counselor have a responsibility to inform Buford's parents?
- Should the counselor have explained the limits of confidentiality to Buford on the first home visit?

◆ **The case of Bettina.** Bettina, who lives at boarding school, makes several suicidal overtures. Because these attempts were judged to be primarily attention-getting gestures, her counselor feels manipulated and does not report them to her parents. During the last of these attempts, however, Bettina seriously hurts herself and ends up in the hospital.

- In this case, do you see any conflict between what is ethically right and what is legally right?
- Did the counselor take the "cry for help" too lightly?

- What are the ethical and legal implications for the counselor in deciding that Bettina's attempts were more manipulative than serious and therefore should be ignored?
- What can a counselor do in a situation in which he or she determines that the attempts are manipulative rather than serious?
- If the counselor told Bettina that she was going to inform the girl's parents about these suicidal attempts and Bettina had responded by saying that she would quit counseling if the counselor did so, what do you think the counselor should do?

Issues involved in end-of-life decisions. Although the cases of Festus, Buford, and Bettina are different, they all raise similar issues of balancing what is ethically right with what is legally required.

- Do counselors have the responsibility and the right to forcefully protect people from the potential harm their own decisions may bring?
- Do helpers have an ethical right to block clients who have clearly chosen death over life? Do counselors have an ethical duty to respect clients' decisions?
- What are a counselor's legal obligations if a client decides to commit suicide?
- What should be done if what seems ethically right is not legal?
- If a course of action is legal but does not seem like the most ethical path to choose, what would you do?
- Once a therapist determines that a significant risk exists, must some action be taken?
- What are the consequences of failing to take steps to prevent clients from ending their lives? Do factors such as the age of the client, the client's level of competence, and the special circumstances of each case make a difference?

Values Pertaining to Sexuality

Examine your values with respect to sexual behavior. Do they tend to be restrictive or permissive? Think about each of the following statements and mark "A" in the space provided if you mostly agree and "D" if you mostly disagree with the statement.

___ Sex belongs in marriage only.
___ Sex is most meaningful as an expression of love and commitment.
___ Recreational sex is fun and doesn't hurt anyone.
___ Sex with multiple partners is okay without protection if you know your partners very well.
___ Safe sexual practices are essential throughout your life.
___ Extramarital sex is okay if you must stay in a failed marriage due to your religious convictions.
___ Premarital sex promotes intimacy in a relationship.
___ Same-gender sex is the right choice for some people.

___ Teenagers should avoid becoming sexually intimate because they are too immature to handle the feelings they will experience.

Can you counsel people who are experiencing conflict over their sexual choices if their values differ dramatically from your own? For example, if you have permissive views about sexual behavior, will you be able to respect the restrictive views of some of your clients? If you think their moral views are giving them difficulty, will you try to persuade your clients to adopt a more liberal view? How will you view the guilt clients may experience? Will you treat it as an undesirable emotion that they need to free themselves of? Conversely, if you have fairly strict sexual guidelines for your own life, will the more permissive attitudes of some of your clients be a problem for you? Can you be supportive of client choices that conflict with your own values? Have you considered where your values regarding sexuality came from? Have you explored them?

◆ **The case of Virginia and Tom.** Virginia and Tom find themselves in a marital crisis when Virginia discovers that Tom has had several affairs during the course of their marriage. Tom agrees to see a marriage counselor. Tom says that he can not see how his affairs necessarily got in the way of his relationship with his wife, especially as they are not going on currently. He believes that what is done is done and that it is pointless to dwell on past transgressions. He is upset over his wife's reaction to learning about his affairs. He says that he loves his wife and that he does not want to end the marriage. His involvements with other women were sexual in nature rather than committed love relationships. Virginia says that she would like to forgive her husband but that she finds it too painful to continue living with him knowing of his activities, even though they are in the past.

Counselor A. This counselor tells the couple at the initial session that from her experience extramarital affairs add many strains to a marriage, that many people tend to get hurt in such situations, and that affairs do pose some problems for couples seeking counseling. However, she adds that affairs sometimes actually have positive benefits for both the wife and the husband. She says that her policy is to let the couple find out for themselves what is acceptable to them. She accepts Virginia and Tom as clients and asks them to consider as many options as they can to resolve their difficulties.

- Is this counselor neutral or biased? Explain.
- Does this approach seem practical and realistic to you? Explain.

Counselor B. From the outset this counselor makes it clear that she sees affairs as disruptive in any marriage. She maintains that affairs are typically started because of a deep dissatisfaction within the marriage and are symptomatic of other real conflicts. With couples therapy, the counselor suggests that Tom and Virginia can get to the basics of their problem. She further says that she will not work with them unless Tom is willing to give up his affairs, because she is convinced that counseling will not work unless he is fully committed to doing what is needed to work on his relationship with Virginia.

- Is this counselor imposing her values?
- Is it appropriate for the counselor to openly state her conditions and values from the outset?
- To what degree do you agree or disagree with this counselor's thinking and approach?
- If, after working with them for a time, the counselor discovers that Tom has begun another affair, what do you think she should do and why?

Counselor C. This counselor views the affairs much as Tom does. She points out that the couple seems to have a basically sound marriage and suggests that with some individual counseling Virginia can learn to get past the affairs.

- With her viewpoint, is it ethical for this counselor to accept this couple for counseling? Should she suggest a referral to another professional? Explain.
- Is there an ethical issue in the counselor ignoring the obvious pain expressed by Virginia?
- Should the counselor have kept her values and attitudes to herself so that she would be less likely to influence this couple's decisions?

Chapter Summary

This chapter has addressed a variety of value-laden counseling situations and issues. Of course, you will encounter many other value questions in your work. Our intent has been to focus attention on the ways your values and those of your clients can affect your counseling relationships.

The role of spiritual and religious values in counseling practice has shifted over the years. There is now widespread interest in the spiritual and religious beliefs of both counselors and clients and in how these beliefs can be an integral part of the therapeutic relationship. Because spiritual and religious values play a vital part in the lives of many who seek counseling, their spiritual values should be viewed as a rich resource in therapy rather than as something to be ignored. In short, spirituality is a major source of strength for many clients, the bedrock for finding meaning in life and an important factor in promoting healing and well-being. Although it is important for counselors to be open to dealing with spiritual and religious issues in counseling, they need to exercise caution about introducing religious themes into counseling. Counselors must guard against making decisions for their clients. A counselor's role is not to prescribe a particular pathway to clients in fulfilling their spiritual needs but to help them clarify ways that their spiritual perspective can lead to enhanced living.

End-of-life decisions are another area in which counselors need to clarify their values. The subject of end-of-life decisions has become increasingly controversial since the Death with Dignity Act became law in Oregon in 1997.

There are arguments both in favor of and in opposition to rational suicide. Generally, the arguments favoring rational suicide center on the premise that terminally ill individuals have a fundamental right to make appropriate decisions about their lives. Counselors have the challenge of clarifying their own beliefs and values pertaining to end-of-life decisions so that they can assist their clients in making decisions within the framework of clients' beliefs and value systems. In this matter, the counselor's role is to assist clients in making the best possible decisions in light of their value system; however, it is essential to be aware of state laws and codes of ethics concerning an individual's freedom to make end-of-life decisions. The counseling profession is faced with formulating ethical and procedural guidelines on right-to-die issues, especially given the advances in medical technology, the aging of the population, and the AIDS epidemic. It is a certainty that counselors increasingly will be expected to assist clients in end-of-life decisions, a fact which demands that counselors assume a proactive stance on this issue.

Counselors cannot be neutral in the area of values and may acknowledge their values when they are related to issues their clients are struggling with. It takes honesty and courage to recognize how your values affect the way you counsel, and it takes wisdom to determine when you are not able to work effectively with a client due to a clash of values. Ongoing introspection and discussions with supervisors or colleagues are necessary to determine how to make optimal use of your values in the therapeutic relationship.

Suggested Activities

1. Have a panel discussion on the topic "Is it possible for counselors to remain neutral with respect to their clients' values?" The panel can also discuss different ways in which counselors' values may affect the counseling process.
2. Invite several practicing counselors to talk to your class about the role of values in counseling. Invite counselors who have different theoretical orientations. For example, you might ask a behavior therapist and a humanistic therapist to talk to your class at the same time on the role of values.
3. For a week or so keep a record of your principal activities. On the basis of what you do and how you use your time, list your values as they are reflected in your record in order of their priority. How do you think these values might influence the way you counsel others?
4. In class, do this exercise in pairs. First, discuss counseling situations that might be difficult for each of you because of a conflict of values. For example, one student might anticipate difficulty working with clients who have fundamentalist religious beliefs. Then choose one of these situations to role-play, with one student playing the part of the client and the other playing the part of the counselor. The client brings up some problem that involves the troublesome value area. It is important for you and your partner to really get into the frame of reference being role-played and to feel the part as much as possible.

5. As a variation on the preceding exercise, assume the role of a client whose values you have difficulty identifying with. For instance, if you think you would have trouble counseling a woman who wanted an abortion, become this client and bring her problem to another student, who plays the part of the counselor.

6. In small groups, each person identifies one specific value that he or she might be inclined to push with a client. Or, identify one of your core beliefs or values, and show how this belief or value could either enhance or inhibit the effectiveness of counseling. Discuss how you might manage this potential value conflict or how you might lessen the chances of imposing one of your values on your clients.

7. Many case examples given in this chapter deal with a wide variety of value issues. In small groups, select two or three of these vignettes and discuss how you, as a group, might address the ethical issues raised in each of these cases. When the small groups are finished with this task, each small group can present the outcomes of the discussion for each case selected.

8. Do this activity in pairs. Talk to your partner about the circumstances in which you would consider referring a client to another professional because of a value conflict between you and your client. Can you think of ways to effectively manage this value conflict other than making a referral?

9. Do this activity in pairs. Talk with your partner about how your spiritual and religious values are likely to influence the manner in which you counsel others. Address topics such as: Would you be inclined to reveal your spiritual or religious values to your clients? Under what circumstances? In certain circumstances, might you be inclined to teach clients about how spirituality could assist them in dealing with their problems? To what degree would you want to include spiritual and religious values in your counseling practice?

10. This activity can be used as a topic for debate in class. End-of-life decisions involve a number of ethical issues. Some counselors believe terminally ill clients have the ultimate right to determine if, how, and when they will end their life. Other counselors believe that their obligation is to assist clients in finding meaning in life regardless of a particular set of circumstances. Divide the class into two groups for a debate: One side will argue for suicide as a free and rational choice, and the other side will argue against the taking of one's life under any circumstances.

11. For this exercise, work in small groups. Discuss the life experiences you have had that you think will enable you to effectively counsel others. You might also talk about limitations in your life experiences that might hinder your understanding of certain clients.

12. Interview some practicing counselors about their experiences with values in the counseling process. You could ask questions such as these: What kinds of clients have you had difficulty working with because of your value system? How do you think your values influence the way you counsel? How are your clients affected by your values? What are the main value issues clients bring to the counseling process?

13. Do this exercise in pairs, with one student acting as the counselor and the other acting as the client. The counselor actively tries to convert the client to some value or point of view that the counselor holds. The job of the counselor is to try to persuade the client to do what the counselor thinks would be best for the client. This exercise can give you a feeling for what it is like to persuade a person to adopt your point of view and what it is like to be subjected to persuasion. Then switch roles.

Ethics in Action CD-ROM Exercises

14. In the *Ethics in Action* CD-ROM, complete the self-inventory on pages 24–25 and bring this to class for discussion.

15. In video role play #4, The Divorce, it is clear that the counselor has an agenda for the client, who has decided to leave her husband and get a divorce. The counselor's line of inquiry is about who will look after the welfare of her children. The client feels misunderstood and does not think the counselor is of help to her. Have one student role-play Gary (the counselor in the video), while another student role-plays his supervisor. As the supervisor, explore the issues you see being played out.

16. In video role play #5, Doing It My Way, Sally (the counselor) is attempting to influence her client to think about the effect of her behavior on her parents. Charlae is seeking increased independence and wants to break away from her parents and be "free." Her father wants her to stay at home, but she wants to live at college in the dorms. Sally suggests that Charlae talk with her parents about this, but she just wants to move out, without any discussion with her parents. Sally is concerned about what Charlae's parents' reaction might be if she moves out without involving her parents in this decision. Charlae says, "I could really care less what they think." Sally wants Charlae to think about the consequences and the effect on her parents and the fact that they have made sacrifices for her. Have one student role-play the counselor, while another student becomes Sally's supervisor. Through role-playing, demonstrate how you might approach the counselor as her supervisor. What would you most want Sally to consider?

17. In video role play #6, The Promiscuous One, the client (Suzanne) is having indiscriminate sexual encounters and her counselor, Richard, expresses concern for her. Suzanne reports meeting a guy in a bar and having sex with him, which she says is the best she has had in a week. He asks if she is protecting herself from pregnancy and/or HIV. She claims she has the greatest life as it is. Suzanne says, "I am not going to get HIV. People are blowing it totally out of proportion." She says she doesn't know why he is so worried about it, for after all, it is her life. Richard then focuses on how Suzanne's behavior plays out the recurring theme of abandonment by her father. She thinks there is no connection. If you were Suzanne's counselor, how would you deal with the situation as she presents it? Is it ethically appropriate for you to strongly influence your client to engage in safe sex practices? Demonstrate how you would approach Suzanne through role playing.

18. In video role play #7, The Affair, the client (Natalie) shares with her counselor that she is struggling with her marriage and is having a long-term affair. Natalie feels alive, youthful, and beautiful when she is with this other person. At home she feels depressed and sees her purpose as being just to serve her husband. For years she has been there for others, but now she has to think about herself. The counselor (Janice) says, "Having an affair is not a good answer for someone—it just hurts everyone. I do not think it is a good idea." How would your values influence your interventions in this situation? Have one student role-play the counselor and show how he or she might work with Natalie. In a second role play, have one student become the counselor's supervisor and demonstrate what issues you might explore with Janice.

19. The CD-ROM contains a number of questions and exercises designed to get you thinking about ways you might deal with the ethical issues involved in these situations. Complete the material for vignettes 4, 5, 6, and 7.

InfoTrac® College Edition Resources

For additional readings, explore InfoTrac College Edition, our online library. Go to *http://www.infotrac.college.com/wadsworth* and select these key word searches:

therap* values
values psych*
spiritual values in psych*
religious values in psych*
end of life decision*
rational suicide

Key words are listed in a form that enables the search engine to locate a wider range of articles in the online university library. Key words should be entered exactly as shown, including asterisks, "W1," "W2," "AND," and other search engine tools.

4

Pre-Chapter Self-Inventory

Directions: For each statement, indicate the response that most closely identifies your beliefs and attitudes. Use the following code:

5 = I *strongly agree* with this statement.
4 = I *agree* with this statement.
3 = I am *undecided* about this statement.
2 = I *disagree* with this statement.
1 = I *strongly disagree* with this statement.

_____1. Well-trained, sensitive, and self-aware therapists who do not impose their own values on clients are better qualified to be multicultural counselors.

_____2. To counsel effectively, I must be of the same ethnic background as my client.

_____3. Basically, all counseling interventions are multicultural.

_____4. I must challenge cultural stereotypes when they become obvious in counseling situations.

_____5. Contemporary counseling theories can be applied to people from all cultures.

_____6. As with any attempt to correct a problem, there exists a possibility of overcorrection in the multicultural movement.

_____7. I will be able to examine my behavior and attitudes to determine the degree to which cultural bias might influence the interventions I make with clients.

_____8. Special guidelines are needed for counseling members of ethnic or racial minority groups.

_____9. Mental health professionals need to take into account the ethnic and cultural differences between themselves and their clients.

____10. The primary function of majority-group counselors is to alert their clients to the choices available to them.

____11. An effective mental health practitioner facilitates assimilation of the minority client into society.

Multicultural Perspectives and Diversity Issues

____12. Ethical practice demands that counselors become familiar with the value systems of diverse cultural groups.

____13. I would have no trouble working with someone from a culture very different from mine, because we would be more alike than different.

____14. If I just listen to my clients, I will know all I need to know about their cultural background.

____15. Client resistance is typically encountered in multicultural counseling and must be overcome before changes can take place.

____16. The ability to observe and understand nonverbal communication is an important component of multicultural counseling.

____17. Establishing a trusting relationship is more difficult when the counselor and the client come from different cultures.

____18. Unless practitioners have been educated about cultural differences, they cannot determine whether they are competent to work with diverse populations.

____19. As a condition for licensure, all counselors should have specialized training and supervised experience in multicultural counseling.

____20. At this point in my educational career, I feel well prepared to counsel culturally diverse client populations.

____21. To be considered competent, I think all counselors need to appreciate the ways that diversity influences the client-counselor relationship and the counseling process itself.

____22. A Christian counselor should refer gay, lesbian, and bisexual clients to another professional.

____23. Gay and lesbian clients are best served by gay and lesbian counselors.

____24. I would have difficulty counseling either a lesbian or gay couple who wanted support in adopting a child.

____25. As a counselor, it is my ethical responsibility to learn about referral resources for gay, lesbian, and bisexual clients and to make appropriate referrals if I do not have the knowledge and skills to work effectively with them.

Introduction

In this chapter we continue discussing values but zero in on the cultural values, beliefs, and assumptions of counselors and examine the ethical implications of how counselors make use of their cultural values in their work. We also discuss the issue of sexual orientation and the values surrounding this topic. The emphasis is on the ethical dimensions of understanding the client's worldview and tailoring the counseling process to the client's cultural context.

One of the major challenges facing counseling professionals is understanding the complex role that cultural diversity plays in their work. In a sense, all counseling interventions are multicultural. Clients and counselors bring very different attitudes, values, culturally learned assumptions, and behaviors to the counseling relationship. One mistake is to deny the importance of these cultural variables in counseling; another is to overemphasize cultural differences to the extent that practitioners lose their naturalness and fail to make contact with their clients.

Cultural sensitivity is not limited to one group but applies to all cultures. There is no sanctuary from cultural bias. All counselors must be vigilant to avoid using their own group as the standard by which to assess appropriate behavior without translating or interpreting that perspective to fit other cultures. African American counselors need to be aware of their possible prejudices toward white clients just as white counselors must be sensitive to their attitudes toward African American clients, and both need to understand how they are being perceived. Indeed, African American counselors also need to be aware of how their own cultural experiences and views are likely to influence their work with African American clients. Greater differences may exist within the same cultural group than between different cultural groups, and we must be intraculturally sensitive as well as multiculturally sensitive.

In this chapter we focus on the ethical implications of a multicultural perspective or lack thereof in the helping professions. To ensure that the terms we use in this chapter will have a precise meaning, we have provided specific definitions (see the box titled Multicultural Terminology). This field is complex and is developing rapidly, and practitioners need to stay abreast of these developments. In this chapter we have chosen to focus on the ethical dimensions of multicultural practice; we do not address separate ethnic groups except by way of providing examples. You are encouraged to expand your knowledge of the topics introduced here by acquiring further information on your own.

The Need for a Multicultural Emphasis

Cultural diversity is a fact of life in today's world, and counselors can no longer afford to ignore the issues involved in counseling culturally diverse populations. Multicultural counseling attempts to clarify the role of sociocultural forces in the origin, expression, and resolution of problems (Axelson, 1999). Das (1995) points out that culture influences every aspect of our lives, for it influ-

Multicultural Terminology

The word *culture* can be interpreted broadly, for it can be associated with a racial or ethnic group as well as with gender, religion, economic status, nationality, physical capacity or handicap, or affectional or sexual orientation. Pedersen (2000) describes culture as including demographic variables such as age, gender, and place of residence; status variables such as social, educational, and economic background; formal and informal affiliations; and the ethnographic variables of nationality, ethnicity, language, and religion. Considering culture from this broad perspective provides a context for understanding that each of us is simultaneously a member of many different cultures. Within group and between group variables define similarities and differences (Pedersen, 2000).

Ethnicity is a sense of identity that stems from common ancestry, history, nationality, religion, and race. This unique social and cultural heritage provides cohesion and strength. It is a powerful unifying force that offers a sense of belonging and sharing based on commonality (Axelson, 1999; Lum, 2000).

Minority group has come to refer to any category of people who have been discriminated against or subjected to unequal treatment and oppression by society largely because of their group membership. These groups have been characterized as subordinate, dominated, and powerless. Thus, minority is often defined by the condition of oppression rather than by numerical criteria. Although the term *minority* has traditionally referred to national, racial, linguistic, and religious groups, it now also applies to women, the aged, gay men, lesbians, bisexuals, and people with disabilities (Atkinson, Morten, & Sue, 1998; Lum, 2000).

Multiculturalism is a generic term that indicates any relationship between and within two or more diverse groups. *Cross-cultural, transcultural,* and *intercultural* are terms with similar meanings. We prefer *multicultural* because it more accurately reflects the complexity of culture but avoids any implied comparison. The multicultural perspective in human-service education takes into consideration the specific values, beliefs, and actions conditioned by a client's ethnicity, gender, religion, socioeconomic status, political views, lifestyle, geographic region, and historical experiences with the dominant culture (Wright, Coley, & Corey, 1989). Multiculturalism provides a conceptual framework that recognizes the complex diversity of a pluralistic society, while at the same time suggesting bridges of shared concern that bind culturally different individuals to one another (Pedersen, 1991, 2000).

Multicultural counseling is any counseling relationship in which the counselor and the client belong to different cultural groups, hold different assumptions about social reality, and subscribe to different worldviews (Das, 1995). Arredondo and her colleagues (1996), who have operationalized a comprehensive set of multicultural competencies, write that multicultural counseling refers to approaches that integrate multicultural and culture-specific awareness, knowledge, and skills into counseling practices.

The United States is a pluralistic society, and all its citizens are ethnic, racial, and cultural beings. Arredondo and her colleagues (1996) suggest that multiculturalism focuses on ethnicity, race, and culture. In contrast, *diversity* refers to individual differences such as age, gender, sexual orientation, religion, and physical ability or disability. Both multiculturalism and diversity have been politicized in the United States in ways that have often been divisive, but these terms can equally represent positive assets in a pluralistic society.

Diversity-sensitive counseling is a concept that includes age, culture, disability, education level, ethnicity, gender, language, physique, race, religion, residential location, sexual orientation, socioeconomic situation, and trauma (Weinrach & Thomas, 1998).

Culture-centered counseling is a three-stage developmental sequence, from multicultural awareness to knowledge and comprehension to skills and applications (Pedersen, 2000).

(continued)

(continued)

Stereotypes are oversimplified and uncritical generalizations about individuals who are identified as belonging to a specific group.

Racism is any pattern of behavior that, solely because of race or culture, denies access to opportunities or privileges to members of one racial or cultural group while perpetuating access to opportunities and privileges to members of another racial or cultural group (Ridley, 1989, 1995). Racism can operate on both individual and institutional levels, and it can occur intentionally or unintentionally.

Although counselors exhibiting these blatantly biased attitudes may be easily identified, many other well-intentioned helpers practice *unintentional racism* (Ridley, 1995). Practitioners who presume that they are free of any traces of racism seriously underestimate the impact of their own socialization. Whether these biased attitudes are intentional or unintentional, the result is harmful for both individuals and society. Pedersen (2000) believes that the key to recognizing unintentional racism lies in the willingness of practitioners to continually reexamine their underlying assumptions.

Note about names: There is some concern about how to refer appropriately to certain racial and ethnic groups. Preferred names tend to change. For instance, some alternate names for one group are Hispanic, Latino (Latina), Mexican American, or Chicana (Chicano). Realizing that there is no one "right" designation to fit any group, practitioners can show sensitivity to the fact that a name is important; they can ask their client how he or she would like to be identified.

ences our view of social and psychological reality. Multicultural counseling is based on a number of premises identified here by Das (p. 45):

- All cultures represent meaningful ways of coping with the problems a particular group faces.
- All counseling can be regarded as multicultural if culture is defined broadly to include not only race, ethnicity, and nationality but also gender, age, social class, sexual orientation, and disability.
- People seek counseling largely because of problems that emerge out of sociocultural conditions.
- Traditional counseling is a particular form of intervention developed in the West to cope with psychological distress.
- All cultures have developed formal or informal ways of dealing with human problems.

The Problem of Cultural Tunnel Vision

A faculty member overheard one of our students inquiring about possibilities for a fieldwork placement in a community agency. The student remarked: "I don't want a placement where I'll have to work with poor people or minority groups." This brief statement revealed much about the student's attitudes and beliefs about both people and the helping professions. If we want students to become more culturally aware, it is essential that we encourage them to seek out people who are different from themselves.

Many students come into training with monocultural tunnel vision. They have had limited cultural experiences, and in many cases they unwittingly impose their values on unsuspecting clients, assuming that everyone shares these values. At times, student helpers from the majority group have expressed the attitude, explicitly or implicitly, that racial and ethnic minorities are unresponsive to professional psychological intervention because of their lack of motivation to change or their "resistance" to seeking professional help.

Students are not alone in their susceptibility to monocultural tunnel vision. Ridley (1995) develops the thesis that, ironic as it may seem, racism has been present in mental health delivery systems for quite some time. Ridley states that studies from the 1950s to the present have documented enduring patterns of racism in mental health care delivery systems. The literature has examined the impact of racism on various racial groups and also the existence of racism in a variety of treatment settings.

The *culturally encapsulated counselor* exhibits monocultural tunnel vision, which is characterized by these traits described by Wrenn (1962, 1985):

- Defines reality according to one set of cultural assumptions
- Shows insensitivity to cultural variations among individuals
- Accepts unreasoned assumptions without proof or ignores proof because that might disconfirm one's assumptions
- Fails to evaluate other viewpoints and makes little attempt to accommodate the behavior of others
- Is trapped in one way of thinking that resists adaptation and rejects alternatives

Years after his formulation of the culturally encapsulated counselor, Wrenn (1985) maintained that cultural encapsulation continued to be a problem for counseling professionals.

A good place for you to begin to develop a multicultural perspective is by becoming more aware of your own culturally learned assumptions. This will provide a context for understanding how diverse cultures share common ground and also how to recognize areas of uniqueness (Pedersen, 2000). Whether you are aware of it or not, cultural factors are an integral part of the counseling process, and culture influences your interventions with clients. Pedersen (1994) puts this challenge well when he writes: "It is no longer possible for good counselors to ignore their own cultures or the cultures of their clients through encapsulation. However, until the multicultural perspective is understood as making the counselor's job easier instead of harder, and increasing rather than decreasing the quality of a counselor's life, little real change is likely to happen" (p. 22).

The Challenges of Reaching Diverse Client Populations

The APA (1993) has developed a set of "Guidelines for Providers of Psychological Services to Ethnic, Linguistic, and Culturally Diverse Populations." Service providers are reminded to be aware of how their own culture, life experiences, attitudes, values, and biases influence them. Additionally, practitioners are challenged to go beyond their cultural encapsulation and ask themselves: "Is it appropriate for me to view these clients any differently than I would if they were from my own ethnic or cultural group?" The APA's guidelines also challenge practitioners to respect the roles of family members and the community structures, hierarchies, values, and beliefs that are an integral part of the client's culture. Providers should identify resources in the client's family and the larger community and use them in delivering culturally sensitive services. For example, an entire Native American family may come to a clinic to provide support for an individual in distress because many of the healing practices found in Native American communities are centered in the family and the community.

Many clients have come to distrust helpers associated with the establishment or with social service agencies because of a history of unequal treatment. These clients may be slow to form trusting relationships with counselors who, because of their role, possess different culturally learned perspectives than they do. Mental health professionals may have difficulty identifying with these clients if they ignore the history behind this distrust. Helpers from all cultural groups need to honestly examine their own assumptions and expectations and attitudes about the helping process. We are all culture-bound to some extent, and it takes a concerted effort for us to monitor our positive and negative biases so that they do not impede the formation of helping relationships.

D. W. Sue and Sue (1999) are convinced that the field of clinical and counseling psychology has failed to meet the particular mental health needs of ethnic minorities. Half of minority clients terminate counseling after only one contact with a therapist. Sue and Sue suggest that a basic reason for this underutilization of services and early termination is the biased nature of the services themselves:

> The services offered are frequently antagonistic or inappropriate to the life experiences of the culturally different client; they lack sensitivity and understanding, and they are oppressive and discriminating toward minority clients. (1999, p. 11)

From an ethical perspective, Sue and Sue maintain that mental health professionals have a moral and professional responsibility (1) to become aware of and deal with the biases, stereotypes, and assumptions that undergird their practice; (2) to become aware of the culturally different client's values and worldview; and (3) to develop appropriate intervention strategies that take into account the social, cultural, historical, and environmental influences of culturally different clients.

The medical model of clinical counseling is often a poor fit for poor people. The child care and transportation challenges alone make it not worth the effort for most people. Clinics in schools on Saturday and in the evening with child care available are part of the answer, and home visits would also benefit this population. Poor people cannot take off work for medical appointments without being docked pay, yet we continue to provide a white, middle-class model that many clients cannot use (John Tweton, personal communication, April 2, 2001).

Sometimes cultural traditions contribute to the underutilization of traditional psychotherapeutic services by minority clients. It may not be an Asian American person's style to seek professional help quickly when faced with a problem. For example, consider Binh's experience of being torn between marrying a person selected by his parents and marrying a woman of his choice. He might first look for a solution within himself through contemplation. If he were unable to resolve his dilemma, he might seek assistance from a family member or a clergy person. Then he might look to some of his friends for advice and support in making the best decision. If none of these approaches resulted in a satisfactory resolution of his problem, Binh might then turn to a mental health professional. The fact that he did not seek counseling services sooner has little to do with resistance or with insensitivity on the part of counselors; Binh was following a route that was congruent with his cultural background.

Some argue that minority clients who use counseling resources may lose their cultural values in the process. Some culturally encapsulated counselors mistakenly assume that a lack of assertiveness is a sign of dysfunctional behavior that should be changed. Merely labeling a behavior dysfunctional reflects a particular value orientation. Practitioners need to consider whether passivity is a problem from the client's culturally learned perspective and whether assertiveness is a useful behavior that the client hopes to acquire.

Learning to Deal with Cultural Pluralism

Multiculturalism is an attitude to be embraced rather than something to be tolerated. To operate monoculturally and monolingually, as if all our clients were the same, is not in accord with reality, and it can result in unethical and ineffective practice. Pedersen (2000) reminds us that culture is complex, yet this complexity can be viewed as friend rather than foe because it helps us avoid searching for easy answers to hard questions.

Becoming multiculturally competent is best conceptualized as a lifelong developmental process that requires continual education and training (D. W. Sue, 1996a). Sue admits that realistically it is not possible to acquire an in-depth understanding of all the different cultural groups. Part of multicultural competence entails recognizing our limitations and is manifested in our willingness to (a) seek consultation, (b) seek continuing education, and (c) make referrals to a professional who is competent to work with a particular client population. Richardson and Molinaro (1996) maintain that when counselors learn about their own culture they are moving in the direction of acquiring multicultural competence. They add: "If a counselor accepts this challenge and engages in self-exploration, then learning about the race, cultures, and experiences of clients becomes a manageable process instead of an overwhelming and threatening one" (p. 241). Travel and cultural immersion are good ways to learn about diverse cultures. Attending a workshop in Mexico and living with a Mexican family for a few weeks can be much more productive than clinical workshops in one's hometown.

Ethics Codes in Multicultural Counseling

Most ethics codes mention the practitioner's responsibility to recognize the special needs of diverse client populations. For example, the preamble to the *Code of Ethics* of the ACA (1995) calls for members to "recognize diversity in our society and embrace a cross-cultural approach in support of the worth, dignity, potential, and uniqueness of each individual." The ACA's nondiscrimination standard states:

> Counselors do not condone or engage in discrimination based on age, color, culture, disability, ethnic group, gender, race, religion, sexual orientation, marital status, or socioeconomic status. (A.2.a.)

The ACA also calls upon counselors to respect differences:

> Counselors will actively attempt to understand the diverse cultural backgrounds of the clients with whom they work. This includes, but is not limited to, learning how the counselor's own cultural/ethnic/racial identity impacts her or his values and beliefs about the counseling process. (A.2.b.)

In addition, specific ACA standards deal with diversity in most areas of theory, practice, training, and research.

In the most recent revision of the NASW *Code of Ethics* (1999), cultural competence and recognition of social diversity are clearly linked to ethical practice. Here are two relevant guidelines:

> Social workers should have a knowledge base of their clients' cultures and be able to demonstrate competence in the provision of services that are sensitive to clients' cultures and to differences among people and cultural groups. (1.05.b.)
>
> Social workers should obtain education about and seek to understand the nature of social diversity and oppression with respect to race, ethnicity, national origin, color, sex, sexual orientation, age, marital status, political belief, religion and mental or physical disability. (1.05.c.)

The APA ethics code (1992) indicates that part of competence implies understanding diversity:

> Where differences of age, gender, race, ethnicity, national origin, religion, sexual orientation, disability, language, or socioeconomic status significantly affect psychologists' work concerning particular individuals or groups, psychologists obtain the training, experience, consultation, or supervision necessary to ensure the competence of their services, or they make appropriate referrals. (1.08.)

Pedersen (2000) contends that the code of ethics of both the APA and the ACA are culturally biased and culturally encapsulated. For example, both contain an unstated bias toward an individualistic perspective, which is not necessarily appropriate for collectivistic cultures. Ethical guidelines appropriate in one cultural context may not be appropriate in contrasting cultural settings. Most ethics codes caution practitioners about establishing dual relationships, which can cloud judgment and result in client exploitation. However, working with clients from a more collectivistic culture or those in a rural community might well require counselors to relate to their clients through many different roles and relationships. Another example is a counselor who might be sanctioned by an ethics committee for promoting dependency for continuing to see a client in therapy for no fee until this client was in a position to pay for the services. The assumption underlying most ethics codes is that there is an absolute standard of right and wrong. This assumption disregards the variety of different cultural contexts for both providers and consumers. To the extent that ethical guidelines are based on the values of one dominant culture, Pedersen argues that they need to be modified. For a more detailed discussion of ethical dilemmas of multicultural counselors, see Pedersen (2000, Chapter 7).

We suggest that you take a few moments to review the ethics codes of one or more professional organizations to determine for yourself the degree to which such codes take cultural, ethnic, and racial dimensions into account. From a multicultural perspective, what are the shortcomings of these codes? To what degree do you think that these codes are culturally encapsulated? What revisions and additions can you think of as a basis for mental health practitioners to function ethically in today's diverse world?

Cultural Values and Assumptions in Therapy

Many therapeutic practices are biased against racial and ethnic minorities and women (D. W. Sue, Ivey, & Pedersen, 1996) and often reflect racism, sexism, and other forms of prejudice. D. W. Sue (1996b) puts this matter bluntly: "Rather than educate or heal, rather than offer enlightenment and freedom, and rather than allow for equal access and opportunities, historical and current practices have restricted, stereotyped, damaged, and oppressed the culturally different in our society" (p. 195). D. W. Sue and Sue (1999) contend that this ethnocentric bias has been destructive to the natural help-giving networks of minority communities. They suggest that helpers need to expand their perception of mental health practices to include support systems such as family, friends, community, self-help programs, and occupational networks.

School counselors and teachers may work in an ethnic minority community yet remain closed to understanding their clients' cultural context. They need to reach out, shop, visit, make home visits, and join community improvement efforts in order to be effective. When they do approach, rather than avoid the community, they are generally received with open arms (John Tweton, personal communication, April 2, 2001).

The diversity-sensitive counseling movement focuses attention on the problems of discrimination, oppression, and racism. The ideas put forward by these practitioners have, in recent years, profoundly changed how counselors conceptualize the helping relationship. But this movement is not without its critics. Weinrach and Thomas (1998) believe the diversity-sensitive counseling movement lacks moderation and attempts to superimpose its agenda on counseling practice. In their view, experts in diversity-sensitive counseling (see, for example, Atkinson, Morten, & Sue, 1998; D. W. Sue & Sue, 1999) have tended to emphasize problems rather than demonstrate how diversity-sensitive counselors might actually conduct counseling sessions with various client populations. Live demonstrations at conventions or videotaped counseling interviews with a variety of diverse populations across the life span with a range of presenting concerns are two suggestions they put forward: "Without videotaped demonstrations, provided by diversity-sensitive counseling experts, it is unreasonable to expect professional counselors to provide effective diversity-sensitive counseling." (p. 119). Although Weinrach and Thomas (1998) are critical of what they consider to be the rhetoric of the diversity-sensitive counseling movement, which at times tends to be extreme and doctrinaire, they do admit that this movement deserves praise because "it has contributed to the profession's awareness of the broad variety of factors that may influence a client's thoughts, feelings, behaviors, and spirituality" (p. 121).

Counselors may misunderstand clients of a different sex, race, age, social class, or sexual orientation. If practitioners fail to integrate these diversity factors into their practice, they are infringing on the client's cultural autonomy and basic human rights, which will reduce the chance of establishing an effective therapeutic relationship. In our opinion, ethical practice demands that practitioners address these diversity factors as they become relevant in the therapy process.

◆ **The case of Lee.** Stacy is a counselor at a high school. A Vietnamese student, Lee, is assigned to her because of academic difficulties. Stacy, who is white, observes that Lee is slow and deliberate in his conversational style, and she immediately signs him up for a class in English as a second language. In the course of their conversations, Lee discloses that his father is directing him toward applying to college and majoring in a pre-med program. Lee is not at all sure that he even wants to attend college. Stacy gives Lee a homework assignment, asking him to talk to his father and tell him that he no longer wants to pursue college plans and is going to follow a direction that appeals to him.

- Was the fact that Lee spoke slowly and deliberately an indication that he was deficient in English? Was the counselor insensitive in recommending an ESL class so hastily?
- Did the therapist's actions reveal respect for the roles of family members, hierarchies, values, and beliefs in the client's culture?
- Was the therapist culturally sensitive by asking Lee to directly confront his father? What alternatives might exist?
- Was Stacy too quick in making her assessments, considering that Lee was sent to the school counselor by a teacher? Would it have made a difference if he had come voluntarily for guidance?
- How would you have handled this situation?

◆ **The case of Cynthia.** An Asian counselor, Ling, has recently set up a private practice in a culturally mixed, upscale neighborhood. A Caucasian housewife, Cynthia, seeks Ling out for counseling. She is depressed, feels that life has little meaning, and feels enslaved by the needs of her husband and small children. When Ling asks about any recent events that could be contributing to her depression, she tells him that she has discussed with her husband her desire to return to school and pursue a career of her choosing. She told her husband that she felt stifled and needed to pursue her own interests. Her husband's response was to threaten a divorce if she followed through with her plans. Cynthia then consulted with her pastor, who pointed out her obligations to her family. Ling is aware of his own cultural biases, which include a strong commitment to family and to the role of the man as the head of the household. Although he shows empathy for Cynthia's struggle, he directs her toward considering postponing her own aspirations until her children have grown up. She surrenders to his direction because she feels guilty about asserting her own needs, and she is also fearful of being left alone. Ling then works with her to find other ways to add meaning to her life that would not have such a radical impact on the family.

- Do you see any evidence of bias or unethical behavior in Ling's approach to this case?
- List some of the potential gender and cultural issues in this case. How might you have addressed each of them?
- Ling did not seem to explore the lack of meaning in Cynthia's life. Would you have done so and why?
- Could Ling have acted any differently and still have been true to himself and his own cultural values?
- What might be the response of a feminist therapist?
- If Ling's client had been from a traditional Asian family, do you think Ling's approach would have been appropriate? Was this approach appropriate for Cynthia?
- Because Ling had different family values from Cynthia's, should he have referred her to another professional?
- Was Cynthia's individual welfare more important than the welfare of her family?
- If Ling had approached you for consultation, what advice might you have given him?
- Given what you know about your values, how might you have worked with Cynthia if she had been your client?

Western Versus Eastern Values

Eastern and Western are not just geographic terms but also represent philosophical, social, political, and cultural orientations. Writers in the field of multicultural counseling allege that most contemporary theories of therapy and therapeutic practices are grounded in Western assumptions, yet most of the world differs from mainstream U.S. culture (Ivey, D'Andrea, Ivey, & Simik-Morgan, 2002; D. W. Sue, Ivey, & Pedersen, 1996). These writers are critical of the strong individualistic bias of contemporary theories and the lack of emphasis on broader social contexts, such as families, groups, and communities. Professional psychological help is not a typical option for many minority groups. In fact, in most non-Western cultures informal groups of friends and relatives provide the supportive network.

Weinrach and Thomas (1998) contend that "existing counseling approaches do not adequately address the needs of a diverse client population" (p. 116).

But Patterson (1985b, 1996) believes Western methods can be useful despite cultural differences. Focusing on the universal factors that link all humanity, he contends that East and West must move toward each other:

> Eastern cultures must change in the direction of greater concern for individual personal development. Western culture must move in the direction of greater concern for the influence of the individual upon others and . . . of cooperation in fostering personal development in others. (1985b, p. 188)

For Patterson, the overemphasis on cultural diversity and training in specific techniques for various cultural groups "ignores the fact that we are rapidly becoming one world, with rapid communication and increasing interrelations among persons from varying cultures, leading to increasing homogeneity and a worldview representing the common humanity that binds all humans together as one species" (1996, p. 230).

Practitioners who draw from any of the contemporary therapeutic approaches would do well to reflect on the underlying values of these therapy models. Many of the therapy systems reflect core value orientations of mainstream U.S. culture, which has its roots in the Anglo-Saxon culture of the English who colonized America. Hogan-Garcia (1999) summarizes the underlying values of this culture as being characterized by an emphasis on the patriarchal nuclear family; "getting things done" and keeping busy; measurable and visible accomplishments; individual choice, responsibility, and achievement; self-reliance and self-motivation; the pragmatic notion of "If an idea works, use it;" change and novel ideas; and equality, informality, and fair play. The degree to which these value orientations fit clients from Eastern cultures needs to be carefully considered by practitioners.

Challenging Counselors' Stereotypical Beliefs

Counselors may think they are not biased, yet many hold stereotypical beliefs that could well affect their practice. Some examples include these statements: "Failure to change stems from a lack of motivation." "People have choices, and it is up to them to change their lives." Many people do not have a wide range of choices due to environmental factors beyond their control. To assume that all these people lack is motivation is simplistic and does not lead to understanding their struggles. Another often held assumption is that "talk therapy" works best. This ignores the fact that in many cultures people rely more on nonverbal expression.

Practitioners who counsel ethnic and racial minority clients without an awareness of their own stereotypical beliefs are likely to cause harm to their clients. Ethical practice in a multicultural context requires that mental health practitioners be aware of and sensitive to the unique cultural realities of their clients. Professionals who practice without this awareness and sensitivity risk engaging in unethical practice (Lee & Kurilla, 1997). Reflect on these issues as you consider the following case examples.

◆ **The case of Mac.** Mac, a successful psychologist, has concerns about much of the multicultural movement. He sees it as more trendy than useful. "I do not impose my values. I do not tell clients what to do. I listen, and if I need to know something, I ask. How am I to know whether a Japanese American client is more American than Japanese or vice versa unless I ask him? My belief is that the client will tell you all you need to know."

- What is your reaction to Mac's attitude?
- How would you determine the level of acculturation of a client?
- What is your reaction to Mac expecting his client to educate him on culture issues?

Commentary. We react not so much to what Mac says as to what is implied by what is said. Certainly, it is important for clients to tell counselors what they need to know. However, Mac seems to downplay the necessity for ongoing education and sensitivity to cultural issues, which might enable him to ask more effective questions. Formal education is not enough; we also need to listen to our clients. However, listening to our clients is not enough; we also need to be formally and informally educated.

◆ **The case of Claudine.** Claudine, a white counselor, takes over as director of a clinic that has a large percentage of Asian immigrants as clients. At a staff meeting she sums up her philosophy of counseling in this fashion: "People come to counseling to begin change or because they are already in the process of change. Our purpose is to challenge them to continue their change. This holds true whether the client is Euro-American, Asian, or some other minority. If clients are slow to speak, our job is to challenge them to speak, because the expectation in American culture is that people deal with problems through talking. Silence may be appropriate in Asian culture, but it does not work in this non-Asian culture. The sooner clients learn this, the better for them."

- To what extent do you agree or disagree with Claudine's assumptions, and why?
- If you disagree with Claudine's dogmatic declaration, do you see any value in the point she is trying to make?

Commentary. Paul Pedersen (2000) would say that Claudine is a culturally encapsulated counselor because she is defining everyone's reality according to her own cultural assumptions and values. She is minimizing cultural differences by imposing her own standards as criteria for judging the behavior of others. In defense of Claudine, there is some truth in her premise regarding a counselor's role in challenging a client to change. However, the key point is that therapists need to first understand the worldview of their clients and then invite them to decide on change that is congruent with their own values and support them as they work through these changes.

Examining Some Common Assumptions

Unexamined assumptions can be harmful to clients, especially assumptions based on cultural biases. What is good for one is not good for all. Let's look at a few of these commonly held beliefs about the therapeutic environment.

Assumptions about self-disclosure. Therapists often assume that clients will be ready to talk about their intimate personal issues, or that self-disclosure is essential for the therapeutic process to work. An example of this assumption is Patterson (1985b, 1996), who contends that unless clients are willing to verbalize and communicate their thoughts, feelings, attitudes, and perceptions there is no basis for empathic understanding by the therapist. He asserts that the inability to self-disclose is something to be overcome, not accepted. Patterson (1996) writes:

> The only way in which the counselor can enter the world of the client is with the permission of the client, who communicates the nature of his or her world to the counselor through self-disclosure. Thus, client self-disclosure is the sine qua non for counseling. Counselor respect and genuineness facilitate client self-disclosure. (p. 230)

Some would contend that this assumption ignores the fact that in some cultures self-disclosure is taboo and that some European ethnic groups stress keeping problems "in the family." Also at issue is how people self-disclose.

D. W. Sue and Sue (1999) point out that most forms of contemporary therapy value one's ability to self-disclose by sharing intimate personal material. The assumption is that self-disclosure is a characteristic of a healthy personality. The converse is that individuals who are reluctant to self-disclose in therapy possess negative traits of being guarded and mistrustful. However, it is unacceptable in some cultures to reveal personal problems because it not only reflects on the person individually but also on the whole family. There are strong pressures on Asian American clients not to reveal personal concerns to strangers or outsiders. Similar pressures have been reported for Hispanic, American Indian, and African American clients. Sue and Sue remind us that therapists who work with clients from a minority background may erroneously conclude that their clients are repressed, inhibited, shy, or passive. It is important for therapists to realize that such clients may in fact be holding true to their cultural background. How much value does "talk" therapy hold for these clients? What are the challenges a counselor faces in working with culturally different groups who emphasize friendship as a precondition to self-disclosure? Indeed, for many clients it seems strange, and even absurd, for them to talk about themselves personally to a professional therapist whom they do not know.

Americans value "cutting to the chase" and getting to the "bottom line." In many cultures a dance, circumlocutions, and certain rituals may precede intimate disclosures. The tendency of an insensitive professional might be to view these behaviors as either resistance or a waste of time. Counselors need to understand that there are many different ways for clients to make themselves known besides talking about private aspects of their lives.

◆ **The case of Lily.** Lily, a licensed counselor, has come to work in a family-life center that deals with many immigrant families. She often becomes impatient over the slow pace of her clients' disclosures. Lily decides to teach her clients by modeling for them. With one of her reticent couples she says: "My husband and I have many fights and disagreements. We express our feelings openly and clear the air. In fact, several years ago my husband had an affair, which put our relationship into a turmoil. I believe it was my ability to vent my anger and express my hurt that allowed me to work through this terrible event."

- What do you think of Lily's self-disclosure? Would such a disclosure be helpful to you if you were her client?
- Might you be inclined to make a similar type of disclosure to your clients? Why or why not?
- In your opinion, when, if ever, would such a disclosure be appropriate?

Assumptions about assertiveness. Many counselors assume that being assertive is better than being nonassertive. Most counselors assume that clients are better off if they can behave in assertive ways, such as telling people directly what they think and what they want. In fact, much of therapy consists of teaching clients the skills to take an active stance toward life. D. W. Sue and Sue (1985) report a widespread view that Asian Americans are nonassertive and passive. They contend, however, that this assumption has not been supported by research. These authors emphasize that certain traditional counseling practices may act as barriers to effective multicultural helping, and they call for the use of intervention strategies that are congruent with the value orientation of Asian American clients.

Assumptions about self-actualization and trusting relationships. Another assumption made by mental health professionals is that it is important for the individual to become a fully functioning person. A counselor may focus on what is good for the individual without regard for the impact of the individual's change on the significant people in that person's life or the impact of those significant people on the client. A creative synthesis between self-actualization and responsibility to the group may be a more realistic goal for some clients.

Another assumption pertains to the development of a trusting relationship. Mainstream Americans tend to form quick, though not necessarily deep, relationships and perhaps more readily talk about their personal lives than do those in other cultures. This characteristic is reflected in most therapeutic approaches. Although clinicians expect some resistance, they assume that clients will eventually be willing to explore personal issues. In many cultures this kind of a relationship takes a long time to develop. Many Asian Americans, Hispanics, and Native Americans have been brought up not to speak until spoken to, especially when they are with the elderly or with authority figures. A counselor may interpret the client's hesitancy to speak as resistance when it is only a sign of respect.

Assumptions about nonverbal behavior. Many cultural expressions are subject to misinterpretation, including appropriate personal space, eye contact, handshaking, dress, formality of greeting, perspective on time, and so forth. Mainstream Americans frequently feel uncomfortable with periods of silence and tend to talk to ease their tension. In some cultures silence may be a sign of respect and politeness rather than a lack of a desire to continue to speak. Silence may be a reflection of boredom or confusion, or it may be an expression of resistance to what the counselor is asking of the client. Itai and McRae (1994) suggest that counselors do well to pay attention to the subtle changes in nonverbal communication by the client so that they are able to understand the true meaning of silence and adopt appropriate counseling interventions to deal with the silence.

Counselors are often systematically trained in a range of microskills that include attending skills, open communication, observational skills, hearing clients accurately, noting and reflecting feelings, and selecting and structuring skills, to mention a few (Ivey & Ivey, 1999). Although these behaviors are aimed at creating a positive therapeutic relationship, individuals from certain ethnic groups may have difficulty responding positively or understanding the intent of the counselor's attitudes and behavior. The counselor whose confrontational style involves direct eye contact, physical gestures, and probing personal questions may be seen as offensively intrusive by clients from another culture.

In Euro-American middle-class culture, direct eye contact is usually considered a sign of interest and presence, and a lack thereof can be viewed as being evasive. However, even in that culture an individual often maintains more eye contact while listening and less while talking. Research indicates that some African Americans may reverse this pattern by looking more when talking and slightly less when listening. Among some Native American and Hispanic groups, eye contact by the young is a sign of disrespect. Some cultural groups generally avoid eye contact when talking about serious subjects (Ivey & Ivey, 1999). Certainly, counselors who interpret every client's lack of eye contact as "resistive" or "pathological" are not understanding or respecting important cultural differences. Clinicians need to acquire sensitivity to cultural differences to reduce the probability of miscommunication, misdiagnosis, and misinterpretation of behavior.

Assumptions about directness. Western therapeutic approaches tend to prize directness, yet in some cultures directness is perceived as a sign of rudeness and should be avoided. The counselor could assume that a lack of directness is evidence of pathology, or at least a lack of assertiveness rather than a sign of respect. Although getting to the point immediately is a prized value in Western culture, clients from other cultures may prefer to delay dealing with their problems, or deal with them more indirectly.

◆ **The case of Miguel.** Miguel, a Latino born in the United States, has completed his Ph.D. and is working at a community clinic in family therapy. In his training he has learned of the concept of triangulation, the tendency of two persons who are in conflict to involve a third person in their emotional system to reduce the stress. Miguel is on the watch for evidence of this tendency. While he is counseling a Latino family, the father says to his son, "Your mother wants you to show her more respect than you do and to obey her more." Miguel says to the mother, "Can you say this directly to your son yourself rather than speaking through your husband?" The room falls silent, and there is great discomfort.

- How might you have handled this situation differently?
- What were Miguel's assumptions?
- Would you assess the above scenario as one of triangulation? Why or why not?

◆ **A personal case history.** A few years ago Marianne Corey and Jerry Corey conducted a training workshop with counselors from a Latin American country. Marianne was accused by a male participant of being too direct and assertive. He had difficulty with Marianne's active leadership style and indicated that it was her place to defer to Jerry by letting him take the lead. Recognizing and respecting our cultural differences, we were able to arrive at a mutual understanding of different values.

Jerry had difficulty with the tardiness of the participants and had to accept the fact that we could not follow a rigid time schedule. Typically we have thought that if people were late or missed a session group cohesion would be difficult to maintain. Because the issue was openly discussed in this situation, however, the problem did not arise. We quickly learned that we had to adapt ourselves to the participants' view of time and they to us as well. To insist on interpreting such behavior as resistance would have been to ignore the cultural context.

Addressing Sexual Orientation

Most of the previous discussion on multiculturalism has focused on issues of race and ethnicity. The concept of human diversity encompasses much more than racial and ethnic factors; it encompasses all forms of oppression, discrimination, and prejudice, including those directed toward age, gender, and sexual orientation. The American Psychiatric Association, in 1973, and the American Psychological Association, in 1975, stopped labeling homosexuality as a form of mental illness. Along with these changes came the assumption that therapeutic practices would be modified to reflect this viewpoint. The mental health system has finally begun to treat the *problems* of gay and lesbian people rather than treating *them* as the problem.

The ethics codes of the ACA, the APA, and the NASW clearly state that discrimination on the basis of minority status—be it race, ethnicity, gender, or sexual orientation—is unethical and unacceptable. Working with lesbian, gay, and bisexual individuals often presents a challenge to counselors who hold traditional values. Counselors who have negative reactions to homosexuality are likely to impose their own values and attitudes. We highlight this topic because it illustrates not only the ethical problems involved in imposing values but also the problems of working with clients who have had different life experiences.

Before counselors can change their therapeutic strategies, they must change their assumptions and attitudes toward sexual orientation. Unless counselors become conscious of their own faulty assumptions and homophobia, they may project their misconceptions and their fears onto their clients. Therapists are challenged to confront their personal prejudices, myths, fears, and stereotypes regarding sexual orientation.

The American Psychological Association's Division 44 (APA, 2000) has developed a set of guidelines for psychotherapy with lesbian, gay, and bisexual clients. Any therapist who may work with lesbian, gay, and bisexual people has a responsibility to understand the special concerns of these individuals and is ethically obligated to develop the knowledge and skills to competently deliver services to these clients. Although space restricts the full discussion this topic deserves, take time to reflect on the 16 guidelines of APA's Division 44 (Committee on Lesbian, Gay, and Bisexual Concerns Joint Task Force on Guidelines for Psychotherapy with Lesbian, Gay, and Bisexual Clients). How might you implement them in your therapeutic practice?

1. Psychologists understand that homosexuality and bisexuality are not indicative of mental illness.
2. Psychologists are encouraged to recognize how their attitudes and knowledge about lesbian, gay, and bisexual issues may be relevant to assessment and treatment and seek consultation or make appropriate referrals when indicated.
3. Psychologists strive to understand the ways in which social stigmatization poses risks to the mental health and well-being of lesbian, gay, and bisexual clients.
4. Psychologists strive to understand how inaccurate or prejudicial views of homosexuality or bisexuality may affect the client's presentation in treatment and the therapeutic process.
5. Psychologists strive to be knowledgeable about and respect the importance of lesbian, gay, and bisexual relationships.
6. Psychologists strive to understand the particular circumstances and challenges faced by lesbian, gay, and bisexual parents.
7. Psychologists recognize that the families of lesbian, gay, and bisexual people may include people who are not legally or biologically related.
8. Psychologists strive to understand how a person's homosexual or bisexual orientation may have an impact on his or her family of origin and the relationship to that family of origin.

9. Psychologists are encouraged to recognize the particular life issues or challenges that are related to multiple and often conflicting cultural norms, values, and beliefs that lesbian, gay, and bisexual members of racial and ethnic minorities face.
10. Psychologists are encouraged to recognize the particular challenges that bisexual individuals experience.
11. Psychologists strive to understand the special problems and risks that exist for lesbian, gay, and bisexual youth.
12. Psychologists consider generational differences within lesbian, gay, and bisexual populations and the particular challenges that lesbian, gay, and bisexual older adults may experience.
13. Psychologists are encouraged to recognize the particular challenges that lesbian, gay, and bisexual individuals experience with physical, sensory, and cognitive-emotional disabilities.
14. Psychologists support the provision of professional education and training on lesbian, gay, and bisexual issues.
15. Psychologists are encouraged to increase their knowledge and understanding of homosexuality and bisexuality through continuing education, training, supervision, and consultation.
16. Psychologists make reasonable efforts to familiarize themselves with relevant mental health, educational, and community resources for lesbian, gay, and bisexual people.

These guidelines have relevance to all mental health professionals, not just to psychologists. Which guidelines might be most helpful for you in challenging your beliefs and attitudes regarding sexual orientation? Are there any specific attitudes, beliefs, assumptions, and values you hold that might interfere with your ability to effectively counsel lesbian, gay, and bisexual clients? If you do become aware of some personal limitations at this time, what kinds of changes would you consider making? How might you challenge certain of your attitudes and assumptions pertaining to any of these guidelines?

Value Issues of Gay and Lesbian Clients

Like any other minority group, lesbians, gay men, and bisexuals are subjected to discrimination, prejudice, and oppression, which manifests itself when gay people seek employment or a place of residence. But lesbian, gay, and bisexual clients also have special counseling needs. For instance, the U.S. Department of Defense does not permit openly homosexual individuals to serve in the military. Lesbians and gay men often bring to counseling the struggle between concealing their identity and "coming out." Dealing with family members is also of special importance to gay couples. They may want to be honest with their parents, yet they may fear hurting them or receiving negative reactions from them. With the reality of the AIDS crisis, gay men often face the loss of friends. Not only do gay men need to deal with death and loss but they may also want to explore their fears of becoming infected. Counselors who work with gay men need to be able to talk with their clients about safe-sex practices. In short, counselors need to listen carefully to their clients and be willing to explore whatever concerns they bring to the counseling relationship.

◆ **The case of Myrna and Rose.** Myrna and Rose are seeking relationship counseling, saying that they are having communication problems. They have a number of conflicts that they both want to work out. They clearly state that they are involved in a lesbian relationship and that their sexual orientation is not an issue they want to explore. They indicate that they are comfortable with their sexual orientation but need help in learning how to communicate more effectively.

Counselor A. This counselor agrees to see the two women and work with them much as she would with a heterosexual couple. The counselor adds that if at any time the uniqueness of their relationship causes difficulties, it would be up to them to bring this up as an issue. She lets them know that if they are comfortable with their sexual orientation she has no need to explore it. What are your reactions to this counselor's approach?

Counselor B. This counselor agrees to see the couple. During the initial session he realizes that he has strong negative reactions toward them. These reactions are so much in the foreground that they interfere with his ability to effectively work with the couple's presenting problem. He tells the two women about his difficulties and suggests a referral. He lets them know that he had hoped he could be objective enough to work with them but that this is not the case.

- Was this counselor's behavior ethical? Is he violating any of the ethical codes in refusing to work with this couple because of their sexual orientation?
- Given his negative reactions, should he have continued seeing the couple, or would this in itself have been unethical?
- Would it be more damaging to the clients to refer them or to continue to see them?
- Is it ethical for the counselor to charge the couple for this session? Explain your point of view.

Counselor C. This counselor agrees to see Myrna and Rose, and during the first session he suggests that they ought to examine their homosexuality. He has concerns about excluding any issues from exploration in determining what the problem really is between them.

- How do you react to the stance of this counselor? Explain.
- Would it have made a difference if, instead of insisting on exploring their sexual orientation, the counselor had said that he had concerns about excluding any issue from possible exploration in therapy?

In reviewing the approaches of these three counselors, which approach would be closest to yours? To clarify your thinking on the issue of counseling gay and lesbian clients, reflect on these questions:

- Therapists often find that the presenting problem clients bring to a session is not their major problem. Does it show the therapist's values to assume that a couple's homosexuality might be the real problem? Is the counselor justified in bringing up homosexuality as a therapeutic issue?
- What are the ethical implications of a heterosexually oriented therapist working with homosexual couples?
- Is it ever an appropriate function for counselors to attempt to sway clients toward a sexual orientation that is deemed "acceptable" by the culture?
- Should the counselor make life decisions for clients, or should the counselor challenge clients to make their own decisions?
- What attitudes are necessary for therapists to be instrumental in helping gay men and lesbians accept their sexual orientations?
- Can a counselor who is not comfortable with his or her own sexuality possibly be effective in assisting homosexual clients to accept their identity?

◆ **The case of Tanya and Liz.** Maxine, a lesbian therapist, is seeing a lesbian couple, Liz and Tanya. It is customary for Maxine to see the partners individually on occasion. During Tanya's first individual session, she confesses to having affairs with several men. Tanya tells Maxine that she sees herself as bisexual, a fact she has not disclosed to Liz. One of the issues introduced by Liz and Tanya was a problem with intimacy. During the individual session, Maxine suggests that this is one more way that Tanya avoids intimacy and begins to explore this issue with her. At the end of the session, Tanya agrees with the therapist's interpretation and agrees to come back for further couples work with Liz.

- If you were the therapist, how would you have handled Tanya's disclosure?
- Do you see anything inappropriate or unethical in Maxine's approach? Why or why not?
- Is this an example of imposition of therapist values? Why or why not?
- How will Maxine deal with the couple now that she shares a secret with Tanya?
- Was Maxine remiss in not exploring these questions: Is Tanya gay with an intimacy issue? Is Tanya bisexual? Is Tanya ambivalent about her sexual orientation?

Counseling Gay Parents and Their Children

You might become involved in counseling a gay parent, a child of a gay parent, a gay or lesbian couple wishing to adopt a child, or a heterosexual former spouse of a gay parent who is fighting for custody of their children. What assumptions and values do you hold that might make it difficult for you to counsel any of these clients? What values do you possess that might facilitate building a relationship with your clients in each of these situations?

◆ **The case of Ruby.** Ruby is counseling Henry, who expresses extremely hostile feelings toward homosexuals and toward people who have contracted AIDS. Henry is not coming to counseling to work on his feelings about gay people; his primary goal is to work out his feelings of resentment over his wife, who left him. In one session he makes derogatory comments about gay people. He thinks they are all deviant and that it serves them right if they do get AIDS. Ruby's son is gay, and Henry's prejudice affects her emotionally. She is taken aback by her client's comments, and she finds that his views are getting in the way as she attempts to work with him. Her self-dialogue has taken the following turns:

- "Maybe I should tell Henry how he is affecting me and let him know I have a son who is gay. If I don't, I am not sure I can continue to work with him."
- "I think I will express my hurt and anger to a colleague, but I surely won't tell Henry how he is affecting me. Nor will I let him know I am having a hard time working with him."
- "Henry's disclosures get in the way of my caring for him. Perhaps I should tell him I am bothered deeply by his prejudice but not let him know that I have a gay son."
- "Because of my own countertransference, it may be best that I refer him without telling him the reason I am having trouble with him."
- "Maybe I should just put my own feelings on a shelf and try to work with him on reducing his prejudice and negative reactions toward gays."

Which of Ruby's possible approaches to Henry do you find yourself most in agreement with? If Ruby came to you as a colleague and wanted to talk about her reactions and the course she should take with Henry, what might you say to her? In reflecting on what you might tell her, consider these issues:

- Is it ethical for Ruby to work on a goal that her client has not brought up?
- To what degree would you encourage Ruby to be self-disclosing with Henry? What do you think she should reveal of herself to him? What do you think she should not disclose? Why?
- Is it ethical for Ruby to continue to see Henry without telling him how she is affected by him?

Specialized Training in Counseling Gay and Lesbian Clients

Practitioners who do not possess knowledge and training about a specific group are ethically required to seek supervision and consultation or make referrals to appropriately trained professionals. It is unethical to counsel gay and lesbian clients without having received specialized training with this population.

Crawford, McLeod, Zamboni, and Jordan (1999) conducted a study to assess psychologists' attitudes toward gay and lesbian parenting. The results of their study suggest that psychologists who participated in the study held affirming attitudes toward gay and lesbian parenting. In addition, these psychologists appeared to be sensitive to the stigmatization and bias gay and lesbian families encounter. The participants indicated their concern about the level of social support these families would receive in managing the stressors associated with parenthood. The findings of this study seem to suggest that most of the participants do not endorse negative stereotypes of gay and lesbian people and do not perceive them to be a threat to the welfare of children reared in the homes of same-gender couples.

Crawford and his colleagues (1999) remind practitioners that they should not provide care outside of their areas of expertise. Practitioners need to have knowledge of the core issues pertaining to same-gender couples, including relationship and parenting concerns. These researchers conclude that before therapists provide mental health services to gay and lesbian people and their children they should complete formal, systematic training on sexual diversity.

One way to increase your awareness of ethical and therapeutic considerations in working with gay and lesbian clients is to take advantage of continuing education workshops sponsored by national, regional, state, and local professional organizations. By participating in such workshops, you can learn about referral resources as well as about specific interventions and strategies that are appropriate for gay and lesbian clients. You may not know the sexual orientation of a client until the therapeutic relationship develops, so even if you do not plan to work with a gay or lesbian population, you need to have a clear idea of your own assumptions, attitudes, and values relative to this issue.

Matching Client and Counselor

Diversity includes culture, religion, race, ability, gender, sexual orientation, education, and socioeconomic level. Is matching client and counselor on the various aspects of diversity desirable? Does the counselor have to share the experiential world of the client to be effective? These are difficult questions to answer, and the research in this area is inconclusive. Some argue that successful multicultural counseling is highly improbable because of the barriers between groups that are involved. Others argue that well-trained counselors, even though they differ from their clients, are capable of providing effective counseling. Pedersen (1991) recognizes the complex diversity of a pluralistic society but also suggests bridges of shared concern that unite culturally different individuals. Counselor and client are both unique and similar. Patterson (1996) asserts that all counseling is multicultural. From his perspective, all clients belong to multiple groups that influence their perceptions, beliefs, attitudes, and behavior. To be effective, counselors must account for these multiple influences on behavior. This perspective allows room for clinicians to effectively work with clients who differ from themselves in a number of significant respects.

Foster (1998) points out that the more disparate the respective worlds of the client and the therapist, the more the therapeutic work will need to involve a collaborative effort to find meaning and understanding. When therapists markedly differ from a client's culture, race, or class, it is imperative that they understand how their own subjectivity, or their cultural countertransference, enters into this relationship. Foster describes a clinician's cultural countertransference as a complex and interacting set of "culturally derived personal life values; academically based theoretical/practical beliefs; emotionally driven biases about ethnic groups; and feelings about their own ethnic self-identity" (p. 256). According to Foster, a cross-cultural therapeutic relationship often involves multiple points of potential dissonance for both the client and the counselor. Both individuals in the therapeutic dyad have diverse assumptions about the world and whether each will be understood by the other. Therapists need to exercise particular caution in applying their assumptions about the world to a client who is culturally different. If therapists lack understanding and insight into the source of their cultural countertransference, the likely result will be impasses, or perhaps even harm, to the therapeutic work. At times, therapists will not be aware of these countertransference attitudes, nor will they recognize the powerful influence their attitudes have on the course of treatment. Although certain subjective attitudes and biases of therapists may not be verbalized, they are frequently perceived by the client. Cross-cultural dyads are not necessarily problematic, but they pose challenges that need to be addressed if mutual understanding is to be achieved.

Another point of view is expressed by Markowitz (1994), who refers to the practices of a therapeutic group in New Zealand. This group believes therapeutic conversations across cultural lines are inherently problematic. In their view, no outsider can overcome his or her own cultural biases and, therefore, will never be able to accurately judge another culture's understanding of what constitutes normal or abnormal, healthy or unhealthy behavior.

C. C. Lee (1997c) points out that one pitfall associated with multiculturalism is that some helping professionals may give up in exasperation, asking: "How can I really be effective with a client whose cultural background is different from mine?" When counselors are overly self-conscious about their ability to work with diverse client populations, they may become too analytical about what they say and do. Counselors who are afraid to face the differences between themselves and their clients, who refuse to accept the reality of these differences, who perceive such differences as problematic, or who are uncomfortable working out these differences are bound to fail. D. W. Sue and Sue (1999) describe culturally competent counselors in this way:

> Mental health practitioners who are willing to address cultural differences directly are those who do not perceive them as impediments. Instead, therapists who view these differences as positive attributes will most likely meet and resolve the challenges that arise in MCT. Such a helper is what we consider to be culturally competent." (p. 232)

Pedersen (1999) sheds light on the topic of matching client and therapist. He proposes that counselors be trained to hear the self-talk of culturally different clients. Pedersen writes about the various alternative identities that constitute our self-talk. Each person has a thousand or more alternative roles or identities that are collected over a lifetime from various sources. What are the implications of this notion of multiple cultures within each of us? When you meet a client for the first time, realize that there are more than two people in your office. There are thousands of people in that room, and learning to hear and understand their "voices" will make you a more responsive and effective therapist. The greater the cultural dissimilarity between you and your client, the more both of you will be challenged to accurately hear the other's inner voices. According to Pedersen, this notion of a thousand "people" surrounding each of us is what makes multicultural counseling an exciting and essential perspective. He believes counselors can be trained to hear the inner voices of their culturally different clients. What is important is for counselors to learn how to pay attention to a client's salient cultural identity as it changes within the context of a single interview.

Many of you may see it as a daunting task to pay attention to the single voice of a client, let alone a thousand voices within a client! Pedersen's (1999) point, however, is basic to the therapeutic task: "Competence is measured by your ability to know what your client is thinking but not saying. To the extent that a client and yourself are culturally different, the task of hearing the client's voices will be more difficult but just as important" (p. 100). Pedersen's views on learning to understand the client's and the therapist's internal dialogue as a crucial part of the therapeutic dyad casts a new light on the possibility of matching client and counselor. More important than striving to discover the ideal match is the task of learning to monitor this internal dialogue and use it as a basic component of the therapy process. Pedersen emphasizes that becoming a multiculturally competent counselor entails more than following a list of rules. The most important aspects of culture-centered counseling can be learned, but not necessarily taught. We can become our own best teachers if we pay attention to the voices within us and within our clients. "If and when we are competent, it is because those inside voices are guiding us toward competence" (p. 100). In our opinion, the voices on both sides of the counseling dyad come from multiple sources, including parents, grandparents, teachers, subcultures, and significant others. If our approach is rigid and concrete, we hear only the spoken content, which diminishes our effectiveness.

It is our position that counselors can learn to work with clients who differ from them in gender, race, culture, socioeconomic background, physical ability, age, or sexual orientation. But our stance is tempered by certain reservations and conditions. First, counselors need to have training in multicultural perspectives, both academic and experiential. Second, as in any other counseling situation, it is important that the client and the counselor agree to develop a working therapeutic relationship. Third, counselors are advised to be flexible in applying theories and techniques to specific situations. The counselor who has an open stance has a greater likelihood of success than someone who rigidly adheres to a single theoretical system.

Fourth, the counselor should be open to being challenged and tested. In multicultural counseling there is a greater likelihood that clients will exhibit suspicion and distrust. Some African Americans perceive Euro-Americans as potential enemies unless proven otherwise. They may use many defenses as survival strategies to protect their true feelings. A Euro-American counselor may be perceived to be a symbol of the establishment. Counselors who see themselves as culturally competent and sensitive may find it difficult to withstand this kind of testing. If counselors become excessively defensive in such situations, they will probably lose the client. If counselors act defensively, they are creating a potential ethical situation that may hurt the client. Clients may feel that they would have to reject their own culture to accept the counselor's values or solutions. To minority clients it may seem that a professional who is not part of the solution to their problem is really part of the problem.

Fifth, it becomes especially important in multicultural counseling situations for counselors to be aware of their own value systems, of potential stereotyping and any traces of prejudice, and of their cultural countertransference. We agree with Foster's (1998) notion of the cultural countertransference of therapists in the sense that therapists need to develop self-understanding of how their values, feelings, attitudes, and biases influence their work with culturally different clients. Earlier we described those culture-bound counselors who are unintentional racists. In some ways, such counselors can be more dangerous than those who are more open with their prejudices. According to Pedersen (2000), unintentional racists must be challenged either to become intentional racists or to modify their racist attitudes and behaviors. The more "overt racism" characteristic of the South is often more accessible than the evasive avoidance of the "liberal North." The key to changing unintentional racism lies in examining basic assumptions. Two forms of covert racism that Ridley (1995) identifies are color blindness and color consciousness. The counselor who says, "When I look at you, I see a person, not a black person" may encounter mistrust from clients who have difficulty believing that. Likewise, a counselor is not likely to earn credibility by saying, "If you were not black, you wouldn't have the problem you're facing." These examples of color blindness and color consciousness are rather extreme, but there are many more subtle variations on these themes. For a thought-provoking analysis of the role of racism in counseling practice, we suggest reading Ridley (1995).

Try to identify your own assumptions as you think about these questions:

- Does a counselor need to share the cultural background of the client to be effective?
- If you were to encounter considerable "testing" from a client who is culturally different from you, how do you think you would react? What are some ways in which you could work therapeutically?
- What experiences have you had with discrimination? How do you think your own experiences could either help or hinder you in working with clients who have been discriminated against?
- What stereotypes are you aware of having?

When counselors identify "unusual behavior" in a client, it is important to determine whether such behavior is unusual within the client's cultural context. Clients may become suspicious if they sense the therapist has already come to a conclusion. Rather than suffering from clinical paranoia, these clients may be reacting to the realities of an environment in which they have suffered oppression and prejudice. In such cases, clients' responses may make complete sense. Counselors who appreciate the context of such perceptions are less likely to pathologize clients and are able to begin working with clients from their experiential framework.

As you read the following case, consider how you could increase your own sensitivity to individuals from cultural groups different from your own.

◆ **The case of John.** John, an African American, comes from a lower-middle-class neighborhood in an eastern city, has struggled to get a college degree, and has finally attained a master's degree in counseling. He is proud of his accomplishments, but he considers himself to be sensitive to his own background and to those who struggle with similar problems. He has moved to the West Coast and has been hired to work in a high school in a neighborhood with a large minority population.

As a high school counselor, John starts a group for at-risk adolescents. His goals for this group are as follows: (1) to instill pride so that group members will see their present environment as an obstacle to be overcome, not suffered with; (2) to increase self-esteem and to challenge group members to fight the negativism they may encounter in their home and school environments; (3) to teach group members to minimize their differences in terms of the larger community (for example, he points out how some of their idioms and ways of speaking separate them from the majority and reinforce differences and stereotypes); and (4) to teach group members how to overcome obstacles in a nonsupportive environment.

John does not work very closely with teachers, administrators, or other school counselors in the district. He views them as being more interested in politics and red tape and as actually giving very little energy to personal counseling in the school. He has little to do with the families of the adolescents, because he sees them as being too willing to accept handouts and welfare and as not being very interested in becoming self-sufficient and independent. He tells his group members: "What you have at home with your families has obviously not worked for you. What you have in this group is the opportunity to change and to have that change appreciated."

- Does John's racial and cultural background and growing experiences qualify him as a multicultural counselor? Why or why not?
- What are John's assumptions?
- What was John's internal dialogue?
- What effect might it have had on his goals if John had become familiar with the environment of this particular group?
- If you were John's colleague, how would you react to his attitude toward you?
- If you were John's supervisor, how would you deal with him?

Commentary. John is a well-intentioned school counselor who demonstrates a lack of sensitivity to the particular needs of this minority community. We disagree with his axiom that simply because he could obtain a graduate degree (against difficult odds) anybody could have the same success. John made no attempt to become aware of the unique struggles or values of the high school students he serves. He stereotyped the parents of his group members in a very indirect, but powerful fashion. Even though John is an African American himself, he imposed values of the majority culture in terms of language and upward mobility. He set up potential conflicts between group members and their families by the way he downplayed and labeled their families' value systems. John acted insensitively to the families of his group members. His basic mistake was his assumption that what worked for him would work for them.

Multicultural Training for Counselors

Although referral is sometimes an appropriate course of action, it should not be viewed as a solution to the problem of inadequately trained counselors. Many agencies have practitioners whose cultural backgrounds are less diverse than the populations they serve. With the increasing number of culturally diverse clients seeking counseling, and with the decreasing number of resources to meet these needs, counselors may not have the luxury of referral. Therefore, we recommend that all counseling students, regardless of their racial or ethnic background, receive training in multicultural counseling and therapy (MCT).

Nuttall, Webber, and Sanchez (1996, p. 131) contend that the heart and soul of a quality multicultural training program depends on the competence, knowledge, and commitment of the faculty. The standards established by the Council for Accreditation of Counseling and Related Educational Programs (CACREP) require that programs provide curricular and experiential offerings in multicultural and pluralistic trends. The CACREP standards call for supervised practicum experiences that include people from the environments in which the trainee is preparing to work. It is expected that trainees will study about ethnic groups, subcultures, the changing roles of women, sexism, urban and rural societies, cultural mores, spiritual issues, and differing life patterns.

Characteristics of the Culturally Skilled Counselor

According to Sue and his colleagues (1998), becoming a multiculturally competent mental health practitioner involves three dimensions. The first dimension deals with the practitioner's attitudes and beliefs about race, culture, ethnicity, gender, and sexual orientation; the need to monitor personal biases; development of a positive view toward multiculturalism; and understanding how one's values and biases may get in the way of effective helping. The second dimension recognizes that a culturally competent practitioner is knowledgeable and understanding of his or her own worldview, possesses specific knowledge of the diverse groups with whom he or she works, and has a basic understanding of sociopolitical influences. The third dimension deals with skills, intervention techniques, and strategies necessary in serving diverse client groups.

Mental health services can be delivered best if practitioners accurately begin with the assumption that their clients are basically psychologically healthy and are experiencing normal developmental struggles. C. C. Lee (1997b) contends that counseling services are enhanced when helpers recognize the cultural dynamics of their clients and have learned how to incorporate naturally occurring support systems into a range of interventions. For Lee, culturally responsive counseling is predicated on making full use of indigenous sources of helping.

A major contribution to the counseling profession has been the development of multicultural competencies, which were initially formulated by D. W. Sue and colleagues (1982) and were later revised and expanded by D. W. Sue, Arredondo, and McDavis (1992). Arredondo and her colleagues (1996) have updated and operationalized these competencies. Sue and his colleagues (1998) have developed multicultural counseling competencies as they apply to individual and organizational development. The essential attributes of culturally competent counselors, compiled from the sources just cited, are listed in the box titled Multicultural Counseling Competencies.

In the early 1980s, D. W. Sue (1996a) requested that both the American Counseling Association and the American Psychological Association endorse the multicultural competencies that he and his colleagues formulated. According to Sue (1996a), defining multicultural competencies has stimulated considerable debate in the counseling profession because these competencies (a) provide a strong rationale for a multicultural perspective in the helping professions, (b) develop specific multicultural standards that define the culturally competent counselor, and (c) advocate a call for action in the implementation of standards for both ACA and APA. These competencies have been endorsed by the Association for Multicultural Counseling and Development (AMCD) and by the Association for Counselor Education and Supervision (ACES). Endorsement of these competencies demonstrates the increased interest among counselor educators and practitioners in actively pursuing cultural competence (D'Andrea & Arredondo, 1996).

◆ **The case of Talib.** Talib, an immigrant from the Middle East, is a graduate student in a counseling program. During many class discussions, his views on gender roles become clear, yet he expresses his beliefs in a respectful and non-dogmatic fashion. Talib's attitudes and beliefs about gender roles are that the man should be the provider and head of the home and that the woman is in charge of nurturance, which is a full-time job. Although not directly critical of his female classmates, Talib voices a concern that these students may be neglecting their family obligations by pursuing a graduate education. Talib bases his views not only on his cultural background but also by citing experts in this country who support his position that the absence of women in the home has been a major contributor to the breakdown of the family. There are

Multicultural Counseling Competencies

I. Counselor Awareness of Own Cultural Values and Biases
   A. With respect to *attitudes and beliefs,* culturally competent counselors:
      - believe that cultural self-awareness and sensitivity to one's own cultural heritage is essential.
      - are aware of how their own cultural background and experiences have influenced attitudes, values, and biases about psychological processes.
      - are able to recognize the limits of their multicultural competencies and expertise.
      - recognize their sources of discomfort with differences that exist between themselves and clients in terms of race, ethnicity, and culture.
   B. With respect to *knowledge,* culturally competent counselors:
      - have specific knowledge about their own racial and cultural heritage and how it personally and professionally affects their definitions of and biases about normality/abnormality and the process of counseling.
      - possess knowledge and understanding about how oppression, racism, discrimination, and stereotyping affect them personally and in their work. This allows individuals to acknowledge their own racist attitudes, beliefs, and feelings.
      - possess knowledge about their social impact on others.
   C. With respect to *skills,* culturally competent counselors:
      - seek out educational, consultative, and training experiences to improve their understanding and effectiveness in working with culturally different populations.
      - are constantly seeking to understand themselves as racial and cultural beings and are actively seeking a nonracist identity.

II. Understanding the Client's Worldview
   A. With respect to *attitudes and beliefs,* culturally competent counselors:
      - are aware of their negative and positive emotional reactions toward other racial and ethnic groups that may prove detrimental to the counseling relationship. They are willing to contrast their own beliefs and attitudes with those of their culturally different clients in a nonjudgmental fashion.
      - are aware of stereotypes and preconceived notions that they may hold toward other racial and ethnic minority groups.
   B. With respect to *knowledge,* culturally competent counselors:
      - possess specific knowledge and information about the particular client group with whom they are working.
      - understand how race, culture, ethnicity, and so forth may affect personality formation, vocational choices, manifestation or psychological disorders, help-seeking behavior, and the appropriateness or inappropriateness of counseling approaches.
      - understand and have knowledge about sociopolitical influences that impinge on the lives of racial and ethnic minorities.
   C. With respect to *skills,* culturally competent counselors:
      - familiarize themselves with relevant research and the latest findings regarding mental health and mental disorders that affect various ethnic and racial groups.
      - become actively involved with minority individuals outside the counseling setting so that their perspective of minorities is more than an academic or helping exercise.

III. Developing Culturally Appropriate Intervention Strategies and Techniques
   A. With respect to *attitudes and beliefs,* culturally competent counselors:
      - respect clients' religious and spiritual beliefs and values, including attributions and taboos, because these affect worldview, psychosocial functioning, and expressions of distress.

(continued)

(continued)

- respect indigenous helping practices and respect help-giving networks among communities of color.
- value bilingualism and do not view another language as an impediment to counseling.

B. With respect to *knowledge*, culturally competent counselors:
- have a clear and explicit knowledge and understanding of the generic characteristics of counseling and therapy and how they may clash with the cultural values of various cultural groups.
- are aware of institutional barriers that prevent minorities from using mental health services.
- have knowledge of the potential bias in assessment instruments and use procedures and interpret findings in a way that recognizes the cultural and linguistic characteristics of clients.
- have knowledge of family structures, hierarchies, values, and beliefs from various cultural perspectives. They are knowledgeable about the community where a particular cultural group may reside and the resources in the community.
- are aware of relevant discriminatory practices at the social and the community level that may affect the psychological welfare of the population being served.

C. With respect to *skills*, culturally competent counselors:
- are able to engage in a variety of verbal and nonverbal helping responses. They are able to send and receive both verbal and nonverbal messages accurately and appropriately. They are not tied to only one method or approach to helping but recognize that helping styles and approaches may be culture bound.
- are able to exercise institutional intervention skills on behalf of their clients. They can help clients determine whether a problem stems from racism or bias in others so that clients do not inappropriately personalize problems.
- are not adverse to seeking consultation with traditional healers or religious and spiritual leaders and practitioners in the treatment of culturally different clients when appropriate.
- take responsibility for interacting in the language requested by the client and, if not feasible, make appropriate referrals.
- have training and expertise in the use of traditional assessment and testing instruments.
- attend to and work to eliminate biases, prejudices, and discriminatory contexts in conducting evaluations and providing interventions and develop sensitivity to issues of oppression, sexism, heterosexism, elitism, and racism.
- take responsibility for educating their clients to the processes of psychological intervention, such as goals, expectations, legal rights, and the counselor's orientation.

For the complete description of these competencies, along with explanatory statements, refer to "Operationalization of the Multicultural Counseling Competencies," by Arredondo, Toporek, Brown, Jones, Locke, Sanchez, and Stadler (1996), in the January edition of the *Journal of Multicultural Counseling and Development.* Also see D. W. Sue and colleagues (1998, Chapter 4) for a detailed listing of multicultural counseling competencies.

many lively discussions between Talib and his classmates, many of whom hold very different attitudes regarding gender roles. Halfway through the semester, his instructor, Dr. Felice Good, asks Talib to come to her office after class. Dr. Good lets Talib know that she has grave concerns about his pursuing a career in counseling in this country with his present beliefs. She encourages him to consider another career if he is unable to change his "biased convictions" about the role of women. She tells him that unless he can open his thinking to more contemporary viewpoints he will surely encounter serious problems with clients and fellow professionals.

- If you were one of Talib's classmates, what would you want to say to him?
- What assumptions underlie Dr. Good's advice to Talib?
- If you were a faculty member, what criteria would you use to determine that students are not suited for a program because of their values?
- How would you approach a person whose views seem very different from your own? How would you respond to Talib?

Commentary. Dr. Good seemed to assume that because Talib expressed strong convictions he was rigid and would impose his values on his clients. She did not communicate a respect for his value system along with her concern that Talib might impose his values on clients. She did not use this situation as a teaching tool in the classroom to explore the issue of value imposition.

Students who express strong values are often told that they should not work with certain clients. As a result, students may hesitate to expose their viewpoints if they differ from the "acceptable norm." In our view, a critical feature of MCT is the personal development of trainees, which includes helping them clarify a set of values and beliefs concerning culture that increases their chances of functioning effectively in multicultural situations. We try to teach students that having strong convictions is not the same as imposing them on others. Students are challenged to become aware of their value systems and be open to exploring them. However, their role is not go into this profession to impose these values on others. Ridley and his colleagues (1994) contend that the scope of training needs to include both the personal and professional development of trainees. In defining a philosophy of MCT, they ask the following questions:

- How far do we go in shifting students' values and beliefs?
- How far do we go in preserving students' values and beliefs?
- How are we to assess the effects of such shifting or preserving of values and beliefs?
- Do we have an ethical responsibility to influence trainees' values and beliefs, or is it an ethical violation of students' rights to their own personal beliefs?
- What are the implications for students who fail to conform to the accepted value system regarding human diversity?

Our Views on Multicultural Training

The first step in the process of acquiring multicultural counseling skills should be that students become involved in a self-exploratory class to help identify their cultural and ethnic blind spots. Ideally, this course would be required of all trainees in the mental health professions and would be taught by someone with experience in multicultural issues. It is our position that it is an ethical obligation of counselor educators to identify, and perhaps even screen out, those students who exhibit and refuse to examine rigid notions of the way people ought to live, regardless of their cultural background. In addition to this introductory course, students could take at least one other course dealing exclusively with multicultural issues and minority groups. Ideally, multicultural counseling will become a part of all courses.

It is also extremely important that a multicultural perspective be integrated throughout the curriculum. When teaching theories and techniques of counseling, for example, instructors can emphasize how such concepts and strategies can be adapted to the special needs of diverse client populations and how some theories may have limited value in working with certain culturally different clients. Wherever possible, representatives of diverse cultures can speak directly to the students about social, economic, and culture-specific factors that may affect mental health treatment. In addition, we support C. C. Lee's (1997b) proposal for comprehensive and ongoing professional development experiences related to multicultural counseling. All counselors must have training in how to account for salient cultural dynamics in the therapeutic process.

Trainees should participate in at least one required internship in which they have multicultural experiences or reframe their experiences from a multicultural viewpoint. Ideally, the agency supervisor will be well-versed in the cultural variables of that particular setting and also be skilled in cross-cultural understanding. Students should also have access to both individual and group supervision on campus from a multiculturally qualified faculty member. Students need to be encouraged to select supervised field placements and internships that will challenge them to work on gender and cultural concerns, developmental issues, and lifestyle differences. They will not learn to become effective multicultural counselors by working exclusively with clients with whom they are comfortable and who are "like them." We agree with C. C. Lee (1997b) that there is a limit to how much can be learned about cultural diversity from courses and workshops. Lee maintains that more can be learned by going out into the community and interacting with diverse groups of people who face a myriad of problems. Through well-selected internship experiences, trainees will not only expand their own consciousness but will also increase their knowledge of diverse groups and will have a basis for acquiring intervention skills.

Finally, we highly recommend that trainees open themselves to people in other cultures through reading and travel. Students can also make use of films and videotapes and can attend seminars and workshops that focus on multicultural issues in the helping professions. Any experiences that will sensitize students to a broad range of life experiences and cultural values will contribute to their effectiveness as counselors. The film *The Color of Fear,* by Lee Mun Wah, is a dramatic challenge to all of us to examine our presumed freedom from prejudice and bias.

As a way of getting the most from your training, we encourage you to accept your limitations and to be patient with yourself as you expand your vision of how your culture continues to influence the person you are today. It is not helpful to overwhelm yourself with all that you do not know. You will not become more effective in multicultural counseling by expecting that you must be completely knowledgeable about the cultural backgrounds of all your clients, by thinking that you should have a complete repertoire of skills, or by demanding perfection. Recognize and appreciate your efforts toward becoming a more effective person and counselor, and remember that becoming a multiculturally competent counselor is an ongoing process. Learning to take small steps is an important part of this process.

Chapter Summary

A number of writers have urged over the last decade that counselors learn about their own culture and become aware of how their experiences affect the way they work with others who are culturally different. By being ignorant of the values and attitudes of a diverse range of clients, therapists open themselves to criticism. Imposing one's own vision of the world on clients not only leads to negative therapeutic outcomes but also constitutes unethical practice.

As we stated in the introduction to this chapter, culture can be interpreted broadly to include racial or ethnic groups, as well as gender, age, religion, economic status, nationality, physical capacity or handicap, or sexual orientation. We are all limited by our experiences in these various groups, but we can increase our awareness by direct contact with a variety of groups, by reading, by special course work, and by in-service professional workshops. It is essential that our practices be accurate, appropriate, and meaningful for the clients with whom we work. This entails rethinking our theories and modifying our techniques to meet clients' unique needs and not rigidly applying interventions in the same manner to all clients. We encourage you to continue to examine your assumptions, attitudes, and values so that you can determine how they might influence your practice.

Suggested Activities

1. Select two or three cultures or races different from your own. What attitudes and beliefs about these cultures did you hold while growing up? How have your attitudes changed, if at all, and what contributed to the changes?
2. What values do you owe primarily to your culture? Have any of your values changed with the passing of time, and if so, how? How might these values influence the way you work with clients who are culturally different from you?
3. What multicultural life experiences have you had? Did you learn anything about your prejudices? What prejudices, if any, did you feel were directed at you? You might bring your experiences to class. Also, we suggest that you interview other students or faculty members who identify themselves as ethnically or culturally different from you. What might they teach you about differences that you as a counselor would need to take into consideration to work more effectively with them?

4. Invite speakers to class to talk about multicultural factors as they relate to values. Speakers representing special concerns of various ethnic groups can address the topic of certain values unique to their group and can discuss the implications of these values for counseling.

5. To what degree have your courses and field experience contributed to your ability to work effectively with people from other cultures? What training experiences would you like to have to better prepare you for multicultural counseling?

6. Divide into groups of four in your class. One person role-plays a minority client. A second person assumes the counselor role. The third person acts as an alter ego for the client, as the anticounselor. The fourth person acts as an alter ego for the therapist, or the procounselor. You might have the minority client be somewhat reluctant to speak. The counselor can deal with this silence by treating it as a form of resistance, using typical therapeutic strategies. During this time the anticounselor expresses the cultural meaning of the silence. The procounselor shares out loud what he or she imagines the counselor might be thinking. Now, devise a way to deal with silence from this frame of reference without using traditional therapeutic techniques.

7. Minorities are often put under strong pressure to give up their beliefs and ways in favor of adopting the ideals and customs of the dominant culture. What do you think your approach would be in working with clients who feel such pressure? How might you work with clients who see their own ethnicity or cultural heritage as a handicap to be overcome?

8. What was your own "internal dialogue" as you read and reflected on this chapter? In small groups, share some of this internal dialogue.

9. In small groups, discuss a few of your assumptions that are likely to influence the manner in which you counsel others. Select one of the assumptions discussed in this chapter from the following list that most applies to you. Explore your attitudes in a small group.

- What assumptions do you make about the value of self-disclosure on the part of clients?
- What are your assumptions pertaining to autonomy, independence, and self-determination?
- To what degree do you assume that it is better to be assertive than to be nonassertive?
- How do you view a fully functioning person?
- What value do you place on being direct?
- What other assumptions can you think of that might either help or hinder you in counseling diverse client populations?

10. In small groups, explore what you consider to be the main ethical issues in counseling lesbian, gay, and bisexual clients. Review the set of guidelines for psychotherapy with lesbian, gay, and bisexual clients given on pages 126 and 127. Which of the 16 guidelines do you think would be most helpful for you in challenging your beliefs and attitudes regarding sexual orientation? Are

there any attitudes, beliefs, or assumptions you hold that might get in the way of your effectively counseling lesbian, gay, and bisexual clients?

11. Select any one of the many cases described in this chapter, and reflect on how you would deal with this case from an ethical perspective. After you select the case that most interests you, review the steps in the ethical decision-making process described in Chapter 1, and then go through these steps in addressing the issues involved in the case.

12. Paul Pedersen (2000) contends that the codes of ethics of both the APA and the ACA are culturally biased and culturally encapsulated. Pederson believes that ethical guidelines appropriate in one cultural context may not be appropriate in contrasting settings. To the extent that ethical guidelines are based on the values of one dominant culture, Pedersen argues that these guidelines need to be modified. Review the ethics codes of one or more professional organizations (APA, ACA, NASW, AAMFT) by looking for specific guidelines that take cultural, ethnic, and racial dimensions into account. To what degree are you satisfied from a multicultural perspective with the ethics codes? If you were on the ethics committee, what kinds of revisions would you want to make that would address ethics and multiculturalism?

13. In small groups, discuss ways for a culturally encapsulated counselor to become more aware of his or her own culturally learned assumptions. Review the list of traits of the culturally encapsulated counselor who exhibits monocultural tunnel vision. What are some of the ways that you might be culturally encapsulated? If you recognize any of these traits in yourself, what do you think you might do about them?

14. *The Color of Fear,* produced and directed by Lee Mun Wah, is an emotional and insightful portrayal of racism in America.* Its aim is to illustrate the type of dialogue and relationships needed if we are to have a truly multicultural society based on equality and trust. After viewing the film in class, share what it brought out in you.

Ethics in Action CD-ROM Exercises

15. In video role play #3, Culture Clash, the client (Sally) directly questions the counselor's background. Sally says she did not expect Richard to be so young, and she wonders how much he knows about Chinese culture. When Richard replies that he can learn, Sally responds that she has come for help and not as a teacher for the counselor. Role-play a situation where a clash between you and a client might develop (such as difference in age, race, sexual orientation, or culture).

16. Refer to the section entitled "Becoming an Effective Multicultural Practitioner" in the *Ethics in Action* CD-ROM. Complete the self-examination of multicultural counseling competencies. Bring your answers into class and

* *The Color of Fear* is available from Stir Fry Productions in Oakland, California. The Stir Fry Productions Company provides trained facilitators (in some areas) to assist with discussion after the film is shown.

explore in small discussion groups what you need to do to become competent as a counselor of clients whose cultural background differs from your own.

InfoTrac® College Edition Resources

For additional readings, explore InfoTrac College Edition, our online library. Go to *http://www.infotrac.college.com/wadsworth* and select these key word searches:

ethic* multicult* couns*
values couns*
values therap*
values psych*
multicult* training couns*
multicultural counseling competencies

Key words are listed in a form that enables the search engine to locate a wider range of articles in the online university library. Key words should be entered exactly as shown, including asterisks, "Wl," "W2," "AND," and other search engine tools.

5

Pre-Chapter Self-Inventory

Directions: For each statement, indicate the response that most closely identifies your beliefs and attitudes. Use the following code:

5 = I *strongly agree* with this statement.
4 = I *agree* with this statement.
3 = I am *undecided* about this statement.
2 = I *disagree* with this statement.
1 = I *strongly disagree* with this statement.

_____1. If there is a conflict between a legal and an ethical standard, a therapist must always adhere to the ethical standard.

_____2. Practitioners who do not use written consent forms are unprofessional and unethical.

_____3. To practice ethically, therapists must become familiar with the laws related to their profession.

_____4. Clients in therapy should not have access to their clinical files.

_____5. Clients should be made aware of their rights at the outset of a diagnostic or therapeutic relationship.

_____6. It is unethical for a counselor to alter the fee structure once it has been established.

_____7. Ethical practice demands that therapists develop procedures to ensure that clients are in a position to make informed choices.

_____8. Therapists have the responsibility to become knowledgeable about community resources and alternatives to therapy and to present these alternatives to their clients.

Client Rights and Counselor Responsibilities

_____9. Before entering therapy, clients should be made aware of the purposes, goals, techniques, policies, and procedures involved.

_____10. It is not necessary to inform clients at the initial counseling session of the limits of confidentiality.

_____11. Therapists have an ethical responsibility to discuss possible termination issues with clients during the initial sessions and to review these matters with them periodically.

_____12. It is primarily the therapist's responsibility to determine the appropriate time for termination of therapy for most clients.

_____13. A therapeutic relationship should be maintained only as long as it is clear that the client is benefiting.

_____14. I would want to be sure that my clients were aware of both the possible benefits and the risks associated with counseling before we began a professional relationship.

_____15. I would keep detailed clinical notes and share these notes with my client because this can be therapeutic.

_____16. When a child is in psychotherapy, the therapist has an ethical and legal obligation to provide the parents with information they request.

_____17. Minors should be allowed to seek psychological assistance regarding pregnancy and abortion counseling *without* parental consent or knowledge.

_____18. Mystification of the client-therapist relationship tends to increase client dependence.

_____19. Involuntary commitment is a violation of human rights, even in those cases where individuals are unable to be responsible for themselves or their actions.

_____20. I should think about specific ways to protect myself from malpractice suits.

Introduction

If we hope to practice in an ethical and legal manner, the rights of clients cannot be taken for granted. In this chapter we deal with ways of educating clients about their rights and responsibilities as partners in the therapeutic process. Special attention is given to the role of informed consent as well as ethical and legal issues that arise when therapists fail to provide for consent. We also deal with some of the ethical and legal issues involved in counseling children and adolescents.

Part of ethical practice is talking with clients about their rights. Depending on the setting and the situation, this discussion can involve the circumstances that may affect the client's decision to enter the therapeutic relationship, the responsibilities of the therapist toward the client, the possibility of involuntary hospitalization, the possibility of being forced to submit to certain types of medical and psychological treatment, matters of privacy and confidentiality, the possible ramifications of a DSM-IV label, and the possible outcomes and limitations of therapy.

Frequently, clients don't realize that they have rights. Vulnerable and sometimes desperate for help, clients may unquestioningly accept whatever their therapist says or does. There may be an aura about the therapeutic process, and clients may have exaggerated confidence in their therapists much like the trust patients often have in their physicians. For most people the therapeutic situation is a new one, and they may be unclear about what is expected of them and what they should expect from the therapist. For these reasons we think the therapist is responsible for protecting clients' rights and teaching clients about these rights. The ethics codes of most professional organizations require that clients be given adequate information to make informed choices about entering and continuing the client-therapist relationship (see the box titled The Rights of Clients and Informed Consent for examples from several ethics codes). By alerting clients to their rights and responsibilities, the practitioner is encouraging them to develop a healthy sense of autonomy and personal power.

In addition to the ethical aspects of safeguarding clients' rights, legal parameters also govern professional practice. When we attend workshops dealing with ethical and legal issues in counseling, we often hear counselors expressing their fears of lawsuits. At times it appears that some counselors are more focused on protecting themselves than on helping their clients. We do not think this legalistic focus brings out the best qualities in practitioners.

You will surely want to protect yourself legally, but we hope you will not allow this reality to immobilize you and inhibit your professional effectiveness. Calfee (1997) informs us that lawsuits brought against mental health professionals are few, but such cases are on the rise. Counseling is a risky venture, and you must become familiar with the laws that govern professional practice. However, we urge you to avoid becoming so involved in legalities that you cease being primarily interested in the ethical and clinical implications of what you do in your practice.

The Rights of Clients and Informed Consent: Some Ethics Codes

American Psychological Association (1992)

Psychologists obtain appropriate informed consent to therapy or related procedures, using language that is reasonably understandable to participants. The content of informed consent will vary depending on many circumstances; however, informed consent generally implies that the person (1) has the capacity to consent, (2) has been informed of significant information concerning the procedure, (3) has freely and without undue influence expressed consent, and (4) consent has been appropriately documented.

National Association of Social Workers (1999)

Social workers should provide services to clients only in the context of a professional relationship based, when appropriate, on valid informed consent. Social workers should use clear and understandable language to inform clients of the purpose of the service, risks related to the service, limits to service because of the requirements of a third-party payer, relevant costs, reasonable alternatives, clients' right to refuse or withdraw consent, and the time frame covered by the consent. Social workers should provide clients with an opportunity to ask questions.

American Counseling Association (1995)

When counseling is initiated, and throughout the counseling process as necessary, counselors inform clients of the purposes, goals, techniques, procedures, limitations, potential risks, and benefits of services to be performed, and other pertinent information. Counselors take steps to ensure that clients understand the implications of diagnosis, the intended use of tests and reports, fees, and billing arrangements. Clients have a right to expect confidentiality and to be provided with an explanation of its limitations, including supervision and/or treatment team professionals; to obtain clear information about their case records; to participate in the ongoing counseling plans; and to refuse any recommended services and be advised of the consequences of such refusal.

The Client's Right to Give Informed Consent

One of the best ways to protect the rights of clients is to develop procedures to help them make informed choices. Informed consent involves the right of clients to be informed about their therapy and to make autonomous decisions pertaining to it. The main purpose of informed consent is to increase the chances that the client will become involved, educated, and a willing participant in his or her therapy. Mental health professionals are required by their ethics codes to disclose to clients the risks, benefits, and alternatives to proposed treatment. The intent of an informed consent document is to define and clarify the nature of the therapeutic relationship. The goal of the informed consent process is to give clients adequate and continuous information so that they may anticipate what they may wish to consent to in treatment (Wineburgh, 1998). Informed consent involves more than a client's signature on a form and is best viewed as an ongoing process. The process of informed consent begins with the intake interview and continues throughout counseling. Informed consent entails a balance between telling clients too much and telling them too little. Although most professionals agree on the ethical principle that it is crucial to provide clients with information about the therapeutic relationship, the manner in which this is done in practice varies considerably among therapists. It is a mistake to overwhelm clients with too much detailed information at once, but it is also a mistake to withhold important information that clients need if they are to make wise choices about their therapy program.

Professionals have a responsibility to their clients to make reasonable disclosure of all significant facts, the nature of the procedure, and some of the more probable consequences and difficulties. All clients have the right to have treatment explained to them. The process of therapy is not so mysterious that it cannot be explained in a way that clients can comprehend how it works. It is essential that clients give their consent *with* understanding. It is the responsibility of professionals to assess the client's level of understanding and to protect the client's free choice. Professionals need to avoid subtly coercing clients to cooperate with a therapy program to which they are not freely consenting. Generally, informed consent requires that the client be competent, have knowledge of what will occur, especially the risks, and be in treatment voluntarily (Anderson, 1996; Bennett et al., 1990; Crawford, 1994).

Legal Aspects of Informed Consent

Three elements are basic to the legal definition of informed consent: capacity, comprehension of information, and voluntariness (Anderson, 1996; Crawford, 1994; Stromberg & Dellinger, 1993). *Capacity* means that the client has the ability to make rational decisions. When this capacity is lacking, a parent or guardian is typically responsible for giving consent. *Comprehension of information* means that therapists must give clients information in a clear way and check to see that they understand it. To give valid consent, it is necessary for clients to have adequate information about both the procedure and the possible consequences. The information must include the benefits and risks of procedures, possible adverse effects from treatment, the risk of forgoing treatment, and available alternative procedures. *Voluntariness* means that the person giving consent is acting freely in the decision-making process and is legally and psychologically able (competent) to give consent. It implies that the professional and the client have discussed the nature of the problem and possible treatments for it. The therapist should explain to competent clients, who have not been ordered by the court to undergo evaluation or treatment, that they are free to withdraw their consent at any time for any reason.

Educating Clients About Informed Consent

It is a good practice for therapists to employ an educative approach by encouraging clients' questions about evaluation or treatment and by offering useful feedback as the treatment process progresses. Here are some questions therapists should answer at the outset of the counseling relationship:

- What are the goals of the therapeutic program?

- What services will the counselor provide?
- What is expected of the client?
- What are the risks and benefits of therapy?
- What are the qualifications of the provider of the services?
- What are the financial considerations?
- How long is the therapy expected to last?
- What are the limitations of confidentiality?
- When might the therapist need to refer a client because of personal values?
- In what situations does the counselor have mandatory reporting requirements?

Informed consent involves disclosure by the practitioner of the necessary information clients will need to make an educated and a free decision of whether or not to become part of a therapeutic relationship. It is essential to give clients an opportunity to raise questions and to explore their expectations of counseling. We view clients as partners with their therapists in the sense that they are involved as fully as possible in each aspect of their therapy. Thus, education about the therapeutic process begins at the intake session and continues to the termination phase. Welfel (2002) points out that it is a myth to assume that clients will understand and remember what they are told initially about informed consent procedures. Another myth is that informed consent is easily completed within the initial session by asking clients to sign forms. Educating clients about the therapeutic process is an ongoing endeavor. The more clients know about how therapy works, including the roles of both client and therapist, the more clients will benefit from the therapeutic experience.

Informed consent is also a means of sharing power with the client, which has clinical as well as ethical significance. Especially in the case of clients who have been victimized, issues of power and control can be central in the therapy process. The process of informing clients about therapy increases the chances that the client-therapist relationship will become a collaborative partnership and that both parties will have a clear idea of what is expected.

Practitioners are ethically bound to offer the best quality of service available, and clients have a right to know that managed care programs, with their focus on cost containment, may have adverse effects on the quality of care available. Prospective clients must be given clear information about the benefits to which they are entitled and clear information about the limits of treatment as the clinician envisions them (Haas & Cummings, 1991). I. J. Miller (1996b) asserts that quality of care is likely to decline under restrictive managed care programs. In her discussion of the ethics of therapy in a managed care environment, Wineburgh (1998) states that informed consent issues are particularly complicated. Clearly, clients have the right to specific information regarding their treatment under managed care and the limitations of their treatment packages. However, professionals are often restricted by managed care organizational contracts from educating clients about treatment allocation decisions. Managed care contracts often have "gag clauses" that prohibit practitioners from sharing any negative information about managed care policies, including options not covered by the plan. (Chapter 10 includes a detailed discussion of the ethical issues associated with managed care.) In the managed care environment, consumers in need of therapy may be denied service, clients who are treated may be systematically undertreated, and those with moderate to severe problems requiring longer term treatment may not receive it. Therapists have an obligation to educate consumers, and managed care programs that promote financial interests to the detriment of quality treatment should be held legally responsible for any adverse impact on clients (Newman & Bricklin, 1991).

Informed Consent in Practice

How do practitioners assist clients in becoming informed partners? Somberg, Stone, and Claiborn (1993) conducted a survey to assess therapists' practices pertaining to informed consent and found that informed consent procedures need to be considered within the context of the therapist's values, orientation, and work setting. Some practitioners use informed consent forms. Others talk with clients and report these discussion in their files. In either case, it is important to note that both the client and the therapist have the option to revise the therapeutic contract at any time. Due to considerations of documentation, ease of administering, and standardization, Somberg and colleagues recommend using a written approach to informed consent.

Bennett and his colleagues (1990) recommend that practitioners record the nature of the consent and suggest that a written consent form include the following information: date of discussion regarding consent; name of the practitioner and the client; a statement affirming that the client understood what was explained to him or her; a statement of the client's right to withdraw from treatment; likely benefits and inherent risks associated with therapy; a description of the kind of treatment that will be provided; issues of confidentiality, privilege, and their limits; and the signature of the client.

Other aspects that might be included in a written informed consent document are: a statement describing the counselor's theoretical orientation and how this will affect treatment, a discussion about the purpose of counseling records and how they will be maintained, clarification pertaining to fees and charges, procedures for filing for insurance reimbursement, the therapist's policies and procedures, and a discussion of how a managed care system will affect the treatment process, if applicable. Consent forms are best viewed as merely one aspect of the ongoing dialogue between the therapist and client about the therapeutic process and its consequences (Bednar et al., 1991). In the context of school counseling, it is generally a good policy to provide informed consent for both individual and group counseling. However, because minors cannot legally give informed consent, the parent or guardian is the one who must sign the informed consent form. In general, through the effective use of informed consent procedures, client misunderstanding is reduced, which also tends to reduce the chances of filing a liability claim. Both the counselor and the client benefit from this practice.

Two Cases for Discussion

We have emphasized the importance of the therapist's role in teaching clients about informed consent and encouraging clients' questions about the therapeutic process. With this general concept in mind, put yourself in the counselor's place in each of the following cases. Identify the main ethical issues in each case, and think about your stance if you were faced with these concerns.

◆ **The case of Dottie.** At the initial interview the therapist, Dottie, does not provide an informed consent form and touches only briefly on the process of therapy. In discussing confidentiality, she states that whatever is said in the office will stay in the office, with no mention of the limitations of confidentiality. Three months into the therapy, the client exhibits some suicidal ideation. Dottie has recently attended a conference at which malpractice was one of the topics of discussion and worries that she may have been remiss in not providing her client with adequate information about her services, including confidentiality and its limitations. She hastily reproduces an informed consent document that she received at the conference and asks her client to sign the form at the next session. This procedure seems to evoke confusion in the client, and he makes no further mention of suicide. After five more sessions, he calls in to cancel an appointment and does not schedule another appointment. Dottie does not pursue the case further.

- What are the ethical and legal implications of the therapist's practice? Explain your position.
- If you had been in Dottie's shoes, what might you have done?
- Would you have contacted this client after he canceled? What are your thoughts about Dottie not doing that?

◆ **The case of Alejandro.** During the initial interview, Simone asks the counselor, Alejandro, how long she might need to be in therapy. Alejandro tells Simone that the process will take a minimum of 2 years of weekly sessions. She expresses dismay at such a lengthy process. Alejandro says that this is the way he works and explains that in his experience significant change is a slow process that demands a great deal of work. He tells Simone that if she cannot commit to this time period he would be willing to give her a referral.

- Did Alejandro take care of the need for informed consent?
- Did Alejandro have an ethical and a professional obligation to explain his rationale for the 2 years of therapy?
- Should Alejandro have been willing to explore alternatives to his approach to therapy, such as the possible values of short-term counseling?
- Given Alejandro's statement of minimum length of therapy, would it have been ethical for him to offer short-term counseling to Simone?

- Would it be ethical for this practitioner to accept clients under a managed care system or with an insurance provider that paid for only a very limited number of sessions?

Checklist for Informed Consent for Treatment

This checklist is from Wheeler and Bertram's (1994) American Counseling Association workshop entitled "Legal Aspects of Counseling: Avoiding Lawsuits and Legal Problems." The following topics are recommended for consideration when developing a written informed consent for treatment document:

1. *Voluntary Participation.* Clients voluntarily agree to treatment and can terminate at any time without penalty.
2. *Client Involvement.* What level of involvement and what type of involvement will be expected from clients?
3. *Counselor Involvement.* What will the counselor provide? How will this be provided? How can the counselor be reached in the event of an emergency?
4. *No Guarantees.* Counselors cannot guarantee results (namely, become happier, less tense or depressed, save the marriage, stop drug use, obtain a good job, and so forth).
5. *Risks Associated with Counseling.* Define what, if any, risks are associated with the counselor's particular approach to counseling.
6. *Confidentiality and Privilege.* Specify how confidentiality will be handled in couple counseling, family counseling, child/adolescent counseling, and group counseling situations. How may confidential and privileged information be released?
7. *Exceptions of Confidentiality and Privilege.* Define specific statutory circumstances where confidentiality and privilege cannot be maintained (namely, abuse reporting).
8. *Counseling Approach or Theory.* What is the counselor's counseling orientation or theoretical belief system? How will that affect treatment?
9. *Counseling and Financial Records.* What will they include? How long will they be maintained? How will they be destroyed?
10. *Ethical Guidelines.* What standards define the counselor's practice? How might a client obtain a copy of these guidelines?
11. *Licensing Regulations.* What license does the counselor hold? How may a client check on the status of the licensee?
12. *Credentials.* What education, training, and experience credential will the counselor need to provide counseling treatment, including any specialty credentials?
13. *Fees and Charges.* What are the specific fees and charges? How will fees be collected? How are financial records maintained?
14. *Insurance Reimbursement.* What responsibility will the counselor take for filing insurance forms? What fees, if any, are associated with insurance filing? How will co-payments be handled?

15. *Responsibility for Payment.* Who is responsible for payment of counseling charges? How will delinquent accounts be handled? What charges will be assessed for delinquent accounts?
16. *Disputes and Complaints.* How will fee or other disputes be resolved? Provide the address and phone number of the state licensing board for complaints if required by state licensing statute.
17. *Cancellation Policy.* How much notice for cancellation of a scheduled appointment is required? What fees will be charged for late cancellation?
18. *Affiliation Relationship.* Describe independent contractor or partnership relationships with other practitioners in the office suite.
19. *Supervisory Relationship.* Describe any required supervisory relationship along with the reason for supervision. Provide supervisor's name and credentials.
20. *Colleague Consultation.* Indicate that, in keeping with generally accepted standards of practice, you frequently consult with other mental health professionals regarding the management of cases. The purpose of consultation is to ensure quality care. Every effort is made to protect the identity of clients.

The Content of Informed Consent

Educating clients about the counseling process, addressing client questions, and clarifying expectations are routes to ethical and effective practice. The challenge is to provide clients with just the right amount of information for them to make informed choices. Providing too much information at the initial meeting can impede clients from becoming active participants in the therapy process. We believe therapy is a collaborative effort, and we emphasize an egalitarian working relationship. As a result, we spend considerable time explaining our view of the therapy process and how it works. By demystifying the therapeutic process, we convey that clients are largely in charge of the direction their therapy will take. Informing clients about the counseling process is an ethical requirement that is part of the code of ethics of all major mental health professions.

One of the main aims of the first meeting is to establish rapport and create a climate of safety in the therapeutic situation. The types and amounts of information, the specific content of informed consent, the style of presenting information, and the timing of introducing this information must be considered within the context of legal requirements, work setting, agency policies, and the nature of the client's concerns. The content of informed consent is also determined by the specific client population being served. It should be added that there is no assurance that practitioners can avoid legal action, even if they do obtain written informed consent. Rather than focusing on legalistic documents, we suggest that you develop informed consent procedures that increase client understanding and foster client-counselor dialogue about the counseling process.

Topics selected for discussion during early counseling sessions are best guided by the concerns, interests, and questions of the client. These questions are often in the minds of new clients:

- How is confidentiality essential, and what are the limits of confidentiality?
- How does the therapeutic process work?
- What is the primary role of the therapist?
- What is expected of the client?
- What is the approximate length of the counseling process?
- How will termination be handled?
- What are clients' and therapists' main rights and responsibilities?
- What are some of the main benefits and risks of therapy?

Of course, not all of these topics can be addressed in the first session. Let's look in more detail at some of the topics about which clients should be informed.

The therapeutic process. Although it may be difficult to give clients a detailed description of what occurs in therapy, some general ideas can be explored. We support the practice of letting clients know that counseling might open up levels of awareness that could cause pain and anxiety. Clients who want long-term counseling need to know that they may experience changes that could produce disruptions and turmoil in their lives. Some clients may choose to settle for a limited knowledge of themselves rather than risking this kind of disruption, and this should be respected. We believe it is appropriate to use the initial sessions for a frank discussion of how change happens, and also the personal and financial costs to the client of such change. Clients should have a knowledge of the procedures and goals of therapy, especially if any unusual or experimental approaches or techniques are to be employed. It is their right to refuse to participate in certain therapeutic techniques. It is important that clients know that they can terminate therapy when they decide to, yet it is advisable to discuss the matter of termination with the therapist.

Background of the therapist. Therapists might provide clients with a description of their training and education, their credentials, licenses, any specialized skills, their theoretical orientation, the types of clients and types of problems in which they have competence, and types of problems that they cannot work with effectively. If the counseling will be done by an intern or a paraprofessional, clients should be aware of this. Likewise, if the provider will be working with a supervisor, this fact should be made known to the client. This description of the practitioner's qualifications, coupled with a willingness to answer any questions clients have about the process, reduces the unrealistic expectations clients may have about therapy. It also reduces the chances of malpractice actions. As a part of this discussion of your background, it is essential that you inform clients in advance of some areas where you may need to refer, especially due to potential value conflicts. Examples of personal convictions include values pertaining to religion, abortion, and end-of-life decisions.

Costs involved in therapy. It is essential to provide information about all costs involved in psychological services at the beginning of these services, including methods of payment. Clients need to be informed about insurance reimbursement and any limitations of their health plan with respect to fees. If fees are subject to change, this should be clear to the client from the beginning. For practitioners who are working with a managed care entity, clients have a right to know that a financial incentive exists to limit the amount or type of service provided (Newman & Bricklin, 1991). Managed care providers have assumed a more active role in the treatment planning process, and these providers impose many limitations on treatment, including the number of sessions allowed and the amount of money that will be reimbursed (Haas & Cummings, 1991).

Most ethics codes have a standard pertaining to establishing fees, as can be seen in these guidelines:

> In establishing fees for professional counseling services, counselors consider the financial status of clients and locality. In the event that the established fee structure is inappropriate for a client, assistance is provided in attempting to find comparable services of acceptable cost. (ACA, 1995)

> Marriage and family therapists make financial arrangements with clients, third party payors, and supervisees that are reasonably understandable and conform to accepted professional practices. (AAMFT, 2001)

> When setting fees, social workers should ensure that the fees are fair, reasonable, and commensurate with the service performed. Consideration should be given to the client's ability to pay. (NASW, 1999, 1.13, a)

> As early as is feasible in a professional or scientific relationship, the psychologist and the patient, client, or other appropriate recipient of psychological services reach an agreement specifying the compensation and the billing arrangements. (APA, 1992)

Dealing with fees can be an ethical issue. Matters of finance are delicate and, if handled poorly, can easily result in a strained relationship between client and therapist. Thus, the manner in which fees are handled has much to do with the tone of the therapeutic partnership.

Some professional codes of ethics recommend a sliding fee standard because the financial resources of clients are variable. In addition to adjusting fees to what clients can afford, many professionals provide services to some clients for little or no financial compensation, making their services available to some who could not otherwise afford help. For example: "Counselors contribute to society by devoting a portion of their professional activity to services for which there is little or no financial return (pro bono)" (ACA, 1995, A. 10. d.).

The length of therapy and termination. Many agencies have a policy limiting the number of sessions provided to clients. These clients should be informed at the outset that they cannot receive long-term therapy. Under a managed care system, clients are often limited to 6 sessions, or a specified amount for a given year, such as 20 sessions. It is a good idea to remind them no later than the next-to-last session that they will not be able to continue with the counseling sessions. Furthermore, clients have the right to expect a referral so that they can continue exploring whatever concerns initially brought them to therapy. If referrals are not possible but the client still needs further treatment, the therapist should explain other alternatives available to the client.

Because practitioners differ with respect to an orientation of long-term versus short-term therapy, it is important to inform clients of the basic assumptions underlying their orientation. In a managed care setting, Richardson and Austad (1991) believe the therapeutic process will be determined largely by the health provider. Under this system, practitioners must have expertise in rapid assessment, identifying the core psychological issues quickly, and matching each client with the most appropriate intervention. They will have to be competent in short-term strategies and be willing to have their work assessed by review committees. Part of informing clients about the therapeutic process entails giving them relevant facts about short-term interventions that may not always be in their best interest. Sometimes short-term interventions are appropriate, but in other situations long-term, intensive therapy may be indicated.

Health maintenance organizations (HMOs) exert considerable influence over basic decisions that affect the therapy process, including length of treatment, number of sessions, and even the content of therapy (D. Smith & Fitzpatrick, 1995). If a health maintenance organization and the therapist disagree about the number of sessions required for effective therapy, the therapist might do well to request in writing from the HMO representative the reasons for not allowing further treatment. Clients have a right to know how their health care program is likely to influence the course of their therapy as well as the limitations imposed by the program.

Some therapists make it a practice to discuss with their clients an approximate length for the therapeutic process, but when the problems that brought the client into therapy are complex and long-standing, predicting the length of treatment is often difficult. Psychodynamic therapists, for example, may be unwilling to discuss the length of treatment during the initial phase because of their conviction that individual differences among clients make such predictions impossible.

Regardless of the therapist's theoretical orientation, clients have a right to expect that their therapy will end when they have realized the maximum benefits from it or have obtained what they were seeking when they entered it. The issue of termination needs to be openly explored by the therapist and the client, and the decision to terminate ultimately should rest with the client.

Kramer (1990) reminds us that termination may do more than signal the end of therapy; it can be a new beginning for clients. Kramer contends that when termination issues are ignored or mishandled the whole of therapy is jeopardized. Termination is a crucial phase of therapy, yet it is also the least understood and most complex of all aspects of therapy. Kramer observes that there is a lack of consensus with regard to every aspect of termination, including the criteria for ending. Furthermore, there are few theoretical and practical guidelines for practitioners to follow as they assist their clients in working through issues pertaining to the termination of their therapy. Responsible practitioners discuss this phase of therapy with clients at critical junctures in the therapy process. It is a good idea for both therapists and clients to be aware that termination does not always mean the end of therapy. Although a therapeutic relationship may end for a time, clients often return for further therapy as new challenges surface, with either the same therapist or another therapist.

Consultation with colleagues. Student counselors generally meet regularly with their supervisors and fellow students to discuss their progress and any problems they encounter in their work. Trainees need to do this at the outset with their clients both verbally and in writing. It is good policy for all counselors to inform their clients that they may be receiving supervision on their cases. Experienced clinicians often have scheduled consultation meetings with their peers to focus on how they are serving clients. Even though it is ethical for counselors to discuss their cases with other counselors, it is wise to routinely let clients know about this possibility. Clients will then have less reason to feel that the trust they are putting in their counselors is being violated. Clinicians can explain that these discussions may well focus on what they are doing and feeling as counselors rather than on their clients as "cases."

Interruptions in therapy. Most ethical codes specify that therapists should consider the welfare of their clients when it is necessary to interrupt or terminate the therapy process. For example, this is the NASW (1999) guideline:

> Social workers who anticipate the termination or interruption of service to clients should notify clients promptly and seek the transfer, referral, or continuation of services in relation to the clients' needs and preferences. (1.16e)

It is a good practice to explain at the first contact with clients the possibilities for both expected and unexpected interruptions in therapy and how they might best be handled. A therapist's absence might appear as abandonment to some clients, especially if the absence is poorly handled. As much as possible, therapists should make plans for any interruptions in therapy, such as vacations or long-term absences. Clients need information about the therapist's method of handling emergencies as part of their orientation to treatment. When practitioners know they will be on vacation, ethical practice entails providing the name and telephone number of another therapist in case of need. Of course, therapists should obtain clients' written consent to provide information to their substitutes (Bennett et al., 1990).

Clients' right of access to their files. It is a good idea to inform clients that counseling records are kept for their benefit. Remley and Herlihy (2001) maintain that clients have a legal right to inspect and obtain copies of records kept on their behalf by professionals. Clients have the ultimate responsibility for decisions about their own health care and also have the right of access to complete information with respect to their condition and care provided. It is a good idea to write about a client in descriptive and nonjudgmental ways, keeping in mind that your client could read these notes or that your records could become public information at some future time. With this possibility in mind, you are advised to be cautious in deciding what to include in your clinical notes.

Professionals have various views about sharing counseling records with a client. Some therapists are reluctant to share their notes, including the diagnosis, with their clients. They may operate on the assumption that their clients are not sophisticated enough to understand their diagnosis and the clinical notes, or they may think that more harm than benefit could result from disclosing such information to clients. Rather than automatically providing clients access to what is written in their files, some therapists give an explanation of the client's diagnosis and the general trend of what kind of information they are recording.

Others are more willing to grant their clients access to information in the counseling records they keep, especially if clients request specific information. ACA's (1995) guideline on this matter is this: "Counselors recognize that counseling records are kept for the benefit of clients, and therefore provide access to records and copies of records when requested by competent clients, unless records contain information that may be misleading and detrimental to the client" (B.4.d.).

Giving clients access to their files seems to be consistent with the consumer-rights movement, which is having an impact on the fields of mental health, counseling, rehabilitation, and education. One way to reduce the growing trend toward malpractice suits and other legal problems is to allow patients to see their medical records, even while hospitalized. Later in this chapter we discuss procedures for keeping records.

Rights pertaining to diagnostic labeling. One of the major obstacles for some therapists to the open sharing of files with clients is the need to give clients a diagnostic classification as a requirement for receiving third-party reimbursement for psychological services. Some clients are not informed that they will be so labeled, what those labels are, or that the labels and other confidential material will be given to insurance companies. Clients also do not have control over who can receive this information, nor are they informed of their right not to be labeled (Mappes et al., 1985). In a managed care system, office workers will have access to specific information about a client, such as a diagnosis. Ethical practice involves informing clients that a diagnosis can become a permanent part of their file. Indeed, a diagnosis can have ramifications in terms of costs of insurance, long-term insurability, and employment. With this information, clients are at least in the position to decline treatment with these restrictions. Some clients have the means to pay for the kind of therapy they want and may choose not to use a third-party payor.

Greenhut (1991) contends that therapists often make clients worse by attaching labels to them. She believes therapy sometimes becomes the exploitation of the exploited. For example, in treating incest survivors, rape victims, and those who have been physically abused, therapists can further oppress these victims by assigning them labels such as co-dependent, narcissistic, eating disordered, and chronically depressed. Greenhut urges therapists to encourage their clients to act on the basis of what they believe is best for themselves and, thus, to move beyond their labels. However, it is important for therapists to have assessment skills and to know that clients' behaviors can fit patterns or categories that may assist in the development of a treatment plan. The danger is in viewing a client entirely in terms of a diagnostic label, or in viewing a disorder as being static, with the end result that the client is left with the notion of being labeled forever.

The nature and purpose of confidentiality. Clients should be educated regarding matters pertaining to confidentiality, privileged communication, and privacy (which we discuss in Chapter 6). Therapists are expected to inform clients of the limitations of confidentiality from the outset of the professional relationship. Doing this not only educates clients but also promotes trust on the client's part. The effectiveness of the client-counselor relationship is built on a foundation of trust. If clients do not trust their therapists, it is not likely that they will engage in significant self-disclosure and self-exploration.

Part of establishing trust involves making clients aware of how certain information will be used and whether it will be given to third-party payors. Clients in a managed care program should be made aware that the confidentiality of their communications will be compromised to some extent. It is especially critical that clients be informed that the managed care organization has the power to limit reimbursement for services. Thus, therapists are often required to release confidential information to determine how much treatment is deemed warranted (Wineburgh, 1998). Clearly, when a practitioner contracts with a third-party payor, a client's records come under the scrutiny and review of the system doing the reimbursing. Some clients may want to safeguard their privacy and confidentiality by seeking treatment that does not involve third-party reimbursement. Clients have a right to be informed of any limits to confidentiality imposed by a managed care plan. Some therapists are concerned that clients will not engage in self-disclosure if they know that confidential information is given to a managed care organization. It is unethical for therapists to withhold the limits of confidentiality from clients in this context (Kremer & Gesten, 1998). All the professional codes have a clause stating that clients have a right to know about any limitations of confidentiality from the outset. For example, NASW (1999) has this guideline:

> Social workers should discuss with clients and other interested parties the nature of confidentiality and limitations of clients' right to confidentiality. Social workers should review with clients circumstances where confidential information may be requested and where disclosure of confidential information may be legally required. This discussion should occur as soon as possible in the social worker-client relationship and as needed throughout the course of the relationship. (1.07e)

If you have clients who will be participating in online counseling, they have a right to know about the limits of confidentiality pertaining to this service. The ACA (1999) *Ethical Standards for Internet On-Line Counseling* state: "Professional counselors inform clients of the limitations of confidentiality and identify foreseeable situations in which confidentiality must be breached in light of the law in both the state in which the client is located and the state in which the professional counselor is licensed."

As you will see in Chapter 6, confidentiality is not an absolute. Certain circumstances demand that a therapist disclose what was said by a client in a private therapy session or disclose counseling records.

Benefits and risks of treatment. Clients should have some information about both the possible benefits and the risks associated with a treatment program. Due to the fact that clients are largely responsible for the outcomes of therapy, it is a good policy to emphasize the role of the client's responsibility. Clients need to know that no promises can be made about specific outcomes, which means that ethical practitioners avoid giving guarantees of cures to clients. Bednar and his colleagues (1991) comment that until more is known about risks it is wise for practitioners to make every attempt to note negative reactions and begin to devise strategies for assisting clients in making more informed choices about their treatment.

Alternatives to traditional therapy. According to the ethics codes of some professional organizations, clients need to know about alternative helping systems. Therefore, it is a good practice for therapists to learn about community resources so they can present these alternatives to a client. Alternatives to psychotherapy include self-help programs, stress management, programs for personal-effectiveness training, peer self-help groups, bibliotherapy, 12-step programs, support groups, and crisis-intervention centers.

This information about therapy and its alternatives can be presented in writing, through an audiotape or videotape, or during an intake session. An open discussion of therapy and its alternatives may, of course, lead some clients to choose sources of help other than therapy. Given the state of psychotherapy research, however, it is difficult to discuss the advantages of alternative treatments and make recommendations (Bednar et al., 1991). For practitioners who make a living providing therapy services, asking their clients to consider alternative treatments can produce financial anxiety. However, openly discussing therapy and its alternatives is likely to reinforce many clients' decisions to continue therapy. Clients have a right to know about alternative therapeutic modalities (such as different theoretical orientations and medication) that are known to be effective with particular clients and conditions.

Tape-recording or videotaping sessions. Many agencies require that interviews be recorded for training or supervision purposes. Clients have a right to be informed about this procedure at the initial session, and it is important that they understand why the recordings are made, how they will be used, who will have access to them, and how they will be stored. Therapists sometimes make recordings because they can benefit from listening to them or by having colleagues listen to their interactions with clients and give them feedback. It is essential for trainees or counselors to secure the permission of clients before making any kind of electronic recording.

The Counselor's Responsibilities in Record Keeping

From an ethical, legal, and clinical perspective, an important responsibility of mental health practitioners is to keep adequate records on their clients. Maintaining thorough clinical notes has a dual purpose: (a) to provide the best service possible for clients, and (b) to provide a basis for safeguarding practitioners in the event of a lawsuit by documenting their decisions and the actions they have taken. At times, therapists may operate on the assumption that keeping clinical records is not an effective use of the limited time they have. Some therapists would rather devote their time in delivering service to clients instead of recording process and progress notes. Remley and Herlihy (2001) assert that it is possible to keep adequate records *and* provide quality treatment. It is a wise policy for counselors to document their actions in crisis situations such as cases involving potential danger of harm to oneself, others, or physical property. At the same time, it is not in the best interests of clients when counselors are more concerned about record keeping as a self-protective strategy rather than devoting their energy to providing quality services to clients. Although keeping records is a basic part of a counselor's practice, Remley and Herlihy suggest that it is critical to balance the need to maintain adequate records with the obligation to provide quality counseling services: "Counselors who find themselves devoting inordinate or excessive amounts of time creating and maintaining records probably need to reevaluate how they are spending their professional time and energy" (p. 109).

Many practitioners believe that accurate and detailed clinical records can provide an excellent defense against malpractice claims, and entire books and monographs are devoted to the subject. Rivas-Vazquez, Blais, Rey, and Rivas-Vazquez (2001) contend that the documentation of clinical services has taken on unprecedented importance for mental health professionals. From their perspective, the main objectives of documentation practices are (a) to structure quality care, (b) to decrease liability exposure, and (c) to fulfill requirements for reimbursement. According to Rivas-Vazquez and his colleagues, the adage, "if it is not documented, it did not happen" has never been more relevant than in today's climate of heightened awareness of potential liability exposure. These authors outline the specific domains required for comprehensive documentation practices. Professional ethics codes also outline the requirements of good record keeping (see the box titled Ethics Codes on Record Keeping). A useful book on this subject is *Documenting Psychotherapy: Essentials for Mental Health Practitioners* (Moline, Williams, & Austin, 1998). Moline and colleagues suggest that the practice of keeping adequate records is more than a way to lessen the

Ethics Codes on Record Keeping

American Psychological Association (1992)

Psychologists create, maintain, disseminate, store, retain, and dispose of records and data relating to their research, practice, and other work in accordance with law and in a manner that permits compliance with the requirements of this Ethics Code.

National Association of Social Workers (1999)

(a) Social workers should take reasonable steps to ensure that documentation in records is accurate and reflective of the services provided. (3.04.a.)

(b) Social workers should include sufficient and timely documentation in records to facilitate the delivery of services and to ensure continuity of services provided to clients in the future. (3.04.b.)

(c) Social workers' documentation should protect clients' privacy to the extent that it is possible and appropriate, and should include only that information that is directly relevant to the delivery of services. (3.04.c.)

(d) Social workers should store records following the termination of service to ensure reasonable future access. Records should be maintained for the number of years required by state statutes or relevant contracts. (3.04.d.)

American Counseling Association (1995)

Counselors maintain records necessary for rendering professional services to their clients and as required by laws, regulations, or agency or institution procedures.

American School Counselor Association (1998)

The professional school counselor:

- maintains and secures records necessary for rendering professional services to the counselee as required by laws, regulations, institutional procedures, and confidentiality guidelines. (A8)

chance of malpractice action: "We firmly believe that good record keeping supports the therapist in conducting professional duties and thus assists in providing appropriate care for clients. This consideration, we believe, outweighs any legal deliberation" (p. ix).

Schaffer (1997) suggests that practitioners who fail to maintain adequate clinical records are putting themselves in great ethical and legal peril. Keeping records is not only required in all settings but is perhaps the least expensive and most effective form of liability insurance as well. Clinicians may not keep notes because they can remember what clients tell them, because they are concerned about violating a client's confidentiality and privacy, because they do not want to assume a legalistic stance in their counseling practice, or because they do not have time to keep notes on their clients. Regardless of the reason for not keeping records, Schaffer claims that it is a serious mistake. Failing to keep records deprives practitioners of evidence they will need to defend themselves should they become involved in a malpractice or disciplinary action. Lack of adequate records may deprive clients of data needed for treatment. For example, clients may need to transfer to another therapist, or the therapist may die or retire. If notes were not kept, both the client and the therapist can be hurt. Because most states and agencies require clinicians to keep records, and because this is a requirement of managed care programs, practitioners have to learn how to write and maintain notes about their client's progress. Ideally, good record-keeping practices will help practitioners provide quality service to their clients.

Even if a mental health provider acts reasonably and keeps good records, there is no complete guarantee that he or she will not be sued. Occasionally a competent practitioner will even be found liable for damages. As unfair as it seems, the law sometimes imposes a legal responsibility on professionals that they did not know they had (Mary Hermann, personal communication, February 25, 2001). By law managed care practitioners are required to keep accurate charts and notes and must provide this information to authorized chart reviewers. Currently, there is no doubt that therapists must maintain client records, but it is unclear what is to be included in such records (Riemersma, 2000). At a minimum, records should contain client-identifying information; the name of the client's primary care physician, or an explanation for the absence of such a name; objective findings from the most recent physical examination; intake sheet; documentation of a mental status exam or assessment; signed informed consent for treatment form; diagnosis and prognosis; the existence of treatment plans, containing specific target problems and goals; statements regarding the client's main presenting problem or problems; previous and present data from psychological tests; documentation of referrals to other providers, when appropriate; signed and dated progress notes; types of services provided; precise times and dates of appointments made and kept; termination summary; the use and completion of a discharge summary; and release of information obtained (Canter et al., 1994).

In some counseling settings, it may be difficult to keep up with record keeping. For example, in school counseling a student-to-counselor ratio of 400-to-1 (or more) is not uncommon. How realistic is it to expect a school counselor to be able to keep detailed notes on every contact with a student? Birdsall and Hubert (2000) indicate that a well-kept record may be useful to demonstrate that the quality of counseling provided was in line with an acceptable standard of care. Keeping records is particularly important in cases involving moderate to severe social or emotional problems. Maintaining records on parent contacts is also essential. School counselors are also cautioned on the importance of safeguarding the confidentiality of any records they keep.

School counselors need to be concerned about both administrative and clinical records. An example of administrative records are the cumulative files that are available to other school personnel. Clinical records are the case notes documenting important events regarding a counseling relationship with a student (Remley & Hermann, 2000). At times, school counselors may need to educate teachers about what to enter into a student's cumulative folder. One of our colleagues reports that he had to ask teachers to rewrite their observational reports to remove judgmental terms such as "lazy" or "bully." School records are open for parents to review as well as other school personnel. It is essential to refrain from making negative comments concerning parents in administrative records. These records also follow the students to other schools and can provide slanted opinions. All school staff and counselors need to stick to the facts and limit their personal judgments (John Tweton, personal communication, April 2, 2001).

Moline, Williams, and Austin (1998) list a number of arguments for keeping records, including these points:

- Record keeping has become a "standard of care" practice set by most professional organizations.
- Adequate clinical records often serve as a counselor's defense against malpractice claims or in the event of being charged with an ethical violation.
- A clinical record can serve clients by reflecting their condition at a particular time.
- Records document that treatment occurred.
- Records can be useful for clients in the event of transferring to a new counselor or school.
- Records can help counselors improve their skills and provide more effective treatment for clients.
- Federal and/or state law may require the practice of record keeping.

School counselors need to understand the provisions of the Family Educational Rights and Privacy Act of 1974. This federal law requires that schools receiving federal funds provide access to all school records to parents of students under the age of 18 and to students themselves once they reach 18. Student records are not to be released to third parties without the written consent of parents of minors, or the written consent of adult students (Remley & Hermann, 2000).

The Committee on Professional Practice and Standards of APA adopted a set of guidelines for record keeping in February 1993 (see Appendix B of Canter et al., 1994). Much of the material that follows is a summary and adaptation of these guidelines.

Case notes should *never* be altered or tampered with after they have been entered into the client's record. Tampering with a clinical record after the fact can cast a shadow on the therapist's integrity in court. Enter notes into a client's record as soon as possible after a therapy session, and sign and date the entry. If you are keeping client notes in a computer, it is essential that your program has a time and date stamp so that if your records are subpoenaed there will be no question of adding or deleting material at a later date.

The content and style of a client's records are often determined by agency or institutional policy, state counselor licensing laws, or other regulatory bodies. The particular setting and the therapist's preference often determine how detailed the records will be. Riemersma (2000) states that there are no hard and fast rules as to the contents of records. She does add that therapists are advised to keep records in such a manner that the records could hold up to scrutiny if challenged.

Remember that the information in the client's record belongs to the client, and a copy may be requested at any time. Thus, it is a prudent policy to write notes in a manner that is honest yet never demeaning of a client. Certainly derogatory remarks do not belong in the client's file. Do not document embarrassing or potentially damaging information about a client. A client's record is not the place for a therapist's personal opinions or personal reactions to the client. If a client misses a session, it is a good practice to document the reasons. In writing progress notes, use clear behavioral language. Focus on describing specific and concrete behavior and avoid jargon. It may help to assume that the contents of a record might someday be read in a courtroom with the client present. Although professional documentation is expected to be thorough, it is best to keep notes as concise as possible. Be mindful of the dictum, "If you did not document it, then it did not happen." Record client and therapist behavior that is clinically relevant. Include in clinical records interventions used, client responses to treatment strategies, the evolving treatment plan, and any follow-up measures taken.

Mental health practitioners bear the ultimate responsibility for what they write, how they store and access records, what they do with these records, and when and how they destroy them (Nagy, 2000). Counselors are ethically and legally required to keep records in a secure manner and to protect client confidentiality. Counselors are responsible for taking reasonable steps to establish and maintain the confidentiality of information based on their own delivery of services, or the services provided by others working under their supervision. Clients' records must be maintained for the period of time required by relevant federal, state, and local laws. Providers have an obligation to keep records for a minimum of 7 years following the termination of a client. Organization policy often prescribes guidelines for maintaining records, including a time frame. In the absence of such laws, the general recommendation is that complete records should be kept for a minimum of 3 years after the last contact with a client. Records, or a summary, should then be maintained for an additional 12 years before disposal. Remley and Herlihy (2001) suggest keeping counseling records for a longer time period than they would normally be kept in cases where counselors have documented actions they have taken to protect themselves. Moline, Williams, and Austin (1998) state that how long records need to be retained is a matter of state law. Because regulations vary from state to state, Moline and her colleagues advise practitioners to find out the specific time period for retention of records that is required by the jurisdiction in which they practice.

Whether records are active or inactive, counselors are expected to maintain and store them safely and in a way in which timely retrieval is possible. Extra care should be taken if information is stored on computer disks. Failure to maintain adequate client records could be the basis of a malpractice claim because it breaches the standard of care expected of a mental health professional (B. S. Anderson, 1996).

It is wise to think about what will happen to your clinical records after your death. The law does not specify how records are to be handled upon a therapist's death, but Riemersma (2000) suggests that you give thought to how you expect your records to be handled before it is too late for you to be involved in the decision making. Here are some questions to consider:

- Who will have access to your records in the event of your death?
- Should your clients be given an opportunity to obtain their records, or should they be given the opportunity to have their records transferred to another therapist?
- Should the records be placed in the custody of another health care professional with the clients so notified?
- Should the records be destroyed immediately, with or without giving your clients the opportunity to retrieve the records?
- Do you have a therapist in the community who is willing to take over your practice in the case of your death?

It is important to find answers to these questions if you want to safeguard your estate, for a client can bring suit against your estate after your death. Even death does not shield us from a malpractice suit!

◆ **The case of Noah.** Noah is a therapist in private practice who primarily sees relatively well-functioning clients. He considers keeping records to be basically irrelevant to the therapeutic process for his clients. As he puts it: "In all that a client says to me in one hour, what do I write down? And for what purpose? If I were seeing high-risk clients, then I certainly would keep notes. Or if I were a psychoanalyst, where everything a client said matters, then I would keep notes." One of his clients, Sue, who had watched a television talk show in which clients rights were discussed, asked to see her file. Noah had to explain his lack of record keeping to Sue.

- What do you think of Noah's philosophy on record keeping? Do you consider it unethical? Why or why not?
- Taking into consideration the kind of clientele Noah sees, is his behavior justified? If you disagree, what criteria would you use in determining what material should be recorded?
- What if a legal issue arises during or after Sue's treatment? How would documenting each session help or not help both the client and the counselor?
- Assuming that some of Noah's clients will move to other locales and see new therapists, does the absence of notes to be transferred to the new therapist have ethical implications? Is it a burden and expense on the clients to have to cover old ground?
- How do you react to Noah's opinion that keeping notes is irrelevant in his practice? Explain.
- If it had no relevance in a court of law, would you still keep notes? Why or why not?

Ethical Issues in Online Counseling

In this section we consider a few of the salient ethical issues in the use of online counseling and the many forms of service delivery via the Internet. The term *behavioral telehealth* has taken root in the current literature. This rapidly developing field involves both potential benefits and risks and, just as with any new practice area, practitioners have a primary duty to consider the best interests of the client, to strive to do no harm, and to adhere to legal requirements (Koocher & Morray, 2000). Ultimately, it is the responsibility of mental health professionals to examine the ethical, legal, and clinical issues related to the use of technology (Maheu & Gordon, 2000).

VandenBos and Williams (2000) agree that mental health professionals must make decisions about how they wish to incorporate delivery of services via the Internet into their practices, but they also maintain that professional associations should develop standards for these services. Likewise, Sampson, Kolodinksy, and Greeno (1997) take the position that it is the responsibility of the professional associations to evaluate and revise their ethical standards to maximize the benefits and minimize the limitations of using online counseling: "the counseling profession cannot afford to wait until the information highway is fully operational to decide how to best use this technology" (p. 211). We agree with the stance taken by these writers who call upon the professional organizations to exert their influence in designing effective guidelines in the use of online counseling and other forms of behavioral telehealth.

At the present time the ethics codes of the APA, NASW, and ACA provide scant mention of ethical issues pertaining to the use of technology. For example, the APA (1992) ethics code contains only a general statement that psychologists should give careful consideration to providing services from a distance. The APA has suggested that future revisions of the ethics code will deal more with psychologists' responsibilities in using technology. With the exception of the confidentiality of client records maintained on computers, ACA's (1995) ethics code does not address the provision of online counseling. However, ACA does have a separate document that is geared specifically to online service delivery (ACA, 1999).

Freeny (2001) makes a case for both professional associations and mental health practitioners to face the challenges involved in electronic therapy:

> The challenge will be for our professional associations to adapt their codes of conduct to the new realities of online therapy with an eye not to preventing it, but to getting it right. In fact, given the therapeutic potential of the Internet, the day may not be far off when failure to integrate online resources into our practices will be considered a form of clinical negligence. (p. 70)

Advantages and Disadvantage of Counseling via the Internet

Most experts agree that what is being currently offered via Internet counseling cannot be considered traditional psychotherapy, yet many think that this form of service delivery may have possibilities for consumers who are reluctant to seek more traditional treatment (Rabasca, 2000a). There are both advantages and disadvantages in using Internet technology to deliver counseling services. Riemersma and Leslie (1999) suggest these advantages for consumers of Internet counseling:

- Some consumers want brief, convenient, and anonymous therapy service.
- Some clients may be reached with online counseling who would not be willing to participate in traditional therapy.
- For persons with physical disabilities, online services may be more accessible.
- This form of counseling is suited to a problem-solving approach, which appeals to many consumers.
- Clients who experience anxiety when talking face-to-face with a therapist, or clients who are extremely shy, may feel more comfortable dealing with their problems by means of a computer.

Sampson, Kolodinsky, and Greeno (1997) identify some benefits to therapists who deliver counseling services online:

- Access to clients in rural areas
- Facilitates assigning, completing, and assessing client homework
- Enhances record keeping
- Expands the pool of referral services
- Increases flexibility in scheduling
- Increases options for supervision and case conferencing
- Enhances collection of research data

Freeny (2001) believes text-based online counseling is uniquely suited to the needs of business travelers. In addition, some clients are far more open in e-mail counseling than they are in face-to-face experiences. Other clients, concerned about the stigma of mental health treatment, prefer this anonymous interaction.

As Freeny (2001) has learned from his practice, online therapy presents a number of therapeutic and ethical concerns, especially with clients in crisis. He underscores the dilemmas clinicians face between honoring the client's desire for anonymity and a therapist's clinical need to be able to respond in an appropriate and timely manner in crisis situations. There are ethical problems involved in using online counseling to deal with a serious crisis, a psychotic individual, or even someone needing a deep emotional experience. To the list of drawbacks, Freeny points out that insurance companies have not recognized online counseling for reimbursement.

The disadvantages of using Internet technology to provide psychological services need to be carefully considered. Simply having technology available does not mean that it is appropriate to employ it. The potential benefits need to be greater than the potential risks for clients to ethically justify any form of technology that is used for counseling purposes. Here are some of the disadvantages we see:

- Inaccurate diagnosis or ineffective treatment may be provided due to lack of behavioral clues.
- Confidentiality and privacy cannot be guaranteed.
- Therapists' duty to warn or protect others is restricted.
- Clients who are suicidal, suffering extreme anxiety or depression, or who are in crisis do not receive adequate immediate attention.

- Anonymity enables minors to masquerade as adults seeking treatment.
- Transference and countertransference issues cannot be addressed.
- Complex long-term psychological problems cannot be successfully treated.

Freeny (2001) admits that there will be errors as electronic therapy develops, yet he maintains that the risks are worth taking, if it means that online care to millions of people can be provided to those who otherwise would not have benefited from mental health services.

Legal Issues and Regulation of Online Counseling

Providing counseling services over the Internet is controversial, and Remley and Herlihy (2001) pose some legal questions about Internet counseling: Is Internet counseling permitted in states in which professionals must be licensed to practice? Where does Internet counseling take place—at the counselor's location, the client's location, or both? Which laws govern the therapeutic process pertaining to issues of mandatory reporting? Remley and Herlihy suggest that counselors who want to offer professional services via the Internet should ensure that they are not violating state laws in either the counselor's state or the client's state. Because online counseling is so new, a host of legal questions will not be addressed until lawsuits are filed pertaining to its use in counseling practice.

Foxhall (2000) states that the most pressing issue regarding behavioral telehealth or Internet counseling is whether it is legal for a mental health practitioner who is licensed in one state to treat a client in another state by telephone or over the Internet. In addition, if therapists do not know where the client is, how can they call for help in the case of an emergency? If a malpractice suit should take place, which state would have jurisdiction? These are some of the thorny problems raised by online counseling.

Up to now, no state legislature has addressed Internet counseling, although some states have begun restricting physician practice across state lines (Foxhall, 2000). Riemersma and Leslie (1999) point out that, under California law, licensed mental health professionals are not prohibited from providing professional services over the Internet or by other technological means, and they are not aware of any malpractice lawsuits involving Internet counseling. However, it is a mistake to conclude that the use of services over the Internet is risk-free. Riemersma and Leslie write that therapists who choose to offer professional services over the Internet will have to give careful thought to ways of limiting their legal liability and to reducing potential harm to their clients.

Competent Counseling Online

Practitioners need to consider their level of competence in delivering services over the Internet, determine what kinds of services they can and cannot appropriately offer, and assess the benefits and risks of this form of service delivery. The ACA's (1999) guidelines regarding the boundaries of competence for online counseling are clear:

> Professional counselors provide on-line counseling services only in practice areas within their expertise and do not provide on-line counseling services to clients located in states in which professional counselors are not licensed.

In addition, the ACA (1999) describes the appropriate use of online counseling:

> Professional counselors develop an appropriate intake procedure for potential clients to determine whether on-line counseling is appropriate for the needs of the client. Professional counselors warn potential clients that on-line services may not be appropriate in certain situations and, to the extent possible, informs the client of specific limitations, potential risks, and/or potential benefits relevant to the client's anticipated use of on-line counseling services. Professional counselors ensure that clients are intellectually, emotionally, and physically capable of using the on-line counseling services, and of understanding the potential risks and/or limitations of such services.

Therapists who choose to counsel clients online should acquire special training regarding counseling via the Internet. Riemersma and Leslie (1999) recommend that therapists address these issues specific to the online counseling environment:

- Evaluate and diagnose a client at the beginning of treatment, ideally through an initial face-to-face session, to determine whether the client is a good candidate for online counseling.
- Require the client to be evaluated by a physician to rule out a physical cause for the client's psychological problem prior to initiating Internet counseling.
- Fully inform the client of the limits and expectations of the online relationship.
- Develop a plan for how emergencies will be dealt with.
- Address with the client, in advance, the limitations involved in confidentiality over the Internet and discuss what actions might be taken in the event that confidentiality is compromised.
- Discuss with the client, in advance, how situations involving technological failure will be handled.

Behavioral health care professionals are using a wide variety of Internet technologies to deliver counseling and therapy, including e-mail. However, neither the appropriateness nor the efficacy of using e-mail for clinical interventions has been proven by empirical research (Rabasca, 2000a). This absence of research data makes it impossible to objectively evaluate the benefits and the efficacy of using e-mail as a clinical intervention (Maheu & Gordon, 2000). Frankel (2000) states that he will not use e-mail to provide services unless all of the following conditions are met: having an existing professional relationship with a client; providing the client with informed consent about the use of e-mail and its attendant confidentiality; and limiting the e-mail exchange to giving a client basic information such as an appointment. Because e-mail is notoriously unsafe in the way that most people use it, Freeny (2001) contends that security and privacy issues in the new mediums of therapy must be disclosed in detail to clients. He adds that practitioners who offer online services should be technically competent enough to coach clients on ways to make sure communications are secure and private.

Freeny (2001) admits that one of the problems presented by the growth of the online advice industry may be beyond our power to change. Consumers have few ways to check the credentials of those offering online counseling, and there is little to distinguish competent therapists from untrained individuals. Freeny states: "The same vulnerable clients who may benefit from easier access to legitimate mental health services may fall prey to charlatans" (p. 70).

This matter of competence and appropriateness of services is more complex than meets the eye. The profession has a long way to go in establishing what specific kinds of counseling or psychological services can be effectively delivered via the Internet. Rabasca (2000b) reports that the jury is still out regarding which technologies are best for delivering which types of services. Little empirical data assessing the efficacy of telehealth capabilities for clinical applications is available, and Maheu and Gordon (2000) recommend that mental health professionals pay close attention to empirical research and current standards of practice before they attempt to deliver counseling or psychotherapy via the Internet.

Commentary. Therapists do not have to choose between Internet counseling and traditional face-to-face counseling. Technology can be used in the service of clients and can address some unique needs, especially if therapists combine online and personal sessions. For example, therapists might require clients to come in for three to six face-to-face sessions to determine their suitability for online counseling and to establish a working therapeutic relationship. This will increase the likelihood that online services will be effective. During these face-to-face sessions, time could be allocated for orienting the client to the counseling process and securing informed consent, taking the client's history, conducting an assessment and formulating a diagnostic impression, collaboratively identifying counseling goals, developing a general treatment plan, and formulating a specific plan of action. As the action plan is carried out following these initial sessions, Internet sessions could be used to monitor specific homework assignments. Depending on the client's needs and situation, there might be face-to-face sessions scheduled at regular intervals along with online counseling. Integrating traditional counseling with online counseling in this way can accommodate consumers who would not take advantage of counseling delivered exclusively by face-to-face sessions due to financial considerations or restrictions imposed by traveling long distances.

From our perspective, counseling services restricted to e-mail or online technology have major limitations. We have serious reservations about the effectiveness of online counseling for clients with deeply personal concerns or interpersonal issues. Most clinical problems involve a complexity of variables that require human-to-human interaction. We do not think online counseling should be used as an exclusive or primary means of delivering services, but it may have value if it is used as a supplement to face-to-face counseling.

Some fields of counseling are better suited for online work than others. For example, career counseling and educational counseling involve gathering information and processing this information. In this endeavor, technology may have some useful applications. Graduate training and continuing education in appropriate technological applications for professional practice are needed (McMinn, Buchanan, Ellens, & Ryan, 1999). Regardless of the kind of technology employed, it is our hope that therapists will always use it as a means to the end of enhancing clients' goals rather than as an end in itself.

Freeny (2001) contends that online counseling "will soon explode into modern clinical treatment, and therapists must have the courage to face up to its implications" (p. 70). What are your thoughts about the use of counseling via the Internet? What do you think the future holds in this area? What implications do you see for the use of technology in the delivery of mental health services? To what degree might you want to be involved in these developments as a part of your practice? What are the challenges that you think most need to be addressed in this area?

Counseling Children and Adolescents

Consistent with the increasing concern over the rights of children in general, more attention is being paid to issues such as the minor's right of informed consent. Here are some of the legal and ethical questions faced by therapists who work with children and adolescents:

- Can minors consent to treatment without parental knowledge and parental consent?
- To what degree should minors be allowed to participate in setting the goals of therapy and in providing consent to undergo it?
- What are the limits of confidentiality in counseling with minors?
- What does informed consent consist of in working with minors?

We will consider some of these questions in this section and focus on the rights of children when they are clients.

The Right to Treatment

The parent's right to information about his or her child is different from a right to have access to a child's records. The general rule is that a parent is entitled to general information from the counselor about the child's progress in counseling. In most states, for a minor to enter into a counseling relationship, it is necessary to have informed parental or guardian consent or for counseling to be court ordered (Lawrence & Kurpius, 2000). However, there are exceptions to this general rule. Informed consent of parents or guardians may not be legally required when a minor is seeking counseling for dangerous drugs or narcotics, for sexually transmitted diseases, for pregnancy and birth control, or for an examination following alleged sexual assault of a minor over 12 years of age

(Lawrence & Kurpius, 2000). The justification for allowing children and adolescents access to treatment without parental consent is that some minors might not otherwise seek needed treatment. Some children and adolescents who seek help when given independent access might not do so without the guarantee of privacy. In the case of school counselors, it is not necessary to obtain parental consent unless a state statute requires this. However, Remley and Herlihy (2001) suggest that parents may have the right to prohibit their children from seeing school counselors.

Counselors who are faced with the issue of when to accept minors as clients without parental consent must consider various factors. Is the parent or the child the primary client? What is the competence level of the minor? What are the potential risks and consequences if treatment is denied? What are the chances that the minor will not seek help or will not be able to secure parental permission for needed help? How serious is the problem? What are the laws pertaining to providing therapy for minors without parental consent? If practitioners need to make decisions about accepting minors without parental consent, they should know the relevant statutes in their state. They would also be wise to consult with other professionals in assessing the ethical issues involved in each case.

Informed Consent of Minors

Minors are not always able to give informed consent. On this matter the guideline provided by the APA (1992) is as follows: "When persons are legally incapable of giving informed consent, psychologists obtain informed permission from a legally authorized person, if such substitute consent is permitted by law." The ACA (1995) guideline suggests including family members in a minor's counseling, if appropriate: "When counseling clients who are minors or individuals who are unable to give voluntary, informed consent, parents or guardians may be included in the counseling process as appropriate. Counselors act in the best interests of clients and take measures to safeguard confidentiality."

Lawrence and Kurpius (2000) recommend that, whenever possible, counselors involve the parents in the initial meeting with their child in order to arrive at a clear, mutual agreement regarding the nature and extent of information that will be provided to them. This policy makes it possible to create clear boundaries for sharing information and establishes a three-way bond of trust. Lawrence and Kurpius state: "Involving the parents in the creation of mutually agreed upon guidelines for disclosure and motivating the minor client to disclose on his or her own are two positive strategies that benefit the parents and the client and protect the counselor" (p. 134).

Although minor clients have an *ethical* right to privacy and confidentiality in the counseling relationship, the law still favors the rights of parents over their children. Parents and guardians usually have a *legal* right to information pertaining to counseling sessions with their children, although a court may hold otherwise because of specific state statutes (Remley & Herlihy, 2001). In cases when parents or legal guardians become involved in the counseling process, counselors must acknowledge that these adults have authority over minors (Remley & Hermann, 2000). However, from an *ethical* perspective, therapists who work with children and adolescents have the responsibility to provide information that will help minor clients become active participants in their treatment. It is a good policy to provide minors with treatment alternatives and to enlist their participation in defining goals for their therapy. There are both ethical and therapeutic reasons for involving minors in their treatment. By giving them the maximum degree of autonomy within the therapeutic relationship, the therapist demonstrates respect for them. Also, it is likely that therapeutic change is promoted by informing children about the process and enlisting their involvement in it.

If children lack the background to weigh risks and benefits and if they cannot give complete informed consent, therapists should still attempt to provide some understanding of the therapy process. If formal consent cannot be obtained, then even partial understanding is better than proceeding with therapy without any attempt to explain the goals and procedures of the process (Margolin, 1982).

At this point we suggest that you think about some of the legal and ethical considerations in providing counseling for minors.

- Many parents argue that they have a right to know about matters that pertain to their adolescent daughters and sons. They assert, for example, that parents have a right to be involved in decisions about abortion. What is your position?
- Some people argue for the right of minors to seek therapy without parental knowledge or consent because needed treatment might not be given to them otherwise. When, if at all, would you counsel a minor without parental knowledge and consent?
- What kinds of information should be provided to children and adolescents before they enter a therapeutic relationship?
- If therapists do not provide minors with the information necessary to make informed choices, are they acting unethically? Why or why not?

Counseling Reluctant Children and Adolescents

Some young people simply resent not having a choice about entering a therapeutic relationship. Adolescents often resist therapy because they become the "identified patient" and the focus is on changing them. These adolescents are frequently aware that they are only *part* of the problem in the family unit. Although many minors indicate a desire to participate in treatment decisions, few are given the opportunity to become involved in a systematic way. The message here is that resistance to therapy can at least be minimized if therapists are willing to openly and nondefensively explore the reasons behind this resistance.

◆ **The case of Frank.** Frank was expelled from high school for getting explosively angry at a teacher who, according to Frank, had humiliated him in front of his class. Frank was told that he would not be readmitted to school unless he sought professional help. His mother called a therapist and explained the situation to her, and the therapist agreed to see him. Although Frank was uncomfortable and embarrassed over having to see a therapist, he was nevertheless willing to talk. He told the therapist that he knew he had done wrong by lashing out angrily at the teacher but that the teacher had provoked him. He said that although he was usually good about keeping his feelings inside, this time he had "just lost it."

After a few sessions, the therapist determined that there were many problems in Frank's family. He lived with an extreme amount of stress, and to work effectively with Frank it would be essential to see the entire family. Indeed, he did have a problem, but he was not the problem. He was covering up many family secrets, including a verbally abusive stepfather and an alcoholic mother. Hesitantly, he agreed that it would be a good idea to have the entire family come in for therapy. When the therapist contacted the family, the other members totally rejected the idea of family therapy. The mother asserted that the problem was with Frank and that the therapist should concentrate her efforts on him. A few days before his next scheduled appointment his mother called to cancel, saying that they had placed Frank in homebound study and that he therefore no longer required counseling.

- What are the ethical responsibilities of the therapist in this situation?
- Should Frank be seen as a condition of returning to school?
- What other strategies could the therapist have used?
- What would you have done differently, and why?
- Should the therapist have seen Frank and the teacher?
- Should the therapist have encouraged Frank to continue his therapy even if his family refused to undergo treatment?

Commentary. One ethical problem in this case was the treatment of the individual as opposed to the treatment of the family. There was an alcoholism problem within the family. Frank's expulsion from school could have been more a symptom of the family dysfunction than of his own disturbance. Indeed, he did need to learn anger management, as both the school and the mother contended, yet more was going on within this family that needed pressing attention. In this case it might have been best for the therapist to stick to her initial convictions of family therapy as the treatment of choice. If the parents would not agree to this, she could have made a referral to another therapist who would be willing to see Frank in individual counseling.

Specialized Training for Counseling Children and Adolescents

Because minors are a special client population, distinct education, training, and supervised practice are required for counselors who expect to work with minor clients (Lawrence & Kurpius, 2000). The ethics codes of the major professional organizations specify that it is unethical to practice in areas for which one has not been trained. Many human-service professionals have been trained and supervised in "verbal therapies," but there are distinct limitations in applying these therapeutic interventions to children. Practitioners who want to counsel children may have to acquire supervised clinical experience in play therapy, art and music therapy, and recreational therapy. These practitioners also must have a knowledge of developmental issues pertaining to the population with which they intend to work. They need to become familiar with laws relating to minors, to be aware of the limits of their competence, and to know when and how to make appropriate referrals. It is essential to know about community referral resources, such as the Child Protective Services.

Counselors working with children and adolescents must also have special training to deal with issues such as confidentiality. Therapists cannot guarantee to minors blanket confidentiality. If the parents or guardians of minors request information about the progress of the counseling, the therapist may be expected to provide some feedback. Remley and Herlihy (2001) state that in some circumstances counselors will determine that parents or guardians must be given information that a minor client has disclosed in a counseling session. For example, if counselors make the judgment that a minor client is at risk of harm (to self or others), they are required to inform the minor's parents. Counselors are called upon to strike an appropriate balance between overdisclosing and underdisclosing to parents, even when a child or adolescent is engaging in risky behavior. If counselors inform parents too quickly in all instances when a minor client is involved in risky behavior, Remley and Herlihy point out that the client will not be likely to disclose significant information in future counseling sessions. However, there is the distinct possibility that counselors could be held legally accountable if a minor client engaged in self-inflicted injury or if he or she harms another person. Counselors also have a duty to protect property when a minor makes a serious threat to destroy it. Because state laws pertaining to confidentiality with minor clients are not uniform, it is essential for counselors to be familiar with the statutes and laws of the jurisdiction in which they practice (Lawrence & Kurpius, 2000).

Information that will or will not be disclosed to parents or guardians must be discussed at the outset of therapy with both the child or adolescent and the parent or guardian. If the matter of confidentiality is not clearly explored with all parties involved, it is almost certain that problems will emerge in the course of therapy.

Involuntary Commitment and Human Rights

The practice of involuntary commitment of people to mental institutions raises difficult professional, ethical, and legal issues. Practitioners must know their own state laws and must be familiar with community resources before taking measures leading to involuntary hospitalization. Good practice involves consulting with professional colleagues to determine the appropriate length and type of treatment (Austin, Moline, & Williams, 1990). The focus of our discussion here is not on specific legal provisions but on the ethical aspects of involuntary commitment.

Under the social policy of "deinstitutionalization," which has gained popularity over the past 25 years, involuntary commitment is sought only after less restrictive alternatives have failed. The main purpose of involuntary hospitalization is to secure treatment for clients rather than to punish them. As it applies to mental health practices, the legal doctrine of using the "least restrictive alternative" requires that treatment be no more harsh, hazardous, or intrusive than necessary to achieve therapeutic aims and to protect clients and others from physical harm (Bednar et al., 1991). Professionals are sometimes confronted with the responsibility of assessing the need to commit clients who pose a serious danger either to themselves or to others. The growing trend is for courts to recognize the therapist's duty to commit such clients. Under most state laws, involuntary civil commitment is based on the following criteria: mental illness, dangerousness to self or others, disability, refusal to consent, treatability, incapacity to decide on treatment, and compliance with the "least restrictive" criterion (Bednar et al., 1991).

Bennett and his colleagues (1990) offer these specific recommendations pertaining to the commitment process:

- Be familiar with your state laws and regulations pertaining to both voluntary and involuntary commitment.
- If you notice that a client's condition is deteriorating, consider consulting with colleagues.
- Carefully consider what you hope to obtain in recommending commitment. Assess the degree to which your client is a danger to self or others.
- Before deciding on a course leading to commitment, consider other options. Also, consider the advisability of referring your client to another professional for evaluation or treatment.
- Ask yourself how commitment might affect the client's attitude toward you as a therapist and toward therapy in general.
- If hospitalization is involuntary, know the procedural steps that must be followed under your state laws.
- Make certain that you can offer reasons for commitment.

Making a decision to commit a client is a serious matter that has implications for you, your client, and members of the client's family. It is essential that you obtain consultation if there is any doubt about the proper course to follow. You need to raise many questions about the appropriateness of choosing commitment over other alternatives. Some writers emphasize practices such as conducting ongoing psychiatric and psychosocial assessments and documenting all examinations and consultations in the client's record. Practitioners are advised to protect themselves from liability associated with involuntary hospitalization by documenting all the steps they take in making this decision (Austin et al., 1990; Bednar et al., 1991).

Imagine yourself as a counselor at a state mental hospital. We are going to describe the worst possible scenario. The ward on which you work is overcrowded, and there are not enough professionals on the staff to provide interventions beyond custodial services. You observe patients who seem to be psychologically deteriorating, and the unattractive surroundings reinforce the attitude of hopelessness that is so prevalent among the patients. You become aware that the rights of patients are often ignored, and you see many of the hospital's practices as destructive. When patients are given medication, for instance, there is rarely a consistent evaluation of the effects of the drug treatment and of whether it should be continued. Moreover, you recognize that some of the people who have been hospitalized against their will really do not belong there, yet institutional procedures and policies make it difficult for them to be released or placed in a more appropriate agency. Finally, although some members of the staff are both competent and dedicated, others who hold positions of power are incompetent.

What do you think you might do if you were involved in this situation? What is your responsibility, and what actions might you take? Check as many of the following statements as you think appropriate:

___ Because I could not change the people in power, I would merely do what I could to treat the patients with care and dignity.
___ I would bring the matter to public attention by writing to newspapers and talking with television reporters.
___ I would attempt to rectify the situation by talking to the top administrators and telling them what I had observed.
___ I would form a support group of my peers for collective action.
___ I would keep my views to myself, because the problem is too vast and complex for me to do anything about it.
___ I would encourage the patients to revolt and demand their rights.
___ I would directly confront the people I thought were incompetent or who were violating the rights of patients and attempt to change them.
___ I would spruce up the environment.

Malpractice Liability in the Helping Professions

How vulnerable are mental health professionals to malpractice actions? What are some practical safeguards against being involved in a lawsuit? In this section we examine these questions and encourage you to develop a prudent approach to risk management in your practice. It is easy to become swept up in a tide of anxiety over the possibility of being sued, but this is certainly not likely to bring out the best in us as practitioners. We hope that our discussion of malpractice will lead you to an increased awareness of the range of professional responsibilities and suggest ways to meet those responsibilities as an ethical practitioner.

What Is Malpractice?

Malpractice is the failure to render professional services or to exercise the degree of skill that is ordinarily expected of other professionals in a similar situation. Malpractice is a legal concept involving negligence that results in injury or loss to the client. Professional negligence can result from unjustified departure from usual practice or from failing to exercise due care in fulfilling one's responsibilities.

Practitioners are expected to abide by legal standards and adhere to the ethics codes of their profession in providing care to their clients. Unless they take due care and act in good faith, they are liable to a civil lawsuit for failing to do their duty as provided by law. The primary problem in a negligence suit is determining which standards of care apply to determine whether a counselor has breached a duty to a client. Counselors are judged according to the standards that are commonly accepted by the profession. Although practitioners need not be infallible, they are expected to possess and exercise the knowledge, skill, and judgment common to other members of their profession. It is a good policy for practitioners to maintain a reasonable view of the realities involved in dealing with high-risk clients. No matter how ethical and careful you try to be, you can still be accused of malpractice. However, the more careful and ethical you try to be, the less likely you are to be successfully sued. The best defense against becoming embroiled in a malpractice suit is to practice quality client care.

Malpractice is generally limited to six kinds of situations: (1) the procedure used by the practitioner was not within the realm of accepted professional practice; (2) the practitioner employed a technique that he or she was not trained to use; (3) the professional did not use a procedure that would have been more helpful; (4) the therapist failed to warn others about and protect them from a violent client; (5) informed consent to treatment was not obtained or not documented; or (6) the professional did not explain the possible consequences of the treatment (B. S. Anderson, 1996).

To succeed in a malpractice claim, these four elements of malpractice must be present: (1) a professional relationship between the therapist and the client must have existed; (2) the therapist must have acted in a negligent or improper manner, or have deviated from the "standard of care" by not providing services that are considered "standard practice in the community"; (3) the client must have suffered harm or injury, which must be demonstrated; and (4) there must be a legally demonstrated causal relationship between the practitioner's negligence or breach of duty and the damage or injury claimed by the client. The burden of proof that harm actually took place is the client's, and the plaintiff must demonstrate that all four elements applied in his or her situation. Let us take a closer look at each of these elements. This discussion is based on an adaptation of the work of several writers (B. S. Anderson, 1996; Austin et al., 1990; Bednar et al., 1991; Bennett et al., 1990; Calfee, 1997; R. L. Crawford, 1994).

1. *Duty.* There are two aspects of establishing a legal duty: one is the existence of a special relationship, and the other is the nature of that special relationship. A duty exists when a therapist implicitly or explicitly agrees to provide mental health services.
2. *Breach of duty.* After the plaintiff proves that a professional relationship did exist, he or she must show that the duty was breached. Practitioners have specific responsibilities that involve using ordinary and reasonable care and diligence, applying knowledge and skill to a case, and exercising good judgment. If the practitioner failed to provide the appropriate standard of care, the duty was breached. This breach of duty may involve either actions taken by the therapist or a failure to take certain precautions.
3. *Injury.* Plaintiffs must prove that they were harmed in some way—physically, relationally, psychologically—and that actual injuries were sustained. Examples of such injuries include wrongful death (suicide), loss (divorce), and pain and suffering. Plaintiffs must show proof of actual injury.
4. *Causation.* Plaintiffs must demonstrate that the professional's breach of duty was the proximate cause of the injury they suffered. The test in this case lies in proving that the harm would not have occurred if it were not for the practitioner's actions or omissions.

In the case of suicide, for example, two factors determine a practitioner's liability: foreseeability and reasonable care. Most important is *foreseeability,* which involves assessing the level of risk. Failing to conduct a comprehensive risk assessment and to document this assessment would be a major error on the therapist's part. If you are not competent to make such an assessment, then a referral is mandatory so that an assessment can be made. Practitioners need to demonstrate that their judgments were based on data observed and that these judgments were reasonable. The second factor in liability is whether *reasonable care* was provided. Once an assessment of risk is made, it is important to document that appropriate precautions were taken to prevent a client's suicide.

Reasons for Malpractice Suits

Violations of confidentiality and sexual misconduct have received the greatest attention in the literature as grounds for malpractice suits. According to Welfel (2002), sexual misconduct, failure to prevent suicide, and incorrect treatment are the major reasons for claims against psychologists. When counselors and psychologists have been asked what kinds of ethical dilemmas they most often face in their work, the most frequently reported area is confidentiality and its limits and applications to various settings (Welfel, 2002). To be liable in the case of confidentiality, psychotherapists must have violated client confidentiality under circumstances outside the legitimate exceptions mandated by ethical guidelines or by state laws. This is a topic that we turn to in Chapter 6. The topic of sexual relationships with clients is taken up briefly in the next section and in some detail in Chapter 7. Swenson (1997) identifies three general problem areas that pose the highest risks of malpractice lawsuits:

- Violations of clients' personal rights (typically related to sex, privacy, or wrongful commitment)
- Failure to protect others from clients (alleged in failure to warn, failure to commit, and wrongful release cases)
- Incompetent treatment of clients (often alleged in suicide cases)

Many areas of a therapist's practice could lead to a legal claim, but the types of professional negligence discussed here are the areas that most often put therapists at legal risk. The discussion of these risk categories is an adaptation of malpractice liability and lawsuit prevention strategies suggested by various writers (B. S. Anderson, 1996; Calfee, 1997; R. L. Crawford, 1994; Stromberg & Dellinger, 1993; Swenson, 1997).

Failure to obtain or document informed consent. Therapists need to recognize that they can be liable for failure to obtain appropriate informed consent even if their subsequent treatment of the client is excellent from a clinical perspective. Although written informed consent may not be needed legally, it is wise to have clients sign a form to acknowledge their agreement with the terms of the proposed therapy. Without a written document, it may be very difficult to ascertain whether counselors communicated clearly and effectively to clients about the therapeutic process and whether clients understood the information. As you recall, earlier in this chapter we discussed the content of informed consent and the importance of making this part of the client's record.

Client abandonment. Courts have determined that the following acts may constitute abandonment: failure to follow up on the outcomes with a client who has been hospitalized; not being able to be reached between appointments; failure to respond to a request for emergency treatment; or failure to provide for a substitute therapist during vacation times. Clients have a case for abandonment when the facts indicate that a therapist unilaterally terminated a professional relationship and that this termination resulted in some form of harm. Under managed care plans, therapists may be accused of abandonment if they terminate when doing so could result in harm to the client.

Marked departures from established therapeutic practices. If counselors employ unusual therapy procedures, they put themselves at risk. They bear the burden of demonstrating a rationale for their techniques. If it can be shown that their procedures are beyond the usual methods employed by most professionals, they are vulnerable to a malpractice action. If it is unlikely that an expert can be found to testify to the acceptability of a certain treatment approach, it would be prudent not to employ this approach (Calfee, 1997).

Practicing beyond the scope of competency. Mental health practitioners have been held liable for damages for providing treatment below a standard of care. If the client relies on the advice given by a professional and suffers damages as a result, the client can initiate a civil action. Professional health care providers should be sure they work only with those clients and deliver only those services that are within the realm of their competence. Accepting a case beyond the scope of a counselor's education and training is not only a breach of ethics but also can result in a malpractice suit. If counselors have any doubts about their level of competency to work with certain cases, they should receive peer input or consultation. If a counselor is accused of unethical practice, the counselor must prove that he or she was properly prepared in that area of practice (Chauvin & Remley, 1996). Counselors who want to augment their skills can participate in continuing education, take additional graduate course work, and work under the direct supervision of a colleague who has clinical experience with such cases (Calfee, 1997).

Misdiagnosis. Giving a diagnosis that the therapist is not qualified or licensed to render could leave the practitioner vulnerable to subsequent liability for malpractice (B. S. Anderson, 1996). It is generally not the court's role to question the therapist's diagnosis. However, in cases where it can be shown through the therapist's records that a diagnosis was clearly unfounded and below the standard of care, a case of malpractice might be successful. In court an expert witness is often questioned to determine whether the therapist used appropriate assessment procedures and arrived at an appropriate diagnosis. It is wise for mental health practitioners to require a prospective client to undergo a complete physical examination, as the results of this examination might have a bearing on the client's diagnosis and affect his or her treatment (Calfee, 1997).

Crisis intervention. Crisis intervention strategies are used in emergency situations. People who need crisis counseling are often close to death or are seriously injured. From a legal perspective, the crisis worker is responsible for harm only if the failure to exercise reasonable care increased the risk of harm to another *and* if that failure increased the risk of harm or left the person in a worse condition than before the intervention (B. S. Anderson, 1996).

Repressed or false memory. Articles in the professional literature on the ethical and legal issues surrounding past memories of child sexual abuse are increasing. B. S. Anderson (1996) cites the example of a jury in Ramsey County, Minnesota, that awarded more than $2.6 million to a woman who claimed she was injured by false memories of abuse induced after her psychiatrist suggested that she suffered from a multiple personality disorder, which most likely was the result of repeated sexual abuse by relatives. Certainly, the style in which a therapist questions a client can influence memories, particularly for young children. Repeated questioning can lead a person to believe in a "memory" that did not occur. A trusted therapist who suggests past abuse as a possible cause of problems or symptoms can greatly influence the client.

What is the best course for you to follow when you suspect that past sexual abuse is related to a client's present problem? How can you best protect the client, the alleged abuser, and other family members, without becoming needlessly vulnerable to a malpractice suit? Anderson (1996, pp. 54–55) recommends following these basic clinical and ethical principles:

- Be attentive to the kinds of questions you ask clients.
- Remain nonjudgmental and demonstrate empathy as you talk to a client about possible memories of abuse.
- Avoid prejudging the truth of the client's reports.
- If a client reports a memory, talk frankly about the clinical uncertainty of such memories at this time.
- Make use of standard assessment and treatment techniques.
- Avoid pressuring the client to believe events that may not have actually occurred.
- Do not suggest to clients that they terminate the relationship precipitously.

If you are not specifically trained in child abuse assessment and treatment, consult with a supervisor or a professional with expertise in this area, or refer the client.

Unhealthy transference relationships. The importance of understanding how transference and countertransference play out in the therapy relationship was considered in Chapter 2. The mere existence of countertransference is not an ethical and legal issue. However, if a therapist's personal reactions to a client cannot be managed effectively, an abuse of power is likely, and this can have both ethical and legal ramifications. In cases involving mishandling of a client's transference or a counselor's countertransference, allegations have included inappropriate socialization with clients, burdening clients with a counselor's personal problems, and putting clients in awkward business situations. When a counselor gets involved in multiple relationships with a client, it is always the client who is more vulnerable to the abuse of power. When a client cannot be served in a professional manner due to a counselor's personal feelings about him or her, it is the therapist's responsibility to seek consultation, to undergo personal therapy, and perhaps to refer the client to another counselor (Calfee, 1997).

Sexual abuse of a client. Related to the topic of unhealthy transference relationships is the area of sexual misconduct, one of the most common grounds for malpractice suits. It is *never* appropriate for therapists to engage in sexual contact with clients or to become sexually and intimately involved with clients. This topic is explored in detail in Chapter 7. A finding of liability against therapists who have engaged in sexual contact with clients is highly likely. Court cases suggest that no act is more likely to create legal problems for therapists than engaging in a sexual relationship with a client. Furthermore, initial consent of the client will not be a defense against malpractice actions. Even in the case of sex between a therapist and a former client, courts do not easily accept the view that therapy has ended. More often than not, the court considers that a therapist has taken advantage of the client by changing a professional relationship into a romantic one (Stromberg & Dellinger, 1993).

Failure to control a dangerous client. Therapists have a duty to intervene in cases where clients pose a grave danger to themselves or to others. However, it is difficult to determine when a given client actually poses a danger to self or others. As Perlin (1997) reminds us, negligence lies in the therapist's failure to warn a third party who is threatened by imminent danger, not in the failure to predict violence. We discuss this topic in greater detail in Chapter 6.

Most states require mental health professionals to warn intended victims of potential harm. Even in states where such a warning is not legally mandated, ethical practice demands a proper course of action on the therapist's part. A therapist can be liable in a wrongful death claim if the therapist failed to diagnose a client's suicidal condition and if the therapist failed to act in a way to prevent the suicide. However, the courts recognize that suicide and assaultive acts are difficult to predict, which means that liability for failing to anticipate such acts is relatively uncommon. Liability may be imposed, however, if the professional's decision can be shown to have departed from accepted professional practice or standards, or when the therapist did not base his or her assessment and treatment on sound clinical principles (Stromberg & Dellinger, 1993).

Risk Management

Risk management is the practice of focusing on the identification, evaluation, and treatment of problems that may injure clients, lead to filing of an ethics complaint, or lead to a malpractice action. One of the best precautions against malpractice is personal and professional honesty and openness with clients. Providing quality professional services to clients is the best preventive step you can take. Although you may not always make the "right choice" in every situation, it is crucial that you know your limitations and remain open to seeking consultation in difficult cases.

Calfee (1997) stresses the importance of understanding risk management techniques that can reduce the practice of unethical behavior and minimize the chance of litigation. She describes risk management as a four-step process whereby practitioners (1) identify potential risk areas, (2) evaluate whether the risk area is serious enough to merit further attention, (3) employ preventive and risk control strategies in their work, and (4) review treatments periodically to ascertain their effectiveness. Here are some additional safeguards against malpractice accusations:

- Make use of informed consent procedures. Realize that there is a wide variation in age of consent, depending on what the client is consenting to.
- Present information to your clients in clear language and check to be sure they understand the information.
- Provide clients with a professional disclosure statement that addresses basic policies and boundary issues in the counseling relationship. Recognize that

the disclosure statement forms a contract between you and your client (Chauvin & Remley, 1996).

- Have a standard of care that can be applied to your services, and communicate this standard to your clients.
- Keep up to date on the ethical and legal standards of care for mental health professionals.
- Explain your diagnosis, the treatment plan, and its risks and benefits in sufficient detail to be sure the client understands it.
- Clearly define issues pertaining to fees at the outset of therapy. If it is your practice to increase your fees periodically, tell clients that fees are subject to change with notice.
- Collect fees for your professional services on a regular basis. A frequent basis of complaints lodged against counselors pertains to fee disputes (Chauvin & Remley, 1996).
- Clients should be informed that they have the right to terminate treatment any time they choose.
- Restrict your practice to clients for whom you are prepared by virtue of your education, training, and experience.
- Refer clients whose conditions are obviously not within the scope of your competence. If you are in doubt, seek peer input to determine whether you are practicing outside the scope of your competency (Austin et al., 1990; Calfee, 1997; Pope & Vasquez, 1998).
- Continue your professional education, even if this is not required by state law.
- Carefully document your clients' treatment plans.
- Maintain adequate business records.
- Develop clear and consistent policies and procedures for creating, maintaining, transferring, and destroying client records (Remley & Herlihy, 2001).
- Recognize your ethical, professional, and legal responsibility to preserve the confidentiality of client records.
- Keep clients' complete records for the time period required in your state.
- Report any case of suspected child abuse as required by law.
- Before engaging in any dual or multiple relationships, seek consultation and talk with your client about the possible repercussions of such a relationship. Explore the dangers to both of you, especially unfulfilled expectations and lack of objectivity (Herlihy & Corey, 1997).
- Exercise caution in situations where you are considering engaging in bartering with clients. Realize that such exchanges can lead to resentment on both your clients' and your part.
- Some would say that it is risky to accept gifts from clients. In deciding whether or not to accept a gift, consider the relevant cultural and clinical issues.
- Although you can be friendly and personal with clients, keep your relationships professional.
- Avoid sexual relationships with either current or former clients and with current supervisees and students.

- Absences on your part may appear to a client to be abandonment. Keep appointments with your clients. If you have to miss a session, be sure to call and make another appointment.
- Be sure to provide coverage for emergencies when you are going away. Consider an answering service so that you can be reached in times of crisis.
- Consult with colleagues, and document the discussions when you are in doubt. Because the legal standard is based on the practices of fellow professionals, the more consensus you have, the better chance you have of prevailing in a suit.
- Before consulting with others about a specific client, obtain consent from the client for the release of information.
- In cases where you have limited experience or encounter cultural barriers, consult with a colleague experienced in treating this population and, if necessary, refer the client (Bennett et al., 1990).
- In accepting or making referrals, carry out your responsibility to obtain or transfer information pertaining to a client (Austin et al., 1990).
- Get training in the assessment of clients who pose a danger to themselves and/or others, or have an experienced and competent therapist to whom you can refer.
- Learn how to assess and intervene in cases in which clients pose a danger to themselves or others. Knowing the danger signs of potentially suicidal and violent clients is the first step toward prevention.
- If you make a professional determination that a client is dangerous, take the necessary steps to protect the client or others from harm (Austin et al., 1990; Bednar et al., 1991; Perlin, 1997).
- Obtain written parental or guardian consent when working with minors. This is generally a good practice even if not required by state law.
- In counseling minors, be aware of sources to whom you can send them when they seek specific information about birth control methods or abortion. Know the laws and regulations pertaining to minors.
- Become aware of local and state laws that limit your practice, as well as the policies of any agency for whom you work. Keep up to date with legal and ethical changes by becoming actively involved in professional organizations.
- Recognize that a counselor is a potential target for a client's anger or transference feelings. Keep the lines of communication open with clients, allowing them to express whatever they feel to you (Chauvin & Remley, 1996).
- Remain alert to the ways that your personal reactions might inhibit your work with a client, and monitor your countertransference.
- Treat your clients with respect by attending carefully to your language and your behavior.
- Avoid undue influence over clients (such as imposing your values or making decisions for clients). Recognize that it is possible for you to unintentionally influence a client in an inappropriate way (Bennett et al., 1990).
- Have a clear theoretical orientation and a rationale for employing techniques as a guide in your practice.

- Create reasonable expectations about what psychotherapy can and cannot do. When initiating a new form of therapy or different method of treatment, make sure that you can support the choice with current professional journal articles attesting to its usefulness (Calfee, 1997).
- Realize that prevention is a less expensive option than a successful defense against a malpractice suit (Swenson, 1997).
- Carry adequate professional-liability insurance.

This list of risk management strategies is long and may seem overwhelming, but our intention is not to make you unduly anxious. This list is to remind you of appropriate actions and to serve as a checklist to expand your awareness of ethical and professional behavior. Most reasonable practitioners will already be taking these steps. The best way to reduce the chance of being sued is to know the ethical and legal standards and to follow them. If you develop too many forms of self-protection, however, the therapeutic relationship may be negatively affected. A client may infer that you are not to be trusted. In turn, your client may be reluctant to engage in the self-disclosure that is so important for successful therapy.

It is worth noting that malpractice claims are not reserved exclusively for the irresponsible practitioner but may also be filed against any practitioner. Clients may make allegations of unethical conduct or file a legal claim due to negligence, even though the counselor may have acted ethically and appropriately. As Williams (2000) has noted, there are false complaints against psychotherapists who become victimized by the "victims." Williams reminds us that risk management is based on the assumption that practitioners can control their exposure to lawsuits and licensing complaints by monitoring their behaviors that reduce the likelihood of litigation. However, reasonable risk management strategies may not be of much use in the face of false accusations. He states: "Psychotherapists must be prepared to face allegations motivated by factors other than a legitimate quest for justice. Greed, vengeance, escape from unwanted treatment, mental illness, false memories, and misunderstandings about the procedures of psychotherapy are all factors that can bring about lawsuits, criminal charges, or licensing board complaints" (p. 81).

Course of Action in a Malpractice Suit

As we have mentioned before, even though you practice prudently and follow most of the guidelines we have given, you may still be sued. In the event that you are sued, consider these recommendations given by Bennett and his associates (1990):

- Treat the lawsuit seriously, even if it represents a client's attempt to punish or control you.
- Do not attempt to resolve the matter with the client directly, because anything you do might be used against you in the litigation.

- Become familiar with your liability policy, including the limits of coverage and the procedures the company will use.
- If a client threatens to sue you or if you receive a subpoena notifying you of a lawsuit, contact your insurance company immediately and contact an attorney as well.
- Never destroy or alter files or reports pertinent to the client's case.
- Promptly retain an attorney. In consultation with your attorney, prepare summaries of any pertinent events about the case that you can use.
- Do not discuss the case with anyone other than your attorney. Avoid making self-incriminating statements to the client, or to his or her attorney, or the press.
- Determine the nature of support available to you from professional associations to which you belong.
- Do not continue a professional relationship with a client who is bringing a suit against you.

If you face going to court, you would do well to have some basic knowledge and take steps to prepare yourself for your appearance. Helpful resources for understanding legal matters pertaining to mental health practices, for avoiding counselor malpractice, and for preparing for court are Remley (1991) and R. L. Crawford (1994).

Legal Liability in an Ethical Perspective

Legal liability and ethical practice are not identical, but they do overlap in many cases. Legal issues give substance and direction to the evolution of ethical issues. Because ethics complaints may lead to civil or criminal lawsuits, Chauvin and Remley (1996) believe the legal aspects of an ethical complaint dictate how counselors must conduct themselves. Thus, counselors need to know the relationship between ethics complaints and lawsuits, how boards process complaints, and the importance of seeking legal consultation.

The public's use of the legal system to resolve grievances against mental health professionals is increasing. Private practitioners are becoming more vulnerable and are likely to find themselves involved in litigation more often than in the past. Consult an attorney about any questionable matters, and purchase professional-liability insurance. This increased scrutiny can have a positive effect, stimulating professionals to offer higher quality and more ethical service. However, increased use of the legal system may also lead to excessive caution on the part of therapists because of their concern about being sued. With the encroachment of malpractice issues into ethical thinking, there is increasing emphasis on doing what is safest for the therapist rather than what is best for the client. No professional is expected to be perfect, but it is beneficial to evaluate what you are doing and why you are practicing as you are.

Chapter Summary

The ethics codes of all mental health organizations specify the centrality of informed consent. Clients' rights can best be protected if therapists develop procedures that aid their clients in making informed choices. Legally, informed consent entails the client's ability to act freely in making rational decisions. The process of informed consent includes providing information about the nature of therapy as well as the rights and responsibilities of both therapist and client. A basic challenge therapists face is to provide accurate and sufficient information to clients yet at the same time not to overwhelm them with too much information too soon. Informed consent can best be viewed as an ongoing process aimed at increasing the range of choices and the responsibility of the client as an active therapeutic partner.

In addition to a discussion of the rights of clients, this chapter has considered the scope of professional responsibility. Therapists have responsibilities to their clients, their agency, their profession, the community, the members of their clients' families, and themselves. Ethical dilemmas arise when there are conflicts among these responsibilities, for instance, when the agency's expectations conflict with the concerns or wishes of clients. Members of the helping professions need to know and to observe the ethics codes of their professional organizations, and they must make sound judgments within the parameters of acceptable practice. We have encouraged you to think about specific ethical issues and to develop a sense of professional ethics and knowledge of state laws so that your judgment will be based on more than what "feels right."

Associated with professional responsibilities are professional liabilities. If practitioners ignore legal and ethical standards or if their conduct is below the expected standard of care, they may be sued. Practitioners who fail to keep adequate records of their procedures are opening themselves to liability. Certainly, it is realistic to be concerned about malpractice actions, and professional practices that can reduce such risks have been described. However, it is our hope that practitioners do not become so preoccupied with making mistakes and self-protective strategies that they render themselves ineffective as clinicians.

Suggested Activities

1. Form small groups in class and create an informed consent document. What does your group think clients must be told either before therapy begins or during the first few sessions? How might you implement your informed consent procedures?

2. Working in small groups in class, explore the topic of the rights clients have in counseling. One person in each group can serve as a recorder. When the groups reconvene for a general class meeting, the recorders for the various groups share their lists of clients' rights on a 3-point scale:

3 = Extremely important
2 = Important
1 = Somewhat important

What rights can your class agree on as the most important?

3. Select some of the open-ended cases presented in this chapter to role-play with a fellow student. One of you chooses a client you feel you can identify with, and the other becomes the counselor. Conduct a counseling interview. Afterward, talk about how each of you felt during the interview and discuss alternative courses of action that could have been taken.

4. Providing clients with access to their files and records seems to be in line with the consumer-rights movement, which is having an impact on the human-service professions. What are your own thoughts on providing your clients with this information? What information would you want to share with your clients? In what ways might you go about providing them with this information? What might you do if there were a conflict between your views and the policies of the agency that employed you?

5. Consider inviting an attorney who is familiar with the legal aspects of counseling practice to address your class. Here are some possible questions for consideration: What are the legal rights of clients in therapy? Legally, what are the main responsibilities of therapists? What are some of the best ways to become familiar with laws pertaining to counselors? What are the grounds for lawsuits, and how can counselors best protect themselves from being sued? What are some future projections concerning the link between the law and ethical counseling practices?

6. Interview practicing counselors about some of their most pressing ethical concerns in carrying out their responsibilities. How have they dealt with these ethical issues? What are some of their legal considerations? What are their concerns, if any, about malpractice suits?

7. Read some of the recent literature on malpractice and on how to reduce the chances of being sued. Students can research different aspects of malpractice and bring the findings to class for a general discussion.

8. In small groups discuss your own concerns about professional liability. How worried are you about being sued someday? What can you do to lessen the chances of being accused of not having practiced according to acceptable standards?

Ethics in Action CD-ROM Exercises

9. In video role play #7, The Affair, a counselor states, "Having an affair is not a good answer for someone—it just hurts everyone. I just don't think it is a good idea." If you held such a view, should this be a part of your informed consent document? In what value areas might you have difficulty maintaining objectivity? Are there situations in which you would want to get your client to adopt your position? What ethical responsibility do you have to inform clients about such values before they decide to work with you?

10. In the video role play #4, on divorce, some interesting points are raised about the rights of clients to know about your values as a counselor if these values influence your approach to counseling them. The client has decided to leave her husband and get a divorce. She tells her counselor that she doesn't want to work on her marriage any more. The counselor responds: "I hate to hear that. What about your kids? Who will be the advocate for them?" She says, "If I am happy, they will be happy. I will take care of my kids." The counselor concludes by asking, "Is divorce the best way to take care of your children?" If you were counseling couples or families, what would you want to tell clients about your values pertaining to matters such as faithfulness in relationships and divorce? In class, role-play a situation in which you are meeting a client (or a couple) for the first session. What would you want to tell them about your role as a counselor? Would you reveal the core values you hold that could either enhance or interfere with their therapeutic progress?

11. In video role play #1, Teen Pregnancy, the client is a 13-year-old who just found out she is pregnant. She begs the counselor not to tell her parents. In this situation, what are the rights of the minor client? What rights do the parents have for access to certain information? What ethical and legal issues are involved in this case? What kind of informed consent process would you implement if you were counseling minors?

InfoTrac® College Edition Resources

For additional readings, explore InfoTrac College Edition, our online library. Go to *http://www.infotrac.college.com/wadsworth* and select these key word searches:

informed W1 consent
informed consent couns*
informed consent therap*
record* couns*
record* therap*
mental health managed care
malpractice liability in psychotherapy
malpractice AND psych*
involuntary commitment
repressed W1 memory W1 syndrome
false memory
online W1 couns*

Key words are listed in a form that enables the search engine to locate a wider range of articles in the online university library. Key words should be entered exactly as shown, including asterisks, "Wl," "W2," "AND," and other search engine tools.

6

Pre-Chapter Self-Inventory

Directions: For each statement, indicate the response that most closely identifies your beliefs and attitudes. Use the following code:

5 = I *strongly agree* with this statement.
4 = I *agree* with this statement.
3 = I am *undecided* in my opinion about this statement.
2 = I *disagree* with this statement.
1 = I *strongly disagree* with this statement.

_____1. I am concerned about what to tell my clients about confidentiality.

_____2. There are no situations in which I would disclose what a client had told me without the client's permission.

_____3. Absolute confidentiality is necessary if effective psychotherapy is to occur.

_____4. If I were working with a client whom I had assessed as potentially dangerous to another person, it would be my duty to warn the possible victim.

_____5. Once I make an assessment that a client is suicidal or at a high risk of carrying out self-destructive acts, it is my ethical and legal obligation to take action.

_____6. Counselors could evoke guilt to discourage a client from suicidal action.

_____7. If a suicidal client does not want my help or actively rejects it, I would be inclined to leave the person alone.

_____8. As a helping professional, it is my responsibility to report suspected child abuse, regardless of when it occurred.

Confidentiality: Ethical and Legal Issues

_____9. The reporting laws pertaining to child abuse sometimes prevent therapy from taking place with the abuser.

____10. I think reporting child abuse should be left to the judgment of the therapist.

____11. To protect children from abuse, strict laws are necessary, and professionals should be penalized for failing to report abuses.

____12. If my client is HIV-positive, I have a legal duty to warn all of the person's identifiable sexual partners if my client refuses to disclose his or her HIV status to them.

____13. In counseling HIV-positive clients, I would be inclined to maintain confidentiality because failing to do so could erode the trust of my clients.

____14. If an HIV-positive client refused to disclose his or her HIV status to a partner, I would explore with my client the reasons for not doing so.

____15. I think that pager communication is a movement toward depersonalization in the therapeutic relationship.

____16. Communication via electronic mail is fraught with privacy problems.

____17. If it became necessary to break a client's confidentiality, I would inform my client of my intended action.

____18. The evaluation and management of suicidal risk is something that I would find stressful.

____19. I view it as unethical for therapists to employ coercive measures aimed at preventing suicide.

____20. I believe that it is easy to invade a client's privacy unintentionally.

Introduction

Perhaps the central right of a client is the guarantee that disclosures in therapy sessions will be protected. As you will see, however, you cannot make a blanket promise to your clients that *everything* they talk about will *always* remain confidential. Consider the ethical and legal ramifications of confidentiality, and inform your clients from the outset of therapy of those circumstances that limit confidentiality.

Landmark court cases have shed new light on the therapist's duty to warn and to protect both clients and others who may be directly affected by a client's behavior. You have both ethical and legal responsibilities to protect innocent people who might be injured by a dangerous client. You also have responsibilities to assess and intervene effectively with clients who are likely to try to take their own lives. To help you think about your position when dealing with potentially dangerous or suicidal clients, we offer some guidelines and case illustrations.

The more you consider the legal ramifications of confidentiality, the clearer it becomes that most matters are not neatly defined. Even if therapists have become familiar with local and state laws that govern their profession, this legal knowledge alone is not enough to enable them to make sound decisions. Each case is unique, for there are many subtle points in the law and at various times conflicting ways to interpret the law. Professional judgment always plays a significant role in resolving cases, from both an ethical and legal perspective.

Confidentiality, Privileged Communication, and Privacy

An important obligation of practitioners in the various mental health professions is to maintain the confidentiality of their relationships with their clients (see the box titled Confidentiality in Counseling Practice for some specific guidelines). This obligation is not absolute, however, and practitioners must develop a sense of professional ethics for determining when the confidentiality of the relationship should be broken. Become familiar with the legal protection afforded by the privileged communications of your clients as well as the limits of this protection.

Confidentiality, privileged communication, and privacy are related concepts, but there are important distinctions among them. Both confidentiality and privileged communication are rooted in a client's right to privacy. Confidentiality is an ethical concept and privileged communication is a legal concept.

Confidentiality

Clients have the right to expect that communications will be kept within the bounds of the professional relationship (Benke, 1998). Mental health professionals have an ethical responsibility and a legal and professional duty to safeguard clients from unauthorized disclosures of information given in the therapeutic relationship. Professionals must not disclose this information

Confidentiality in Counseling Practice

American Psychological Association (1992)

Psychologists have a primary obligation and take reasonable precautions to respect the confidentiality rights of those with whom they work or consult, recognizing that confidentiality may be established by law, institutional rules, or professional or scientific relationships.

American School Counselor Association (1998)

The professional school counselor informs the counselee of the purposes, goals, techniques and rules of procedure under which she/he may receive counseling at or before the time when the counseling relationship is entered. Notice includes confidentiality issues such as the possible necessity for consulting with other professionals, privileged communication, and legal or authoritative restraints. The meaning and limits of confidentiality are clearly defined to counselees through a written and shared statement of disclosure. (A2a.)

National Association of Social Workers (1999)

Social workers should protect the confidentiality of all information obtained in the course of professional service, except for compelling professional reasons. The general expectation that social workers will keep information confidential does not apply when disclosure is necessary to prevent serious, foreseeable, and imminent harm to a client or other identifiable person. In all instances, social workers should disclose the least amount of confidential information necessary to achieve the desired purpose; only information that is directly relevant to the purpose for which the disclosure is made should be revealed. (1.07 c)

American Counseling Association (1995)

When counseling is initiated and throughout the counseling process as necessary, counselors inform clients of the limitations of confidentiality and identify foreseeable situations in which confidentiality must be breached.

American Association for Marriage and Family Therapy (2001)

Marriage and family therapists have unique confidentiality concerns because the client in a therapeutic relationship may be more than one person. Therapists respect and guard confidences of each individual client.

except when authorized by law or by the client to do so. Hence, there are limitations to the promise of confidentiality. Court decisions, for example, have underscored the therapist's duty to warn and to protect the client or others, even if it means breaking confidentiality. Also, because confidentiality is a client's right, psychotherapists may legally and ethically reveal a client's confidences in those cases where a client waives this right. It needs to be emphasized that confidentiality belongs to the client, and counselors generally do not find it problematic to release information when the client requests that they do so. Challenges arise, however, when third parties demand that counselors release confidential information that clients do not want released (Glosoff, Herlihy, & Spence, 2000).

The APA (1992) ethics code provides the following guidelines for disclosure of confidential information:

> Psychologists disclose confidential information without the consent of the individual only as mandated by law, or where permitted by law for a valid purpose, such as (1) to provide needed professional services to the patient or the individual or organizational client, (2) to obtain appropriate professional consultations, (3) to protect the patient or client or others from harm, or (4) to obtain payment for services, in which instance disclosure is limited to the minimum that is necessary to achieve the purpose.

Privileged Communication

Privileged communication is a legal concept that protects against forced disclosure in legal proceedings that would break a promise of privacy. Privilege is the client's right to prevent a mental health professional from revealing confidential communications in a legal proceeding (Benke, 1998). Only privileged communication that is established by statute can protect clients from disclosure in a legal proceeding (Glosoff et al., 2000). All states have enacted into law some form of psychotherapist-client privilege, but the specifics of this privilege vary from state to state. These laws ensure that clients' disclosures of personal and sensitive information will be protected from exposure by therapists in legal proceedings. In other words, therapists can refuse to answer questions in court or refuse to produce a client's records in court. This privilege belongs to the client and is designed for the client's protection rather than for the protection of the mental health professional, regardless of his or her license (DeBell & Jones, 1997). In short, both confidentiality and privilege belong to the client, not the practitioner, and it is the client who can waive his or her privacy. If a client knowingly and rationally waives this privilege, the professional has no legal grounds for withholding the information. Professionals are obligated to disclose information that is necessary and sufficient when the client requests it, but only the information that is specifically requested and only to the individuals or agencies that are specified by the client.

The basic principles of privileged communication have been reaffirmed by case law. On June 13, 1996, the United States Supreme Court ruled that communications between licensed psychotherapists and their clients in the course of diagnosis or treatment are privileged and therefore protected from forced disclosure in cases arising under federal law. The Supreme Court ruling in *Jaffee v. Redmond* (1996), written by Justice John Paul Stevens, states that "effective psychotherapy depends upon an atmosphere of confidence and trust in which the patient is willing to make frank and complete disclosure of facts, emotions, memories, and fears." According to Newman (1996), the high court's ruling recognizes the societal value of psychotherapy and the importance of confidentiality to successful treatment. This decision may signal the broadening of a trend toward stronger privileged communication statutes.

Generally speaking, the legal concept of privileged communication does not apply to group counseling, couples counseling, marital and family therapy, or child and adolescent therapy. Members of a counseling group can assume that they could be asked to testify in court concerning certain information revealed in the course of a group session, unless there is a statutory exception. Similarly, couples therapy and family therapy are not subject to privileged communication statutes in many states. In the case of child and adolescent clients, there are restrictions on the confidential character of disclosures in the counseling relationship. No clear judicial trend has emerged for communications that are made in the presence of third persons. It is best for therapists to assume that such communications are not privileged by law. Therapists should inform their clients of the ethical need for confidentiality and the lack of legal privilege concerning disclosures made in the presence of third persons (B. S. Anderson, 1996). Although confidentiality is not *legally* protected in the presence of a third person, from an *ethical* perspective, confidentiality is still applicable when three or more clients are involved.

It is a good policy to inform clients about confidentiality and its exceptions from the beginning of the professional contact and to then be open to discussing this matter as the situation may warrant later in the professional relationship. Clients have a right to be informed about any limitations on confidentiality in group work, child and adolescent therapy, couples and family therapy, and organizational consulting (Nagy, 2000).

Glosoff, Herlihy, and Spence (2000) stress that counselors need to stay abreast of both statutes and case law. They give the following suggestions for counselors who are asked to divulge confidential client information in a legal proceeding:

- Make use of informed consent statements regarding the parameters of confidentiality.
- Inform clients of the situation and involve them in the process.
- Take reasonable steps to protect client confidentiality.
- If information is required to be disclosed, provide only minimal disclosure.
- With permission, contact the client's attorney.
- Document all action taken and what information was disclosed.
- Make it a practice to consult with colleagues regarding clinical judgments and with attorneys regarding legal obligations.

Privacy

Privacy, as a matter of law, refers to the constitutional right of an individual to decide the time, place, manner, and extent of sharing oneself with others (Stromberg and his colleagues, 1993). In discussing some basic issues pertaining to privacy, Everstine and his colleagues (1980) raise the following questions:

- To what extent should beliefs and attitudes be protected from manipulation or scrutiny by others?
- How can it be decided who may intrude on privacy and in what circumstances privacy must be maintained?
- Assuming that privacy has been violated, what can be done to ameliorate the situation?

- Do people have a right to waive their privacy, even when their best interests might be threatened?

Practitioners should exercise caution with regard to the privacy of their clients. It is easy to invade a client's privacy unintentionally. Examples of some of the most pressing situations in which privacy is an issue include an employer's access to an applicant's or an employee's psychological tests, parents' access to their child's school and health records, and a third-party payor's access to information about a client's diagnosis and prognosis. It is of paramount importance to respect the privacy of your clients and to always exercise caution in discussing your work publicly. Nagy (2000) states that you must not reveal identifying information about clients, orally or in writing, or even the fact that they consult you, without their formal consent. He adds that you need to understand state and federal laws pertaining to privacy and the rules of your employment setting as well, and how they might affect your work in therapy, research, consulting, and supervision.

Most professional codes of ethics contain guidelines to safeguard a client's right to privacy. An example of such a standard is the APA (1992) ethics code: "In order to minimize intrusions on privacy, psychologists include in written and oral reports, consultations, and the like, only information germane to the purpose for which the communication is made."

One other area where privacy is an issue involves practitioners who also teach courses, offer workshops, write books and journal articles, and give lectures. If these practitioners use examples from their clinical practice, it is of the utmost importance that they take measures to adequately disguise their clients' identities. Additionally, those who teach counseling courses need to explain to their students that they should adequately disguise identities of their clients in any reports they give in class. Of course, students' personal comments in class are also to be kept confidential.

We think it is a good practice to inform clients if you are likely to use your clinical experience in writing or in lectures. One relevant guideline on this issue of privacy is given by the NASW (1999): "Social workers should respect clients' right to privacy. Social workers should not solicit private information from clients unless it is essential to providing service or conducting social work evaluation or research. Once private information is shared, standards of confidentiality apply."

Privacy Issues With Telecommunication Devices

The use of the telephone, answering machines, voice mail, pagers, faxes, cellular phones, and e-mail can pose a number of potential ethical problems regarding the protection of privacy of clients. Mental health practitioners need to exercise caution in discussing confidential or privileged information with anyone over the telephone. Remley and Herlihy (2001, pp. 124–125) offer these guidelines for counselors using the telephone:

- Do not acknowledge that clients are receiving services or give out information regarding clients to unknown callers.
- Strive to verify that you are actually talking to the intended person when you make or receive calls in which confidential information will be discussed.
- Be aware that there is no way to prevent your conversation from being recorded or monitored by an unintended person.
- Be professional, brief, and very careful in talking about confidential information over the telephone.
- Avoid making any comments that you would not want your client to hear or that you would not want to repeat in a legal proceeding.

There are also privacy issues involved in using answering machines, voice mail, pagers, and cellular telephones. Remley and Herlihy (2001) offer a number of suggestions as a way to protect the privacy of clients:

- In using answering machines in your office, do not allow unauthorized persons to hear answering machine messages as they are being left or retrieved.
- If you use voice mail or an answering service, ensure that your access codes are not disclosed to unauthorized persons.
- When you leave a recorded message, there is no way for you to know that the intended person will be the one who retrieves your message. A family member may retrieve a personal message you left for a client.
- If you are talking to a client by cellular phone, assume that he or she is not in a private place. Also, realize that your conversation may be intercepted by an unauthorized person.
- If you use a pager, exercise caution in retrieving a message. In sending a pager message to a client, be mindful of ensuring your client's privacy by exercising the same caution you would if you were sending answering machine or voice mail messages.

Not only are there privacy concerns in pager communication, but there are consequences to the therapeutic relationship as well. In their study of the implications of pager use for the therapeutic relationship, DiVerde-Nushawg and Walls (1998) found that clinicians who did not use pagers were those who placed primary emphasis on the value of the therapeutic relationship as the agent of change. DiVerde-Nushawg and Walls warn: "Pager communication is another movement toward depersonalization within the therapy relationship —the same experience of depersonalization that prompts some individuals into therapy in the first place" (p. 372).

Using fax machines to send confidential material is another source of potential invasion of a client's privacy. It is the counselor's responsibility to make sure fax transmissions arrive in a secured environment in such a way as to protect confidential information. Before sending a confidential fax, it is a good idea to make a telephone call to ensure that the appropriate person will be able to retrieve this information in a safe and sensitive manner (Cottone & Tarvydas, 1998).

Communication via electronic mail is fraught with potential privacy problems. If you use e-mail to make contact with your clients, realize that there are a number of ethical and legal issues, one of which is the impossibility of ensuring client confidentiality. It should not be assumed that e-mail is private, because e-mail messages can easily be accessed by people other than their intended recipients (Shapiro & Schulman, 1996). Avoid sending clients e-mail messages at their workplace because employees have no right to privacy in that situation. Since there is no reasonable expectation of confidentiality for e-mail, clients need to have input regarding how they want communication to be handled so that their privacy is protected.

This discussion of privacy may appear to be mere common sense, but we have become so accustomed to relying on technology that careful thought is not always given to subtle ways that privacy can be violated. Exercise caution and pay attention to ways that you could unintentionally breach the privacy of your clients when using these modern forms of communication. As was mentioned in the previous chapter, your clients have a right to confidentiality and privacy warnings as a part of the informed consent process. Apprise your clients of potential problems of privacy regarding a wide range of technology such as storing client notes in a computer, use of cellular phones and cordless phones, answering machines, voice mail, and e-mail. It is a wise policy to discuss with your clients how communication via these avenues can best be handled. Discuss with them how they might best contact you between office visits and how you might leave messages for them. Take preventive measures so that both you and your clients have an understanding and agreement about these important concerns.

Privacy in a Small-Town Private Practice*

I practiced for many years as a marriage and family therapist in a small community. This situation presented a set of ethical considerations involving safeguarding the privacy of clients. First, it was important that I choose an office that afforded privacy to clients as they entered and left. I considered leasing space in a small professional building in the center of town, but I quickly discovered that people would be uncomfortable making themselves that visible when seeking psychological help. A home office, which was remote from the center of the village, worked out well. However, I had to carefully schedule clients, allowing ample time between sessions so clients who might know each other would not meet in the office. When an office is located within a home, it is essential that a professional atmosphere be provided. Clients have a right to expect privacy and should not have to deal with intrusions by the therapist's family members.

I discussed with my clients the unique variables pertaining to confidentiality in a small community. I informed them that I would not discuss professional concerns with them should we meet at the grocery store or the post office, and I

*This example is presented from the private practice of Marianne Corey.

respected their preferences regarding interactions away from the office. Knowing that they were aware that I saw many people from the town, I reassured them that I would not talk with anyone about who my clients were, even when I might be directly asked. Another example of protecting my clients' privacy pertained to the manner of depositing checks at the local bank. Because the bank employees knew my profession, it would have been easy for them to identify my clients. Again, I talked with my clients about their preferences. If they had any discomfort about my depositing their checks in the local bank, I arranged to have them deposited elsewhere.

Now consider the following questions:

- What other ethical issues do you think apply to practicing in a small community?
- Can you apply any of the principles illustrated in this example to having a private practice in a large city or working in a community mental health center?
- Is there room for flexibility in setting guidelines regarding social relationships and outside business contacts with clients in a small community?

Confidentiality and Privacy in a School Setting

Protecting confidentiality and privacy is a major concern in school counseling. Even though students are minors, they have a right to know what information will and will not be kept confidential from their first contact with a school counselor. Birdsall and Hubert (2000) warn school counselors of their responsibility to safeguard a student's right to privacy when teachers or principals ask counselors to divulge confidences of students. The balance between student rights and parent or guardian rights is another ethical issue in school counseling. When minors are unable to give informed consent, parents or guardians provide this informed consent, and they may need to be included in the counseling process. Parents and guardians have some legal right to request information about counseling sessions, but minors have an ethical right to expect confidentiality in the relationship. School counselors have an ethical responsibility to ask for client permission to release information. School counselors should clearly inform their counselees of the limitations of confidentiality and how and when confidential information may be shared. The ASCA (1998) guideline regarding parents is that the school counselor "informs parents of the counselor's role with emphasis on the confidential nature of the counseling relationship between the counselor and counselee."

School counselors face a host of ethical challenges in protecting the confidentiality of the students they counsel. Although they may be required to provide certain information to parents and school personnel, they need to do so in a manner that will minimize intrusion of the child or adolescent's privacy and in a way that demonstrates respect for the counselee.

Laws regarding confidentiality in school counseling differ. In some states, therapists in private practice are required to demonstrate that attempts have been made to contact the parents of children who are younger than 16, whereas school counselors are not required to do so. Schools that receive federal funding are generally bound by the provisions of the Family Educational Rights and Privacy Act of 1994 (FERPA). It is essential that school counselors exercise discretion in the kind and extent of information they reveal to parents or guardians about their children. Counselors working in schools are not required by FERPA to make their personal records available or to disclose the substance of confidential counseling sessions to parents (B. S. Anderson, 1996).

◆ **The case of Donna.** Donna, a school counselor, shifted her career from private practice to counseling in an elementary school. She was particularly surprised by the differences between private practice and school counseling with respect to confidentiality issues. She remarked that she was constantly fielding questions from teachers such as: "Whom do you have in that counseling group?" "How is Johnny doing?" "It's no wonder this girl has problems. Have you met her parents?"

Although Donna talked to the teachers about the importance of maintaining a safe, confidential environment for students in counseling situations, she would still receive questions from them about students, some of whom were not in their classes. In addition to the questions from teachers, Donna found that she had to deal with inquiries from school secretaries and other staff members, some of whom seemed to know everything that was going on in the school. They would ask her probing questions about students, which she, of course, was not willing to answer. For example, although she would not tell a secretary whom she was counseling, a teacher might have told the secretary that she was seeing one of his students. One secretary asked her: "Why are you working with Jimmy Smith? He doesn't have as many problems as some of the other students!"

Donna observed that principals and parents also asked for specific information about the students she was seeing. She learned the importance of talking to everyone about the need to respect privacy. If she had not exercised care, it would have been easy for her to say more than would have been ethical to teachers, staff members, and parents. She also learned how critical it was to talk about matters of confidentiality and privacy in simple language with the schoolchildren she counseled.

If you were an elementary school counselor, how might you address these questions?

- If you were asked some of the questions that were posed to Donna, how would you respond?
- How might you protect the privacy of the students and at the same time avoid alienating the teachers and staff members?
- How might you explain the meaning of confidentiality and privacy to teachers? staff members? parents? administrators? the children?

Ethical and Legal Ramifications of Confidentiality and Privileged Communication

The ethics of confidentiality rest on the premise that clients in counseling are involved in a deeply personal relationship and have a right to expect that what they discuss will be kept private. The compelling justification for confidentiality is that it is necessary to encourage clients to develop the trust needed for full disclosure and for the other work involved in therapy. Surely no genuine therapy can occur unless clients trust that what they say is confidential.

When it does become necessary to break confidentiality, it is a good practice to inform the client of the intention to take this action and also to invite the client to participate in the process. This step may preserve the therapeutic relationship and create the opportunity to resolve the issue between the individuals concerned (Mappes et al., 1985). For example, most states now have statutes that require professionals who suspect any form of child abuse or elder abuse to report it to the appropriate agencies, even when the knowledge was gained through confidential communication with clients. The failure to report often includes substantial fines, and even imprisonment (Ahia & Martin, 1993). Professionals who report suspected child abuse are immune from prosecution for breaching confidentiality.

Exceptions to confidentiality and privileged communication. The circumstances under which confidentiality cannot be maintained are not clearly defined by accepted ethical standards, and therapists must exercise their own professional judgment. When assuring their clients that what they reveal will ordinarily be kept confidential, therapists should point out that they have obligations to others besides their clients. All of the major professional organizations have taken the position that practitioners must reveal certain information when there is clear and imminent danger to an individual or to society; therapists are bound to act in such a way as to protect others from harm. ASCA's (1998) ethical standard states that "The professional school counselor keeps information confidential unless disclosure is required to prevent clear and imminent danger to the counselee or others or when legal requirements demand that confidential information be revealed. Counselors will consult with other professionals when in doubt as to the validity of an exception" (A2b.).

It is the responsibility of therapists to clarify the ethical and legal restrictions on confidentiality. Consider these exceptional circumstances in which it is permissible to share information with others in the interest of providing competent services to clients:

- When the client consents to disclosure
- When reimbursement or other legal rules require disclosure
- When clerical assistants handle confidential information, as in managed care
- When the counselor consults with experts or peers
- When the counselor is working under supervision
- When other mental health professionals request information and the client has given consent to share
- When other professionals are involved in a treatment team and coordinate care of a client

Remley and Herlihy (2001) provide a detailed discussion of exceptions to confidentiality and privileged communication. Among the conditions that warrant disclosure of information shared in the counseling relationship are these legally mandated exceptions to confidentiality and privileged communication:

- Disclosure is ordered by a court
- Clients file complaints against their counselors
- Clients claim psychological damage in a lawsuit
- Civil commitment proceedings are initiated

Remley and Herlihy underscore the importance of consultation whenever you are in doubt about your obligations regarding confidentiality or privileged communication.

The limitations of confidentiality may be greater in some settings and agencies than in others. If clients are informed about the conditions under which confidentiality may be compromised, they are in a better position to decide whether to enter counseling. If clients are involved in involuntary counseling, they can decide what they will disclose in their sessions. It is generally accepted that clients have a right to understand in advance the circumstances under which therapists are required or allowed to communicate information about the client to third parties. Unless clients understand the exceptions to confidentiality, their consent to treatment is not genuinely informed.

If you breach confidentiality in an unprofessional manner (in the absence of a recognized exception), you open yourself to both ethical and legal sanctions, including expulsion from a professional association, loss of certification, license revocation, and a malpractice suit. To protect yourself against such liability, Ahia and Martin (1993) recommend taking the following actions. As part of the written informed consent process, let your clients know about all counseling procedures and policies, including confidentiality and its exceptions. Become familiar with all applicable ethical and legal guidelines pertaining to confidentiality, including state privilege laws and their exceptions, child, elder, and disabled abuse reporting requirements, and the parameters of the duty-to-warn exceptions in your state.

◆ **The case of Larry.** Larry, 14 years old, is sent to a family guidance clinic by his parents. During the first session the counselor sees Larry and his parents together. She tells the parents in his presence that what she and Larry discuss will be confidential and that she will not feel free to disclose information acquired through the sessions without his permission. The parents seem to understand that confidentiality is necessary for trust to develop between their son and his counselor.

At first Larry is reluctant to come in for counseling. Eventually, as the sessions go on, he discloses that he has a serious drug problem. Larry's parents know that he was using drugs at one time, but he has told them that he is no longer using them. The counselor listens to anecdote after anecdote about Larry's use of illegal drugs, about how "I get loaded at school every day," and about a few brushes with death when he was under the influence of drugs. Finally, she tells Larry that she does not want the responsibility of knowing he is experimenting with illegal drugs and that she will not agree to continue the counseling relationship unless he stops using them. At this stage she agrees not to inform his parents, on the condition that he quit using drugs, but she does tell him that she will be talking with one of her colleagues about the situation.

Larry apparently stops using drugs for several weeks. However, one night when he is under the influence of PCP he has a serious automobile accident. As a result of the accident, Larry is paralyzed for life. Larry's parents angrily assert that they had a legal right to be informed that he was unstable to the point of committing such an act, and they file suit against both the counselor and the agency.

- What is your general impression of the way Larry's counselor handled the case?
- Do you think the counselor acted in a responsible way toward herself? the client? the parents? the agency?
- If you were convinced that Larry was likely to hurt himself or others because of his drug use and his emotional instability, would you have informed his parents, even at the risk of losing Larry as a client? Why or why not?
- Which of the following courses of action might you have taken if you had been Larry's counselor? Check as many as you think are appropriate:

  ___ State the legal limits on you as a therapist during the initial session.
  ___ Consult with the supervisor of the agency.
  ___ Refer Larry for psychological testing to determine the degree of his emotional disturbance.
  ___ Refer Larry to a psychiatrist for treatment.
  ___ Continue to see Larry without any stipulations.
  ___ Insist on a session with Larry's parents as a condition of continuing counseling.
  ___ Inform the police or other authorities.
  ___ Document your decision-making process with a survey of pertinent research.

- What potential ethical violations do you see in this case?

◆ **Three short cases.** The following cases deal with ethical and legal aspects of confidentiality. What do you think you would do in each of these situations?

1. You are a student counselor. For your internship you are working with college students on campus. Your intern group meets with a supervisor each week to discuss your cases. One day, while you are having lunch in the campus cafeteria with three other interns, they begin to discuss their cases in detail, even mentioning names of clients. They joke about some of the clients they are seeing, while nearby are other students who may be able to overhear this conversation. What would you do in this situation?

___ I would tell the other interns to stop talking about their clients where other students could overhear them and to continue their conversation in a private place.
___ I would bring the matter up in our next practicum meeting with the supervisor.

___ I would not do anything because the students who could overhear the conversation would most likely not be that interested in what was being said.

2. You are leading a counseling group on a high school campus. The members have voluntarily joined the group. In one of the sessions several of the students discuss the drug use on their campus, and two of them reveal that they sell illegal substances to their friends. You discuss this matter with them, and they claim that there is nothing wrong with using these drugs. They argue that most of the students on campus use drugs, that no one has been harmed, and that there isn't any difference between using drugs (which they know is illegal) and relying on alcohol. What would you do in this situation?

___ Because their actions are illegal, I would report them to the police.
___ I would do nothing because their drug use doesn't seem to be a problem for them, and I would not want to jeopardize their trust in me.
___ I would report the situation to the school authorities but keep the identities of the students confidential.
___ I would let the students know that I planned to inform the school authorities of their actions and their names.
___ I would not take the matter seriously because the laws relating to drugs are unfair.
___ I would explore with the students their reasons for making this disclosure.

3. You are counseling children in an elementary school. Barbara is referred to you by her teacher because she is becoming increasingly withdrawn. After several sessions Barbara tells you that she is afraid that her father might kill her and that he frequently beats her. Until now she has lied about obvious bruises on her body, claiming that she fell off her bicycle and hurt herself. She shows you welts on her arms and back but tells you not to say anything to anyone because her father has threatened a worse beating if she tells anyone. What would you do in this situation?

___ I would respect Barbara's wishes and not tell anyone what I knew.
___ I would report the situation to the principal and the school nurse.
___ I would immediately go home with Barbara and talk to her parents.
___ I would report the matter to the police.
___ I would ask Barbara why she was telling me about the beatings if she did not want me to reveal them to anyone else.
___ I would tell Barbara that I had a legal obligation to make this situation known to the authorities but that I would work with her and not leave her alone in her fears.

The Duty to Warn and to Protect

Mental health professionals, spurred by the courts, have come to realize that they have a double professional responsibility: to protect other people from potentially dangerous clients and to protect clients from themselves. In this section we look first at therapists' responsibilities to warn and to protect potential victims and then at the problems posed by suicidal clients.

The Duty to Protect Potential Victims

Practitioners need to integrate legal and professional issues into their clinical practices in such a manner that care of clients is not compromised. Bednar and his colleagues (1991) maintain that counselors must exercise the ordinary skill and care of a reasonable professional in (1) identifying those clients who are likely to do physical harm to third parties, (2) protecting third parties from those clients judged potentially dangerous, and (3) treating those clients who are dangerous. They recommend that practitioners "take reasonable precautions in *record keeping* and collegial *consultations* that will most dramatically reduce the chances of successful malpractice suits" (p. 59). It is, in fact, this standard—what a *reasonable* professional in the community would do under similar circumstances—that often determines professional liability in a malpractice suit.

One of the most difficult tasks therapists must grapple with is deciding whether a particular client is dangerous. Although practitioners are not generally legally liable for their failure to render perfect predictions of violent behavior of a client, a professionally inadequate assessment of client dangerousness can result in liability for the therapist, harm to third parties, and inappropriate breaches of client confidentiality. Therapists faced with potentially dangerous clients should take specific steps to protect the public and to minimize their own liability. They should take careful histories, advise clients of the limits of confidentiality, keep accurate notes of threats and other client statements, seek consultation, and record steps they have taken to protect others. Indeed, it is extremely difficult to decide when breaching confidentiality to protect potential victims is justified. Most states permit (if not require) therapists to breach confidentiality to warn or protect victims. In addition, many states grant therapists protection from being sued for breaching confidentiality if the therapist can demonstrate that he or she acted in good faith to protect third parties (Stromberg, Schneider, & Joondeph, 1993). Ahia and Martin (1993) state that there is clearly no exact way to determine who is a reasonably identifiable victim who must be warned of the dangerous behavior of a client. Counselors are advised to consult with a supervisor or an attorney because they may be subject to liability for either failing to warn those entitled to warnings or warning those who are not entitled.

The responsibility to protect the public from dangerous acts of violent clients entails liability for civil damages when practitioners neglect this duty by (1) failing to diagnose or predict dangerousness, (2) failing to warn potential victims of violent behavior, (3) failing to commit dangerous individuals, or (4) prematurely discharging dangerous clients from a hospital (APA, 1985). The first two of these legally prescribed duties are illustrated in the case of *Tarasoff v. Board of Regents of the University of California* (1976), which has been the subject of extensive analysis in the psychological literature. The other two duties are set forth in additional landmark court cases.

The *Tarasoff* case. In August 1969 Prosenjit Poddar, who was a voluntary outpatient at the student health service on the Berkeley campus of the university, was in counseling with a psychologist named Moore. Poddar had confided to Moore his intention to kill an unnamed woman (who was readily identifiable as Tatiana Tarasoff) when she returned from an extended trip in Brazil. In consultation with other university counselors, Moore made the assessment that Poddar was dangerous and should be committed to a mental hospital for observation. Moore later called the campus police and told them of the death threat and of his conclusion that Poddar was dangerous. The campus officers did take Poddar into custody for questioning, but they later released him when he gave evidence of being "rational" and promised to stay away from Tarasoff. He was never confined to a treatment facility. Moore followed up his call with a formal letter requesting the assistance of the chief of the campus police. Later, Moore's supervisor asked that the letter be returned, ordered that the letter and Moore's case notes be destroyed, and asked that no further action be taken in the case. Tarasoff and her family were never made aware of this potential threat.

Shortly after Tarasoff's return from Brazil, Poddar killed her. Her parents filed suit against the Board of Regents and employees of the university for having failed to notify the intended victim of the threat. A lower court dismissed the suit in 1974, the parents appealed, and the California Supreme Court ruled in favor of the parents in 1976, holding that a failure to warn an intended victim was professionally irresponsible. The court's ruling requires that therapists breach confidentiality in cases where the general welfare and safety of others is involved. This was a California case, and courts in other states are not bound to decide a similar case in the same way.

Under the *Tarasoff* decision, the therapist must first accurately diagnose the client's tendency to behave in dangerous ways toward others. This first duty is judged by the standards of professional negligence. In this case the therapist did not fail in this duty. He even took the additional step of requesting that the dangerous person be detained by the campus police. But the court held that simply notifying the police was insufficient to protect the identifiable victim (Laughran & Bakken, 1984).

In the first ruling, in 1974, the lower court cited a "duty to warn," but this duty was expanded by the 1976 California Supreme Court ruling, which said: "When a therapist determines, or pursuant to the standards of his profession should determine, that his patient presents a serious danger of violence to another, he incurs an obligation to use reasonable care to protect the intended victim against such danger."

Benke (1998) states that the legal implications of *Tarasoff* are that the psychotherapist has a duty to warn and to protect—*and* to predict dangerousness. A mental health professional has a duty to warn, to protect, and to predict only when the client has communicated to the therapist a serious threat of physical violence against a reasonably identifiable victim or victims. In dealing with situations pertaining to dangerousness, it is critical to consult with other mental health professionals and to use their input in making the best decision possible.

Therapists can protect others through traditional clinical interventions such as reassessment, medication changes, referral, or hospitalization. Other steps therapists may take include warning potential victims, calling the police, or informing the state child protection agency. Negligence lies in the practitioner's failure to warn a third party of imminent danger, not in failing to predict any violence that may be committed. Stromberg, Schneider, and Joondeph (1993) indicate that courts and legislatures tend to be sympathetic toward interns in the mental health professions in terms of predicting violence, identifying potential victims, and requiring therapists to protect third parties. In fact, few reported decisions have found mental health professionals actually liable for failing to protect a threatened third party. Because psychology is not an exact science, predicting the likelihood of future dangerousness cannot be done in a highly reliable manner.

The *Tarasoff* decision made it clear that client confidentiality can be readily compromised; indeed, "the protective privilege ends where the public peril begins" (cited in Perlin, 1997). Issues of the welfare of the individual client are balanced against concerns for the welfare of society. As Bednar and his colleagues (1991) indicate, the mental health professional is a double agent. Therapists have ethical and legal responsibilities to their clients, and they also have legal obligations to society. These dual responsibilities sometimes conflict, and they can create ambiguity in the therapeutic relationship. State courts and legislatures vary in their interpretations of *Tarasoff,* and practitioners remain uncertain about the nature of their duty to protect or to warn. However, the codes of ethics of most mental health professions incorporate this general concept, and it is generally assumed that the duty to warn and to protect is a national legal requirement.

In their assessment of *Tarasoff,* Knapp and VandeCreek (1982) make the point that variations in state laws make the procedures involved in the "duty to warn" a difficult matter. In the *Tarasoff* case, the identity of the victim was known. However, therapists are often concerned about legal responsibility when the identity of the intended victim is unknown. What are the therapist's obligations in cases of generalized statements of hostility? What is the responsibility of the therapist to predict future violence? Knapp and VandeCreek (1982) recommend that "psychotherapists need only follow reasonable standards in predicting violence. Psychotherapists are not liable for the failure to warn when the propensity toward violence is unknown or would be unknown by other psychotherapists using ordinary skill" (pp. 514–515). Their point is that therapists should not become intimidated by every idle fantasy, for every impulsive threat is not evidence of imminent danger. In their opinion recent behavioral acts can best predict future violence. In addition to warning potential victims, Knapp and VandeCreek suggest that practitioners consider other alternatives to diffuse the danger and, at the same time, satisfy their legal duty. They recommend seeking consultation with other professionals who have expertise in dealing with potentially violent people and documenting the steps taken.

In his assessment of *Tarasoff*, Fulero (1988) suggests that the issues raised by the decision are likely to continue generating litigation, legislation, and controversy for some time to come. To clarify the soundness of their professional practices, it is suggested that clinicians seek consultation. As mentioned earlier, therapists are not liable for a negative outcome unless their actions fall below the expected standard of care. Therapists can be deemed negligent for failing to protect potential victims in cases where a court finds that other therapists of average skill, exercising reasonable care, would have predicted the client's violent actions (Stromberg, Schneider, & Joondeph, 1993).

Not all states have embraced the *Tarasoff* doctrine. In 1999 the members of the Texas Supreme Court unanimously rejected the *Tarasoff* duty (*Thapar v. Zezulka*, 1999). Basing its decision on the Texas statute governing the legal duty of mental health professionals to protect clients' confidentiality, the court found that it was unwise to impose a duty to warn on mental health practitioners.

The *Bradley* case. A second case illustrates the duty not to negligently release a dangerous client. In *Bradley Center v. Wessner* (1982) the patient, Wessner, had been voluntarily admitted to a facility for psychiatric care. Wessner was upset over his wife's extramarital affair. He had repeatedly threatened to kill her and her lover and had even admitted to a therapist that he was carrying a weapon in his car for that purpose. He was given an unrestricted weekend pass to visit his children, who were living with his wife. He met his wife and her lover in the home and shot and killed them. The children filed a wrongful death suit, alleging that the psychiatric center had breached a duty to exercise control over Wessner. The Georgia Supreme Court ruled that a physician has a duty to take reasonable care to prevent a potentially dangerous patient from inflicting harm (Laughran & Bakken, 1984).

The *Jablonski* case. A third legal ruling underscores the duty to commit a dangerous individual. The intended victim's knowledge of a threat does not relieve therapists of the duty to protect, as can be seen by the decision in *Jablonski v. United States* (1983). Meghan Jablonski filed suit for the wrongful death of her mother, Melinda Kimball, who was murdered by Philip Jablonski, the man with whom she had been living. Earlier, Philip Jablonski had agreed to a psychiatric examination at a hospital. The physicians determined that there was no emergency and thus no basis for involuntary commitment. Kimball later again accompanied Jablonski to the hospital and expressed fears for her own safety. She was told by a doctor that "you should consider staying away from him." Again, the doctors concluded that there was no basis for involuntary hospitalization and released him. Shortly thereafter Jablonski killed Kimball. The Ninth U.S. Circuit Court of Appeals found that failure to obtain Jablonski's prior medical history constituted malpractice. The essence of *Jablonski* is a negligent failure to commit (Laughran & Bakken, 1984).

The *Hedlund* case. The decision in *Hedlund v. Superior Court* (1983) extends the duty to warn to anyone who might be near the intended victim and who might also be in danger. LaNita Wilson and Stephen Wilson had received psychotherapy from a psychological assistant, Bonnie Hedlund. During treatment Stephen Wilson told the therapist that he intended to harm LaNita Wilson. He later did assault her, in the presence of her child. The allegation was that the child had sustained "serious emotional injury and psychological trauma."

In keeping with the *Tarasoff* decision, the California Supreme Court held (1) that a therapist has a duty first to exercise a "reasonable degree of skill, knowledge, and care ordinarily possessed and exercised by members [of that professional specialty] under similar circumstances" in making a prediction about the chances of a client's acting dangerously to others and (2) that therapists must "exercise reasonable care to protect the foreseeable victim of that danger." One way to protect the victim is by giving a warning of peril. The court held that breach of such a duty with respect to third persons constitutes "professional negligence" (Laughran & Bakken, 1984).

In the Hedlund case the duty to warn of potentially dangerous conduct applied to the mother, not to her child, against whom no threats had been made. However, the duty to exercise reasonable care could have been fulfilled by warning the mother that she and her child might be in danger.

The *Jaffee* case. In *Jaffee v. Redmond* (1996) the U.S. Supreme Court ruled that communications between licensed psychotherapists and their clients are privileged and therefore protected from forced disclosure in cases arising under federal law. The 7–2 decision in this case represented a victory for mental health organizations because it extended the confidentiality privilege.

An on-duty police officer, Mary Lu Redmond, shot and killed a suspect while attempting an arrest. The victim's family sued in federal court, alleging that the victim's constitutional rights had been violated. The court ordered Karen Beyer, a licensed clinical social worker, to turn over notes she made during counseling sessions with Redmond after the shooting. The social worker refused, asserting that the contents of her conversations with the police officer were protected against involuntary disclosure by psychotherapist-client privilege. The court rejected her claim of psychotherapist-client privilege, and the jury awarded the family $545,000.

The Court of Appeals for the Seventh Circuit then reversed this decision and concluded that the trial court had erred by refusing to afford protection to the confidential communications between Redmond and Beyer. Jaffee, an administrator of the victim's estate, appealed this decision to the Supreme Court.

The Supreme Court upheld the appellate court's decision, clarifying for all federal court cases, both civil and criminal, the existence of the privilege. The Court recognized a broadly defined psychotherapist-client privilege and further clarified that this privilege is not subject to the decision of a judge on a case-by-case basis. The Court's decision to extend federal privilege (which already applied to psychologists and psychiatrists) to licensed social workers leaves the door open for inclusion of other licensed psychotherapists, such as licensed professional counselors, mental health counselors, and licensed marriage and family therapists. The issues in this case are critical for psychotherapists, and it is expected that this decision will have far-reaching consequences for licensed psychotherapists and their clients (Hinnefeld & Towers, 1996; Morrissey, 1996; Newman, 1996; Seppa, 1996).

In discussing the impact on the law of the *Jaffee v. Redmond* case, Shuman and Foote (1999) indicate that the case is not constitutionally based. Instead, *Jaffee* is an interpretation of the Federal Rules of Evidence that apply in actions tried in federal courts. Thus, *Jaffee* applies only in federal cases, both civil and criminal, governed by the Federal Rules of Evidence.

Knapp and VandeCreek (1997) discuss the impact of the *Jaffee* decision and possible future directions for the therapist-client privilege in federal and state courts. Knapp and VandeCreek conclude that more work needs to be done in extending equal protection to clients across all states. In that way therapists will better be able to inform their clients about the limits to confidentiality. Glosoff, Herlihy, Herlihy, and Spence (1997) support this point of view saying there needs to be a consistent definition of privilege, because therapists may be liable in a legal claim for breach of duty if they neglect to *accurately* describe the limits of confidentiality to their clients. DeBell and Jones (1997) state that *Jaffee* does not appear to cover couples, family, and group therapy. It might be reasonable to argue that couple and family therapy are no different than individual therapy in this regard, but a problem arises when one party is willing to divulge or requests the therapist to divulge the information. Likewise with group therapy, it is essential that group therapists be familiar with the laws of their own states in regard to privilege in group therapy (DeBell & Jones, 1997).

Implications of Duty to Warn and to Protect for School Counselors

In her doctoral dissertation on legal issues in counseling, Hermann (2001) describes the multiple interpretations of the *Tarasoff* duty and the lack of case law as it pertains to the duty to warn and protect in situations of potential violence in school settings. The basic standard of care for school counselors is clear; courts have uniformly held that school personnel have a duty to protect students from foreseeable harm (Hermann & Remley, 2000). School personnel may need to act on student reports of their peers' plans related to intended violence. Furthermore, school officials may be held accountable if a student's writing assignments contain evidence of premeditated violence.

Preventing students from harming other students seems to be implicit in the duty of school personnel, but whether warning students of threats of violence against them can be considered to be a part of this duty has yet to be determined (Hermann & Remley, 2000). In August of 2000, a Kentucky court dismissed the claims filed against school personnel by victims' families in a school shooting incident in West Paducah, Kentucky (Glaberson, 2000). Even though this Kentucky court had evidence that the student perpetrator kept knives under his bed, showed students his guns when he brought them to school, and wrote homicidal thoughts in his writing assignments, the court found that the perpetrator was the only responsible party for the shootings.

In the short space of one month in 2001, two major shooting sprees took place within the same school district in San Diego, California. Both of these events resulted in heavy national media coverage and raised the question of how these tragedies might have been prevented. In the first event the boy doing the shooting had told a couple of his friends of his intentions, and they searched his knapsack for a gun, which they could not find. The shooter insisted he was joking, and his friends failed to report the matter because they did not want to get him in trouble. He later killed 2 and injured 13 others on the campus. In the second incident, no one was killed, but several were injured. In this case, the student had made prior threats of violence.

School counselors are increasingly being forced to deal with threats of violence by students (Isaacs, 1997). Costa and Altekruse (1994) recommend that school counselors make an assessment of dangerousness according to the student's plans for implementing the violent act and the student's ability to carry out the act. Waldo and Malley (1992) advise gathering the necessary information to make a determination about the student's potential dangerousness, and when faced with potential dangerousness, counselors should consult with other mental health professionals and with legal counsel about the state's most recent position on *Tarasoff*-type cases. Given the context of emerging case law and the violent climate of today's schools, Hermann and Remley (2000) assert that school counselors would do well to take every threat of violence seriously. School counselors might find themselves legally responsible for preventing students from bringing about harm to others by acting on any evidence indicating that a student may be violent and warning others of threats of violence made against them.

Many schools are now searching students for weapons, which has resulted in protests from some of infringing on students' constitutional rights. On this point, Hermann and Remley (2000) report that in the wake of public outrage at school violence constitutional rights are being restricted at the schoolhouse gates: "As school violence and school security increase, students are likely to continue to engage in court battles against educators seeking lost constitutional protections. And educators face even more litigation as those injured seek to find someone to blame for the unfortunate societal phenomenon of guns and violence in schools" (p. 439).

The central ethical concern surrounding this issue involves the commitment of mental health professionals to develop organized prevention efforts in response to school violence. Although many psychologists are involved in assessing and treating at-risk youth for violent behavior, Evans and Rey (2001) report that efforts are not often directed toward organized prevention of violence and delinquency. Not only are psychologists being asked to shed light on the community's understanding of the causes of high profile incidences of violence, but they are increasingly being asked what they might do to help prevent youth violence, both in and out of the school. Evans and Rey believe practicing psychologists represent a critical resource to school districts in designing and implementing a comprehensive violence prevention program. They outline a collaborative program between a model school and a mental health clinic that can be replicated in a variety of settings.

Guidelines for Dealing With Dangerous Clients

Most counseling centers and community mental health agencies now have guidelines regarding the duty to warn and protect when the welfare of others is at stake. These guidelines generally specify how to deal with emotionally disturbed individuals, violent behavior, threats, suicidal possibilities, and other circumstances in which counselors may be legally and ethically required to breach confidentiality.

The question raised by these documents is, "What are the responsibilities of counselors to their clients or to others when, in the professional judgment of the counselor, there is a high degree of probability that a client will seriously harm another person or destroy property?" Many counselors find it difficult to predict when clients pose a serious threat to others. Clients are encouraged to engage in open dialogue in therapeutic relationships, and many clients express feelings or thoughts about doing physical harm to others. But few of these threats are actually carried out, and counselors should not be expected to routinely reveal all threats. Breaking confidentiality can seriously harm the client-therapist relationship as well as the relationship between the client and the person "threatened." Such disclosures should be carefully evaluated; counselors should exercise reasonable professional judgment and apply practices that are commonly accepted by professionals in the specialty.

In most cases therapists will not have advanced warning that a client is dangerous. Therefore, it is essential for therapists to be prepared for the eventuality of dangerousness and to know in advance what specific steps to take. We suggest preparing by taking these steps:

- Examine your informed consent document. Is it clear in terms of the forfeiture of privilege because of a threat of violence to self or others?
- Know how to contact the legal counsel of your professional organization.
- Familiarize yourself with professionals who are experienced in dealing with violence. Such experts can be located through your professional organization.
- If there is any hint of violence in the client's history, request clinical records from previous therapists, if they exist.
- Take at least one workshop in the assessment and management of dangerous clients.
- Determine that the limits of your professional liability insurance are adequate.

If you have prepared yourself for the eventuality of a dangerous client, you will have a better sense of what to do in these circumstances.

If a client poses a serious danger of violence to others, the counselor is obliged to exercise reasonable care to protect the would-be victims. Costa and

Altekruse (1994) conclude that the duty to warn and to protect presents a major challenge to counselors. Generally, the duty to warn and to protect is indicated when these three conditions are present: (a) a special relationship exists between client and therapist, (b) a reasonable prediction of harmful conduct (based on a history of violent behavior) is made, and (c) a potential victim can be identified.

Some additional guidelines for risk containment in duty to warn and protect cases are described by Monahan (1993):

- Become educated in risk assessment, stay current with developments in the field, and be conversant with the relevant laws.
- For cases that raise particular concerns about violence, consider intensification of treatment or hospitalization. Seek consultation from experienced colleagues or consultants.
- Record the source, content, and date of significant information on risk and the rationale and dates of all actions taken to prevent violence.
- Develop policy statements and feasible guidelines for handling risk, and subject these guidelines to clinical and legal review.

Truscott, Evans, and Mansell (1995) present a model for clinical decision making to determine the best interventions for dealing with dangerous outpatient clients, which takes into account the degree of risk of violence and the strength of the therapeutic alliance. They suggest a periodic informal assessment of the therapeutic alliance and maintenance of detailed case notes pertaining to the alliance. Some specific aspects of the therapeutic relationship to be assessed include the level of trust between client and counselor, the client's perception of feeling understood and accepted, indication of working toward shared goals, and notes on the helpfulness of therapy and the value of the therapeutic process.

From the vantage point of limiting therapist exposure to duty to protect liability, Monahan (1993) emphasizes the role of documentation as a risk management strategy. Documentation should include a brief statement of the rationale for the actions taken. If a therapist becomes involved in a malpractice suit, what is not in the written record is difficult, if not impossible, to prove. Unrecorded warnings to a client's family member that he or she has been threatened with harm are of no value when that person is dead as a result of the threatened violence. As was mentioned in Chapter 5, under no circumstances should clinicians alter client records. If asked under oath whether any part of the records have been altered and such entries later come to light, the clinician is guilty of perjury, a criminal offense. Monahan writes: "It is, in short, much better to admit that you did not keep good records and hope that the jury believes you when you tell them what happened than to manufacture good records after the fact at the cost of your own integrity and credibility" (p. 248).

Now let's explore two case examples. As you think about these cases, ask yourself how you would assess the degree to which Marvin and Kevin are potentially dangerous. What would you do if you were the therapist in each case?

◆ **The case of Marvin.** Marvin has been seeing Robin, his counselor, for several months. One day he comes to the therapy session inebriated and very angry. He has just found out that a close friend is having an affair with his wife. He is deeply wounded over this incident. He is also highly agitated and even talks about killing the friend who betrayed him. As he puts it, "I am so damn mad I feel like getting my gun and shooting him." Marvin experiences intense emotions in this session. Robin does everything she can to defuse his rage and to stabilize him before the session ends. The session continues for about 2 hours (instead of the usual hour), and she asks him to call her a couple of times each day to check in. Before he leaves, she contracts with him that he will not go over to this man's house and that he will not act out his urges. Because of the strength of the therapeutic relationship, she assessed Marvin as not being a violent person and decided not to follow through with the duty to warn. He follows through and calls her every day. When he comes to the session the following week, he admits to still being in a great deal of pain over his discovery, but he no longer feels so angry. As he puts it, "I am not going to land in jail because of this jerk!" He tells Robin how helpful the last session was in allowing him to get a lot off his chest.

- Do you think Robin followed the proper ethical and legal course of action in this case?
- Did she fulfill her responsibilities by making sure that Marvin called her twice a day?
- Some would say that she should have broken confidentiality and warned the intended victim. What do you think? Explain your reasoning.
- What criteria could you use to determine whether the situation is dangerous enough to warn a potential victim? What is the fine line between overreacting and failing to respond appropriately in this kind of case?
- If Robin had sought you out for consultation in this case immediately after the session at which Marvin talked about wanting to kill his friend, how would you have advised her?

◆ **The case of Kevin.** Kevin is a high school student who seems to have the potential for violence. During his sessions with you, he talks about his impulses to hurt others and himself, and he describes times when he has seriously beaten his girlfriend. He tells you that she is afraid to leave him because she thinks he will beat her even more savagely. He later tells you that sometimes he gets so angry that he comes very close to killing her. You believe Kevin is very likely to seriously harm and possibly even kill the young woman. Which of the following would you do? Check all that apply.

___ I would notify Kevin's girlfriend that she might be in grave danger.
___ I would notify the police or other authorities.
___ I would keep Kevin's threats to myself, because I could not be sure that he would act on them.
___ I would seek a second opinion from a colleague.
___ I would inform my director or supervisor.

___ I would refer Kevin to another therapist.
___ I would arrange to have Kevin hospitalized.

Would it make a difference if Kevin showed real promise in therapy and seemed to really want to change his behavior?

The Duty to Protect Suicidal Clients

In the preceding discussion we emphasized the therapist's obligation to protect others from dangerous individuals. The guidelines and principles outlined in that discussion often apply to the client who poses a danger to self, but some courts have found there is not the same duty in cases of suicide as in cases of violence (Mary Hermann, personal communication, February 25, 2001). As part of the informed consent process, therapists must inform clients that they have an ethical and legal obligation to break confidentiality when they have good reason to suspect suicidal behavior. Even if clients argue that they can do what they want with their own lives, including taking them, therapists have a legal duty to protect suicidal clients. The crux of the issue is knowing when to take a client's hints seriously enough to report the condition. Certainly not every mention of suicidal thoughts or feelings justifies extraordinary measures.

The evaluation and management of suicidal risk is a source of great stress for most therapists. It brings to the surface many troublesome issues that clinical practitioners must face, such as their degree of influence, competence, level of involvement with a client, responsibility, legal obligations, and ability to make life-or-death decisions. Mental health professionals have a legal duty to make accurate assessments in cases involving potential harm to self. Determinations are difficult to make, but counselors are expected to recognize the warning signs. Although every suicidal threat must be taken seriously, counselors are expected to exercise professional judgment and may determine that a client who mentions suicide is not currently at risk (Remley & Sparkman, 1993).

Remley and Herlihy (2001) state that counselors can be accused of malpractice for neglecting to take action to prevent harm when a client is likely to commit suicide, yet they are also liable if they overreact by taking actions that violate a client's privacy when there is not a justifiable basis for doing so. The law does not require practitioners to always make correct assessments of suicide risk, but the law does require that therapists make assessments from an informed position and that they carry out their professional obligations in a manner comparable to what other reasonable professionals would do in similar situations. If a counselor makes a determination that a client is at risk for suicide, the counselor should take the least intrusive steps necessary to prevent the harm (Remley & Herlihy, 2001).

School Counselor Liability for Student Suicide

Suicide by a student is perhaps the greatest tragedy on a campus, and one that shocks the entire school community. Recognizing signs of potential suicide and preventing suicide certainly have to be among the major challenges a school counselor faces.

In a study of school counselors' concerns about student suicide, King, Price, Telljohann, and Wahl (1999) found that only 38% of the high school counselors surveyed believed they could determine if a student was at risk for committing suicide. King, Price, Telljohann, and Wahl (2000) also studied (1) whether high school counselors knew the risk factors associated with suicidal behavior, and (2) whether these counselors knew the appropriate steps to take in intervening with a student who expressed suicidal ideation, had a specific plan, and had the lethal means to carry out the plan. King and colleagues (2000) found that the majority of the high school counselors surveyed were knowledgeable about risk factors of adolescent suicide and knew the appropriate steps to take when a student gave indications of suicidal ideation. Many of the respondents also reported that they did not believe they could identify a student at risk for suicide. This discrepancy may result from the reality of the very large numbers of students that school counselors are assigned, which makes it difficult for counselors to have personal knowledge about the majority of the students for whom they are responsible. King and colleagues (2000) made a number of suggestions based on their findings:

- Counselors need to educate school employees, especially teachers, about the risk factors associated with adolescent suicide.
- Counselors might institute peer assistance programs to help identify students at risk for suicide.
- It would be useful for school counselors to have increased access to training programs geared to acquiring information about student suicide.
- Given the legal duty to protect students who may pose a danger to themselves, school counselors would do well to take the initiative in obtaining continuing education on recent developments in the field of student suicide to help limit their legal liability.
- Professional journals and professional conferences need to continue highlighting the issue of student suicide.
- Counselor education programs need to better prepare future school counselors to recognize students at risk for suicide.

In school settings, courts have found a special relationship between school personnel and students. Hermann (2001) has documented this, and our discussion is based on her work. One of the first cases that addressed school counselor liability for student suicide was *Eisel v. Board of Education* (1991). In this case, 13-year-old Nicole was involved in Satanism. Nicole made a suicide pact with another student, who subsequently shot Nicole and then shot herself. Fellow students had told their school counselor that Nicole wanted to take her own life. When the school counselor confronted Nicole about her suicidal intentions, she denied making any such statements. The counselor did not attempt to contact Nicole's parents. In *Eisel* the court found that school counselors have a duty to use reasonable means to attempt to prevent a suicide when they know about a student's suicidal intentions. The reasoning of the court was that an adolescent is more likely to share thoughts of suicide with friends than with a school counselor, teacher, or parent. The court found that reasonable care would have included notifying Nicole's parents that their daughter was at risk for suicide. Although the suicide occurred off the school premises, the court held that legally the school could be held liable for failure to exercise reasonable care to prevent a foreseeable injury.

Even if the risk of the student actually committing suicide is remote, the possibility may be enough to establish a duty to contact the parents and inform them of the potential for suicidal behavior. Courts have found that the burden involved in making a telephone call is minor considering the risk of harm to a student who is suicidal. In short, school personnel are advised to take every suicide threat seriously and to take every precaution to protect the student.

The courts have also addressed the need for training school employees in suicide prevention. The *Wyke v. Polk County School Board* (1997) case involved a 13-year old named Shawn, who attempted suicide two times at school before finally killing himself at home. School officials were aware of the suicide attempts, yet they failed to notify Shawn's mother. During the trial, several experts in the field of suicide prevention testified about the need for suicide prevention training in schools, including mandatory written policies requiring parental notification, holding students in protective custody, and arranging for counseling services. The experts who testified at the trial believed the school board failed to provide adequate training for school personnel. Without training, school personnel will most likely underestimate the lethality of suicidal thoughts, statements, and attempts. The conclusion of this expert testimony was that Shawn would not have committed suicide if the employees had been adequately trained. Persuaded by this input, the court held that the school could be found negligent for failing to notify the decedent's mother.

This discussion is not meant to overwhelm those of you who are aiming for a career as a school counselor. Instead, our intention is to provide you with some basic knowledge regarding your ethical and legal obligations to respond in a professional manner in situations where students may pose a danger to themselves or others. Continuing education in this area is of the utmost importance, as is the willingness to seek appropriate consultation when you become aware of students who are at risk.

Guidelines for Assessing Suicidal Behavior

Although it is not possible to prevent every suicide, it is possible to recognize the existence of common crises that may precipitate a suicide attempt and reach out to people who are experiencing these crises. Counselors must take the "cry for help" seriously. Therapists need to have the necessary knowledge and skills to intervene once they make an assessment that a client is suicidal (Fujimura, Weis, & Cochran, 1985). Several researchers have suggested factors to consider when making an assessment (Fujimura et al., 1985; Peruzzi & Bongar, 1999; Pope, 1985b; Sommers-Flanagan & Sommers-Flanagan, 1995; Wubbolding, 1996). In an assessment interview, especially focus on evaluating depression, suicide ideation, suicide intention, and suicide plans. In crisis counseling, assess your clients for suicidal risk during the early phase of therapy, and keep alert to this issue during the course of therapy. Danger signs, such as those listed here, should be evaluated:

- Take direct verbal warnings seriously, as they are one of the most useful single predictors of a suicide.
- Pay attention to previous suicide attempts, as these are the best single predictor of lethality.
- Identify clients suffering from depression, a characteristic common to all suicide victims. Sleep disruption, which can intensify depression, is a key sign. For people with clinical depression the suicide rate is about 20 times greater than that of the general population.
- Be alert for feelings of hopelessness and helplessness, which seem to be closely associated with suicidal intentions. Explore the client's ideational and mood states. Individuals may feel desperate, guilt-ridden, and worthless.
- Explore carefully the interpersonal stressor of loss and separation, such as a relationship breakup or the death of a loved one.
- Monitor severe anxiety and panic attacks.
- Determine whether the individual has a plan. The more definite the plan, the more serious is the situation. Suicidal individuals should be asked to talk about their plans and encouraged to explore their suicidal fantasies.
- Identify clients who have a history of severe alcohol or drug abuse, as they are at greater risk than the general population. Alcohol is a contributing factor in one fourth to one third of all suicides.
- Be alert to client behaviors such as giving away prized possessions, finalizing business affairs, or revising wills.
- Determine whether clients have a history of previous psychiatric treatment or hospitalization. Clients who have been hospitalized for emotional disorders are more likely to be inclined to suicide.
- Assess the client's support system. If there is no support system, the client is at greater risk.

In addition to these factors, be aware of the categories of people who have an increased risk of suicide. Suicide is the 8th leading cause of death in the United States. For the elderly, it is the 13th, and for young people between the ages of 15 and 24, it is the 3rd leading cause of death (Rosenberg, 1999). Men are 3 times more likely than women to commit suicide (the rate rises rapidly until age 35 and is also high for men over 65). Single people are twice as likely as married people to commit suicide. And finally, factors such as unemployment increase the risk of suicide.

Wubbolding (1996) states that even veiled threats of suicide should be taken seriously and discussed in a clear and explicit manner. He suggests raising the following six generic questions as an approach to assessment of lethality and to open a frank discussion of whether further intervention is necessary:

- Are you thinking about killing yourself?

- Have you attempted suicide in the past?
- Do you have a plan?
- Do you have the means available to you?
- Will you make a no-suicide agreement to stay alive?
- Is there anyone close to you who could prevent you from killing yourself and to whom you could speak if you feel suicidal?

Once these questions have been asked and answered, the final decision about the degree of suicidal risk is a subjective one that demands professional judgment. Consultation is critical when you determine a high risk for suicide, and Peruzzi and Bongar (1999) make the following recommendation: "Given the highly stressful nature of working with a suicidal patient, a clinician can gain much relief by conferring with a trusted colleague. We recommend a formal consultation that is documented in the patient record as a risk management strategy, yet enough cannot be said about reviewing one's assessment and treatment plan in such a difficult clinical situation" (p. 579).

According to Sommers-Flanagan and Sommers-Flanagan (1995), two processes offer safeguards against malpractice liability in suicidal cases: consultation and documentation. Consultation gives professionals working with suicidal clients the support they need in dealing with the most stressful of all clinical activities. Consultation also provides feedback about the degree to which standards of practice are being met. Documentation is especially important when working with suicidal individuals, and practitioners who conduct suicide assessments should document these steps in the process:

- Conduct a thorough assessment
- Obtain a relevant history
- Obtain previous treatment records
- Directly evaluate suicidal thoughts
- Consult with one or more professionals
- Discuss the limits of confidentiality with the client
- Implement appropriate suicide interventions
- Provide resources to the client
- Contact authorities and family members if a client is at high risk for suicide

The case for suicide prevention. Suicidal individuals often hope that somebody will listen to their cry. Many are struggling with short-term crises, and if they can be given help in learning to cope with the immediate problem, their potential for suicide can be greatly reduced.

Therapists have the responsibility to prevent suicide if they can reasonably anticipate it. Once it is determined that a client is at risk, the professional is legally required to break confidentiality and take appropriate action. Liability generally arises when a counselor fails to act in such a way as to prevent the suicide or when a counselor does something that might contribute to it.

Expectations for action by mental health professionals dealing with suicidal clients differ depending on the setting. In school settings, the law imposes a duty to take precautions to protect students who may be suicidal. A similar standard exists in hospital settings. However, legal opinions are not consistent when addressing suicidal clients in outpatient settings. It should be noted that successful lawsuits have been brought against therapists who did not follow standard procedures to protect a client's life (Austin et al., 1990). The following are recommendations for managing suicidal behavior (see Austin et al., 1990; Bednar et al., 1991; Bennett et al., 1990; Bonger, 1991; Fujimura et al., 1985; Peruzzi & Bongar, 1999; Pope, 1985b; Pope & Vasquez, 1998; Rosenberg, 1999; Sommers-Flanagan & Sommers-Flanagan, 1995; Wubbolding, 1996):

- Know your personal limits; recognize the stresses involved in working with suicidal clients and the toll that they take on you personally.
- Work with the suicidal client to create a supportive environment.
- Attempt to secure a contract from the client that he or she will not try to commit suicide, either intentionally or unintentionally.
- Periodically collaborate with colleagues and ask for their views regarding the client's condition; realize that even for experienced practitioners two perspectives are better than one.
- Specify your availability to your clients; let them know how they can contact you during your absences.
- Obtain training for suicide prevention and for crisis-intervention methods.
- Keep up to date with current research, theory, and practice.
- Realize that you may have the responsibility to prevent suicide if the act can be reasonably foreseen.
- Recognize the limits of your competence and know when and how to refer.
- Consider hospitalization, weighing the benefits, the drawbacks, and the possible effects. If the client does enter a hospital, pay particular attention to the increased risk of suicide immediately after discharge.
- Be clear and firm with the client, and do not allow yourself to be manipulated by threats. Give clear messages to the client.
- For services that take place within a clinic or agency setting, ensure that clear and appropriate lines of responsibility are explicit and are fully understood by everyone.
- Work with clients so that dangerous instruments are not within easy access. If the client possesses any weapons, make sure that they are in the hands of a third party.
- Consider increasing the frequency of the counseling sessions.
- Work with clients' strengths and desires to remain alive.
- Attempt to communicate realistic hopes.
- Be willing to communicate your caring. Suicidal people sometimes interpret the unwillingness of others to listen as a sign that they do not care. People may be driven to suicide by an avoidance of the topic on the part of the listener. Remember that caring entails some specific actions and setting of limits on your part.
- As much as possible, involve the client in the decisions and actions being taken. It is important for clients to share in the responsibility for their ultimate decisions.

- Attempt to develop a supportive network of family and friends to help clients face their struggles. Discuss this with clients and enlist their help in building this resource of caring people.

As we have consistently mentioned, it is a good idea to document in writing the steps you take in crisis cases, for documentation may be necessary to demonstrate that you actually used sound professional judgment and acted within acceptable legal and ethical parameters. Remember that clients are ultimately responsible for their own actions and that there is only so much that you can reasonably do to prevent self-destructive actions. Even though you take specific steps to lessen the chances of a client committing suicide, the client may still take this ultimate step.

The case against suicide prevention. Now that we have looked at the case for suicide prevention, we explore another point of view. Szasz (1986) challenges the statement that mental health professionals have an absolute professional duty to try to prevent suicide. He presents the thesis that suicide is an act of a moral agent who is ultimately responsible, and he opposes coercive methods of preventing suicide, such as forced hospitalization. Szasz argues that by attempting to prevent suicide mental health practitioners often ally themselves with the police power of the state and resort to coercion, therein identifying themselves as foes of individual liberty and responsibility. When professionals assume the burden of responsibility of keeping clients alive, they deprive their clients of their rightful share of accountability for their own actions. It is the client's responsibility to choose to live or to die. According to Szasz, if clients seek professional help for their suicidal tendencies, the helper has an ethical obligation—and in some cases a legal obligation—to provide the help being sought. However, if clients do not seek such help and actively reject it, the professional's duty is either to persuade them to accept help or to leave them alone. Here is the core of Szasz's argument in his own words:

> Because I value individual liberty highly and am convinced that liberty and responsibility are indivisible, I want to enlarge the scope of liberty and responsibility. In the present instance, this means opposing policies of suicide prevention that minimize the responsibility of individuals for killing themselves and supporting policies that maximize their responsibility for doing so. In other words, we should make it more difficult for suicidal persons to reject responsibility for deliberately taking their own lives and for mental health professionals to assume responsibility for keeping such persons alive. (p. 810)

Szasz is not claiming that suicide is always good or that it is a morally legitimate option; rather, his key point is that the power of the state should not be used to prohibit an individual from taking his or her own life. The right to suicide implies that we must abstain from empowering agents of the state to coercively prevent it.

A new dimension has been added to the suicide prevention debate with the passage of Oregon's Right to Die legislation, which enables a person following standard guidelines with physician assistance to hasten the advent of death.

Basic to this proposition is the assumption that not every person contemplating suicide is mentally incompetent. In other words, an argument has been made for rational suicide. (See Chapter 3 for more on this topic.)

Your stance on suicide prevention. Considering the arguments for and against suicide prevention, what is your stance on this complex issue? You may want to review the discussion on personal values in Chapter 3 when considering this issue. Where do you stand with respect to your ethical obligations to recognize, evaluate, and intervene with potentially suicidal clients? To what degree do you agree with the guidelines discussed in this chapter? Which guidelines make the most sense to you? Do you take a contrary position on at least some cases of suicide? How do you justify your position? To what extent do you agree or disagree with the contention of Szasz that current policies of suicide prevention displace responsibility from the client to the therapist and that this needlessly undermines the ethic of self-responsibility? What are your thoughts on Oregon's Right to Die law? After clarifying your own values underlying the professional's role in assessing and preventing suicide, reflect on the following cases of clients who are contemplating suicide. If they were your clients, what actions would you take?

◆ **The case of Ivan.** Ivan is a member of a weekly group. At the 16th meeting he unexpectedly tells the group that he has often thought of suicide, although he has never developed a detailed plan. But suicide is weighing heavily on his mind, and it frightens him. Consider three possible responses that a group leader could make to Ivan.

Counselor A: This is a surprise. I would like you to tell me more about what is going on in your life now. Perhaps you can address the members in the group and give each person a reason why life is not worth living. This will give you an opportunity to explore at a deeper level the meaning of your suicidal thinking. [At the end of the session, the therapist adds] Ivan, you are ultimately responsible for your life, but I would like to make myself available to you to explore and understand what you are experiencing. I think you could also use this group as a tool to help you in this struggle.

Counselor B: Ivan, this is news to me! I am very willing to work with you on your suicidal ideation, but I hold you responsible for your life. If you choose to kill yourself, that is your responsibility. If you choose to challenge yourself and live, that, too, is your responsibility. I refuse to burden myself with the responsibility of your life.

Counselor C: Ivan, this really surprises me! If I had known this, I would not have put you in the group. I would like to switch you from group treatment to individual treatment twice a week. Furthermore, I will check in with you by telephone every day, and I would like you to call me at any time if you become frightened by your impulses. Perhaps later on, when you have worked through this problem, you may be able to be in a group again.

In reviewing these three approaches, consider your own stance:

- Are any legal issues involved in this case? If so, what are they?
- Which approach are you most likely to take, and why?
- Imagine yourself as Ivan. Which of these approaches would you find most helpful? least helpful? Why?

◆ **The case of Emmanuel.** Emmanuel is a middle-aged widower who complains of emptiness in life, loneliness, depression, and a loss of the will to live any longer. He has been in individual therapy for 7 months with a clinical psychologist in private practice. Using psychodiagnostic procedures (both objective tests and projective techniques), she has determined that Emmanuel has serious depressive tendencies and is potentially self-destructive. In their sessions he explores the history of his failures, the isolation he feels, the meaninglessness of his life, and his feelings of worthlessness and depression. With her encouragement he experiments with new ways of behaving in the hope that he will find reasons to go on living. Finally, after 7 months of searching, he decides that he wants to take his own life. He tells his therapist that he is convinced he has been deluding himself in thinking that anything in his life will change for the better and that he feels good about deciding to end his life. He informs her that he will not be seeing her again.

The therapist expresses her concern that Emmanuel is very capable of taking his life at this time because so far he has not been able to see any light at the end of the tunnel. She acknowledges that the decision to commit suicide is not a sudden one, for they have discussed this wish for several sessions, but she lets him know that she wants him to give therapy more of a chance. He replies that he is truly grateful to her for helping him to find his answer within himself and that at least he can end his life with dignity in his own eyes. He says firmly that he does not want her to attempt to obstruct his plans in any way. She asks that he postpone his decision for a week and return to discuss the matter more fully. He tells her he isn't certain whether he will keep this appointment, but he agrees to consider it.

The therapist does nothing further. During the following week she hears from a friend that Emmanuel has committed suicide.

- What do you think of the way the therapist dealt with her client?
- What might you have done differently if you had been Emmanuel's therapist?
- How do you think your viewpoint regarding suicide would influence your approach with Emmanuel?
- Which of the following actions might you have pursued if you had been Emmanuel's counselor?

___ Committed him to a state hospital for observation, even against his will, for 72 hours

___ Consulted with another professional as soon as he began to discuss suicide as an option

___ Respected his choice of suicide, even if you did not agree with it

___ Informed the police and reported the seriousness of his threat

___ Informed members of his family of his intentions, even though he did not want you to

___ Bargained with him in every way possible in an effort to persuade him to keep on trying to find some meaning in life

Discuss in class any other steps you might have taken in this case.

Concluding thoughts. In his discussion of malpractice liability for the suicidal client, Swenson (1997) writes that suicidal clients, like dangerous clients, pose a high risk for therapists. Although prediction of both danger to others and to self is difficult, courts impose liability on therapists who predict incorrectly. Swenson adds, "Even an hour of therapy can create a special relationship with a therapist and consequent duties to competently attempt to predict who will commit suicide and to take preventive steps. Although there is no *Tarasoff* duty to warn the next of kin of suicidal patients, therapists must warn if it is the best way to prevent the suicide" (p. 188). Given this caution, are you inclined to modify your stance on the issue of suicide prevention? If so, how?

Protecting Children From Harm

Whether you work with children or adults in your practice, you are expected to know how to assess potential abuse and then to report it in a timely fashion. Privileged communication does not apply in cases of child abuse and neglect. If children disclose that they are being abused or neglected, the professional is required to report the situation. If adults reveal in a therapy session that they are abusing or have abused their children, the matter must generally be reported.

In 1974 Congress enacted the National Child Abuse Prevention and Treatment Act (PL 93-247), which defines child abuse and neglect as follows:

> Physical or mental injury, sexual abuse or exploitation, negligent treatment, or maltreatment of a child under the age of eighteen or the age specified by the child protection law of the state in question, by a person who is responsible for the child's welfare, under circumstances which indicate that the child's health or welfare is harmed or threatened thereby.

If you have reason to suspect abuse or neglect, the law requires you to report the situation under penalty of fines and imprisonment.

Increasingly, states are enacting laws that impose liability on professionals who fail to report abuse or neglect. States also provide immunity by law from civil suits that may arise from reporting suspected child abuse and neglect if the reports are made in good faith. Some states require that professionals complete continuing education workshops on assessment of abuse and proper reporting as a condition of license renewal.

Mandatory reporting laws differ from state to state (Youngstrom, 1991b). In Pennsylvania, for example, therapists are required to file a report if the client is a child who appears to be the victim of abuse. If the client is the abuser, however, the mandatory reporting law does not apply. In New York, therapists must report abuse whether they learn about the situation from the child in therapy, the abuser who is in therapy, or a relative. In 1989 Maryland changed its law, and it now requires therapists to report both present and past cases of child abuse that have been revealed by adult clients in therapy.

How effective are state laws in inducing professionals to report suspected child abuse? Many professionals do not adhere to mandatory reporting laws. In a study to assess psychologists' decisions to report suspected child abuse, Kalichman and Craig (1991) found that the age of the child, the child's behavior during a clinical interview, and the type of abuse influenced their decisions. These investigators cite studies suggesting that clinicians may decide not to report because of concerns about the potential negative effect that reporting may have on therapy. Their review indicates that clinicians are hesitant to report unless they are fairly certain that abuse is occurring.

A study on confidentiality and its relation to child abuse reporting indicated that respondents were inconsistent in their procedures for informing clients of the limits of confidentiality (Nicolai & Scott, 1994). The findings of this study suggest the need to reassert the importance of providing clients with detailed information about the limits of confidentiality from the onset of therapy. Nicolai and Scott maintain that continuing education and peer-review processes should emphasize the ethical and legal obligations pertaining to child abuse reporting. The focus on training and supervision needs to be on both the associated risks as well as the benefits involved in reporting child abuse.

Although therapists are likely to accept their professional responsibility to protect innocent children from physical and emotional mistreatment, they may have difficulty determining how far to go in making a report. It is often difficult to reconcile ethical responsibilities with legal obligations. Therapists may feel that they have been placed in the predicament of either behaving unethically (by reporting and thus damaging the therapy relationship) or illegally (by ignoring the mandate to report all cases of suspected child abuse). Sometimes therapists are uncertain about when they need to report an incident. Is it necessary to report adult clients who admit having abused a child years ago or who were abused as minors themselves? The laws of some states now require therapists to report disclosures by adult clients about child sexual abuse that occurred years before treatment.

A graduate student in counseling informed us that in her internship she learned that child abuse should be viewed in a cultural context. What constitutes "abuse" in American culture may not be viewed as abuse in another culture. Also, the language used to describe abuse differs from culture to culture. This student told us that she conducted an intake session and called the Child Protective Services because an African American woman was talking about "whooping her kids" repeatedly. The Child Protective Services worker told the student that this was a cultural term and was not necessarily indicative of abuse. This illustration reminds us of the importance of taking into account the client's culture in making an assessment of child abuse. However, a lawyer, who reviewed this book made the observation that although it is interesting that culture may affect how child abuse is viewed there is no evidence that the law makes such a distinction (Mary Hermann, personal communication, February 25, 2001).

Clinicians must develop a clear position regarding child abuse assessment and reporting. To clarify your ethical stance in dealing with the duty to protect children (and vulnerable adults) from abuse, consider these questions:

- Would you consider cultural factors in determining whether a situation indicates actual abuse? How would you account for cultural differences in assessing abuse?
- Can you make a determination of child abuse without seeing the child? If a parent from another culture uses the term "whooping," how would you go about determining what the word implied?
- Some state laws require reporting all child abuse, regardless of when it occurred. What are your thoughts about such laws? Do they always serve to protect children from abuse?
- Can you think of ways in which you could file a report on an adult abuser and continue working with the client therapeutically?
- What struggles, if any, have you encountered with respect to following the laws regarding reporting child abuse?
- If you follow the law in all cases, are you also following an ethical course? What potential conflicts are there between doing what is legal and what is ethical?
- In what situations might encouraging the client to participate in reporting abuse actually enhance the therapeutic relationship?
- If an adult admits having abused a child, what are your thoughts about a therapist who argues that keeping the client in therapy is the best way to help him or her work through this problem, even if it means failing to report the abuse to authorities?
- Do you think therapists should have some flexibility in deciding when it would be best to make a report? What policies might be in the best interests of the abused child?

To help you clarify your position with respect to situations involving child abuse, consider the following three case examples. In the first case, ask yourself how far you should go in reporting suspected abuse. Does the fact that you have reported a matter to the officials end your ethical and legal responsibilities? In the second case, how might you respond to parents who inquire about their son's progress? In the third case, look for ways to differentiate between what is ethical and what is legal practice. Ask yourself what you would be inclined to do if you saw a conflict between ethics and the law.

◆ **The case of Martina.** Martina, a high school counselor, has reason to believe that one of her students is being physically abused. As part of the abuse, critical medication is being withheld from the student. Martina reports the incident to Child Protective Services and gives all the information she has to the caseworker. She follows up the phone conversation with the caseworker with a written report. A week later, the student tells her that nothing has been done.

- Has Martina adequately fulfilled her responsibility by making the report? Does she have a responsibility to report the agency for not having taken action?
- If the agency does not take appropriate action, does Martina have a responsibility to take other measures?
- Would it be ethical for Martina to take matters into her own hands and to call for a family session or make a house call, especially if the student requests it?
- Does Martina have an obligation to inform the administration? Does the school have a responsibility to see that action is taken?

◆ **The case of Rupe.** Rupe, a 16-year-old high school student, is being seen by the school psychologist, Vernon, at the request of his parents. His school work has dropped off, he has become withdrawn socially, and he has expressed to his parents that he has thought of suicide, even though he has not made a specific plan. After the psychologist has seen Rupe for several weeks of individual counseling, his concerned parents call and ask how he is doing. They wonder whether they should be alert to possible suicide attempts. Rupe's parents tell Vernon that they want to respect confidentiality and are not interested in detailed disclosures but that they want to find out if they have cause for worry. Without going into detail, Vernon reassures them that they really do not need to worry.

- Is Vernon's behavior ethical? Would it make a difference if Rupe were 25 years old?
- Does Vernon have an ethical obligation to inform Rupe of the conversation with his parents?
- If the parents were to insist on having more information, does Vernon have an obligation to say more?
- If Vernon provides details to the parents, does he have an obligation to inform Rupe before talking with his parents?
- Other than doing what this school psychologist did, do you see other courses of action?
- If Rupe were indeed suicidal, what ethical and legal obligations would Vernon have toward the parents? Would he have to inform the school principal?

◆ **The case of Sally.** One night, in a moment of rare intoxication, a father stumbles into his 12-year-old daughter's bedroom and briefly fondles her. Sally's cries bring her mother into the room, and the incident does not go further. Later, the father does not recall the incident. There has been no previous history of molestation. During therapy the family is able to talk openly about the incident and is working through the resulting pain. Because of this incident, the father has enrolled in a substance abuse program. The family is adamant that this situation should not be reported to social services. The therapist knows that the statute in her state clearly specifies that she is required to report this incident, even if it had happened in the past and no further incidents had occurred. Listen to the inner dialogue of the therapist as she debates the pros and cons of reporting the incident, and think about your reactions to each course of action she considers:

> There are many hazards involved if I don't report this incident. If this family ever broke up, the mother or daughter could sue me for having failed to report what happened. I would be obeying the law and protecting myself by reporting it, and I could justify my actions by citing the requirement of the law.
>
> But this occurred on one occasion, and the father was intoxicated. The daughter was frightened by the incident, but she seems to be able to talk about it in the family now. If I obey the law, my actions may be more detrimental to the family than beneficial.
>
> But the law is there for a reason. It appears that a child has been abused—that is no minor incident—and there was trauma for some time afterward.
>
> What is the most ethical thing to do? I would be following the law by reporting it, but is that the most ethical course in this case? Is it the best thing for this family now, especially as none of the members want it reported? My ethical sense tells me that my interventions should always be in the best interests of all three members of this family.
>
> I am required to report only if I suspect or believe that abuse has occurred. Some could argue that no abuse has taken place, which is what the parents seem to indicate by their behavior.
>
> The family is now in therapy with me. If I do make a report, the family might terminate therapy. Is reporting this situation worth risking that chance?
>
> Child protective agencies are often overburdened, and only the most serious cases may be given attention. Because no abuse is presently going on, I wonder if this case will be followed up. Will it be worth risking the progress that has been made with this family?
>
> As an alternative to reporting this matter to the authorities, I could document a clinical plan of action that addresses therapeutic interventions with the father and also the well-being of the others. This course of action might be the best way to meet my legal and ethical obligations in this particular case.
>
> Before I act, perhaps I should consult an attorney for advice on how to proceed. Or I could call Child Protective Services to find out what I must do. Maybe I should call the Board of Ethics of my professional organization and get some advice on how to proceed.
>
> I don't know what action to take. Maybe I should consult with a colleague before I take any definite action.

Commentary. This case illustrates some of the difficulties counselors can find themselves in when their inner ethical sense conflicts with the law or an ethics code. This counselor must struggle with herself to determine whether she will follow her clinical intuitions by doing what she thinks is in the best interests of this family or whether she will do what is required by the law. If she simply reported this case, she would be taking the most conservative route. Her actions would be characterized by compliance with the law and adherence to the ethics code of her profession. However, she may not be putting ethical considerations in the forefront.

If the therapist called the ethics committee of her professional organization or a colleague, she would be acting on a slightly higher level of ethical functioning because of her willingness to consult. Consulting colleagues is always recommended in cases such as this one. The consultation process would help from a legal perspective as well. If other professionals agreed with her course of action, she would have a good chance of demonstrating that she had acted in good faith and that she had met the professional standards of her peers. In addition, consulting colleagues would provide her with one or more different perspectives on a difficult case.

The therapist is acting on the highest level of ethical functioning in examining all the factors and special circumstances of this family before acting. She is struggling to act appropriately, not just to protect herself, and is truly concerned with the best interests of everyone in the family. The welfare of the family members does not require her to violate the law, yet it does require her to think beyond merely obeying the law. It would be good for her to keep in mind that she has the legal obligation to report the situation.

It may still be possible for her to continue her therapeutic relationship with the family even if she decides to make a report. If this therapist approached you for consultation, what suggestions would you give her? What are your views about this case? What might you do if you were the therapist in this situation?

Confidentiality and HIV/AIDS-Related Issues

AIDS affects a large population with diverse demographics and will continue to gain prominence as a public health and social issue. All mental health practitioners will inevitably come in contact with people who have AIDS, with people who have tested positive as carriers of the virus, or with people who are close to these people.

People who have tested HIV-positive (and those who have contracted AIDS) are usually in need of short-term help. They need to find a system to support them through the troubled times they will endure. Those who are HIV-positive live with the anxiety of wondering whether they will come down with this incurable disease. Many of these individuals also struggle with the stigma attached to AIDS. They live in fear not only of developing a life-threatening disease but also of being discovered and rejected by society and by friends and loved ones. In addition to feeling different and stigmatized, they typically have a great deal of anger, which is likely to be directed toward others, especially those who have given them the virus. Those at risk are often angry at health professionals as well. Because such clients are particularly vulnerable to being ostracized and suffering discrimination, it is critical that professionals obtain their informed consent and educate them about their rights and responsibilities.

Therapists need to be very clear in their own minds about the limits of confidentiality, matters of reporting, and their duty to warn and to protect third parties, and they need to communicate their professional responsibilities to their clients from the outset. If therapists decide that they cannot provide competent services to HIV-infected people, it is ethically appropriate that they refer these clients to professionals who can provide assistance. We recommend that you review the earlier discussion in this chapter regarding the therapist's duty to warn and to protect as it applies to people who have AIDS or are HIV-positive.

As a counselor you may indeed work with clients who are HIV-positive. You might accept a client and establish a therapeutic relationship only to find out months later that this person had recently tested positive. If this were the case, would it be ethical to terminate the professional relationship and make a referral? Would the ethical course be to become informed so that you could provide competent help? What would be in the best interests of your client? If you are counseling HIV-positive individuals, do you have a duty both to your clients and to their sexual partners? Do you have an ethical responsibility to warn and protect third parties in cases of those who are HIV-positive and who are putting others at risk by engaging in unprotected sex or needle sharing? If you do your best to convince your client to disclose his or her HIV status to a partner, and if your client refuses to share this information, what course of action might you take? As you think about these questions, we hope you will consider your ethical responsibilities to respond to this population *before* you encounter possible difficult situations. The three cases described here are designed to help you clarify your position on the ethical dimensions of counseling clients who have AIDS or are HIV-positive.

◆ **The case of Al and Wilma.** Al and Wilma are seeing Sarina for marital counseling. After a number of sessions Wilma requests an individual session, in which she discloses that she has tested HIV-positive as a result of several extramarital alliances. Sarina finds herself in a real dilemma: She has concerns for the welfare of the couple, but she is also concerned about Wilma's painful predicament, especially because Wilma has a sincere desire to make her marriage work. Part of Sarina's quandary is that she did not tell the couple her policy about handling confidentiality for private sessions.

- Does Sarina have a duty to warn Al? Why or why not?
- Would such a duty supersede any implied confidentiality of the private session?
- What are some of the potential ethical violations in the manner in which Sarina handled this case?
- Would it be more therapeutic for Sarina to persuade Wilma to disclose her condition to Al rather than taking the responsibility for this disclosure herself?
- If Wilma refused to inform her husband, should Sarina discontinue therapy with the couple? If she were to discontinue working with them, how might she ethically explain her decision?
- If she felt obligated to continue therapy with the couple, how would she handle the secret, and what would be the ethical implications of her practices?
- Are there factors in this situation that would compel Sarina to treat Wilma's secret differently from other major secrets in couples therapy?

◆ **The case of Paddy.** Paddy has been seeing a counselor for several months to deal with his depression. He comes to one session in a state of extreme anxiety. He has been in a gay relationship with Christopher for 15 years. On a recent business trip Paddy had a sexual encounter with another man. Paddy is now worried that he may have contracted HIV, but he refuses to be tested. He is terrified of confirming his fear that he is HIV-positive. The counselor encourages Paddy to challenge his fears and be tested. He also encourages him to discuss this matter with Christopher. Paddy steadfastly refuses to consider either of the counselor's suggestions. When the counselor asks Paddy what he wants from him, he replies that he wants to be reassured that he is merely overreacting. He also would like to get over feeling depressed most of the time.

- What are the ethical dilemmas in this case?
- Are there any legal ramifications?
- How would you work with Paddy? Would you try to convince him to be tested, and would this be ethical? Would you try to persuade him to tell Christopher, and would your persuasion be ethical?
- What kind of referral might you make? What if Paddy refused a referral you suggested but insisted on continuing to see you?
- How would you help him achieve his stated goal for seeing you? Do you have enough information to accomplish that goal?
- What values of yours might come into play in dealing with this situation?
- If Paddy consented to being tested and was found to be HIV-positive but still refused to disclose this fact to his partner, what ethical and legal concerns would now come into play? How would you proceed with this new information?
- If Paddy did not have a life-threatening disease but instead contracted a sexually transmitted disease (genital herpes), would your course of action be any different? If so, how might you proceed differently?

◆ **The case of Hershel.** Hershel is a vice-president in a large company. He is married and has young children. Hershel's job necessitates transcontinental travel several times a year. During these trips he spends time with a lover. On his last trip he confided that one of the men that he had recently been sexually involved with had received an HIV-positive diagnosis. Hershel is panic stricken and seeks the help of a counselor, Blanche, who immediately recommends that he be tested. He follows her recommendation, and his test results are negative. He is elated and now sees no reason to continue therapy. Blanche makes no attempt to persuade him to explore other issues. She has no expertise in the treatment of AIDS clients and lacks essential knowledge pertaining to the latest AIDS research.

- Blanche appeared to take the ethical course in suggesting that Hershel be tested for AIDS, but was one test sufficient? What else needed to be done?
- Given this therapist's level of knowledge about AIDS, should she have referred Hershel?

- Although he was symptom-free and may not have transmitted the virus to his wife, there is a chance that he could be carrying the virus and that symptoms might not develop until much later. Given these facts, do you think that he presented a clear and imminent danger to his wife or to other sexual partners?
- Did the therapist have a duty to warn his wife of the potential life-threatening situation to which she was now exposed?
- Did the therapist have a duty to notify the authorities, and if so, which authorities?
- If Hershel had disclosed to Blanche that he and his wife were planning on having more children, how might that have affected the complexity of this case?
- Did Blanche have an obligation to persuade him to discontinue his potentially life-threatening behavior?
- Did Blanche have an obligation to get him to discuss the matter with his wife because of the risk to her health?
- If Hershel had come to see you, what course of action would you have taken?

Ethical and Legal Considerations in AIDS-Related Cases

In the past few years much has been written about the conditions under which confidentiality might be breached in AIDS-related therapy situations. Up to now, courts have not applied the duty to warn to cases involving HIV infection, and therapists' legal responsibility in protecting sexual partners of HIV-positive clients remains unclear. Practitioners have few legal guidelines to help them determine when or how to inform a potential victim of the threat of HIV transmission (Erickson, 1993). Despite the lack of legal guidance on this issue, Erickson contends that there is some basis to consider this an exception to confidentiality issue. Calculated risks can be taken to ensure that unsuspecting individuals are protected from the definite possibility of infection by a contagious, fatal disease.

In the last revision of its ethics code, the ACA (1995) added a guideline pertaining to the ethical responsibility of practitioners who might deal with HIV-positive clients who are unwilling to inform their sexual or needle-sharing partners of their HIV status. ACA's standard pertaining to contagious, fatal diseases reads:

> A counselor who receives information confirming that a client has a disease commonly known to be both communicable and fatal is justified in disclosing information to an identifiable third party, who by his or her relationship with the client is at a high risk of contracting the disease. Prior to making a disclosure the counselor should ascertain that the client has not already informed the third party about his or her disease and that the client is not intending to inform the third party in the immediate future. (B.1.d.)

This guideline places the responsibility on the counselor for examining a number of issues and eventually arriving at the best decision in a given case. The ACA guideline states that you *may be ethically justified* in breaching confidentiality to a third party who is at risk, yet you are not necessarily *obligated* to take this course of action. In fact, this is an example of where what is ethically appropriate may conflict with what is legally acceptable. Until a landmark court case determines a precedent, mental health professionals will have to continue to struggle with doing what they think is morally and ethically right without any guarantee of legal protection.

Duty to protect versus confidentiality. Earlier in this chapter we discussed the principles involved in situations where therapists may have a duty to warn and to protect innocent victims. The literature reveals some attempts at applying the *Tarasoff* decision to AIDS-related cases (Ahia & Martin, 1993; Cohen, 1997; Erickson, 1993; Gray & Harding, 1988; Hoffman, 1991a; Knapp & VandeCreek, 1990; Lamb, Clark, Drumheller, Frizzell, & Surrey, 1989; McGuire, Nieri, Abbott, Sheridan, & Fisher, 1995; Melton, 1988; Morrison, 1989; Totten, Lamb, & Reeder, 1990). The duty to warn and to protect may arise when a counselor has reason to believe that an HIV-positive client intends to continue to have unprotected sex, or to share needles, with unsuspecting but reasonably identifiable third parties (Ahia & Martin, 1993).

The HIV-positive duty to warn decision is one of the more controversial and emotion-laden issues practitioners might encounter. The complexity of this issue and a corresponding lack of case law may account for the large number of calls for help to the APA office on AIDS (Werth & Carney, 1994). For practitioners who work with HIV-positive clients, the choice is often between protecting the client-therapist relationship and breaching confidentiality to protect at-risk populations. This situation can put practitioners in a moral, ethical, legal, and professional dilemma. The duty to warn and to protect third parties is especially difficult because counselors face not only ethical and legal issues surrounding confidentiality of client communications but also specific statutory prohibitions against disclosure of HIV information (Ahia & Martin, 1993; VandeCreek & Knapp, 1994).

State laws differ regarding HIV and the limits of confidentiality, and the law is often different for medical professionals than for licensed psychotherapists. According to Pennsylvania law, therapists may not break confidentiality to warn that a client poses a threat to others through HIV/AIDS. Instead, therapists are expected to persuade clients to change their behavior voluntarily (VandeCreek & Knapp, 1994). Some state laws forbid any disclosure of HIV status to third parties, and others allow some disclosure to at-risk third parties by physicians and psychiatrists but not by other mental health professionals. Under many state laws, therapists who disclose a person's HIV-status to an unauthorized third party are subject to criminal charges and to malpractice action as well. Other states have yet to address this issue by statute.

Two thirds of the states have enacted legislation specifying limits to confidentiality regarding an individual's HIV status (Melchert & Patterson, 1999). Montana is the only state that protects mental health practitioners from liability in making good faith disclosures to third parties at risk for HIV infection. In Texas, all therapists are given protection against liability for disclosing this information to a spouse. Although therapists may be morally obligated to warn third parties who are at risk for HIV infection, Melchert and Patterson (1999) report that no state requires health care professionals to make such warnings. Furthermore, very few states (Montana and Texas) offer legal protection against liability for practitioners who break client confidentiality to warn third parties at risk. Therapists need to carefully consider any applicable state laws that might restrict or guide reporting options.

Melton (1988) believes the core ethical and legal issue is the duty to protect third parties from HIV infection with minimal violation of the client's privacy. Cohen (1997) contends that the HIV dilemma can be resolved by referring to legal precedent, state statutes, and professional codes of ethics. Counselors who disclose information about their client's HIV status to endangered third parties will break client-counselor confidentiality. However, counselors who keep this confidentiality may fail to prevent serious and preventable harm to the third party. Cohen (1997) proposes these ethical guidelines for deciding when to disclose confidential information about a client's HIV status:

- When there are sufficient factual grounds for considering risk of harm to the third party to be high
- When the third party is at risk of death or substantial bodily harm
- When the harm to the third party is not likely to be prevented unless the counselor makes the disclosure
- When the third party cannot reasonably be expected to foresee or comprehend the high risk of harm to self

Because preserving client confidentiality is a serious moral, ethical, and legal obligation, Cohen (1997) states that the case for breaching confidentiality must be strong before disclosure is justifiable.

Do *Tarasoff* principles apply in AIDS-related psychotherapy? McGuire and colleagues (1995) assert that *Tarasoff* guidelines may be helpful in identifying critical factors in the ethical dilemma of having a client who is HIV-positive and who refuses to disclose his or her HIV status or otherwise warn sexual partners. They suggest that therapists should be extremely cautious regarding breaching confidentiality and should first consider less intrusive means of dealing with HIV-positive clients who indicate that they are not using safe sex practices and are not warning their partners of their HIV status. Several researchers have addressed breaching confidentiality related to the danger to others posed by HIV-positive clients (Ahia & Martin, 1993; Erickson, 1993; Lamb et al., 1989; McGuire et al., 1995). They provide these recommendations for therapists:

- All limits to confidentiality should be discussed with the client at the onset of treatment. When this is done early in the therapeutic relationship, it is less likely that therapists will lose clients because of breaching confidentiality. The implications of disclosing confidentiality, as well as other alternatives, can be explored with HIV-positive clients within the counseling context at this time.

- Therapists must be aware of the state laws regarding their professional interactions with HIV-positive clients and know the HIV confidentiality law of their state. Therapists should be aware that some state laws prohibit warning identifiable third parties of partners who are HIV-positive.
- Therapists need to keep current with regard to relevant medical information related to the transmission of HIV, know which sexual practices are safe and which are not, and encourage their clients to practice safe sex. Because sharing a contaminated needle is another major means of HIV transmission, therapists should be up to date on approaches to drug education.
- Practitioners can seek training for intervening in the crises facing HIV-positive clients and those with AIDS.
- Therapists need to be aware of their own attitudes, biases, and prejudices as they relate to individuals who are at a higher risk of becoming infected.
- Therapists should speak directly and openly with their clients about their concerns regarding the danger of certain behaviors and the risk to third parties. They can use the therapeutic process to educate their clients as to the effects their behavior can have on others, teach safe sex practices, obtain commitments from the client to notify partners, and offer help in communicating information to partners.
- If the client continues to resist using safe sex practices or refuses to inform partners, then the therapist needs to determine what course of action to follow.
- Practitioners should consult with knowledgeable peers or attorneys, or both, to determine that their intended course of action is ethically and legally sound.
- If all other options have been exhausted and the therapist has decided to breach confidentiality by warning an identified partner, the client should generally be informed of this intention, and the therapist should attempt to obtain the client's permission.
- In disclosing HIV information, therapists need to follow the statutory guidelines and safeguard the client's privacy as much as possible.

Several writers have applied *Tarasoff* as a framework for examining decisions about breaking confidentiality and protecting third parties (Lamb et al., 1989; McGuire et al., 1995; Totten et al., 1990). Therapists have a duty to protect when the following three conditions are met:

- There must be a *special client-therapist relationship* that entails the practitioner's responsibility for the safety of the client and also of other parties whom the therapist knows to be threatened by the client.
- *Clear and imminent danger* must exist. It is important to be certain that the client is HIV-positive. The degree of dangerousness of a client who has tested HIV-positive depends on several factors: the client's medical diagnosis, the extent to which the person engages in high-risk behaviors, and the use of safe sex techniques aimed at reducing the chances of transmission of the virus. Assessing dangerousness calls for an in-depth discussion of the client's drug use and sexual practices.

- There must be an *identifiable victim.* The duty to protect would probably extend to partners of an exclusive relationship but would not include anonymous partners unknown to the therapist. HIV-positive clients may have been sexually involved with many people in the past and may now have multiple sexual partners. This matter is complicated by the fact that the virus can remain dormant for years. Who are the potential victims? How should the therapist decide whom to inform?

Totten and her colleagues (1990) found that some clinicians used the criteria of degree of dangerousness and identifiability of a third party in determining when to break confidentiality. These researchers found that dangerousness appeared to be a more relevant factor than identifiability of a victim. Those clinicians who had had professional contact with people with HIV or AIDS were less likely to favor breaking confidentiality than those practitioners who had not had such contact.

If an HIV-infected individual is engaging in high-risk behavior with an identifiable, unsuspecting partner, then it appears that the three criteria under the *Tarasoff* decision may be met. However, many states have not adopted *Tarasoff,* which places the professional responsibility on each practitioner to examine his or her personal and professional values in weighing the ethical, legal, and moral implications of any proposed course of action.

Special Training on HIV-Related Issues

Mental health professionals have an ethical obligation to be knowledgeable about HIV and AIDS so they can ask the right questions. You can start by reading about AIDS-related issues and by attending a workshop on the subject. You can also contact one of the many clinics throughout the country, which are useful resources for treatment and referrals. In many communities, groups of volunteers have been organized to work with AIDS clients.

Werth and Carney (1994) emphasize the importance of incorporating HIV-related issues into graduate student training. They cite several surveys that show that most students are not receiving HIV-related training in their graduate programs and are unprepared to handle ethical, legal, and professional issues pertaining to HIV situations. Specifically, on the topic of the duty to protect versus confidentiality, they find the reaction of their students is to breach confidentiality too soon, without giving adequate consideration to other alternatives or to the potential consequences. In training students in this area, Werth and Carney review case scenarios, discuss the implications of the *Tarasoff* case, and review ethical and legal cases. They pose the following questions for discussion:

- What is the therapist's role (watchdog, change agent, client advocate)?
- To whom does the therapist have a primary responsibility?
- How is this situation similar or different from the *Tarasoff* case?
- What options and courses of action are available?
- Where can the therapist go for consultation?

Erickson's (1993) challenge to the profession is still relevant: "Society must come to view AIDS as a deadly disease, rather than a stigma, and must grapple with the legal and ethical issues involved. But, until society responds, and clear legal and ethical guidelines are established, each mental health counselor must carefully consider all pertinent professional issues and then make an individual decision for appropriate action" (pp. 129–130).

In summary, dealing responsibly with the dilemmas posed in this section demands an awareness of the ethical, legal, and clinical issues involved in working with clients with AIDS. There are no simple solutions to the many complex issues practitioners may face, and this topic is surely one of the more challenging ones. Consulting with both colleagues and attorneys is an excellent practice that can help you make appropriate decisions.

Chapter Summary

Along with their duties to clients, therapists also have responsibilities to their agency, to their profession, to the community, to the members of their clients' families, and to themselves. Ethical dilemmas arise when there are conflicts between responsibilities. Members of the helping professions should know and observe the ethics codes of their professional organizations and make sound judgments that are within the parameters of acceptable practice. We have encouraged you to think about specific ethical issues and to develop a sense of professional ethics and knowledge of state laws so that your judgment will be based on more than what "feels right."

Court decisions have provided an expanded perspective on the therapist's duty to protect the public. As a result of the *Tarasoff* case, therapists are now becoming aware of their responsibility to the potential victims of a client's violent behavior. This duty spans interventions from warnings to threatened individuals to involuntary commitment of clients. Therapists are vulnerable to malpractice action when they demonstrate negligent failure to diagnose dangerousness, negligent failure to warn a known victim once such a diagnosis has been made, negligent failure to commit a dangerous person, or negligent failure to keep a dangerous client committed.

Therapists also have a duty to protect clients who are likely to injure or kill themselves. Practitioners must develop skills in making accurate assessments of potentially suicidal persons. Once a client is diagnosed as a danger to himself or herself, the therapist is responsible for preventing suicide by acting in professionally acceptable ways. A dissenting opinion on this issue is that of Szasz (1986), who challenges the assumption that therapists should be held accountable for a client's decision to die. He believes suicide is an ultimate right and responsibility of the client and that it is unethical for therapists to employ coercive measures aimed at preventing it.

All states have laws that require professionals to report child abuse whenever they suspect or discover it in the course of their professional activities.

Clients have a right to know that therapists are legally and ethically bound to breach confidentiality in situations involving child abuse.

The duty to protect has also been applied to HIV/AIDS cases. Because state laws vary on breaching confidentiality to warn victims of a client's HIV status, practitioners are advised to know their state laws and to consult professional colleagues, and perhaps an attorney, before they take the action of informing an identified partner of an HIV-infected client. This should be the last option, implemented only after less obtrusive measures have failed.

Suggested Activities

1. In small groups discuss the cases and guidelines presented in this chapter on the duty to protect victims from violent clients. If you found yourself faced with a potentially dangerous client, what specific steps might you take to carry out this duty?
2. Structure a class debate around the arguments for and against suicide prevention. Failure to prevent suicide is one of the main grounds for successful malpractice suits against mental health professionals and institutions (Szasz, 1986). Consider debating a specific case of a client who is terminally ill with AIDS and decides that he wants to end his life because of his suffering and because there is no hope of getting better. Divide the class into teams for an exchange on the therapist's responsibility to prevent this suicide.
3. Ask several students to investigate the laws of your state pertaining to confidentiality and privileged communication and present their findings to the class. What kinds of mental health providers in your state can offer their clients privileged communication? What are the exceptions to this privilege? Under what circumstances are you legally required to breach confidentiality? Regarding confidentiality in counseling minors, what state laws should you know?
4. In small groups discuss specific circumstances in which you would break confidentiality, and see whether you can agree on some general guidelines.
5. Discuss some ways in which you can prepare clients for issues pertaining to confidentiality. How can you teach clients about the purposes of confidentiality and the legal restrictions on it? Examine how you would do this in various situations, such as school, group work, couples and family counseling, and counseling with minors.
6. In a class debate, have one side take the position that absolute confidentiality is necessary to promote full client disclosure. The other side can argue for a limited confidentiality that still promotes effective therapy.

Ethics in Action CD-ROM Exercises

7. Refer to role play #6, The Promiscuous One, and think of ways to reenact a role play with different students demonstrating a variety of ways to deal with this woman who is having unprotected casual sexual encounters. If she told you that she just found out that she is HIV-positive—and that she absolutely

does not intend to reveal this news to her husband—what would your stance be? Would you protect the client's confidentiality? Or would you see this as a duty to warn and protect case? Devise alternative role plays showing a variety of approaches for dealing with the ethical and legal dimensions in this case.

InfoTrac® College Edition Resources

For additional readings, explore InfoTrac College Edition, our online library. Go to *http://www.infotrac.college.com/wadsworth* and select these key word searches:

confidentiality psych*
privileged W1 communication
privacy couns*
privacy psych*
limits W2 confidentiality
duty to warn
duty to protect
suicid* client*
suicid* therap*
suicide W1 prevention
child abuse
confid* HIV
confid* AIDS

Key words are listed in a form that enables the search engine to locate a wider range of articles in the online university library. Key words should be entered exactly as shown, including asterisks, "W1," "W2," "AND," and other search engine tools.

7

Pre-Chapter Self-Inventory

Directions: For each statement, indicate the response that most closely identifies your beliefs and attitudes. Use the following code:

5 = I *strongly agree* with this statement.
4 = I *agree* with this statement.
3 = I am *undecided* about this statement.
2 = I *disagree* with this statement.
1 = I *strongly disagree* with this statement.

_____1. A good therapist gets involved in the client's case without getting involved with the client emotionally.

_____2. Touching, whether erotic or not, is best avoided in counseling, because it can easily be misunderstood by the client.

_____3. Therapists who touch clients of only one sex are guilty of sexist practice.

_____4. Although it may be unwise to form social relationships with clients while they are in counseling, there should be no ethical or professional prohibition against social relationships after counseling ends.

_____5. If I were a truly ethical professional, I would never be sexually attracted to a client.

_____6. If I were counseling a client who was sexually attracted to me, I might refer this client to another counselor.

_____7. I might be inclined to barter my therapeutic services for goods if a client could not afford my fees.

_____8. If a client initiated the possibility of exchanging services in lieu of payment, I would consider bartering as an option.

_____9. Sexual involvement with a client is never ethical, even after therapy has ended.

Managing Boundaries and Multiple Relationships

____10. Topics such as nonerotic touching, dealing with sexual attractions, and sexual dilemmas should be addressed throughout the counselor's training program.

____11. Unethical behavior is anything that results in harm to the client.

____12. If another professional was doing something I considered to be unethical, I would report him or her to the state licensing agency.

____13. It is essential that I monitor my own behavior and think of ways to lessen the chances of unethical behavior on my part.

____14. I would never accept a gift from a client, for doing so constitutes crossing appropriate boundaries.

____15. It is essential to consider the cultural context in deciding on the appropriateness of bartering, accepting gifts, and the counselor assuming multiple roles with a client.

____16. Dual or multiple relationships are almost always problematic and therefore should be considered unethical.

____17. Because dual relationships are so widespread, they should not be considered as either inappropriate or unethical in all circumstances but should be decided on a case-by-case basis.

____18. I would have no trouble accepting a close friend as a client if we had a clear understanding of how our personal relationship could be separated from our professional one.

____19. As long as my client felt comfortable about developing a social relationship with me once therapy was over, I would have little difficulty forming such a relationship.

____20. It will be relatively easy for me to establish clear and firm boundaries with my clients.

Introduction

Ethical problems are often raised when counselors blend their professional relationship with a client with another kind of relationship. The ethics codes of most professional organizations have increasingly paid attention to the potential for crossing boundaries and not acting in the best interests of clients when dual or multiple relationships occur. Because of the complex nature of combining various roles and relationships, the term *multiple relationships* is often more accurate than *dual relationships* in capturing the many forms that can occur.

Dual or multiple relationships occur when professionals assume two or more roles at the same time or sequentially with a client. This may involve assuming more than one professional role (such as instructor and therapist) or blending a professional and nonprofessional relationship (such as counselor and friend or counselor and business partner). Other examples of dual relationships include bartering therapy for goods or services, providing therapy to a relative or a friend's relative, socializing with clients, attending a social event of a client, accepting gifts from clients, becoming emotionally or sexually involved with a client or former client, or combining the roles of supervisor and therapist. Mental health professionals must learn how to effectively and ethically manage multiple relationships, including dealing with the power differential that is a basic part of most professional relationships, managing boundary issues, and striving to avoid the misuse of power (Herlihy & Corey, 1997).

Sometimes it is difficult to understand the rationale behind prohibitions, and some boundary limitations may seem arbitrary. Many of the ethics codes are based on reactions to violations rather than being well-thought-out codes based on the diagnosis of the client and the nature of the so-called dual relationship. Codes can provide some guidelines, but good judgment, the willingness to reflect on one's practices, and being aware of one's motivations are critical dimensions of an ethical practitioner. Mental health professionals often fail to heed warning signs in their relationships with clients. They may not have paid sufficient attention to the potential problems involved in boundary crossings, or they may have innocently crossed boundaries that led to problems for both the client and themselves.

The underlying theme of this chapter is the need for therapists to be honest and self-searching in determining the impact of their behavior on clients. Some of the issues and cases we present may seem clear-cut to you, but others are not. In ambiguous cases it becomes a personal challenge to make an honest appraisal of your behavior and its effect on clients. Consider this key question: Whose needs are being met, the therapist's or the client's? To us, behavior is unethical when it reflects a lack of awareness or concern about the impact of the behavior on clients. Some counselors may place their personal needs above the needs of their clients, engaging in more than one role with clients to meet their own financial, social, or emotional needs.

This chapter deals with the subject of boundary issues in counseling practice, dual and multiple relationships, role blendings, a variety of nonsexual dual relationships, and sexual issues in therapy. We also examine the more subtle aspects of sexuality in therapy, including sexual attractions and the misuse of power. Multiple relationship issues cannot be resolved with rules alone; therapists must think through the ethical and clinical dimensions involved in a wide range of boundary concerns.

Dual and Multiple Relationships in Perspective

During the 1980s sexual relationships between therapists and clients received considerable attention in the professional literature. Sexual relationships with clients are clearly unethical, and all of the major professional ethics codes have specific prohibitions against them. Additionally, most states have declared such relationships to be a violation in law. However, *nonsexual* relationships have also received increased interest (see Herlihy & Corey, 1997). The codes of ethics of most professional organizations warn of the potential hazards of dual and multiple relationships (see the box titled Ethical Standards for Dual and Multiple Relationships). These codes typically take a dim view of becoming involved in dual relationships, and the standards caution professionals against any involvement with clients that might impair their judgment or result in exploitation or harm to clients.

Differing perspectives. There is a wide range of viewpoints on dual relationships. If you are intent on clarifying your position on this issue, you will encounter conflicting advice. Some writers focus on the problems inherent in dual relationships. St. Germaine (1993) maintains that although dual relationships are not always harmful to clients it is essential for professionals to recognize the potential for harm associated with any kind of blending of roles. She mentions that errors in judgment may occur when a professional's self-interest becomes involved. Pope (1985a) and Pope and Vasquez (1998) contend that dual relationships tend to impair the therapist's judgment, increasing the potential for conflicts of interest, exploitation of the client, and blurred boundaries that distort the professional nature of the therapeutic relationship. Pope and Vasquez note that therapists often try to justify, trivialize, or discount their practices of engaging in more than one role with clients. Therapists may block out awareness of the potential for serious harm; may focus on the beneficial aspects of such relationships; may assert that these practices are widely prevalent, inevitable and unavoidable, and reflect tradition; and may emphasize the right of clients to enter into relationships of their choice. Such rationalizations enable the professional to evade responsibility for designing acceptable alternative approaches.

Those who take a more moderate view see the entire discussion of dual relationships as subtle and complex, defying simplistic solutions or absolute answers. In many situations, it is not possible to remain within the context of a single role. Tomm (1993) believes standards in the ethics codes that address dual relationships tend to be narrow and deceptive. He makes an excellent

Ethical Standards for Dual and Multiple Relationships

The standard of the AAMFT *Code of Ethics* (2001) dealing with dual relationships cautions therapists to avoid exploitation:

> Marriage and family therapists are aware of their influential position with respect to clients, and they avoid exploiting the trust and dependency of such persons. Therapists, therefore, make every effort to avoid conditions and multiple relationships with clients that could impair professional judgment or increase the risk of exploitation. When the risk of impairment or exploitation exists due to conditions or multiple roles, therapists take appropriate precautions. (4.1.)

The ACA *Code of Ethics and Standards of Practice* (1995) encourages counselors to avoid dual relationships when possible:

> Counselors are aware of their influential positions with respect to clients, and they avoid exploiting the trust and dependency of clients. Counselors make every effort to avoid dual relationships with clients that could impair professional judgment or increase the risk of harm to clients. (Examples of such relationships include, but are not limited to, familial, social, financial, business, or close personal relationships with clients.) When a dual relationship cannot be avoided, counselors take appropriate professional precautions such as informed consent, consultation, supervision, and documentation to ensure that judgment is not impaired and no exploitation occurs. (A.6.a.)

The NASW *Code of Ethics* (1999) focuses on factors of risk of exploitation or potential harm to clients:

> Social workers should not engage in dual or multiple relationships with clients or former clients in which there is a risk of exploitation or potential harm to the client. In instances when dual or multiple relationships are unavoidable, social workers should take steps to protect clients and are responsible for setting clear, appropriate, and culturally sensitive boundaries. (1.06.c.)

Although the *Ethical Standards of the National Organization for Human Services Education* (NOHSE, 2000) point to the unequal power and status in the helping relationship, dual or multiple relationships are not prohibited:

> Human service professionals are aware that in their relationships with clients, power and status are unequal. Therefore, they recognize that dual or multiple relationships may increase the risk of harm to, or exploitation of, clients, and may impair their professional judgment. However, in some communities and situations it may not be feasible to avoid social or other nonprofessional contact with clients. Human services professionals support the trust implicit in the helping relationship by avoiding dual relationships that may impair professional judgment, increase the risk of harm to clients, or lead to exploitation.

The APA (1992) standard on multiple relationships points to the potential for impairing a professional's objectivity:

> In many communities and situations, it may not be feasible or reasonable for psychologists to avoid social or other nonprofessional contacts with persons such as patients, clients, students, supervisees, or research participants. Psychologists must always be sensitive to the potential harmful effects of other contacts on their work and on those persons with whom they deal. A psychologist refrains from entering into or promising another personal, scientific, professional, financial, or other relationship with such persons if it appears likely that such a relationship reasonably might impair the psychologist's objectivity or otherwise interfere with the psychologist's effectively performing his or her functions as a psychologist, or might harm or exploit the other party. (1.17.a.)

observation when he points out that simply avoiding dual relationships does not prevent exploitation. Counselors can misuse their power and influence in a variety of ways that can harm clients. Tomm contends that maintaining interpersonal distance focuses on the power differential, promotes an objectification of the therapeutic relationship, and tends to promote a vertical hierarchy in the relationship.

From a psychoanalytic perspective, Hedges (1993) maintains that transference, countertransference, resistance, and interpretation necessarily involve some form of dual relationship. He points out the beneficial aspects of therapy that can be a consequence of a dual relationship.

Dual relationships are inherent in the work of all helping professionals, regardless of work setting or client population. Despite certain clinical, ethical, and legal risks, some blending of roles is unavoidable, and it is not necessarily unethical or unprofessional. Although the codes of ethics of most professions warn against engaging in dual relationships, not all such relationships can be avoided, nor are they necessarily harmful (Herlihy & Corey, 1997). For example, "mentoring" involves blending roles, yet both mentors and learners can certainly benefit from this relationship.

Designing safeguards to protect clients. After reviewing the literature on the topic of dual and multiple relationships, Herlihy and Corey (1997) conclude that there is no clear consensus regarding nonsexual relationships in counseling. It is the responsibility of practitioners to monitor themselves and to examine their motivations for engaging in such relationships. In rural areas, for instance, mental health practitioners may find it more difficult to maintain clear boundaries than do those who work in large cities. They may have to blend several professional roles and functions, and they may attend the same church or community activities as the clients they serve. In an isolated area a priest or a minister may seek counseling for a personal crisis from the only counselor in the town—someone who also happens to be a parishioner.

Schank and Skovholt (1997) conducted interviews with psychologists who lived and practiced in rural areas and small communities. They found that all of the psychologists in their study acknowledged concerns involving professional boundaries. Some of the major themes were the reality of overlapping social or business relationships, the effects of overlapping social relationships on members of the psychologist's own family, and the dilemma of working with more than one family member as clients or with clients who have friendships with other clients. Although the psychologists knew the content of the ethics codes, they admitted that they often struggled in choosing how to apply those codes to the ethical dilemmas they faced in rural practice.

Sleek (1994) also describes ethical dilemmas that plague rural practice. For example, if a therapist shops for a new tractor, he risks violating the letter of the ethics code if the only person in town who sells tractors happens to be a client. However, if the therapist were to buy a tractor elsewhere, this could strain relationships with the client because of the value rural communities place on loyalty to local merchants. Or consider clients who wish to barter goods or services for counseling services. Some communities operate substantially on swaps rather than on a cash economy. This does not necessarily have to become problematic, yet the potential for conflict exists in the therapeutic relationship if the bartering agreements do not work well.

In the same vein, Kitchener and Harding (1990) contend that dual relationships range from those that are potentially seriously harmful to those that have little potential for harm. They maintain that even in cases where there is a low risk of damage, practitioners have an obligation to evaluate the risk and act responsibly.

Identifying boundary violations. Certain behaviors of professionals have the potential for creating a dual relationship, but they are not inherently considered to be dual relationships. Examples of these behaviors include accepting a client's invitation to a special event such as a graduation; bartering goods or services for professional services; accepting a small gift from a client; attending the same social, cultural, or religious activities as a client; or giving a supportive hug after a difficult session. Some writers (Gabbard, 1994, 1995, 1996; Gutheil & Gabbard, 1993; D. Smith & Fitzpatrick, 1995) caution that engaging in boundary crossings paves the way to boundary violations and to becoming entangled in complex multiple relationships. Gutheil and Gabbard (1993) distinguish between boundary crossings (changes in role) and boundary violations (exploitation of the client at some level). A *boundary crossing* is a departure from commonly accepted practices that could potentially benefit clients, whereas a *boundary violation* is a serious breach that results in harm to clients. They note that not all boundary crossings should be considered boundary violations. Interpersonal boundaries are fluid; they may change over time and may be redefined as therapists and clients continue to work together. Yet behaviors that stretch boundaries can become problematic if boundary crossings lead to a pattern of blurring of professional boundaries. When this occurs, there is a real potential for harm. The key is to take measures to prevent boundary crossings from becoming boundary violations. The prevention of boundary violations by practitioners should be based on early detection and thorough individual assessment (Twemlow, 1997).

Establishing and maintaining appropriate boundaries. Consistent yet flexible boundaries are often therapeutic and can help clients develop trust in the therapy relationship. Borys (1994) suggests that many clients require the structure provided by clear and consistent boundaries. Such a structure is like "a buoy in stormy, chaotic seas; that is, the only stable object to cling to for miles" (p. 270).

Strasburger, Jorgenson, and Sutherland (1992) contend that therapists who push nonsexual boundaries are more likely to become sexually involved with clients. They recommend avoiding this slippery slope to prevent sexual misconduct. Inherent in the concept of the "slippery slope" is the warning that clinicians need to exercise caution before entering into all types of multiple relationships, even if they are not harmful in themselves.

Lamb and Catanzaro (1998) summarize areas where nonsexual relationships can prove to be ethically questionable. Particularly problematic boundary behaviors include social, financial, or workplace relationships with current or former clients; business relationships with current or former clients; multiple relationships with clients, students, or supervisees; and physical touch of current or former clients, students, or supervisees.

Role blending. A concept related to that of maintaining appropriate boundaries is *role blending*. Certainly, blending some roles is indefensible, such as blending the roles of therapist and lover or therapist and business partner. But other roles that professionals play involve an inherent duality. For example, counselor educators serve as instructors, but they also act as therapeutic agents for their students' personal development. At different times, counselor educators may function in the role of teacher, therapeutic agent, mentor, evaluator, or supervisor. The roles supervisors play are another example. Although supervision and psychotherapy are two different processes, they share some common aspects. The supervisor may need to assist supervisees in identifying ways that their personal dynamics are blocking their ability to work effectively with clients. Herlihy and Corey (1997) assert that role blending is inevitable in the process of educating and supervising counselor trainees and that this role blending can present ethical dilemmas that involve a loss of objectivity or conflicts of interest. They state that role blending is not necessarily unethical, but it does call for vigilance on the part of the professional to ensure that exploitation does not occur.

Functioning in more than one role involves thinking through potential problems before they occur and building safeguards into practice. Whenever a potential for negative outcomes exists, professionals have a responsibility to design safeguards to reduce the potential for harm. Herlihy and Corey (1997) and St. Germaine (1993) identify the following measures aimed at minimizing the risks inherent in dual or multiple relationships:

- Maintain healthy boundaries from the outset.
- Secure the informed consent of clients and discuss with them both the potential risks and benefits of dual relationships or any kind of blending of roles.
- Remain willing to talk with clients about any potential problems and conflicts that may arise.
- Consult with other professionals to resolve any dilemmas; those who exploit, rarely, if ever, consult.
- Seek supervision when dual relationships become particularly problematic or when the risk for harm is high.
- Document any dual relationships in clinical case notes.
- When necessary, refer clients to another professional.

In *Boundary Issues in Counseling: Multiple Roles and Responsibilities* Herlihy and Corey (1997) identify ten key themes surrounding multiple roles in counseling. We present these themes here as a summary of critical issues in thinking about dual and multiple relationships.

1. Multiple relationship issues affect virtually all mental health practitioners, regardless of their work setting or clientele.
2. All professional codes of ethics caution of the potential exploitation in dual relationships. The newer codes tend to acknowledge the complex nature of these relationships.
3. Not all multiple relationships can be avoided, nor are they necessarily always harmful.
4. Multiple role relationships challenge us to monitor ourselves and to examine our motivations for our practices.
5. Whenever you consider becoming involved in a dual or multiple relationship, seek consultation from trusted colleagues or a supervisor.
6. Few absolute answers exist to neatly resolve dual or multiple relationship dilemmas.
7. The cautions for entering into dual or multiple relationships should be for the benefit of our clients or others served rather than to protect ourselves from censure.
8. In determining whether to proceed with a dual or multiple relationship, consider whether the potential benefit outweighs the potential for harm. To the extent possible, include the client in making this consideration.
9. It is the responsibility of counselor preparation programs to introduce boundary issues and explore multiple relationship questions. It is important to teach students ways of thinking about alternative courses of action.
10. Counselor education programs have a responsibility to develop their own guidelines, policies, and procedures for dealing with multiple roles and role conflicts within the program.

We find it useful to frame the discussion of dual or multiple relationships within the context of boundaries. It might be helpful to professionals to determine whether or not they maintain healthy boundaries in their personal lives. Professionals often get into trouble when their boundaries are poorly defined and when they attempt to blend roles that do not mix well. A gradual erosion of boundaries can lead to very problematic multiple relationships that bring harm to clients. Gabbard (1994) cites the well-known "slippery slope" phenomenon as one of the strongest arguments for carefully monitoring boundaries in psychotherapy. But Twemlow (1997) argues that the concept of exploitation is often used far too broadly so that it now includes prohibiting all nontraditional methods of treatment: "It has become clear to me that an individual assessment is the cornerstone of a logical and sensitive answer to the question of whether a particularly slippery slope has truly been slippery for the particular patient" (p. 360).

The ban on nonsexual dual relationships. Within the last 10 years the trend in state licensure boards has been to prohibit all dual relationships, including nonsexual dual relationships (O'Laughlin, 2001). Some state licensure rules prohibit therapists from engaging in any kind of dual relationship that *may* impair the professional judgment of the therapist or that *may* be potentially exploitive of clients. According to O'Laughlin, prohibiting relationships that are *potentially* exploitive or that *might* impair objectivity or competency gives licensing boards a great deal of power and raises serious concerns about violating constitutional freedoms.

Here are two examples of dual relationships that were subject to disciplinary actions against licensed practitioners:

- A licensed marriage and family therapist was charged with failing to maintain clear boundaries and engaging in a dual relationship with a client. The therapist simultaneously maintained a professional relationship and a close personal relationship with the client, which included social, religious, and familial behavior. It was found that this impaired the therapist's judgment and resulted in the exploitation of the client, to her extreme detriment (California Association of Marriage and Family Therapists, 2001, p. 40).
- A licensed clinical social worker was required to surrender her license after being charged with participating in dual relationships with a client. The therapist had related to the client as a personal and social friend, invited the client to a dinner party, exchanged gifts with the client, and confided personal information to the client (California Association of Marriage and Family Therapists, 2001, p. 40).

Zur (1999) points out that some therapists will exploit dual relationships with clients regardless of prohibitions by licensure boards. Further, he contends that avoiding all dual relationships puts therapists in unrealistic and inappropriate power positions vis-à-vis their clients and leads to increased isolation of therapists. Appropriate dual relationships, in contrast, are essential to some therapeutic approaches, and these relationships can alter the power differential between therapist and client in ways that enhance the healing process.

Even more disturbing than the absolute ban on dual relationships with current clients is the ban on social, business, or financial relationships until 24 months has passed since the last professional [illegible] O'Laughlin (2001) contends that this broad prohibition is too extreme: "Simply engaging in a dual relationship without some exploitation or deception does not violate the client's trust and therefore should not be considered a breach of fiduciary duty" (p. 729). He adds that "not every dual relationship creates a conflict of interest and not all conflicts of interest will inevitably result in a breach of the client's trust" (p. 729). O'Laughlin concludes that rather than prohibiting dual relationships what should be prohibited is exploitation of clients.

What are the ethics involved in nonsexual posttherapy relationships between therapists and former clients? In their study on this topic, Anderson and Kitchener (1996) found little consensus among professionals regarding how ethical these contacts are. Some therapists believe the client-therapist relationship continues in perpetuity; however, the majority of study participants suggested that posttherapy relationships were ethical if a certain time period had elapsed. Others proposed that such relationships were ethical if the former client decided not to return to therapy with that therapist and if the posttherapy relationship did not seem to hinder later therapy with other therapists.

Salisbury and Kinnier (1996) found that many counselors have engaged in posttermination friendships under certain circumstances, and fully 70% of their study participants believed that posttermination friendships were ethical approximately 2 years after termination of the professional relationship.

Commentary. Prohibiting all forms of multiple relationships does not seem to be a sound answer to the problem of exploitation of clients. Zur (1999) writes that during his graduate school training he was warned over and over never to engage in any kind of dual relationship. Here are some of the "nevers" he heard: never indulge in boundary crossing, never touch a client, never go to coffee or have lunch with a client, never treat a spouse or a friend of a client, never meet clients in social situations, and never join the same synagogue or church as a client. We agree with Zur's (2000a) contention that the professions have gone too far in the direction of discouraging practitioners from engaging in any form of dual relating.

Think about the circumstances in which you may decide to stretch the boundaries. How might certain dual or multiple relationships be unavoidable at times, and what can you do in these situations? What kinds of relationships might place you in professional jeopardy? Consider how condemning bartering or refusing to attend a social event of a client could complicate the therapeutic relationship. In your struggle to determine what constitutes appropriate boundaries, you are likely to find that certain role blendings are inevitable. Therefore, it is crucial to learn how to manage boundaries, how to prevent boundary crossings from turning into boundary violations, and how to develop safeguards that will prevent exploitation of clients.

Controversies on Boundary Issues

We appreciate Lazarus's (1998, 2001) reasonable perspective on boundaries. Lazarus states that a general proscription against dual relationships has led to unfair and inconsistent decisions by state licensing boards, brought sanctions against practitioners who have done no harm, and sometimes impeded a therapist's ability to perform optimum work with a client. He argues for a case-by-case, nondogmatic evaluation of boundary questions when deciding whether to enter into a secondary relationship: "The therapist is to be fully accountable and must ponder issues such as potential risks of harming the patient, possible conflicts of interest, whether or not a dual relationship will impair the therapist's judgment, if the patient's rights or autonomy will be infringed upon, and whether the therapist will gain a personal advantage over the client" (1998, p. 24). Lazarus (1994a, 2001) contends that some well-intentioned ethical standards can be transformed into artificial boundaries that result in destructive prohibitions and undermine clinical effectiveness. Moreover, he believes some dual relationships can enhance treatment outcomes. In this section we present Lazarus's key arguments along with some responses to those ideas.

When taken too far, Lazarus (1994a, 2001) argues that some well-intentioned guidelines can backfire. He admits that he has socialized with some clients, played tennis with others, taken walks with some, respectfully accepted small gifts, and given gifts (usually books) to clients. Lazarus emphasizes that he is clearly opposed to any form of disparagement, exploitation, abuse, harassment, or sexual contact with clients. Indeed, certain boundaries are essential. Rather than being driven by rules, however, Lazarus calls for a process of negotiation in many areas of nonsexual multiple relationships that some would contend are in the forbidden zone. Lazarus (2001) emphasizes that boundary crossings should not be undertaken without serious consideration. "A clear rationale is necessary, a risk-benefit analysis may need to be factored in, roles and expectations should be quite clear, and possible power differentials must be kept in mind" (p. 16).

Lazarus's (1994a) keynote article caused a good deal of controversy, as can be seen by the number of authors who were invited to respond. These authors included Bennett, Bricklin, and VandeCreek (1994), Borys (1994), L. S. Brown (1994), Gabbard (1994), Gottlieb (1994), and Gutheil (1994).

Bennett, Bricklin, and VandeCreek (1994) remind us of the unfortunate reality that too many practitioners have difficulty distinguishing where appropriate boundary lines should be drawn. They point out that beyond a few clear prohibitions most ethics codes offer little real guidance. Bennett and his colleagues agree with Lazarus that competent therapists will use clinical judgment rather than a cookbook approach when working with clients, but they fear that less experienced therapists will misinterpret his position as granting them license to minimize the importance of respecting boundary issues in therapy.

In her response, Borys (1994) takes Lazarus to task for associating ethics and boundaries with traits such as rigidity, dehumanization, artificiality, and the absence of flexibility. She sees it as a mistaken notion to equate confusing clear boundaries with coldness. Instead, Borys draws a parallel between good parents and good therapists—both need to set limits in a firm but nonauthoritarian fashion and still be empathic and warm.

In her response to Lazarus's article, L. S. Brown (1994) maintains that the goal of ethical decision making is to take a position where potential for abuse and exploitation are minimized. She recognizes how easy it is for therapists to misuse the power they have and suggests that therapists consider the impact of their behavior on clients. Brown questions the clinical purpose of Lazarus's extraoffice encounters with his clients—playing tennis, eating meals, and going for walks—and wonders if he has taken into account the entire therapeutic relationship before deciding to engage in any of these extraoffice contacts. Brown takes the position that violations of boundaries tend to profoundly imbalance the power of an already power-imbalanced relationship by placing the needs of the more powerful person, the therapist, in a paramount position.

Gabbard (1994) fears that Lazarus is "teetering on the precipice." Failing to establish clear boundaries can be very dangerous to both the client and the therapist. Gabbard sees boundaries as providing safety for clients: "Professional boundaries provide an envelope within which a warm, empathic holding environment can be created" (p. 285). He further states that the established guidelines (or boundaries) of the mental health professions are aimed at minimizing the opportunity for therapists to use their clients for their own gratification.

Gottlieb (1994) asserts that Lazarus "argues his point to the extreme and in the process trivializes serious ethical and clinical issues" (p. 287). Gottlieb criticizes Lazarus for ignoring literature of ethical decision making that provides clear guidelines to help therapists protect clients, discounting the historical context in which risk management has developed, failing to apply basic ethical principles to clinical practice, and disregarding the subtle ways ethical decisions affect clinical outcome. Gottlieb believes clients appreciate a clear structure that is explained from the outset of therapy. He adds that using informed consent procedures when ethical issues arise in the midst of treatment can serve as grist for the therapeutic mill.

Gutheil (1994) criticizes Lazarus for not considering the potential impact of his interventions on the client. He also stresses his belief that sound risk management is not antithetical to spontaneity, warmth, humanitarian concerns, or flexibility of approach, as Lazarus contends. One of Gutheil's main points is that sound and valid risk management principles need to rest on a solid clinical foundation.

In Lazarus's rejoinder (1994b) he comments that the major difference between his views and those of the respondents is that they dwell mainly on the potential *costs and risks,* whereas he focuses mainly on the potential *advantages* that may occur when certain boundaries are transcended. Elsewhere Lazarus (2001) asserts that there is a widespread sense of mass hysteria where clinicians and licensing boards incorrectly assume that consumers are protected by declaring all forms of dual relationships as harmful, exploitive, and inevitably resulting in sexual misconduct. He writes: "Too many therapists see only a negative and hazardous side to all dual relationships. They claim that harm is inevitable, faulty clinical judgments will ensue, and in terms of risk-management, great dangers lurk behind every corner" (p. 16). Lazarus thinks that professionals who hide behind rigid boundaries often fail to be of genuine help to their clients.

Commentary. In much of the literature on boundaries focus is put in negative terms. Phrases such as "protecting the client," "minimizing the potential for abuse and exploitation," "teetering on the precipice," and "the slippery slope phenomenon" abound. The assumption seems to be that without ethical rules and regulations all practitioners would be violating the rights of clients. We are in strong agreement with Lazarus that this focus on the negative, emphasizing what the practitioner cannot do, leads to rigid thinking. Greenspan (1995) expresses sentiments similar to our thinking, and she is doubtful that the admonition to eschew all dual relationships achieves the objective of protecting clients while promoting healing. Elsewhere Greenspan (1994) states: "The standard of care itself conspires against the genuine meeting of persons that is the real *sine qua non* of healing. It keeps patient and professional separate even when they do not wish to be. It makes authenticity feel like a bad and dangerous thing" (pp. 199–200). Zur's (2000a) statement that the real focus ought to be on preventing exploitation to the client is especially relevant here. For instance, consider some of the advantages of out-of-office encounters between school counselors and students. By attending a student's school play, musical recital, or sports event, the counselor can do a lot to build a relationship with a student. We recommend that counselors ask this question: "In what way is what I am contemplating in the best interests of the client?"

Imagine that you were required to videotape all your sessions with clients and maintain them as your records. Would your behavior with your clients be different in any way? What do you do now that you might hesitate to do if your colleagues were to view your videotaped sessions? Would you be pleased to have your work with the client be published in the local newspaper? If you are an ethical practitioner, you should be comfortable with oversight from your peers. If you would not be comfortable, take time to examine your assumptions about dual relationships.

Consider the client population with whom you are dealing as this will certainly influence the kinds of boundaries of which you need to be sensitive. Not all clients are alike. Age, diagnosis, and culture are key elements that need to be considered in establishing boundaries. A second element is the character of the therapist. Lamb and Catanzaro (1998) maintain that situations that test boundaries are frequent, sometimes ambiguous, and are influenced by training and orientation. In our opinion, the therapist's character and values have more influence than training and orientation. Consider how boundaries were respected in your family of origin and how you manage boundaries in your own personal life. How sensitive are you to the boundaries of others in your personal life? If we establish and maintain appropriate boundaries in our personal lives, it is unlikely that we would be indifferent to boundaries in our professional lives, or would unwittingly ignore them.

Before you read about the various forms of multiple relationships therapists may encounter, clarify your thinking on these issues:

- What do you think of Lazarus's contention that certain boundaries can diminish therapeutic effectiveness? Can you think of any?
- What are your reactions to Lazarus's claim that some dual relationships tend to enhance treatment outcomes?
- Do you think nonsexual dual relationships necessarily lead to exploitation, sex, or harm?
- Do you think the ethics codes of the various professional organizations as they pertain to boundary issues and multiple relationships are too rigid and may compromise therapeutic effectiveness?
- What kinds of boundaries do you maintain in your personal life?
- Might certain dual relationships alter the power differential between you and your clients in such a manner as to facilitate better health and healing?
- How can you assess the impact your interventions and behavior have on your clients?

- Would you allow your fear of a malpractice suit to alter the way you deal with boundaries with clients? If so, is this an ethical issue itself?
- What topics pertaining to managing boundaries, multiple roles, and multiple relationships would you want to address with your clients from the initial session?

As you read the rest of this chapter, imagine yourself in these situations. What challenges might you encounter in managing multiple relationships?

Bartering for Professional Services

When a client is unable to afford therapy, he or she may offer a bartering arrangement. For example, a mechanic might exchange work on a therapist's car for counseling sessions. However, if the client was expected to provide several hours of work on the therapist' car in exchange for one therapy session, this client might become resentful over the perceived imbalance of the exchange. If the therapist's car was not repaired properly, the therapist might harbor resentment against the client. This could damage the therapeutic relationship. In addition, problems of another sort can occur with dual relationships, especially when clients clean house, perform secretarial services, or do other personal work for the therapist. Clients can easily be put in a bind when they are in a position to learn personal material about their therapists. The client might feel taken advantage of by the therapist, which could damage his or her therapy. Certainly, many problems can arise from these kinds of exchanges for both therapists and clients.

Ethical Standards on Bartering

Most ethics codes now address the complexities of bartering (see the box titled Ethics Codes and Standards for Bartering). We agree with the general tone of these standards, although we would add that bartering should be evaluated within a cultural context. In some cultures and in certain communities, bartering is an accepted practice.

Before bartering is entered into, both parties should talk about the arrangement, gain a clear understanding of the exchange, and come to an agreement. It is also important that problems that might develop be discussed and that alternatives be examined. Using a sliding scale to determine fees or making a referral are two possible alternatives that might have merit. Bartering is an example of a dual relationship that we think allows some room for practitioners to use their professional judgment and to consider the cultural context in which they practice.

Forester-Miller (1997) writes about the difficulties involved in avoiding dual relationships in rural communities. She reminds counselors that values and beliefs may vary significantly between urban dwellers and their rural counterparts and suggests that counselors need to work to ensure that they

Ethics Codes and Standards for Bartering

The APA ethics code (1992) includes a standard that discourages bartering as a general rule but also delineates circumstances when psychologists might become involved in such an arrangement:

> Psychologists ordinarily refrain from accepting goods, services, or other nonmonetary remuneration from patients or clients in return for psychological services because such arrangements create inherent potential for conflicts, exploitation, and distortion of the relationship. A psychologist may participate in bartering *only* if (1) it is not clinically contraindicated, and (2) the relationship is not exploitative. (1.18.)

The AAMFT ethics code (2001) offers this guideline on bartering:

> Marriage and family therapists ordinarily refrain from accepting goods and services from clients in return for services rendered. Bartering for professional services may be conducted only if: (a) the supervisee or client requests it, (b) the relationship is not exploitative, (c) the professional relationship is not distorted, and (d) a clear written contract is established. (7.5.)

NASW (1999) has the following guideline on bartering:

> Social workers should avoid accepting goods or services from clients as payment for professional services. Bartering arrangements, particularly involving services, create the potential for conflicts of interest, exploitation, and inappropriate boundaries in social workers' relationships with clients. Social workers should explore and may participate in bartering only in very limited circumstances where it can be demonstrated that such arrangements are an accepted practice among professionals in the local community, considered to be essential for the provision of service, negotiated without coercion and entered into at the client's initiative and with the client's informed consent. Social workers who accept goods or services from clients as payment for professional services assume the full burden of demonstrating that this arrangement will not be detrimental to the client or the professional relationship. (1.13.b.)

Like the codes of other professional associations, ACA's (1995) code also discourages bartering:

> Counselors ordinarily refrain from accepting goods or services from clients in return for counseling services because such arrangements create inherent potential for conflicts, exploitation, and distortion of the professional relationship. Counselors may participate in bartering only if the relationship is not exploitive, if the client requests it, if a clear written contract is established, and if such arrangements are an accepted practice among professionals in the community. (A.10.c.)

are not imposing values that come from a cultural perspective different from that of their clients. She uses bartering as an example of one way of providing counseling services in some regions to individuals who could not otherwise afford counseling. Forester-Miller gives an example of adapting her practices in the Appalachian culture, where individuals pride themselves on being able to provide for themselves and their loved ones. Forester-Miller once counseled an adolescent girl whose single-parent mother could not afford her usual fee, nor could she afford to pay a reduced fee, as even a small amount would be a drain on this family's resources. When Forester-Miller informed the mother that she would be willing to see her daughter for free, the mother stated that this would not be acceptable to her. However, she asked the counselor if she would accept a quilt she had made as payment for counseling the daughter. The mother and the counselor discussed the monetary value of the quilt and decided to use this as payment for a specified number of counseling sessions. Forester-Miller reports that this was a good solution because it enabled the adolescent girl to receive needed counseling services and gave the mother an opportunity to maintain her sense of pride that she could pay her own way.

Making a Decision About Bartering

Bartering is not prohibited by ethics or law. As a therapist, it is your choice to accept or reject a bartering arrangement. Woody (1998) argues against the use of bartering for psychological services. He suggests that it could be argued that bartering is below the minimum standard of practice. If you enter into a bartering agreement with your client, you will have the burden of proof to demonstrate that (a) the bartering arrangement is in the best interests of your client; (b) is reasonable, equitable, and undertaken without undue influence; and (c) does not get in the way of providing quality psychological services to your client. Because bartering is so fraught with risks for both client and therapist, Woody believes prudence dictates that it should be the option of last resort. He concludes that bartering is a bad idea and should be avoided: "No matter how carefully a bartering agreement is structured, the psychologist remains vulnerable" (p. 177). Even if the client needs special financial arrangements or suggests bartering as a solution to his or her financial problem, the therapist is always left with the liability. Woody also takes a dim view of providing *pro bono* services in cases of financial hardship.

Therapists who are considering entering into a bartering arrangement would do well to consider Hall's (1996) recommendations prior to establishing such an arrangement:

- Evaluate whether the bartering arrangement will put you at risk of impaired professional judgment or have a negative impact on your performance as a therapist.
- Determine the value of the goods or services in a collaborative fashion with the client at the outset of the bartering arrangement.
- Determine the appropriate length of time for the barter arrangement.
- Document the bartering arrangement, including the value of the goods or services and a date on which the arrangement will end or be renegotiated.

Woody (1998) presents some additional guidelines to clarify the bartering arrangements:

- Minimize any unique financial arrangements.
- If bartering is used for psychological services, it is better to exchange goods rather than services.
- Both you and your client should reach a written agreement for the compensation by bartering.
- If a misunderstanding begins to develop, the matter should be dealt with by a mediator, not by you and your client.

To these recommendations we add the importance of consulting with experienced colleagues, a supervisor, or your professional organization if you are considering some form of bartering in lieu of payment for therapy services. At this juncture we highly recommend a straightforward discussion with your client about the pros and cons of bartering in your particular situation. With your client's permission, it might be a good idea to tape-record this discussion so that you both can refer to the discussion later, if necessary. Once potential problems have been identified, consult with colleagues about alternatives you and your client may not have considered. Schank and Skovholt (1997) remind us that we all have our blind spots, and trusted colleagues can help us become aware of them and constructively examine them. Ongoing consultation and discussion of cases, especially in matters pertaining to boundaries and dual roles, provide a context for understanding the implications of certain practices.

Your stance on bartering. If you had a client who could not afford to pay even a reduced fee, might you be inclined to engage in bartering goods for your services? What kind of understanding would you need to work out with your client before you agreed to a bartering arrangement? Would your decision be dependent on whether you were practicing in a large urban area or a rural area? How might you take the cultural context into consideration when making your decision?

Consider these cases and apply the ethical standards we have summarized to your analysis. What ethical issues are involved in each case? What potential problems do you see emerging from these cases? What alternatives to bartering can you think of?

◆ **The case of Barbara.** Barbara is 20 years old and has been in therapy with Sidney for over a year. She has developed respect and fondness for her therapist, whom she sees as a father figure. She tells him that she is thinking of discontinuing therapy because she has lost her job and simply has no way of paying for the sessions. She is obviously upset over the prospect of ending the relationship, but she sees no alternative. Sidney informs her that he is willing to continue her therapy even if she is unable to pay. He suggests that as an exchange of services she can become the baby-sitter for his three children. She gratefully accepts this offer. After a few months, however, Barbara finds that the situation is becoming difficult for her. Eventually, she writes a note to Sidney telling him that she cannot handle her reactions to his wife and their children. It makes her think of all the things she missed in her own family. She writes that she has found this subject difficult to bring up in her sessions, so she is planning to quit both her services and her therapy.

- What questions does this case raise for you?
- How might you have dealt with this situation?
- Was it unethical for the therapist to suggest that Barbara do baby-sitting for him? In doing so, to what degree did Sidney take into consideration the nature of the transference relationship?
- Do you see any solutions for this dilemma?

◆ **The case of Olive.** Olive is a massage therapist in her community. Her services are sought by many professionals, including Gerard, a local psychologist. In the course of a massage session, she confides in him that she is experiencing difficulties in her marriage. She would like to discuss with him the possibility of exchanging professional services. She proposes that in return for marital therapy she will give both he and his wife massage treatments. An equitable arrangement based on their fee structures can be worked out. Gerard might make any one of the following responses

Response A: That's fine with me, Olive. It sounds like a good proposal. Neither one of us will suffer financially because of it, and we can each benefit from our expertise.

Response B: Well, Olive, I feel OK about the exchange, except I have concerns about the dual relationship.

Response C: Even though our relationship is nonsexual, Olive, I do feel uncomfortable about seeing you as a client in marital therapy. I certainly could refer you to a competent marital therapist.

- What are your thoughts on these responses?
- What are your thoughts about Olive's proposal? What are the ethical implications in this case?
- If you were in this situation, how would you deal with Olive?

Giving or Receiving Gifts

Few of the codes of ethics of various professional organizations specifically address the topic of giving or receiving gifts in the therapeutic relationship, but the AAMFT (2001) does have such a guideline: "Marriage and family therapists do not give to or receive from clients (a) gifts of substantial value or (b) gifts that impair the integrity or efficacy of the therapeutic relationship" (3.10.).

Lavish gifts certainly present an ethical problem, yet we can go too far in the direction of trying to be ethical and, in so doing, actually damage the therapeutic relationship. Some therapists include a policy statement on matters such as not accepting gifts from clients in their informed consent document, so that there will not be a question on this matter. Rather than establishing a hard and fast rule, our preference is to evaluate each situation on a case-by-case basis. A number of factors need to be considered in making a decision of whether or not to accept gifts from clients. Let's examine a few of these areas in more detail.

- *What is the monetary value of the gift?* Most mental health professionals would agree that accepting a very expensive gift would be inappropriate and unethical. It would also be problematic if a client offered tickets to the theater or a sporting event and wanted you to accompany him or her to this event.
- *What are the clinical implications of accepting or rejecting the gift?* It is important to know when accepting a gift from a client is clinically contraindicated and be willing to explore this with your client. Certainly, knowing the motivation for a client's overture is critical to making a decision. For example, a client

may be seeking your approval, and the main motivation for giving you a gift is to please you. Accepting the gift without adequate discussion would not be helping your client in the long run.

- *When in the therapy process is the offering of a gift occurring?* Is it at the beginning of the therapy process? Is it at the termination of the professional relationship? It is more problematic to accept a gift at an early stage of a counseling relationship because doing so may be a forerunner to creating lax boundaries.
- *What are your own motivations for accepting or rejecting a client's gift?* Some counselors will accept a gift simply because they do not want to hurt a client's feelings, even though they are not personally comfortable doing so. Counselors may accept a gift because they are unable to establish firm and clear boundaries. Other counselors may accept a gift because they actually want what a client is offering.
- *What are the cultural implications of offering a gift?* The cultural context does play a role in evaluating the appropriateness of accepting a gift from a client. D. W. Sue (1997a) points out that in Asian cultures gift giving is a common practice to show gratitude and respect and to seal a relationship. Although such actions are culturally appropriate, Western-trained professionals may believe that accepting a gift would distort boundaries, change the relationship, and create a conflict of interest. According to Sue, if the therapist were to refuse the gift, it is likely that this client would feel insulted.

One of the reviewers of this book stated that students sometimes give school counselors a gift. Such gifts are usually inexpensive, if purchased, or are something made in an art or shop class. He indicates that he could accept the gift and display the gift in his office. If you were a school counselor, would you be inclined to accept inexpensive gifts? Would you display a gift in your office? How would you respond if other students (your clients) or teachers asked you who made the gift that is on display? Under what circumstances, if any, might you be inclined to give a student a gift?

◆ **Tomoko's case.** Tomoko, a Japanese client, presents a piece of jewelry to her counselor, Joaquin. Tomoko says she is grateful for all that her counselor has done for her and that she really wants him to accept her gift, which has been in her family for many years. In a discussion with the counselor, Tomoko claims that giving gifts is a part of the Japanese culture. Joaquin discusses his dilemma, telling Tomoko that he would like to accept the gift but that he has a policy of not accepting gifts from clients. He reminds her of this policy, which was part of the informed consent document she signed at the beginning of the therapeutic relationship. Tomoko is persistent and lets Joaquin know that if he does not accept her gift she will feel rejected. She is extremely grateful for all Joaquin has done for her, and this is her way of expressing her appreciation.

Put yourself in this situation with Tomoko. What aspects would you want to explore with your client before accepting or not accepting her gift?

- Do you see a difference between accepting a gift during therapy or at the end of therapy?

- Would it be important to consider your client's cultural background in accepting or not accepting the gift?
- What might you say to Tomoko if she told you that in her culture it is expected that you will reciprocate in some way if you accept her gift?
- How would you deal with Tomoko if she were insistent that you recognize her token of appreciation?
- If you find that clients frequently want to give you gifts, might you need to reflect on what you are doing to promote this pattern?

Social Relationships With Clients

Do social relationships with clients necessarily interfere with therapeutic relationships? Some would say no, contending that counselors and clients are able to handle such relationships as long as the priorities are clear. They see social contacts as particularly appropriate with clients who are not deeply disturbed and who are seeking personal growth. Some peer counselors, for example, maintain that friendships before or during counseling are actually positive factors in establishing trust.

Other counselors take the position that counseling and friendship should not be mixed. They argue that attempting to manage a social and professional relationship simultaneously can have a negative effect on the therapeutic process, the friendship, or both. Here are some reasons for discouraging the practice of accepting friends as clients or of becoming socially involved with clients: (1) counselors may not be as confrontive as they need to be with clients they know socially; (2) counselors' own needs to be liked and accepted may lead them to be less challenging, lest the friendship or social relationship be jeopardized; (3) counselors' own needs may be enmeshed with those of their clients to the point that objectivity is lost; and (4) counselors are at greater risk of exploiting clients because of the power differential in the therapeutic relationship.

Cultural considerations. The cultural context can play a role in evaluating the appropriateness of dual relationships that involve friendships in the therapy context. D. W. Sue (1997a) makes it clear that some cultural groups may value multiple relationships with helping professionals. Some of Sue's points are worth considering in determining when multiple relationships might be acceptable:

- In some Asian cultures it is believed that personal matters are best discussed with a relative or a friend. Self-disclosing to a stranger (the counselor) is considered taboo and a violation of familial and cultural values. Thus, some Asian clients may prefer to have the traditional counseling role evolve into a more personal one.
- Clients from many cultural groups prefer to receive advice and suggestions from an expert. They perceive the counselor to be an expert, having higher status and possessing superior knowledge. To work effectively with

these clients, the counselor may have to play a number of different roles, such as advocate, adviser, change agent, and facilitator of indigenous support systems. Yet counselors may view playing more than one of these roles as engaging in dual or multiple relationships. (See Chapter 13 for a more extensive discussion of alternatives to traditional roles for professionals who work in the community.)

Sue (1997a) admits that the guidelines that discourage multiple relationships are well-intentioned and basically sound, yet he emphasizes that they must not be rigidly applied to all situations. For him, it is essential to take into consideration community characteristics, multicultural redefinitions of counseling roles, and cultural perceptions of helping practices.

Differing perspectives. In a survey of dual relationships between therapist and client (Borys & Pope, 1989), psychologists, psychiatrists, and social workers rated the following practices as being "never ethical":

- Accepting a client's invitation to a special occasion (6.3%)
- Becoming friends with a client after termination (14.8%)
- Inviting clients to an office or clinic open house (26.6%)
- Going out to eat with a client after a session (43.2%)
- Inviting a client to a personal party or social event (63.5%)

Although forming friendships with former clients may not be unethical, the practice may be unwise. The safest policy is probably to avoid developing social relationships with former clients. O'Laughlin (2001) reports that some state licensing boards view social relationships with former clients much the same as sexual relationships with former clients. Some state regulations have posttherapy bans on both of these relationships for at least 2 years after the termination of therapy. This social relationship restriction bars a therapist and a client from dating, becoming friends, or getting married.

In the long run, former clients may need you more as a therapist at some future time than as a friend. If you develop a friendship with a former client, then he or she is no longer eligible to use your professional services. Additionally, it is possible that in many situations the imbalance of power never changes. Even in the social relationship, you are either seen as a therapist, or you behave as a therapist. Counselors should be aware of their own motivations, as well as the motivations of their clients, when allowing a professional relationship to evolve into a personal one. We question therapists who rely upon their professional position as a way to meet their social needs. Furthermore, therapists who are in the habit of developing relationships with former clients may find themselves overextended and come to resent the relationships they sought out or consented to. Perhaps the crux of the situation involves the therapist being able to establish clear boundaries regarding what he or she is willing to do. Consider this case example.

◆ **The case of a counselor intern.** Imagine that you are an intern in a college counseling center, and one of your clients says to you: "I like working with you, but I find the office environment cold and unappealing. I wonder if it is possible to meet somewhere else? Maybe we could meet in the park nearby. I would feel more comfortable."

- Would you agree to meet your client outside the office?
- Would your client's age and gender affect your decision?

Later, your client invites you to a party. The client says: "It would mean a lot to me for you to come."

- What are your immediate reactions?
- What would you say to your client? How would you support your decision?
- What effect do you think meeting your client on a social basis would have on the therapeutic process?

Commentary. Certainly, there are problems when professional and social relationships are blended. Such arrangements demand a great deal of honesty and self-awareness on the part of the therapist. No matter how clear the therapist is on boundaries, if the client cannot understand or cannot handle the social relationship, such a relationship should not be formed—with either current or former clients. When clear boundaries are not maintained, both the professional and the social relationship can sour. Clients may well become inhibited during therapy out of fear of alienating their therapist. They may fear losing the respect of a therapist with whom they have a friendship. They may censor their disclosures so that they do not threaten this social relationship.

Your position on socializing with clients. There are many types of socializing, ranging from dating a client to having a cup of tea or coffee with a client. There are differences between a social involvement initiated by a client and one instigated by a therapist. Another factor to consider is whether the social contact is ongoing or occasional. The degree of intimacy is also a factor. For instance, there is a difference between meeting a client for coffee as opposed to a candlelight dinner. In thinking through your own position on establishing a dual relationship with a current client, consider the nature of the social function, the nature of your client's problem, the client population, the setting where you work, the kind of therapy being employed, and your theoretical approach. If you are psychoanalytically oriented, you are likely to adopt stricter boundaries and will be concerned about polluting the transference relationship should you blend any form of socializing with the therapy. If you are a behavior therapist helping a client to stop smoking, it may be possible to have social contact at some point. Weigh the various factors and consider this matter from both the client's and the therapist's perspective.

Ethics codes do not address the issue of friendships with former clients. What are your thoughts on this topic? What are the therapist's obligations to former clients? Should the focus be on all relationships with former clients or only those that are exploitative? Should ethics codes address nonromantic and nonsexual posttherapy relationships specifically? Under what circumstances might such relationships be unethical? When do you think these relationships might be considered ethical?

Sexual Attractions in the Client–Therapist Relationship

Are sexual attractions to be expected in therapy? In a pioneering study, "Sexual Attraction to Clients: The Human Therapist and the (Sometimes) Inhuman Training System," Pope, Keith-Spiegel, and Tabachnick (1986) developed the theme that there has been a lack of systematic research into the sexual attraction of therapists to their clients. This silence gives the impression that therapists are incapable of being sexually attracted to those they serve or that the phenomenon is a regrettable aberration limited to the few who sexually act out with clients. If therapists do experience sexual attractions toward clients, many feel that they are guilty of therapeutic errors. Pope and his colleagues provide clear evidence that attraction to clients is a prevalent experience among both male and female therapists and investigated the following questions:

- What is the frequency of sexual attraction to clients by therapists?
- Do therapists feel guilty or uncomfortable when they have such attractions?
- Do they tend to tell their clients about their attractions?
- Do they consult with colleagues?
- Do therapists believe their graduate training provided adequate education on attraction to clients?

Pope and his colleagues (1986) studied 585 respondents, and only 77 reported never having been attracted to any client. The vast majority (82%) reported that they had never seriously considered actual sexual involvement with a client. An even larger majority (93.5%) reported never having had sexual relations with their clients. Therapists gave a number of reasons for having refrained from acting out their attractions to clients, including a need to uphold professional values, a concern about the welfare of the client, and a desire to follow personal values. Fears of negative consequences were mentioned, but they were less frequently cited than values pertaining to client welfare. With respect to the client's being aware of the therapist's attraction, 71% believed that the client was probably not aware. Most therapists (81%) believed that the attraction had been mutual. Over half (55%) indicated that they had received no education on the subject of sexual attraction to clients in their graduate training and internships; 24% had received "very little"; 12% had received "some"; and 9% thought they had received adequate preparation in dealing with sexual attraction to clients. Those who had some graduate training in this area were more likely to have sought consultation (66%) than were those with no such training.

According to Pope, Sonne, and Holroyd (1993), the tendency to treat sexual feelings as if they are taboo has made it difficult for therapists to acknowledge and accept attractions to clients. They found that the most common reactions of therapists to sexual feelings in therapy were these:

- Surprise, startle, and shock
- Guilt
- Anxiety about unresolved personal problems
- Fear of losing control
- Fear of being criticized
- Frustration at not being able to speak openly—or at not being able to make sexual contact
- Confusion about tasks
- Confusion about boundaries and roles
- Confusion about actions
- Anger at the client's sexuality
- Fear or discomfort at frustrating the client's demands

Given these reactions, it is not surprising that many therapists want to hide rather than to acknowledge and deal with sexual feelings by consulting a colleague or by bringing this to their own therapy.

There is a distinction between finding a client sexually attractive and being preoccupied with this attraction. Surely it can happen that we find ourselves being physically attracted to some clients more than others. However, as therapy proceeds, this generally becomes less and less of an issue, and the attraction in no way determines how we treat our clients. If you find yourself sexually attracted to your clients, it is important that you examine these feelings. If you are intensely attracted often, you need to deal with this issue in your own therapy and supervision. If this frequently happens, consider these questions: What is going on in my own life that may be creating this intense sexual attraction? What am I not taking care of in my personal life?

Educating counselor trainees to deal with sexual attractions. Too many training programs spend too little time addressing the prohibition or on how to deal with sexual attraction to clients (Hamilton & Spruill, 1999; Housman & Stake, 1999; Pope, 1987; Pope et al., 1986; Pope et al., 1993; Rodolfa, Kitzrow, Vohra, & Wilson, 1990; Samuel & Gorton, 1998; Vasquez, 1988; Wiederman & Sansone, 1999). Moreover, little attention has been given to the ethical aspects of nonerotic physical contact (see Holub & Lee, 1990, in a later section in this chapter).

Although transient sexual feelings are normal, intense preoccupation with clients is problematic. Pope, Keith-Spiegel, and Tabachnik (1986) found that 57% of the psychologists in their study sought consultation or supervision when attracted to a client. Housman and Stake (1999) found that 50% of the doctoral students in their study reported having experienced a sexual attraction to a client; only half of these students had chosen to discuss the attraction with a supervisor. Seeking help from a colleague or supervision or personal therapy can give therapists access to guidance, education, and support in handling their feelings. Pope, Sonne, and Holroyd (1993) believe that exploration of sexual feelings about clients is best done with the help, support, and encouragement of others. They maintain that practice, internships, and peer supervision groups are ideal places to talk about this issue but that this topic is rarely raised.

Counselors need to ask themselves how they support their choices clinically, and they especially need to ask how they are able to set boundaries when sexual attraction occurs. Heiden (1993) writes that counselors must ask themselves about how they treat clients in different ways, especially with reference to time spent, intimacy, and touch. It is well for counselors to think about how their own needs for intimacy are being met by clients and about ways to set boundaries when sexual attraction to a client occurs.

In their national survey of education for prevention of therapist-client sexual misconduct, Samuel and Gorton (1998) conclude that there is a trend toward increased education during internship programs. They recommend education not only during graduate training but in later continuing education settings and at points of licensure and re-licensure.

Housman and Stake (1999) surveyed sexual ethics training and student understanding of sexual ethics in clinical psychology doctoral programs and found that 94% of the students had received sexual ethics training. Programs provided an average of 6 hours of training. Other of their findings call attention to the importance of addressing sexual issues in therapy early in students' training. Sexual feelings for clients are common among students as well as professional practitioners. It was concluded that most students in training do not understand that sexual attractions for clients are normal. Housman and Stake's findings suggest that only half the students who are attracted will seek supervision. They note that even if students refrain from acting on their sexual feelings for clients, they may withdraw emotionally from their clients to avoid feelings they believe are unacceptable. It is crucial that students acknowledge these feelings to themselves and their supervisors and take steps to deal effectively with them.

Housman and Stake (1999) state that in addition to supervisory consultations, clinical programs should provide all students with some form of planned experiential training for developing skills in clarifying boundaries and setting limits with clients. As a part of this experiential training, Housman and Stake recommend discussion of videotaped scenarios portraying client and therapist sexual feelings, role-playing of common scenarios that could result in sexual misconduct, and opportunities to discuss personal cases. They emphasize the importance of broadening sexual ethics training to address both the emotional and cognitive aspects of attractions in the therapeutic relationship.

Wiederman and Sansone (1999) concur that deliberate attention to sexuality issues during training is required for the development of competent mental health professionals. Ideally, this training would involve accurate information and firsthand experience. Stake and Oliver (1991) recommend a multifaceted approach, including changes in legal codes, consumer education, and training for therapists. They suggest that the best approach is for training programs to include the topic of sexual misconduct as a basic component of ethics education and to provide continuing education for therapists. Hamilton and Spruill (1999) believe it is crucial to increase students' awareness of sexual attraction before they begin seeing clients. They recommend including this topic as a basic component in a preparatory clinical skills course. This training needs to create the expectation that sexual attractions will arise in therapy and to create an atmosphere of trust in which students feel as free as possible to disclose these feelings and experiences in their supervision. If students are not presented with normalizing information, they are likely to continue to regard sexual feelings as proof of a troubled therapy relationship. Hamilton and Spruill (1999) conclude: "Feelings of sexual attraction must be openly discussed as a normal reaction to the type of closeness that characterizes psychotherapy, and appropriate therapeutic boundaries must be clearly explained and strictly enforced" (p. 325).

We think training programs have a responsibility to help students identify and openly discuss their concerns pertaining to sexual dilemmas in counseling practice. Prevention of sexual misconduct is a better path than remediation. Gutheil (1989), for example, suggests that students should receive explicit instruction on the ethical, legal, and clinical issues pertaining to sexual abuses. Holub and Lee (1990) recommend that these issues be addressed in clinical supervision, in ethics seminars, in continuing education programs, in in-service training, and formally by ethics committees. They also recommend that trainees experience personal therapy as a way to better clarify their own needs and motivations. It is the responsibility of training programs to help students identify and openly discuss their concerns about sexual attractions. Ignoring this subject in training sends a message to students that the subject should not be talked about, which will inhibit their willingness to seek consultation when they encounter sexual dilemmas in their practice.

Suggestions for dealing with sexual attractions. Bennett, Bryant, VandenBos, and Greenwood (1990) and Gill-Wigal and Heaton (1996) offer these suggestions on how therapists can deal with powerful attractions to clients:

- Acknowledge the feelings of attraction to yourself.
- Explore the reasons you are attracted to a client. Ask if there is something about this person that meets some of your needs.
- Never act out feelings of attraction. Be careful of actions that might foster the attraction, such as sitting close to the client, hugging the client, or prolonging the sessions.
- Seek out an experienced colleague, supervisor, or personal therapist who might be able to help you decide on a course of action.
- Seek personal counseling, if necessary, to help you understand your feelings about this client and to uncover the issues in your life that may be triggering them.
- Monitor boundaries by setting clear limits on physical contact, self-disclosure, and client requests for personal information.
- If you are unable to resolve your feelings appropriately, terminate the professional relationship and refer the client to another therapist. Be sure to make this your problem, not your client's problem.

Put yourself in this situation. Imagine that you are sexually attracted to one of your clients. You are aware that your client has sexual feelings toward you and would be willing to become involved with you. You often have difficulty paying attention during sessions because of your fantasies. How would you interpret this situation?

- I can easily hide these feelings from the client.
- I must discuss this immediately with my client, with a strong recommendation for referral.
- My own needs have become more important than my client's needs.
- I need to consult with a colleague.
- I have serious problems.

What course of action do you think you would take in this situation?

- I can ignore my feelings for the client and my client's feelings toward me and focus on other aspects of the relationship.
- I will tell my client of my feelings of attraction, discontinue the professional relationship, and then begin a personal relationship.
- I will openly express my feelings toward my client by saying: "I'm glad you find me an attractive person, and I'm attracted to you as well. But this relationship is not about our attraction for each other, and I'm sure that's not why you came here."
- If there was no change in the intensity of my feelings toward my client, I would arrange for a referral to another therapist.
- I would consult with a colleague or seek professional supervision.

Can you think of another direction in which you might proceed? Why would you choose this direction?

◆ **The case of Adriana.** Adriana's husband, a police officer, was killed in the line of duty, leaving her with three school-age boys. She seeks professional help from Clint, the school social worker, and explores her grief and other issues pertaining to one son who is acting out at school. She seems to rely on the social worker as her partner in supporting her son. After 2 years the son is ready to move on to high school. She confesses to Clint that she is finding it increasingly difficult to think of not seeing him anymore. She has grown fond of him. She finds herself constantly thinking about him, and she wonders if they could continue to see each other socially, maybe even romantically.

At first Clint is taken aback. But he also realizes that throughout the relationship he has come to admire and respect Adriana, and he discloses his fondness for her. He explains to her that because of their professional relationship he is bound by ethical guidelines not to become involved with parents socially or romantically. He proposes to her that they not see each other for a year. If their feelings persist, he will then consider initiating a personal relationship. Adriana expresses her disappointment at the year's delay but agrees to the stipulation.

- What are your thoughts about Clint's way of handling the situation?
- If Clint was attracted to Adriana but had withheld this information for therapeutic reasons, how would you react?
- What if Clint has no feelings of attraction or desire to continue any sort of relationship but said what he did to avoid a difficult ending? If you were in a similar situation and did not want to pursue the relationship, how might you deal with your client's disclosure?

Sexual Relationships: Ethical and Legal Issues

The issue of erotic contact in therapy is not simply a matter of whether or not to have sexual intercourse with a client. Even if you decide intellectually that you would not engage is such intimacies, it is important to realize that the relationship between therapist and client can involve varying degrees of sexuality. Therapists may have sexual fantasies, they may behave seductively with their clients, they may influence clients to focus on romantic or sexual feelings toward them, or they may engage in physical contact that is primarily intended to arouse or satisfy their sexual desires. Their behavior is clearly sexual in nature. Sexual overtones can distort the therapeutic relationship and become the real focus of the sessions. It is crucial that practitioners learn to differentiate between having sexual feelings and acting on them. Olarte (1997) makes the point that as therapists none of us is immune from the possibility of engaging in an inappropriate relationship with a client. We need to be aware of the effects of our sex-related socialization patterns and how they may influence possible countertransference reactions.

During the past decade a number of studies have documented the harm that sexual relationships with clients can cause. As you will see in Chapter 9, there has also been considerable writing on the damage done to students and supervisees when educators and supervisors enter into sexual relationships with them. Later in this section we discuss the negative effects on clients that typically occur when the client-therapist relationship becomes sexualized.

Ethical Standards on Sexual Contact With Clients

Virtually all of the professional organizations now have a specific statement prohibiting sexual intimacies in the therapeutic relationship (see the box titled Sexual Contact and the Therapeutic Relationship). If therapists have had a prior sexual relationship with a person, many of the ethical codes also specify that they should not accept this person as a client. It is clear from the statements of the major mental health organizations that these principles go beyond merely condemning sexual relationships with clients. The existing codes are explicit with respect to sexual harassment and sexual relationships with clients, students, and supervisees. However, they do not, and maybe they cannot, define some of the more subtle ways that sexuality may be a part of professional relationships.

Sexual Contact and the Therapeutic Relationship

- "Sexual intimacy with clients is prohibited" (AAMFT, 2001).
- "Counselors do not have any type of sexual intimacies with clients and do not counsel persons with whom they have had a sexual relationship" (ACA, 1995).
- "Psychologists do not engage in sexual intimacies with current patients or clients" (APA, 1992).
- "Psychologists do not accept as therapy patients or clients persons with whom they have engaged in sexual intimacies" (APA, 1992).
- "Social workers should under no circumstances engage in sexual activities or sexual contact with current clients, whether such contact is consensual or forced" (NASW, 1999, 1.09, a).
- "Social workers should not provide clinical services to individuals with whom they have had a prior sexual relationship. Providing clinical services to a former sexual partner has the potential to be harmful to the individual and is likely to make it difficult for the social worker and individual to maintain appropriate professional boundaries" (NASW, 1999, 1.09, d).

Sexual contact with current clients is explicitly prohibited in the codes of ethics of the various professional organizations. Yet even with this clear proscription, sexual boundary violations have been documented in various groups of health professionals (Olarte, 1997). Sexual misconduct is considered to be one of the more serious of all ethical violations for a therapist, and it is also one of the most common allegations in malpractice suits. Therapist-client sexual contact is arguably the most disruptive and potentially damaging boundary violation (D. Smith & Fitzpatrick, 1995).

The Scope of the Problem

In her review of research on the sexually abusive therapist, Olarte (1997) notes that a majority of sexual boundary violations (approximately 88%) occur between male therapists and female clients. Sixty-five percent of offending therapists reported being "in love" with their clients, 33% were repeat offenders, 40% regretted instances of sexual contact with clients, and 41% consulted colleagues. Therapists who engage in sexual misconduct are typically described as being in a "lovesick" state, which tends to cloud their judgment. The typical composite of a therapist who becomes involved in sexual boundary violations is a middle-aged man who is experiencing personal distress, is isolated professionally, and overvalues his healing abilities. His methods are unorthodox, and he inappropriately discloses personal information that is irrelevant to therapy.

Many professional journals review disciplinary actions regarding therapists who violate ethical and legal standards. A cursory review of these sections in the journals reveals that most therapists who are subject to disciplinary actions have been charged with sexual misconduct. These cases provide a picture of how therapists can manipulate clients to meet their own sexual or emotional needs.

• A licensed psychologist was charged with gross negligence in using vulgar language with clients and suggesting that they hug and/or kiss him on the cheek, even though doing so made his clients uncomfortable (California Department of Consumer Affairs, Board of Psychology, 1999, pp. 12–13).

• A licensed psychologist, who was a professor, was charged with gross negligence and unprofessional conduct in using his position as a professor to take advantage of a student that involved both giving the student a back massage and inappropriate sexually touching (California Department of Consumer Affairs, Board of Psychology, 1999, pp. 12–13).

• A licensed clinical social worker was charged with gross negligence in the performance of clinical social work, engaging in sexual relationships with a client, and dual relationships. The therapist commenced a professional relationship with a client that evolved into a social and friendship relationship. The therapist admitted to her client that she loved her, in response to a similar statement by the client. At the therapist's invitation, the client attended a birthday party for the therapist, at which time the therapist introduced her client to other clients. She also offered to loan her client money so that she could attend graduate school. Later the therapist attended a housewarming party given by her client. The therapist subsequently engaged in sexual relations with another client. The client abruptly terminated counseling. About 2 weeks after counseling ended, the therapist and client became lovers and remained lovers for about a year and a half, when the client ended this relationship (California Association of Marriage and Family Therapists, 1996a, p. 18).

• A licensed counselor treated a female client for about 10 years. The counselor asked his client how she felt about taking her clothes off during therapy sessions. She indicated that she would feel very embarrassed. About 3 months later, he urged her to remove her clothing, proposing to use "Reichian" therapy. The client removed her clothes, except her underwear, but told her counselor about her discomfort in doing this. He assured her that this technique would help her in dealing with her sexual problems. Later, she agreed to take off all her clothes and was nude during her sessions. This occurred between 6 and 12 times and constituted gross negligence on the counselor's part (California Association of Marriage and Family Therapists, 1996b, p. 25).

• A licensed marriage, family, and child counselor permitted and encouraged a client's therapy relationship to develop into a personal and sexual relationship, including hugging, kissing, and sexual intercourse. The therapist also provided the client with marijuana and alcohol in the course of his personal relationship with her, despite his knowledge that some of the problems for which she was in therapy were related to drugs and alcohol. The therapist also loaned the client about $1,000 (California Association of Marriage and Family Therapists, 1996b, p. 26).

• A licensed counselor told a female client that she needed to have and to express her oedipal sexual feelings toward her father as a child in a safe place, that he would be that safe place, that she should have sexual feelings for someone other than her father, and that she needed to be sexually attracted to him. During a session in the early phase of her therapy, the counselor instructed the client to sit on his lap and tell him what she wanted to do with him sexually. Later the counselor kissed the client on the mouth. Although she did not experience this kiss as sexual, she did not feel it was right. The therapist later tried to convince her that the kiss was on the cheek and not on the lips. She eventually terminated therapy because she felt that the situation surrounding the kiss operated against any therapeutic gain in continuing therapy with this counselor (California Association of Marriage and Family Therapists, 1996c, p. 34).

As serious as sexual misconduct is, it is a mistake to overemphasize this form of boundary violation as the only kind of behavior associated with professional impairment. There is a tendency for ethics boards to be reactive and perhaps overreactive. Sexual violations are currently given priority consideration, and rightly so, yet there are many other violations, including client abandonment, suicide, misuse of the power differential with the student in academic settings, and financial ruin resulting from a business relationship with a treating therapist (Orr, 1997). All these are instances that may be considered egregious violations, at least by the persons who have experienced them. Orr writes:

> It is also important to understand the etiology of violation and exploitation. Often, this etiology is best understood in the personality and circumstances of the violator. And, in addition to recognizing the history and personality characteristics of the individual violator, we may also profit from examining our educational settings and training institutes as possible sources for the modeling of boundary violation and exploitation. (p. 294)

◆ **The case of Wayne.** A recently divorced 29-year-old high school counselor, Wayne, is assigned the senior class. An attractive 17-year-old senior girl, Kelly, works in the counseling office as a student assistant. She eventually comes to see Wayne as a father figure and becomes infatuated with him. Later during her senior year of high school, Kelly and Wayne share their sexual attraction and fondness for each other. Wayne goes out of his way to get her accepted at the state university, where he has performed consulting activities. After Kelly graduates from the university they get married.

- What potential ethical and legal issues are involved in this case?
- Is the fact that Wayne used his influence to get Kelly accepted in a university itself an ethical concern?
- Assuming Kelly and Wayne wait until she is no longer a student at the high school, and assuming she has now turned 18, do you still see ethical or legal issues involved?
- If Wayne were to seek you out for consultation regarding this case, what input might you give him?

At-Risk Therapists

In their study on sexual boundary violations, Jackson and Nuttall (2001) note that it is critical for clinicians to become aware of their own history and the impact it may have on their relationships with clients. They contend that, although sexual exploitation of clients by therapists is the result of a complex set of factors, one of these factors is a childhood history of severe sexual abuse in the background of offending male therapists. Jackson and Nuttall provide the following recommendations to minimize the likelihood of sexual transgressions by clinicians:

- Learn to recognize sexual attractions and how to deal with these feelings constructively and therapeutically.
- Seek professional support during times of personal loss or crisis.
- Make it a practice to examine and monitor feelings and behaviors toward clients.
- Know the difference between sexual attraction to clients and acting out.
- Learn about the possible adverse consequences for clients and therapists who engage in sexual activity.
- Establish and maintain clear boundaries with clients by dealing with a client's sexual advances firmly and consistently.
- Terminate the therapeutic relationship when sexual feelings obscure objectivity.

In addition to abiding by these recommendations, Jackson and Nuttall conclude that therapists can minimize their potential for sexual boundary violations through a process of self-examination and being willing to seek ongoing support. They urge high-risk clinicians to avoid the isolation of private practice, closely monitor their boundaries with clients, obtain ongoing professional supervision, and seek their own therapy to address any remaining abuse-related issues.

Harmful Effects of Sexual Contact With Clients

Studies continue to demonstrate that clients who are the victims of sexual misconduct suffer dire consequences. Erotic contact is totally inappropriate and is an exploitation of the relationship by the therapist. Sexual contact with clients is viewed by most practitioners as being unprofessional, unethical, and clinically harmful. Not only does sexualizing a therapy relationship result in harm to clients, but therapists who engage in sexual activity with clients (or former clients) risk negative consequences for themselves, both personally and professionally. Among these consequences are being the target of a lawsuit, being convicted of a felony, having their license revoked, being expelled from professional organizations, losing their insurance coverage, and losing their jobs. Therapists may also be placed on probation, be required to undergo their own psychotherapy, be closely monitored if they are allowed to resume their practice, and be required to obtain supervised practice.

Bouhoutsos, Holroyd, Lerman, Forer, and Greenberg (1993) suggest that when sexual intercourse begins therapy as a helping process ends. When sex is involved in a therapeutic relationship, the therapist loses control of the course of therapy. Sexual contact is especially disruptive if it begins early in the relationship and if it is initiated by the therapist. Of the 559 clients in their study who became sexually involved with their therapists, 90% were adversely affected. This harm ranged from mistrust of opposite sex relationships to hospitalization and, in some cases, suicide. Other effects of sexual intimacies on clients' emotional, social, and sexual adjustment included negative feelings about the experience, a negative impact on their personality, and a deterioration of their sexual relationship with their primary partner. Bouhoutsos and her colleagues conclude that the harmfulness of sexual contact in therapy validates the ethics codes barring such conduct and provides a rationale for enacting legislation prohibiting it.

Coleman and Schaefer (1986) describe other negative outcomes of inappropriate sexual contact in therapy, including depression and other emotional disturbances, impaired social adjustment, and substance abuse. Many clients found that their primary relationships deteriorated. Even though these clients felt that their emotional problems had increased, they also found it more difficult to seek out further therapy because of their previous negative experience. According to Coleman and Schaefer, the psychological and covert forms of abuse may be more damaging than overt abuse. In cases involving overt actions there is no question about the ethical violation, and clients often feel justified in considering themselves abused. With either psychological or covert abuse, however, clients are likely to feel confusion, guilt, and shame. Olarte (1997) identifies these harmful effects of sexual boundary violations: distrust of the opposite sex, distrust for therapists and the therapeutic process, guilt, depression, anger, feeling of rejection, suicidal ideation, and low self-esteem. It is generally agreed that sexual boundary violations remain harmful to clients no matter how much time elapses after termination of therapy.

Pope (1988) describes a syndrome that is associated with sexual contact between therapist and client, which bears a striking relationship to the rape syndrome, the battered-spouse syndrome, and responses to child abuse. Some aspects of the therapist-client syndrome are ambivalence, guilt, emptiness and isolation, sexual confusion, an impaired ability to trust, identity and role confusion, suppressed rage, increased suicidal risk, and cognitive dysfunction. After an extensive survey of the research on the harmful consequences of sexual intimacies with clients, Pope concludes that awareness of this problem can help professionals avoid the temptation to act out sexual attractions to clients. This awareness can challenge mental health professionals to create effective measures to ensure that clients are protected from exploitative therapists, and it can help other professionals recognize and respond therapeutically to victims who have experienced distress over this abuse.

The APA's Committee on Women in Psychology (1989) asserts that sexual relationships between therapists and clients are never the fault of the client, that such relationships are never appropriate or helpful in therapy, and that therapists can never be excused for sexual misconduct. This committee contends that sexual contact destroys the objectivity that is necessary for effective therapeutic relationships and that it damages not only clients' trust in the therapist but also their trust in other people, including other therapists. The negative impact may be apparent almost immediately, but often it does not become evident until later. Clients typically feel taken advantage of and may discount the value of any part of their therapy. They may become embittered and angry, and they may terminate therapy with psychological scars. The problem is compounded if they are deterred from initiating therapy with anyone else because of their traumatic experience.

Legal Sanctions Against Sexual Violators

Clients have sued therapists who engaged in sex with them. Therapists found guilty of sexual malpractice have been given sanctions, have been expelled from their professional organizations, have had their licenses revoked or suspended by the state, and have been ordered to undergo therapy to resolve their problems. Austin, Moline, and Williams (1990) reviewed relevant court cases and came to the conclusion that therapists who had engaged in sex with their clients had few arguments they could use in court. Courts have rejected claims of consent by clients, mainly because of the vulnerability of clients and the power of the transference relationship.

Some states have legal sanctions in cases of sexual misconduct in the therapeutic relationship. Sexual activity with a client is a felony in the states of Colorado, Wisconsin, Minnesota, Missouri, Texas, Washington, Michigan, and Florida, to mention a few. In Minnesota it is a felony to have sexual contact with a client during the therapy session, and in certain cases the counselor may be found guilty of sexual misconduct even if the contact occurred outside the session. Client consent cannot be used as a defense.

Some states have passed legislation making it easier to remove licenses in situations involving sexual misconduct. In those states it is no longer necessary to prove that damage has resulted from sexual intimacy with a therapist; the only question is whether the sexual misconduct occurred (Holroyd & Bouhoutsos, 1985). These laws place the ultimate ethical and legal burden of responsibility to avoid sexual relationships squarely on the licensed professional. Consistent with such laws is the position of Coleman and Schaefer (1986) that the counselor must take responsibility for setting appropriate sexual boundaries for the client, communicate these boundaries, and keep the relationship professional rather than personal. Professionals cannot argue that their clients seduced them. Even if clients behave in seductive ways, it is clearly the professional's responsibility to maintain appropriate boundaries. Regardless of the client's pathology, the responsibility to hold to ethical standards in a therapy relationship rests solely with the therapist (Olarte, 1997).

Ethical Sanctions

The procedures for filing and processing ethical complaints against psychologists are codified and are dealt with by the state professional associations and by the APA's Committee on Scientific and Professional Ethics and Conduct. Sanders and Keith-Spiegel (1980) summarize the investigation of one psychologist who was accused of becoming sexually involved with his female client after 2 years of therapy. The psychologist promptly terminated the therapeutic relationship, according to the client, yet no attempt was made to resolve the therapeutic issues remaining. The sexual relationship continued for about a year, on a weekly basis, until it was finally cut off by the client because of her guilt and disgust over the situation. The psychologist made two attempts to resume the affair, but the client refused to become involved.

Although the psychologist at first flatly denied the client's charges, he eventually admitted that they were true. He also said that he loved his client, that he was struggling with a midlife crisis, and that he was having severe marital problems. He added that he was willing to seek personal therapy to work on his problems.

The state psychological association voted to monitor this psychologist's personal therapy and have his practice reviewed for 1 year. In his hearing before the APA's ethics committee, the therapist gave a progress report on his personal therapy and attempted to convince the committee members that the insights he had gained would preclude any recurrence of this sort of ethical violation. The committee offered a stipulated resignation from the APA for 5 years, after which he might reapply if no further ethical violations had been brought to the association. Consider these questions:

- Should this psychologist have been allowed to continue his professional practice? Why or why not?
- If you had been a member of the ethics committee that reviewed this case, what action would you have recommended, and why?
- If the psychologist was aware that he had fallen in love with his client and wanted to become sexually involved with her (yet had not done so), what ethical course of action could he have taken? Is termination of the professional relationship enough?

Assisting Victims in the Complaint Process

The number of complaints of sexual misconduct against therapists has risen dramatically, but individuals are still reluctant to file complaints for disciplinary action against their therapists, educators, or supervisors (Gottlieb, 1990; Hotelling, 1991; Howard, 1991; Riger, 1991). Many clients do not know that sexual contact between counselors and client is unethical and illegal. They are often unaware that they can file a complaint, and they frequently do not know the avenues available to them to address sexual misconduct. Hotelling (1988) describes ethical, legal, and administrative options for individuals who have been victims of professional misconduct. Clients can file an ethical complaint with a professional association or with the therapist's licensing board. Another option is to lodge a complaint with the counselor's employer. There are also legal alternatives: civil suits or criminal actions. A malpractice suit on civil grounds seeks compensatory damages for the client for the cost of treatment and for the suffering involved. Each option has both advantages and disadvantages, and it is ultimately up to clients to decide what is best for them.

Mental health professionals have an obligation to help increase public awareness about the nature and extent of sexual misconduct and to educate the public about possible courses of action. Gottlieb (1990) describes some institutional barriers within the profession that lead women to feel intimidated and deterred. He suggests the need to establish an organizational structure to help them. Howard (1991) focuses on the need for written policies and consistent, accessible grievance procedures for addressing sexual violations. Asserting that the profession has an obligation to do more than merely process ethical complaints, Gottlieb (1990) encourages creation of a Committee for Complaint Assistance within each state or provincial professional association. The main goal of the committee would be to reach out to clients, students, and trainees who have been abused by professionals. Another function would be to educate the public and the profession.

Sexual Relationships With Former Clients

What are the ethics of beginning a sexual relationship once therapy has ended? Gutheil (1989) asserts that many professionals wrongly operate on the assumption that sexual relationships are permissible if a client's therapy has ended or if there is a termination with a referral. To avoid a possible legal or ethical conflict, Gutheil emphasizes that practitioners should not establish a social or sexual relationship with either a present or a past client. But what do the ethics codes have to say with respect to sexual relationships with former clients? (See the box titled Sexual Relationships with Former Clients for specific statements on this topic.)

The American Counseling Association, the American Psychological Association, and the American Association for Marriage and Family Therapy all agree that sexual contact before 2 years after termination is unethical. The National Association of Social Workers does not specify a time period. All four of these organizations state that in the exceptional circumstance of sexual relationships with former clients—even after a 2-year interval—the burden of demonstrating that there has been no exploitation clearly rests with the therapist. The factors that need to be considered include the amount of time that has passed since termination of therapy, the nature and duration of therapy, the circumstances surrounding termination of the professional-client relationship, the client's personal history, the client's competence and mental status, the foreseeable likelihood of harm to the client or others, and any statements or actions of the therapist suggesting a romantic relationship after terminating the professional relationship.

With regard to posttermination sexual relationships, the question that is always unclear is when the professional relationship actually terminated (Foster, 1996). Foster summarizes some points made by Gary Schoener, who raises some very useful questions to help practitioners evaluate posttermination relationships:

- What was the length and level of therapeutic involvement?
- How much transference, dependency, or power inequity remains after termination?

Sexual Relationships With Former Clients

- "Counselors do not engage in sexual intimacies with former clients within a minimum of two years after terminating the counseling relationship. Counselors who engage in such relationships after two years following termination have the responsibility to examine and document thoroughly that such relations did not have an exploitative nature, based on factors such as duration of counseling, amount of time since counseling, circumstances of termination, client's personal history and mental status, adverse impact on the client, and actions by the counselor suggesting a plan to initiate a sexual relationship with the client after termination" (ACA, 1995).
- "Psychologists do not engage in sexual intimacies with a former therapy patient or client for at least two years after cessation or termination of professional service" (APA, 1992).
- "Social workers should not engage in sexual activities or sexual contact with former clients because of the potential for harm to the client. If social workers engage in conduct contrary to this prohibition or claim that an exception to this prohibition is warranted due to extraordinary circumstances, it is social workers—not their clients—who assume the full burden of demonstrating that the former client has not been exploited, coerced, or manipulated, intentionally or unintentionally" (NASW, 1999, 1.09, c).
- "Sexual intimacies with former clients is likely to be harmful and is therefore prohibited for two years following the termination of therapy or last professional contact. In an effort to avoid exploiting the trust and dependency of clients, marriage and family therapists should not engage in sexual intimacy with former clients after the two years following termination or last professional contact. Should therapists engage in sexual intimacy with former clients following two years after termination or last professional contact, the burden shifts to the therapist to demonstrate that there has been no exploitation or injury to the former client or to the client's immediate family" (AAMFT, 2001, 1.5).

- Was there any deception or coercion, intentional or unintentional by the therapist indicating that sex is generally acceptable after termination of therapy?
- Was there an actual termination? Was the decision to terminate a mutual one? Did the therapist end the professional relationship to make it possible to enter into a romantic or sexual relationship with a client?
- Who initiated posttermination contact?
- What was the extent of the discussion of the pros and cons of engaging in a romantic or sexual relationship?
- What kind of consultation, if any, took place?

Some counselors maintain: "Once a client, always a client." Although a blanket prohibition on sexual intimacies, regardless of the time that has elapsed since termination, might clarify the issue, some would contend that this is too extreme of a measure. Others point out that there is a major difference between an intense, long-term therapy relationship and a less intimate, brief-term one. A blanket prohibition ignores these distinctions.

Although the question of whether sexual relationships with former clients are ever acceptable has not been resolved, there appears to be a trend toward strongly discouraging, if not prohibiting, this behavior. For example, an ethics code task force of the American Psychological Association is debating the merits of the current standard that prohibits sexual intimacy for 2 years once a therapeutic relationship ends. The task force is proposing a "perpetuity rule" that would prohibit sexual relationships no matter how much time has elapsed since the last client visit. According to the APA's task force, an absolute ban on posttermination sexual relationships more clearly addresses the inherent power imbalance, which is not erased with termination. Furthermore, the task force decided that the public image of the profession would be strengthened by an ethical standard that imposes a lifetime ban on sexual intimacy with former clients (Martin, 1999).

Few of the codes of ethics of the various professions currently have an absolute ban on sexual relationships after the end of a therapy relationship. Yet all these codes have guidelines to consider even after the specified time period has elapsed. In exceptional circumstances when a therapist is considering becoming involved in a personal relationship with a former client, it is essential that the therapist be willing to seek consultation or personal therapy to explore his or her motivations and the possible ramifications of transforming a professional relationship into a personal one. Bennett and his colleagues (1990) offer several suggestions to those considering initiating a relationship with a former client:

- Be aware that developing a personal relationship with a former client is illegal in some jurisdictions and that therapists have been sued for malpractice for engaging in this practice.
- Reflect on the reasons for termination. If you, the client, or both of you experienced an attraction before ending therapy, was the professional relationship terminated for an appropriate reason or so that a sexual relationship could develop?
- Ask yourself about the potential benefits and risks of developing a personal relationship with a former client.
- Before initiating such a relationship, consider discussing the matter with a colleague.

What is your position? At this point, reflect on your own stance on the controversial issue of forming sexual relationships once therapy has ended. Consider these questions in clarifying your position:

- Should counselors be free to formulate their own practices about developing sexual relationships with former clients? Give your reasons.
- Does the length and quality of the therapeutic relationship have a bearing on the ethics involved in such a personal relationship? If a client was in therapy for several years and struggled with an intense transference relationship with her therapist, for example, would it be ethical for them to establish a personal relationship 2 years after her therapy had ended? If a client saw her counselor for only six sessions to learn how to cope with stress, would it be ethical for them to get involved personally 2 years after her final session?

- Would you favor changing the ethics codes to include an absolute ban on posttermination sexual relationships regardless of the length of time elapsed? Why or why not?
- Are sexual relationships with former clients unethical regardless of the elapsed time or the type of therapy? Are there any exceptions that might justify developing an intimate relationship with a former client?
- What guidelines can you come up with to determine the ethics of personal relationships with former clients?
- Although it might not be illegal in your state, is it wise to engage in sex with former clients?
- React to the statement, "Once a client, always a client."

Commentary. We question whether the enhancement of psychology's image should be the guiding force in making ethical decisions. Also, we believe the statement "Once a client, always a client" is a dogmatic pronouncement that should be subject to research and discussion. In proposing an absolute ban on all sexual relationships with former clients there is no mention of the client's diagnosis. Does this imply that a diagnosis is irrelevant? There is also no mention of length of therapy or of the type of therapy offered. Is a client who is seen for two sessions to be considered on equal footing with a client who may have been in therapy for 5 years? Clearly there is concern when a therapist marries a former client and, indeed, doing so might be unwise. Yet making all actions that may be unwise into "clearly unethical actions" seems unjustified.

A Special Case: Nonerotic Physical Contact With Clients

Although we contend that acting on sexual feelings and engaging in erotic contact with clients is unethical, we do think that nonerotic contact is often appropriate and can have significant therapeutic value. It is important to stress this point, because some counselors perceive a taboo against touching clients. Therapists may hold back when they feel like touching their clients compassionately. They may feel that touching can be misinterpreted as sexual or exploitative; they may be afraid of their impulses or feelings toward clients; they may be afraid of intimacy; or they may believe that to express closeness physically is unprofessional. With the current attention being given to sexual harassment and lawsuits over sexual misconduct in professional relationships, some counselors are likely to decide that it is not worth the risk of touching clients at all, lest their intentions be misinterpreted. Although touching does not necessarily constitute a dual relationship, we include this discussion here because certain kinds of touching can lead to dual relationships. A therapist's touch can be a genuine expression of caring, or it can be done primarily to gratify the therapist's own needs.

There are two sides to the issue of touching: Some practitioners support it, and others do not. Some clinicians oppose any form of physical contact between counselors and clients on the grounds that it can promote dependency, can interfere with the transference relationship, can be misread by clients, and can become sexualized. However, in writing about a men's therapy group, Rabinowitz (1991) cites research findings indicating that appropriate touching can foster self-exploration, increase verbal interaction, increase the client's perception of the expertness of the counselor, and produce more positive attitudes toward the counseling process.

Holub and Lee (1990) assert that the decision to touch or not to touch clients involves more than considering its effectiveness in helping clients or engaging them in therapy. They maintain that this decision should also include deliberating over the correctness, motivations, and interpretations of the touching. The power differential between therapist and client should be considered, and touching often elicits different feelings in men than it does in women. The practice of male therapists' touching only female clients might be interpreted as sexist or at least as poor judgment.

Rabinowitz (1991) describes some therapeutic values of embracing in a men's group. He states that it may be safer for a hug to occur in group therapy rather than in individual counseling because there are witnesses to the context of the touching, leaving less room for misinterpretation. However, counselors are still responsible for being sensitive to each member of the group and for avoiding meeting their own needs at the expense of the members. Rabinowitz adds: "Despite the cultural taboo for men to engage in physical touching, the act of embracing another man, in the context of the therapy group, does seem to encourage the expression of deeper feelings and lessen the isolation men often feel in our competitive society" (p. 576).

If touching is consistently and actively used in therapy, Bennett and his colleagues (1990) suggest that it is wise to explain this practice to clients and their families, if appropriate, before therapy begins. They recommend that practitioners consider how clients are likely to react to touching and that they ask themselves these questions:

- How well do I know the client?
- What makes me think that touch is indicated?
- Could the touch be misinterpreted by the client (or the client's family) as a sexual overture?
- Is touching appropriate in this circumstance?

In our view, it is critical to determine whose needs are being met when it comes to touching. If it comes from the therapist alone, and not from the context of the therapeutic relationship, it needs to be carefully examined. If touching occurs it should be a spontaneous and honest expression of the therapist's feelings. It should not be done as a technique. It is unwise for therapists to touch clients if this behavior is not congruent with what they feel. A nongenuine touch will be detected by clients and could erode their trust in the relationship. Counselors need to be sensitive to those circumstances when touching could be counterproductive. There are times when touching clients can distract them from what they are feeling, or when clients do not want to be touched. This is often the case with clients who come from a background of physical and/or sexual abuse. There are also times when a touch that is given at the right moment can convey far more empathy than words can. Therapists need to be aware of their own motives and to be honest with themselves about the meaning of physical contact. They also need to be sensitive to factors such as the client's readiness for physical closeness, the client's cultural understanding of touching, the client's reaction, the impact such contact is likely to have on the client, and the level of trust that they have built with the client.

Care needs to be taken so that we do not throw out the baby with the bath water. It appears that many therapists will not touch a client, other than for a handshake, for fear of misinterpretation of their motives. Although practitioners need to formulate clear guidelines and consider appropriate boundaries, touch can be a therapeutic means to healing. It is sad that the legal climate discourages the appropriate use of this medium of reaching clients.

Think about your position on the ethical implications of the practice of touching as part of the client-therapist relationship by answering these questions:

- What criteria could you use to determine whether touching your clients was therapeutic or countertherapeutic?
- Do you think some clients may never be ready to engage in touching in therapy?
- How could you honestly answer the question, "Are my own needs being met at the expense of my client's needs?" What might you do if you hugged a client whom you felt needed this kind of physical support and the client suggested that you were meeting your own needs?
- To what degree do you think your professional training has prepared you to determine when touching is appropriate and therapeutic?
- What factors should you consider in determining the appropriateness of touching clients? (Examples are age, gender, the type of client, the nature of the client's problem, and the setting in which the therapy occurs.)
- Imagine your first session with a same-sex client who is crying and in a state of crisis. Might you be inclined to touch this person? Would it make a difference if the client asked you to hold him or her? Would it make a difference if this client were of the opposite sex? of the same sex?
- If you are favorably inclined toward the practice of touching clients, are you likely to restrict this practice to opposite-sex clients? to same-sex clients? to clients of either sex to whom you are attracted? Explain.
- What would you do if your client wanted a hug, but you were resistant to doing it? How would you explain yourself to the client?

◆ **The case of Ida.** Tu Chee is a warm and kindly counselor who routinely embraces his clients, both male and female. One of his clients, Ida, has had a hard life, has had no success in maintaining relationships with men, is now approaching her 40th birthday, and has come to him because she is afraid that she will be alone forever. She misreads his friendly manner of greeting and assumes that he is giving her a personal message. At the end of one session when he gives his usual embrace, she clings to him and does not let go right away. Looking at him, she says: "This is special, and I look forward to this time all week long. I so much need to be touched." He is surprised and embarrassed. He explains to her that she has misunderstood his gesture, that this is the way he is with all of his clients, and that he is truly sorry if he has misled her. She is crestfallen and abruptly leaves the office. She cancels her next appointment.

- What are your thoughts on this counselor's manner of touching his clients?
- If Tu Chee explained at the outset of therapy that his touching was part of his style, would that have been more acceptable?
- Was the manner in which he dealt with Ida's embrace ethically sound?
- What would you had done with Ida's cancellation of her appointment?

Commentary. In our opinion, this case is a good example of a situation where the counselor was more concerned with the bind he was in, rather than the bind his client was in. The nature of a therapist's work is to take care of the client's difficulty first. How could he have done it better?

Dealing With Suspected Unethical Behavior in Dual Relationships

In our classes and workshops many students have raised the question, "What should I do when I suspect other therapists are engaging in questionable behavior?" To sharpen your thinking on this question, reflect for a few moments on the possibility of your being involved in the following situations:

- You are aware that a clinical supervisor has made it a practice to have sexual relationships with several of her supervisees. Some of these students are friends of yours, and they tell you that they felt pressure to comply because they were in a vulnerable position. What would you do?
- You know a student intern who initiates social relationships with his clients. He says that his clients are consenting adults, and he argues that by dating them he actually gets to know them better, which helps him in his role as a therapist. What would you do?
- Several of your friends tell you that a counseling professor makes it a practice to date former students. When colleagues confronted him in the past, he maintained that all of these students were adults, that none of them were his students when he dated them, and that what he did in his private life was strictly his own business. What is your view of his behavior? If his behavior were not known to his colleagues, would you report him? Why or why not?
- You have heard unsettling reports from several clients about another therapist in an agency where you work. They say that he touches them frequently and that he behaves seductively. When you confront this therapist, he becomes defensive, telling you that he is not hung up on touching and that he likes to express his feelings spontaneously. What would you say to him? If you felt you were not getting through to him, what might you do next?

Unethical Behavior by Colleagues

- "Counselors expect professional associates to adhere to the Code of Ethics. When counselors possess reasonable cause that raises doubts as to whether a counselor is acting in an ethical manner, they take appropriate action" (ACA, 1995, H.2.a.).
- "When counselors have reasonable cause to believe that another counselor is violating an ethical standard, they attempt to first resolve the issue informally with the other counselor if feasible, providing that such action does not violate confidentiality rights that may be involved" (ACA, 1995, H.2.d.).
- "When an informal resolution is not appropriate or feasible, counselors, upon reasonable cause, take action such as reporting the suspected ethical violation to state or national ethics committees, unless this action conflicts with confidentiality rights that cannot be resolved" (ACA, 1995, H.2.e.).
- "Social workers should take adequate measures to discourage, prevent, expose, and correct the unethical conduct of colleagues" (NASW, 1999, 2.11.).
- "Human service professionals respond appropriately to unethical behavior of colleagues. Usually this means initially talking directly with the colleague and, if no resolution is forthcoming, reporting the colleague's behavior to supervisory or administrative staff and/or to the professional organization(s) to which the colleague belongs" (NOHSE, 2000, Statement 24).
- "When psychologists believe that there may have been an ethical violation by another psychologist, they attempt to resolve the issue by bringing it to the attention of that individual if an informal resolution appears appropriate and the intervention does not violate any confidentiality rights that may be involved" (APA, 1992, 8.04.).

- Imagine yourself as a student in a training program. One of your professors makes inappropriate advances to you. How might you react? What would you do?

You may wonder whether it is your place to judge the practices of other practitioners. Even if you are convinced that the situation involves clear ethical violations, you may be in doubt about the best way to deal with it. Should you first discuss the matter with the person? Assuming that you do and that the person becomes defensive, should you take any other action or simply drop the matter? When would a violation be serious enough that you would feel obligated to bring it to the attention of an appropriate local, state, or national committee on professional ethics? Most professional organizations have specific ethical standards that clearly place the responsibility for confronting recognized violations squarely on members of their profession. Ignoring an ethical violation is considered to be a violation in itself (see the box titled Unethical Behavior by Colleagues).

The APA's (1992) ethics code makes it clear that professionals have an ethical obligation to be familiar with the ethics code. Furthermore, not being aware of the code or misunderstanding an ethical standard is not an adequate defense to a charge of unethical conduct. Professionals also have an obligation to deal with colleagues when they suspect unethical conduct—first by informally dealing with the person, and if that does not work, then using more formal methods of addressing the situation. Generally, the best way to proceed when you have concerns about the behavior of colleagues is to tell them directly. Then, depending on the nature of the complaint and the outcome of the discussion, reporting a colleague to a professional board would be one of several options open to you.

In a survey of APA-approved clinical training programs, graduate students were asked what they *should* do in a hypothetical situation in which a friend and colleague had violated APA ethical principles; they were then asked what they *would* do (Bernard & Jara, 1986). Approximately half of these students said they would not live up to their own interpretation of what the ethics codes required of them as professionals. Bernard and Jara contend that the problem in training professionals is not how to communicate ethics codes to students but rather how to motivate them to apply their knowledge of ethical standards. "Psychologists need to carefully examine this question and to arrive at ways to reorder priorities so that their responsibility to monitor their own practices is taken more seriously" (p. 315).

It is sometimes easier to see the faults in others and to judge their behavior than to examine our own behavior. Make a commitment to continually reflect on what you are doing personally and professionally. Being your own judge is more realistic and more valuable than being someone else's judge.

Chapter Summary

Sexual relationships with clients are obviously detrimental to their welfare. However, it is important that you not overlook some of the more subtle and perhaps insidious behaviors of the therapist that may in the long run cause as much damage to clients.

It is unwise, unprofessional, unethical, and in many states illegal to become sexually involved with clients. This is not to say that as a counselor you are not also human or that you will never be attracted to certain clients. You are probably imposing an unnecessary burden on yourself if you believe that you should not have such feelings for clients or if you try to convince yourself that you should not have more feeling toward one client than toward another. What is important is how you decide to deal with these feelings as they affect the therapeutic relationship. Referral to another therapist is not necessarily the best solution, unless it becomes clear that you can no longer be effective with a certain client. Instead, you may recognize a need for consultation or, at the very least, for an honest dialogue with your colleagues. If for some reason your feelings of attraction become known to the client, it is essential that the client be assured that they will not be acted upon. If this creates a problem for the client, a referral should be discussed.

Becoming a therapist does not make you perfect or superhuman. You are likely to make mistakes. We want to stress the importance of reflecting on what you are doing and on whose needs are primary. A willingness to be honest in your self-examination is your greatest asset in becoming an ethical practitioner.

As was mentioned earlier, it is always good to keep in mind whether you would act differently if your colleagues were observing you.

Suggested Activities

1. Investigate the ethical and legal aspects of dual relationships as they apply to the area of your special professional interests. Look for any trends, special problems, or alternatives. Once you have gathered some materials and ideas, consider presenting your findings in class.

2. Some say that dual relationships are inevitable, pervasive, and unavoidable and have the potential to be either beneficial or harmful. Form two teams and debate the core issues. Have one team focus on the potential benefits of dual relationships and argue that they cannot be dealt with by simple legislative or ethical mandates. Have the other team argue the case that dual relationships are unethical because they have the potential for bringing harm to clients and that there are other and better alternatives.

3. Write a brief journal article on your position on dual relationships in counseling. Take some small aspect of the problem, develop a definite position on the issue, and present your own views. Consider submitting this article to one of the professional journals. If your article is accepted, you are already on the road to professional writing. If your article is rejected, you have had the experience of writing a position paper and actually going through the process of submission and review. Consider doing this project jointly with one of your professors.

4. What are your views about forming social relationships with clients during the time they are in counseling with you? after they complete counseling?

5. What guidelines would you employ to determine whether nonerotic touching was therapeutic or countertherapeutic? Would the population you work with make a difference? Would the work setting make a difference? How comfortable are you in both receiving and giving touching? What are your ethical concerns about touching?

6. Take some time to review the ethics codes of the various professional associations as they apply to two areas: (a) dual relationships in general and (b) sexual intimacies with present or former clients. Have several students team up to analyze different ethics codes, make a brief presentation to the class, and then lead a discussion on the code's value.

7. Review the discussion on sexual relationships with former clients. Form two teams, and debate the issue of whether sexual and romantic relationships with former clients should be allowed after a specific length of time.

8. What unethical behaviors by your colleagues do you think you would report, if any? How might you proceed if you knew of the unethical practice of a colleague?

9. Form small groups to explore the core issues involved in some of the cases in this chapter. Role-play the cases, and then discuss the implications.

Acting out the part of the therapist and the client is bound to enliven the discussion and give you a different perspective on the case. Feel free to embellish on the details given in the cases.

10. Divide the class into a number of small groups, and brainstorm one case other than the ones we have presented in this chapter. The case should illustrate some ethical dilemma in the general area of dual relationships. Come up with a title for your case, creative names for the therapist and the client, and interesting points that will make the case a good discussion tool. Each group can act out its case in class and lead a general discussion.

Ethics in Action CD-ROM Exercises

11. Using segment 3 of the CD-ROM (boundary issues), bring your completed responses to the self-inventory to class for discussion.

12. In video role play #8, The Picnic, the client (Lucia) would like to meet with the counselor (John) at the park down the street for their counseling sessions so she can get to know him better and feel closer to him. She could bring a lunch for a picnic. John is concerned about creating an environment that would help Lucia the most, but as she says, "That (meeting in the park) would really help me."

Assume your client tells you: "I'd like to meet for your sessions at the park so that I can feel more comfortable." Through role playing, demonstrate how you would establish and maintain boundaries with this client.

13. In video role play #9, The Friendship, at the last therapy session the client (Charlae) says she would like to continue their relationship because they have so much in common and she has shared things with the counselor (Natalie) that she has not discussed with anyone else. Natalie informs Charlae that this puts her in a difficult situation and she feels awkward. Charlae says, "What if we just go jogging together a couple of mornings a week?"

Assume your client would like to meet with you socially and this is the final therapy session. Via role playing, demonstrate how you would handle such a request from a former client who is interested in developing a social relationship with you.

14. In video role play #10, The Disclosure, the counselor (Conrad) shares with the client (Suzanne) that he has been thinking about her a lot and that he is attracted to her. Suzanne responds with, "You are kidding, right?" She says she came to him because of having problems with men taking advantage of her and not respecting her. She has bared her soul to him and now she feels devalued. Suzanne suggests possibly seeing another counselor, but Conrad thinks they can work it out.

What are your thoughts about the way the counselor (Conrad) shared his feelings with the client? If you were sexually attracted to a client, what course of action would you follow? Role-play the way you would deal with a client who disclosed to you that he or she found you "quite attractive." Assume that you also found this client "quite attractive."

15. In video role play #11, The Architect, the client (Janice) lost her job and can no longer pay for counseling sessions. She suggests providing architecture services for work on his house. The counselor (Jerry) suggests they discuss the pros and cons and that he wants to be sure that this is in her best interests. He mentions the code of ethics that discourages bartering. Jerry talks about issues of value and timeliness of services.

Put yourself into this scene. Assume your client lost her job and could no longer pay for therapy. She suggests a bartering arrangement for some goods or services you value. Role-play how you would deal with her. What issues would you want to explore with your client?

16. In video role play #12, Tickets for Therapy, the client (John) shows his appreciation for his counselor (Marianne) by giving her tickets to the theater. John says, "I got tickets for you so you can go and enjoy it and have a good time." Marianne talks about why she cannot accept the tickets, in spite of the fact that she is very appreciative of his gesture.

Put yourself in the counselor's place. What issues would you explore with John? Might you accept the tickets, under any circumstances? Why or why not? Demonstrate, through role playing, what you would say to the client.

InfoTrac® College Edition Resources

For additional readings, explore InfoTrac College Edition, our online library. Go to *http://www.infotrac.college.com/wadsworth* and select these key word searches:

dual relationship* couns*
dual relationship* psych*
multiple relationships
barter* couns*
barter* psych*
gift psych*
gift therap*
social W1 relationship* client*
social W1 relationship* therap*
sexual W1 attraction client*
sexual W1 relationship client*
touching psych*

Key words are listed in a form that enables the search engine to locate a wider range of articles in the online university library. Key words should be entered exactly as shown, including asterisks, "W1," "W2," "AND," and other search engine tools.

8

Pre-Chapter Self-Inventory

Directions: For each statement, indicate the response that most closely identifies your beliefs and attitudes. Use the following code:

5 = I *strongly agree* with this statement.
4 = I *agree* with this statement.
3 = I am *undecided* about this statement.
2 = I *disagree* with this statement.
1 = I *strongly disagree* with this statement.

_____1. Counselors are ethically bound to refer clients to other therapists when working with them is beyond their professional training.

_____2. Ultimately, practitioners must create their own ethical standards.

_____3. Possession of a license or certificate from a state board of examiners shows that a person has therapeutic skills and is competent to practice psychotherapy.

_____4. Professional licensing protects the public by setting minimum standards of preparation for those who are licensed.

_____5. The present processes of licensing and certification encourage the self-serving interests of the groups in control instead of protecting the public from incompetent practice.

_____6. Continuing education course work should be a requirement for renewal of a license to practice psychotherapy.

Professional Competence and Training

_____7. It is unethical for counselors to practice without continuing their education.

_____8. Institutions that train counselors should select trainees on the basis of both their academic record and the degree to which they possess the personal characteristics of effective therapists (as determined by current research findings).

_____9. The arguments for licensing psychotherapists outweigh the arguments against licensing.

____10. Candidates applying for a training program have a right to know the criteria for selecting trainees.

____11. Once students are admitted to a graduate training program, that program should assess them at different times to determine their suitability for completing the degree.

____12. Trainees who display rigid and dogmatic views about human behavior should not be allowed to continue in a training program.

____13. It is unethical for a program to train practitioners in only one therapeutic orientation without providing an unbiased overview of other theoretical systems.

____14. The process of licensing tends to pit professional specializations against one another.

____15. I might not seek out workshops, seminars, courses, and other postgraduate learning activities if continuing education were not required to maintain my license to practice.

Introduction

In this chapter we focus on the ethical and legal aspects of professional competence and the education and training available for mental health professionals. We discuss issues related to professional licensing and certification as well as approaches to continuing education.

Ability is not an easy matter to assess. Competence is a process rather than something that is achieved once and for all. To maintain their competence in a meaningful way, practitioners need to be interested in keeping up to date in their field. They need to enhance their skills and find ways to meet the needs of new populations. Areas such as eating disorders, sexual abuse, substance abuse, gerontological counseling, and AIDS all present challenges for ongoing education for practitioners. Continuing education is particularly important in emerging areas of practice.

Practitioners can develop competence both as a generalist and as a specialist. A generalist is a practitioner who is able to work with a broad range of problems and client populations. A specialist is a worker who has developed competence in a particular area of practice such as drug and alcohol counseling, eating disorders, or career development.

Counselor training is given special attention because of the unique ethical issues involved. Indeed, ethical issues must be considered from the very beginning, starting with admission and screening procedures for graduate programs. One key issue is the role of training programs in safeguarding the public when it becomes clear that a trainee has problems that are likely to interfere with professional functioning.

Therapist Competence: Ethical and Legal Aspects

In this section we examine what therapist competence is, how we can assess it, and what some of its ethical and legal dimensions are. We explore these questions: What ethical standards exist that offer guidance in determining competence? What ethical issues are involved in training therapists? To what degree is professional licensing an accurate and valid measure of competence? What are the ethical responsibilities of mental health professionals to continue to upgrade their knowledge and skills?

Perspectives on Competence

We begin this discussion of competence with an overview of specific guidelines from various professional associations. They are summarized in the box titled Professional Codes of Ethics on Competence. These guidelines leave several questions unanswered. What are the boundaries of one's competence, and how do professionals know when they have exceeded them? How can practitioners determine whether they should accept a client if they question their experience and training? What should be the minimal degree required for entry level to

Professional Codes of Ethics on Competence

American Association for Marriage and Family Therapy (2001)

Marriage and family therapists do not diagnose, treat, or advise on problems outside the recognized boundaries of their competencies.

American Psychological Association (1992)

Psychologists provide services, teach, and conduct research only within the boundaries of their competence, based on their education, training, supervised experience, or appropriate professional experience.

National Association of Social Workers (1999)

Social workers should accept responsibility or employment only on the basis of existing competence or the intention to acquire the necessary competence. (4.01.a.)

Social workers should strive to become and remain proficient in professional practice and the performance of professional functions. Social workers should critically examine, and keep current with, emerging knowledge relevant to social work. Social workers should routinely review professional literature and participate in continuing education relevant to social work practice and social work ethics. (4.01.b.)

American Counseling Association (1995)

Counselors practice only within the boundaries of their competence, based on their education, training, supervised experience, state and national professional credentials, and appropriate professional experience. Counselors will demonstrate a commitment to gain knowledge, personal awareness, sensitivity, and skills pertinent to working with a diverse client population.

professional counseling? To be competent to practice with a variety of client populations, does a counselor have to be both a generalist and a specialist?

These questions become more complex when we consider the criteria used in evaluating competence. In our opinion, assessing competence is an extremely difficult task. What are the criteria for the assessment? How do you measure the competence and objectivity of the assessors? Many people who complete a doctoral program lack the skills or knowledge needed to carry out certain therapeutic tasks. Obviously, a degree alone does not guarantee competence for any and all psychological services. Practitioners must also assess how far they can safely go with clients and when to refer them to other specialists. Similarly, it is important to learn when to consult another professional if the counselor has not had extensive experience working with a particular problem.

However, if you were to refer all the clients with whom you encountered difficulties, you would probably have few clients. As a beginning counselor, you are not alone if you have doubts about your general level of competence. In fact, it is not at all unusual for even highly experienced therapists to wonder seriously at times whether they have the personal and professional abilities needed to work with some of their clients. It is more troubling to think of therapists who rarely question their competence. Thus, difficulty working with some clients does not by itself imply incompetence, nor does lack of difficulty imply competence.

One way to develop or upgrade your skills is to work with colleagues or professionals who have more experience than you do. You can also learn new skills by going to conferences and conventions, by taking additional courses in areas you do not know well and in theories that you are not necessarily drawn to, and by participating in workshops that combine didactic work with supervised practice. The feedback you receive can give you an additional resource for evaluating your readiness to undertake certain therapeutic tasks. In addition to having a basic preparation as a generalist, you might also want to acquire advanced training in a specialty area, a topic we deal with later in this chapter.

Making Referrals

It is crucial for professionals to know from the outset the boundaries of their own competence and to refer clients to other professionals when working with them is beyond their professional training or when personal factors would interfere with a productive working relationship. With rare exceptions, you should be able to determine whether you are competent to treat a given client by the end of the initial interview. Both you and your client need to know if therapy is limited to a specified number of sessions. The client should be made aware of this knowledge at the intake session.

Because the counseling process can be unpredictable at times, counselors will sometimes encounter situations where the ethical path to follow is to refer a client due to a lack of competence in a particular area. For example, consider the case of Quan whose presenting problem was anxiety pertaining to academic success in college. This was within the scope of her counselor's training. However, later in the course of therapy Quan became very depressed and engaged in self-mutilation and other forms of self-destructive behavior. Quan's counselor recognized that these symptoms and behavior reflected a problem area that was outside the scope of his expertise. He recognized that ethical practice required him to make a referral to another professional who was competent to treat Quan's problems. Of course, before taking this action he would seek consultation and perhaps obtain supervision from an expert. He would not be in a position of being able to continue to counsel Quan if her symptoms were medical in nature and if her behavior posed a threat to her life.

Possessing the expertise to effectively work with a client's problem is one benchmark, but other circumstances might also make you wonder if a referral is in order. You and a client may decide that because of value conflicts or for some other reason your relationship is not productive. The client may want to continue working with another person rather than discontinue counseling. For these and other reasons, you will need to develop a framework for evaluating when to refer a client, and you will need to learn how to make this referral in such a manner that your client will be open to accepting your suggestion rather than being harmed by it. We hope you would not see referring a client with whom you have difficulty as a cure-all. Clients can be negatively affected when you refer them too quickly. If you recognize a pattern of frequent referrals, then you may need to examine your perception of your level of competence. In a way, consider a referral as a final intervention after you have exhausted other interventions including consulting. Most codes of ethics have a standard pertaining to conditions for making a referral, for example:

> Social workers should refer clients to other professionals when other professionals' specialized knowledge or expertise is needed to serve clients fully or when social workers believe they are not being effective or making reasonable progress with clients and additional service is required. (NASW, 1999, 2.06.a.)

◆ **The case of Helen.** To make the art of referral more concrete, consider the following exchange between a client and her counselor. Helen is 45 years old and has seen a counselor at a community mental health center for six sessions. She suffers from periods of depression and frequently talks about how hard it is to wake up to a new day. In other respects it is very difficult for Helen to express what she feels. Most of the time she sits silently during the session. The counselor decides that Helen's problems warrant long-term therapy that he doesn't feel competent to provide. In addition, the center has a policy of referring clients who need long-term treatment to therapists in private practice. The counselor therefore approaches Helen with the suggestion of a referral:

Counselor: Helen, during your intake session I let you know that we are generally expected to limit the number of our sessions to six visits. Since today is our sixth session, I'd like to discuss the matter of referring you to another therapist.

Helen: Well, you said the agency generally limits the number of visits to six, but what about exceptions? I mean, after all, I feel as if I've just started with you, and I really don't want to begin all over again with someone I don't know or trust.

Counselor: I can understand that, but you may not have to begin all over again. I could meet with the therapist you'd be continuing with to talk about what we've done these past weeks.

Helen: I still don't like the idea at all. I don't know whether I'll see another person if you won't continue with me. Why won't you let me stay with you?

Counselor: I think you need more intensive therapy than I'm trained to offer you, and, as I've explained, I'm expected to do only short-term counseling.

Helen: Intensive therapy! Do you think that my problems are that serious?

Counselor: It's not just a question of you having serious problems. I am concerned about your prolonged depressions, and we've talked about my concerns over your suicidal fantasies. I'd just feel much better if you were to see someone who is trained to work with depression.

Helen: I think you've worked with me just fine. If you won't let me come back, then I'll just forget counseling.

This exchange reflects a common problem. What do you think of the way Helen's counselor approached his client? Is it possible that the counselor was not clear enough regarding the limitation of six visits? Would you have waited until the sixth session to remind her of termination? Would you have done anything differently? If you were Helen's counselor, would you agree to continue seeing her if she refused to be referred to someone else? Why or why not?

Ethical Issues in Training Therapists

Training is a basic component of practitioner competence. Our discussion of the central ethical and professional issues in training is organized around questions pertaining to selection of trainees, content of training programs, best approaches to training, and student evaluation.

Selection of Trainees

A core ethical and professional issue involves formulating policies and procedures for selecting appropriate candidates for a training program. Here are some issues to consider:

- What criteria should be used for admission to training programs?
- Should the selection of trainees be based solely on traditional academic standards, or should it take into account the latest findings on the personal characteristics of effective therapists?
- To what degree is a candidate for training open to learning and to considering new perspectives?
- Does the candidate have problems that are likely to interfere with training and with the practice of psychotherapy?
- What are some ways to increase applications to programs by diverse groups of candidates?
- How open are training programs to diversity? How open are they to including people who will challenge us as trainers?
- Which populations do you desire to work with, and which do you not want as clients? Why?
- What is the importance of a thorough orientation to a program?
- How do you determine the mental fitness of a candidate?
- When the selection committee has made a careful analysis of the applicant and determined that the applicant was not suitable because of serious psychological impairment, how willing is the administration to support the committee's decision? If there is a lack of administrative support, what is the responsibility of the relevant professional organization to intervene?

Training programs have an ethical responsibility to establish clear selection criteria, and candidates have a right to know the nature of these criteria when they apply. Although grade-point averages, scores on the Graduate Record Examination, and letters of recommendation are often considered in the selection process, relying on these measures alone does not provide a comprehensive picture of a candidate. Many programs ask candidates to write a detailed essay that includes their reasons for wanting to be in the program, their professional goals, an assessment of their personal assets and liabilities, and life experiences that might be useful in their work as counselors. We recommend conducting group interviews with candidates. A number of programs have both faculty members and graduate students on the reviewing committee. If many sources are considered and if more than one person makes the decision about whom to select for training, there is less likelihood that people will be screened out on the basis of a personal bias of one individual.

As part of the screening process, ethical practice implies that candidates are given information about what will be expected of them if they enroll in the program. Just as potential therapy clients have a right to informed consent, students applying for a program have a right to know the material they will be expected to learn and the manner in which education and training will take place. With this kind of knowledge, students are better equipped to decide if they want to make a commitment to a program.

Screening is a two-way process. As faculty screen candidates and make decisions on whom to admit, candidates may also be screening the program to decide if this is right for them. Here is the ACA (1995) guideline on orientation:

> Prior to admission, counselors orient prospective students to the counselor education or training program's expectations, including but not limited to the following: (1) the type and level of skill acquisition required for successful completion of the training, (2) subject matter to be covered, (3) basis for evaluation, (4) training components that encourage self-growth or self-disclosure as part of the training process, (5) the type of supervision settings and requirements of the sites for required clinical field experiences, (6) student and supervisee evaluation and dismissal policies and procedures, and (7) up-to-date employment prospects for graduates. (F.2.a.)

◆ **The case of Leo.** Julius is on a review committee in a graduate counseling program. Leo has taken several introductory courses in the program, and he has just completed an ethics course with Julius. It is clear to this professor that Leo displays a rigid and dogmatic approach to human problems, particularly in areas such as interracial marriage, same-sex relationships, and abortion. Over the course of the semester, Leo appeared to be either unwilling or unable to modify his thinking. When challenged by other students in the class about his views, Leo argued that certain behaviors were simply "never proper" and that it was the task of the counselor to point this out to clients. In meeting with the committee charged with determining whether candidates should be advanced in the program, Julius expresses his strong concern about retaining Leo in the program. His colleagues share this concern, and Leo is denied advancement.

- What concerns, if any, do you have about the manner in which this case was handled? Were any of Leo's rights violated?
- Was it clear to Leo that when he expressed his ideas in his classes they could be held against him? Is there an ethical issue in that situation?

- Could the committee determine so early in the program that Leo would not change his ideas in the course of his education?
- Were any other avenues open in dealing with him short of disqualifying him from the program?
- If his values reflected his minority cultural background, would that make a difference? Would the committee be culturally insensitive for rejecting him from the program?
- What if Leo said that when he eventually obtained his license he intended to work exclusively with people from his cultural and religious background? Should he be denied the opportunity to pursue a degree in counseling if his career goal was to work with a specific population that shared his views and values?
- Using the criteria seemingly espoused by this selection committee, would a minister from a fundamentalist background who was attempting to get a master's degree in counseling be rejected?
- If you were on the committee, how would you handle candidates who seemed to exhibit racism, homophobia, and absolutist thinking?

Content of a Program

What is the content of a training program, and how is it decided? Is the curriculum determined by the preferences of the faculty, or is it based on the needs of the people being served, or both? Lazarus (1990) writes that "most graduate programs socialize their students into delimited schools of thought" (p. 351). In his lectures, Lazarus often warns of the limitations of rigidly following a particular theory and then stretching clients to fit its preconceptions rather than adapting the techniques that flow from a theory to fit the unique needs of each client. He argues that a multimodal, systematic, technically eclectic model can point the way to a genuinely scientific approach to the training of therapists. Thus, training programs would do well to offer students a variety of therapeutic techniques and strategies that can be applied to a wide range of problems with a diverse clientele.

Some programs are structured around a specific theoretical orientation in two ways: first, by the school itself having a specific orientation, and second, by insisting that students subscribe to one theory at some point in their training. Other programs have a broader content base and are aimed at training generalists who will be able to step into future positions that present evolving challenges. Some think that all specialty training should be abolished. They are concerned about training practitioners in only one therapeutic orientation (without also providing unbiased introductions to other models). There is merit in an analytically trained therapist's learning about alternative approaches such as behavior therapy or a systemic model. By the same token, a behavior therapist and a systemic therapist need to be able to recognize the role of transference and countertransference in the therapeutic process. It is important that therapists know when a particular approach is contraindicated, especially if it is their own specialty. From an ethical perspective, counselor educators and trainers are expected to present varied theoretical positions:

> Counselors present varied theoretical positions so that students and supervisees may make comparisons and have opportunities to develop their own positions. Counselors provide information concerning the scientific bases of professional practice. (ACA, 1995, F.2.f.)

We recommend that students be exposed to the major contemporary counseling theories and that they be taught to formulate a rationale for the therapeutic techniques they employ. It is a good idea to teach students the strengths and limitations of these contemporary counseling theories. Some writers point out the limitations of basing training mainly on these standard counseling models and call for training in alternative theoretical positions that apply to diverse client populations (D. W. Sue, Ivey, & Pedersen, 1996). For an overview of the contemporary counseling theories see G. Corey, 2000c; Corsini and Wedding, 2000; Ivey, D'Andrea, Ivey, and Simek-Morgan, 2002; Seligman, 2001; and Sharf, 2000.

In deciding what to teach, certain questions are worth considering:

- Is the curriculum inclusive of cultures, or is it culturally biased?
- Is there a universal definition of mental health, or is mental health culturally defined?
- Should therapy help clients adjust to their culture? Or might it encourage them to find ways of making the changes they want within their culture?
- Does the curriculum give central attention to the ethics of professional practice?
- Is it ethical to leave out training in ethics? Is it enough to hope that ethical issues will be addressed through the supervision process alone?
- What is the proper balance between academic course work and supervised clinical experience?
- What core knowledge should be taught in counselor education programs?
- What is the appropriate balance between basic preparation and advanced specialization?

In training programs for various mental health professions, general content areas are part of the core curriculum. For example, in counseling programs the following areas are typically required for all students: professional orientation, human growth and development, social and cultural foundations, counseling theory and practice, group counseling, lifestyle and career development, appraisal of individuals, and research and evaluation.

It is our opinion that training programs need to be designed so that students can acquire a more thorough understanding of themselves as well as acquire theoretical knowledge. Ideally, students will be introduced to various content areas, will acquire a range of skills they can utilize in working with diverse clients, will learn how to apply theory to practice through supervised fieldwork experiences, and will learn a great deal about themselves personally. A good program does more than impart knowledge and skills essential to the helping process. In a supportive and challenging environment, the program encourages students to build on their life experiences and personal strengths and provides opportunities for expanding their awareness of self and others.

Ethics deserves prominent attention in any program geared to educating and training mental health practitioners. (But we are aware of an APA-accredited doctoral program in clinical psychology in which a separate ethics course is not required!) Although ethics is supposedly incorporated in a number of required courses, seminars, and practicum and internship experiences, we believe the lack of systematic coverage of ethical issues will hinder students, both as trainees and later as professionals. The topics we address in this book deserve a separate course as well as infusion throughout all courses and supervised fieldwork experiences.

How Can We Best Train?

Programs geared to educating and training counselors should be built on the foundation of the natural talents and abilities of the students. Ideally, as we have said, counselor educators and supervisors teach students the knowledge and skills they need to work effectively with diverse populations. In addition, students need a core set of attitudes and values that are congruent with carrying out their role as helping professionals. In his provocative article "Can Psychotherapists Transcend the Shackles of Their Training and Superstitions?" Lazarus (1990) contends that formal education and training in psychological diagnosis and treatment often undermine the natural talents and skills of trainees. In illustrating his point, he describes a friend who was "an absolute natural when it came to understanding people and showing genuine warmth, wisdom, and empathy" (p. 352). When Lazarus brought his own problems to his friend, he found the experience to be "amazingly therapeutic." After his friend obtained a Ph.D. in psychology, however, Lazarus was able to receive only "a string of platitudes and labels." He maintains that as his friend took courses in assessment, diagnosis, and treatment, his natural talents were destroyed. Of course, Lazarus does not believe that training necessarily erodes natural talent, but he does warn that "one of the main shackles under which many therapists labor comes from the almost endless list of proscriptions that they are handed" (p. 353).

We think Lazarus (2001) makes an excellent point in calling for training programs "to avoid instilling a fear of lawsuits in students and terrorizing them about the dangers of running afoul of licensing agencies." Lazarus writes: "Some therapists create such highly sanitized treatment environments that they lose sight of human and humane concerns. Instead of producing frightened conformists, our training programs should focus on turning out caring and enterprising helpers who have the confidence to think for themselves" (p. 16).

In our view, one of the best ways to teach students how to effectively relate to a wide range of clients, many of whom will differ from themselves, is for faculty to model healthy interpersonal behavior. It is imperative that counselor educators and supervisors display cohesive relationships among themselves and treat students in a collegial manner with respect. This is not always the case, however. In some programs the faculty performs somewhat like a dysfunctional family with behavioral characteristics of power plays, unaddressed interpersonal conflict, and even hostile behavior. Conflict among faculty members may be obvious, and students are sometimes drawn into these rivalries, being expected to side with a particular faculty member. In an effective program, differences are discussed openly, and there is an atmosphere of genuine respect and acceptance of diversity of perspectives. If a faculty practices the principles they teach, they are demonstrating powerful lessons about interpersonal relating that students can apply to their personal and professional lives.

- What would you do if you found yourself in a program characterized by dysfunctional behavior?
- How would you react to a student who said, "I don't care what they do; I just want to get my degree and get out of here"?
- If you were concerned about the ethics of this program as a student, what actions would be open to you besides quitting?

Effective programs combine academic and personal learning, weave together didactic and experiential approaches, and integrate study and practice. A program structured exclusively around teaching academics does not provide important feedback to students on how they function with clients. In experiential learning and in fieldwork, problem behaviors of trainees will eventually surface and can be ameliorated. Evaluation is an important component of this process. The policies and procedures pertaining to how students will be evaluated and how decisions will be made about their advancement or dismissal from a program should be known by all students. Evaluation criteria is the topic we turn to next.

Evaluation Criteria

Evaluation of knowledge and skills. Every training institution has an ethical responsibility to screen candidates so that the public will be protected from incompetent practitioners. Programs clearly have a dual responsibility: to honor their commitment to the students they admit and also to protect future consumers who will be served by those who graduate. Just as the criteria for selecting applicants to a program should be clear, the criteria for successful completion and the nature of the evaluation process need to be spelled out as clearly and objectively as possible.

Lamb, Cochran, and Jackson (1991) recommend that trainees be informed about evaluation criteria and procedures as part of the orientation to the program. It should be made known to students "When, how, by whom, and by what form" their evaluations will occur (p. 291). Lamb and colleagues also recommend that the evaluation criteria include the following broad aspects of professional functioning: (a) knowledge and application of professional standards; (b) competency; and (c) personal functioning (such as self-awareness, use of supervision, and coping with stress). The code of ethics of the NASW, APA,

Evaluating Student Performance

The NASW (1999) deals with performance evaluation thusly:

> Social workers who have the responsibility for evaluating the performance of others should fulfill such a responsibility in a fair and considerate manner and on the basis of clearly stated criteria. (3.03)

The APA (1992) provides these guidelines for assessing student and supervisee performance:

> In academic and supervisory relationships, psychologists establish an appropriate process for providing feedback to students and supervisees. (6.05a)
>
> Psychologists evaluate students and supervisees on the basis of their actual performance on relevant and established program requirements. (6.05b)

The ACA (1995) addresses the evaluation process in counselor education and training programs in this way:

> Counselors clearly state to students and supervisees, in advance of training, the levels of competency expected, appraisal methods, and timing of evaluations for both didactic and experiential components. Counselors provide students and supervisees with periodic performance appraisal and evaluation feedback throughout the training program. (F.2.c.)

and ACA outline standards for performance evaluation, and we strongly support these statements (see the box titled Evaluating Student Performance). In addition to evaluating candidates when they apply to a program, we favor periodic reviews to determine whether trainees should be retained.

Students need feedback on their progress so they can build on their strengths or remediate problem areas. Ideally, trainees will also engage in self-evaluation to determine whether they are "right" for the program and the program is suitable for them. The first goal of an evaluation of candidates is to correct problems. If shortcomings are sensitively pointed out to trainees in a timely way, they can often correct them.

Assessing graduate students to determine whether they have the knowledge and skills required to function effectively as practitioners is essential. Forrest, Elman, Gizara, and Vacha-Haase (1999) identify categories of professional competence that might be considered as a part of the evaluation process: academic skills, assessment skills, clinical judgment, clinical skills, ethics, interpersonal skills, intrapersonal skills, response to supervision, and theoretical skills. One approach to evaluating trainees' professional competence is to require an oral examination judged by experienced professionals in the community who have no other connection to the university. Many states require a similar oral examination to obtain a license as a mental health professional. This type of comprehensive exam would help protect clients by ensuring that beginning counselors are adequately trained and prepared to enter private or agency practice.

Evaluation of interpersonal skills. Evaluating trainees' knowledge and skills is important, but it is also essential to evaluate trainees' professional behavior and performance. It is most important to identify personal characteristics and interpersonal behaviors that are likely to influence trainees' ability to effectively deliver mental health services. The research literature on evaluative processes to identify trainees with problems remains minimal. There is a lack of clear, shared, and consistent language to represent the different types of problematic behaviors (Forrest et al., 1999). Sometimes students have personal characteristics or problems that interfere with their ability to function effectively, yet when this is pointed out to them, they may deny the feedback they receive. A program has an ethical responsibility to take action and not simply pass on a student with serious academic or personal problems. ACA's *Code of Ethics* (1995) addresses this issue:

> Counselors, through ongoing evaluation and appraisal, are aware of the academic and personal limitations of students and supervisees that might impede performance. Counselors assist students and supervisees in securing remedial assistance when needed, and dismiss from the training program supervisees who are unable to provide competent service due to academic or personal limitations. Counselors seek professional consultation and document their decisions to dismiss or refer students or supervisees for assistance. Counselors assure that students and supervisees have recourse to address decisions made, to require them to seek assistance, or to dismiss them. (F.3.a.)

Forrest and her colleagues (1999) summarize the ethical obligation of faculty members and clinical supervisors in overseeing trainees' work:

> Ethical standards mandate that educators and trainers:
> (a) attend to the possibility that their trainees' personal problems might lead to harm of others; (b) make sure that trainees are not harming clients or others under their care; (c) attend to the possibility that trainees may misuse their influence; (d) evaluate whether trainees are performing services responsibly, competently, and ethically; (3) articulate a clear set of professional standards; and (f) evaluate trainees based on these relevant and established requirements. (p. 636)

Given the increased awareness of possible damage caused by counselors who do not possess the personal qualities of effective counselors, it is reasonable to assume that faculty will have to serve as gatekeepers for the profession (Lumadue & Duffey, 1999). In their review of the literature, Forrest et al. (1999) found these common categories for dismissal: poor academic performance, poor clinical performance, poor interpersonal skills, and unethical behavior. Psychological reasons for dismissal included factors such as emotional instability, personality disorder, psychopathology, and unprofessional demeanor.

Many mental health educators and administrators are hesitant to dismiss students. This is especially true if the concerns are about personal characteristics or problematic behavior, even in cases where the faculty are in agreement regarding the lack of suitability of a given student. Some of the barriers to taking the action of dismissing students from a program include difficulties in giving clear evidence to support the decision to dismiss a student; the lack of adequate procedures in place to support a dismissal decision; concern about the psychological distress for faculty and students; concern about the heightened resistance and defensiveness in the trainee; the potential for receiving criticism from other faculty or supervisors who were not involved in the trainee's remediation; and lack of administrative support (Forrest et al., 1999).

Perhaps the major deterrent to dismissing a student is the fear of legal reprisal by that student. After their review of the literature on evaluating the competence of trainees, Forrest and her colleagues (1999) came to the conclusion that "we are struggling to understand and implement our responsibilities as gatekeepers for professional quality control" (p. 679). From our perspective, faculty who are in the business of training counselors should be credited with the ability to have accurate perceptions and observations pertaining to personality characteristics that are counterproductive for becoming effective counselors. If a student has good grades but has serious unresolved personal conflicts or demonstrates dysfunctional interpersonal behavior, action needs to be taken. Dismissal from a program is a measure of last resort. We would hope this option would not be employed unless all other attempts at remediation had failed.

Professional training programs can be held legally liable for turning out incompetent practitioners (Custer, 1994). If those who graduate from a program are proven to be incompetent, the program can be sued. If it can be demonstrated that a program failed to adequately train an individual, the university is responsible for the harm the graduate inflicts on clients. Custer describes a lawsuit involving a master's level counselor who graduated from Louisiana Tech's College of Education. A female therapy client filed suit against Louisiana Tech, claiming that the program allowed an incompetent practitioner to graduate from the program. The client claimed that her life had been destroyed by incompetent therapy. The claim was that the program itself was inadequate in that it simply did not adequately prepare her counselor. The counselor was named in the malpractice action along with her supervisor and the university. The initial lawsuit was settled in 1994 for $1.7 million. A case such as this makes it clear that specific competency standards for retaining and graduating counseling students are not only useful but necessary.

Donigian (1991) takes the provocative position that the consumer's trust in the profession is violated if counselors are not psychologically prepared for the challenges they will confront as they undertake their work. He suggests that preparation programs should take responsibility for evaluating students' emotional and psychological readiness to become practitioners.

If faculty groups assume the role of examining and evaluating both the academic and personal fitness of students to graduate, who evaluates and examines the examiners? Assume that several advanced students approach the dean of their graduate school to express their concern about the seeming discrepancies between what they are experiencing in their internships and supervised sessions and what they are being taught in their counseling classes. They complain that their professors live in an ivory tower, and they point out that most of their professors are not practitioners. The dean replies that all of the faculty members are properly credentialed. Although they are not seeing clients, they have had practical experience in the past.

- Is it important for those who teach and train students in the mental health professions to have current hands-on experience with clients?
- Every program evaluates students and their suitability for the helping professions. Is it equally important to evaluate the evaluators and their suitability to make such assessments?

◆ **The case of a discouraged professor.** Prudence was a student at a university with a 48-unit master's degree program in counseling. This core degree and a few additional classes qualified a graduate to apply for the licensed professional counselor examination once the required supervised internship hours were completed. Prudence was identified by the faculty to have a level of affect that could be termed as a complete lack of empathy. In counseling dyads, group process experiences, and classroom exercises it became clear that Prudence was unable to make empathic connection. Academically, Prudence received good grades; she completed the reading, wrote satisfactory papers, and took examinations as well as most. It was in the behavioral dimension—such as reflective listening, being able to establish client rapport, and demonstrating empathic understanding—that her lack of skill was noted.

Prudence progressed through most of the graduate program and entered an intensive group process course, which was a requirement of the program. The professor in this didactic training environment noted Prudence's barriers to building effective counseling relationships and made two or three interventions. These interventions included direct discussion with Prudence as well as referral and recommendation for personal counseling. At the end of the semester, Prudence's behaviors and skills had not improved, and by some measures they had actually deteriorated. The grade for the group process class was the only grade Prudence needed to complete her degree program. After many hours of soul searching, the professor decided that this student should not be allowed to advance because her lack of empathic understanding and her typically bizarre responses in counseling dyads made her, as a potential counseling professional, a risk to others. He gave Prudence a failing grade, which meant that Prudence would not receive her degree without successfully repeating the group process class.

Prudence responded by suing both the professor and the university. An investigation was completed at the university by the academic senate. In addition to the professor and the student, several members of the faculty and many individuals from the group process class were called as witnesses. The senate overruled the professor's grade and awarded a master's degree in counseling to Prudence. Today she is a licensed professional counselor.

Discouraged by the lack of support from the university, the professor reduced his teaching to part time and retired at the first available opportunity. In reflecting on this case, what implications can you draw?

- If this student was able to pass all of her other courses, was it justified to block her from a master's degree based on her performance in this one group process course?
- What are your thoughts about the actions taken by the administration?

- Is it the responsibility of professional accrediting agencies to intervene in a situation such as this?

Professional Licensing and Credentialing

Most states have established specific requirements of supervised practice beyond the receipt of a master's or doctoral degree for licensing and certification in areas such as clinical social work, clinical or counseling psychology, rehabilitation counseling, mental health counseling, and couples and family therapy. Most licenses are generic in nature, meaning the holder of the license is assumed to have minimal competence in the general practice of counseling or clinical work. In this section we focus on some of the issues pertaining to competence both as a generalist and in an advanced specialization: basic assumptions of the practice of licensing, arguments for and against licensing and certification for mental health professionals, professional jealousy and turf battles, and the value of professional collaboration.

Purposes of Legislative Regulation of Practice

Sweeney (1995) describes credentialing as an approach to identifying individuals by occupational group, involving at least three methods: registry, certification, and licensure. In its simplest form, *registry* is generally a voluntary listing of individuals who use a title or provide a service. Registration represents the least degree of regulation of practice. Both certification and licensure involve increased measures designed to regulate professional practices.

Although licensing and certification differ in their purposes, they have some features in common. Both require applicants to meet specific requirements in terms of education and training and acceptance from practicing professionals. Both also generally rely on tests to determine which applicants have met the standards and deserve to be granted a credential.

Certification is a voluntary attempt by a group to promote a professional identity. Certification confirms that the practitioner has met a set of minimum standards established by the certification agency. Some types of certification are required for practicing in a certain setting. For example, in most states school counselors must obtain a certificate in order to practice. Although certification gives practitioners the right to use a specific title, it does not ensure quality practice, nor does it govern practice (Hosie, 1995).

Unlike certification, *licensure* statutes determine and govern professional practice. Licensure acts, sometimes called practice acts, specify what the holder of the license can do and what others cannot do (Remley, 1995). Licensure is generally viewed as the most desirable form of legislative regulation of professional practice because it tends to highlight the uniqueness of an occupation and restricts both the use of the title and the practice of an occupation (Sweeney, 1995).

Licensure and certification assure the public that practitioners have completed minimum educational programs, have had a certain number of hours of supervised training, and have gone through some type of evaluation and screening. Licenses and certifications do not, and probably cannot, ensure that practitioners will competently do what their credentials permit them to do. The main advantages of licensure and certification are the protection of the public from grossly unqualified and untrained practitioners and the formal representation to the public that practitioners are part of an established profession.

Most licenses and credentials are generic; that is, they usually do not specify the clients or problems practitioners are competent to work with, nor do they specify the techniques that they are competent to use. A licensed psychologist may possess the expertise needed to work with adults yet lack the training necessary to work with children. The same person may be qualified to do individual psychotherapy yet have neither the experience nor the skills required for family counseling or group therapy. Most licensing regulations do specify that licensees are to engage only in those therapeutic tasks for which they have adequate training, but it is up to the licensee to put this rule into practice. Such a broad definition of practice also applies to many other professions.

Arguments for and Against Professional Licensing and Credentialing

Four main arguments have been put forth in favor of legislation to regulate the delivery of mental health services. The first is that the public is protected by setting minimum standards of service and holding professionals accountable if they do not measure up. This argument contends that the consumer would be harmed by the absence of such standards because incompetent practitioners can cause long-term negative consequences. Second, the regulation of practitioners is designed to protect the public from its ignorance about mental health services. This argument rests on the assumption that the consumer who needs psychological services typically does not know how to choose an appropriate practitioner or how to judge the quality of services received. Most people do not know the basic differences between a licensed professional counselor, a licensed psychologist, a psychiatrist, a licensed clinical social worker, and a licensed marital and family therapist. Third, because insurance companies frequently reimburse clients for the services of licensed practitioners, licensing means that more people can afford mental health care. Finally, there is the view that licensing allows the profession to define for itself what it will and will not do. In fact, licensure itself is perceived to enhance the profession and is a sign of maturity.

The arguments for licensure revolve around the contention that the consumer's welfare is better safeguarded with legal regulation than without it. Those who challenge this assumption often maintain that licensing is designed to create and preserve a "union shop" and that it works more as a self-serving measure that creates monopolistic helping professions than as a protection for the public from misrepresentation and incompetence (Davis, 1981). Others are skeptical when it comes to setting up criteria for regulating mental health practitioners. Carl Rogers (1980) maintained that as soon as criteria are set up for certification the profession inevitably becomes frozen in a past image. He noted that there are as many certified charlatans as there are uncertified competent practitioners. Another drawback to licensing, from his viewpoint, is that professionalism builds up a rigid bureaucracy.

We have observed that the process of licensing often contributes to professional specializations' pitting themselves against one another. Instead of fostering a collaborative spirit between licensed clinical social workers and licensed marriage and family therapists or between licensed psychologists and licensed professional counselors, the licensing process of each group too often promotes working in the opposite direction. We wonder if the protection of consumers is the main motivation of some licensing boards or whether their motivation may be to limit the number of practitioners. Furthermore, the examinations used to determine competence may have questionable validity. Although we are not opposed to the concept of professional licensing, we do have serious concerns about the criteria and the processes that are often used to determine who is competent to practice and the manner in which candidates are assessed.

Specialties Within the Mental Health Professions

Some training programs offer specialty training and encourage students to enroll in a specific track at all levels of education, from associate of arts to doctoral programs. For example, students can be trained and certified as substance abuse counselors in associate of arts programs. At the master's level counseling program, students can specialize in a given area such as school counseling, rehabilitation counseling, or marriage and family counseling. Doctoral programs offer specializations in community and multicultural counseling, organizational development, and human development, to mention a few. At the doctoral level specializations also exist within each of the major mental health professions of social work, marriage and family therapy, clinical psychology, counseling psychology, and counselor education.

Should states adopt legislation to regulate the practice of counseling specializations? There are some who argue in favor of specialty licensing and others who argue against it. Although Remley (1995) sees a need to recognize counselors who possess specialized knowledge and training, he opposes state regulation of the practice of counseling specializations as being not in the best interests of either the public or the profession. Remley contends that only the general practice of counseling should be regulated by the state; specialty practice should be addressed through credentialing. Hosie (1995) challenges the assumption that specialties are necessary to provide competent practice to specific client types. He makes a case for basic preparation required to be a competent generalist rather than viewing advanced specialization as necessary for employment as a counselor and for competent practice with clients.

Professionals who argue for the need for specializations within the counseling field point to the current realities and complexities of counseling practice in diverse settings, with various client problems, and with a range of client populations. Practitioners who have expressed concern over certification of specialties are asking for a basis to bring unity to the counseling field. It is our hope that consumers do not get forgotten in the heated debates surrounding certification and licensure issues and professional specialties. Also, we hope these issues will not separate professionals.

The process of registration, certification, and licensure can promote a sense of professional identity. It can also be the basis for professional jealousy over turf and can lead to restrictive regulation that is motivated by competition for access to the marketplace. How has interprofessional bickering manifested itself? According to Cummings (1990), professional psychology has struggled with the psychiatric profession to retain its turf in the areas of hospital privileges, licensure to prescribe drugs, and inclusion in Medicare. Cummings asserts that a major contribution of psychology to the other mental health professions was designing and implementing the freedom-of-choice amendments to state insurance codes. Psychology has made great strides in expanding mental health services to the elderly and to residents of rural areas through revisions in Medicare regulations.

Just as psychology has struggled with psychiatry for turf, clinical psychologists often contend that their scientific discipline makes them preeminent over other disciplines (Cummings, 1990). Some writers warn about the dangers of competition to the welfare of the client; they contend that such fighting among professions can lead to an erosion in the quality of services and that those who stand to suffer most are the consumers (Garcia, 1990; Ivey & Rigazio-DiGilio, 1991). Brooks and Gerstein (1990) also decry the competition within and among the various professional fields, and they urge professionals to join forces and collaborate. They add that interprofessional bickering must cease if mental health professionals, their associations, and the respective licensing boards are to achieve their goal of delivering the best services possible. The more that money is a factor, the more vigorous the "ideological" turf battles are bound to become.

Continuing Education and Demonstration of Competence

Most professional organizations support efforts to make continuing education a mandatory condition of relicensing (see the box titled Ethical Guidelines for Continuing Education). Professionals are encouraged to engage in ongoing education and training in their specializations. According to Nagy (2000), this means that professionals should stay on top of new developments in their area and keep their skills sharp. They can do this by reading books and journals, attending workshops and conventions, giving presentations, participating in a peer consultation group, and doing whatever is necessary to continue growing personally and professionally.

Most mental health professionals are required to demonstrate, as a basis for relicensure or recertification, that they have completed a minimal number of continuing education activities. As a condition for relicensure as a social worker, psychologist, or a marriage and family therapist, most states now require specific courses and a minimum number of hours of continuing education. For

Ethical Guidelines for Continuing Education

APA's (1992) *Ethical Principles* has the following guideline on maintaining professional expertise:

> Psychologists who engage in assessment, therapy, teaching, research, organizational consulting, or other professional activities maintain a reasonable level of awareness of current scientific and professional information in their fields of activity, and undertake ongoing efforts to maintain competence in the skills they use. (1.05)

NASW's *Code of Ethics* (1999) has this guideline on continuing education and staff development:

> Social work administrators and supervisors should take reasonable steps to provide or arrange for continuing education and staff development for all staff for whom they are responsible. Continuing education and staff development should address current knowledge and emerging developments related to social work practice and ethics. (3.08.)

ACA's *Code of Ethics* (1995) states the following on continuing education:

> Counselors recognize the need for continuing education to maintain a reasonable level of awareness of current scientific and professional information in their fields of activity. They take steps to maintain competence in the skills they use, are open to new procedures, and keep current with the diverse and/or special populations with whom they work. (C.2.f.)

AAMFT's *Code of Ethics* (2001) has this standard:

> Marriage and family therapists pursue knowledge of new developments and maintain competence in marriage and family therapy through education, training, or supervised experience. (3.1.)

example, licensed psychologists and marriage and family therapists in California are required to complete a 4-hour course in ethics and the law as a part of the 36 hours of continuing education for every renewal period (which occurs every 2 years).

Individual practitioners have an ethical responsibility to seek out ways to keep current with new developments in their field, and administrators of mental health agencies also have responsibilities to provide continuing education activities for the staff. Some of these activities can take the form of in-service workshops and training at the agency site; other activities will require therapists to go outside the agency.

To assume that our skills never deteriorate or that we know everything we need to know upon graduation is naive. If we rarely or never seek continuing education, how are we to justify this lack of initiative? Learning never ceases; new clients present new challenges. New areas of knowledge and practice demand ongoing education. Even recent graduates may have significant gaps in their education that will require them to take workshops or courses in the future. You may also need to seek supervision in working with various client populations or to acquire skills in certain therapeutic modalities. For example, your job may require you to conduct groups, yet your program may not have included even one group course in the curriculum. When continuing education is tailored to your personal and professional needs, it can keep you on the cutting edge of your profession.

Consider the following case of a therapist who believes that competence can be attained once and for all.

◆ **The case of Conrad.** Dr. Conrad Hadenuf has been a licensed psychologist for 20 years and has always maintained a busy practice. He sees a wide variety of clients. As a condition of license renewal, he is required to attend a 15-hour retraining program on substance abuse. He is indignant. "I have a Ph.D., I have 3,000 hours of supervised experience, and I have years of experience with all sorts of problems," he says. "This is just a money-making gimmick for those who want to generate workshops!" Knowing that he has no choice if he wants to retain his license, Conrad grudgingly attends the workshop, sits in the back of the room, takes no notes, takes longer breaks than scheduled, and leaves as soon as the certificates of attendance are available.

- What are your reactions to Conrad's statements? Is his rationale for not wanting to participate in the workshops justified?
- Although Conrad might claim that he has no desire to deal with substance abuse, can he realistically say that he will never be confronted with clients with substance abuse problems?
- How do you view mandated continuing education as a condition for license renewal?
- Are practitioners being ethically responsible to their clients if they never actively participate in the required continuing education courses?

Clarifying your stance. We hope you have thought about ways to maintain and enhance your competence. Use the following questions to clarify your thinking on the issues we have raised. What is your own strategy for remaining professionally competent?

- What effects on individual practitioners do you think the trend toward increased accountability is likely to have? How might this trend affect you?
- Do you think it is ethical to continue practicing if you do not continue your education? Why or why not?
- What are some advantages and disadvantages to using continuing education programs solely as the basis for renewing a license? Is continuing education enough? Explain.
- What are your reactions to competence examinations (oral and written) for entry-level applicants and as a basis for license renewal? What kinds of examinations might be useful?
- Should evidence of continuing education be required (or simply strongly recommended) as a basis for recertification or relicensure?
- If you support mandatory continuing education, who do you think is in the best position to determine the nature of this education? What standards could be used in making this judgment?

- What kinds of continuing education would you want for yourself? Through what means do you think you can best acquire new skills and keep abreast of advances in your field?

Review, Consultation, and Supervision by Peers

Peer review. Peer review is an organized system by which practitioners within a profession assess one another's services. Peer review provides some assurance to consumers that they will receive competent services. In addition to providing peer review, colleagues can challenge practitioners to adopt a fresh perspective on problems they encounter in their practice. Regarded as a means rather than an end in itself, peer review has as its ultimate goals not only to determine whether a practitioner's professional activity is adequate but also to ensure that future services will be acceptable. Peer review continues a tradition of self-regulation.

Peer-consultation groups. Borders (1991) described the value of structured peer groups that foster the development of skills, conceptual growth, participation, instructive feedback, and self-monitoring. Peer-supervision groups are useful for counselors at all levels of experience. For trainees, peer groups offer a supportive atmosphere and help them learn that they are not alone with their concerns. For counselors in practice, they provide an opportunity for continued professional growth.

Peer-consultation groups can also function as an informal and voluntary form of review in which individual cases and ethical and professional issues are examined (G. J. Lewis, Greenburg, & Hatch, 1988). These groups provide additional safeguards to consumers and a greater measure of accountability. Furthermore, being part of a peer-consultation group offers reassurance to practitioners who are concerned about malpractice litigation.

Consider your own stance as you answer these questions about peer review and peer consultation:

- Can you think of both advantages and disadvantages to basing license renewal strictly on peer-review procedures?
- Who determines the qualifications of the peer reviewer? What criteria should be used to determine the effectiveness of counseling practice?
- What are your thoughts about a peer consultation group for yourself? If you would like to be involved in such a group, how might you take the initiative to form one?

Commentary. Before closing this discussion of competence, we want to mention the danger of rarely allowing yourself to experience any self-doubt and being convinced that you can handle any therapeutic situation. Some therapists feel this way. They tell themselves they have it made and attend conventions reluctantly. Sidney Jourard (1968) made a comment many years ago that still seems timely. Jourard warns about the delusion that one has nothing new to learn. He maintains that exciting workshops or contact with challenging colleagues can keep therapists growing. He urges professionals to find colleagues whom they can trust so that they can avoid becoming "smug, pompous, fat-bottomed and convinced that they have the word. [Such colleagues can] prod one out of such smug pomposity, and invite one back to the task" (p. 69).

We support the view that supervision is a useful tool throughout one's career. Along with Jourard, we also see the development of competence as an ongoing process, not a goal that counselors ever finally attain. This process involves a willingness to continually question whether you are doing your work as well as you might and to search for ways of becoming a more effective person and therapist.

Chapter Summary

Clients' welfare is directly affected by ethical issues in the training of therapists, in the debate over whether professional licensure and credentialing are adequate signs of competence, and in the importance of continuing one's education. Counselors must acquire new knowledge and skills throughout their professional career. This is particularly true for practitioners wishing to develop a specialty area dealing with certain client populations or problems.

A core ethical and professional issue in training involves the question of how to develop policies and procedures for selecting the candidates who are best suited for the various mental health professions. The challenge is to adopt criteria for choosing people who have the life experiences that will enable them to understand the diverse range of clients with whom they will work. The personal characteristics of trainees, such as attitudes and beliefs, are critical in deciding whom to admit to training programs.

Another important issue is the effectiveness of professional licensing and credentialing as a sign of an individual's competence. Although most practitioners will need to acquire competence as generalists, the counseling profession has been characterized by the emergence of specialty areas of practice. These areas of specialization need to be clarified without destroying the unity within the profession.

The issues are complex, yet the goal is to focus licensure and certification more on protecting consumers than on protecting professional specializations. Increased collaboration among the various mental health professions can enhance this process. Isolation too often creates turf battles and professional jealousies that benefit no one.

Suggested Activities

1. Invite several practicing counselors to talk to your class about the ethical and legal issues they encounter in their work. You might have a panel of practitioners who work in several different settings and with different kinds of clients.

2. In small groups explore the topic of when and how you might make a referral. Role-play a referral, with one student playing the client and another the counselor. After a few minutes the "client" and the other students can give the "counselor" feedback on how he or she handled the situation.

3. In small groups explore what you think the criteria should be for determining whether a therapist is competent. Let a student role-play an "incompetent" therapist and defend himself or herself. Make up a list of specific criteria, and share it with the rest of the class. Are you able as a class to come up with some common criteria?

4. Several students can look up the requirements for licensure or certification of the major mental health specializations in your state. What are some of the common elements? Present your findings to the class.

5. Work out a proposal for a continuing education program. In small groups, develop a realistic model to ensure competency for professionals once they have been granted a license. What kind of design most appeals to you? a peer-review model? competency examinations? taking courses? other ideas?

6. Assume that you are applying for a job or writing a résumé to use in private practice. Write up your own professional disclosure statement in a page or two. Bring your disclosure statements to class and have fellow students review what you have written. They can then interview you, and you can get some practice in talking with "prospective clients." This exercise can help you clarify your own position and give you valuable practice for job interviews.

7. As a class project several students can form a committee to investigate some of the major local and state laws that apply to the practice of psychotherapy. You might want to ask mental health professionals what major conflicts they have experienced between the law and their professional practice.

8. Form a panel to discuss procedures for selecting appropriate applicants for your training program. Your task as a group is to identify specific criteria for candidates. Consider these questions: In addition to grade-point averages, scores on the Graduate Record Examination, and letters of recommendation, what other criteria might you establish? What life experiences would your group look for? What personal qualities are essential? What attitudes, values, and beliefs would be congruent with becoming a counseling professional? What personal characteristics, if any, would you use as a basis for rejecting an applicant? What process should the program use in making selections? Would you recommend individual interviews? interviews conducted in small groups?

9. Assume that you are a graduate student who is part of the interviewing team for applicants for your training program. Identify six questions to pose to all applicants. What are you hoping to learn about the applicants from your questions?

10. Interview professors or practitioners in schools, agencies, or work settings that interest you. Ask them what they most remember about their training programs. What features were most useful for them? What training do they wish they had had more of, and what would they like to have had less of? How adequately do they think their graduate program prepared them for the work they are now doing? What continuing education experiences do they most value?

11. Form a small group for role playing a licensing board that will interview candidates for a professional license. Meet out of class for the time it takes to draw up a list of questions to pose to the "practitioners" who will be examined by your group. Several students in the class can volunteer to sit for the interview.

12. Consider the advantages of forming a peer-support group within one of your own classes. Several of you could make a commitment to meet to explore ways to get the most from your training and education. The group could also study together and exchange ideas for future opportunities.

Ethics in Action CD-ROM Exercises

13. Reflect on all of the role-playing situations enacted in the *Ethics in Action* CD-ROM. Putting yourself in the place of the counselor, can you think of any situations in which you would determine that a referral is in the best interests of your client? Consider situations such as sharp value differences between you and your client, a lack of multicultural competence in a particular case, a client to whom you were sexually attracted, or a client who cannot pay you because of losing employment. Select an area where you could envision yourself making a referral and role-play this with another student as the client. Assume that your client does not want to accept the referral and insists on remaining with you.

InfoTrac® College Edition Resources

For additional readings, explore InfoTrac College Edition, our online library. Go to *http://www.infotrac.college.com/wadsworth* and select these key word searches:

psychotherapist competence
training therap*
continuing education for mental health workers
education mental health
education psych*
training AND psychotherapy AND research
techniques in couns*
professional AND licensing AND mental health
professional AND licensing AND couns*
professional AND licensing AND psych*
credentialing mental health

Key words are listed in a form that enables the search engine to locate a wider range of articles in the online university library. Key words should be entered exactly as shown, including asterisks, "W1," "W2," "AND," and other search engine tools.

9

Pre-Chapter Self-Inventory

Directions: For each statement, indicate the response that most closely identifies your beliefs and attitudes. Use the following code:

5 = I *strongly agree* with this statement.
4 = I *agree* with this statement.
3 = I am *undecided* about this statement.
2 = I *disagree* with this statement.
1 = I *strongly disagree* with this statement.

_____1. To protect the client, the supervisor, and the supervisee, ethical guidelines are needed to govern the conduct of counselor supervisors.

_____2. Supervisors should be held legally accountable for the actions of the trainees they supervise.

_____3. Supervisors have the responsibility to monitor and assess a trainee's performance in a consistent and careful manner.

_____4. Working under supervision is one of the most important components of my development as a competent practitioner.

_____5. Supervisors must be sure that trainees fully inform clients about the limits of confidentiality.

_____6. Supervision is best focused on my progress as a practitioner rather than on the client's problems.

_____7. Ideally, supervisory sessions are not aimed at providing therapy for the trainee.

_____8. It is clearly unethical for counselor educators to date their students or other students who are involved in the training program.

_____9. It is acceptable for a supervisor or educator to date former students, once they have completed the program.

Issues in Supervision and Consultation

____10. Supervisees and trainees have a right to know what is expected of them and how they will be evaluated. They also have a right to periodic feedback and evaluation from supervisors so that they have a basis for improving their clinical skills.

____11. It is unethical for counseling supervisors to operate in multiple roles such as mentor, adviser, teacher, and evaluator.

____12. Ethically, supervisors need to clarify their roles and to be aware of potential problems that can develop when boundaries become blurred.

____13. It is unethical for supervisors or counselor educators to provide therapy to a current student or supervisee.

____14. Personal information that trainees share in supervision should remain confidential and never be shared with other faculty members.

____15. Supervisors have a role in advocating for their supervisees and clients in the educational and training settings within which they practice.

____16. Before initiating a contract, consultants may ethically investigate the goals of the agency to determine whether they can support them.

____17. When consultants become aware of value clashes that cannot be resolved, ethical practice dictates that they decline to negotiate a contract.

____18. Consultants need to make an ethical determination whether they are sufficiently trained to offer the services they contract to perform.

____19. In consulting it is almost impossible to avoid dual relationships, because the work involves blending teaching skills and counseling skills as needed in the situation.

____20. Ethical practice requires that consultants inform their consultees about the goals and process of consultation, the limits to confidentiality, the voluntary nature of consultation, the potential benefits, and any potential risks.

Introduction

Supervision is an integral part of training helping professionals and is one of the ways in which trainees can acquire the competence needed to fulfill their professional responsibilities. Supervision is perhaps the most important component in the development of a competent practitioner. It is within the context of supervision that trainees begin to develop a sense of their professional identity and to examine their own beliefs and attitudes regarding clients and therapy. Supervision is a process that involves a supervisor overseeing the professional work of a trainee with three major goals: (1) to enhance the skills and knowledge of the supervisee, (2) to ensure the welfare of the supervisee's clients, and (3) to serve a gatekeeping function for the profession.

As we mentioned in Chapter 8, professional competence is not attained once and for all. Remaining a competent professional demands not only continuing education but also a willingness to obtain periodic supervision when faced with ethical or clinical dilemmas. By consulting experts, practitioners show responsibility in obtaining the assistance necessary to provide the highest quality of care for clients. As practitioners, we can never know all that we might like to know, nor can we attain all the skills required to effectively intervene with all client populations or all types of problems. This is where the processes of supervision and consultation come into play.

Counselors are often expected to function in the roles of both supervisor and consultant. To carry out these roles ethically and effectively, they must have proper training in both areas. The skills used in counseling are not necessarily the same as those needed to adequately supervise trainees or to advise other helping professionals, which implies a need for specific training in how to supervise. Supervision is a well-defined area that is rapidly becoming a specialized field in the helping professions with a developing body of research and an impressive list of publications, and ethical and professional standards are an integral part of the profession of supervision. This chapter explores dilemmas frequently encountered in the fields of supervision and consultation and provides some guidelines for ethical and legal practice in these areas.

Ethical and Legal Issues in Clinical Supervision

The relationship between the clinical supervisor and the trainee (or student) is of critical importance in the development of competent and responsible therapists. If we take into consideration the dependent position of the trainee and the similarities between the supervisory relationship and the therapeutic relationship, the need for guidelines describing the rights of trainees and the responsibilities of supervisors becomes obvious. Although specific guidelines for ethical behavior between a supervisor and trainee have not been delineated in the ethics codes of all professional associations, the Association for Counselor Education and Supervision (ACES) has developed "Ethical Guidelines for Counseling Supervisors" (ACES, 1993, 1995), which address issues such as client welfare and rights, supervisory role, and program administration role. The National Association of Social Workers created "Guidelines for Clinical Social Work Supervision" (NASW, 1994b), which addresses the purpose and intent of supervision, qualifications of supervisors, conduct of supervision, legal issues, and ethical issues.

Some critical ethical issues in supervision are balancing the rights of the clients, the rights and responsibilities of supervisees, and the responsibilities of supervisors to both supervisees and their clients. Tyler and Tyler (1997) maintain that many of the ethical standards pertaining to the client-therapist relationship also apply to the supervisor-supervisee relationship. Informed consent regarding supervision is as essential as informed consent in counseling (which was discussed in Chapter 5). It is beneficial to discuss the rights of supervisees from the beginning of the supervisory relationship, in much the same way as the rights of clients are addressed early in the therapy process. If this is done, the supervisee is empowered to express expectations, make decisions, and become an active participant in the supervisory process. Tyler and Tyler propose a "Bill of Rights" for supervisees that defines the parameters of the supervision process, creates an equitable and mutual relationship, and ensures quality supervision. Specific rights of supervisees include these:

- The right to a supervisory session free from interruptions and distractions.
- The right to be fully informed of supervisors' approaches to supervision.
- The right to confidentiality with regard to supervisee's disclosure as well as that of clients, except as mandated by law.
- The right to continual access to any records maintained during the supervisory relationship.
- The right to offer feedback to supervisors concerning the helpfulness of supervision.
- The right to receive timely feedback, assessment, and evaluation from the supervisor.
- The right to seek consultation from other professionals as necessary.

The Supervisor's Roles and Responsibilities

Supervisors have a responsibility to provide training and supervised experiences that will enable supervisees to deliver ethical and effective services. Supervisors must be well trained, knowledgeable, and skilled in the practice of clinical supervision (Vasquez, 1992). If they do not have training in clinical supervision, it will be difficult for supervisors to ensure that those they supervise are functioning effectively and ethically.

Supervisors are ultimately responsible, *both ethically and legally,* for the actions of their trainees. Therefore, they are cautioned not to supervise more trainees than they can responsibly manage at one time. They must check on trainees' progress and be familiar with their caseloads. Just as practitioners keep case records on the progress of their clients, supervisors should maintain records pertaining to their work with trainees. Supervisees have a right to begin their supervisory experience knowing the conditions that dictate their status and progress. Supervisees need to clearly understand what their responsibilities are and what the supervisors' responsibilities are (Bernard & Goodyear, 1998). Trainees have a right to know what is expected of them and what processes and procedures will be used to evaluate their performance. Furthermore, trainees have an ethical and legal right to periodic feedback and evaluation so that they have a basis for improving their clinical skills (ACA, 1995; ACES, 1993, 1995; NASW, 1994b).

Counseling or clinical supervisors have a position of influence with their supervisees; they operate in multiple roles as teacher, evaluator, counselor, model, mentor, and adviser. It is essential that supervisors monitor their own behavior so as not to misuse the inherent power in the supervisor-supervisee relationship. According to Sherry (1991), supervisors are ethically vulnerable for three main reasons: (1) the power differential between the participants, (2) the "therapylike" quality of the supervisory relationship, and (3) the conflicting roles of the supervisor and supervisees. He points to the multiple roles supervisors are expected to play. Although the requirements of these roles overlap in some cases, they may also conflict. Supervisors are faced with the responsibility of protecting the welfare of the clients, the supervisees, the public, and the profession. Sherry maintains that the clients' welfare comes first, followed by that of the supervisees. Because supervision is like therapy in some ways, Sherry reminds us that there is a risk of harm to both the client and the supervisee from a supervisor's blurred objectivity, impaired judgment, or exploitation. Supervisors are responsible for ensuring compliance with relevant legal, ethical, and professional standards for clinical practice (ACES, 1993, 1995). The main purpose of ethical standards for clinical supervision is to provide behavioral guidelines to supervisors, protect supervisees from undue harm or neglect, and to ensure quality client care (Bernard & Goodyear, 1998). Supervisors can demonstrate these ethical guidelines through the behavior they model in the supervisory relationship.

Responsibilities to supervisees and their clients. Here are some responsibilities of supervisors to supervisees and some specific ways in which supervisors can promote counselor development:

- State the specific objectives of supervision.
- Formulate a sound supervisory contract that clarifies the expectations and parameters of the supervision agreement.
- Negotiate mutual decisions, rather than make unilateral decisions, about the needs of the trainee.
- Perform the role of teacher, counselor, or consultant as appropriate.
- Clarify the supervisory role.
- Integrate knowledge of supervision with one's personal talents or areas of expertise.
- Meet with supervisees on a regular basis to give ongoing evaluation and feedback.

- Evaluate the supervisee's role and conceptual understanding of the therapeutic process.
- Promote the supervisee's ethical and legal knowledge and behavior.
- Interact with counselor trainees in a manner that facilitates their self-exploration, problem-solving ability, and confidence.
- Provide supervisees with guidance in the assessment and treatment of their clients.
- Recognize issues of cultural diversity, including ethnicity/race, gender, sexual orientation, age, disabilities, and religion, and integrate that recognition into their work with trainees.
- Assist supervisees in recognizing their personal limitations so as to protect the welfare of their clients.
- Be aware of the clients being treated by supervisees.
- Teach and model ethical and professional behavior.
- Be familiar with the techniques being employed by the trainees.
- Be sensitive to possible cues that might indicate a client is at risk.
- Maintain confidentiality of clients.
- Maintain the confidentiality of supervisees, and explain the parameters of confidentiality in the supervisory relationship.
- Maintain documentation of supervision.

Supervisors have an evaluative role, and at times faculty members need to be apprised of students' progress. However, personal information that supervisees share in supervision should generally remain confidential. At the very least, supervisees have a right to be informed about what will and will not be shared with others on the faculty. Because supervisors best teach by modeling, it is essential that they demonstrate ethical standards for practice. They need to put ethics in the foreground of their supervisory practices, which can best be done by treating supervisees in a respectful, professional, and an ethical manner. One of the best ways for supervisors to model professional behavior for supervisees is to deal appropriately with confidentiality issues pertaining to supervisees. The primary responsibility of supervisors is to model what they hope to teach (Bernard & Goodyear, 1998).

Methods of supervision. The standards of the APA (1992), NASW (1994b,1999), ACA (1995), and ACES (1993, 1995) require that supervisors demonstrate a conceptual knowledge of supervisory methods and techniques and that they be skilled in using this knowledge to promote the development of trainees. It is essential that supervisors have a clearly developed model of supervision and the methods they employ. We believe that the most important element in the supervisory process is the kind of person the supervisor is. The methods and techniques supervisors use are more likely to be helpful if an effective and collaborative working relationship with supervisees has been established. In much the same way that effective therapists create a climate in which clients can explore their conflicts, supervisors need to establish a collaborative relationship that encourages trainees to reflect on what they are doing.

Fogel (1990), who considers herself a "rebellious supervisor," makes an urgent plea to teach trainees the value of doubting and of creative innovation:

> My whole purpose in supervision has been to create such a safe environment that the trainee can function in his/her own style and feel cherished enough to ask for help when the going gets rough. We can then reflect, explore options, and discover together the process which feels suited to the trainee's present psychic state and skills. (p. 61)

Supervision can be accomplished in a variety of ways. Here Feist (1999) describes some commonly used methods of supervision:

- *Self-report* is one of the most widely used supervisory methods, yet it may be the least useful. This procedure is limited by the supervisee's conceptual and observational ability.
- *Process notes* has the advantages of the self-report but adds a written record explaining the content of the session and the interactional processes.
- *Audiotapes* are a widely used procedure that yields direct and useful information about the supervisee.
- *Videotape* recording allows for an assessment of the subtleties of the interaction between the supervisee and the client.
- *Live supervision,* which is conducted by the supervisor during the supervisee's session with a client, provides the most accurate information about the therapy session.

Styles of supervision. Supervisees at different stages in their professional development may require different styles of supervision. Overholser (1991) points out that an important element in the supervisory process is balancing a directive style and a permissive one. A supervisor's task is to strive for an optimal level of challenge and support. The hope is that the supervisor will promote autonomy without overwhelming the supervisee. Although supervisees may need more direction when they begin their training, it is a good idea to foster a reflective and questioning approach that leads to self-initiated discovery. Overholser applies the Socratic method to supervision, assuming that trainees achieve more insight when they discover a relationship on their own rather than having it explained to them. The Socratic supervisor functions more as a catalyst for exploration than as a lecturer and helps trainees realize that the answers lie within themselves.

When we supervise, we focus on the dynamics between ourselves and our trainees, as well as the dynamics between supervisees and their clients. Here we see a parallel process operating between a counseling model and a supervisory model. Supervisees can learn ways to conceptualize what they are doing with their clients by reflecting on what they are learning about interpersonal dynamics in the supervisory relationship. Although the trainee's ability to assess and treat a client's problems is important, in supervision we are more concerned with the interpersonal aspects that are emerging. In our view, supervisors do well to look beyond the cases trainees bring to the supervisory sessions and focus on the interpersonal dimensions.

As supervisors we oversee the work of our supervisees and help them refine their own insights and clinical hunches. Rather than placing the emphasis on teaching supervisees by giving them information, we strive to help them identify their intuitions and insights. Instead of using our words with supervisees' clients, we hope supervisees will find their own words and develop their voice. Our style of supervision is reflected by the questions we explore: What are you wanting to say to your clients? What direction do you think is most appropriate to take with your clients? What is going on with you as you listen to your clients? How are you reacting to your clients? How is your behavior affecting them? Which clients bring out your own resistances? How are your values manifested by the way you interact with your clients? How might our relationship, in these supervisory sessions, mirror your relationships with your clients? Are you feeling free enough to bring into these supervisory sessions any difficulties you are having with your clients?

Although we see supervision as a separate process from psychotherapy and do not attempt to make training sessions into therapy sessions, the supervisory process can be therapeutic and growth producing. One of the most important goals for clinical supervisors is to promote the supervisee's self-awareness and ability to recognize personal characteristics that could have a negative impact on the therapeutic relationship (Vasquez, 1992). We might add that this goal of promoting self-awareness and independence of supervisees may be inhibited by the emphasis on the supervisor's legal responsibilities and the threat of being involved in a malpractice suit. Because supervisors are responsible for whatever happens to the supervisees' clients, some supervisors may tend to be more directive and controlling. As a way to resolve this dilemma, supervisors might discuss this struggle with their supervisees and with colleagues. Being concerned about liability issues should not prevent supervisors from giving their best efforts to guiding their supervisees.

Ethical Practices of Clinical Supervisors

Ladany, Lehrman-Waterman, Molinaro, and Wolgast (1999) reviewed the literature identifying key ethical guidelines for clinical supervision and conducted a study that examined ethical practices of supervisors. The results of the study indicate that 51% of the 151 supervisees sampled reported what they considered to be at least one ethical violation by their supervisors. The ethical guidelines most frequently violated involved adequate performance evaluation, confidentiality issues relevant to supervision, and ability to work with alternative perspectives. Let's examine some specific ethical guidelines included in the study along with the results.

- *Performance evaluation and monitoring supervisee activities.* It is expected that the supervisor will review actual counseling sessions via videotape or audiotapes and will read the supervisee's case notes; the supervisor should provide ongoing feedback to supervisees. In evaluating supervisors, this was the most frequent ethical violation reported by the supervisees. One third of the study participants perceived that their supervisors did not provide adequate evaluations of their counseling performances.

- *Confidentiality in supervision.* Supervisors are to appropriately handle confidentiality issues in the supervisory relationship. Eighteen percent of the supervisees reported that confidentiality issues were not handled appropriately by their supervisors.
- *Ability to work with alternative perspectives.* Eighteen percent of the supervisees reported that their supervisors were not receptive to theoretical approaches other than their own.
- *Session boundaries and respectful treatment.* Supervisors are to demonstrate respect for supervisees by establishing and maintaining appropriate boundaries. Of all of the participants, 13% reported that their supervisors did not ensure adequate session conditions or respect.
- *Orientation to professional roles.* It is expected that the role and responsibilities of the supervisor and supervisee will be clearly defined. Nine percent of respondents reported that their supervisors never explained the roles and responsibilities of the supervisee and the supervisor.
- *Expertise/competency issues.* The supervisor has the responsibility for making appropriate disclosures to the supervisee when the supervisor or supervisee does not possess the competence to deal with a particular case or situation. Nine percent of the supervisees viewed their supervisors as lacking competence regarding the clients the supervisees were treating.
- *Disclosure to clients.* It is the responsibility of supervisors to ensure adequate disclosure of the supervisee's training status to the supervisee's clients. Eight percent of the supervisees reported that their supervisors did not address the issue of how they were to disclose their student status to clients. In some instances, a supervisee was instructed to refer to himself or herself as staff and not as a student or trainee.
- *Modeling ethical behavior and responding to ethical concerns.* Eight percent of the supervisees reported that modeling and responding to ethical concerns were not provided by their supervisors.
- *Crisis coverage and intervention.* In the event of a crisis, the supervisor is to provide adequate communication with the supervisee and is to provide appropriate supervisory support and guidance. Although crisis intervention methods are taught in the classroom, it is in the context of supervision where the practical reality of crisis work is best learned. Seven percent of the supervisees contended that crisis procedures and policies were not explained to them by supervisors or by the agency where they were doing their fieldwork.
- *Multicultural sensitivity toward clients and supervisees.* It is the responsibility of supervisors to deal appropriately with racial, ethnic, cultural, sexual orientation, and gender issues concerning both clients and supervisees. Seven percent of the supervisees reported that their supervisors were multiculturally insensitive in reference to clients and also that they were multiculturally insensitive to them as supervisees.
- *Dual roles.* It is the responsibility of the supervisor to handle role-related conflicts in an appropriate and ethical manner. Supervisees may be affected by

the multiple roles in which supervisors are engaged, and this blending of roles may influence the supervision process. In this study, 6% of the supervisees reported ethical violations pertaining to dual roles.

- *Termination and follow-up issues.* Supervisors have the responsibility of ensuring the continuity of a client's care and of preventing abandonment of a client. Five percent of supervisees believed their supervisors did not handle termination and follow-up issues appropriately.
- *Differentiating supervision from psychotherapy.* In the supervisory relationship, it is expected that a supervisee's personal issues will be dealt with appropriately and that referrals will be made to a therapist when a supervisee experiences a personal problem that interferes with providing adequate care to the client. According to the participants in this study, only 5% believed that their supervisor failed to adhere to this ethical guideline.
- *Sexual issues.* One percent of the supervisees reported that their supervisors were inappropriate regarding sexual or romantic issues in the supervisory relationship.

Ladany and his colleagues (1999) conclude that clinical supervisors may be in need of education and training regarding ethical guidelines in supervision. Their findings also indicate that supervisors' unethical behaviors often are not noticed or monitored by the agency in which they are employed.

Legal Aspects of Supervision

Three legal considerations in the supervisory relationship are informed consent, confidentiality and its limits, and liability. First, supervisors must see that trainees provide the information to clients that they need to make informed choices. Clients must be fully aware that the counselor they are seeing is a trainee, that he or she is meeting on a regular basis for supervisory sessions, that the client's case may be discussed in group supervision meetings with other trainees, and that sessions may be taped or observed. As Bernard and Goodyear (1998) indicate, by virtue of supervision, supervisors have a relationship with the trainee's clients. Therefore, it is necessary that the client be informed of that relationship in detail. Supervisees' clients certainly should be informed that the counselor is working with supervision and what this involves.

Cobia and Boes (2000) suggest that supervisors make use of professional disclosure statements for supervision so that supervisees are informed of the potential benefits, risks, and expectations of entering into the supervisory relationship. In much the same way that therapists provide their clients with a professional disclosure statement, it is wise for supervisors to inform supervisees about the relevant aspects of the supervision process. McCarthy, Sugden, Koker, Lamendola, Maurer, and Renninger (1995) discuss a practical guide to informed consent in clinical supervision. They recommend addressing the following areas in a written informed consent document: purpose of supervision, professional disclosure statement, practical issues, supervision process, administrative issues, ethical and legal issues, and statement of agreement. McCarthy and her colleagues view informed consent as a crucial aspect of clinical supervision. They suggest that this process is best implemented through written documents and discussion between supervisees and supervisors. By attending to informed consent in the supervision process, the professional development of supervisees will be enhanced, and quality client care will be fostered.

Second, supervisors have a legal and ethical obligation to respect the confidentiality of client communications. Supervision involves discussion of client issues and review of client materials, and it is essential that supervisees respect their clients' privacy by not talking about their clients outside of the context of supervision. By their own behavior, supervisors have a responsibility to model for supervisees appropriate ways of talking about clients and keeping information protected and used only in the context of supervision (Bernard & Goodyear, 1998). Supervisors must make sure that both supervisees and their clients are fully informed about the limits of confidentiality, including those situations in which supervisors have a duty to warn or a duty to protect.

Third, supervisors ultimately bear legal responsibility for the welfare of those clients who are counseled by their trainees. In addition to being ethically vulnerable, supervisors are legally vulnerable to the work performed by those they are supervising. It is incumbent upon supervisors to understand the legal ramifications of their supervisory work. To carry out their ethical and legal responsibilities, supervisors are required to be familiar with each case of every supervisee. Failure to do this is to invite legal action. This requirement may not be practical in the sense that supervisors cannot be cognizant of all details of every case, but they should at least know the direction in which the cases are being taken. Also, university training programs have a responsibility to clients to make some kind of formal assessment of each trainee before allowing the person to counsel clients. Harrar and his colleagues (1990) indicate that supervisors bear both direct liability and vicarious liability. *Direct liability* can be incurred if supervisors are derelict in the supervision of their trainees, if they give trainees inappropriate advice about treatment, or if they give tasks to trainees that exceed their competence. *Vicarious liability* pertains to the responsibilities that supervisors have because of the actions of their supervisees. From both a legal and ethical standpoint, trainees are not expected to assume final responsibility for clients; rather, their supervisors are legally expected to carry the decision-making responsibility and liability.

Just as therapists are vulnerable to clients who may decide to press forward with malpractice actions, so are supervisors open to malpractice litigation against them by the supervisees' clients. Guest and Dooley (1999) point out that supervisors are aware of their vulnerability for malpractice litigation against them due to the actions of supervisees. This has resulted in the reluctance of some professionals to agree to take on supervisory functions. Guest and Dooley suggest that supervisors would do well to practice risk management in supervision much as they do in their therapy practice with clients.

Competence of Supervisors

Today clinical supervisors are more vulnerable and at risk for ethical and legal liability than they were 20 years ago. Yet only recently has the standard for qualifying to be a clinical supervisor included formal course work and supervision of one's work with supervisees. Currently, most psychology and counselor education programs offer a course in supervision at the doctoral level, and some programs provide training for supervisors at the master's level (Polanski, 2000). However, many supervisors do not have formal training in supervision and may rely on the model of supervising they experienced when they were in supervision themselves. Supervisors who are unable to demonstrate that they have achieved competence in clinical supervision are at risk in the litigious environment of today's clinical practice (Miars, 2000).

From both an ethical and legal standpoint, it is essential that supervisors have the education and training to adequately carry out their roles. Course work in theories of supervision, working with difficult supervisees, working with culturally diverse supervisees, and methods of supervision provide a good foundation. The counselor licensure laws in a number of states (Arkansas, Louisiana, Ohio, South Carolina, and Texas) now stipulate that licensed professional counselors who practice supervision are required to have relevant training experiences and course work in supervision. Licensed professional counselors in Ohio who are applying for status as counseling supervisors are required to have a minimum of 3 years of practice as a licensed counselor prior to their application (Polanski, 2000). In California the supervised hours of marriage and family therapy interns and psychology interns are not recognized unless the supervisor has been in practice for at least 2 years and has had a least one continuing education course in supervision. Beginning in 2001, social workers and psychologists in California are required to complete formal course work in supervision to be qualified to function as clinical supervisors. For practitioners to qualify as supervisors in Oregon, a three-credit semester course or a 30-hour continuing education course is minimal, and supervision of supervision is highly desirable (Miars, 2000). Besides course work, counselors need to be provided with training in supervision. Unfortunately, many who function as supervisors do not have the academic training and background to deal with the challenges they will face as supervisors. It is essential that these supervisors acquire the specific knowledge and skills they lack through continuing education.

Polanski (2000) makes a case for teaching supervision at the master's level. Course work in supervision for counselors entering the field can teach them how to ask for what they need and influence their own supervision experiences. They are able to learn about the importance of mutuality in the supervision relationship. In short, students receiving this training become more educated consumers of supervision, and they have a better understanding of the practice of supervision when they take such a role in the future.

In addition to specialized training in methods of supervision, supervisors also need to have an in-depth knowledge of the specialty area in which they will provide supervision. Storm (1994) contends that this expertise is often lacking in those supervising trainees in marriage and family therapy. Most supervisors working with these trainees lack an academic background in marriage and family therapy. Storm concludes that the unique context of this specialty practice creates difficulties for untrained supervisors as they attempt to carry out their roles in an ethical and effective manner. It is unethical for supervisors to offer supervision in areas that are beyond the scope of their practice. On this matter, the NASW (1999) ethical guideline is clear: "Social workers who provide supervision or consultation should have the necessary knowledge and skill to supervise or consult appropriately and should do so only within their areas of knowledge and competence" (3.01a). When supervisees are working outside the area of competence of the supervisor, it is the responsibility of the supervisor to arrange for competent clinical supervision of the cases in question (Cobia & Boes, 2000).

Little research into outcomes related to either the supervisee or the supervisee's clients has been done. This means that the picture of the "good" supervisor that emerges from research is derived primarily from findings regarding supervisee satisfactions and preferences. The good supervisor is one the supervisees most prefer, respond to positively, find satisfactory, and are able to trust. Some of the personal attributes that have been consistently identified as helpful in supervisors include humor, empathy, respect, genuineness, ability to confront, immediacy, concern for supervisee growth and well-being, concern for clients' welfare, availability for self-reflection, flexibility, courage, tolerance, and openness to various styles of learning. In short, good supervisors tend to be available, accessible, affable, and able. The general picture of the good supervisor reveals an individual who is a technically competent professional, with good human relations skills and effective organizational-managerial skills.

Supervision for School Counselors

In their article on clinical supervision in the schools, Crespi, Fischetti, and Butler (2001) state that the viability of clinical supervision as a tool to enhance school counseling has received little attention. With increasing numbers of problems and a greater responsibility for the mental health needs of children and adolescents, it makes sense for schools to carefully examine ways to develop clinical supervision programs dealing with treatment issues. Crespi and colleagues write about the advantages of clinical supervision as an approach to enhancing skills and providing a valuable means of professional development, some of which are as follows:

- Clinical supervision can provide a means for creating an interdisciplinary discussion of children's and adolescents' mental health and for utilizing an array of interventions with different children with different problems.
- Supervision could provide the much needed support and guidance school counselors need when they deal with difficult situations.
- Supervision offers a consistent vehicle to upgrade and refine assessment and counseling skills, and as well, it offers a framework from which to review case interventions.

One excellent way to build supervision opportunities in school settings is to establish community linkages between local schools and university faculty. Faculty in counselor preparation programs are in a good position to advise and educate school counselors on innovative developments in counseling that can be applied to schools.

Multicultural Issues in Supervision

Ethical supervision must include the ways in which individual differences can influence the process. The ACA's (1995) standards dealing with supervision and training call for counselor educators and supervisors to demonstrate knowledge of individual differences with respect to gender, race, ethnicity, culture, sexual orientation, disability, and age and to understand the importance of these characteristics in supervisory relationships and training. *Multicultural supervision* encompasses a broad definition of culture that includes race, ethnicity, socioeconomic status, sexual orientation, religion, gender, and age (Fukuyama, 1994). Supervisors who are functioning ethically and competently are cognizant of and address the salient issues that apply to multicultural supervision (Bernard, 1994). The topic of competence in supervision is incomplete without taking into consideration the role of cultural factors in the supervisory relationship and the competence of supervisors in this area. Bernard and Goodyear (1998) identified the following dimensions of a good model of multicultural supervision: (a) a pluralistic philosophy, (b) cultural knowledge, (c) consciousness raising, (d) experiential training, (e) contact with racial and ethnic minorities, and (f) practicum or internship with minorities. Certainly, supervisors have an ethical responsibility to become aware of the complexities of a multicultural society (see Chapter 4).

Racial issues in supervision. There is a price to be paid for ignoring racial and ethnic factors in supervision. If supervisors do not assist supervisees in addressing racial issues, their clients may be denied the opportunity to explore these issues in their therapy. D. A. Cook (1994) calls for routinely including discussions of racial identity attitudes as part of both therapy and supervisory relationships. The supervisor's recognition of racial issues can serve as a model for supervisees in their counseling relationships. Reflecting on racial interactions in supervision offers a cognitive framework for supervisees to generalize to their counseling practices. Cook suggests that supervisors might raise these questions: "When did you notice the client's race?" "How did this affect you?" "What did you do in response to the client's race?" According to Cook, unspoken assumptions regarding race and cultural influences of those involved in the supervision process can affect all aspects of supervision including establishment of the relationship and expectations for supervision, assignment of clients, conceptualization of clients and treatment planning, recommendations for client referrals, and the evaluation of supervisees.

Priest (1994) focuses on the supervisor's role in enhancing the supervisee's respect for diversity. Because of the power dynamics inherent in the supervisory relationship, Priest believes it is the supervisor's responsibility to serve as the catalyst for facilitating discussions about multicultural issues. He points out that too often supervisors emphasize client similarities and minimize racial and cultural differences. If trainees do not understand the cultural context in which their clients live, Priest believes the chances are increased that trainees' behavior will result in clients' prematurely terminating counseling.

Toward multiculturally effective supervision. In her pilot study to define the issues in multicultural supervision with visible ethnic minority trainees, Fukuyama (1994) explored critical incidents in multicultural supervision. Respondents were asked how to make supervision more multiculturally sensitive and effective. Here are some of their suggestions:

- Have supervisors initiate discussion of multicultural issues as a basic part of supervision.
- Provide increased training for supervisors in working with multicultural issues, including opportunities to tape supervision sessions for self-reflection.
- Provide more supervisors with multicultural experience.
- Involve all personnel within an agency in multicultural training.
- Train supervisors to develop a genuine respect for and acceptance of cultural diversity. Caution them about the problems involved in trying to be "politically correct" and overemphasizing diversity issues.
- Provide a training model for "prejudice reduction" that could be used with trainees' clients to help them deal with racism and prejudice.
- Discuss multicultural issues in an intern seminar under the supervisor's guidance.

Fukuyama (1994) found two emerging themes in multicultural supervision: culture and cultural differences, and racism and racial identity issues. It is essential that supervisors receive training in multicultural issues, including having course work, practical experiences in supervision, research activities, and multicultural counseling (Fukuyama, 1994; Priest, 1994).

Constantine (1997) proposes a framework to facilitate learning multicultural competencies in supervision relationships. Semi-structured questions are used to assist trainees in identifying their own cultural group identities and acknowledging the extent to which these identities influence their interactions in both supervision and counseling relationships. Ideally, this framework is introduced during the early stages of the supervision relationship because it helps to establish rapport between supervisors and supervisees. It also highlights the importance of paying attention to multicultural issues in the supervision process, and it sensitizes students to ethical issues. In using Constantine's framework, supervisors and supervisees discuss their responses to this series of questions:

- What are the main demographic variables that make up my cultural identity?
- What worldviews—assumptions and values—do I bring to the supervision relationship based on my cultural identity?
- What value systems are inherent in my approach to supervision? What strategies and techniques do I use in supervision?
- What knowledge and skills do I possess about the worldviews of supervisors/supervisees who have different cultural identities from me?
- What are some of the issues and challenges I face in working with supervisors/supervisees who are culturally different from me? How do I address these issues?
- In what ways would I like to improve my abilities in working with culturally diverse supervisors/supervisees?

Although this framework was initially developed for use in the early stages of the supervision process, Constantine (1997) states that it can be used to help supervisors and supervisees continue their discussion of multicultural concerns and differences throughout the supervisory relationship.

Implications for training and supervision. Bernard (1994) suggests the following parameters of training and supervision to achieve multicultural competence:

- Supervisees must be at least as multiculturally sensitive as their clients, and supervisors must be at least as multiculturally competent as their supervisees.
- Training programs need to determine a trainee's readiness for clinical experience and for entry-level practice.
- Supervisors need to understand both developmental supervision models and racial identity models. It is essential that supervisors acquire skills in knowing when and how to challenge supervisees on multicultural issues.
- Supervisors themselves need to seek consultation if they hope to enhance their own multicultural development.

On a more personal note, one of our former students, who is now in a doctoral program in counseling, shared her views with us about the importance of including multicultural considerations in supervision. She reported an experience in a group supervision session with a fellow student (an Asian American whom we will call Hoa). The supervisor, who was generally a sensitive person, perceived Hoa's quiet nature in a negative light and questioned her level of empathy. Hoa attributed her style of relating to colleagues and clients to her cultural background. This is but one example of how supervisors may hold assumptions that are out of their awareness that can be detrimental to both supervisees and to their clients. This also illustrates the need for supervisors to be sensitive to their blind spots, which can often be achieved by participating in their own supervision.

To develop the knowledge and skills to work effectively in multicultural counseling situations, trainees need to understand their own level of racial and cultural identity. Furthermore, they need to recognize how their attitudes and behaviors affect their clients. Good supervision will enable trainees to explore the impact that diversity issues may have on their counseling style.

Gender issues in supervision: Feminist supervision. Carta-Falsa and Anderson (2001) describe a collaborative model of clinical supervision that is based on genuine dialogue between supervisor and supervisee. In this active collaborative supervision, the supervisee is seen as resourceful, with the supervisor's role to reinforce the strengths of the supervisee. In this new paradigm, power is shared between the supervisor and supervisee. Together they participate in acquiring, sharing, and reshaping knowledge. According to Carta-Falsa and Anderson (2001), this collaborative spirit leads to an empowered relationship that is characterized by a sense of safety. This sense of trust and security forms the basis for increased risk taking, higher levels of performance, and greater individual confidence. This model is very similar to the feminist approach to supervision, which also addresses the role of power in the supervisory relationship.

Gender issues occupy a central place in the supervision process. Both feminist supervision and multicultural supervision pay attention to the power dynamic in the supervisory relationship as well as to the relationship between client and counselor. For example, instead of the supervisor telling supervisees what to do, the supervisor can help supervisees think about their clients in new ways, formulate their own interpretations, and devise their own interventions. Porter and Vasquez (1997) describe the feminist supervision model and emphasize the collaborative aspects of supervision:

> Feminist supervision is a collaborative, respectful process, personal but unintrusive, balanced between supervisory responsibility and supervisee autonomy. Feminist supervision emphasizes an open discussion and analysis of power dynamics, and targets the best interests of the supervisee. It is a process that remains focused on the social context of the lives of the client, supervisee, and supervisor. (p. 169)

Porter and Vasquez (1997, pp. 162–167) identify nine principles that guide feminist supervision:

1. Feminist supervisors are proactive in analyzing power dynamics and differentials between supervisor and supervisee, model the use of power in the service of the supervisee, and vigilantly avoid abuses of power. This principle is a hallmark of feminist supervision as it addresses the power dynamics of the supervisory relationship. It is the supervisor's responsibility to address the power differential in the supervisory relationship and, to the extent possible, minimize it.

2. Feminist supervision is based on a mutually respectful and collaborative relationship. This does not imply an equal relationship, however, because supervisors do have evaluative responsibilities. Supervisees are provided with informed consent, and diversity perspectives are encouraged. To the extent possible, supervisees develop learning goals and objectives and choose client populations with whom to work.

3. Feminist supervisors facilitate reflexive interactions and supervisee self-examination by modeling openness, authenticity, reflexivity, and the value of lifelong learning and self-examination. Supervisors are willing to explore their own motivations, attitudes, and potential countertransference that could affect the supervisory relationship.

4. Supervision occurs in a social context that attends to and emphasizes the diversity of women's lives and context. Unfortunately, the world does not attend to women's lives equally with men's lives. One of the tasks of feminist supervision is to balance the need for attention to and redefinition of women's gender roles without excluding or demonizing men.

5. Feminist supervisors attend to the social construction of gender and the role of language in maintaining a gendered society. Feminist supervisors are attuned to external factors as well as internal dynamics that influence the client's concerns. For example, if a client has an eating disorder, supervisors will suggest that it is important to consider societal messages about women's bodies. Feminist supervisors look for the supervisee's social constructions of gender that might influence their work with their clients. An example here would be a supervisee who assumes that a female client is dysfunctional if she does not conform to the traditional view of a woman as mother, caretaker, and homemaker.

6. Another hallmark of feminist supervision is that supervisors advance and model the principle of advocacy and activism. Supervisors guide their supervisees into thinking about their role and power in influencing the systems in which they work. Feminist supervisors are aware of the fine balance between imposing their beliefs and being apolitical in supervision.

7. Feminist supervisors maintain standards that ensure their supervisees' competent and ethical practice. Supervisors help their supervisees to appreciate the complex nature of ethical dilemmas, and they discuss ways to prevent ethical breaches. Furthermore, they assume responsibilities for challenging sexist and racist attitudes and behaviors of their supervisees, including the negative use of stereotypes and the misuse of diagnoses.

8. Feminist supervisors attend to the developmental shifts occurring in the supervisory process and provide input as a function of the skill level, developmental level, and maturational level of the supervisee. Supervisors encourage both accountability and independence on the part of their supervisees as they develop maturity and competencies. Supervisors monitor their own authoritarian supervisory practices.

9. Feminist supervisors advocate for their supervisees and clients in the educational and training settings within which they practice. Supervisors recognize that the feminist tenet of working for social change often originates in their own institution.

With which of these principles do you find yourself in most agreement? Do you see any distinction between these feminist principles and the principles of any effective approach to supervision? Are there any distinct aspects to feminist supervision? In your view, how are the concerns of the feminist supervision model reflecting broader multicultural concerns? To what degree is supervision ethical if it does not take into consideration gender issues and cultural issues?

Multiple Roles and Relationships in the Supervisory Process

The ACES standards (1993, 1995) state that counseling supervisors are expected to possess the personal and professional maturity to play multiple roles. Although multiple roles and relationships are common in the context of training and supervision, it is essential for supervisors to thoroughly discuss and process issues relevant to these multiple roles with their supervisees (Ladany et al., 1999). Ethically, supervisors need to clarify their roles and to be aware of potential problems that can develop when boundaries become blurred. As Herlihy and Corey (1997) point out, unless the nature of the supervisory relationship is clearly defined, both the supervisor and the supervisee may find themselves in a difficult situation at some point in their relationship. If the supervisor's objectivity becomes impaired, the supervisee will not be able to make maximum use of the process. If the relationship evolves into a romantic one, the entire supervisory process becomes confounded, with the supervisee sooner or later alleging exploitation.

The crux of the issue of multiple-role relationships in the training and supervisory process is the potential for abuse of power. Like therapy clients, students and supervisees are in a vulnerable position and can be harmed by an educator or supervisor who exploits them, misuses power, or crosses appropriate boundaries. The ACA (1995) standard is relevant to this discussion:

> Counselors clearly define and maintain ethical, professional, and social relationship boundaries with their students and supervisees. They are aware of the differential in power that exists and the student's or supervisee's possible incomprehension of that power differential. Counselors explain to students and supervisees the potential for the relationship to become exploitative. (F.1.b.)

In their study of faculty-student relationships, Bowman, Hatley, and Bowman (1995) assessed both faculty and student perceptions regarding dual or multiple relationships in mentoring, friendships, monetary interactions, informal social interactions, and romantic-sexual relationships. They admit that certain multiple relationships are unavoidable in most training programs. Rather than viewing multiple relationships as inherently unethical, Bowman and her colleagues propose that it is best to examine the behavior of the persons who are involved in these relationships. Apart from sexual dual relationships with students and supervisees, which are clearly unethical, a wide range of dual and multiple relationships exist that are part and parcel of supervision and training of therapists. It is misleading to mix these nonsexual dual or multiple relationships with unethical sexual relationships. At its best, professional training is responsible for teaching skills that enable the supervisor to ethically manage situations involving multiple roles and relationships.

Burian and O'Connor Slimp (2000) point out that multiple-role relationships may at first appear benign, and sometimes even beneficial, yet they pose some risks to interns and training staff. For example, the mentoring that occurs between faculty and students (and between supervisors and supervisees) often includes social elements, which can be beneficial to the trainee. Burian and O'Connor Slimp's decision-making model pertaining to social multiple-role relationships between interns and their trainers is designed to raise awareness of the issues involved in these relationships and provide a basis for evaluating their potential for harm. These authors suggest ending or postponing the social relationship if more than a minimal risk of harm exists. The ultimate ethical responsibility rests with the individual with the greatest power.

In their discussion of faculty-student dual relationships, Biaggio, Paget, and Chenoweth (1997) note that overlapping roles are to be expected. They add that faculty-student relationships are not static. Students progress from the beginning stages, to graduation, and to becoming colleagues with faculty members. Biaggio and her colleagues present three general guidelines for faculty to attend to in maintaining ethical relationships with students. First, faculty need to recognize the potential for harm in dual relationships with their students, and they need to be aware that they hold a position of power and authority over students. Because dual and overlapping relationships are unavoidable in educational settings, careful monitoring is essential so that students are not harmed.

Second, a framework is necessary for evaluating appropriate and inappropriate conduct. An ethical relationship with a student is one in which these conditions are met: (a) educational standards are maintained, (b) educational experiences are provided for the student, and (c) care is taken to avoid exploitation of the student.

Third, emphasis is placed on establishing and maintaining a climate for ethical relationships between faculty and students. Perhaps most important is that faculty and administrators model appropriate and ethical relationships with other professionals, students, and clients. When faculty model ethical behavior, they bring about increased awareness of ethical concerns in both educational and professional settings.

Both faculty and supervisors play a critical role in helping counselor trainees understand the dynamics of balancing multiple roles and managing dual relationships. Although students may learn about dual relationships during their academic work, it is generally not until they are engaged in fieldwork experiences and internships that they are required to grapple with these boundary issues (Herlihy & Corey, 1997).

Supervisors must not exploit students and trainees or take unfair advantage of the power differential that exists in the context of training. Managing multiple roles ethically is the responsibility of the supervisor. We think supervisors have a much better chance of managing boundaries in their professional work if they are able to take care of their boundaries in their personal lives. Supervisors who are able to establish appropriate personal and professional boundaries are in a good position to teach students how to develop appropriate boundaries for themselves. Next we look at sexual dual relationships in training and supervision.

Sexual Intimacies During Professional Training

In their national survey on sexual intimacy in counselor education and supervision, G. M. Miller and Larrabee (1995) found that counseling professionals who were sexually involved with a supervisor or an educator during their training later viewed these experiences as being more coercive and more harmful to a working relationship than they did at the time the sex occurred. Perceptual changes took place over time with respect to how students were affected by becoming sexually involved with people who were training them, which raises questions about their willingness to freely consent to such relationships and how prepared they were to deal with the ethics of such intimacies. Moreover, it seems clear that educators and supervisors have professional power and authority long after direct training ends.

Hammel, Olkin, and Taube (1996), who studied student-educator sex in doctoral training programs in psychology, also found that respondents were, in retrospect, more likely to view sexual relationships as coercive, ethically problematic, and a hindrance to the working relationship compared to how they viewed them at the time they occurred. Clear power differentials exist between educators and students. The typical relationship is between an older male professor and a younger female graduate student. Both G. M. Miller and Larrabee (1995) and Hammel and his colleagues (1996) take the position that engaging in sexual behavior with students and supervisees is highly inappropriate and contrary to the spirit of the ethics codes of most professional organizations and educational institutions (see the box titled Sexual Relations Are Prohibited between Supervisor and Trainee). Additionally, Hammel and his colleagues make a strong recommendation for the APA to take a more encompassing stand against sexual relationships during training and to forbid them outright. Miller and Larrabee (1999) suggest that educators and supervisors be aware of their position of power and function as professional role models. They add that, because of the detrimental impact of sexual involvements during training, educators and supervisors ought to refrain from any sexual involvements with students and supervisees.

Supervisory relationships have qualities in common with instructor-student and therapist-client relationships. In all of these professional relationships, it is the professional who occupies the position of greater power. Thus, it is the professional's responsibility to establish and maintain appropriate boundaries and to explore with the trainee (student, supervisee, or client) ways to prevent potential problems associated with boundary issues. If problems do arise, the professional has the responsibility to take steps to resolve them in an ethical manner.

Sexual Relations Are Prohibited Between Supervisor and Trainee

- "Supervisors should not participate in any form of sexual contact with supervisees. Supervisors should not engage in any form of social contact or interaction which would compromise the supervisor-supervisee relationship. Dual relationships with supervisees that might impair the supervisor's objectivity and professional judgment should be avoided and/or the supervisory relationship terminated" (ACES, 1993).
- "Counselors do not engage in sexual relationships with students or supervisees and do not subject them to sexual harassment" (ACA, 1995, F.1.c.).
- "Social workers should not engage in any dual or multiple relationships with supervisees in which there is a risk of exploitation of or potential harm to the supervisee" (NASW, 1999, 3.01.c.).
- "Marriage and family therapists do not engage in sexual intimacy with students or supervisees during the evaluative or training relationship between the therapist and student or supervisee. Should a supervisor engage in sexual activity with a former supervisee, the burden of proof shifts to the supervisor to demonstrate that there has been no exploitation or injury to the supervisee" (AAMFT, 2001).
- "Psychologists do not engage in sexual relationships with students or supervisees in training over whom the psychologist has evaluative or direct authority, because such relationships are so likely to impair judgment or be exploitative" (APA, 1992, 1.19.b.).

The core ethical issue is the difference in power and status between educator and student or supervisor and supervisee and the exploitation of that power. When supervisees first begin counseling, they are typically naive and uninformed with respect to the complexities of therapy. They frequently regard their supervisors as experts, and thus, they have a dependence on their supervisors that may make it difficult to resist sexual advances. Supervisees may disclose personal concerns and intense emotions during supervision, much as they might in a therapeutic situation. The openness of supervisees and the trust they place in their supervisors can be exploited by supervisors who choose to satisfy their own psychological or sexual needs at the expense of their supervisees.

Assume that you are a trainee and that your clinical supervisor consistently harasses you sexually, both verbally and behaviorally. During your individual supervision sessions the supervisor frequently acts flirtatious toward you. You get the distinct impression that your evaluations will be more favorable if you "play the game." What course of action might you take in such a situation? Is there a difference between sexual harassment and consensual sexual relationships, or are all sexual advances in unequal power relationships really a form of sexual harassment? Can there ever be consensual sex with such a power differential?

◆ **The case of Augustus.** Augustus meets weekly with his professor, Amy, for individual supervision. With only 3 weeks remaining in the semester, Augustus confesses to having a strong attraction to Amy and says he finds it difficult to maintain professional distance with her. Amy discloses that she, too, feels an attraction. But she is sensitive to the professional boundaries governing their relationship, and she tells him it would be inappropriate for them to have any other relationship until the semester ends. She lets him know that she would be open to further discussion about a dating relationship at that point. Even though he will still be in the program, Amy says that she will no longer have a supervisory role with him, nor will she be evaluating his status in the program.

- What are your thoughts on this situation? List them and explain.
- Do you think Amy handled her attraction to Augustus in the best way possible? Explain your response.
- If you were a colleague of Amy's and heard about this situation from another student, what would you do?
- Is the fact that Amy will no longer be supervising Augustus sufficient to eliminate the imbalance of power in the relationship? Do you think it would be appropriate for them to date each other while he is still a student in the program? after he graduates?

Commentary. We wonder how Amy's sexual attraction toward Augustus affected her supervision prior to acknowledging these feelings. We also wonder about her motivation for disclosing her attraction with only three supervisory sessions remaining. The sexual attractions were most likely influencing supervision, even before being acknowledged. Rather than disclosing her feelings of attraction, it would have been more appropriate for Amy to seek consultation once she became aware of her attraction.

Trainees do need to have a safe environment in which they can discuss sexual attractions they may be having for their clients. They need to be reassured that these feelings in themselves are human and harmless but that acting on them is always inappropriate and unethical.

Ethical Issues in Combining Supervision and Counseling

Supervisors play multiple roles in the supervision process, and the boundaries between therapy and supervision are not always clear. In the literature on supervision, there seems to be basic agreement that the supervision process should concentrate on the supervisee's professional development rather than on personal concerns and that supervision and counseling have different purposes. However, there is a lack of consensus and clarity about the degree to which supervisors can ethically deal with the personal issues of supervisees. Supervisory relationships are a complex blend of professional, educational, and therapeutic relationships. This complex process can become increasingly complicated when supervisors are involved in certain multiple roles with trainees. It is the supervisor's responsibility to help trainees identify how their personal dynamics are likely to influence their work with clients, yet it is not the proper role of supervisors to serve as personal counselors for supervisees. Combining the roles of supervising and counseling often presents conflicts (Corey & Herlihy, 1996c; Pope & Vasquez, 1998; Whiston & Emerson, 1989).

As personal problems or limitations become evident, training professionals are ethically obliged to encourage and challenge trainees to face and deal with these barriers that could inhibit their potential as helpers (Herlihy & Corey, 1997). However, this discussion should emanate from the work of the trainee with the client. Sometimes the personal concerns of the supervisee are part of the problem presented in supervision. In such cases, the safety and welfare of the client would require the supervisor to pay some attention to the supervisee's personal issue. Supervision could involve assisting the supervisee in identifying personal concerns so that these concerns do not become the client's problem. Although discussing a trainee's personal issues may appear to be similar to therapy, the purpose is to facilitate the trainee's ability to work successfully with clients. When personal concerns are discussed in supervision, the goal is not to solve the trainee's problem. This generally requires further exploration in personal therapy that is beyond the scope of supervision. If the trainee needs or wants personal therapy, the best course for a supervisor to follow is to make a referral to another professional. We now consider two specific cases.

◆ **The case of Hartley.** During a supervision hour, Hartley confides to his supervisor that his 5-year personal relationship has just ended and that he is in a great deal of pain. As he describes in some detail what happened, he becomes very emotional. Hartley expresses his concern about his ability to work with clients, especially those who are struggling with relationships. Here are how five supervisors might have dealt with Hartley's concerns:

Supervisor A: I'm sorry you're hurting, but I feel the need to use this time to help you work with your clients. I can see no way for you to refer your clients at this point without serious repercussions for them.

Supervisor B: [After listening to Hartley for some time and acknowledging his pain] I know it is difficult for you to work with your clients. I know you are in therapy, and I suggest that you increase the frequency of your sessions to give you an opportunity to deal with your own pain.

Supervisor C: That must be very painful. Do you want to talk about it? Because what is going on with you interferes with your ability to be present with clients, I think it is essential that we work with your pain. [The more the supervisor works with Hartley's pain, the more they tap into other problems in his life. Three weeks later the supervision time still involves Hartley's hurt and crisis.]

Supervisor D: I see you are very affected by the changes in your life. I am glad that you can see how this may affect your work with clients. Can we spend a little time discussing how your experience may create a problem in your dealings with clients?

Supervisor E: This is obviously very difficult and emotional for you. What specifically are you afraid may happen with you when helping clients with similar problems?

- Which of the five responses comes closest to your own, and why?
- How might you have responded to Hartley?

- Do you think any of these five responses crossed the boundary between supervision and personal therapy? Explain.

◆ **The case of Greta.** Ken is a practicing therapist as well as a part-time supervisor in a counseling program. One of his supervisees, Greta, finds herself in a personal crisis after she learns that her mother has been diagnosed with terminal cancer. Much of her internship placement involves working with hospice patients. She approaches Ken and lets him know that she feels unable to continue doing this work. He is impressed with her therapeutic skills and thinks that it would be most unfortunate for her to interrupt her education at this point. He also assumes that he can more effectively deal with her personal crisis because of their trusting relationship. For the next four supervision sessions, Ken focuses almost exclusively on Greta's personal problems. As a result of his help, Greta recovers her stability and is able to continue working with the hospice patients, with no apparent adverse effects for either them or her.

- What are your thoughts on the problem and the solution Ken chose? Explain.
- What are your reactions to Ken blending the roles of supervisor and counselor?
- What potential ethical issues, if any, would you see if Ken had recommended that Greta temporarily discontinue her field placement and enter therapy with him in his private practice?
- If Ken recommended that Greta see another therapist for her personal therapy but she refused on the ground that he knew her best, would that make a difference?
- Do you see another way of dealing with this situation?
- Is it ever appropriate for supervisors to blend the roles of supervisor and therapist? Why or why not?

Commentary. It is our position that the emphasis of supervision needs to be on the enhancement of supervisees' work with their clients. Because we believe in the notion of countertransference, we think trainees' own issues can be stimulated by their clients. Therefore, the task of supervision sometimes involves attending to the personal dynamics of supervisees. We see this as a necessary part of supervision. For instance, with Greta, we would attend to the pain that is triggered by her work, yet we would not explore in an in-depth way the unfinished business she might have with her mother. With Hartley, we would be sensitive to his pain, yet we would not pursue the historical roots of his problem. Supervision requires a focus on the here and now. Past concerns are more appropriately explored in personal therapy.

Educators Who Counsel Students

There is no clear answer to the ethical question raised by counselor educators who provide counseling for their students. As we mentioned in Chapter 2, many professional programs strongly recommend, if not require, a personal therapeutic experience. Some programs expect students to undergo individual therapy for a time, and other programs provide a growth-group experience. At the very least, students have a right to know of these requirements before they make a commitment to begin a program. Further, we believe students should generally be allowed to decide what type of therapeutic experience is most appropriate for them.

Many professional codes have a standard that addresses the ethical issue of educators and supervisors who offer their services as therapists to students and supervisees. For example, the AAMFT (2001) code states: "Marriage and family therapists do not provide therapy to current students or supervisees" (4.2). The practice of faculty members' providing counseling for students for a fee is highly questionable. Some situations are not so clear-cut, however. Once students complete a program, for example, what are the ethics of a psychology professor taking them on as clients? Can it still be argued that the prior role as educator might negatively affect the current role as therapist? If the former student and the professor/therapist agree that there are no problems, is a therapeutic relationship ethically justified? To clarify your position on this issue, reflect on this case.

◆ **The case of Brent.** A psychology professor, Hilda, teaches counseling classes, supervises interns, and also provides individual therapy at the university counseling center. One of her graduate students, Brent, approaches her with a request for personal counseling. Even though she tells him of her concern over combining roles, he is persuasive and adds that he trusts her and sees no problem in being both her student and her counselee.

- What issues, if any, ethical or otherwise, do you see in this case?
- Would it make a difference if Brent had approached her for counseling after he had completed the course with her?
- Would the situation take on a different dimension if the professor had a private practice and charged Brent a fee for her service?
- Assume that Hilda was leading a therapy group during the semester and that Brent wanted to join the group. Is being a client in a group different from being an individual client?
- Do you see any potential for exploitation in this case?
- Would it make a difference if there was a lack of availability of other counseling resources in the area?

Clarifying your stance. What is your position on the potential ethical and legal issues raised in these brief scenarios?

- Your supervisor does not provide what you consider to be adequate supervision. You are left mainly on your own with a difficult caseload. The staff members where you work also have overwhelming caseloads. When you do get time with a supervisor, he or she also seems overwhelmed with responsibilities. Thus, you do not get enough time to discuss your cases. What would you be inclined to do?

- You have a conflict with your supervisor over the most ethical way to deal with a client. What would you do?
- You do not get adequate feedback on your performance as a trainee. At the end of the semester your supervisor gives you a negative evaluation. What potential ethical and legal issues might be involved? What might you do or say?
- Do you think it is unethical for supervisors to initiate social or sexual relationships with trainees after they have graduated (and when the supervisors have no professional obligations to the trainees)? Explain your position.
- If during the course of your supervision you became aware that personal problems were interfering with your ability to work effectively with clients, what would you be inclined to do?
- What are the main problems with multiple relationships in supervision? What potential problems do you see, and how might you resolve them? Do you think all such relationships in supervision should be minimized or even avoided entirely?
- What possible benefits, if any, do you see when supervisors combine a multiplicity of roles such as teacher, mentor, counselor, consultant, evaluator, and supervisor?

Ethical and Professional Issues in Consultation

Consultation is becoming a specialized professional process, and it is being carried out by many different groups in diverse work settings. Wallace and Hall (1996) offer this definition of consultation, which generalizes across the various psychological groups involved in delivering consulting services:

> Psychological consultation involves a broad helping approach in which qualified psychological consultants help consultees (1) resolve work-related issues pertaining to individuals, clients, or programs that they are responsible for, (2) become active agents in achieving solutions to problems, or (3) strengthen consultees' work-related competencies to address similar issues in the future. (p. 10)

For the most part, professionals who function in the role of consultants are involved in collaborative forms of consultation that aim at improving the mental health of individuals and the functioning of organizations (Brown, 1993). Consultants often work with individuals and small groups in schools, agencies, and businesses and share expertise with others in the helping professions so that they can better serve their own clients. This process is aimed at helping people work more effectively on the individual, group, organizational, or community level. Consultants assist consultees with immediate problems and also try to improve their ability to solve future problems.

Based on a survey of the literature on the nature of consultation, Dougherty (2000, pp. 11–12) found general agreement on these common characteristics of consultation:

- The consultant provides indirect service to the client by providing direct service to consultees to better serve their own clients.
- Participation in the consultation process should be voluntary by all the parties involved.
- Consultees have the freedom to decide what they will do with the suggestions and recommendations of the consultant.
- The relationship between the consultee and the consultant, at its best, is a collaboration of peers who are equal in power.
- Consultation is a temporary process. Depending on the type, consultation may range from a single session to multiple sessions.
- Consultation is primarily aimed at problems with work or caretaking as opposed to personal concerns (such as the consultee's marital discord or depression). For example, consultants might provide training workshops for counselors and social workers in an agency. The focus of consultation could be on learning to recognize and deal effectively with job-related stress that can easily interfere with one's professional functions.
- Consultants can take on a variety of roles depending on the nature of consultation and the desired outcomes of consultation.
- Consultation typically occurs in an organizational context.

The Need for Ethical Standards for Consultants

The ethics codes of most helping professions offer only limited guidelines for the practice of consultation. Consultants are faced with many ethical and legal dilemmas, and they carry a heavy responsibility for their actions and the decisions they make. Wallace and Hall (1996) believe that most writers in the field of psychological consulting agree that a consultants' code of ethics is urgently needed. The existing ethics codes of the various professional organizations do not sufficiently address the complexity of ethical issues consultants encounter, nor do these codes provide clear directions for consultants. It would be a step forward if consultants had a set of ethical standards to ensure that consumers received professional service.

Wubbolding (1991) mentions several pitfalls facing consultants and offers some useful guidelines for responsible practice:

- Consultants need to identify their *real client,* for the expectations of the manager and of the participants are frequently quite different.
- The cultural context in which consultation occurs is important. In Asian cultures, for example, consultants may be expected to assume a more directive role in their dealings with consultees.
- Creating a job for oneself is a pitfall that a consultant needs to monitor. The goal is to help people acquire skills that will lead to independence rather than to create a niche for the consultant.
- Even though the optimal consultant-consultee relationship is an equal one, the potential for dual relationships exists; these can be problematic from both a business and a professional perspective.

Dougherty (2000) describes a number of ethical and professional issues that pertain to consultation in the human-services professions: values, multicultural issues, consultant competence and training, the consultation relationship, the rights of consultees, and consultation in groups. We now look more closely at each of these ethical issues in consultation. Our discussion is based on material from a variety of sources (Dougherty, 2000; Jackson & Hayes, 1993; Newman, 1993; Remley, 1993; Wallace & Hall, 1996).

Values issues in consulting. A major professional issue for consultants is the degree to which their personal values will have an impact on their actions and decisions in the consultation process. It is essential that consultants understand how their values influence the practice of consultation.

Ethical practice demands that consultants investigate the goals of an agency before agreeing upon a contract to offer consultation services so that they can determine whether or not they can fulfill the terms of the contract (Wallace & Hall, 1996). When consultants become aware of differences in values that cannot be resolved, or a clear difference in expectations, the ethical course to follow is to decline the contract. This approach prevents arriving at an insoluble value conflict in the middle of the consulting contract. Because of a difference between the values of the consultant and the agency hiring the consultant, referral is sometimes in order.

Value conflicts can arise at any stage of the consultation process. Consulting involves multiple parties with diverse and often competing interests and priorities, and it can be expected that value conflicts will occur among various sectors within an organization. Because consultation generally occurs in a systems context, what is good for an agency or an organization may not always be good for the individuals employed in that system (Wallace & Hall, 1996). The challenge of dealing with the balance between the system as a whole and the individuals within it often demands a stance of openness on the consultant's part in addressing different values and in making key choices. It is critical that difficult choices be made *with* consultees rather than *for* them by the consultant acting alone.

Multicultural issues in consultation. Most ethics codes make specific mention of the practitioner's responsibility to consider the cultural context of delivering professional services. Ethical practice entails the willingness of consultants to demonstrate sensitivity to and respect for cultural differences that apply when they offer services to diverse clients in a variety of settings. If consultants do not take into consideration diversity issues, the quality of their services is bound to be negatively affected. The NASW (1999) has a relevant guideline: "Social workers who provide supervision or consultation are responsible for setting clear, appropriate, and culturally sensitive boundaries" (3.01b).

Just as cultural awareness is critical in the practice of counseling, so is it basic to effective consultation. Jackson and Hayes (1993) state that a broader multicultural training program is needed for consultants. Consultants need training in diverse worldviews, an awareness of differences in reasoning patterns, an understanding of variations in communication patterns, and an awareness of one's capabilities to effect change. If students are not exposed to training in the multicultural dimensions of consultation, they will have only a limited ability to reach members of diverse racial, ethnic, and cultural backgrounds. Jackson and Hayes conclude: "To continue down the existing training and consulting path using monocultural philosophies and strategies, consultants, along with the profession of consultation, will be seen as ineffective, nonresponsive, and potentially identified as nonessential" (p. 147).

Competence and training in consultation. It is imperative that consultants have adequate education and training to perform the services for which they intend to contract. Furthermore, they are ethically bound to assume responsibility for keeping abreast of theoretical and technical developments in their field. The codes of ethics of the ACA (1995) and the APA (1992) recommend that consultants deliver only those services that they are competent to perform. Consultants should present their professional qualifications to avoid misrepresenting themselves. Consultants need to recognize their own personal and professional limitations, which entails knowing and appreciating the boundaries of their competence. Prior to accepting a consulting role, consultants need to decide whether their competence is adequate for a particular project. If consultants realize that they do not have the competence to undertake an assignment, they should decline providing consultation services and make an appropriate referral. Furthermore, consultants need to be reasonably certain that the organization employing them has the resources to give the kinds of help that its clients need and that referral resources are available.

Closely related to the issue of competence is determining whether consultants have an adequate level of training to perform contracted services. Consultants can maintain a high level of professionalism by continuing their education, by attending professional conferences, by consulting with more experienced colleagues, and by obtaining the relevant credentials or licenses for the profession in which they expect to serve as a consultant. Wallace and Hall (1996) indicate that consultants are ethically obligated to keep current in the field by being aware of training alternatives, recent research, and both innovative and tested consulting strategies, methods, techniques, and instruments.

Relationship issues in consulting. The consultant-consultee-client relationship is a complex one that needs to be considered in the context of the organization in which the consulting is occurring. The consultee's interests and needs are paramount. The consulting relationship is based on an understanding and agreement between the consultant and the consultee on what the problem is, the goals for change, and the predicted outcomes of the interventions selected (ACA, 1995). Consultants are expected to establish a clear contract with well-defined limits, respect their contract, and communicate its terms to all who are participating in consulting activities. Any changes in the contract should be made only through explicit agreement with staff members and the administration.

Some writers recommend using a written consultation contract as a basis for setting the stage for a successful consulting relationship (Remley, 1993). An alternative to a formal, written contract is a letter of understanding in which the consultant summarizes and confirms the expectations of the consultation agreement (Wallace & Hall, 1996). Both consultants and consultees gain from written documents that spell out the essentials of the agreement, including the nature of the consultation relationship, goals, practical aspects, fees, confidentiality matters, and informed consent issues. The more specific a written contract is, the more useful the document will be to both parties. According to Remley (1993), contracts are best structured in this way:

- Clearly specify the work to be completed by the consultant.
- Identify any work products expected from the consultant.
- Establish a time frame for completing the work.
- Identify lines of authority and the person to whom the consultant is responsible.
- Establish compensation arrangements, including the method of payment.
- Specify any special arrangements agreed upon by the parties.

A good contract is a form of legal protection for both the consultant and the consultee. It can also assist both parties in developing a clear understanding of the terms of the consultation agreement and can be used as a source of reference if misunderstandings emerge at any stage in the consultation process.

An ethical consultant places top priority on the consultee's freedom of choice. Consultants have a responsibility to protect the freedom of consultees by declining to become involved in activities that require discussion of highly personal issues. If the consultation process is structured by a clear contract, inappropriate dual relationships are unlikely to develop.

Newman (1993) reminds us that consultants need to exert special care in maintaining appropriate boundaries, even if consultees request counseling. If it becomes evident that a consultee needs personal counseling, refer the consultee for appropriate professional help. Ethical practice dictates that consultants monitor their interventions to avoid creating dependency or otherwise misusing their power.

Dougherty (2000) takes the position that it is best for consultants to be cautious about engaging in dual professional relationships. If a mistake is made, he suggests that it is a better practice to be conservative and engage in only one professional relationship. Because maintaining two professional roles in the consulting relationship can be particularly hazardous to consultants and their consultees, Dougherty recommends avoiding such relationships whenever possible. He states: "It is my opinion that the benefits of serving in two professional roles in the consultation relationship are outweighed by the potential conflicts" (p. 157).

Rights of consultees. Two central issues involving the rights of consultees are confidentiality and informed consent. Just as in any other professional relationship, absolute confidentiality cannot be guaranteed. The matter of who will have access to the consultant's findings needs to be established before gathering data. Consultants can remind staff members and administrators of the limits of confidentiality established during contract negotiations. Newman (1993) suggests that at a minimum consultants make certain that consultees clearly understand what and how information will be used, by whom, and for what purposes.

Consultants who work in schools may need to break confidentiality when there is abusive behavior on a consultee's part, such as a teacher's consistent violation of a school's policy regarding corporal punishment. Likewise, consultants who work in a residential care facility need to assume responsibility for protecting the residents, yet they may also have to report certain incidents or situations to others in the facility. In all settings, those who are participating in the consultation process have a right to know about the limits of confidentiality. It is the consultant's job to ensure that all participants clearly understand the parameters of confidentiality.

Ethical practice requires that consultants inform their consultees about the goals and purpose of consultation, the limits to confidentiality, the potential benefits, any potential risks, and the potential outcomes of intervention. Basic to informed consent is the notion that individuals have the freedom to choose from among various options, one of which is the freedom to decline to participate in the consultation process (Newman, 1993). As was mentioned in Chapter 5, informed consent is not exclusively accomplished at the outset of a relationship but is best achieved through a continuing discussion of relevant issues. It is a good policy for consultants to put themselves in the place of their consultees and ask themselves what they would want to know. All who are participating have a right to know about the nature and purpose of the consultation process.

Issues involving consulting in groups. Consultation is increasingly being done between a consultant and a group of consultees. The ethical guidelines for group work discussed in Chapter 12 apply here to the process of consulting in groups. When consultants use group process approaches, it is essential that they be competent in group consultation. Those who participate in consultation in groups have a right to know what will be expected of them. Matters such as self-disclosure, privacy, the boundary between work-related concerns and personal concerns, and the limits of confidentiality are all particularly important.

Three Case Examples of Consulting

◆ **The case of Lynn.** The principal of a school hires Lynn, a psychologist in private practice, to conduct a communications workshop focusing on improving interpersonal relationships between the faculty and the administration. The workshop is a 2-day intensive group experience involving all teachers and the three administrators in the school. Participants are encouraged to openly express their concerns and difficulties and to focus on possible strategies for improving working conditions. The workshop seems to go well.

The following week, the principal calls Lynn and asks for a meeting. The principal agrees that the workshop seemed successful and says she would be interested in Lynn's assessment of the key faculty members whom she needs to pay closer attention to. She would like to know more about the natural leaders and the potential troublemakers. Lynn is asked to go through the list of teachers and make an assessment of each person's potential to be troublesome or helpful.

- What potential ethical issues, if any, are involved in this case?
- As the principal attended the workshop and basically heard everything, would it be permissible for Lynn to give her professional assessment of each person?
- The consultation contract was between the principal and Lynn. What rights, if any, does that fact give the principal?
- What are your reactions to the after-workshop meeting between Lynn and the principal?
- Does informed consent require that all participants know exactly how the information they share will be used?

◆ **The case of Delilah.** An airline management group is concerned about the loss of working hours because of on-the-job stress. Delilah is hired to provide stress management skills to solve the problem. The contract calls for her to teach specific strategies such as relaxation, diet, exercise, aerobics, and visualization, with the stated goal of reducing stress and improving efficiency. In the process of teaching employees how to cope with stress, she discovers that many outside personal problems are contributing to their stress. She decides to alter her strategy to include several hours of group counseling to address the personal problems of the participants. In addition, she gives the participants three sources of referral for further professional help.

- Can a consultant unilaterally change the provisions of a contract?
- Should Delilah ignore the personal problems that are contributing to inefficiency on the job because this information was not available to her when the contract was designed?
- Does management have any rights to insist on the contract being strictly adhered to? What if management contends that personal problems are best dealt with separately and financed by the employees or their insurance company?
- Is Delilah now involved in a dual relationship as consultant and counselor? Explain your position.

◆ **A case of a hidden agenda.** A state-funded agency employs a team of consultants to conduct human-relations training and staff development. Over time, these consultants earn a reputation for working effectively with the lower-level staff. The director of the agency expresses a desire for the consultants to "work on" key members of the upper-level staff who are identified as being particularly troublesome to the agency. The stipulation is that the focus on these key members is not to be disclosed; rather, the impression to be given is that the team is working to improve the overall efficiency of the staff.

- If the consultants accept this contract as it is written, are they being unethical?
- If this hidden agenda is successfully carried out, overall efficiency will be enhanced and the entire agency benefits. Does the end justify the means?
- Assume that a hidden agenda becomes evident to you during the course of a consulting workshop you are giving. What would be the ethical thing to do? Would you disclose to the members that you suspect a hidden agenda? Would you confront the director who had hired you?

Chapter Summary

Supervision and consultation are two roles counselors are often asked to assume. It is clear that special training is needed to effectively perform the many functions required in these activities. Some of the key ethical issues associated with supervision and consultation involve carrying out professional roles and responsibilities, maintaining clear boundaries between roles, and avoiding the problems created by dual or multiple relationships.

Supervision is one way in which trainees learn how to apply their knowledge and skills to particular clinical situations. It is essential that supervisees receive regular feedback so that they have a basis for honing their skills. Effective supervision deals with the professional as a person and as a practitioner. It is not enough to focus on the trainee's skills, for the supervisory relationship is a personal process. Thus, the supervisee's dynamics are equally important in this process. Although supervision aims at honing the skills of trainees, the welfare of those served by trainees is the primary consideration. Supervisors have both legal and ethical responsibilities to clients, who have a right to competent service regardless of the supervisee's level of training (Welfel, 2002).

Consultation, much like supervision, is a growing professional specialization that can be carried out with individuals and in small groups with diverse client populations in various work settings. Consultants help human-services workers deliver services to their clients more effectively, but they are not legally responsible for consultees' clients. Thus, they focus on work-related concerns. Ethical and professional issues pertaining to consultation can be broken down into these areas: values, multicultural issues, competence and training, the consulting relationship, the rights of consultees, and consulting in groups.

Suggested Activities

1. Role-play a situation that involves a supervisor asking supervisees to get involved in therapy situations that are beyond the scope of their training and experience. One student in class can play the role of a persuasive supervisor who thinks students will learn best by "jumping into the water and learning how to swim—or sink." The supervisor can ask trainees to work with a

family, lead a therapy group alone, or work with abused children. After the role play, discuss the ethical and clinical issues involved with a focus on ways to deal with inadequate supervision.

2. Set up another role-playing situation. In this case, the supervisor is difficult to reach and rarely keeps his or her appointments with the supervisees. One student can role-play the inaccessible supervisor, and several others can assume the roles of students who need to meet with their supervisor to discuss difficult cases.

3. Investigate some of the community agencies in your area to learn what supervision they offer to interns and to newly hired practitioners. Several students can form a panel to share the results.

4. Form an ethics committee in class to review these two cases dealing with supervision:

- A supervisor has made sexual offers to several supervisees.
- A supervisor is accepting supervisees as clients in his or her private practice, and the supervisor makes it a practice to date former students in the program.

The ethics committee can present its case in class with appropriate courses of action for each problem area. The others in the class can interact with the committee by providing alternative viewpoints.

5. Interview a consultant to discover how this person was trained and what professional activities he or she typically performs. It would be useful for various students to interview consultants in different settings, such as businesses, public schools, agencies, and private practice. Ask the consultants to share some of the ethical dilemmas they have faced in their work. How did they deal with them?

6. Design a role-playing situation that involves consultation. At least one student assumes the role of consultant. A number of students can play the role of consultees who are seeking help from the consultant. Again, think of diverse settings to add some variety. Afterward, discuss the process involved.

7. Interview several clinical supervisors to determine what they consider to be the most pressing ethical and legal issues in the supervisory relationship. Here are some questions you might ask supervisors: What are the rights of trainees? What are the main responsibilities of supervisors? To what degree should supervisors be held accountable for the welfare of the clients who are counseled by their trainees? What kind of specialized training have they had in supervision? Who is the proper focus of supervision—the client? the trainee? What are some common problems faced by supervisors in effectively carrying out their duties?

8. Assume that you are in a field placement as a counselor in a community agency. The administrators tell you that they do not want you to inform your clients that you are a student intern. They explain that your clients might feel that they were getting second-class service if they found out that you were in training. What would you say and do if you found yourself as an intern in this situation? Would it be ethical to follow this directive and not inform your clients that you are a trainee and that you are receiving supervision? Do you

agree or disagree with the rationale of the administrators? Might you accept the internship assignment under the terms outlined if you could not find any other field placements?

Ethics in Action CD-ROM Exercises

9. Reflect on all of the role-playing situations enacted in the *Ethics in Action* CD-ROM. Put yourself in the place of the counselor. Would you seek input from a supervisor in any of these situations? Consider situations such as working with a pregnant teenager who urges you not to tell her parents; becoming aware of countertransference with a client; having a sharp value difference between you and your client; finding yourself attracted to a client; having difficulty establishing and maintaining boundaries with a client. Select the one vignette in the video that you think would be most challenging. A small group of students can offer you peer supervision as you role-play the counselor who is struggling with a particularly difficult ethical situation. Ask another student to role-play the counselor with an ethical issue you would find challenging. Assume the role of the supervisor of this counselor. What questions would you ask of the counselor? What kinds of suggestions might you offer?

InfoTrac® College Edition Resources

For additional readings, explore InfoTrac College Edition, our online library. Go to *http://www.infotrac.college.com/wadsworth* and select these key word searches:

clinical W1 supervision
ethic* clinical superv*
legal clinical superv*
clinical superv* role*
clinical superv* responsib*
clinical supervis* competence
multicult* supervision
multiple roles AND relationships in superv*
ethic* AND consultation AND psych*

Key words are listed in a form that enables the search engine to locate a wider range of articles in the online university library. Key words should be entered exactly as shown, including asterisks, "W1," "W2," "AND," and other search engine tools.

10

Pre-Chapter Self-Inventory

Directions: For each statement, indicate the response that most closely identifies your beliefs and attitudes. Use the following code:

5 = I *strongly agree* with this statement.
4 = I *agree* with this statement.
3 = I am *undecided* about this statement.
2 = I *disagree* with this statement.
1 = I *strongly disagree* with this statement.

_____1. It is best that I adhere to a definite theory of counseling.
_____2. I would rather combine insights and techniques derived from various theoretical approaches to counseling than base my practice on a single model.
_____3. People are basically capable of and responsible for changing their behaviors.
_____4. What happens in counseling sessions is more my responsibility than it is my client's.
_____5. I would find it difficult to work for an agency if I were expected to perform functions that I didn't think were appropriate to counseling.
_____6. I should have the power to define my own role and professional identity as a mental health practitioner.
_____7. Clients should always select the goals of counseling.
_____8. I would be willing to work with clients who did not seem to have any clear goals or reasons for seeking counseling.
_____9. Competent diagnosis is necessary for planning appropriate treatment.

Issues in Theory, Practice, and Research

____10. The drawbacks associated with diagnosis in counseling outweigh the values.

____11. Testing can be a very useful adjunct to counseling.

____12. The medical model of mental health can be applied effectively in counseling and psychotherapy.

____13. The theory I hold and the techniques I employ need to be compatible with the demands of a managed care system.

____14. Skill in using a variety of techniques is one of the most important qualities of a therapist.

____15. Theories of counseling can limit counselors by encouraging them to pay attention only to behavior that fits their particular theory.

____16. Counselors should develop and modify their own theory of counseling as they practice.

____17. There are major shortcomings in applying most of the contemporary counseling theories to diverse ethnic and cultural groups, such as Asian Americans, Latinos, Native Americans, and African Americans.

____18. Although people are not responsible for creating their problems, I believe they are responsible for finding ways to deal effectively with these problems.

____19. It can be unethical for practitioners to fail to do some type of assessment and diagnosis, especially with high-risk (suicidal or dangerous) clients.

____20. It is critical to take cultural factors into consideration in assessment and diagnosis if the therapist hopes to gather accurate data and come up with a valid perspective on a client.

Introduction

Therapists' theoretical positions and conceptual views influence their actual practice. Ideally, theory should help practitioners make sense of what they hear in counseling sessions. Another way of thinking about this issue is to imagine a client asking you to explain your view of counseling in clear and simple terms. Could you tell your client what you most hoped to accomplish and how you would go about it? Ethical practice is grounded in a solid theoretical and research base. Practitioners who operate in a theoretical vacuum, with little or no interest in the practical applications of psychotherapeutic research, may be engaging in behavior that is ethically questionable or at least not very helpful.

This chapter addresses a variety of interrelated ethical issues, such as why a theory has both practical and ethical implications, the goals and techniques that flow from one's theoretical orientation, the role of diagnosis and testing in the therapeutic process, ethical considerations in the practice of managed care, and ethics in research. We examine the impact that managed care is having on counseling practice, and we especially look at the balance between cost-containment measures and providing quality care to consumers. We consider the ethical and legal implications of managed care as they apply to informed consent, appropriate levels of care, and outcome expectations for short-term interventions on a range of client problems.

Professional counselors need to be able to conceptualize what they are doing in their counseling sessions and why they are doing it. Too often practitioners are unable to explain why they use certain counseling procedures. When you first meet a new client, for example, what guidelines would you use in structuring what you have heard? What do you want to accomplish at this initial session? Rank in order of importance the following factors that you would be interested in knowing about your client:

___ The presenting problem (the reason the client is seeking counseling)
___ The client's style of coping with demands, stresses, and conflicts
___ Early experiences as a child, particularly in relation to parents and siblings
___ Ego strength
___ Functional strengths and weaknesses
___ History of successes and failures
___ Developmental history
___ The client's struggle with current choices
___ The client's cultural background
___ Goals and agenda for counseling
___ Current support system
___ Motivation to change
___ Level of reality testing

Now examine how you ranked these items. What theoretical approach would your rankings seem to indicate? You might consider how open you are to challenging your theoretical stance and how this openness or lack of it might influence the therapeutic outcome for your clients. Think about how your theoretical viewpoint influences your decisions on questions such as these: What are your goals for counseling? What techniques would you use to reach your goals? What is the proper place of diagnosis and testing in the counseling process? How do you make provisions for cultural diversity in your assessment and treatment plans? How flexible are you in your approach? Does research have a place in your counseling practice? What connections do you see between theory, practice, and research?

Developing a Counseling Stance

Developing a counseling stance is more complicated than merely accepting the tenets of a given theory. We believe the theoretical approach you use to guide your practice is an expression of you as a person and an outgrowth of your life experience. Further, because a theory of counseling is often an expression of the personality of the theorist, a theoretical approach becomes more useful and meaningful once you have taken a critical look at the theorist who developed it as well as its key concepts. Uncritically following any single theory can lead you to ignore some of the insights that your life and your work open up to you. This is our bias, of course, and many would contend that providing effective therapy depends on following a given theory. Ultimately your counseling stance must be appropriate for the type of counseling you do and the unique needs of your clients.

Theories of counseling are based on worldviews, each with its own values, biases, and assumptions of how best to bring about change in the therapeutic process (Ivey, D'Andrea, Ivey, & Simek-Morgan, 2002). As we discussed in Chapter 4, contemporary theories of therapeutic practice are grounded in assumptions that are part of Western culture, and they emphasize choice, the uniqueness of the individual, self-assertion, and ego strength. Many of these assumptions are inappropriate for evaluating clients from non-Western cultures that focus on interdependence, downplay individuality, and emphasize being in harmony with the universe. From an Asian perspective, for example, basic life values are associated with a focus on inner experience and an acceptance of one's environment.

Whereas the Western therapeutic approaches are oriented toward individual change, non-Western approaches focus more on the social framework than on development of the individual. The Western model of therapy has limitations when it is applied to many ethnic and cultural groups, such as Asian Americans, Latinos, Native Americans, and African Americans. It is not customary for many client populations to seek professional help, and they will typically turn first to informal systems such as family, friends, and the community.

D. W. Sue, Ivey, and Pedersen (1996) believe we need to develop a theory that enables us to work with various cultures. In addition to dealing with the feeling, thinking, and behaving dimensions familiar to Western theorists, a multicultural approach emphasizes the social and cultural context of human existence. This approach takes into account that we are all biological, spiritual, and political beings as well.

When developing or evaluating a theory, a major consideration is the degree to which that perspective helps you understand and organize what you are doing with clients. Does your framework provide a broad base for working with diverse clients in different ways, or does it restrict your vision and cause you to ignore variables that do not fit the theory? Does your theory allow for cultural differences? To what degree are you flexible? If you hold steadfastly to one theory, you might expect your clients to conform to your expectations. It is important, therefore, to evaluate what you are emphasizing in your counseling work. The following questions may help you make this evaluation:

- Where did you acquire your theory? Did you incorporate many of the views of your instructors or training supervisors? Has one theory intrigued you to the point that it is the sole basis for your orientation?
- Does your theory evolve and change as you gain clinical experience with a variety of clients?
- Do you embrace a particular theory because it is a justification of your own experiences and values? What does your approach stress, and why does it appeal to you?
- To what degree does your theory challenge your own previous frame of reference? Does it cause you to test your hypotheses, beliefs, and assumptions? Does it encourage you to think of alternatives?
- To what degree does your theory reinforce your present worldview? Does it force you to extend your thinking, or does it merely support your assumptions?
- Do you have a responsibility to know many theories and techniques to better serve diverse clients?
- Does your theory have research to support its effectiveness?
- Is your theory a dogma, or is it the way that you work best and have best results? Do you include your theoretical model in your informed consent document?
- Does your theory make room for cultural factors? Can you apply your theory to a wide range of clients, many of whom will have different expectations in seeking help? Does the range of interventions available to you based on your theoretical orientation accommodate cultural diversity?
- How do your own life experiences influence your counseling approach? In what ways have your life experiences caused you to modify your theoretical viewpoint? In what ways has your work with clients helped modify your theory?
- Does ethical practice demand having a rationale for the interventions you make?

Your assumptions about the nature of counseling and the nature of people have a direct impact on your manner of practice. The goals that you think are important in therapy, the techniques and methods you employ to reach these goals, the way in which you see the division of responsibility in the client-therapist relationship, your view of your role and functions as a counselor, and your view of the place of diagnosis and testing in the therapeutic process are all largely determined by your theoretical orientation.

Practicing counseling without an explicit theoretical rationale is somewhat like flying a plane without a map and without instruments. A theoretical orientation (or a counseling stance) is not a rigid structure that prescribes specific steps of what to do in a counseling situation; rather, it is a set of general guidelines that counselors can use to make sense of what they are doing.

The Division of Responsibility in Therapy

Many beginning counselors deprive their clients of their rightful responsibility for their therapy by anxiously taking too much of this responsibility on themselves. If clients do not progress fast enough, these counselors may blame themselves for not knowing enough, not having the necessary skill and experience, or not being sensitive or caring enough. They may worry constantly about their adequacy as counselors and transmit this anxiety to their clients. If only they were better therapists, their clients would be changing in more positive directions. Overly anxious counselors frequently fail to see the role their clients play in the outcome of their own therapy, whether for better or for worse.

Counselors do well to bring up the question of responsibility during the initial sessions and to encourage clients to begin thinking about their part in their own therapy. One way to clarify the shared responsibility in a therapeutic relationship is by a contract. A contract is based on a negotiation between the client and the therapist to define the therapeutic relationship. A contract (which can be an extension of the informed consent process discussed in Chapter 5) tends to encourage the client and the therapist to specify the goals of the therapy and the methods likely to be employed in obtaining these goals. Other aspects of a contract include the length and frequency of sessions, the duration of therapy, the cost and method of payment, provisions for renegotiating the contract, any factors limiting confidentiality, the extent of responsibility for each partner, and ways of determining the outcomes of the therapeutic relationship. Most probably the therapist has the greater responsibility in the initial phase of therapy. However, as therapy progresses, the responsibility becomes more balanced between counselor and client. For certain populations, such as children, legal and ethical considerations need to be taken into account in designing the contract.

If you work within a managed care system, the HMO or PPO provider determines many of these issues, including what kinds of problems are acceptable for treatment, how long treatment will last, the number of sessions, and the focus of the work. Under this system, practitioners must be accountable to the managed care company by demonstrating that specific objectives have been met. At the very least, therapists need to discuss with clients how being involved with managed care will influence the division of responsibility among the HMO, the client, and the therapist. Ethical issues in managed care is a topic we address more fully in a later section in this chapter.

From our own perspective, therapy is a collaborative venture of the client and the therapist. Both have serious responsibilities for the direction of therapy, and this needs to be clarified during the initial stages of counseling. Counselors who typically decide what to discuss and are overdirective run the risk of perpetuating their clients' dependence. Clients should be encouraged from the start to assume as much responsibility as they can. Directive therapies, such as the cognitive-behavioral approaches, emphasize client-initiated contracts and homework assignments as ways in which clients can fulfill their commitment to change. These devices help to keep the focus of responsibility on clients by challenging them to decide what they want from therapy and what they are willing to do to get what they want.

As you consider the range of viewpoints on the division of responsibility in therapy, think about your own position on this issue. What is your responsibility, both to your client and to yourself? What do you expect from your client? Do you burden yourself with the total responsibility for what happens in therapy?

Deciding on the Goals of Counseling

Therapy without a goal is unlikely to be effective, yet too often practitioners fail to devote enough time to thinking about the goals they have for their clients and the goals clients have for themselves. In this section we discuss possible aims of therapy, how goals are determined, and who should determine them. Counselors' answers to these questions are directly related to their theoretical orientations. When considering therapeutic goals, it is important to keep in mind the cultural determinants of therapy. The aims of therapy are specific to a particular culture's definition of psychological health. In describing their theory of multicultural counseling and therapy, D. W. Sue, Ivey, and Pedersen (1996) develop a number of propositions that are considered to be basic assumptions underlying their metatheory. Two of these assumptions have particular relevance for the topic of therapeutic goals. Sue and his colleagues claim that multicultural counseling is more effective when counselors use modalities and define goals that are consistent with the life experiences and cultural values of the client. They stress that no single approach is equally effective in working with all client populations. The ultimate goal of training practitioners to be multiculturally competent, regardless of their theoretical orientation, is to expand the range of therapeutic strategies they can apply to culturally diverse client groups. A second proposition of their multicultural theory pertains to its basic goal, which is the liberation of consciousness. This approach goes beyond the limitations of the traditional goals of Western psychotherapy and emphasizes the family, group, and cultural aspects of counseling. Ultimately, this theory considers the person-in-relation and the cultural context as essential aspects in developing appropriate goals for the helping process. This topic was addressed in Chapter 4.

In most counseling approaches, effective counseling does not result when the therapist imposes goals; rather, goals should be determined by the client and the therapist working together. However, some therapists believe they know what is best for their clients and try to persuade their clients to accept certain goals. Others are convinced that the specific aims of counseling ought to be determined entirely by their clients. Who sets the goals of counseling is best understood in light of the theory you operate from, the type of counseling you offer, the setting in which you work, and the nature of your clientele. Your theoretical orientation influences generic goals, such as insight versus behavior change, and if you are not clear about your general goals, your techniques may be random and arbitrary. Other factors can also affect the determination of goals. For example, if you work with clients in a managed care system, the goals will need to be highly specific, limited to reduction of problematic symptoms, and often aimed at teaching coping skills. If you work in crisis intervention, your goals are likely to be short term and practical, and you may be very directive. If you are working with children in a school, you may combine educational and therapeutic goals. As a counselor with elderly people in an institution, you may stress coping skills and ways of relating to others in this environment. What your goals are and how actively you involve your client in determining them will depend to a great extent on the type of counseling you provide and the type of client you see.

◆ **The case of Leon.** Leon, a 45-year-old aeronautical engineer who is married and has three children, has been laid off after 20 years of employment with the same company. He shows signs of depression, has lost weight, and was referred to you by his primary physician. He has had no previous history of depression, but his father committed suicide at age 50. Leon is not close to his mother or siblings and describes his marriage as lackluster at best. He expresses, without much affect, feelings of abandonment at being terminated after so many years of dedicated service.

How would you assess and work with Leon if he were your client? Consider these questions:

- Would Leon's age, ethnicity, and culture be significant factors for you to consider in developing a treatment plan?
- What specific goals would you have in mind as you develop a treatment plan for Leon?
- Would your approach call for a suicide assessment? Why or why not?
- Would your approach call for a medical assessment for the possible need for medication?
- How do you see Leon's support system, and how significant would that be in setting goals?
- To what degree would you involve Leon in creating goals?

- Would you consider Leon's unemployment a significant factor in this case? Would your goals include dealing with that reality?
- How would you assess the outcomes of your work with Leon? What would need to change for you to deem your work with Leon successful? In what ways might you involve Leon in assessing outcomes?

The Use of Techniques in Counseling

Your view of the use of techniques in counseling is closely related to your theoretical model. What techniques, procedures, or intervention methods would you use, and when and why would you use them? Out of anxiety over not knowing what to do in a given counseling situation, counselors may try technique after technique in an indiscriminate fashion. Practitioners should have a rationale for using particular methods of intervention and need to have training in the proper use of techniques. We question the benefit to the client of an overreliance on technique.

Lambert and Cattani-Thompson (1996) reviewed studies on counseling effectiveness and found little evidence of specific efficacy for particular techniques or counseling theories. However, a number of significant implications for counseling practice did come to light. For example, some specific techniques appear to be more effective with particular symptoms and disorders, especially for certain behavioral disorders. However, Lambert and Cattani-Thompson assert that successful client outcome is largely determined by client characteristics, such as motivation, severity of symptoms, and acceptance of personal responsibility for change. Other predictors of successful outcomes of counseling involve client-therapist relationship factors. Practitioners would do well to pay attention to the way they interact with clients and the manner in which they participate in the therapy, providing high levels of empathy, respect, and collaboration. It appears that the techniques counselors employ, although important, are less crucial to therapy outcomes than are the interpersonal factors operating in the client-counselor relationship.

The purpose of techniques is to facilitate movement in a counseling session, and your techniques really cannot be separated from your personality and your relationship with your client. When practitioners fall into a pattern of mechanically employing techniques, they are not responding to the particular individuals they are counseling. To avoid this pitfall, it is useful to pay attention to the ways you use techniques. You may try a technique you have observed someone else using very skillfully only to find that it does not work well for you. In essence, your techniques need to fit your therapeutic style, and they should be tailored to the specific needs of your client. When working with culturally diverse client populations, it is clinically and ethically imperative that you use interventions that are consistent with the values of your client. It is best to adapt your techniques to the needs of your clients rather than to expect your clients to fit your techniques.

Diagnosis as a Professional Issue

Assessment and diagnosis are integrally related to your counseling stance. Depending on the theory from which you operate, a diagnostic framework may occupy a key role or a minimal role in the therapeutic process. Cognitive-behavioral therapies place heavy emphasis on the role of assessment as a prelude to the treatment process. The rationale is that specific therapy goals cannot be designed until a thorough picture is formed of the client's past and present functioning. The relationship-oriented approaches tend to view the process of assessment and diagnosis as external to the immediacy of the client-counselor relationship, a process that can remove the therapist from understanding the subjective world of the client. The developmental counseling and therapy model (DCT) is based on the assumption that greater attention needs to be paid to environmental and contextual issues. This approach is grounded on the premise that the individual develops within a family in a community and cultural context (Ivey & Ivey, 1998). Regardless of the particular theory espoused by a therapist, both clinical and ethical issues are associated with the use of assessment procedures and diagnosis as part of a treatment plan.

Assessment consists of evaluating the relevant factors in a client's life to identify themes for further exploration in the counseling process. Diagnosis, which is sometimes part of the assessment process, consists of identifying a specific psychological or behavioral problem based on a pattern of symptoms. This diagnosis enables the therapist to plan treatments tailored to the special needs of the client.

There are different kinds of diagnosis. *Medical diagnosis* is the process of examining physical symptoms, inferring causes of physical disorders or diseases, providing a category that fits the pattern of a disease, and prescribing an appropriate treatment. *Psychodiagnosis* (or *psychological diagnosis*) is a general term covering the process of identifying an emotional or behavioral problem and making a statement about the current status of a client. This process also includes identification of possible causes of the person's emotional, psychological, and behavioral difficulties, suggestions for appropriate therapy techniques to deal effectively with the identified problem, and estimates of the chances for a successful resolution.

Differential diagnosis is the process of distinguishing one form of disease or psychological disorder from another by determining which of two (or more) diseases or disorders with similar symptoms the person is suffering from. The fourth edition of the American Psychiatric Association's (1994) *Diagnostic and Statistical Manual of Mental Disorders* (DSM-IV) is the standard reference for distinguishing one form of psychological disorder from another. DSM-IV is the most widely used system for identifying, classifying, and describing mental and emotional disorders in the world (Wylie, 1995).

Whether diagnosis should be part of psychotherapy is a controversial issue. Some mental health professionals see diagnosis as an essential step in any treatment plan, but others view it as an inappropriate application of the medical model of mental health to counseling and therapy (Sleek, 1996). Some contend that clients in managed care systems can no longer trust their therapists' motives, so they are faced with making significant life decisions without professional guidance (Shore, 1996). The constant refrain of those who oppose a diagnostic model is that DSM labels and stigmatizes people; yet those who designed DSM assert that it classifies mental illnesses, not people (Wylie, 1995). Although you may not yet have had to face the practical question of whether to diagnose a client, you will probably need to come to terms with this issue at some point in your work. Making a diagnosis is likely to be an integral part of your job responsibilities, especially if you are employed in an agency setting. Let us briefly review some of the arguments for and against the use of diagnosis in therapy. Then you can consider how valuable diagnosis is from your point of view.

Arguments for Psychodiagnosis

Practitioners who favor the use of diagnostic procedures in therapy generally argue that such procedures enable the therapist to acquire sufficient knowledge about the client's past and present behavior to develop an appropriate plan of treatment. Diagnosing a client can be likened to putting together a jigsaw puzzle—it involves piecing together small bits of information to build an overall picture of the individual (Sleek, 1996). This approach stems from the medical model of mental health, according to which different underlying causal factors produce different types of disorders.

Psychoanalytically oriented therapists favor psychodiagnosis, because this form of therapy was patterned after the medical model of mental health and stresses understanding the past situations that have contributed to a dysfunction. Some psychological assessment devices used in psychodiagnosis involve projective techniques that rest on psychoanalytic concepts.

For different reasons, practitioners with a behavioristic orientation also favor a diagnostic stance. Although they may not follow the medical model, these practitioners value observation and other objective means of appraising both a client's specific symptoms and the factors that have led up to the client's malfunctioning. Such an appraisal, they argue, enables them to use the techniques that are appropriate for a particular disorder and to evaluate the effectiveness of the treatment program.

Those who argue for the usefulness and necessity of diagnosis often make some of the following points:

- There is no third-party reimbursement without an acceptable diagnosis. For example, under a managed care system, formulating a diagnosis is a basic first step to qualify for further therapy sessions.

- To function effectively in most mental health agencies, practitioners need to be skilled in understanding and utilizing diagnostic procedures.
- In working with a professional team, diagnosis is essential so that all team members have a common language and a common frame of reference.
- It may be difficult to formulate a meaningful treatment plan without clearly defining the specific problems that need to be addressed. Diagnosis points the way to appropriate treatment strategies for specific disorders and is helpful in predicting the course of the disorder.
- Diagnosis alerts therapists to the existence of a possible organic problem, which would necessitate a medical assessment (for instance, a thyroid deficiency).
- Therapists have a legal, professional, and ethical obligation to assess whether clients may pose a danger to themselves or to others. They also need to screen for organic disorders, bipolar disorders, and psychotic states.
- Diagnosis provides a framework for research into various treatment approaches. Responsible delivery of psychological services depends on data-based clinical outcome studies; accurate diagnosis is necessary to these outcome studies.

In his article on ethical concerns about diagnosis, Hamann (1994) makes a case for the usefulness of diagnosis:

> When I take my car to the mechanic, I expect him or her not to fix my brakes if my transmission is faulty. If I go to my family doctor with a complaint of chest pain, I do not want him or her to treat me for a broken leg. In the same manner, I do not believe professionals providing clinical care can simply treat without first determining what is the problem. Clearly, treatment varies depending on the disorder. As clinicians we must be able to diagnose accurately before we can treat effectively. (p. 259)

In his experience with both public and private mental health agencies, Hamann (1994) has found that all clinicians have the responsibility for diagnosing. Practitioners who work in an agency setting have the initial contact with most clients. They are expected to take a history as part of the intake session to arrive at a diagnosis. Such clinicians often have a caseload of at least 100 clients, and they are expected to define the client's problem and develop a treatment plan to alleviate the problem—typically in one session. From Hamann's perspective, graduate programs involved in training therapists need to teach diagnosis. Because mental health agencies assume that those they employ will be proficient in diagnosis, training programs have a responsibility to see that students acquire competence in understanding a diagnostic framework.

Ivey and Ivey (1998) propose reframing DSM-IV by paying special attention to the interface of multicultural issues, origin of problems, and treatment. The Iveys suggest that diagnostic systems need more balance and that attention must be focused on the reality of human experience. In their developmental counseling and therapy model, psychological distress is viewed as the result of biological and developmental factors. Although the stressor may be located within the individual, this model calls for inclusion of the broader systemic and cultural contexts as a basis for meaningful assessment. For example, the distress of depression is generally the result of the interaction of the person in the environment. Depression in women or in ethnic minority group members may result from cultural racism or sexism. Individuals who have been discriminated against may experience depression as a result of environmental factors. From the developmental perspective, the inclusion of culture-related issues such as race, ethnicity, gender, sexual orientation, and spirituality is essential for accurate assessment and diagnosis. Ivey and Ivey argue that "a diagnosis that is not culture-centered with awareness of multiple contextual issues is incomplete at best and potentially dangerous and misleading" (p. 336).

Although you may not find diagnosis necessary or useful in your practice, it is important to know enough about diagnosis to refer a client. For example, once you have made a diagnosis of a client who is chronically depressed with possible suicidal tendencies, you are in a position to make an appropriate referral if you do not have the competence to deal with this problem area.

Those who support traditional forms of diagnosis agree that present classification systems have limitations and that some of the problems mentioned by the critics of diagnosis do exist. Rather than abandoning diagnostic classifications altogether, however, they favor updating diagnostic manuals to reflect improvements in diagnosis and treatment procedures.

Arguments Against Psychodiagnosis

Many professionals see diagnosis as an essential component of psychotherapy, but others view it as unnecessary or harmful. Rogers (1961) consistently maintained that diagnosis was detrimental to counseling because it tended to pull clients away from an internal and subjective way of experiencing themselves and to foster an objective and external conception of themselves. The result was an increased tendency toward dependence, with clients acting as if the responsibility for changing their behavior rested with the expert and not with themselves.

Person-centered therapy is grounded in the belief that clients are in the best position to understand and resolve their personal difficulties. Existential or relationship-oriented therapists generally fall into this group of clinicians who see diagnosis as restrictive or who resist diagnosis in their practice. Here are some of the arguments against diagnosis:

- Diagnosis is typically done by an expert observing a person's behavior and experience from an external viewpoint, without reference to what they mean to the client.
- Diagnostic categories can minimize the uniqueness of the client.
- Reducing people to the sum of their symptoms ignores natural capacities for self-healing.
- Because the emphasis of DSM-IV is on pathology, deficits, limitations, problems, and symptoms, individuals are not encouraged to find and utilize their strengths, competencies, and abilities.

- Diagnosis can lead people to accept self-fulfilling prophecies or to despair over their condition.
- Diagnosis can narrow therapists' vision by encouraging them to look for behavior that fits a certain disease category.
- DSM-IV is based on the assumption that distress in a family or social context is the result of individual pathology, whereas a systemic approach views the source of the distress as being within the entire system.
- Although DSM-IV makes some reference to ethnic, cultural, environmental, and class factors in understanding and interpreting dysfunctional behavior, it deals largely with culture-bound syndromes and does not adequately take into account culture, age, gender, and other ways of viewing health and sickness.
- The best vantage point for understanding another person is through his or her subjective world, not through a general system of classification.
- Many therapists do not possess the competence to use DSM-IV diagnosis appropriately.

Our Position on Assessment and Psychodiagnosis

Both assessment and diagnosis, broadly construed, are legitimate parts of the therapeutic process. The kind of diagnosis we have in mind is the result of a collaborative effort by the client and the therapist, also referred to as co-diagnosis. Both should be involved in discovering the nature of the client's difficulty, a process that commences with the initial sessions and continues until therapy is terminated. Even practitioners who oppose conventional diagnostic procedures and terminology unavoidably make an assessment of clients based on questions such as these:

- What brought the client into therapy?
- What are the client's resources for change?
- What are the client's strengths and vulnerabilities?
- What does the client want from therapy, and how can it best be achieved?
- What should be the focus of the sessions?
- What factors are contributing to the client's problems, and what can be done to alleviate them?
- In what ways can an understanding of the client's cultural background shed light on developing a plan to deal with the problems?
- What specific family dynamics might be relevant to the client's present struggles and interpersonal relationships?
- What kind of support system does the client have?
- What are the prospects for meaningful change?

From our perspective, assessment and diagnosis can help the practitioner conceptualize a case and implement treatment. The clinician and the client can discuss key questions as part of the therapeutic process. Counselors will develop hypotheses about their clients, and they can talk about these conjectures with them. Diagnosis does not have to be a matter of categorizing clients;

rather, counselors can think more broadly, describe behavior, and think about its meaning. In this way, diagnosis becomes a process of thinking *about* the client *with* the client. Diagnosis can be viewed as a general descriptive statement identifying a client's style of functioning. The therapist can develop hunches about a client's behavioral style and perhaps even share these observations with the client as a part of the therapeutic process.

We favor a collaborative approach to assessment, one that includes the client as a therapeutic partner. After the initial assessment of the client is completed, a decision can be made whether to refer the individual for alternative or additional treatment. If the client is accepted by the therapist, the two can discuss the assessment results. This information can be used in exploring the client's difficulties and in selecting treatment goals. Assessment and diagnosis can be linked directly to the therapeutic process, forming a basis for developing methods of evaluating how well the therapist's procedures are working to achieve the client's goals.

It is not so much a simple question of whether to diagnose or not. Using DSM-IV nomenclature is a reality that most practitioners must accept, especially if they work within a managed care system. For therapists who must work with a diagnostic framework, the challenge is to use diagnosis as a means to the end of providing quality service to clients rather than as an end in itself that leads to a justification for treatment. As one clinician put this struggle: "It's hard *not* to think in terms of DSM when I have to use it every day for managed care. The language seeps into my brain, into the way I look at clients, even when I know better" (Wylie, 1995, p. 68).

Clarifying your stance. What is your position on diagnosis? The following questions may help you clarify your thinking on this issue:

- After reviewing the arguments for and against psychodiagnosis, what position do you tend to support? Why?
- Some contend that clients have a right to know their diagnoses as part of informed consent. What do you think of this practice?
- If you omit telling the client the diagnosis, how do you explain that omission from your informed consent?
- Some maintain that clients should not be told their diagnoses because of dangers of their living up to a self-fulfilling prophecy. What is your thinking on this matter?
- If you were working for an agency that relied on managed care programs, how would you deal with the requirement of quickly formulating a diagnosis and a treatment plan? How would you work with the limitations of being able to see clients for no more than six visits?
- Some writers have taken the position that practitioners should take a stand against classification and coding for the purpose of third-party payments unless clients know of their diagnoses and agree to provide this information to insurance companies. Do you see an ethical issue in this practice?

- Do you agree or disagree that therapists who do not accept the medical model, yet who provide diagnoses for reasons of third-party payments, are compromising their integrity? Are there any ethical issues here?
- What ethical and professional issues can you raise pertaining to diagnosis? In your view what is the most critical issue?

Ethical and Legal Issues in Diagnosis

Ethical dilemmas are often created when diagnosis is done strictly for insurance purposes, which often entails arbitrarily assigning a client to a diagnostic classification, sometimes merely to qualify for third-party payment. Many insurance carriers will not pay for treatment that is not defined as an "illness" for which treatment is medically necessary. Wylie (1995) gives the example of the V-codes, a grab bag of diagnostic leftovers at the back of DSM-IV that rarely qualify for reimbursement. If a therapist treats a couple for marital difficulties and submits a claim with a V-code diagnosis, chances are that the claim will be rejected. Some therapists may agree to see a couple or a family but submit a claim for an individual as the "identified patient," using an acceptable DSM diagnosis. According to Wylie (1995), not only is this practice technically unethical and inaccurate but it may be illegal.

Hamann (1994) stresses that under no circumstances should clinicians compromise themselves regarding the accuracy of a diagnosis to make it "fit" criteria accepted by an insurance company. This behavior is not only unethical but is also fraudulent. Some practitioners who are opposed to a diagnostic framework take the path of least resistance and give every client the same diagnosis. A related matter is the fact that many insurance companies pay only for psychological services that have been approved under an acceptable diagnosis. Presumably, clients who consult therapists regarding problems that do not fit a standard category will not be reimbursed for their psychotherapy.

With some managed care mental health companies, a therapist may call the company with a diagnosis. A technician then looks up "appropriate" treatment strategies to deal with the identified problem (if, indeed, the diagnosis even meets the criteria for reimbursement). This raises significant ethical issues. In such cases important treatment decisions may be made by a nonprofessional who has never seen the client.

Practitioners who submit claims to managed care companies must often wrestle with practical versus ethical decision making. If a therapist submits an honest diagnosis, but one not classified as an illness in DSM, there will be no reimbursement. However, if the diagnosis is selected mainly on the basis that it is one the company will accept, the therapist runs the risk of deceptive practice. "Therapists are forever trying to fit their diagnosis to the procrustean bed of official DSM terminology and managed care's interpretation of it" (Wylie, 1995, p. 32).

Competence is another central ethical issue in making assessments. If therapists do not understand how to work within a diagnostic framework, it is possible that they will develop inappropriate treatment plans. Unless practitioners have full diagnostic pictures of their clients, they cannot be certain that they are ethically providing the most appropriate treatment. For example, unless a practitioner knows that a client has had a manic episode, he or she may proceed incorrectly by treating depression alone. We also think it is an ethical (and sometimes legal) obligation of therapists to be mindful that a medical evaluation is many times indicated. This is especially true in dealing with problems such as organic disorders, schizophrenia, manic-depression, and suicidal types of depression. Students need to learn the clinical skills necessary to do this type of screening and referral, which is a form of diagnostic thinking.

Practitioners may cause harm to clients if they begin to treat their clients in restrictive ways because they have diagnosed them on the basis of a pattern of symptoms. Therapists can actually behave toward clients in ways that make it very difficult for the clients to change. Furthermore, it is essential that practitioners who use the DSM-IV be trained in its use. This training requires learning more than diagnostic categories; it involves knowing personality theory, psychopathology, and seeing how they relate to therapeutic practice. Now let us look at two specific cases where diagnosis and treatment options had to be evaluated.

◆ **The case of Irma.** Irma has just accepted her first position as a counselor in a community agency that is part of a managed care system. An agency policy requires her to conduct an intake interview with each client, determine a diagnosis, and establish a treatment plan—all in the first session. Once a diagnosis is established, clinicians have a maximum of five more sessions with a given client. After 3 weeks, she lets a colleague know that she is troubled by this timetable. Her colleague reassures her that what she is doing is acceptable and that the agency's aim is to satisfy the requirements of the HMO. Irma does not feel reassured and cannot justify making an assessment in so short a time.

- Do you share Irma's concern? Are there ethical difficulties with this agency's policies?
- Is it ever justified to provide a person with a diagnosis mainly for the purpose of obtaining third-party payment? How can you ethically satisfy the demands of insurance companies that a psychiatric disorder be identified and treated?
- If Irma retains her convictions, is she ethically obliged to discontinue her employment at this agency? What other alternatives, if any, do you see for her situation?
- In the course of a client's treatment, if the original diagnosis becomes obsolete, would you continue to use that diagnosis simply because your client wishes to see you?

◆ **The case of Bob.** Bob displays symptoms of anxiety and lethargy. After 12 weeks of treatment, Felicita realizes that her client has all the symptoms of a major depression and that he is showing no improvement. She is inclined to double the number of weekly sessions to accelerate her client's progress.

- What do you think of Felicita's plan? Is it justified?
- Should she have done a more thorough assessment earlier in the treatment? Might the results have indicated alternative treatments?
- Is Felicita obligated to refer Bob for a psychiatric evaluation to determine whether or not antidepressant medication is indicated? Is she obliged to refer him if he so desires?
- What are her ethical obligations if he refuses to see a psychiatrist?
- Do you see any other ethical issues in this case?

Cultural Issues in Diagnosis

In its ethics code ACA (1995) recognizes that cultural sensitivity is essential in making a proper diagnosis:

> Counselors recognize that culture affects the manner in which clients' problems are defined. Clients' socioeconomic and cultural experience is considered when diagnosing mental disorders. (E.5.b.)

The APA's (1992) *Ethical Principles* also provides general guidance in applying the assessment process with special populations:

> Psychologists attempt to identify situations in which particular interventions or assessment techniques or norms may not be applicable or may require adjustments in administration or interpretation because of factors such as individuals' gender, age, race, ethnicity, national origin, religion, sexual orientation, disability, language, or socioeconomic status. (2.04.c.)

If counselors fail to consider ethnic and cultural factors in certain patterns of behavior, a client may be subjected to an erroneous diagnosis. Due to the methods used to identify meaning in diagnosis, the cultural and gender aspects of the presenting problem frequently are not considered (Sinacore-Guinn, 1995), and certain behaviors and personality styles may be labeled neurotic or deviant simply because they are not characteristic of the dominant culture. Being adept at psychodiagnosis requires cultural sensitivity; without it the value of your diagnoses will be limited.

Itai and McRae (1994) recommend caution in diagnosis as it applies to cross-cultural situations, especially when English is not the client's primary language. Some cultural differences are easily misunderstood and misdiagnosed. Itai and McRae give the example of Japanese Americans to whom appearing foolish or crying in front of people would mean a loss of face. A therapist could inappropriately assign a DSM diagnosis of "Avoidant Personality Disorder" if the cultural imperative of not displaying emotion in public were not considered. Japanese Americans tend to let their parents make important decisions for them. Such clients could be misdiagnosed as "Dependent Personality Disorder" if the therapist did not understand the value placed on interdependence, respect, and conformity in Japanese culture.

The APA's (1993) guidelines for serving culturally diverse populations address the importance of modifying assessment and treatment approaches to meet the needs of ethnic minorities, recommending that providers of psychological services "need knowledge and skills for multicultural assessment and intervention" (p. 45), "recognize ethnicity and culture as significant parameters in understanding psychological processes" (p. 46), and "consider not only differential diagnostic issues but also the cultural beliefs and values of the client and his/her community in providing intervention" (p. 46).

DSM-IV also incorporates cautions so that misdiagnoses are less likely with culturally diverse populations:

> Diagnostic assessment can be especially challenging when a clinician from one ethnic or cultural group uses the DSM-IV classification to evaluate an individual from a different ethnic or cultural group. A clinician who is unfamiliar with the nuances of an individual's cultural frame of reference may incorrectly judge as psychopathology those normal variations in behavior, belief, or experience that are particular to the individual's culture. (American Psychiatric Association, 1994, p. xxiv)

Whenever clinicians assess clients with different ethnic or cultural backgrounds, it is important to be aware of unintentional bias and to keep an open mind to the possibility of distinctive ethnic and cultural patterns.

Using Tests in Counseling

As is true of diagnosis, the proper use of testing in counseling and therapy is the subject of some debate. Generally, those who use therapeutic approaches that emphasize an objective view of counseling are inclined to use testing procedures as tools to acquire information about clients or as resources that clients themselves can use to help them in their decision making. Therapists who employ person-centered and existential approaches tend to view testing in much the same way that they view diagnosis—as an external frame of reference that is of little use to them in counseling situations.

We think the core issue is not whether you will use tests but rather under what circumstances and for what purposes. Tests are available that measure aptitude, ability, achievement, intelligence, values and attitudes, vocational interests, or personality characteristics. Unfortunately, these tests are often misused. They may be given routinely, given without providing feedback to clients, used for the wrong purposes, or given by unqualified testers. Here are some questions that will help you think about the circumstances under which you might want to use tests for counseling purposes.

- What do you know about the tests you may use? It is important for counselors to be familiar with any tests they use and to have taken these tests themselves. They should know the purpose of each test and how it measures what it purports to measure. Sometimes mental health workers find that they are expected to give and interpret tests as a basic function of their job. If they have not had adequate training in this area, they are in an ethical bind. In-service training and continuing education programs are ways of gaining competence in using psychological assessment devices.

• Do you follow the codes of ethics with respect to competence in working with tests? The ACA (1995) indicates the importance of a counselor recognizing the limits of competence to use and interpret tests: "Counselors recognize the limits of their competence and perform only those testing and assessment services for which they have been trained." The APA's *Ethical Principles* (1992) stresses the importance of competence in assessment:

> Psychologists who develop, administer, score, interpret, or use psychological assessment techniques, interviews, tests, or instruments do so in a manner and for purposes that are appropriate in light of the research on or evidence of the usefulness and proper application of the techniques. (2.02.a.)

• How much involvement should clients have in the selection of tests? Should counselors assume the responsibility, or should clients decide whether they want to take certain tests? Are you ethically required to provide informed consent when administering tests?

• Do you know why you want to use a particular test? Does your agency require that you administer certain tests? Are you giving tests because they will help you understand a client better? Do you administer tests mainly when clients request them? Whatever your reasons, you should be able to state them clearly.

• When clients request testing, do you explore their reasons? Some clients may think that a test will provide them with answers in making important decisions. Clients need to be aware that tests are merely tools that can provide useful information they can then explore in their counseling sessions. They also need to know clearly what the tests are designed for. These points are particularly relevant in testing culturally diverse populations.

• How do you view test results? Do you believe test scores are true indicators of what is going on with the client? A true test score is only a theoretical possibility, but the standard error of measurement provided with every test is often overlooked. When test scores are understood as indicating a range of possibilities, they are often helpful in providing a guideline for future work.

• How do you integrate test results into the counseling sessions? In general, it is best to give test *results*, not simply test *scores*. In other words, explore with your clients the meaning the results have for them. Evaluate your clients' readiness to receive and accept certain information and be sensitive to the ways in which clients respond to the information provided. The interpretation and discussion of test data should be understandable and relevant to the needs of ethnically and culturally diverse client populations (APA, 1993).

• Are you concerned about maintaining the confidentiality of test results? Results may be handled in different ways, depending on the purpose and type of each test. Nevertheless, your clients need to feel that they can trust you and that test results will neither be used against them nor revealed to people who have no right to this information.

• Are you critical in evaluating tests? Too often mistakes are made because counselors have unquestioning faith in tests. Know the limitations of the tests you use, and keep in mind that a test can be useful and valid in one situation but inappropriate in another. On this point, the APA (1993) guidelines for working with diverse populations caution psychologists to consider the validity of a given test and to interpret test data in the context of the cultural and linguistic characteristics of the individual being tested. Be aware of the reference population of the test, and recognize the possible limitations of such an instrument with other populations.

The ACA (1995) has developed a number of specific standards governing the ethical use of tests in counseling. Clients being tested should know what the test is intended to discover, how it relates to their situation, and how the results will be used. Test results should be placed in proper perspective and read in the context of other relevant factors. Furthermore, in interpreting tests it is essential for counselors to recognize the effects of socioeconomic, ethnic, linguistic, and cultural factors that might affect scores. The ACA warns counselors to proceed with caution when testing culturally diverse client populations and to avoid inappropriate testing that may be outside the client's socialized behavioral or cognitive patterns.

Clients from culturally diverse backgrounds may react to testing with suspicion if tests have been used to discriminate against them in schools and employment. To minimize such negative reactions, it is a good practice to explore a client's views and feelings about testing and to work with him or her in resolving attitudes that are likely to affect the outcome of a test. ACA's guideline on diversity in testing reinforces the need for caution when interpreting tests:

> Counselors are cautious in using assessment techniques, making evaluations, and interpreting the performance of special populations not represented in the norm group on which an instrument was standardized. They recognize the effects of age, color, culture, disability, ethnic group, gender, race, religion, sexual orientation, and socioeconomic status on test administration and interpretation and place test results in proper perspective with other relevant factors. (E. 8.)

Many clients seek tests in the hope of finding "answers." It is important to explore why a person wants to take a battery of tests and to teach the person the values and limitations of testing. If that is done, there is less chance the tests will be undertaken in a mechanical fashion or that unwarranted importance will be attributed to the results. Perhaps the most basic ethical guideline for using tests is to keep in mind the primary purpose for which they were designed: to provide objective and descriptive measures that can be used by clients in making better decisions. Additionally, it is wise to remember that tests are tools that should be used in the service of clients, not against clients.

Counseling in a Managed Care Environment

Mental health professionals are challenged to deal with some unique ethical issues if they work in a managed care environment. MacCluskie and Ingersoll (2001) point out one of the challenges for delivering services in a sensitive and ethical manner in a managed care environment:

> This is not to imply that managed care is unethical care; only that in the context of managed care, the motives for decision making are primarily economic. Economic parsimony does not necessarily constitute unethical behavior unless it sacrifices the sufficiency or quality of care in the process. This is precisely where some observers have criticized managed care and managed care companies in general. (pp. 102–103)

Until the 1980s mental health services were generally purchased through a traditional fee-for-service delivery system, wherein practitioners controlled both the supply and the demand dimensions of service delivery (Cummings, 1995). Practitioners decided what clients needed, how and when to treat them, and how long therapy would last. Individual practitioners billed insurance carriers on a fee-for-service basis, and there was little incentive for practitioners to reduce costs by increasing their efficiency and effectiveness. With large numbers of health care professionals entering the marketplace, the general expectation was that fees would fall. However, the opposite has been the case, and fees have risen.

Rapidly escalating costs, especially in inpatient care, have led third-party payors to demand more effective cost and quality controls (see Acuff et al., 1999; Broskowski, 1991; Cooper & Gottlieb, 2000; Cummings, 1995; Glosoff, Garcia, Herlihy, & Remley, 1999; Haas & Cummings, 1991; Hering, 2000; Hersch, 1995; Karon, 1995; I. J. Miller, 1996c, 1996d; Newman & Bricklin, 1991). Managed care offered a plan to businesses that would reduce the costs of care (Hersch, 1995). The creation of managed care was a business decision. Offering a system that promised a reduction in health care costs was easy to sell to businesses. The development of managed care was helped by the failure of mental health professionals to control rising costs of health care services.

Psychological fees are often exorbitant, which means that only a small number of people can afford them. On a personal note, consider the case of a student we know who wanted to enter couples therapy. She inquired about the fee schedule and was given this overview by the therapist:

> For a 90-minute session with a couple my fee is $290. I like to see the couple together for the first session to get a sense of how you interact as a couple. Then I see each partner individually for the second and third sessions. In the fourth session, I meet with you as a couple to establish your goals for therapy.

At this point the process has cost the couple $1,160, and if they are lucky, they have identified the goals for their work. This is a good example of an approach to treatment that has contributed to the rise of cost-containment systems for mental health services. As intrusive and arbitrary as managed care can be, it may well be that therapists have otherwise priced themselves out of business.

Fee-for-Service Care Versus Managed Care

Under fee-for-service care, some therapists operate from the assumption, "the longer, the better." The managed care dictum appears to be "the shorter, the better." In both systems, clients are vulnerable to the judgment of others (in the first instance the solo practitioner and in the second the HMO provider) regarding length of treatment, nature of treatment, techniques to be used, and content of treatment sessions. In the fee-for-service approach, individual practitioners determine the costs and the length of treatment without any outside review. To think that this system is not abused would be naive. However, it is equally obvious that managed care does not focus on the best interests of the client. As the managed care model stresses time-limited interventions, cost-effective methods, and a focus on preventive rather than curative strategies, this shift in values has, as Cummings (1995) points out, brought forth a fundamental redefinition of the role of the therapist. I. J. Miller (1996b) reports that one major problem with managed care is that clients receiving therapy are undertreated, which leads to underdiagnosing important conditions, dangerously restricting hospital admissions, failing to make referrals, and providing insufficient follow-up. Other writers state that mental health practitioners and managed care companies appear to be worlds apart in their respective set of work values.

Managed care is driven by economics, like any other business. Current managed care practice is characterized more by an interest in reducing costs than by quality of service. Managed care systems are primarily interested in cost containment as a route to profitability and are concerned only secondarily with consumer needs and preferences. Equally untenable are health care professionals' attitudes that the pursuit of profit has no place in the effective delivery of psychological services (Davis & Meier, 2001; Karon, 1995).

Shore (1996) states that managed care makes people powerless, depriving them of basic rights of choice, privacy, and decision making: "Managed care is simply a search on behalf of employers for the cheapest health plan—a search, by the insurer, for the least possible treatment performed by the cheapest, least-trained clinician" (p. 324). It is clear that financial considerations are driving decisions and that the costs of medical care have soared. But does managed care cure the problem or simply create a new problem? What about what is best for the client? Again, Shore is critical of managed care, stating: "Managed care favors clinicians who generate a profit and cause no trouble. Skill, training, and ethics matter less than compliance with managed care procedures" (p. 324).

In her discussion of the ethical issues in managed care, Austad (1996) points out that those who oppose managed care contend that it is inherently unethical because it gives providers a financial incentive to withhold treatment. Furthermore, the financial incentives inherent in managed care tempt both the practitioner and the payor to underserve clients in these ways:

- Deny and limit access to long-term therapy
- Narrow the clients' choice of a therapist
- Disrupt the continuity of care
- Rely on less-qualified providers to provide services
- Use less-qualified providers to review care
- Breach client confidentiality by giving reviewers too much personal information about clients
- Base practices on a business ethic instead of a professional ethic

Despite these problems, Austad is not opposed to managed care, and she makes a convincing case about the myth of long-term psychotherapy as the standard for ideal therapy.

Austad (1996) contends that long-term therapy poses real problems for the fair distribution of psychological services to those who need care. Taking the position that what is good for the individual must be tempered by the common good, Austad urges the profession to develop therapy models that provide care to the largest number who need treatment. She believes it is better to give some therapy to those who need it rather than to provide abundant therapy to only a select few. Austad argues that short-term therapy can be highly effective, that it is not inferior to long-term treatment, and that brief therapy enables more people to be served. She concludes with this statement:

> A change from an individual ethic to a societal ethic will lead to a change from long-term dominance to temporal eclecticism. And this change will command greater accessibility and universality for behavioral health care. Let us develop a societal ethic of psychotherapy whereby both patients and therapists know that they should take what they need and leave the rest for others. (p. 275)

Of interest in the discussion of the ethics of managed care is the lack of any strong voice coming from the professional organizations. Although the codes of ethics of these organizations all have guidelines pertaining to the priority of client welfare and competent services, they are essentially silent on the ethics of certain operations of managed care companies. The question we consider to be at the core of this conflict is this: Who is taking care of the client's interests?

Critical Ethical Issues Associated With Managed Care

Counselors who work in a managed care context face a number of ethical concerns. In a review of recent literature, we identified four major areas where ethical dilemmas most commonly surface in a managed care system: (1) informed consent, (2) confidentiality, (3) abandonment, and (4) utilization review. The following discussion is based on key points from a variety of sources (Acuff et al., 1999; Cooper & Gottlieb, 2000; Davis & Meier, 2001; Glosoff et al., 1999; Haas & Cummings, 1991; Hering, 2000; Karon, 1995; MacCluskie & Ingersoll, 2001; Newman & Bricklin, 1991; Younggren, 2000).

Informed consent. Informed consent is an ongoing process. If you are a practitioner who works within a managed care setting, you need to address these questions:

- What can I do to maintain both ethical standards and high-quality services?
- What concerns are there regarding the ethics of such systems themselves?
- What kinds of information does my client have a right to know prior to entering into a professional relationship with me?

Informed consent assumes particular importance under a managed care system, and informed consent forms should state that the managed care company may request a client's diagnosis, results on any tests given, a wide range of clinical information, treatment plans, and perhaps even the entire clinical record of a client. Clinicians who work in a managed care system are ethically bound to ensure that clients understand any policies or arrangements with managed care systems that are pertinent to treatment before entering into a therapeutic relationship (Glosoff et al., 1999).

Acuff and her colleagues (1999) point out that some managed care organizations make it a practice not to provide full, complete, and accurate information to their subscribers. Many clients are not fully aware of how the complexities of managed care arrangements affect their benefits and rights, and it is a mistake to assume that new clients have complete information regarding how the managed care system affects their specific benefit package. For this reason, the informed consent procedure must be very clear (Cooper & Gottlieb, 2000).

Clients have a right to know that there may be other forms of treatment—possibly ones that may be more helpful—that are being denied to them solely for cost-containment reasons. They have a right to know if the therapist is versed in brief therapy, that an outside person is likely to judge what kind of treatment will be given and how many sessions will be allowed, the specific limitations of the plan they are participating in, and who decides the time of termination of therapy. Ethical practice demands that providers inform clients of all of these issues pertaining to their treatment, but managed care practices often fall short of full disclosure.

Confidentiality. Traditionally, confidentiality is considered an ethical and legal duty imposed on therapists to protect client disclosures, as you recall from Chapter 5. Within a managed care context, however, confidentiality may no longer be presumed in the therapeutic relationship. Davis and Meier (2001) observe: "While maintaining confidentiality has always been a cornerstone of counseling and psychotherapy, for some managed care companies it is unfamiliar terrain" (p. 42). Managed care shifts the traditional basis for limits on confidentiality to matters pertaining to cost containment (Cooper & Gottlieb, 2000). In exploring confidentiality in managed care, Acuff and her colleagues (1999) contend that without the assurance of confidentiality it is reasonable to assume that many people will not seek treatment, and clients in therapy may withhold crucial information. Although there have always been exceptions to confidentiality, the demand for client information inherent in managed care far exceeds traditional limitations to confidentiality. At the very least, clients should be aware that managed care contracts may require therapists to reveal sensitive client information to a third party who is in a position to authorize initial or additional treatment. Practitioners can no longer assure their clients of confidential therapy at any level. Practitioners have no control over confidential information once it leaves their offices, and many managed care contracts require a practitioner to submit all treatment records before payment is issued. Because of these restrictions on confidentiality, therapists have an obligation to inform clients from the outset of therapy about the relevant limits of confidentiality under their managed care policy (Acuff et al., 1999; Cooper & Gottlieb, 2000).

Hering (2000) has argued that managed care has resulted in the erosion of the traditional sense of confidentiality. HMOs have wide access to client disclosures, and clients cannot be assured that much of what they say will remain confidential. Hering asserts that the managed care company is mainly concerned with cost containment and only gives lip service to a therapist's autonomy and professional judgment. In short, managed care, without any legal intervention, without any research, without any input from professional organizations, has redefined confidentiality.

Abandonment. The codes of ethics of professional organizations state that mental health practitioners do not abandon clients. Traditionally, the matter of termination of therapy is a collaborative effort involving both the client and the therapist. Under managed care programs, termination is generally a matter decided by the managed care provider. Termination does not come out of a collaborative process but out of company policy. Clients may have a sense of abandonment if their therapy ends abruptly. It is the responsibility of therapists to inform clients that the request for additional sessions may or may not be granted by their managed care provider.

In many HMOs, clients are limited to 20 sessions annually, with lifetime cost caps, and they may be denied the care they need if it extends beyond their benefits. Even though a client's policy may allow for up to 20 therapy sessions, the client may be authorized for only 6 sessions. It is essential to apply for additional sessions well in advance of the last authorized visit (Cooper & Gottlieb, 2000). Although these limitations may make financial sense, this situation can become ethically problematic. Haas and Cummings (1991) note that this policy shifts the risk to the therapist. Therapists are ethically and legally obligated to offer a standard of care to clients, and they are not to abandon them. This puts therapists who work with managed care in the position of referring clients if continued therapy is needed.

Although the cost-containment practices of managed care are not necessarily unethical, Acuff and her colleagues (1999) believe that such practices can lead to client abandonment:

> Unfortunately, the industrialization of health care has created financial incentives to limit treatment even when, in the psychologist's opinion, treatment is clinically indicated and the patient desires more treatment. These arrangements may limit the ability of psychologists and patients to work collaboratively to complete treatment successfully within a realistic time frame. (p. 571)

As an alternative to ending treatment with a client who clearly needs further treatment, therapists could offer *pro bono* services. However, this might put an unrealistic strain on their ability to survive financially. If referral resources are not readily available, and if therapists are not willing to abandon clients, how can therapists protect their financial interests and still serve the best interests of their clients?

It is anticipated that more consumers of mental health services will file both ethical and legal complaints against therapists because of their willingness to terminate therapy due to decisions made by HMOs (Glosoff et al., 1999). Practitioners are ultimately responsible to their clients in an HMO system, even if the decisions are made by the managed care system.

Utilization review. Under managed care plans all treatment is monitored. Utilization review refers to the use of predefined criteria to evaluate treatment necessity, appropriateness of therapeutic intervention, and therapy effectiveness. This process may take place before, during, and after treatment (Cooper & Gottlieb, 2000). Acuff and her colleagues (1999) state that utilization management and review involves making decisions regarding types of treatment, setting, and the duration of treatment. They point out that ideally the needs of the client should remain paramount, yet these needs should be met in a cost-effective manner. Utilization review of clients is generally done by way of a written document that is periodically sent to the company. One disadvantage of this form of review is the possibility of the loss of confidentiality, because paper reviews are sent by mail or electronic means. The disadvantage of telephone reviews is finding the time to make the call and then waiting to actually make the connection (Davis & Meier, 2001). One additional potential problem pertaining to utilization review is the competence of the person doing the reviewing. Is the reviewer also a clinician? If not, what makes the individual competent to make a clinical decision?

Other ethical issues. Other common problems that must be addressed include matters of financial incentives; diagnosis and assessment; competence; limited client choice of diverse providers; and teaching, training, and supervision of students (Glosoff et al., 1999). Competence is a critical issue. Therapists must be capable of providing time-limited, effective services. Furthermore, therapists will have to assume a pragmatic and theoretically eclectic orientation, as they will need to demonstrate flexibility in the use of effective techniques in dealing with a variety of problems. Therapists who are not competent in short-term interventions should probably avoid involvement in a managed care program. In this system, brief therapy is the norm, regardless of the problem. If counselors are not trained in brief therapy methods, and if clients will not be well served by a limited number of sessions, then counselors need to have skills in making appropriate referrals.

A critical ethical issue involves the divided loyalties therapists experience in attempting to do what is best for the client and the obligation to contain costs and restrict intervention to short-term, highly focused goals. It is important that the welfare of the client does not get put on the back burner in the interests of preserving the financial integrity of the system. Karon (1995) reminds us that competent and ethical therapists are primarily concerned with the well-being of their clients, which is an entirely different criterion from cost effectiveness.

Karon (1995) considers psychotherapy under managed health care "a growing crisis and a national nightmare." Although Karon admits that there are legitimate ways to save money without impairing the quality of care, he emphasizes that doing so requires careful thought and research; managed care companies are largely ignoring such reasonable and reasoned approaches. Stating that the aim of managed care is to provide as little psychological care as possible, while giving the appearance of providing adequate mental health care, Karon contends that ethical therapists are bound to encounter dilemmas. In a system where the median number of sessions is five or six, no matter what problem is presented, medication is often relied on to obviate the need for long-term therapy. Davis and Meier (2001) make a further observation of what may ensue from the practices of some managed care companies: "A danger exists that a new hierarchy of psychotherapy will develop with the most skilled therapists unavailable to those with managed care coverage that is not clinician friendly" (p. 52).

Managed Care and Malpractice

Mental health managed care increases the potential for misdiagnosis, negligent treatment, and abandonment of the client. According to Stromberg and Dellinger (1993), two core issues of malpractice apply to managed care: standard of care and therapist liability. Is the standard of care by which a therapist's service is measured different, or lower, in a managed care plan? Some may argue that clients who participate in a less expensive health plan—one that offers only limited coverage for psychological services—should not be in a position to sue therapists who terminate treatment after a predetermined number of sessions. To date, there is no evidence that courts recognize a lower standard of competence for managed care versus fee-for-service care. This means that therapists who work under managed care must still do the best they can to provide the kind of service clients require. Moreover, practitioners have a responsibility to anticipate the limited nature of services, and they should discuss the implications of this with their clients.

Are health care professionals liable for decisions to limit care that are specified by managed care plans? Some court rulings have established an ambiguous but important obligation for therapists: Although therapists need not disregard the utilization review standards of the managed care plan, they are likely to be legally required (1) to provide emergency psychological services regardless of payment, and (2) to energetically seek approval for additional services that the client genuinely needs.

A recent ruling by a federal court has implications for therapists who work with managed care companies. Believed to be the first of its kind involving a managed behavioral health care company, the 1996 lawsuit alleged that CIGNA Behavioral Health, Incorporated terminated therapists, purportedly without cause, when therapists requested more sessions for their clients than the managed care company was willing to provide. In their lawsuit, the plaintiffs claimed that in limiting the number of sessions provided the managed care company was substituting its judgment for the therapist's professional judgment, contrary to client welfare and public policy, and that these policies unlawfully prevented psychologists from exercising appropriate standards of care and clinical judgment. Nessman and Herndon (2000) report that this ruling has implications beyond this particular case and CIGNA: "In essence, a federal court determined that if a managed-care company uses 'no cause' terminations to retaliate against providers who advocate for their patients to secure needed care, this would be an illegal act in violation of public policy" (pp. 20–21).

It is clear that managed care has both ethical and legal implications for professional practice. Ethically, therapists must not abandon their clients, and they have a responsibility to render competent services. Legally, it appears that practitioners employed by a managed care unit are not exempt from malpractice suits if clients claim that they did not receive the standard of care they required. Therapists cannot use the limitations of the managed care plan as a shield for failing to render crisis intervention, to make appropriate referrals, or to request additional services from the plan.

The Future of Mental Health Care Delivery

Most who write about managed care seem to agree that the system is here to stay and that therapists will need to become trained or retrained in a body of knowledge and skills applicable to time-efficient and cost-effective therapies. All mental health providers are facing and will continue to face major changes in the manner in which their services are delivered. Clearly, accommodations must be made if professionals expect to survive in the era of managed care. Hersch (1995) notes the initial negative and defensive reactions on the part of practitioners and calls upon psychologists to use their existing organizational structures to form working alliances with other professional groups, consumer groups, and employers to influence the direction of health care reform. He concludes:

> If psychologists mobilize their resources constructively, they can occupy important leadership roles in reshaping the health care system in ways that enhance psychology's opportunities to serve the public's welfare. (p. 25)

Various writers have forecast the future of mental health services under managed care. Here is a sampling of their thoughts:

> Overall, experts agree that managed care, in some form, is here to stay, at least in the foreseeable future . . . It is expected that practitioners will be doing more group therapy, especially psychoeducational groups. Finally, we anticipate that there will be an increase in the effort to use manualized therapy for various diagnostic categories to standardize practice and reduce cost. (Cooper & Gottlieb, 2000, p. 229)

> Managed care works in its present form because we let this dictatorial system keep us feeling helpless and powerless. We have been shamed into abdicating control to a ruthless corporate authoritarian, whose value system is based soley on the profit motive . . . It is time to stand up and take responsibility for our fear. Let us do what we would advise our own clients to do: empower ourselves before managed care owns any more of us than it already does. (Hering, 2000, p. 38)

> In summary, the future doctoral practitioner will be an innovative clinician, a creative researcher, an inspired supervisor, a knowledgeable health psychologist, a caring skilled manager, and an astute business person. (Cummings, 1995, p. 15)

We certainly are not wise enough to predict the future of the therapy enterprise under a managed care paradigm. However, we wonder whether managed care might be improved, from an ethical dimension, if clients were included in the review process of their assessment and the appropriateness for treatment. Under both the old and the new systems clients have had relatively little voice in decisions that are made about them. Under the old system a solo practitioner might tell them, "Your problem will require at least 2 years of therapy, or longer." With the new system the client is likely to hear, "Your treatment will be limited to six sessions." Regardless of the structure underlying the delivery of services, we believe ethical practice demands that clients be given the maximum voice possible in agreeing to basic aspects of their treatment and in participating in the process of making decisions about the course of their therapy.

Clarifying your stance. If you are currently in training to become a mental health services provider, you will surely confront some of these issues. Clarify your position by answering these questions about working in a managed care environment.

- What are the major ethical problems you might face under a managed care program?
- Is your role being determined or restricted by managed care? To what degree are you willing to accept the requirements imposed by a managed care approach?
- How might your ability to establish a working relationship with your clients be affected under managed care?
- How would you educate your clients about the benefits and limitations inherent in a managed care plan? Can you think of ways to increase the chances that your clients will have a voice in the process of their therapy?
- What steps can you take to become competent in rendering cost-effective treatments that do not compromise the welfare of your clients?

Ethical Issues in Psychotherapeutic Research

Most of the questions we have raised in this chapter have a direct relationship to a therapist's therapeutic approach. Specialized techniques, the balance of responsibility in the client-therapist relationship, the functions of the therapist, and the goals of treatment are all tied to a therapist's theoretical orientation. But at some point you will probably ask: Does my psychotherapeutic approach or technique work? To answer this question, you need to rely on the findings of psychotherapeutic research.

Although the ethical implications of conducting research in counseling and psychotherapy are vast, we want to address a few selected issues and encourage you to think about your responsibilities in this area. Consider these questions:

- In conducting research in a counseling setting, is it necessary that participants always give their informed consent? Can you think of situations in which it might be justified not to obtain informed consent for the sake of a better research design?
- Is it ever ethical to use deception in psychological research? Is deception justified if the participants are given accurate details after the research study is completed?
- Can practitioners be considered ethical if they practice without conducting any research on the techniques they use or without having them empirically validated?

Ethics and Research: Some Situations

Considering the vast number of studies on psychotherapeutic research, there is little discussion in the literature of the ethical problems encountered in designing and conducting studies. Yet critical ethical issues in this field deserve the careful attention of investigators (Imber et al., 1986). In this section we consider some of these issues, including informed consent, using deception in psychological research, withholding treatment, using placebos, research with training and personal-growth groups, and cultural diversity in research. For further reading in this area we recommend Sales and Folkman (2000).

Situations involving informed consent. We define informed consent as the participant's assent to being involved in a research study after having received full information about the procedures and their associated risks and benefits. In the process of informing research participants about what will be expected of them, it is important to use simple and clear language in addition to any technical language that may be required. Nagy (2000) lists the following elements as being basic to informed consent:

- Description of the research
- Voluntary participation
- Consequences of refusing to participate or dropping out
- Information that would affect one's willingness to participate
- Answering questions raised by participants

The APA (1992) guideline stresses outlining the responsibilities of both researcher and participant:

> Prior to conducting research (except research involving only anonymous surveys, naturalistic observations, or similar research), psychologists enter into an agreement with participants that clarifies the nature of the research and the responsibilities of each party. (6.10)

NASW's (1999) code of ethics focuses on informed consent issues regarding research participants:

> Social workers engaged in evaluation or research should obtain voluntary and written informed consent from participants, when appropriate, without any implied or actual deprivation or penalty for refusal to participate, without undue inducement to participate, and with due regard for participants' well-being, privacy and dignity. Informed consent should include information about the nature, extent, and duration of the participation requested and disclosure of the risks and benefits of participation in the research. (5.02.e.)

Informed consent is important for a variety of reasons: it protects people's autonomy by allowing them to make decisions about matters that directly concern them; it guarantees that the participants will be exposed to certain risks only if they agree to them; it decreases the possibility of an adverse public reaction to experimenting with human subjects; and it helps researchers scrutinize their designs for inherent risks (Lindsey, 1984). The researcher might be guided by asking: "What would clients who are interested in their own welfare need to know before making a decision?" With these points in mind consider the following situation to determine the ethics of the researcher's behavior.

◆ **The case of Hannah.** Hannah is committed to designing research procedures to evaluate the process and outcome of her treatment programs. She is convinced that to obtain valid data she must keep the research participants ignorant in many respects. Thus, she thinks it is important that the clients she sees be unaware that they are being studied and be unaware of the hypotheses under investigation. Although she agrees that some ethical issues may be raised by her failure to inform her clients, she believes that good research designs call for such procedures. She does not want to influence her clients and thus bias the results of her study, so she chooses to keep information from them. She contends that her practices are justified because there are no negative consequences or risks involved with her research. She further contends that if she is able to refine her therapeutic techniques through her research efforts with her clients, both they and future clients will be the beneficiaries.

- What are your thoughts about Hannah's ethics and the rationale she gives for not obtaining informed consent?
- Assume that she was interested in studying the effects of therapists' reinforcement of statements by clients during sessions. If the clients knew she was using certain procedures and studying certain behaviors, would it bias the results?
- If the value of the research seems to be greater than the risks involved to participants, do you think researchers are justified in not obtaining the informed consent of participants?

Commentary. Although some of Hannah's contentions have merit, we do not think the ends are justified by the means she employs. Further, although she might be justified in withholding some of the details of her research studies (or the hypotheses under investigation), it seems unethical for her to fail even to mention to her clients that she is actually doing research with them as part of her therapeutic approach. Because Hannah's clients are investing themselves both emotionally and financially in their therapy, they have the right to be informed about procedures that are likely to affect them. Furthermore, they have the right to agree or refuse to be a part of her study. Her approach does not allow them to make that choice.

Situations involving deception. Individuals who participate in a research project have a right to know what they will be voluntarily agreeing to. One of APA's (1992) guidelines on deception in research is this: "Psychologists never deceive research participants about significant aspects that would affect their willingness to participate, such as physical risks, discomfort, or unpleasant emotional experiences" (6.15.b.). ACA's (1995) standard on deception reads: "Counselors do not conduct research involving deception unless alternative procedures are not feasible and the prospective value of the research justifies the deception. When the methodological requirements of a study necessitate concealment or deception, the investigator is required to explain clearly the reasons for this action as soon as possible" (G.2.b.).

The case against deception in psychological research has been strongly made, and ethics codes prohibit deception that undermines an individual's rights. Deception violates the individual's right to voluntarily choose to participate, abuses the trusting relationship between experimenter and subject, contributes to deception as a societal value, is contrary to the professional roles of educator or scientist, and will eventually erode trust in the profession of psychology (Adair, Dushenko, & Lindsay, 1985). With these points in mind, consider the following situation and determine whether deception is justified.

◆ **The case of Vincent.** Vincent, a family therapist, routinely videotapes his initial session with families without their knowledge. He does so because he wants to have a basis for comparing the family's behavior at the outset with their behavior at the final session. He assumes that if the family members knew they were being videotaped at the initial session they would behave in self-conscious and fearful ways. At the beginning of therapy he does not think they could handle the fact of being taped. Yet he likes to have families look at themselves on videotape at their final session, at which time he tells them that he taped their initial session and explains why he did not inform them of this procedure.

- Because Vincent eventually does tell families that they were taped at the initial session, do you think he is guilty of deception? Explain.
- To what degree do you think the practice of taping clients without their knowledge affects the trust level in the therapeutic relationship? Are the possible benefits of this practice worth the potential risks to the practitioner's reputation?

Commentary. Vincent's policy of videotaping clients without their knowledge and consent is ethically questionable. Most of the professional codes of the national organizations explicitly state that such a practice is to be avoided. Because the therapeutic relationship is built on goodwill and trust, we oppose any practices that are likely to jeopardize that trust.

Situations involving withholding treatment. Is it ethical to withhold treatment from a particular group so that it can be used as a control group? Consider this situation.

◆ **The case of Hope.** Hope works with people diagnosed as depressive psychotics in a state mental hospital. In the interest of refining therapeutic interventions that will help depressed clients, she combines therapy and research procedures. Specifically, she employs cognitive-behavioral approaches in a given ward. Her research design specifies treatment techniques for a particular group of patients, and she carefully monitors their rate of improvement as part of the treatment program. Hope says that she believes in the value of cognitive-behavioral approaches for depressive patients, yet she feels a professional and ethical obligation to empirically validate her treatment strategies. For her to know whether the treatment procedures alone are responsible for changes in the patients' behaviors, she deems it essential to have a comparable group of patients who do not receive the treatment. When she is challenged on the ethics of withholding treatment from a particular group of patients on the ward, she justifies her practice on the ground that she is working within the dictates of sound research procedures.

- Some researchers contend that they are necessarily caught in ethical dilemmas if they want to use a control group. Do you see an apparent contradiction between the demands of sound research methodology and sound ethical practice?
- Do you think Hope was acting ethically in withholding treatment so that she could test her therapeutic procedures? Would it be better for her to simply forget any attempts at empirical validation of her procedures and devote her efforts to treating as many patients as she can?
- Would it be ethical for her to use procedures that are untested?

◆ **A modification of the case.** In a second case Hope uses placebo controls. That is, rather than merely denying treatment to a group or keeping members on a waiting list, she meets with a control group whose members think they are receiving therapy but actually are not receiving standard treatment. In short, the group is led to believe that it is benefiting from therapy.

- What are the ethics of using placebos in counseling and clinical research?
- Does the placebo approach by its very nature constitute deception of patients?
- Can you think of any situations that justify the use of this approach?

Situations involving research with training and personal growth. In many graduate programs it is common for trainees in counseling internships to participate in personal-growth groups. Sometimes these groups are integrated with training or supervision groups in which the interns are encouraged to explore their own personal issues that arise in conjunction with their placements in the field.

◆ **The case of Wesley.** Wesley makes it a practice to conduct research on the process and outcomes of the personal-growth groups he leads for counselor trainees. To begin with, all the students in his graduate counseling program are required to attend the sessions of a personal-growth group for a full academic year. In addition to leading these growth groups for trainees, he also teaches theory courses and supervises students writing master's theses and doctoral dissertations. His primary theoretical orientation is Gestalt therapy, with an emphasis on other experiential and role-playing techniques. He expects the students to come to the sessions and be willing to work on personal concerns. These personal concerns often pertain to issues that arise as a result of problems they encounter with difficult client situations in their internship. At the beginning of the group Wesley asks students to take psychological tests that assess traits such as openness, dogmatism, degree of self-acceptance, level of self-esteem, and other dimensions of personality that he deems to be related to one's ability to counsel others. He again administers these same devices at the end of the year so that he has a comparison. During the year he asks a group of experts to observe his trainees in the group sessions at various points. This is done so that outsiders can assess the level of growth of individuals at different points as well as get a sense of the progress of the group as a whole.

As part of informed consent, Wesley tells the trainees what he is attempting to evaluate during the year, and he discusses fully with them the rationale for using outsiders to observe the group. He also promises the students that he will meet with them individually at any time during the semester if they want to discuss any personal issues. He also meets with them individually at the end of the group to discuss changes in scores on the psychological tests. As a way to correct for his bias in the investigation, he submits his research design to a university committee. The function of this committee is to review his design for any ethical considerations and to give him suggestions for improving his study.

- Do you think it is ethical for a program to require student attendance at personal-growth groups? Is it ethical for the leader of such a group to also have these same students in academic classes and to evaluate and supervise them?
- What research practices, if any, would you say are ethically questionable?
- Do you think it is ethically sound to have observers as a part of the design? The students know about these outsiders, but the observers will be part of the process even if some students do not like the idea. Do you see pressure being exerted? If so, is it justified in this case?
- What recommendations can you make for improving Wesley's research design as well as improving the quality of the learning experience for the students?

Cultural Diversity Aspects of Research

Although research is considered basic to the development of theory, cultural factors are often neglected in both research and theory. It is critical that research designs be based on culturally sensitive principles. ACA's (1995) guideline on the use of human subjects is as follows: "Counselors plan, design, conduct, and report research in a manner consistent with pertinent ethical principles, federal and state laws, host institution regulations, and scientific standards governing research with human subjects. Counselors design and conduct research that reflects cultural sensitivity appropriateness" (G.1.a.). Another guideline is given on diversity: "Counselors are sensitive to diversity and research issues with special populations. They seek consultation when appropriate" (G.1.f.).

The APA's "Guidelines for Providers of Psychological Services to Ethnic, Linguistic, and Culturally Diverse Populations" (1993) calls for a conceptual framework that will enable service providers to organize and accurately assess the value and utility of current and future research involving diverse ethnic and cultural populations. These guidelines include an exploration of several research issues:

- The impact of ethnic and racial similarity in the counseling process
- Minority groups' use of mental health services
- The relative effectiveness of directive and nondirective styles of therapy
- The role of cultural values in treatment
- Appropriate counseling models
- Competence in skills for working with specific ethnic populations

In a discussion of new approaches to cultural diversity, C. C. Lee (1997b) contends that research evidence must guide counseling. Based on reviews of what has been accomplished in research on cross-cultural counseling, he proposes the following three areas for future research:

- New process and outcome research in the area of multicultural counseling. Evaluation of culturally responsive methods must be made an integral part of practice in various settings.
- Normal human development research from a cross-cultural perspective. New studies might focus on coping skills among diverse groups of people.
- Research on intragroup differences due to factors such as level of ethnic identity, level of acculturation, and socioeconomic status.

Inventory of Your Position on Research

As a way of concluding this discussion, we suggest that you clarify your own thinking on the matter of balancing scientific rigor with ethical rigor. If you agree more than you disagree with the following statements, place an "A" in the space provided; if you disagree more than you agree, place a "D" in the space. After you have finished the inventory, discuss some of your answers with fellow students.

___ 1. To use therapeutic techniques or interventions that lack a sufficient research base is irresponsible and unethical.
___ 2. Deception is sometimes a necessary aspect of psychological research.
___ 3. Failure to obtain the informed consent of participants in research is always unethical.
___ 4. If a research study contains any risks to the participants, its design should be changed, for by its very nature it is unethical.
___ 5. The use of placebo groups can be justified. If these controls are not used, practitioners will have difficulty evaluating the efficacy of the intervention they use.
___ 6. Researchers will ultimately get the best results if they are open and honest about the research design with the participants in the study.
___ 7. If individuals are "debriefed" afterward, deception during the study can be justified.
___ 8. Practitioners should use no techniques that have not been empirically shown to be of value.
___ 9. To produce sound research studies of therapy, we must be willing to tolerate some ethical violations.
___ 10. It is ethical to justify research in educational settings solely on the basis of the potential benefits of the research itself.

Chapter Summary

Issues in theory, practice, and research are necessarily interrelated. From an ethical perspective, therapists need to anchor their practices to both theory and research. Without a theoretical foundation, practitioners are left with little rationale to formulate therapeutic goals and develop techniques to accomplish these goals. Practitioners are sometimes impatient when it comes to articulating a theory that guides practice. Some are riveted to concrete techniques to deal with every conceivable problem clients may present. However, a good theory is highly practical, for theoretical concepts help clinicians understand what they are doing. Just as clinicians sometimes have little use for theory, some do not see the practical applications of research. Without understanding how to translate current research findings into their practices, therapists have little basis for deciding what techniques to use with different clients. Thus, an appreciation of how theory and research can enhance how therapists function may result in ethical and effective practice.

We do not advocate that you subscribe to one established theory; therapeutic techniques from many theoretical approaches may be useful in your practice. However, it is important that you develop clear views pertaining to these questions: How does change come about? What is your view of human nature? How does the therapeutic relationship lead to change? What is the role of diagnosis and assessment as a prelude to designing a treatment plan? When might tests be useful in the counseling process? How do you determine what techniques are appropriate in working with a given client? Can you adapt your techniques to short-term treatment? How can research help you determine the degree to which treatment is working? Ideally, your theoretical orientation will serve as a basis for reflecting on matters such as goals in counseling, the division of responsibility between the client and the counselor in meeting these goals, and techniques that are most appropriate with specific clients in resolving a variety of problems.

Suggested Activities

1. Do this exercise in dyads. Describe your theoretical stance, and tell your partner how you view human nature. How will this view determine the way you counsel?

2. How do you determine for yourself the proper division of responsibility in counseling? How might you avoid assuming responsibility that you think belongs to your client? How might you ensure that you will accept your own share of responsibility?

3. If you were applying for a job as a counselor and were asked, "What are the most important goals you have for your clients?" how would you respond?

4. In class, debate the role of diagnosis in therapy. Have one person make a case for diagnosis as a valuable part of the therapeutic process, and have the other person argue against the use of diagnosis. Or have a class discussion on trends in diagnosis, its uses and abuses, and its purpose and value.

5. Suppose a client came to you and asked you to administer a battery of interest, ability, and vocational tests. How would you respond? What questions would you ask the client before agreeing to arrange for the testing?

6. What is your position on the use of techniques in counseling? When do you think they are appropriate? How can you determine for yourself whether you are using techniques as gimmicks to allay your anxiety or as extensions of your personal style as a counselor?

7. Interview at least one practicing therapist and discuss how his or her theoretical orientation affects that therapist's practice. Ask the practitioner the kinds of questions that were raised in this chapter. Bring the results of your interview to class.

8. Suppose you were applying for a job in a community mental health center. How would you respond to these questions during the interview:

- Many of our clients represent a range of diverse cultural and ethnic backgrounds. To what degree do you think you will be able to form positive therapeutic relationships with clients who are culturally different from you?
- How do you think your own acculturation will influence the way you counsel ethnically and culturally diverse clients?
- Can you think of any factors that might get in the way of forming trusting relationships with clients who are culturally different from you?

9. In dyads, have one person argue that a thorough assessment (diagnosis) is not necessary with a majority of clients in outpatient counseling. The other

person can argue that without a thorough assessment of each client it is not ethically possible to proceed with an appropriate treatment plan.

10. What interventions might you make during your initial session in getting to know your client? How would you structure future sessions? Explore the following questions:

- Would you begin with a detailed case history? Why or why not?
- Do you consider a comprehensive assessment and a diagnosis necessary prerequisites to counseling? Why or why not?
- Are tests important as a prerequisite to counseling? Would you decide whether to test, or would you allow your client to make this decision?
- How much would you structure the session to obtain current information about your client's life? How much would you want to know about your client's past?
- How would you incorporate a cultural perspective into your work? How would your client's cultural and ethnic background influence the development of your relationship?
- Who would set the goals of therapy? Who would be primarily responsible for what was discussed? Why?
- Who would take the greater responsibility for directing the initial session? To what degree would you encourage your client to structure the session?
- Would you develop a contract with your client specifying what the client could expect from you, what the client wanted from counseling, and what the client was willing to do to meet these goals? Why or why not?
- Would you be inclined to use directive, action-oriented techniques, such as homework assignments? Why or why not?
- What aspects of the client's life would you stress?

11. Videotape or tape-record sessions with several clients. Instead of focusing your attention on what your client said or did, examine your own responses and how you relate to clients.

- Do you ask many questions? If so, are the questions mainly to get information or are they open-ended ones designed to challenge your client?
- Are you asking questions just to keep the sessions moving?
- Do you tend to give advice and work quickly toward solutions? Or do you allow your client to explore feelings in depth rather than focusing on solutions to problems?
- How much support and reassurance do you give? Do you allow your clients to fully express what they are feeling before you offer support?
- Do you challenge your clients when you think they need it? Do your interventions get them to think about what they are saying on a deeper level?
- Who does most of the talking?
- Do you reflect back to your clients what you hear them saying? If so, is your reflection done mechanically, or does it encourage a deeper self-exploration? Do you check to be sure you are hearing what your client means to express?

- Do you make many interpretations, telling your clients what you think certain behaviors mean? Or do you leave it to your clients to discover what their behaviors mean from their own perspectives?
- Do you use techniques primarily to get clients moving, or do you use interventions aimed at enabling clients to explore thoughts or feelings that they bring up?
- Do you use techniques that you are comfortable using? Have you experienced these techniques yourself as a client?
- Are the procedures you use drawn from one counseling approach? Or do you borrow techniques from various approaches and use them when they seem appropriate?
- When you use a particular technique, does it seem mechanical to you? Or do you feel that your techniques are appropriate and unforced?
- Do you see your favorite techniques as being applicable to all clients?
- How do your clients generally respond to the techniques you use? Do they react negatively to any of your counseling methods?

Monitoring your own work in light of these questions can help you discover your counseling style, understand the interventions you make, and evaluate the impact these counseling procedures have on your clients. This willingness to reflect on the effects your interventions have on clients is of the utmost importance.

InfoTrac® College Edition Resources

For additional readings, explore InfoTrac College Edition, our online library. Go to *http://www.infotrac.college.com/wadsworth* and select these key word searches:

psychodiagnosis
ethical issue* AND diagnosis
ethical issue* test* couns*

Key words are listed in a form that enables the search engine to locate a wider range of articles in the online university library. Key words should be entered exactly as shown, including asterisks, "W1," "W2," "AND," and other search engine tools.

11

Pre-Chapter Self-Inventory

Directions: For each statement, indicate the response that most closely identifies your beliefs and attitudes. Use the following code:

5 = I *strongly agree* with this statement.
4 = I *agree* with this statement.
3 = I am *undecided* about this statement.
2 = I *disagree* with this statement.
1 = I *strongly disagree* with this statement.

_____1. A person who comes from a troubled family is generally a poor candidate to become a good family therapist.

_____2. I would never divulge in a family session any secrets given to me privately by one of the members.

_____3. In practicing couples counseling, I would also be willing to see them for individual sessions in addition to conjoint therapy.

_____4. Counselors have an ethical responsibility to encourage spouses to leave partners who are physically or psychologically abusive.

_____5. I would not be willing to work with a couple if I knew that one of the individuals was having an affair unbeknownst to the other.

_____6. It is ethical for family therapists to use pressure and even coercion to get a reluctant client to participate in family therapy.

Ethical Issues in Couples and Family Therapy

_____7. Therapists who feel justified in imposing their own values on a couple or a family can do considerable harm.

_____8. In couples or family therapy I would explain about confidentiality at the first session.

_____9. Most family therapists, consciously or unconsciously, proselytize for maintaining a family way of life.

_____10. There are ethical problems in treating only one member of a family.

_____11. I would be willing to work with a single member of a family and eventually attempt to bring the entire family into therapy.

_____12. Before accepting a family for treatment, I would obtain supervised training in working with families.

_____13. Before working with families, I need to explore issues in my own family of origin.

_____14. Skill in using family therapy techniques is far more important to success in this area than knowing my own personal dynamics.

_____15. I favor requiring continuing education in the field of couples and family therapy as a condition for renewal of a license in this area.

Introduction

Much of the practice of couples and family therapy rests on the foundation of systems theory. This theory views psychological problems as arising from within the individual's present environment and the intergenerational family system. Symptoms are believed to be an expression of dysfunctions within the system, which are often passed along through numerous generations. That the identified client's problem might be a symptom of how the system functions, not just a symptom of the individual's maladjustment and psychosocial development, was a revolutionary notion. The family systems perspective is grounded on the assumptions that a client's problematic behavior may (1) serve a function or purpose for the family, (2) be a function of the family's inability to operate productively, or (3) be a symptom of dysfunctional patterns handed down across generations. However, other theoretical frameworks also guide the practice of family therapy, including Bowen's multigenerational family therapy, Satir's human validation process model, Whitaker's experiential approach, structural family therapy, strategic family therapy, and the social construction models of family therapy (Corey, 2001c).

Goldenberg and Goldenberg (2000) urge therapists to view all behavior, including the symptoms expressed by the individual, within the context of the family and society. Although traditional approaches to treating the individual have merit, it might be incumbent upon therapists to expand their perspectives by considering clients as members of their family, community, and society. The Goldenbergs claim that a systems orientation does not preclude dealing with the individual but does broaden the traditional emphasis to address the roles individuals play in the family.

The systems perspective views the family as a functioning entity that is more than the sum of its members. The family provides the context for understanding how individuals behave. Actions by any individual member influence all the other members, and their reactions have a reciprocal effect on the individual. For instance, an acting-out child may be expressing deep conflicts between the mother and the father and may actually be expressing the pain for an entire family. Family therapists often work with individuals, the couple, and parents and children to get a better understanding of patterns that affect the entire system and to develop strategies for change.

Although contemporary couples and family therapists usually base their clinical practice on a foundation of systems theory, the majority of family therapists integrate concepts and techniques from various theoretical orientations to produce their own blend of methods based on their training, personality, and the population of families they serve (Hanna & Brown, 1999). Nichols and Schwartz (1998) also maintain that family therapy is moving toward integration. They believe that it does not make sense to study only one model and to neglect the insights of others.

Many master's programs in counseling now offer a specialization in relationship counseling or couples and family therapy. Components of the training program in couples and family therapy include the study of systems theory, an examination of family of origin, the use of live supervision, and an emphasis on ethical and professional issues specific to working with couples and families.

Many of the ethical issues we have already discussed take on special significance when therapists work with more than one client. Most graduate programs in couples and family therapy now require a separate course in ethics and the law pertaining to this specialization, with an increased emphasis on ethical, legal, and professional issues unique to a systems perspective. Some specific areas of ethical concern for family therapists that we will discuss in this chapter include therapist responsibility, confidentiality, client privilege, informed consent and the right to refuse treatment, therapist values, and training and supervision. The professional practice of couples and family therapy is regulated by state laws, professional specialty guidelines, ethics codes, peer review, continuing education, managed care, and consultation (Goldenberg & Goldenberg, 2000). We now turn to a discussion of the implications for the practice of family therapy in the ethics codes developed by the AAMFT (2001).

Ethical Standards in Couples and Family Therapy

The AAMFT *Code of Ethics* (2001) provides a framework for many of the ethical issues we will consider in this chapter. In addition to the AAMFT code, two useful resources are the *Ethical Casebook for the Practice of Marriage and Family Counseling* (Stevens, 1999) and the *American Association for Couples and Family Therapy Ethics Casebook* (Brock, 1998). Both of these casebooks address a variety of situations encountered by marriage and family therapists. We begin our discussion by providing the AAMFT's (2001) code in each of eight core areas, followed by a brief discussion of what this means for therapists.

1. *Responsibility to clients.* "Marriage and family therapists advance the welfare of families and individuals. They respect the rights of those persons seeking their assistance, and make reasonable efforts to ensure that their services are used appropriately."

As the focus of therapy shifts from the individual to the family system, a new set of ethical questions is raised: Whose interests should the family therapist serve? To whom and for whom does the therapist have primary loyalty and responsibility? the identified patient? the separate family members as individuals? the family as a whole? By agreeing to become involved in family therapy, the members can generally be expected to place a higher priority on the goals of the family as a unit rather than on their own personal goals. Other questions can also be raised: Should the therapist work with one client and then eventually attempt to bring the entire family into therapy? What is the proper course in cases involving reluctant children and adolescents?

2. *Confidentiality.* "Marriage and family therapists have unique confidentiality concerns because the client in a therapeutic relationship may be more than one person. Therapists respect and guard confidences of each individual client."

Confidentiality assumes unique significance in the practice of couples and family therapy. This issue arises within the family itself in deciding how to deal with secrets. Incest, extramarital affairs, contagious diseases, or physical or psychological abuse of a partner or children may be involved. Should the therapist attempt to have families reveal all their secrets? What are the pros and cons of revealing a family secret when some members are likely to suffer from extreme anxiety if it is disclosed? Family therapists have different perspectives on maintaining confidentiality. Some treat all information they receive from a family member just as if the person were in individual therapy. Others refuse to see any member of the family separately, claiming that doing so fosters unproductive alliances and promotes the keeping of secrets. Still others tell family members that they will exercise their own judgment about what to disclose from an individual session in a couples or family session.

3. *Professional competence and integrity.* "Marriage and family therapists maintain high standards of professional competence and integrity."

This principle implies that therapists will seek professional help when their own personal problems are likely to negatively affect their professional work or impair their clinical judgment. It also implies that they keep abreast of developments in the field through continuing education and clinical experiences. A single course or two in a graduate counseling program is hardly adequate preparation for functioning ethically and effectively as a counselor with couples or families. Here are some questions that can be productively explored: How can therapists know when their own personal problems are likely to hamper their professional work? What are some ways in which therapists can best maintain their level of competence? How can therapists use their values in a constructive fashion?

4. *Responsibility to students and supervisees.* "Marriage and family therapists do not exploit the trust and dependency of students and supervisees."

The code cautions practitioners to avoid multiple relationships, which are likely to impair clinical judgment. As you saw in Chapter 7, perspectives differ on how best to handle dual relationships. Ryder and Hepworth (1990) suggest that the AAMFT dual relationship prohibition is undesirable because of the complex nature of such relationships in couples and family therapy. Not only are multiple relationships virtually impossible to eliminate, they contend, but even if it were possible, it would be a bad idea. Ryder and Hepworth are against making these complex relationships overly simple by legislation. Instead, they recommend that training and supervision include preparing students to deal with such complexity as well as teaching them how to deal with issues such as exploitation and power. Rather than condemning dual and multiple relationships as being harmful to clients, Tomm (1993) suggests that they can lead to increased counselor authenticity and can actually enhance the therapy process. Thus, prohibiting dual and multiple relationships is not the solution to the exploitation of clients or the misuse of power.

At this point you might consider these questions: What are your views about dual relationships as they apply to couples and family therapy? Do you agree with the AAMFT guideline that cautions against forming dual or multiple relationships? What are some multiple relationships that you might be faced with in working with couples or families? How would you weigh the potential benefits and the associated potential risks of such multiple relationships?

5. *Responsibility to research participants.* "Investigators respect the dignity and protect the welfare of research participants, and are aware of federal and state laws and regulations and professional standards governing the conduct of research."

Researchers must carefully consider the ethical aspects of any research proposal, making use of informed consent procedures and explaining to participants what is involved in any research project. If there is a conflict between research purposes and therapeutic purposes, how would you resolve it? What are some multicultural considerations in doing research in this area? Can couples and family therapists who do not conduct research be considered ethical? What obstacles do you see to doing research in this area?

6. *Responsibility to the profession.* "Marriage and family therapists respect the rights and responsibilities of professional colleagues and participate in activities which advance the goals of the profession."

Ethical practice requires measures of accountability that meet professional standards. It is expected that couples and family therapists will contribute time to the betterment of society, including donating services. What would you say about the ethics of those therapists who do not contribute any of their professional time without a fee? What do you see as your ethical obligation to advance the goals of your profession? What activities do you participate in (or expect to participate in) for professional advancement?

7. *Financial arrangements.* "Marriage and family therapists make financial arrangements with clients, third party payers, and supervisees that are reasonably understandable and conform to accepted professional practices."

Couples and family therapists do not accept payment for making referrals and do not exploit clients financially for services. They are truthful in representing facts to clients and to third parties regarding any services rendered. Ethical practice dictates a disclosure of fee policies at the onset of therapy. What steps would you take to inform your clients about your fee policies? What are some examples of your fee policies? Would you charge for missed appointments? What would you say about the ethics of a practitioner who charged a fee for making a referral to another professional? What are some ways in which clients can be exploited financially?

8. *Advertising.* "Marriage and family therapists engage in appropriate informational activities, including those that enable the public, referral sources, or others to choose professional services on an informed basis."

Ethical practice dictates that practitioners accurately represent their competence, education, training, and experience in couples and family therapy. Professional standards are used in announcing services. Therapists do not advertise themselves as specialists (for example, in sex therapy) without being able to support this claim by virtue of their education, training, and supervised experience. How would you propose to advertise your services? How might you promote yourself as a couples and family practitioner?

A number of ethical and legal considerations are unique to couples and family therapy. Because couples and family therapists focus on the family system as the client rather than on the individual's dynamics, potential ethical dilemmas can arise from the first session (Smith, Carlson, Stevens-Smith, & Dennison, 1995). Because of the increased complexity of their work, couples and family therapists are faced with more potential ethical conflicts than are practitioners who specialize in individual therapy. Therapists who work with cohabitating couples or multiple family members often encounter dilemmas that involve serving one member's best interest at the expense of another member's interest. Couples and families frequently seek professional assistance because of their conflicting goals and interests. In the interventions, therapists need to consider that the status of one partner or family member does not improve at the expense of the other partner or another family member. Gladding, Remley, and Huber (2001) maintain that therapists can respond to ethical dilemmas over conflicting interests of multiple individuals by identifying the couple or family system as the focus of treatment rather than a single individual as the primary "client." Therapists who function as an advocate of the system avoid becoming an agent of any one partner or family member. Working within a framework that conceptualizes change as affecting and being affect by all family members, practitioners are able to define problems and consider plans for change in the context of the family system.

Some other ethical concerns faced by couples and family counselors are addressed by Huber (1994, p. 61):

- Can therapists automatically assume the right to define couples' and families' presenting problems in terms of their own therapeutic orientation?
- How much concerted effort can therapists exert in convening all significant family members for therapy sessions?
- Should willing individual relationship partners or several family members seeking assistance go untreated because one individual refuses to participate?
- Under what situations, if any, should therapists impose their control on couples and families? If so, to what extent should they impose it in seeking change in the relationship system?
- How much intrasystem stress should be engendered or allowed to materialize in the pursuit of change?
- What are the ethical implications inherent in employing paradoxical procedures?
- How can the impact of working with couples and families within the larger context of service agency constraints be pursued ethically?

Contemporary Professional Issues

In this section we identify a few of the current professional issues in the practice of couples and family therapy. These include the personal, academic, and experiential qualifications necessary to practice in the field.

Personal Characteristics of the Family Therapist

In Chapter 2 we addressed the significance of the personal characteristics of the therapist as a major factor in creating an effective therapeutic alliance. Self-knowledge is particularly critical for family therapists, especially with regard to family-of-origin issues. When therapists work with a couple or a family, or with an individual who is sorting out a family-of-origin issue, their perceptions and reactions are bound to be influenced by their own family-of-origin issues. Therapists who are unaware of their own vulnerabilities are likely to misinterpret their clients or steer clients in a direction that will not arouse their own anxieties. Therapists who are aware of their own emotional issues are less likely to get entangled in the problems of their clients.

Many trainers of family therapists hold that a practitioner's mental health, as defined by relationships with his or her family of origin, has implications for professional training. It is assumed that trainees can benefit from an exploration of the dynamics of their family of origin because it enables them to relate more effectively to the families they will meet in their clinical practice.

Getz and Protinsky (1994) take the position that personal growth is an essential part of training for couples and family counselors and that knowledge and skills cannot be separated from a helper's internal dynamics and use of self. They write: "Trainees can and should be referred for personal therapy, but their issues, when identified as affecting their work, are addressed preferably in training" (p. 183). Getz and Protinsky point to growing clinical evidence that a family-of-origin approach to supervision is a necessary dimension of training for therapists who want to work with families. They contend that the reactions of therapists to their clients' stories tend to reactivate therapists' old learned patterns of behavior and unresolved problems. Through studying their own family of origin, students are ultimately able to improve their ability to counsel families.

In writing on the personal training of family therapists, Aponte (1994) describes his person/practice model, which is based on the premise that therapy is a personal encounter within a professional framework. Although he acknowledges that theory and technique are essential to the professional practice of family therapy, he stresses that the process is affected wholly through the relationship between therapist and client. Above all, therapists must be skilled and sensitive clinicians. Knowledge and skills are of limited practical value if therapists are not able to use themselves as persons constructively in sessions with couples and families. For Aponte, training the person of the therapist calls for trainees to examine their personal issues in relation to the therapy they do: "The touching of therapists' and clients' lives in therapy beckons therapists to gain mastery of their personal selves in their clinical relationships" (p. 4).

Educational Requirements for Family Therapy

Professionals who practice couples and family therapy come from diverse academic backgrounds. In an attempt to provide uniform structure to evaluate the quality of a professional's education and training, the AAMFT (1994) has established minimal educational standards and a set of training guidelines. To qualify for *clinical membership*, candidates must possess a master's or doctoral degree in couples and family therapy, or its equivalent, preferably from an AAMFT-accredited educational institution. They are expected to have successfully completed appropriate graduate course work in both couples and family studies and couples and family therapy, to have had 2 years of professional work experience in couples and family therapy, and to have successfully completed at least 200 hours of supervision with a minimum of 1,000 hours of work with couples and family cases.

All couples and family training programs acknowledge that both conceptual knowledge and clinical skills are necessary to become a competent family therapist. As training programs have evolved, major didactic and experiential components have been identified. Family therapy training programs use three primary methods of training: (1) didactic course work, (2) the use of master therapist videotapes plus trainee tapes for postsession viewing by the trainees and supervisors; and (3) regular supervision by an experienced family supervisor, who together with trainees, may watch the session behind a one-way mirror or through videotaped sessions (Goldenberg & Goldenberg, 2000). In addition to these methods of training, trainees are now likely to be exposed to a variety of current issues in the field of family therapy. Some of these include (a) gender-sensitive models aimed at overcoming trainee gender bias and sex-role stereotyping; (b) a raised consciousness concerning the role of cultural and ethnic factors in influencing the outlooks and behaviors of individuals and families; (c) a knowledge of family law; and (d) an introduction to social constructionist perspectives on alternative therapist roles and the collaborative nature of family therapy (Goldenberg & Goldenberg, 2000). It is a good practice for students to gain experience in working with a variety of families from different ethnic and socioeconomic backgrounds who have various presenting problems. A program offering both comprehensive course work and clinical supervision provides the ideal learning situation.

Experiential Qualifications for Family Therapy

In training couples and family therapists, primary emphasis should be given to the quality of supervised practice and clinical experience. Academic knowledge comes alive in supervised practicum and internship experiences, and trainees learn how to use and sharpen their intervention skills. It is through direct clinical contact with families, under close supervision, that trainees develop their own styles of interacting with families. A variety of supervisory methods can be employed to assist trainees in learning by doing, including the use of audiotapes, videotapes, written process notes, co-therapy, corrective feedback by telephone, live supervision, and calling the trainee out of the family session for consultation.

Most graduate programs employ both didactic and experiential methods and supervised practice. Didactic methods include classroom lectures, readings, demonstrations, films and videotapes of family therapy sessions, role playing, and discussion. Clinical experience with families is of limited value without regularly scheduled supervisory sessions. Live supervision can be conducted by a supervisor who watches and guides the sessions behind a one-way mirror and offers useful feedback and consultation to the trainee on how he or she is working with a family (Goldenberg & Goldenberg, 2000). Family therapy trainees can also profit from the practice of co-therapy, which provides trainees with opportunities to work closely with a supervisor or a colleague. A great deal of the supervision can take place immediately after and between sessions.

Experiential methods include both personal therapy and working with issues of one's own family of origin. A rationale for personal therapeutic experiences is that such exploration enables trainees to increase their awareness of transference and countertransference, which assists trainees in relating more effectively to the families they will meet in their clinical practice.

If counselors are seeing families as part of their work, and if their program did not adequately prepare them for competence in intervening with families, they are vulnerable to a malpractice suit for practicing outside the boundaries of their competence. Those practitioners who did not receive specialized training as students need to involve themselves in postgraduate in-service training or special workshops.

◆ **The case of Ludwig.** Ludwig is a counselor whose education and training have been exclusively in individual counseling. Ella comes to him for counseling, but, after more than a dozen sessions with Ella, Ludwig realizes that much of her difficulty lies not just with her but with her entire family system. By this time Ludwig has established a strong working relationship with Ella. Because he has no experience in family therapy, he ponders what to do. He thinks of referring Ella to a colleague who is well trained in family therapy, but he realizes that doing so could have a detrimental effect on her. One of Ella's problems has been a sense of abandonment by her parents. He wants to avoid giving her the impression that he, too, is abandoning her. He decides to stay with her and work with her individually. Much of the time is spent trying to understand the dynamics of the family members who are not present.

- Do you agree with Ludwig's clinical decision? Do you agree with his rationale?
- From your perspective, would it have made a difference if he had consulted with Ella? Would it have made a difference if he had consulted with or obtained supervision from a colleague?
- Even though Ludwig was not trained as a family therapist, what if he had decided to see the entire family and attempted to do family therapy for the benefit of his client? Would you be inclined to do that?
- What if Ludwig had been trained in family systems but, when he suggested family sessions to Ella, she refused? What would you do if faced with such a dilemma?

- Assume that Ludwig decided to see each family member individually to learn how each viewed the family system. In this process he discovered a great discrepancy between Ella's description of the family and what the other family members said. Ludwig became convinced that his client was either misreading the family or was not presenting an accurate description of her problem. What is your opinion of his analysis? Does it raise any concerns for you?

Values in Couples and Family Therapy

In Chapter 3 we explored the impact of the therapist's values on the goals and direction of the therapeutic process. We now consider how values take on special significance in counseling couples and families. Values pertaining to marriage, the preservation of the family, divorce, traditional and nontraditional lifestyles, gender roles and the division of responsibility in the family, child rearing, and extramarital affairs can all influence the therapist's interventions. Counselors who, intentionally or unintentionally, impose their values on a couple or a family can do considerable harm.

It is crucial for therapists to understand how they might be biased against an individual or family whose views differ radically from their own. There are several ways that family therapists might make undue use of their influence because of their particular biases, values, or attitudes: They may take sides with one member of the family against another; they may impose their values on family members; or they may proselytize for maintaining a current marriage.

The value system of therapists has a crucial influence on their formulation and definition of the problems they see in a family, the goals and plans for therapy, and the direction the therapy takes. Ethical issues are raised in establishing criteria of psychosocial dysfunction, assessing the problems of the identified patient in the family context, and devising treatment strategies. Values occupy a central place in creating models of adaptive and maladaptive family functioning and in treating the family in such a manner as to meet the needs of all its members (Block & Harari, 1996).

In their discussion of the valuing components of the professional practice of couples and family therapy, Gladding, Remley, and Huber (2001) agree with the assumption that the *content* of values is important and cannot be ignored, yet they place emphasis on the *process* of valuing. They note that too often values are represented as static positions construed as right or wrong. Instead, Gladding and his colleagues view the valuing process as involving the values, beliefs, and resultant actions they encompass. This process requires continual reconsideration and reclarification. They draw a comparison between the valuing process applied to couples and family therapy with a similar process therapists use to understand cultural diversity. Respect for a client's culture or ethnicity involves initial acceptance of differences, exploration of those differences, and subtle explanations of how a given ethnic group's customs differ from the larger culture. In a like manner, therapists have the role of assisting couples and families to negotiate the values they want to retain, modify, or discard. Gladding and colleagues put this point as follows:

> The focus of marriage and family therapists is to find out what their clients are trying to conserve, and participate in their attempts to conserve it while seeking to maintain that balance of fairness necessary for more satisfying experiences. (p. 250)

We want to emphasize again that it is not the function of any therapist to make decisions for clients. Family therapists should not decide how members of a family should change. The role of the therapist is to help family members see more clearly what they are doing, to help them make an honest evaluation of how well their present patterns are working for them, and to help and encourage them to make necessary changes.

In this section we invite you to think about your own values and to reflect on the impact that they are likely to have on the interventions you make with couples and families. To assist you in formulating your personal position on these issues, consider these two cases that raise value issues that could affect the course of therapy.

◆ **The case of Sharon.** Sharon is a 25-year-old client who says, "I'm never going to get married because I think marriage is a drag. I don't want kids, and I don't want to stay with one person forever." Here are the inner dialogues of four therapists regarding her case.

Therapist A: She seems very selfish to me. With her attitude, it's probably a good idea that she doesn't intend to get married. I wonder why she is in therapy, anyway?

Therapist B: Well, she doesn't have to be married. Mental health doesn't necessarily require that one be married. I certainly would want to communicate to her that remaining single is acceptable. But I would like to explore with her how she went about making this decision.

Therapist C: Why is she so opposed to marriage? I wonder if she is talking more about her family than marriage?

Therapist D: I feel sorry for her. She must have had some very painful experiences growing up. She must have had a terrible relationship with her father that prevents her from forming healthy relationships now. If I can only get to the underlying problem, I know she will be able to overcome her negative experiences.

- What is your reaction to Sharon's statement?
- What is your reaction to each of the therapist's responses to her?
- What implied value is each therapist expressing?
- Why would you want to challenge (or accept) Sharon's decision?
- In what ways do you think you might work with Sharon differently from the four therapists? If you don't feel comfortable with a commitment to marriage and a family yourself, do you think you could be objective enough to help her explore some of the possibilities she might be overlooking?

◆ **The case of Frank and Judy.** During the past few years Frank and Judy have experienced many conflicts in their marriage. Although they have made attempts to resolve their problems by themselves, they have finally decided to seek the help of a professional marriage counselor. Even though they have been thinking about divorce with increasing frequency, they still have some hope that they can achieve a satisfactory marriage.

We will present the approaches of three couples counselors, each holding a different set of values pertaining to marriage and the family. As you read these responses, think about the degree to which they represent what you might say and do if you were counseling this couple.

Counselor A. This counselor believes it is not her place to bring her values pertaining to the family into the sessions. She is fully aware of her biases regarding marriage and divorce, but she does not impose them or expose them in all cases. Her primary interest is to help Frank and Judy discover what is best for them as individuals and as a couple. She sees it as unethical to push her clients toward a definite course of action, and she lets them know that her job is to help them be honest with themselves.

- What are your reactions to this counselor's approach?
- Do you think it is possible for this counselor to keep her values out of the therapy process?

Counselor B. This counselor has been married three times herself. Although she believes in marriage, she is quick to maintain that far too many couples stay in their marriages and suffer unnecessarily. She explores with Judy and Frank the conflicts that they bring to the sessions. The counselor's interventions are leading them in the direction of divorce as the desired course of action, especially after they express this as an option. She suggests a trial separation and states her willingness to counsel them individually, with some joint sessions. When Frank brings up his guilt and reluctance to divorce because of the welfare of the children, the counselor confronts him with the harm that is being done to them by a destructive marriage. She tells him that it is too much of a burden to put on the children to keep the family together at any price.

- Do you see any ethical issues in this case? Is this counselor exposing or imposing her values?
- Do you think she should be a marriage counselor, given her bias and her background of three divorces?
- What interventions made by the counselor do you agree with? What are your areas of disagreement?

Counselor C. At the first session this counselor states his belief in the preservation of marriage and the family. He feels that many couples take the easy way out by divorcing too quickly in the face of difficulty. He says that most couples have unrealistically high expectations of what constitutes a "happy marriage." The counselor lets it be known that his experience continues to teach him that divorce rarely solves any problems but instead creates new problems that are often worse. The counselor urges Frank and Judy to consider the welfare of their three dependent children. He tells the couple of his bias toward saving the marriage so they can make an informed choice about initiating counseling with him.

- What are your personal reactions toward the orientation of this counselor?
- Do you agree with him stating his bias so obviously?
- What if he were to keep his bias and values hidden from the couple and accept them into therapy? Do you think he could work objectively with this couple? Why or why not?

Commentary. This case illustrates that the value system of the counselor determines the direction counseling will take. The counselor who is dedicated to preserving marriage and family life is bound to function differently from the counselor who puts primary value on the welfare of individual family members. What might be best for one family member is not necessarily in the best interests of the entire family. It is essential, therefore, for counselors who work with couples and families to be aware of how their values influence the goals and procedures of therapy. Ethical practice should challenge clients to look at their own values and to choose a course of action that is best for them.

Gender-Sensitive Couples and Family Therapy

Gender-sensitive couples and family therapy attempts to help both women and men move beyond stereotyped gender roles. Sexist attitudes and patriarchal assumptions are examined for their impact on family relationships. With this approach, family therapy is conducted in an egalitarian fashion, and both therapist and client work collaboratively to empower individuals to choose roles rather than to be passive recipients of gender-role socialization.

Both women and men are recipients of stereotyping and countertransference by therapists. All therapists need to be aware of their values and beliefs about gender. In Chapter 4 we discussed the importance of counselors' being aware of how their culture has influenced their personality. The ways in which people perceive gender likewise have a great deal to do with their cultural background. A challenge to all family therapists is to be culturally sensitive, gender sensitive, and to avoid imposing their personal values on individuals, couples, and families.

Challenging Traditional Gender Roles

Counselors who work with couples and families can practice more ethically if they are aware of the history and impact of gender stereotyping as it is reflected in the socialization process in families. Effective practitioners must continually evaluate their own beliefs about appropriate family roles and responsibilities, child-rearing practices, multiple roles, and nontraditional vocations for women and men. Counselors also must have the knowledge to help their clients explore educational, vocational, and emotional goals that they previously deemed unreachable. The principles of gender-aware therapy have relevance for counselors as they help clients identify and work through gender concepts that have limited them.

L. S. Brown (1990) makes the point that a clinician's own countertransference responses to gender issues affect the assessment process, which further influences the way therapy is conducted. Some of her guidelines for incorporating gender concerns in assessment and therapy include inquiring into the meaning of femininity or masculinity for the client and guarding against the inappropriate imposition of gender-stereotyped values regarding healthy functioning.

Effective communication between therapists and their clients is often undermined by stereotypical views about how women and men think, feel, and behave. Counselors must be alert to the particular issues women and men struggle with and the ways their own views about gender might restrict clients to traditional roles. Counseling professionals offer help to both women and men in exploring and challenging the stereotyped expectations that they behave in certain limited ways. Women may need assistance in overcoming internal barriers to autonomy, raising their self-esteem, and overcoming dependency. Men may need assistance in learning new ways to take responsibility for their own emotional lives.

Learning to make autonomous choices does not mean that women have to deny their needs for connection, and choosing to take care of oneself does not imply being unconcerned about others. Similarly, for men, learning to be more relational and sharing one's inner life does not mean a loss of independence and strength.

Feminist Perspective on Family Therapy

Some feminist therapists have been critical of the clinical practice of family therapy, contending that it has been filled with outdated patriarchal assumptions and grounded on a male-biased perspective of gender roles and gender-defined functions within the family. Feminists assert that our patriarchal society subjugates women, blames them for inadequate mothering, and expects them to accept their contribution to their problem.

Feminism focuses on the gendered use of power in relationships, and feminist therapists encourage a personal commitment to challenge gender inequity. They espouse a vision of a future society that values equality between women and men. Examining the power differential in their relationships often helps partners demystify the gendered differences between them. Feminist family therapists share a number of roles, each of which is based on a specific value orientation: They make their values and beliefs explicit so that the therapy process is clearly understood; they strive to establish egalitarian roles with clients; they work toward client autonomy and client empowerment; and they emphasize commonalities among women. In short, they do have an agenda to challenge traditional gender roles and the impact this socialization has on a relationship and a family.

Feminist therapists do not take a neutral stance with respect to gender roles and power in relationships. They advocate for definite change in the social structure, especially in the area of equality, power in relationships, the right to self-determination, freedom to pursue a career outside the home, and the right to an education.

Although we support some of the goals of the feminist approach to family therapy, we do not think it is the role of any therapist to impose any set of values on women or men. For example, what if a woman chooses to make her primary commitment to her children and decides she does not want to get professionally involved outside the home? What about a woman who recognizes that she is sacrificing some of her personal educational or career ambitions for the sake of others? What if a woman clearly recognizes the hierarchy in her family, yet does not choose to risk upsetting her husband? From our perspective, feminist family therapists need to take care lest their agenda takes precedence over the agenda of the individuals within a family.

Therapists can best function in the interests of both female and male clients by challenging them to examine self-contradictions. The therapist's task is to help clients decide who and what they want to be, not what the therapist thinks they should be. Feminist therapists state that all therapists have values and that they believe it is important to be clear with clients about these values. This is different, however, from imposing values on clients. An imposition of values is inconsistent with viewing clients as their own best experts. Clients should be encouraged to make their own choices, and their choices need to be supported by their therapist.

A Nonsexist Perspective on Family Therapy

Regardless of their particular theoretical orientation, it is incumbent upon family therapists to take whatever steps are necessary to account for gender issues in their practice and to become nonsexist family therapists. Margolin (1982) provides a number of recommendations on how to be a nonsexist family therapist and how to use the therapeutic process to challenge the oppressive consequences of stereotyped roles and expectations in the family. One recommendation is that family therapists examine their own behavior for unwitting comments and questions that imply that the wife and husband should perform specific roles and hold a specific status. For example, a therapist can show bias in subtle and nonverbal ways, such as looking at the wife when talking about rearing children or addressing the husband when talking about any important decisions that need to be made. Further, Margolin contends that family therapists are particularly vulnerable to the following biases: (1) assuming that remaining married would be the best choice for a woman, (2) demonstrating less interest in a woman's career than in a man's career, (3) encouraging couples to accept the belief that child rearing is solely the responsibility of the mother, (4) showing a different reaction to a wife's affair than to a husband's, and (5) giving more importance to satisfying the husband's needs than to satisfying the wife's needs. She raises two important questions dealing with the ethics of doing therapy with couples and families:

- How does the therapist respond when members of the family seem to agree that they want to work toward goals that (from the therapist's vantage point) are sexist in nature?
- To what extent does the therapist accept the family's definition of gender-role identities rather than trying to challenge and eventually change these attitudes?

As you read the case examples that follow, consider your own values. What are your values pertaining to gender, and how do these values influence your perception of these cases? How do you think your values might affect your manner of counseling in each case?

◆ **The case of Marge and Al.** Marge and Al come to marriage counseling to work on the stress they are experiencing in rearing their two adolescent sons. The couple direct the focus toward what their sons are doing and not doing. In the course of therapy, the counselor learns that both Marge and Al have full-time jobs outside the home. In addition, Marge is a full-time mother and homemaker, but her husband refuses to share any domestic responsibilities. Marge doesn't question her dual career. Neither Marge nor Al shows much interest in exploring the division of responsibilities in their relationship. Instead, they focus the sessions on getting advice about how to handle problems with their sons.

- What would you do with their presenting problem, their trouble with their sons? What else might the behavior of the sons imply?
- Is it ethical for the therapist to focus only on the expressed concerns of Marge and Al? Does the therapist have a responsibility to challenge this couple to look at how they have defined themselves and their relationship through assumptions about gender roles?
- If you were counseling this couple, what might you do? How do you think your values would influence the interventions you might make in this case?

As you think about this case and the following one, ask yourself how your values regarding traditional wives and mothers might affect your relationship with clients like Marge and Melody.

◆ **The case of Melody.** Melody, 38, is married and has returned to college to obtain a teaching credential. During the intake session she tells you that she is experiencing conflicting feelings and is contemplating some major changes in her life. She has met a man who shares her interest and enthusiasm for school as well as many other aspects of her life. She is considering leaving her husband and children to pursue her own interests for a change.

Which of the following reactions reflect how you think? Would you verbalize them?

- "Perhaps this is a phase you are going through. It happens to a lot of women who return to college. Maybe you should slow down and think about it."
- "You'll never forgive yourself for leaving your children."

"You may have regrets later on if you leave your children in such an impulsive fashion."

- "Many women in your position would be afraid to do what you are thinking about doing."
- "I hate to see you divorce without having some marriage counseling first to determine whether that is what you both want."
- "Maybe you ought to look at the prospects of living alone for a while. The idea of moving out of a relationship with your husband and right into a new relationship with another man concerns me."

If Melody were your client, what values of yours would influence your interventions?

◆ **The case of Naomi.** The White family (consisting of wife, husband, four children, and the wife's parents) has been involved in family therapy for several months. During one of the sessions, Naomi (the wife) expresses the desire to return to college to pursue a degree in law. This wish causes tremendous resistance on the part of every other member of her family. The husband says that he wants her to continue to be involved in his professional life and that, although he admires her ambitions, he simply feels that it would put too much strain on the entire family. Naomi's parents are shocked by their daughter's desire, viewing it as selfish, and they urge her to put the family's welfare first. The children express their desires for a full-time mother. Naomi feels great pressure from all sides, yet she seems committed to following through with her professional plans. She is aware of the sacrifices that would be associated with her studies, but she is asking for everyone in the family to make adjustments so that she can accomplish some goals that are important to her. She is convinced that her plans would not be detrimental to the family's welfare. The therapist shows an obvious bias by giving no support to Naomi's aspirations and by not asking the family to consider making any basic adjustments. Although the therapist does not openly say that she should give up her plans, his interventions have the result of reinforcing the family's resistance.

- Do you think this therapist is guilty of furthering gender-role stereotypes? Do his interventions show an interest in the well-being of the entire family?
- Are there any other potential ethical issues in this case? If so, what are they?
- Being aware of your own bias regarding gender roles, how would you work with this family?
- Assume that the therapist had an obvious bias in favor of Naomi's plans and even pushed the family to learn to accept her right to an independent life. Do

you see any potential ethical issues in this approach? Do you think a therapist can remain neutral in this kind of case? Explain your stance.

Responsibilities of Couples and Family Therapists

Margolin (1982) argues persuasively that difficult ethical questions confronted in individual therapy become even more complicated when a number of family members are seen together. She observes that the dilemma with multiple clients is that in some instances an intervention that serves one person's best interests could burden another family member or even be countertherapeutic. Under the family systems model, for example, therapists do not focus their responsibility on the individual but on the family as a system. Such therapists avoid becoming agents of any one family member, believing that all family members contribute to the problems of the whole family. Ethical practice demands that therapists declare the nature of their commitments to each member of the family.

Therapist responsibilities are also a crucial issue in counseling with couples. This is especially true when the partners do not have a common purpose for seeking counseling. When one person wants divorce counseling and the other is coming to the sessions under the expectation of saving the marriage or improving the relationship, who is the primary client? How do therapists carry out their ethical responsibilities when the two persons in the relationship have different expectations?

In addition to clinical and ethical considerations, Margolin (1982) mentions legal provisions that can decide when the welfare of an individual takes precedence over that of a relationship. A clear example of a therapist's legal obligations is a case of child neglect or child abuse. The law requires family therapists to inform authorities if they suspect such abuse or become aware of it during the course of therapy. Even though reporting this situation may have negative consequences for the therapist's relationships with some members of the family, the therapist's ethical and legal responsibility is to help the threatened or injured person. It is clear that in some situations interventions to help an individual become more important than the goals of the family as a system, and clients should be informed of these situations during the initial session. In cases where there are conflicts between ethical and legal dimensions of practice, it is especially important for family therapists to know when to seek consultation.

At times couples and family therapists struggle over the issue of when to consult with another professional. This is especially true of situations in which a person (or couple or family) is already involved in a professional relationship with a therapist and seeks the counsel of another therapist. What course of action would you take if a husband sought you out for private counseling while he and his wife were also seeing another therapist for marriage counseling? Would it be ethical to enter into a professional relationship with this man without the knowledge and consent of the other professional? What might you do or say if the husband told you that the reason for initiating contact with you was to get another opinion and perspective on his marital situation and that he did not see any point in contacting the other professional?

◆ **An open-ended case.** A couple is seeing a therapist for marriage counseling. The husband decides to quit the joint sessions and begins private sessions with another therapist. The wife remains in individual therapy with the original therapist. In the course of individual therapy, the husband comes to realize that he does not want to terminate the marriage after all. He persuades his wife to come with him for a joint session with his therapist to pursue the possibility of keeping the marriage intact.

- What are the ethical obligations of the husband's therapist? Does she have responsibility for consulting with the wife's therapist?
- Do the two therapists need to get permission from their clients to consult with each other?
- Would it be ethical for the husband's therapist to do marital therapy with the couple, ignoring the work being done by the wife's therapist?

Confidentiality in Couples and Family Therapy

The principle of confidentiality as it applies to couples and family therapists entails that practitioners do not disclose what they have learned through the professional relationship except (1) when mandated by law, such as in cases of physical or psychological child abuse, incest, child neglect, or abuse of the elderly; (2) when it is necessary to protect clients from harming themselves or to prevent a clear and immediate danger to others; (3) when the family therapist is a defendant in a civil, criminal, or disciplinary action arising from the therapy; or (4) when a waiver has previously been obtained in writing. If therapists use any material from their practice in teaching, lecturing, and writing, they take care to preserve the anonymity of their clients.

Therapists have differing views on the role of confidentiality when working with families. One view is that therapists should not divulge in a family session any information given to them by individuals in private sessions. In the case of couples counseling, some practitioners are willing to see each spouse for individual sessions. Information given to them by one spouse is kept confidential. Other therapists, however, reserve the right to bring up certain issues in a joint session, even if one person mentioned the issue in a private session.

Some therapists who work with entire families go further. They have a policy of refusing to keep information secret that was shared individually. Their view is that secrets are counterproductive for open family therapy. Therefore, "hidden agendas" are seen as material that should be brought out into the open during a family session. Still another view is that therapists should inform their clients that any information given to them during private sessions will be divulged as they see fit in accordance with the greatest benefit for the couple or the family. These therapists reserve the right to use their professional judgment about whether to maintain individual confidences. In our opinion this latter approach is the most flexible; it avoids putting the counselor in the awkward position of having to either divulge secrets or keep secrets at the expense of the welfare of the family. Therapists who have not promised confidentiality have more options and thus must carefully consider the therapeutic ramifications of their actions.

As a part of the informed consent process, it is absolutely essential to ethical practice that couples and family therapists clarify their position regarding confidentiality from the outset. The informed consent statement must include clarification as to who is the client and how personal matters that are expressed by a family member to the counselor on an individual basis will be dealt with during the course of family therapy (Smith, 1999). Family members can then decide whether to participate in therapy and how much to disclose to the therapist. For example, a husband might disclose less in a private session if he knew that the therapist might bring these disclosures out in joint sessions.

◆ **A case of therapist quandary.** A husband is involved in individual therapy to resolve a number of personal conflicts, of which the state of his marriage is only one. Later, his wife comes in for some joint sessions. In their joint sessions much time is spent on how betrayed the wife feels over having discovered that her husband had an affair in the past. She is angry and hurt but has agreed to remain in the marriage and to come to these therapy sessions as long as the husband agrees not to resume the past affair or to initiate new ones. Reluctantly, the husband agrees to her demands. The therapist does not explicitly state her views about confidentiality, yet the husband assumes that she will keep to herself what she hears in both the wife's private sessions and his private sessions. During one of the joint sessions, the therapist does state her bias. She says that maintaining or initiating an affair is counterproductive if they both want to work on improving their marriage. The therapist states a strong preference that they agree not to have extramarital affairs.

In a later individual session the husband tells the therapist that he has begun a new affair. He brings this up privately with his therapist because he feels some guilt over not having lived up to the agreement. But he maintains that the affair is not negatively influencing his relationship with his wife and has helped him to tolerate many of the difficulties he has been experiencing in his marriage. He also asks that the therapist not mention this in a joint session, for he fears that his wife will leave him if she finds out that he is involved with another woman.

Think about these questions in deciding on the ethical course of action:

- The therapist has not explicitly stated her view of confidentiality. Is it ethical for her to bring up the husband's new affair in a joint session?

- How does the therapist handle her conviction regarding affairs in light of the fact that the husband tells her that it is actually enhancing, not interfering with, the marriage?
- Should the therapist attempt to persuade the husband to give up the affair? Should she persuade the client to bring up this matter himself in a joint session? Is the therapist colluding with the husband against the wife by not bringing up this matter?
- Should the therapist discontinue therapy with this couple because of her strong bias? If she does suggest termination and referral to another professional, might not this be tantamount to admitting to the wife that the husband is having an affair? What might the therapist say if the wife is upset over the suggestion of a referral and wants to know the reasons?

Informed Consent in Couples and Family Therapy

In Chapter 5 we examined the issue of informed consent and clients' rights within the framework of individual therapy. Informed consent is a critical ethical issue in the practice of couples and family therapy. Before each individual agrees to participate in family therapy, it is essential that the counselor provide information about the purpose of therapy, typical procedures, the risks of negative outcomes, the possible benefits, the fee structure, the limits of confidentiality, the rights and responsibilities of clients, the option that a family member can withdraw at any time, and what can be expected from the therapist. When therapists take the time to obtain informed consent from everyone, they convey the message that no one member is the "identified patient" who is the source of all the family's problems. Although getting the informed consent of each member of the family is ideal from an ethical point of view, actually carrying out this practice may be difficult. The more thorough and clear the preparation and informed consent process is, the easier it is for families to make decisions regarding their treatment, and as well, the more control the therapist has over future potential problems.

Clients have a right to know that the family system will be the focus of the therapeutic process and to know about the practical implications of this theoretical perspective. Informed consent can be more complex than it appears. Many times families enter counseling with one person in the family being perceived as the one with the problem or the person causing the family distress. After therapy commences, however, the entire family becomes the focus of the therapist's intervention. Did these family members truly consent to become clients, or did they perceive their role as consultants? Family members should have opportunities to raise questions and know as clearly as possible what they are getting involved in when they enter family therapy.

Kaplan (2000) uses an informed consent brochure as a basis for establishing a solid therapeutic relationship among participants in family therapy. Here are some of the steps in this informed consent procedure:

- Construct a thorough informed consent brochure.
- Ask the couple or family to arrive early before the first session so they have time to read the brochure.
- Ask the family if they have any questions about the therapeutic process based on their reading of the informed consent brochure.
- Review the policies and rules about confidentiality.
- Request from each family member a written acknowledgment that he or she has reviewed and understood the contents of the brochure.
- Give the family the brochure to take home for further reference.
- Ask about the brochure at the beginning of the second session.

This structured informed consent procedure increases the chances of instilling a sense of trust that is foundational for future therapy sessions.

As a part of any informed consent document, it is essential that the therapist's policy be spelled out regarding the conditions for family therapy to begin. For instance, some family therapists will conduct family sessions even if certain members will not attend. Other family therapists consider it essential that all members of the family participate in the therapy process. This latter bias raises ethical questions about exerting pressure on an individual to participate, even if that person is strongly against being involved. Although coercion of a reluctant person is generally viewed as unethical, many therapists strongly suggest that a reluctant family member participate for a session or two to determine what potential value there might be in family therapy. Some resistance can arise from a family member's feeling that he or she will be the main target of the sessions. This resistance can be lessened and perhaps even eliminated in a short period of time if the therapist refuses to allow the family to use one member as a scapegoat.

There is no professional agreement on whether it is necessary to see all the family for therapy to take place, but we believe it is particularly important when it comes to therapy with children. In so many instances the child is the first family member presented for therapy. This can put an inordinate burden on the child. Including the whole family in therapy provides more protection for the child, and as the whole system corrects itself, the family can become a source of support for the child.

Chapter Summary

The field of couples and family therapy is rapidly expanding and developing. With an expansion in educational programs comes the need for specialized training and experience. A thorough discussion of ethical issues must be part of all such programs. A few of these issues are determining who is the primary client, dealing with confidentiality, providing informed consent, counseling with minors, and exploring the role of values in family therapy.

The job of the therapist is to help a couple or a family explore and clarify their own values, not to influence them to conform to the therapist's value system. Likewise, a key ethical issue is the impact of the therapist's life experiences on his or her ability to practice effectively and objectively. For instance, if family therapists are bogged down by their own unfinished business with their family of origin or unresolved conflicts in their current family, it is not likely that they will be able to be therapeutic agents for other families. Therapists who are using their work as a way to fulfill their own needs or who have intense countertransference reactions toward particular family members may be blocking a family's progress. The ethical issues are clear in these cases.

As is true regarding all ethical issues, there is a significant relationship between sound ethical practices and clinical decision making. Family therapists may sometimes experience confusion, for example, regarding the ethical aspects of deciding who will attend family sessions. It is obvious, however, that such decisions cannot be made without a solid foundation in clinical theory and methodology. With increased knowledge and practical experience, therapists can make these ethical decisions with greater certainty. Being open to periodic supervision, seeking consultation when necessary, and being willing to participate in one's own therapy are some ways in which couples and family therapists can refine their clinical skills.

Suggested Activities

1. In the practice of couples and family therapy, informed consent is especially important. As a class discussion topic, explore some of these issues: What are the ethical implications of insisting that all members of a family participate in family therapy? What kind of information should a family therapist present from the outset to all those involved? Are there any ethical conflicts in focusing on the welfare of the entire family rather than on what might be in the best interests of an individual?
2. Investigate the status of regulating professional practice in couples and family therapy in your state. What are the academic and training requirements, if any, for certification or licensure in this field?
3. In a small group, discuss the major ethical problems facing couples and family therapists. Consider issues such as confidentiality, enforced therapy involving all family members, qualifications of effective family therapists, imposing the values of the therapist on a family, and practicing beyond one's competence.
4. Design a project to study your own family of origin. Interview as many relatives as you can. Look for patterns in your own relationships, including problems you currently struggle with, that stem from your family of origin. What advantages do you see in studying your own family as one way to prepare yourself for counseling families?

5. Imagine that you are participating on a board to establish standards—personal, academic, and experiential—for family therapists. What do you think the minimum requirements should be to prepare a trainee to work with families? What would your ideal training program for couples and family therapists look like?

Ethics in Action CD-ROM Exercises

6. In video role play #4, The Divorce, the client (Janice) has made a decision to leave her husband and get a divorce. She says she does not want to work on her relationship anymore. The counselor (Gary) says he hates to hear that. Janice has not been happy for a long time, and she is tired of her husband's temper and his moods. Gary brings up the kids and asks who will be the advocate for them. Janice thinks that if she is happy they will be happy. She says she will take care of the kids, but that she has to do something with her life. Gary concludes by asking, "Is divorce the best way to take care of them?"

Put yourself in this situation with a client similar to Janice. Assume that your client is experiencing a great deal of ambivalence about getting a divorce, even though she tells you she is convinced that her marital situation is hopeless. She pleads with you to tell her whether she should remain married or get a divorce. What approach might you take? If your client expects you to provide her with an answer, because she is coming to you as the expert, what would you do? Have one student role-play the confused client who is searching for an answer and ask several students to give different ways of proceeding with this client.

7. Now let's assume that the client in video role play #4 is struggling with staying versus leaving her husband. Using the responses of Counselors A, B, and C in the text for the case of Frank and Judy (see pages 405–407), three students can role-play the counselors and interact with the client in the video.

InfoTrac® College Edition Resources

For additional readings, explore InfoTrac College Edition, our online library. Go to *http://www.infotrac.college.com/wadsworth* and select these key word searches:

ethic* family therap*
couples counseling ethical issues
value* marriage therapy
gender sensitive AND therapy
confidentiality in marital and family therapy

Key words are listed in a form that enables the search engine to locate a wider range of articles in the online university library. Key words should be entered exactly as shown, including asterisks, "W1," "W2," "AND," and other search engine tools.

12

Pre-Chapter Self-Inventory

Directions: For each statement, indicate the response that most closely identifies your beliefs and attitudes. Use the following code:

5 = I *strongly agree* with this statement.
4 = I *agree* with this statement.
3 = I am *undecided* about this statement.
2 = I *disagree* with this statement.
1 = I *strongly disagree* with this statement.

_____1. Groups are a second-rate therapeutic approach, used mainly as a way to cut costs.

_____2. Ethical practice requires that prospective group members be carefully screened and selected.

_____3. It is important to prepare members so that they can derive the maximum benefit from the group.

_____4. Requiring people to participate in a therapy group raises ethical issues.

_____5. It is unethical to allow a group to exert pressure on one of its members.

_____6. Confidentiality is less important in groups than it is in individual therapy.

_____7. Socializing among group members is almost always undesirable because it interferes with the functioning of the group.

Ethical Issues in Group Work

_____8. One way of minimizing psychological risks to group participants is to negotiate contracts with the members.

_____9. A group leader has a responsibility to teach members how to translate what they have learned in the group to their outside lives.

_____10. It is unethical for counselor educators to lead groups of their students in training.

_____11. Group psychotherapy cannot be conducted in an ethical manner over the Internet except in very limited circumstances.

_____12. It is the group leader's responsibility to make prospective members aware of their rights and responsibilities and to demystify the process of a group.

_____13. Group members should know that they have the right to leave the group at any time.

_____14. Before people enter a group, it is the leader's responsibility to discuss with them the personal risks involved, especially potential life changes, and help them explore their readiness to face these risks.

_____15. It is a sound practice to provide written ethical guidelines to group members in advance and discuss them in the first meeting.

Introduction

We are giving group work special attention, as we did with couples and family therapy, because it raises unique ethical concerns. Practitioners who work with groups face a variety of situations that differ from those encountered in individual therapy. Groups have been increasing in popularity, and in many agencies and institutions they are the primary form of therapy. Along with this increased use of groups, there has been a rising ethical awareness.

Research confirms that group treatment is more effective than no treatment, yet group therapy does not appear to be superior to other forms of therapy. According to Steenbarger and Budman (1996), group therapy is attractive to managed care organizations, and to some therapists, because it is a more cost-effective form of counseling. Thus, managed behavioral health care is likely to make group therapy a more viable option in the future.

Although there are some distinct advantages to group therapy, this mode of therapy appears to be underutilized because clients, and some therapists, view group therapy as a second-choice form of treatment. If groups are to flourish, group practitioners face the challenge of educating the public and health care professionals about this therapeutic approach. Clients are less frequently referred for group therapy than they are to individual treatment, and when clients are referred they may not always follow through and join a group (Trull & Phares, 2001).

In our view, groups are often *the* treatment of choice, not a second-rate therapeutic approach. Many of the problems that bring people to counseling are rooted in interpersonal issues and involve difficulties forming or maintaining intimate relationships. Clients may be at a loss in knowing how to live well with the ones they love, they often believe that their problems are unique, and they see few options to change their life situation. Groups provide a natural laboratory that demonstrates to people that they are not alone and that there is hope for creating a different life. Groups are powerful because long-term problems of group members may be played out in the group sessions, giving group members opportunities to try out different solutions.

Our illustrations of important ethical considerations in this chapter are drawn from a broad spectrum of groups, including therapy groups, counseling groups, personal-growth groups, psychoeducational groups, and structured groups. Obviously, these groups differ with respect to their member population, purpose, focus, and procedures, as well as in the level of training required for the facilitators of these groups. Although these distinctions are important, all groups face some common concerns: training group leaders, co-leadership issues, the ethical issues surrounding group membership, confidentiality in groups, uses and abuses of group techniques, and issues concerning termination and follow-up. We address these issues in this chapter.

Training and Supervision of Group Leaders

For competent group leaders to emerge, training programs must make group work a priority. Unfortunately, in some graduate training programs not even one group course is required. If a group course is required, it usually covers both the didactic and experiential aspects of group process.

With proper training in group work, competent practitioners will know their limitations and recognize the kinds of groups they are able to lead. Practitioners will familiarize themselves with referral resources and refrain from working with client populations that need special help beyond their level of competence. Competent group counselors will be able to explain to their clients the theory behind their group work and how their theory influences their practice. They will be able to present in clear language to the members the goals of the group and the relationship between the way they lead the group and their goals. Effective group workers are able to conceptualize the group process and to relate what they do in a group to this model. Furthermore, responsible group workers need to be keenly aware of the importance of continuing their education. Beginning therapists, as well as experienced professionals, attend conventions and workshops, take courses, read, seek consultation and supervision, and get involved in special training programs from time to time.

Professional Training Standards*

The Association for Specialists in Group Work (ASGW) revised the "Professional Standards for the Training of Group Workers" (ASGW, 2000), taking under consideration the seminal "Best Practice Guidelines" (ASGW, 1998) and the "Principles for Diversity-Competent Group Workers" (ASGW, 1999). The ASGW training standards specify two levels of competencies and related training. First is a set of *core knowledge* and *skill competencies* that provide the foundation on which *specialized* training is built. At a minimum, one group course should be included in a training program, and it should be structured to help students acquire the basic knowledge and skills needed to facilitate a group. These group skills are best mastered through supervised practice, which should include a minimum of 10 hours of observation and participation in a group experience.

Once counselor trainees have mastered these core knowledge and skills domains, they can acquire training in group work specializations in one or more of these four areas: (1) task and work groups, (2) psychoeducational groups, (3) group counseling, and (4) group psychotherapy. The ASGW standards detail specific knowledge and skill competencies for these specialties and recommend the number of hours of supervised training necessary for each.

*Adapted from "Professional Standards for the Training of Group Workers," adopted January 22, 2000, in *The Group Worker: Association for Specialists in Group Work, 29*(3), (Spring 2000), 1–10. The ASGW is a division of the American Counseling Association, 5999 Stevenson Avenue, Alexandria, VA 22304.

The ASGW's (2000) training standards are the foundation for training group workers. The standards of the Council for Accreditation of Counseling and Related Educational Programs (CACREP, 1994) that deal with group work reflect much of this material. Attempts have been made to implement the ASGW recommendations with the CACREP standards, outlining supervised clinical experience obtained in both practicum and internship programs. The CACREP standards require experience in individual and group counseling under supervision and, consistent with the ASGW training standards, indicate that at least one fourth of the direct service practicum be devoted to group work.

Whether core training in group work reflects minimal CACREP standards or the more specific ASGW standards, this training alone is not sufficient to prepare counselors for conducting groups on their own. Practitioners must still acquire training in a particular specialization in group work (Conyne, 1996). The current trend in training for group workers focuses on learning group processes by becoming involved in supervised experiences. Both direct participation in planned and supervised small groups and clinical experience in leading various groups under careful supervision are needed to equip leaders with the skills to meet the challenges of group work.

Our Views on Training

Professional codes, legislative mandates, and institutional policies alone will not ensure competent group leadership. Group counselor trainees need to confront the typical dilemmas they will face in practice and learn ways to clarify their views on these issues. This can best be done by including ethics in the trainees' academic program as well as discussing ethical issues that grow out of the students' experiences in practicum, internship, and fieldwork. We have found that one effective way to teach ethical decision making is by presenting trainees with case vignettes of typical problems that occur in group situations and encouraging discussion of the ethical issues and pertinent guidelines. We tell both students and professionals who attend our workshops that they will not have the answers to many of the dilemmas they encounter in practice. Ethical decision making is an ongoing process that takes on new forms and increased meaning as practitioners gain experience. What is critical is that group leaders develop a receptivity to self-examination and to questioning the professionalism of their group practice.

We highly recommend at least three experiences as adjuncts to a training program for group workers: (1) personal (private) psychotherapy; (2) experience in group therapy, group counseling, or a personal-growth group; and (3) participation in a supervision and training group.

Personal psychotherapy. As we discussed in Chapter 2, personal therapy for trainees can be most helpful in enhancing both their personal lives and their professional development. We agree with Yalom (1995) that extensive self-exploration is necessary if trainees are to perceive countertransference feelings, recognize blind spots and biases, and use their personal attributes effectively in groups. Although videotaping, working with a co-leader, and supervision all are excellent sources of feedback, Yalom maintains that personal therapy is usually necessary for fuller understanding and correction. We think that group leaders should demonstrate the courage and willingness to do for themselves what they expect members in their groups to do: Expand their awareness of self and the effect of that self on others.

Self-exploration groups. As an adjunct to formal course work and internship training, participation in a therapeutic group can be extremely valuable. In addition to helping interns resolve personal conflicts and develop increased self-understanding, a personal-growth group can be a powerful teaching tool. One of the best ways to learn how to assist group members in their struggles is to work as a member of a group yourself. Yalom (1995) strongly recommends a group experience for trainees. Some of the benefits, he suggests, are experiencing the power of a group, learning what self-disclosure is about, coming to appreciate the difficulties involved in self-sharing, learning on an emotional level what one knows intellectually, and becoming aware of one's dependence on the leader's power and knowledge. He cites surveys indicating that 60% to 70% of group therapy training programs offer some type of personal-group experience. About half of these programs offer an optional group, and the other half a mandatory group.

Participation in a training and supervisory group. We have found that workshops help group trainees develop the skills necessary for effective intervention. Also, interns can learn a great deal about their response to criticism, their competitiveness, their need for approval, their concerns over being competent, and their power struggles. In working with both university students learning about group approaches and professionals who want to upgrade their skills, we have found an intensive weekend workshop to be an effective format.

As you consider the training of group leaders, ponder these questions for yourself:

- What makes you qualified to lead groups? What are the criteria for determining the competence of group leaders?
- What are some differences between a training group and a therapy group? Can you think of safeguards to minimize the potential risks of combining experiential and didactic methods?
- Does ethical practice demand that group leaders receive some form of personal therapy? Should this be group therapy or experience in a personal-growth group?
- How important are continuing education and training once trainees have completed a professional program?
- What are your reactions to the suggestions we offered for the training of group workers?

Co-Leadership

If you decide to lead groups, you will probably work with a co-leader at some time. We think there are many advantages to the co-leader model. The group can benefit from the insights and feedback of two leaders. The leaders can complement and balance each other. They can grow by discussing what goes on in the group and by observing each other's style, and together they can evaluate what has gone on in the group and plan for future sessions. Also, co-leaders can share the responsibilities. While one leader is working with a particular member, the other can be paying attention to others in the group.

The choice of a co-leader is crucial and can have ethical implications. A group can suffer if its leaders are not working effectively together. If much of the leaders' energies are directed at competing with each other or at some other power struggle or hidden agenda, there is little chance that the group will be effective.

Selection of a co-leader should involve more than attraction and liking. Each of the leaders should be secure enough that the group won't have to suffer as one or both of them try to "prove" themselves. We surely don't think it is essential that co-leaders always agree or share the same perceptions or interpretations; in fact, a group can be given vitality if co-leaders feel trusting enough to express their differences of opinion. Mutual respect and the ability to establish a relationship based on trust, cooperation, and support are most important. Also, each person should be autonomous and have his or her own style yet be able to work with the other leader as a team.

In our view it is essential for co-leaders to spend some time together immediately following a group session to assess what has happened. Similarly, we believe that they should meet at least briefly before each session to talk about anything that might affect their functioning in the group.

At this point we ask you to draw up your own guidelines for selecting a co-leader:

- What are the qualities you would look for in a co-leader?
- What kind of person would you not want to lead with?
- If you found that you and your co-leader clashed on many issues and approached groups very differently, what do you think you would do?
- What ethical implications are involved when a great deal of time during the sessions is taken up with power struggles and conflicts between the co-leaders?
- In what ways could you be most helpful to your co-leader?
- What kind of help would you expect to receive from your co-leader?

Ethical Issues in Group Membership

How can group leaders make potential members aware of the services they are providing? What information do clients have a right to expect before they decide to attend a group? People have a right to know what they are getting into before they make a commitment to become a part of any group. Informed consent requires that leaders make the members aware of their rights (as well as their responsibilities) as group participants.

◆ **A case of informed consent.** A group leader operates on the assumption that giving members information about her groups will ultimately be counterproductive. She does not tell them about the nature of the group process, the procedures she may use, or the best ways to get the maximum benefit from the group. She is concerned that members would focus on meeting her expectations. She does not emphasize defining goals and believes that members' uncertainty about what they want from the group will be good material to explore as part of the group process.

- Is this leader behaving unethically in not providing members with information about the goals of the group or the procedures she may use?
- What are some of the potential problems of providing too much information about a group before members enroll?
- What information do you think a member should have before deciding whether to participate in a group?

Screening and Selection of Group Members

Group leaders are faced with the difficult task of determining who should be included in a group and who should not. Are groups appropriate for all people? To put the question in another way, is it appropriate for *this* person to become a participant in *this* type of group, with *this* leader, at *this* time?

Assuming that not everyone will benefit from a group experience—and that some people may be psychologically harmed by certain group experiences—is it unethical to fail to screen prospective group candidates? Many group leaders do not screen participants, for various reasons. Some practitioners are theoretically opposed to the notion of using screening as a way of determining who is suitable for a group, and some maintain that they simply do not have the time to carry out effective screening. Others believe that ethical practice demands careful screening and preparation of all candidates.

Unless careful selection criteria are employed, Yalom (1995) argues that group therapy clients may end up discouraged and may not be helped. He maintains that it is easier to identify the people who should be excluded from group therapy than those who should be included. Citing clinical studies, he lists the following as poor candidates for a heterogeneous outpatient intensive-therapy group: brain-damaged people, paranoid individuals, hypochondriacs, those who are addicted to drugs or alcohol, acutely psychotic individuals, and antisocial personalities. In terms of criteria for inclusion, he contends that the client's level of motivation to work is the most important variable. From his perspective, groups are useful for people who have problems in the interpersonal domain, such as loneliness, inability to make or maintain intimate contacts, feelings of unlovability, fears of being assertive, and dependency issues.

Clients who lack meaning in life, who suffer from diffuse anxiety, who are searching for an identity, who fear success, and who are compulsive workers might also profit from a group experience. The "Best Practice Guidelines" of ASGW (1998) identifies the group leader's responsibility for screening prospective group members:

> Group Workers screen prospective group members if appropriate to the type of group being offered. When selection of group members is appropriate, Group Workers identify group members whose needs and goals are compatible with goals of the group.

Screening is most effective when the leader interviews the members and the members also have an opportunity to interview the leader. While prospective group members are being screened, they should be deciding whether they want to work with a particular leader and whether the group in question is suitable for them. Group candidates should not passively allow the matter to be decided for them by an expert. Practitioners should welcome the opportunity to respond to any questions or concerns prospective members may have, and they should actively encourage prospective members to raise questions about matters that will affect their participation. In some settings it is impractical to screen members prior to forming a group. In situations where it is not possible to conduct screening interviews, one alternative is to use the initial session to screen participants and to present informed consent guidelines.

Preparing Group Participants

To what extent are group counselors responsible for helping participants to benefit from their group experience? Many practitioners do very little to prepare members systematically for a group. In fact, we know of some group workers who are opposed to systematic preparation on the ground that it would inhibit a group's spontaneity and autonomy. Others take the position that members must be provided with some structure to derive the maximum gains.

Yalom (1995) advocates exploring group members' misconceptions and expectations, predicting early problems, and providing a conceptual framework that includes guidelines for effective group behavior. He views this preparatory process as more than the dissemination of information. He contends that it reinforces the therapist's respect for the client, demonstrates that therapy is a collaborative venture, and shows that the therapist is willing to share his or her knowledge with the client. This cognitive approach to preparation has the goals of providing a rational explanation of the group process, clarifying how members are expected to behave, and raising expectations about what the group can accomplish.

In our training workshops we have seen much resistance that can be attributed to ignorance of group process and a misunderstanding of goals. Our preparation procedures apply to all types of groups, with some modifications.

At both the screening session and the initial group meeting, we explore the members' expectations, clarify goals and objectives, discuss procedural details, explore the possible risks and values of group participation, and discuss guidelines for getting the most from a group experience (G. Corey, Corey, Callanan, & Russell, 1992; M. Corey & Corey, 2002). As part of member preparation, we include a discussion of the values and limitations of groups, the psychological risks involved in group participation, and ways of minimizing these risks. We also allow time for dealing with misconceptions that people have about groups and for exploring any fears or resistances the members may have. In most of our groups, members do have certain fears about what they will experience, and until we acknowledge these fears and talk about them very little productive work can occur. Further, we ask members to spend time before they come to the group defining for themselves what they most want to achieve. To make their goals more concrete, we usually ask them to develop a contract that entails areas of concern on which they are willing to work in the group. We also ask them to do some reading and to write about their goals and about the significant turning points in their lives.

At this point, we ask you to write down some things you might do to prepare people for a group. What ethical concerns do you have regarding preparation? What do you think would occur if you did little in the way of preparing group members?

Involuntary Participation

Should group membership always be voluntary? Are there situations in which it is ethical to require or coerce people to participate in a group? How is informed consent especially critical in groups where attendance is mandatory?

Obviously, voluntary participation is an important beginning point for a successful group experience. Members will make significant changes only to the extent that they actively seek something for themselves. Unfortunately, not all groups are composed of clients who have chosen to be there. In some community agencies and inpatient facilities, the main therapeutic vehicle may be group therapy. People receiving services may be required to attend group sessions, sometimes several times a week. This situation is somewhat akin to compulsory education—people can be forced to attend but not to learn.

When group participation is mandatory, much effort needs to be directed toward fully informing members of the nature and goals of the group, procedures to be used, the rights of members to decline certain activities, the limits of confidentiality, and what effect their level of participation in the group will have on critical decisions about them outside of the group. When attendance at group sessions is mandatory, group leaders must be certain that group members understand their rights and their responsibilities.

In the case that follows, consider the ethical issues involved in mandated group therapy, the failure to give members enough information to make decisions, and the use of pressure.

◆ **A case of an involuntary group.** In a prison group an inexperienced leader senses that little progress is being made. In an attempt to lessen the members' resistance, she tells them that she does not want anybody to be part of the group who is not willing to participate freely in the sessions. She neglects to inform them that their refusal to attend group sessions will be documented and will be a factor in the decision about their release. Thus, the members are operating under the assumption that they have freedom of choice, yet they have not been given the information they need to make a real choice.

- Does this leader's desire for an effective group justify her practice? Why or why not?
- Do you think members can benefit from a group experience even if they are required to attend? Why or why not?
- What strategy might this leader have used to foster more effective group participation while still giving the members true freedom of choice?
- From an ethical perspective, is it required that members of an involuntary group give consent? To what degree should members be informed about the consequences of the quantity or quality of their participation in a group?

Freedom to Leave a Group

Once members make a commitment to be a part of a group, do they have the right to leave at any time they choose? Procedures for leaving a group should be explained to all members during the initial session. Ideally, the leader and the member cooperate to determine whether a group experience is proving to be productive or counterproductive. We take the position that clients have a responsibility to the leader and to other members to explain why they want to leave. There are several reasons for this policy. It can be deleterious to members to leave without having been able to discuss what they considered threatening or negative in the experience. Further, it is unfortunate for members to leave a group because of a misunderstanding about some feedback they have received. Such a termination can be harmful to group cohesion, for the members who remain may think that they caused a particular member's departure. We tell our members that they have an obligation to attend all sessions and to inform us and the group should they decide to withdraw. If members even consider withdrawing, we encourage them to bring this up for exploration in a session. We do not think it is ethical to use undue pressure to keep these members, and we are alert to other members' pressuring a person to stay.

Psychological Risks

The fact that groups can be powerful catalysts for personal change means that they are also risky. Although we don't think groups should be free of risks, ethical practice demands that group practitioners inform prospective participants of the potential hazards involved in the group experience. However, merely informing participants does not absolve leaders of all responsibility. Group leaders have an ethical responsibility to take precautionary measures to reduce unnecessary psychological risks. ACA's (1995) guideline is this: "In a group setting, counselors take reasonable precautions to protect clients from physical or psychological trauma" (A.9.b.). Certain safeguards can be taken during the course of a group to avoid disastrous outcomes. Here are some of the risks that participants should know about (M. Corey & Corey, 2002, pp. 72–75):

- Members may experience major disruptions in their lives as a result of their work in the group.
- Group participants are often encouraged to be completely open. In this quest for complete self-revelation, privacy is sometimes invaded.
- A related risk is group pressure. The participants' right not to explore certain issues or to stop at a certain point should be respected. Also, members should not be coerced into participating in an exercise.
- Scapegoating is another potential hazard in groups. Unchallenged projection and blaming can have dire effects on the target person.
- Confrontation can be used or misused in groups. Harmful attacks on others should not be permitted under the guise of "sharing."
- Even though a counselor may continue to stress the necessity not to discuss with outsiders what goes on in the group, there is no guarantee that all members will respect the confidential nature of their exchanges.

One way to minimize psychological risks in groups is to use a contract, in which leaders specify what their responsibilities are and members specify their commitment to the group by declaring what they are willing to do. If members and leaders operate under a contract that clarifies expectations, there is less chance for members to be exploited or damaged by a group experience.

Of course, a contract approach is not the only way to reduce potential risks, nor is it sufficient in itself to do so. One of the most important safeguards is the leader's training in group process. Group counselors have the major responsibility for preventing needless harm to members. To fulfill this role, group leaders should have a clear grasp of the boundaries of their competence. As a rule, leaders should conduct only those types of groups for which they have been sufficiently prepared. A counselor may be trained to lead a personal-growth or consciousness-raising group but be ill-prepared to embark on a therapy group. Sometimes people who have attended a few intensive groups become excited about doing this type of group as leaders, even though they have had little or no training or supervision. Oftentimes they are in over their heads and unable to cope with what emerges in the group. Working with an experienced co-leader is one good way to learn and also a way to reduce potential risks.

Confidentiality in Groups

The ethical, legal, and professional aspects of confidentiality (discussed in Chapter 6) have a different application in group situations. Are members of a group under the same ethical and legal obligations as the group leader not to disclose the identities of other members or the content of what was shared in the group? The legal concept of privileged communication generally does not apply in a group setting, unless there has been a statutory exception. Therefore, group counselors have the responsibility of informing members of the limits of confidentiality within the group setting, their responsibilities to other group members, and the absence of legal privilege concerning what is shared in a group (Anderson, 1996). One of the clear ethical responsibilities of members is to respect the communications of others in the group.

How to encourage confidentiality. The ASGW (1998) "Best Practice Guidelines" state the following regarding confidentiality:

> Group Workers define confidentiality and its limits (for example, legal and ethical exceptions and expectations; waivers implicit with treatment plans, documentation, and insurance usage). Group Workers have the responsibility to inform all group participants of the need for confidentiality and potential consequences of breaching confidentiality; they must explain that legal privilege does not apply to group discussions (unless provided by state statute).

Although most writers on ethical issues in group work make the point that confidentiality cannot be guaranteed, they also talk about the importance of teaching group members to avoid breaking confidences. Confidentiality in group situations is difficult to enforce. Because members cannot assume that anything they say or hear in the group will remain confidential, they should be able to make an informed choice about how much to reveal.

It is our position that leaders need periodically to reaffirm to group members the importance of not discussing with outsiders what has occurred in the group. In our own groups we talk with each prospective member about the necessity of maintaining confidentiality to establish the trust and cohesion required if participants are to reveal themselves in significant ways. We discuss this point during the screening interviews, again during the pregroup or initial meetings, at times during the course of a group when it seems appropriate, and again at termination. Most people do not maliciously attempt to hurt others by talking with people outside the group about specific members. However, it is tempting for members to share their experiences with other people, and in so doing they sometimes make inappropriate disclosures. Because of this tendency to want to share with outsiders, we repeatedly caution participants in any type of group about how easily and unintentionally the confidentiality of the group can be compromised.

If you were to lead any type of group, which of the following measures might you take to ensure confidentiality? Check any of the statements that apply:

___ I would repeatedly mention the importance of confidentiality.

___ I would require group members to sign a statement saying that they fully understand their commitment to maintain the confidential character of the group.

___ I would let members know that they would be asked to leave the group if they violated confidentiality.
___ I would have a document describing the dimensions of confidentiality to which all the members could refer.
___ With the permission and knowledge of the members, I would tape-record all the sessions.
___ I would say very little about confidentiality and leave it up to group members to decide how they would deal with the issue.

Exceptions to confidentiality. Group counselors have a responsibility to define clearly what confidentiality means, explain its importance, and inform members of the difficulties involved in enforcing it. Although group counselors are expected to stress the importance of confidentiality and set a norm, they are also expected to inform members about its limits. For example, if members pose a danger to themselves or to others, the group leader would be ethically and legally obliged to breach confidentiality. The other limitations for confidentiality, which were discussed in Chapter 6, also apply to group work.

It is a good practice for group workers to give a written statement to each member outlining the nature, purposes, and limitations of confidentiality and acknowledging specific situations that would require the breaching of confidences. It seems that such straightforwardness with members from the outset does a great deal to create trust, for at least members know the consequences of certain revelations to the group.

Of course, it is imperative that those who lead groups become familiar with the state laws that have an impact on their practice. For instance, since 1967, all states have had mandatory child abuse reporting laws. Several states also have mandatory elder abuse and dependent adult abuse reporting laws. The great majority of states currently have laws requiring counselors to report clients' threats to harm themselves or others.

If you lead a group at a correctional institution or a psychiatric hospital, you may have to record in a member's chart certain behaviors or verbalizations that he or she exhibits in the group. At the same time, your responsibility to your clients requires you to inform them that you are documenting their verbalizations and behaviors and that this information is accessible to other staff.

Confidentiality with minors. Do parents have a right to information that is disclosed by their children in a group? The answer to that question depends on whether we are looking at it from a legal, ethical, or professional viewpoint. State laws differ regarding counseling minors. It is important for group leaders to be well aware of the laws related to working with minors in the state where they are practicing. Circumstances in which a minor may seek professional help without parental consent, defining an emancipated minor, or the rights of parents (or legal guardians) to have access to the records regarding the professional help received by their minor child vary according to state statutes.

Before any minor enters a group, it is a good practice to obtain written permission from the parents. Such a statement should include a brief description of the purpose of the group, the importance of confidentiality as a prerequisite to accomplishing these purposes, and your intention not to violate any confidences. Although it may be useful to give parents information about their child, this can be done without violating confidences. It is helpful to inform and discuss with minors their concerns in advance about confidentiality and how it will be maintained. Such practices can strengthen the child's trust in the counselor.

Group leaders have a responsibility in groups that involve children and adolescents to take measures to increase the chances that confidentiality will be kept. It is important to work cooperatively with parents and legal guardians as well as to enlist the trust of the young people. It is also useful to teach minors, using a vocabulary that they are capable of understanding, about the nature, purposes, and limitations of confidentiality. It is a good idea for leaders to encourage members to initiate discussions on confidentiality whenever this becomes an issue for them.

Confidentiality and online group therapy. Humphreys, Winzelberg, and Klaw (2000) take the position that online group psychotherapy cannot ethically be conducted over the Internet, except in very limited circumstances. Internet group therapy involves typing, recording, copying, and distributing all the "interactions" that take place online. This makes ensuring clients' privacy and confidentiality a very difficult matter. In addition, individuals cannot be reliably identified over the Internet. A person with access to a client's computer could sign into online group therapy by using the password and the name of the actual client. The implications for lack of confidentiality and privacy are obvious here. Because of the difficulty of maintaining the confidential nature of a group, we are opposed to online group therapy on both ethical and clinical grounds.

Humphreys, Winzelberg, and Klaw (2000) state that some kinds of peer groups and self-help groups do utilize Internet technology, but they add that the astonishing growth in the technology has outpaced the development of formal ethical guidelines for practitioners involved in online groups. Humphreys and colleagues write about a therapist's ethical responsibilities in self-help groups, discussion groups, and support groups that operate on the Internet, and they offer practical strategies for avoiding ethical problems.

Values in Group Counseling

Group counselors should be aware of their own values and the potential impact they have on the interventions they are likely to make. However, group counselors are sometimes timid about making their values known lest they influence the direction members are likely to take. Group counselors must consider when it might be appropriate to expose their beliefs, decisions, life experiences, and values. The key issue is that leaders should not short-circuit the members' exploration. Rather, the leader's central function is to help members find answers that are congruent with their own values.

From our perspective, the leader's function is to challenge members to evaluate their behavior to determine how it is working for them, not to advise members on the proper course to adopt. If members come to the realization that what they are doing is not serving them well, it is appropriate for the leader to challenge them to develop alternative ways of behaving that will enable them to reach their goals. Group leader behaviors that are hallmarks of ethical, professional, and effective practice include (a) demonstrating acceptance of the person of the client; (b) avoiding responding to sarcastic remarks with sarcasm; (c) educating the members about group process; (d) being honest with members rather than harboring hidden agendas; (e) avoiding judgments and labeling of members, and instead describing the behavior of members; (f) stating observations and hunches in a tentative way rather than dogmatically; (g) letting members who are difficult know how they are affecting them in a nonblaming way; (h) detecting their own countertransference reactions; (i) avoiding misusing their power; (j) providing both support and caring confrontations; and (k) avoiding meeting their own needs at the expense of the members (M. Corey & Corey, 2002).

Diversity Issues in Group Work

Being diversity-competent is more complex in meaning than "respecting other people." To fully assimilate the meaning into our personal and professional beings, it is important for us to have a common understanding of the principles on which diversity-competence is built. To that end, understanding and respecting differences in people is included in the ACA's (1995) code of ethics:

> Counselors will actively attempt to understand the diverse cultural backgrounds of the clients with whom they work. This includes, but is not limited to, learning how the counselor's own cultural, ethnic, racial identity impacts her/his values and beliefs about the counseling process. (A.2.b)

Most of the ethical codes of the various professional organizations now give some attention to applying these principles when working with culturally diverse clients, and the ASGW (1999) addresses diversity issues in various aspects of group work. These principles emphasize the practitioner's responsibility to have a general understanding of the cultural values of his or her clients, so interventions are congruent with their worldviews.

Guidelines for competence in diversity issues in group practice are discussed in a variety of sources, some of which include ACA (1995), ASGW (1999), APA (1993), DeLucia-Waack (1996), Arredondo and colleagues (1996), and D. W. Sue, Arredondo, and McDavis (1992). Based on these sources, we have adapted the following guidelines for group practice:

- Group counselors acknowledge that ethnicity and culture influence behavior.

- Group counselors consider the impact of adverse social, environmental, and political factors in assessing problems and designing interventions.
- Group counselors acquire the knowledge and skills necessary for effectively working with the diverse range of members in their groups. They seek consultation, supervision, and further education as ways of filling in any gaps or keeping themselves current.
- Group counselors are aware of how their own cultural backgrounds, attitudes, values, beliefs, and biases influence their work. In their practices, they develop sensitivity to issues of oppression, sexism, and racism.
- Group counselors respect the roles of family and community hierarchies within a client's culture.
- Group counselors respect members' religious and spiritual beliefs and values.
- Group counselors assist members in determining those instances when their difficulties stem from others' racism or bias, so they do not inappropriately personalize problems.
- Group counselors inform members about basic values that are implicit in the group process (such as self-disclosure, reflecting on one's life, and taking risks).

An awareness of cultural diversity is particularly important for group work. In Chapter 4 we discussed the characteristics of the culturally competent counselor. If group counselors do not understand how their cultural backgrounds influence their own thinking and behavior, there is little chance they can work ethically and effectively with group members who are culturally different from themselves.

The self-awareness, knowledge, and skill competencies described in Chapter 4 certainly apply to practitioners who work in groups. In working with groups characterized by diversity, counselors need to be aware of the assumptions they make about ethnic and cultural groups, and they are challenged to adapt their practices to the needs of the members. It is essential that the goals and processes of the group match the cultural values of the members of that group. Counselors need to be watchful of tendencies to treat people on the basis of stereotypes. It is critical that leaders become aware of their biases based on age, disability, ethnicity, gender, race, religion, or sexual orientation.

Ivey, Pedersen, and Ivey (2001) present the idea of multicultural intentionality, or the ability to work effectively with many varying types of individuals with diverse cultural backgrounds. To the key components of awareness, knowledge, and skills, they add the characteristics of humility, confidence, and recovery skills as critical to effective group leadership. These attributes mean that leaders do not have to possess all the answers, that they can learn from their mistakes, and that they can develop confidence in their ability to become flexible with challenging situations. The ability to recover from mistakes gracefully is more important than not making any mistakes.

This is a good time to reflect on your own characteristics that will enable you to become a diversity-competent group leader. What awareness, knowledge, and skills do you already possess that you can build on to help you develop the ability to work well with multicultural groups? To what degree are you able to respect the values and worldviews of group participants who may be very different from you? We suggest that you refer to the discussion of value conflicts in Chapter 3 and consider specific areas in which you might be inclined to impose your values in the groups you lead. Reflect on any tendencies you may have to lead your clients in a certain direction and think about ways to minimize the chances of imposing your values on them.

Uses and Abuses of Group Techniques

Group techniques can be used to facilitate the movement of a group and to deepen and intensify certain feelings. We think leaders should have a clear rationale for using each technique. This is an area in which theory can be a useful guide for practice.

Techniques can also be abused or used in unethical ways. Here are some ways leaders might employ techniques unethically:

- Using techniques with which they are unfamiliar
- Using techniques to serve their own hidden agenda or to enhance their power
- Using techniques whose sole purpose is to create an intense atmosphere because of the leader's need for intensity
- Using techniques to pressure members

We use these guidelines in our practice to avoid abusing techniques in a group:

- Techniques used should have a therapeutic purpose and be grounded in some theoretical framework.
- The client's self-exploration and self-understanding should be fostered.
- Techniques are devised for each unique client situation, and they assist the client in exploring some form of new behavior.
- Leaders need to modify their techniques so that they are suitable for the client's cultural and ethnic background.
- Techniques are not used to cover up the leader's incompetence; rather, they are used to enhance the group process.
- Techniques are introduced in a timely and sensitive manner, and they are abandoned if they are not working.
- The tone of a leader is consistently invitational; members are given the freedom either to participate in or to skip a given experiment.
- Leaders restrict their use of techniques to those interventions in which they have received training and supervision.

Although it is unrealistic to expect that leaders will always know exactly what will result from an intervention, they should know how to cope with unexpected outcomes. For example, guided fantasies into times of loneliness as a child or physical exercises designed to release anger can lead to intense emotional experiences. If leaders use such techniques, they must be ready to deal with any emotional release. It is essential that group counselors become aware of the potential for encouraging catharsis to fulfill their own needs. Some leaders may enjoy seeing people express anger because they would like to be able to do so themselves. They may push members to get into contact with angry feelings by developing techniques to bring out such feelings and to focus the group on anger. Although these are legitimate feelings, for surely most of us are at times angry, expressing anger in the group may satisfy the leader's agenda rather than being therapeutic for the member. This question ought to be raised frequently: "Whose needs are primary, and whose needs are being met—the members' or the leader's?"

Therapist Competence

How can leaders determine whether they are competent to use a certain technique? Although some leaders who have received training in the use of a technique may hesitate to use it (out of fear of making a mistake), other overly confident leaders may not have any reservations about trying out new techniques. It is useful if leaders have experienced these techniques as members of a group and have a clear rationale for using them. Group counselors need to be able to articulate a theoretical orientation that guides the interventions they make in their groups.

◆ **A case of an inexperienced leader.** An inexperienced group leader has recently graduated from a master's degree program in counseling. As a part of his job as a community mental health counselor, he organizes a weekly 2-hour group. He realizes that his training in group approaches is limited, so he decides to attend a weekend workshop on body therapy. He does some intense personal work himself at the workshop, and he comes away impressed with the power of what he has experienced. He is eager to meet his group on Tuesday evening so that he can try out some of these techniques. (He has not been trained in these techniques in graduate school, nor is he receiving any direct supervision in the group that he is leading.)

At the next session of the group a member says, "I feel a lot of pain and anger, and I don't know how to deal with these feelings." The leader intervenes by having the member lie down. He pushes on the client's abdomen and encourages her to scream, kick, shout, and release all the feelings that she has been keeping locked up inside of her. The client becomes pale, and her breathing becomes shallow and fast. She describes tingling sensations in her arms, a numbness, and a tight mouth, and she says that she is scared and cannot breathe. The leader encourages her to stay with it and get out all those pent-up feelings that are choking her up. At the same time others in the group seem frightened, and some are angry with the leader for pushing the client.

- Do you think a leader is competent to use body-oriented techniques after one weekend workshop?
- Was this leader's behavior dangerous, unethical, or both? If the leader had had a qualified supervisor at the session, would your answer be different?

- How can a group leader determine when he or she is adequately trained in the use of a technique?

Unfinished Business

Another major issue pertaining to the use of group techniques relates to providing immediate help for any group member who shows extreme distress during or at the end of a group session, especially if techniques were used to elicit intense emotions. Although some "unfinished business" promotes growth, there is an ethical issue in the use of a technique that incites strong emotional reactions if the client is abandoned at the end of a session because time has run out. Leaders must take care to allow enough time to deal adequately with the reactions that were stimulated in a session. It is unwise to introduce techniques in a session when there is not enough time to work through the feelings that might result or in a setting where there is no privacy or where the physical setup would make it harmful to employ certain techniques.

Our position on the ethical use of techniques is that group leaders need to learn about potential adverse effects. One way for group leaders to learn is by taking part in groups themselves. By being a group member and first experiencing a range of techniques, a therapist can develop a healthy respect for using techniques appropriately to meet clients' needs. In our training workshops for group leaders we encourage spontaneity and inventiveness in the use of techniques, but we also stress the importance of striking a balance between creativity and irresponsible bravado. The reputation of group work has suffered from the actions of irresponsible practitioners, mostly those who use techniques randomly without a clear rationale or without any sense of the potential outcome of techniques. If the group leader has a sound academic background, has had extensive supervised group experience, has participated in his or her own therapy or personal-growth experience, and has a basic respect for clients, he or she is not likely to abuse techniques.

The Consultation and Referral Process

Group counselors need to be aware of their limitations in working with certain types of clients. The willingness to consult with other professionals demonstrates good faith on the practitioner's part. For example, diversity-competent group workers are willing to seek consultation with traditional healers and religious or spiritual healers in the treatment of a diverse range of problems of individual members. Group workers actively seek out educational experiences that foster their knowledge and understanding of skills for facilitating groups across differences (ASGW, 1998, 1999). It is a good practice for leaders to explain to members their policies about consultation. When are they likely to consult? What measures do they take to protect confidentiality? Are they willing to have between-session consultations with group members? When and how might they refer? Here are some guidelines pertaining to the consultation and referral process:

- It is a good idea for members to bring the issues that were discussed during between-session consultations into the group, if appropriate.
- Group counselors can seek consultation and supervision when they are faced with ethical concerns or difficulties that interfere with their carrying out their leadership functions.
- Leaders need to develop a sensitivity to making appropriate referrals.
- Leaders should learn about the resources within the community and help members make use of these resources.

As we discussed earlier, one way to protect against a malpractice suit is to demonstrate that consultation procedures were used in dealing with an ethical dilemma. If group leaders consult supervisors or other professionals, they are demonstrating good clinical practice, adhering to ethical guidelines, and minimizing their chances of malpractice.

Issues Concerning Termination

The final phase in the life of a group is critical, for this is when members have the task of consolidating their learning. At this time members need to be able to express what the group experience has meant to them and to state where they intend to go from here. For many group members endings are difficult because they realize that time is limited in their group. The ending of a group often triggers other losses that members have experienced. Thus, the termination of a group may involve a grieving process. It is important for leaders to focus on the feelings of loss that may permeate the atmosphere. These feelings need to be identified and explored, although they probably cannot be alleviated. Members need to face the reality of termination and learn how to say goodbye. If the group has been truly therapeutic, the members will be able to extend their learning outside the group, even though they may well experience a sense of sadness and loss.

The Termination Phase

The termination phase of a group provides an opportunity for members to clarify the meaning of their experience, to consolidate the gains they have made, and to make decisions about the new behaviors they want to carry away from the group and apply to their everyday lives. The following professional issues are involved in the termination of a group:

- What responsibilities do group leaders have for assisting participants to develop a conceptual framework that will make sense of, integrate, and consolidate what they have learned in their group?
- To what degree is it the leader's responsibility to ensure that members are not left with excessive unfinished business at the end of the group?

- How can group leaders help participants translate what they have learned as a result of the group into their daily lives? Should leaders assume that this translation will occur automatically, or must they prepare members for generalizing their learning?

Typically, the final phase of group work is the one that leaders handle most ineptly, partly owing to their lack of training and partly because of their own resistance to termination. Avoiding acknowledgment of a group's termination may reflect discomfort on the leader's part in dealing with endings and separations. When termination is not dealt with, the group misses an opportunity to explore concerns that may affect many members, and the clients' therapy is jeopardized. When learning is not conceptualized, the ability to extend the meaning of the experience to real life is severely diminished.

Follow-Up and Evaluation

Throughout the life of a group, group leaders assist members in assessing their own progress and monitor their style of modeling. In this sense, evaluation is an ongoing process whereby members are taught how to determine if the group is helping them attain their personal goals. But group counselors also must assess both the process and the outcomes of their groups. Once a group has ended, follow-up group sessions provide an opportunity to do this. In our opinion, follow-up activities are useful to the members and to the group counselor as well. Both short-term follow-up (after 1 month) and long-term follow-up (after 3 months to a year) can be invaluable measures of accountability.

If members know that they will be coming together to evaluate their progress toward their goals, they will be more willing to work actively at making changes. Participants can develop contracts during the final sessions involving actions to be taken between the termination and the follow-up session (or sessions). These sessions are valuable not only because they offer the leader an opportunity to evaluate the effectiveness of the group but also because they provide members with the opportunity to gain a more realistic assessment of the group's impact. Members have a chance to express and work through their reactions to the group experience, and they can report on the degree to which they have fulfilled their contracts since they left the group. Group members also have a chance to receive additional feedback and reinforcement from the other members. (For more discussion on termination issues, see M. Corey & Corey, 2002.)

Chapter Summary

Along with the growing popularity of group approaches to counseling and therapy comes a need for ethical and professional guidelines for those who lead groups. There are many types of groups, and there are many possible uses of groups in various settings. In this chapter we have discussed some issues that are related to most groups: How does a leader's theoretical view of groups influence the way a group is structured? What are some key elements in recruiting, screening, selecting, and preparing group members? What ethical, professional, legal, and practical issues concerning confidentiality are involved in any type of group? To what degree should participants be prepared for a group before the group begins? What are some ethical issues in the selection and training of group leaders? In what ways can group techniques be used or abused? What responsibility do group leaders have in terms of follow-up and evaluation? With respect to these and other issues, we have stressed the importance of formulating your own views on ethical practice in leading groups.

Suggested Activities

1. Replicate the initial session of a group. Two students can volunteer to be co-leaders, and approximately 10 other students can become group members. Assume that the group is a personal-growth group that will meet for a predetermined number of weeks. The co-leaders' job is to orient and prepare the members by describing the group's purpose, giving an overview of group process concepts, and talking about ground rules for effective group participation. If time allows, members can express any fears and expectations they have about being involved in the group, and they can also raise questions they would like to explore. This exercise is designed to give you practice in dealing with concerns that both group leaders and members often have at the beginning of a group.
2. Practice conducting screening interviews for potential group members. One person volunteers to conduct interviews, and another student can role-play a potential group member. Allow about 10 minutes for the interview. Afterward, the prospective client can talk about what it was like to be interviewed, and the group leader can share his or her experience. This exercise can be done with the entire class watching, in small groups, or in dyads.
3. As part of your job, suppose you are expected to lead a group composed of people who are required to be part of the group and who really don't want to be there. How will the nature of the group affect your approach? What might you do differently with this group compared with a group of people who want the experience? This is a good situation to role-play in class, with several students playing the reluctant members while others practice dealing with them.
4. You are leading a counseling group with high school students on their campus. One day a member comes to the group obviously under the influence of drugs. He is incoherent and disruptive. How do you deal with him? What might you say or do? Discuss in class how you would deal with this situation, or demonstrate how you might respond by having a fellow student role-play the part of the adolescent.
5. Again, assume that you are leading a high school counseling group. An angry father who gave written permission for his son's participation comes to your office and demands to know what is going on in your group. He is con-

vinced that his son's participation in the group is an invasion of family privacy. As a group leader, how would you deal with his anger? To make the situation more real and interesting, have someone role-play the father.

6. Selecting a good co-leader for a group is important, for not all matches of co-leaders are productive. Form dyads and negotiate with your partner to determine whether the two of you would be effective if you were to lead a group together. You might discuss matters such as potential power struggles, competitiveness, compatibility of views and philosophy, your differing styles and how they might complement or interfere with each other, and other issues that you think would have a bearing on your ability to work as a team.

7. Form a panel in class to explore the uses and abuses of group techniques. The panel can look at specific ways in which group techniques can be used to enhance learning, as well as ways in which they can be misused.

InfoTrac® College Edition Resources

For additional readings, explore InfoTrac College Edition, our online library. Go to *http://www.infotrac.college.com/wadsworth* and select these key word searches:

training of group W1 leader*
supervision AND group W1 leader*
co-leadership in group work
confidentiality AND groups
values in group counseling

Key words are listed in a form that enables the search engine to locate a wider range of articles in the online university library. Key words should be entered exactly as shown, including asterisks, "W1," "W2," "AND," and other search engine tools.

13

Pre-Chapter Self-Inventory

Directions: For each statement, indicate the response that most closely identifies your beliefs and attitudes. Use the following code:

5 = I *strongly agree* with this statement.
4 = I *agree* with this statement.
3 = I am *undecided* about this statement.
2 = I *disagree* with this statement.
1 = I *strongly disagree* with this statement.

_____1. It is important to include people from the client's environment in his or her treatment.

_____2. Counselors need to take an active role in seeking solutions to the social and political conditions related to human suffering.

_____3. Mental health experts would do well to devote more of their energies to preventing emotional and behavioral disorders rather than just treating them.

_____4. With increasing attention being paid to the community mental health approach, the role of the professional needs to expand to include a variety of indirect services to clients as well as direct clinical services.

_____5. The use of nonlicensed workers is a valuable and effective way to deal with the shortage of professional help.

_____6. Nonlicensed workers who receive adequate training and close supervision are capable of providing many of the direct services that professionals now provide.

_____7. In working with a variety of client groups in the community, it is essential for community workers to be skilled in out-of-office strategies and roles such as change agent, outreach, consulting, and advocacy.

_____8. Human-service workers can be more helpful if they understand the community in which they operate, including its needs, assets, and issues.

Ethical Issues in Community Work

_____9. It is possible to work within the framework of a system and still do the things I am convinced are most important.

____10. When I think of my experience in working in an agency or an institution, I feel a sense of hope about initiating significant change in that organization.

____11. I frequently have good ideas and proposals, and I see myself as being willing to do the work necessary to translate these plans into actual programs.

____12. Ethical practice requires that we look for ways to involve and mobilize resources in the community for identifying problems and finding solutions.

____13. Although I might be unable to bring about major changes in an institution or system, I do feel confident that I can make changes within the boundaries of my own position.

____14. I can see that I might fall into complacency and rarely question what I am doing or how I could do my work more effectively.

____15. It would be unethical to accept a position with an agency whose central aims I disagreed with philosophically.

____16. Human-service workers should be able to identify indigenous leaders in the community and work with them to improve conditions in the community.

____17. A central role in human services is the development of leadership among community members.

____18. As a professional working in the community, one of my main goals is to assist people in the community to develop their power and become increasingly self-reliant.

____19. As a counselor I am part of a system, and I have a responsibility to work toward changing those aspects of the system that I think need changing.

____20. I feel a personal need for meaningful contact with colleagues so that I do not become excessively narrow in my thinking.

Introduction

Working with people who come for "individual" counseling is only one way in which professionals can use their skills to promote mental and emotional health. Professional helpers can foster real and lasting changes if they have an impact on the total milieu of people's lives in a "systems" approach. The aspirations and difficulties of clients intertwine with those of many other people and, ultimately, with those of the community at large. In this chapter we focus on the community itself as the client.

Modern psychotherapeutic approaches were largely developed from psychoanalytic therapy. For the first half of the last century the psychoanalytic model dominated the therapeutic scene. However, other therapeutic systems developed—humanistic, behavioral, and cognitive-behavioral approaches—many as a reaction to the perceived limitations of the psychoanalytic approach. By the 1950s systemic family therapy began to take root, but it was still considered a revolutionary approach to treatment. Family systems theory posits that the identified client's problem might be a symptom of how the system functions, not just a symptom of the individual's internal dynamics. The assumption of the systems model is that families can best be helped by treating the whole family system. About the same time, the community mental health movement came into existence, which takes the family systems perspective a step further and holds that the entire community is the best focus of treatment. By looking at the whole community it is possible to discover the strengths within the community and to develop ways to bring these strengths to work for the community. Feminist therapy, an offshoot of the women's movement of the 1960s, also addresses the need to consider the social and cultural context that contributes to a person's problems in order to understand that person. It is our contention that individual, family, community, and feminist perspectives all have a place as each one addresses a specific and complementary need that is not addressed by the others. These systems need not compete with one another; the field is enriched by all approaches.

In this chapter, we discuss the idea that counseling and psychology have special responsibilities in the community. The foundation of all ethical practice is promoting the welfare of clients. More often than not, ethical practice requires that we look at the community as a whole to identify problems and find solutions. If practitioners who work in the community ignore community needs because such needs seem overwhelming, this poses ethical concerns. Certainly, community agency practitioners who do not accept the critical challenges facing the community are not demonstrating a spirit of aspirational ethics. Practitioners can make ripples within segments of the community even in small ways if they are committed to becoming change agents. It is essential that community workers focus on the capabilities and strengths within a community, for doing so empowers people in the community.

We use the term *community agency* broadly to include any institution—public or private, nonprofit or for-profit—designed to provide a wide range of social and psychological services to the community. Likewise, when we speak of a *community counselor,* we refer to a diverse pool of human-service workers whose primary duties include serving individuals within the community in a variety of community groups. Community workers include, but are not limited to, social workers, psychologists, psychiatrists, nurses, counselors, couples and family therapists, and human-service workers with varying degrees of education and training.

Whether or not you work in a community agency setting, you can benefit by knowing how to work with community resources. Examine your own commitment to community counseling by thinking about these questions:

- What sense do you have of the social and psychological needs in your community and whether or not they are met?
- What are the special needs of low-income people?
- What are some pressing economic needs in addition to mental health concerns?
- If clients ask what resources are available to assist them, would you know where to refer them?
- What forces within your community exacerbate the problems individuals and groups are experiencing?
- What are the main assets available to assist people in your community?
- What factors contribute to the strength and development of your community?
- What are the prevailing attitudes of people in your community about the range of mental health services available to them?
- What role do you play or want to play in improving your community?
- Do you believe you have a broader responsibility to address the conditions that create problems for individuals who come to see you?

We begin this chapter by looking at the community mental health movement. Whereas the traditional approach to understanding and treating human problems focuses on resolution of internal conflicts as a pathway to individual change, the community approach focuses on ways of changing the environmental factors causing individual problems. A community orientation requires practitioners to design interventions that go beyond the office. Counselors trained in individual therapy who work in the community need to develop a more expansive notion of who the client is. This perspective is based on the premise that the community itself is the most appropriate focus of attention, rather than the individual. The "community as client" is a notion that Homan (1999a) emphasizes:

> Just like an individual or a family, a community has resources and limitations. Communities have established coping mechanisms to deal with problems. To promote change in a community, the community must believe in its own ability to change and must take responsibility for its actions or inactions. (p. 20)

We also examine an issue of particular importance to the community worker, namely, how the system affects the counselor and how to survive while working in a system. In examining the counselor's relationship to both the community and the system, we address the ethical dimensions of practice. If counselors do not acquire alternative roles, are they effectively reaching those

Ethical Responsibilities to the Community and to Society

National Organization for Human Service Education (2000)

Human service professionals keep informed about current social issues as they affect the client and the community. They share that information with clients, groups and community as part of their work. (Statement 11)

Human service professionals act as advocates in addressing unmet client and community needs. Human service professionals provide a mechanism for identifying unmet client needs, calling attention to these needs, and assisting in planning and mobilizing to advocate for those needs at the local community level. (Statement 13)

Human service professionals advocate for the rights of all members of society, particularly those who are members of minorities and groups at which discriminatory practices have historically been directed. (Statement 16)

National Association of Social Workers (1999)

Social workers should engage in social and political action that seeks to ensure that all persons have equal access to the resources, employment, services, and opportunities that they require in order to meet their basic human needs and to develop fully. Social workers should be aware of the impact of the political arena on practice, and should advocate for changes in policy and legislation to improve social conditions in order to meet basic human needs and promote social justice. (6.04.a.)

Social workers should act to expand choice and opportunity for all persons, with special regard for vulnerable, disadvantaged, oppressed, and exploited persons and groups. (6.04.b.)

who most need assistance? What are some strategies for becoming more responsive to the needs of the community? Is taking a proactive stand on social issues that affect communities functioning at an aspirational level? The ethics codes of professional practice reinforce the practitioner's responsibility to the community and to society (see the box titled Ethical Responsibilities to the Community and to Society).

The Community Mental Health Orientation

Central to the community mental health movement is the notion of community control of psychological services and an emphasis on prevention, early detection, and making services available to underserved populations (Trull & Phares, 2001). The need for diverse and readily accessible treatment programs has been a key factor in the development of the community mental health orientation, which is based on the premise that problem solving does not take place in a vacuum, isolated from the larger social and political influences of society. Environmental factors cause or contribute to the problems of many groups in society, and a process that considers both the individual and the environment is often most beneficial to clients.

Some writers advocate strategies that include sociopolitical factors. Changing client populations, society's pressing problems, and the impact of advanced technology challenge mental health counselors to develop problem-solving techniques that draw from various disciplines (Brooks & Gerstein, 1990; Cohen & Cohen, 2000; Ezell, 2001; Gerstein & Brooks, 1990; Herr, 1991; Ivey & Rigazio-DiGilio, 1991; MacCluskie & Ingersoll, 2001). For example, community psychology is an approach to mental health that emphasizes the role of social and environmental forces in both the creation and solution of problems. The focus of community psychology is on preventing rather than curing problems (Trull & Phares, 2001). J. A. Lewis, Lewis, Daniels, and D'Andrea (1998) define community counseling as "a comprehensive helping framework of intervention strategies and services that promotes the personal development of all individuals and communities" (p. 5). They describe the activities that make up a comprehensive community counseling model as having the following four components: (1) direct client services, (2) indirect client services, (3) direct community services, and (4) indirect community services. Let's examine each of these component separately.

1. *Direct client services* focus on outreach activities to a population that might be at risk for developing mental health problems. Community counselors provide help to clients either facing crises or dealing with ongoing stressors that impair their coping ability. By reaching out to those schools and communities that would be receptive to help, community workers can offer a variety of personal, career, family, and counseling services to at-risk groups (Lewis and colleagues, 1998). This population would also include referrals from the courts, from probation departments, and mandated therapy for drug and alcohol abuse.

2. *Indirect client services* consist of client advocacy, which involves active intervention for and with an individual or a group. The community agency works to empower disenfranchised groups that have become isolated from the mainstream community. These include, but are not limited to, the unemployed, the homeless, people with disabilities, and persons living with AIDS. Counselors need to become advocates, speaking up on their clients' behalf and actively intervening in their client's situation (Lewis and colleagues, 1998). Advocacy consists of those focused efforts to change existing policy or to influence proposed policy on behalf of specific underrepresented groups (Ezell, 2001). The advocacy process is best conceived of as a way to assist groups who typically do not have power to move in the direction of acquiring tools to find and use resources, both within the community and within themselves.

3. *Direct community services* in the form of preventive education are geared to the population at large. Examples of these programs include life planning workshops, value clarification seminars, interpersonal skills training, and teaching parents about their legal rights and responsibilities. Because the emphasis is on prevention, these programs help people develop a wider range of competencies. The focus of preventive programs is on teaching effective living and problem-solving competencies.

4. *Indirect community services* are attempts to change the social environment to meet the needs of the population as a whole and are carried out by influencing public policy. Community counseling deals with the victims of poverty,

sexism, and racism, which typically leave people feeling powerless. The focus is on promoting systemic change by working closely with those is the community who develop public policy. The overall goal is the reduction of health problems, both mental and physical.

Community counseling calls for practitioners who (a) are familiar with resources within the community that they can refer clients to, when necessary; (b) have a basic knowledge of the cultural background of their clients; (c) possess skills that can be used as needed by clients; (d) have the ability to balance various roles as professionals; and (e) have the willingness to be advocates for policy changes in the community.

Roles of Counselors Working in the Community

Ideally, all mental health professionals have an interest in promoting change not only in their individual clients but also within the community at large. In reality, however, all of us have different areas of interest and expertise. Some professionals are most effective as private clinicians, and others are more effective as community workers and advocates. No matter what setting we choose for our work, we must be aware of the broader context of human problems. The challenge is to think beyond the needs of the individual to the needs of the community at large, in much the same way as practitioners would include the family when addressing the needs of the child. In other words, it is essential to view the client in context.

As we indicated in Chapter 4, to meet the needs of many ethnic and culturally diverse clients, traditional counselors need to develop a different vision and master different skills. Counselors may need to do more outreach work with their clients, working in a public-housing tract, at a hospital bedside, at the workplace, or in other places where clients conduct their lives. The outreach approach may include both developmental and educational efforts, such as skills training, stress management, and consultation. In addition to helping clients solve their individual problems, community counselors also attempt to change the dysfunctional system that is producing problems for individuals, families, and communities. The focus is on looking at the problem in context rather than dealing only with the problem within the individual.

Alternative Counselor Roles

Rather than operating in a singular role, as is the case with many traditional counselors, the emphasis of the community perspective is on alternative ways of helping clients. D. W. Sue, Ivey, and Pedersen (1996) stress the importance of flexibility when working in a community with many culturally different groups. Counselors' roles in these communities frequently involve larger social units, systems interventions, and prevention programs. Sue and his colleagues (1996) recommend that counselors who work in the community emphasize these strategies:

- Recognize that no one person or group has a monopoly on the helping process.
- Use community resources as a way to enrich therapy.
- Supplement informal methods with formal methods of helping.
- Recognize that client problems are often best defined as residing in the family, group, or community.
- Work with client problems in their cultural context and attend to the network of support systems surrounding the client.

Atkinson, Thompson, and Grant (1993) state that the role of psychotherapist is frequently inappropriately applied when working with racial or ethnic minority clients. Atkinson and his colleagues believe the conventional role of psychotherapist is appropriate "only for a client who is highly acculturated and now wants relief from an existing problem that has an internal etiology" (p. 269). Other writers have criticized conventional approaches to therapy because they place undue responsibility on the client for his or her plight. At the extreme, some interventions blame client problems entirely on the individual without regard to contributing environmental factors. Community-oriented counseling emphasizes the necessity for recognizing and dealing with environmental conditions that often create problems for ethnically diverse client groups. Atkinson, Morten, and Sue (1998) suggest these alternative roles for counselors who work in the community: advocate, change agent, consultant, adviser, facilitator of indigenous support systems, and facilitator of indigenous healing methods. In selecting a role and strategies to use with racial or ethnic minority clients, Atkinson, Morten, and Sue (1998) believe it is useful to take into account the client's level of acculturation, the locus of the problem etiology, and the goal of counseling. It is ethically incumbent on counselors who work in the community to assume some or all of these roles as needed to benefit their clients.

Advocate. Because ethnic minority clients are often oppressed to some degree by the dominant society, they can be helped by counselors who are willing to speak on their behalf. Counselors especially need to function as advocates for clients who are low in acculturation and who need remediation of a problem that results from discrimination and oppression.

Change agent. Functioning in the role of change agents, counselors confront and bring about change within the system that contributes to, if not creates, many of the problems clients face. Homan (1999a) makes a case for helpers assuming the role of change agent: "I believe that community change efforts clearly relate to professional practice. We need to see this as part of our job. This is something we should do within our professional role, not outside of it" (p. 47). In this role, counselors assist clients in recognizing oppressive forces in the community as a source of their problem. Counselors also teach clients strategies for dealing with these environmental problems. As change agents, community workers assist clients in developing power, particularly political power, to bring about change in the clients' social and physical environment. A change agent recognizes that healthy communities produce healthy people. The main purpose of community change is fostering healthy communities (Homan, 1999a). As a change agent one must sometimes educate organizations to change their culture to meet the needs of the community. As one community worker discovered, a counselor taking part in a community collaborative can often help accomplish this (Honie Abramowicz, personal communication, November 18, 2000).

Consultant. Operating as consultants, counselors can encourage ethnic minority clients to learn skills they can use to interact successfully with various forces within their community. In this role, the client and the counselor cooperate in addressing unhealthy forces within the system. As consultants, counselors can work with racial and ethnic minority clients to design preventive programs to reduce the negative impact of racism and oppression. The role of a consultant can be seen as the role of a teacher. Often the "teacher" is less of a threat and more socially acceptable to members of non-Western cultures than the "counselor," even though the same professional may be performing both functions. Getting an education enhances status worldwide, whereas "telling family secrets" to a mental health expert does not (Paul Pedersen, personal communication, November 17, 2000).

Adviser. This role is similar to that of consultant, except the counselor as adviser initiates the discussion with clients about ways to deal with environmental problems that contribute to their personal problems. For example, recent immigrants may need advice on immigration paperwork, coping with problems they will face in the job market, or problems that their children may encounter at school.

Facilitator of indigenous support systems. All cultural groups have some form of social support aimed at preventing or remediating psychological and social problems. Many ethnically diverse clients, people in rural environments, and older people would not consider seeking professional help in the traditional sense. However, they are willing to turn to social support systems within their own communities. Counselors need to be aware of cultural factors that may be instrumental in contributing to a client's problem or resources that might help alleviate or solve the client's problem. Counselors can play an important role by encouraging clients to make full use of resources within their own communities, including community centers, extended families, neighborhood social networks, and ethnic advocacy groups. Churches of all denominations can be powerful influences in low-income, minority, and ethnic communities. Community workers can work with church leaders to influence social policy and community change. Churches are often able to provide for immediate needs as well as advocate for more long-term community change. By directing clients to indigenous support systems, practitioners can do a great deal to aid clients.

Facilitator of indigenous healing systems. Mental health practitioners need to learn what kinds of healing resources exist within a client's culture. In many cultures professional counselors have little hope of reaching individuals with problems because these people are likely to put their trust in traditional healers. If counselors are aware of indigenous resources, they can refer a client to a folk or spiritual healer from his or her culture. At times it may be difficult for helpers to adopt the worldview of their clients. In such instances it could be helpful to work with an indigenous healer.

Alternative therapies have increased in popularity for a number of reasons. Alternative therapies are generally less expensive, and insurance companies are increasingly recognizing them for third-party payments. Furthermore, the client is more directly involved as a participant in healing, it is less invasive, more gentle and natural, relies on self-healing capabilities, and values the subjective dimension of the therapeutic process (Paul Pedersen, personal communication, November 17, 2000). Clients may not have to choose between conventional therapy and indigenous healing. Practitioners can structure their activities to complement or augment, rather than replace, traditional healing resources.

Some Tasks of Community Counseling

Too often counselors ignore the fact that before people can move toward growth and actualization their basic needs must be met. Psychotherapy can no longer afford to be tailor-made for the upper middle class. People who are unable to afford the services of professionals in private practice are entitled to adequate treatment. The community counseling approach serves people of all ages and backgrounds and with all types and degrees of problems. To be able to effectively serve this variety of client populations, practitioners need to develop culturally diverse competencies (Hogan-Garcia, 1999). In community counseling, practitioners may find themselves performing some or all of these duties:

- Supporting the needs of minority groups in the community
- Assisting client groups to become true partners with professionals in the development and delivery of services
- Promoting community organization and development activities as fundamental agency responsibilities and seeing that this is reflected in agency budgets
- Actively reaching out to people with special needs and initiating programs aimed at preventing problems rather than merely treating them
- Drawing on and improving the skills of community workers and laypeople to help meet the many different needs of clients
- Developing strategies to deal effectively with drug and alcohol abuse, child sexual and physical abuse, and domestic violence
- Developing strategies that will empower the disenfranchised in the community

- Consulting with a variety of social agencies about programs in gerontology, welfare, child care, and rehabilitation, and helping community workers apply psychological knowledge in their work
- Evaluating human-service programs to assess agency intervention efforts
- Advocating and assisting with public and private initiatives that promote the total well-being of clients
- Working with members of a particular community to develop and build on community assets to promote communities and instill self-reliance

Homan (1999a, p. 51) describes some other options for counselors who hope to empower client groups. He admits that counselors may not be able to exert a major role in changing the conditions of the client, but they can take these specific actions that will help the client:

- Assist clients in understanding the forces in the environment that are causing or contributing to their distress and help clients develop skills to confront these forces.
- Identify those in a community who can assume a major role in fostering change, which could include bringing similarly affected clients together or referring clients to other programs or other professionals.
- Bring the existence of harmful conditions to the attention of those who are in a position to act on that awareness.

Educating the Community

There are many reasons people do not make use of available mental health resources. They may not be aware of their existence; they may not be able to afford these services; they may have misconceptions about the nature and purpose of counseling; they may be reluctant to recognize their problems; they may harbor the attitude that they should be able to take charge of their lives on their own; or they may perceive that these resources are not intended for them because the services are administered in a culturally insensitive way. One of the major barriers to clients not making use of social and psychological services is that access to these services is confusing and sometimes humiliating.

One goal of the community approach is to educate the public and attempt to change the attitudes of the community about mental health and the attitudes of those who deliver mental health services. Many people still cling to a very narrow definition of mental illness. They make a clear demarcation between people whom they perceive as "abnormal" and those whom they perceive as "normal." Widespread misconceptions include the notion that once people suffer from any kind of emotional disturbance they can never be cured, the idea that people with emotional and behavioral disorders are merely deficient in "willpower," and the belief that the mentally ill are always dangerous and should be separated from the community lest they "contaminate" or harm others. Professionals face real challenges in combating these misconceptions. Unless practitioners actively work to present counseling services in a way that is understandable to and respectful of the community at large, many people who could benefit from professional help will not seek it.

Influencing Policymakers

Mental health programs can help communities work toward solutions for societal problems such as poverty, the plight of the homeless, AIDS, absent parents, child abuse, drive-by shootings, gang activities, crime, domestic violence, unemployment, tension and stress, alienation, addictions to drugs and alcohol, delinquency, and neglect of the elderly. The challenges facing community workers are often overwhelming, especially with current constraints on funding and the bureaucratic malaise. How can even those most dedicated community workers continue to develop social programs if they are constantly faced with the likelihood that their programs will be cut back or canceled? There is little room for staff members to come up with innovative social programs when the agencies themselves are concerned with mere survival. Yet one way community workers can initiate change is by organizing within an agency or even several agencies and developing a collective voice. Practitioners who assume the role of change agents might assist a community by organizing political action to influence the state and national government to fulfill its responsibilities to smaller communities. This action may involve providing funds, technical assistance, legal protection, or other support a smaller community requires to flourish (Homan, 1999a).

A real challenge to society is to spend at least as much of the government budget on prevention as is spent on punishment. In a recent election in California, voters approved a proposition that requires probation and treatment, not incarceration, for possession or use of controlled substances. This legislation was passed in an environment where there is strong support for the three-strikes program, which requires incarceration for a third felony offense. Much of the credit for bringing this issue to the voters' attention must go to the efforts of those in the helping professions who were willing to work to influence policymaking as a way to bring about change in addressing a social problem.

◆ **The case of a nonprofit agency designed to educate the community.** The Coalition for Children, Adolescents and Parents (CCAP) is a community agency aimed at the prevention of adolescent pregnancy. This of a small grassroots agency in Orange County, California, applies outreach strategies to educate the community as a way to meet a critical need in the community (Hogan-Garcia & Scheinberg, 2000). For the past 20 years, CCAP has served as a model of how to involve the community in a project to enhance the community. From its inception, a high priority has been given to hiring a multiethnic staff that could serve and mirror the community. The staff is committed to understanding each other, rather than allowing their differences to separate them, and staff members meet frequently for cultural sharing as a way to better understand each other and themselves. Those who work at the agency have opportunities to critically examine their ethnocentric assumptions about the world and the community. All the members of the agency staff are committed to clarifying and understanding personal values, beliefs, and behaviors. Because the individuals on the staff believe in the value of understanding cultural diversity, they are able to serve as a bridge between the mainstream and minority communities.

One of the early projects designed by CCAP involved outreach and education in the Latino community to prevent the spread of HIV. A Latina staff member conducted interviews with 30 mothers in the community regarding their understanding of HIV, human sexuality, and teen pregnancy. From this contact with these mothers, a group of leaders (comadres) was formed to educate the community. The women who served as leaders met for monthly meetings, which were held at a neighborhood center. Eventually, the women invited their husbands into the classes. This project was funded by an external source, and the agency was required to report to the funders about the outcomes of the project. Hogan-Garcia and Scheinberg (2000) summarize these outcomes thusly:

> By the end of the contract year, the agency had exceeded the expectations of funders with the project and the Comadres Project had spread the word about HIV prevention to friends, neighbors, and family members. The empowerment of disenfranchised women and men continued beyond the contract term. CCAP staff continued to meet with and follow this special group of friends. Three women went back to school, a group of the women formed a Spanish-speaking PTA group, and one went on to become a school board member. (p. 28)

In 2000 the agency served more than 12,000 clients, providing after-school recreational services, tutoring, academic enrichment programs, physical examinations, parenting education, conflict resolution, cultural diversity training, school-based group counseling, a homeless shelter, drug abuse prevention, and child care training. This agency is an example of an effective collaboration that is committed to ensuring that the members of the community have a full voice in determining the nature of community services.

The projects that are a part of CCAP are based on a set of culturally competent practice principles, which have been described by Hogan-Garcia and Scheinberg (2000):

- Be willing to examine your assumptions and personal values.
- In an agency, bring together an ethnically diverse staff and board.
- Develop and maintain positive relationships with key people in the community.
- Ask community members about their perceptions of what is needed in the community.
- Bring community members and agency staff together in genuine dialogue.
- Design a program based on the community's definition of their needs.
- In implementing a program, be sensitive to the pace of the community.
- Advocate for the needs of the community and serve as a bridge between cultural groups.

- Translate the progress of the community in terms that the funders of the project will understand.

Consider whether you have the skills necessary to operate in this kind of community counseling environment.

- Are you open to learning first-hand about other cultures?
- Do you think ethnic diversity of staff members is necessary for a community agency to be successful?
- Would you value this kind of ongoing self-evaluation?

◆ **The case of Maribel.** Maribel is the director of a community clinic in an inner-city neighborhood. Her agency provides birth control counseling and funding for abortion for low-income women. As the time approaches for her to submit her request for financing to the state government, she is contacted by a local politician who is adamantly opposed to abortion. He informs her that if she requests funding for abortion he will do everything in his power not only to deny the money but also to reduce the overall funding for the agency. Faced with the prospect of radically reduced funds, Maribel omits her request for money for abortion services.

- In light of the threats that were made, did Maribel act in the best interest of her community? Can you see any justification for her action? Do you think that her decision was the best possible one in this situation?
- What if Maribel seemed to go along with the politician's request, but later on, when the funding for the other programs was acquired, she diverted some of the money for abortion services? Would this be ethical? Would Maribel be breaking the law?
- How ethically bound was Maribel to disclose the coercive attempts of the influential politician, even though it was only her word against his?
- What would you have done in her place?

◆ **The case of Natalie.** Natalie is an intern with a community agency that provides counseling services to local elementary schools. She facilitates a group for children with behavioral problems. On one occasion the principal overheard one of the students expressing strong anger. The principal assumed control of the group, got into a verbal exchange with the child, and suspended him from school. When Natalie appealed to her clinical director, he angrily told her: "Back off, and don't you dare challenge the principal." He let her know in no uncertain terms that if she were to take action against the principal the contract of providing counseling services to the school would be jeopardized, with the subsequent loss of funding to the clinic.

- What are the possible ethical considerations in this case?
- If you were Natalie, what would you do?
- If you were her supervisor, what would you say to her? What would you feel obligated to do, if anything?

How You Can Become Involved in the Community

Consider your responsibility to teach clients to use the resources available to them in their communities. Here is a list of things you might do to link clients to the environment in which they live. Rate each of these activities, using the following code:

A = I would do this *routinely.*
B = I would do this *occasionally.*
C = I would do this *rarely.*

___ 1. I would familiarize myself with available community resources so that I could refer my clients to appropriate sources of further help. I would follow up to see whether clients had been helped.
___ 2. With my clients' permission, I would contact people who had a direct influence on their lives.
___ 3. I would try to arrange sessions with clients and significant others so that they could explore ways of strengthening relationships.
___ 4. As part of the counseling process, I would teach my clients how to take advantage of support systems already available in the community.
___ 5. I would work actively with groups that were trying to help themselves.
___ 6. I would work actively with groups that were trying to bring about change in the community.
___ 7. I would encourage efforts to make the community's helping network more responsive.
___ 8. I would use community leaders in setting up liaisons with other professional practitioners and agencies.
___ 9. I would train key people of various cultural groups in peer-counseling skills so that they could work with groups that might not seek professional services from an agency.
___ 10. I would help organize support for politicians who were actively involved in helping the community.
___ 11. I would work with agencies to determine which services need to be offered and how they might best be offered.

If you plan on going into one of the mental health professions, you are likely to spend some time working in a community agency setting, and you will be working with many different facets within the community. If you were to work in such a setting at this time, consider the following questions:

- What can you learn that would help you to become an effective agent for change in the community?
- What skills do you already have that can be applied to community change?
- What specific skills will you need to acquire?
- What fears would you have of working in the community?
- How might you translate your idealism into a practical set of strategies aimed at bringing about constructive change within the community?

The Value of Nonlicensed Workers

The question of how best to deliver services to the people who are most in need of them is a controversial one. It is clear that there are not enough professionally licensed practitioners willing to meet the demand for psychological assistance to the underprivileged. Moreover, mental health services have not always been made available to those unable to pay. Faced with these realities, many in the mental health field have concluded that nonlicensed people could be given the training and supervision they need to provide some psychological services.

Until recently, all such nonlicensed workers were called paraprofessionals. However, Woodside and McClam (1998) state that the concept of the paraprofessional is now outdated because an advanced degree is no longer necessary for professional status. The formerly labeled paraprofessionals have demonstrated a positive influence in the human-service field and have been able to effectively carry out roles and assume responsibilities that were not anticipated. Clients often did not distinguish between paraprofessionals and professionals, but treated both with respect (Woodside & McClam, 1998).

Until a better designation is developed, we refer to two categories of community workers—licensed professionals and nonlicensed professionals. Licensed mental health professionals have a graduate degree and may assume roles of practitioners, supervisors, and consultants. Examples of these licensed professionals include clinical social workers, counselors, psychologists, and marriage and family therapists. Nonlicensed professionals may have a graduate degree, an undergraduate degree, an associate of arts degree, a certificate of competence in some aspect of human services, or some formal training from experts in the field. These nonlicensed workers have a variety of job titles, a few of which include community support worker, human-services worker, social work assistant, alcohol or drug abuse counselor, mental health technician, child care worker, community outreach worker, and case manager (Woodside & McClam, 1998). Another example of nonlicensed workers are volunteers from the community who receive training and supervision in therapeutic intervention with a wide range of clients. These volunteers work on hot lines, co-lead groups, and engage in other supportive activities.

Former patients can also be employed to meet the increasing demand for mental health services. Former addicts can assume a mentoring role in substance abuse programs to help others who are addicted to drugs. Besides helping to alleviate the shortage of personnel, these nonlicensed practitioners may actually be more effective in reaching certain clients because they have experienced similar problems and learned to deal with them successfully.

Service agencies have discovered that nonlicensed professionals can indeed provide some services as effectively as licensed professionals, for much less cost. Tan (1997) asserts that these helpers are able to provide support by fostering a sense of community and decreasing the isolation that many clients experience: "Paraprofessional helpers can make unique and significant contributions in treatment planning and implementation, and paraprofessionals and psychologists can work collaboratively to benefit their communities" (p. 371). Trull and Phares (2001) also believe that there is a vital role for nonlicensed professionals in the mental health field today and that they are very effective in some settings.

Not all mental health professionals are enthusiastic about the increased reliance on nonlicensed professionals. Some point to the danger that inadequately trained helpers might do more harm than good. Others contend that the poor will receive inferior service. Still others fear that more and more nonlicensed professionals will be allowed to practice without supervision and necessary training. Some fear that their own jobs or income may be jeopardized if nonlicensed professionals are allowed to provide services similar to those rendered by licensed professionals.

A large part of the success of community mental health programs will depend on these nontraditional workers' receiving the training and supervision they need to develop skills for effective intervention. In some instances, these nonlicensed workers may aid licensed practitioners, who are often trained in psychotherapeutic techniques but do not have sufficient experience or training in working with various racial, ethnic, and socioeconomic groups.

A nontraditional training program. The Community Based Block (CBB) at San Diego State University offers a 1-year master's degree in counseling to train nonlicensed counselors with an interest in working in underserved communities. Although this program does not make students eligible for licensure, it does equip students to address specific diversity needs within the community. This 1-year program contains a clinical practicum, fieldwork, and theory/practice courses. Although personal therapy is not required of the students, it is strongly recommended, and it is a factor used to evaluate students' readiness for seeing clients in the fieldwork program. The top priority of the program is diversity, and faculty members seek diverse students who have an interest in working in the community with diverse client populations.

During the admission process, considerable emphasis is given to the group interviews, and students are typically asked how their growing up has influenced them with respect to their views on race, gender, and sexual orientation. Both students in the program and faculty are included in the selection interviews. Once candidates have been selected, the year begins with a weekend residential retreat in the mountains. The retreat is the basis for formulating the goals for the coming year, and all students have an opportunity to get to know one another. Although we would ordinarily not be supportive of a 1-year master's program, this training program illustrates how community workers without a doctorate or a license can make a significant contribution in addressing critical needs within the community.

Expanding professional roles. The trend toward the increased use of nonlicensed workers means that licensed mental health professionals will have to assume new and expanding roles. Mental health professionals can expect to spend less time providing direct services to clients and more time teaching, supervising, and consulting with community workers. Leading in-service workshops for nonlicensed and volunteer workers, educating the public about the nature of mental health, consulting, working as agents for change in the community, designing new programs, conducting research, and evaluating existing programs may all become part of the job for licensed professionals.

Acting in the role of consultant enables mental health professionals to offer a wide array of assistance on individual, group, institutional, and community levels. Much of the work of consulting in agencies deals with training nonlicensed workers and even lay volunteers. For example, Marianne Corey provided training for lay helpers in a church group who did grief counseling. This consulting took the form of teaching volunteers basic listening and attending skills, ways to assess their limitations, and how and when to make appropriate referrals.

Working Within a System

One of the major challenges for counselors who work in the community is to learn how to make the system work for the clients they serve and, secondarily, work for themselves so that in the process they do not lose their ability to work effectively with clients. One of the reasons that working in a system can put an added strain on the counselor is that those providing financing may require monumental amounts of paperwork to justify continued funding. Another source of strain is the counselor's relationships with those who administer the agency or institution, who may have long forgotten the practicalities involved in providing direct services to clients. Conversely, practitioners who deal with clients directly may have little appreciation for the intricacies with which administrators must contend in managing their programs. If communication is inadequate, as it often is, tension is inevitable.

Case Management in a Community Setting

The emergence of case management as a dominant force in human-services delivery presents new ethical challenges. More often referred to today as "case coordination" or "program coordination," these programs often target "consumers" rather than "clients." Case management is guided by the principles of fairness, accountability, collaboration, advocacy for individuals' needs, effective and efficient delivery of services, treatment of the whole person, and individual empowerment. True to this holistic stance, the overall goal of program coordination/case management is to promote, restore, or maintain the independent functioning of consumers (clients) in the least-restrictive, community environment.

Because of the collaborative and holistic nature of case management both within and between human-service agencies, the interdisciplinary approach plays a pivotal role in the provision of assessment, planning, resource information, monitoring, and evaluation of client services. Depending on the range and complexity of human services offered, interdisciplinary teams include professionals from many disciplines, each representing a service the consumer may need. However, the effectiveness of the interdisciplinary team approach is very much dependent on the professionalism, respect, and cooperation between team members. For instance, a team that is dominated by one discipline or one team member can be detrimental to human-services delivery. When team members lack professional skills and resource knowledge to make appropriate interventions, recommendations, and referrals, clients may be harmed. Sometimes case managers are seen as lowest on the totem pole in the interdisciplinary team process, and their professional opinions are least valued. Case managers with large caseloads may, in turn, perceive the interdisciplinary team as a time-consuming intrusion rather than an essential resource in providing holistic service delivery, especially to clients with complex problems. Time and efficiency considerations can also play a role in the careless exclusion of clients and their families from the interdisciplinary process deliberations, which is a failure to honor the principle of empowering the client. Similarly, in the interest of time and job security, the case manager may ignore client advocacy responsibilities.

Cooperation and collaboration between human-service agencies can be particularly challenging. Typically, each community agency has specific eligibility criteria (often state or federally mandated), a specific range of services, and a limited budget. Depending on the financial health of the agency budget, the eligibility criteria are interpreted in a less or more strict manner, forcing consideration of the principle of fairness as it is applied to agency applicants. The principle of fairness must also be considered with regard to cooperation between agencies in the provision of client services. For example, with limited budgets, there are concerted efforts to shift responsibility to the "other" agency —a "turf war" of sorts—even when that agency is less professionally equipped to provide the service in question.

Nowhere today is the application of the case management system of human-services delivery more pronounced than in Health Maintenance Organizations (HMOs). Although it is generally accepted that case management has provided accountability and a level of fairness to the health care, some criticisms are raised. One criticism is that necessary health services are often denied by a case manager within the HMO organization. Furthermore, the HMO case manager is acting as a gatekeeper, rationing medicine to paying clients in order to promote and protect large corporate profits.

Consider these questions as they pertain to the ethical issues associated with case management as a way to deliver human services in a community agency:

- In delivering services, is staying within budget just as important as service to clients?
- Is it right to break rules (federal, state, agency) for the welfare of the individual client?
- Should I always consult with agency management when I see the necessity of breaking rules?

- Is it fair that I may jeopardize my job or promotion if I advocate for client needs?
- Should client files be accessible to all agency professional staff on the agency computer network in the interests of efficiency?
- Should client autonomy be honored more than professional codes or agency policies and procedures?
- Should I resign from my position as an agency worker if my work assignments are beyond my professional capabilities?
- Should I be a "whistle blower" when agency management or staff engage in unethical or illegal behavior?

The Challenge of Maintaining Integrity in an Agency Environment

Many professionals struggle with the issue of how to work within a system while retaining their integrity and vitality. When all attempts to bring about change in the system fail, the worker might consider a change of attitude. When people focus on what cannot be changed, they promote powerlessness and helplessness. Focusing on the things that can be changed fosters a sense of personal power that may allow for progress. Although working in an organization is oftentimes frustrating, counselors also need to know that their attitude can be a problem. Blame, whether of clients or institutions, is not an effective agent of change.

Practitioners need to evaluate the options they have in responding to unacceptable circumstances. Homan (1999a) raises some thought-provoking questions in this regard:

- If you respond to the presence of disturbing social conditions within your midst by attempting to mainly soften the pain they cause, does this imply tolerance for these problems in the system?
- If you genuinely believe that your efforts make a difference, should you accept limitations on your efforts?
- To what degree is it your ethical responsibility to work toward shaping the system that shapes your practice?

Homan suggests that simply tolerating problems within a system is rarely gratifying and that workers gain professional satisfaction by actively taking steps to promote positive changes:

> I believe that you do have options for challenging the circumstances that lead to the problems you confront. And I believe that you have options for creating conditions that permit you to do effective work. In my experience, workers who have acted thoughtfully and purposefully to confront and resolve systemic problems have produced many positive results. (p. 57)

Recognizing the need for action is the first step toward responding to unacceptable circumstances. Once a problem has been identified, Homan (1999a) suggests that you have four basic responses to choose from:

- You can change your perception by identifying the situation as acceptable.

- You can leave the situation, either by emotionally withdrawing or by physically leaving.
- You can recognize the situation as unacceptable and then decide to adjust to the situation.
- You can identify the situation as unacceptable and do what you can to change it.

Each of these actions has consequences for both you and your clients. If you recognize that you do have choices in how you respond to unacceptable situations, you may be challenged to take action to change these circumstances. From an ethical perspective, you are expected to alert your employer to circumstances that may impair your ability to reach clients. ACA's (1995) standard states: "Counselors alert their employers to conditions that may be potentially disruptive or damaging to the counselor's professional responsibilities or that may limit their effectiveness" (D.1.c.).

We support Homan's ideas of how to respond to problems in a system. However, sometimes a worker's physical and mental health may be at risk in a dysfunctional system. In such a case, the only viable option might be to withdraw from the system to prevent serious health problems or burnout.

◆ **The case of Toni.** For 13 years Toni has worked with women in recovery in a community agency that is funded by a grant. To prevent burnout she and her co-workers organized a support group among the community workers in the agency. Her group consists of about 15 people, some of whom are case managers, treatment counselors, nurses, social workers, and supervisors. They meet at the agency during work hours twice a month for up to 2 hours. During these sessions the workers have opportunities to talk about difficult clients or stressful situations they are facing on the job or in their personal lives. Personal concerns sometimes have an impact on workers' abilities to function professionally, and members are able to use the support within the group as a way to deal with personal issues. Toni looks forward to the meetings because of the opportunity to interact with people who have the same type of work situation. Besides the camaraderie, these meetings help to alleviate the effects of stress on the job (Toni Wallace, personal communication, November 18, 2000).

- If you worked for this agency, would you want to join this group?
- If you chose not to be part of this group, how would you feel about working in this agency?
- Do you think members of this group might have more power within the agency than workers who are not in the group?

Commentary. The agency did not offer this service; rather, the workers took the initiative to form this group because of a felt need. Once the workers presented this group to their supervisor, she was quite willing to allow them to meet as part of continuing education. This group, which has been meeting for about 4 years, is an example of how a group of workers can organize their efforts to deal with the demands of working in a community agency.

Toni and her co-workers created a support system and a sense of camaraderie rather than giving into feeling isolated and powerless. They also became a unit of influence in the agency, giving them some sense of power. A prime ingredient in burnout is a feeling of powerlessness. In this case, without any outside influence, the staff empowered itself to make a difference.

Relationships Between Counselor and Agency

If you are working in an agency, we hope you will reflect on your attitudes and your stance toward the agency. First, there is the matter of your attitudes. Why are you working in a particular agency? Are you committed to the welfare of the community? How do you take care of yourself? How do you motivate yourself? Second, consider the agency's role in the community. Is the agency committed to the welfare of clients and the community? Or is it an agency committed to self-preservation? When the interests of the agency supercede the interests of the community, the ethical issues are much the same as when a practitioner's interests supercede the client's interests.

The ethical violations in a community agency are more complex and difficult to resolve than violations pertaining to individual counseling. If a worker is not motivated, the system may tolerate this lack of motivation. If the system violates the rights of the client (community), then this is a real challenge to address. We are aware of a community agency that relied heavily on court referrals, and time and again this agency placed clients in a program of extended therapy, without authorization from the courts, solely to generate money. Many agency workers must have known of this condition, yet the issue was not brought out by agency personnel. Eventually clients began to complain about the procedures in the agency. If an agency worker were to have reported this situation, he or she might conceivably have been fired. There is no easy solution to the problem of a system abusing clients, but clearly, the underprivileged who seek help in agencies need to be protected. Correcting such an abuse that may be systemwide demands the willingness of those involved in the system to practice aspirational ethics and take action.

To take an active role in their agency, counselors must know how to work effectively within the system. In addition to their degrees, training, and professional competencies, counselors working in the community need to learn how to best deal with the rules and regulations of their agency. Counselors typically have little say in the formulation of agency policies, yet they are limited in what they can do by the agency's rules and regulations. The system may be so cumbersome and difficult for clients to work with that the counselor must assist clients in obtaining resources through lobbying, advocacy, referrals, and networking.

As a counselor, you need to decide how you will work within the system and how you can be most effective. Investigate an agency's philosophy before you accept a position, and determine whether the agency's norms, values, and expectations coincide with what you expect from the position. If you are not able to support the philosophy and policies of that agency, you are almost certain to experience conflicts. An ACA (1995) ethical standard calls upon practitioners to work with their employers to change situations that impede professional functioning: "Counselors strive to reach agreement with employers as to acceptable standards of conduct that allow for changes in institutional policy conducive to the growth and development of clients" (D.1.l.).

Dissatisfied counselors may decide to subvert the agency in as many ways as they can. Others conform to institutional policies out of a fear of losing their position. Some find ways to make compromises between institutional demands and their personal requirements. Others find it impossible to retain their personal and professional dignity and still work within an institutional framework. It will be up to you to find your own answers to questions such as these:

- To what degree is my philosophy of helping compatible with the agency where I work?
- How can I meet the requirements of an institution and at the same time do what I most believe in?
- What stance will I take in dealing with a system?
- In what ways can I work to change a particular system?
- At what point does the price of attempting to work within an organized structure become too high?
- Can I work within an institutional framework and still retain my mental health?
- What special ethical obligations am I likely to face in working in a system?

Moving toward empowerment. We encourage you to think about the following questions to clarify your position on ways in which you could increase your chances of assuming power within the system:

- What questions would you want to raise in a job interview?
- What ideas of yours have been opposed?
- What would you do if the organization for which you worked instituted a policy to which you were strongly opposed?
- What would you do if you believed strongly that certain changes needed to be made in your institution but your colleagues disagreed?
- What would you do if your supervisor continually blocked most of your activities despite your efforts to keep him or her informed of the reasons for them?
- How would you attempt to make contact with your colleagues if members of the staff seemed to work largely in isolation from one another?
- If the staff seemed to be divided by jealousies, hostilities, or unspoken conflicts, what do you think you would do?
- What do you consider to be the ethics involved in staying with a job after you have done everything you can to bring about change, but to no avail?

Now let's look at some examples that illustrate issues discussed in this chapter. Try to imagine yourself in each of these situations, and ask yourself how you would deal with them.

◆ **The case of Ronnie.** Ronnie, an African American student, moved with his family into a mostly white community and attends high school there. Almost immediately he becomes the butt of racial jokes and experiences social isolation. A teacher notices his isolation and sends him to the school counselor. It is evident to the counselor that Ronnie is being discriminated against, not only by many of the students but also by some of the faculty. The counselor has no reason to doubt the information provided by Ronnie because she is aware of racism in the school and in the community. She determines that it would be much more practical to help Ronnie learn to ignore the prejudice than to try to change the racist attitudes of the school and the community.

- What do you think of the counselor's decision? What are its ethical ramifications? Does she have an obligation to work to change community attitudes?
- To what set of values might the counselor be responding?
- What would you do in this situation?
- Does a school system have an ethical obligation to attempt to change attitudes of a community that discriminate against some of its citizens?
- By not addressing the problem, is the counselor part of the problem?

Commentary. In this case, the counselor may be experiencing a conflict of values and may fear reprisals if she acts on values that are not shared by many in the community. She may want to do what is needed to promote the well-being of her client, yet she may be struggling with self-doubts and with anxiety about not being accepted by the faculty. If you were consulting with this counselor, what might you say to her?

◆ **The case of Adriana.** Adriana works in a community mental health clinic, and most of her time is devoted to dealing with immediate crises. The more she works with people in crisis, the more she is convinced that the focus of her work should be on preventive programs designed to educate the public. Adriana comes to believe strongly that there would be far fewer clients in distress if people were effectively contacted and motivated to participate in growth-oriented educational programs. She develops detailed, logical, and convincing proposals for programs she would like to implement in the community, but they are consistently rejected by the director of her center. Because the clinic is partially funded by the government for the express purpose of crisis intervention, the director feels uneasy about approving any program that does not relate directly to this objective.

If you were in Adriana's place, what do you think you would do? Check the following courses of action that you would be likely to take?

___ I would do what the director expected and complain that the bureaucratic structure inhibited imaginative programs.

___ I would continue to work toward a compromise and try to find some way to make room for my special project. I would work with the director until I convinced her to permit me to launch my program in some form.

___ If I could not do what I deemed important, I would look for another job.

- ___ I would involve clients in setting the direction for the proposal and providing the necessary support to secure approval.
- ___ I would examine the director's responses and try to incorporate them into my approach.
- ___ I would get several other staff members together, pool our resources, and look for ways to implement the program as a group.
- ___ With my director's approval, I would try to obtain a grant for a pilot program in the community.

◆ **The case of Dermot.** Dermot is a social worker in a school district. He is expected to devote most of his time to checking on children who are habitually truant and to do social welfare work with dependent families. Although he understood the job description before he accepted the position, he now feels that his talents could be put to better use if he were allowed to do intensive counseling with families as units. Referral sources in the area are meager, and the families he works with cannot afford private treatment. Although he has the training to do the type of family counseling he thinks is sorely needed, his school administrator makes it clear that any kind of therapy is outside the province of the school's responsibility. Dermot is told to confine himself to tracking down truant children and processing forms. If you were in Dermot's position, what do you think you would do?

- ___ Prior to taking action, I would think about what the administrator needs in order to become an ally rather than an opponent.
- ___ I would present a written plan to the local school board, showing that family counseling was needed and that public facilities were inadequate to meet this need.
- ___ I would go ahead and do family counseling without telling my administrator.
- ___ I wouldn't make waves, because I wouldn't want to lose my job.

◆ **The case of Maria.** Maria is a 14-year-old Hispanic female honor student at Traymore High School. She discovered that she is pregnant and feels she would be better off dead than being a teenage mom. She has witnessed how her friends and relatives who were teenage parents were doomed to live a life of poverty. Maria's parents had her when they were teenagers, and she knows they will never allow her to have an abortion. Maria went to see the school social worker to talk about how she was feeling. The social worker educated Maria on the different options she had in regard to her pregnancy. Maria stated that she wanted to abort her pregnancy. If her parents would not allow her to have an abortion, Maria said she would kill herself. With Maria's permission, the social worker arranged to talk with Maria and her parents. Maria father stated he would not hear of Maria's having an abortion. Maria then stated with conviction how she would kill herself. The social worker believed Maria would act on her threat of suicide.

- If you were the social worker, what would you do to protect Maria from harming herself?
- What cultural variables would you consider in your interventions?
- Knowing what Maria told you about her parent's values, would you have involved them in this case? Why or why not?
- Would you use Maria's threat of suicide to influence her parents, or would you ignore this threat?
- Would you try to involve Maria's family priest in this situation?

◆ **The case of Andres.** Andres is 14 years old and is brought to the school social worker because of chronic truancies. Andres explains to the social worker that he does not see the use of getting a high school diploma because he never knows when he might be killed. He further explains that his entire family are gang members and the older members of his family are in the Mexican Mafia. Andres tells the social worker he would like to get out of the gang and live a normal kid's life but that he has no other choice than to remain in the gang. Andres told the social worker that he could not walk down certain streets because rival gangs would attempt to kill him. If he told his family he wanted out of the gang, he would alienate himself from his family, and they might have him killed.

- What approach would you be tempted to take with Andres, and why?
- What cultural variables would you include in approaching this case?
- What, if anything, would you do about the perceived threat to Andres' life?
- Is there anything in this case that is reportable?
- If you could think of no way to help Andres, what would you do?

Some Concluding Thoughts About Ethical Thinking

We have raised some of the ethical and professional issues you are likely to encounter in your counseling practice and tried to stimulate you to think about your own guidelines for professional practice. If one fundamental question can serve to tie together all the issues we have discussed, it is this: Who has the right to counsel another person? This question can be the focal point of your reflection on ethical and professional issues. It can also be the basis for self-examination whenever you have concerns about clients. At times you may be troubled and feel that you have no right to counsel others, perhaps because your own life is not always the model you would like it to be for your clients. Yet occasional self-doubt is far less damaging, in our view, than a failure to question. Complacency will stifle your growth as a counselor; honest self-examination, although more difficult, will make you a more effective therapist.

Developing a sense of professional and ethical responsibility is a task that is never really finished. There are no final or universal answers to many of the questions we have posed. For ourselves, we hope we never fall into the deadening trap of thinking that we "have it made" and no longer need to reexamine our assumptions and practices. We have found in our own practice that the issues raised in this book have demanded periodic reflection and an openness to change. Thus, although we hope you have given careful thought to your own ethical and professional guidelines, we also hope you will be willing to rethink your positions as you gain more experience.

Take time now to retake the self-assessment at the end of Chapter 1, which surveys your attitudes about ethical and professional issues. Cover your initial answers when you complete the self-assessment, and compare your responses now to see whether your thinking has changed. In addition, we suggest that you circle the 10 questions that are most significant to you or that you are most interested in pursuing further. Bring these to class, and discuss them in small groups. As a way to review this book and the course you are completing, write down a few of the most important things you have learned. You might also write down some of the questions that this book and your course have left unanswered for you. Form small groups and exchange ideas with other students. This can be an excellent way to get some sense of the most crucial areas and topics that were explored by your fellow students and a fine way to wrap up the course.

Once the course is over, where can you go from here? How can you maintain the process of reflection that you have begun? One excellent way to keep yourself alive intellectually is to develop a reading program. Begin by selecting some of the books listed in the References and Selected Readings, and dip into this book again from time to time. It can be valuable to reread particular chapters as you take courses that deal with issues considered here. In addition, periodically reexamining your responses can stimulate your thinking and provide a measure of your professional and intellectual growth. We hope you will find other ways to make this book meaningful as you continue your search for your own direction.

Chapter Summary

The primary focus of this chapter has been on the importance of working in the community as a change agent. The community mental health orientation is one way to meet the increasing demand for psychological services. Too often mental health professionals have been denied the opportunity to devise programs that address the diverse needs of the community. Over the past few years some alternatives to conventional therapy have arisen, creating new roles for counselors who work in a community agency setting.

You may be looking forward to a full-time career in a system. We think it is essential to consider how to make the system work *for* you and your clients rather than *against* you and your clients. If you treat people in a system as allies, the chances that they will support your proposals for change are increased. If you treat people as opponents, they are more likely to become your enemies and block actions you take to make changes in the system.

We challenge you to think of ways to accept the responsibility of surviving and working effectively in an organization and thus increasing your power as a person. Finally, we ask you to reflect on the major causes of disillusionment that often accompany working in a system and to find creative ways to remain vital as a person and as a professional.

Suggested Activities

1. In small groups explore specific ways of becoming involved in the community or using community resources to assist you in working with your clients. After you have explored these issues, the class can reconvene to pool ideas.

2. Have several students who are interested in the use of nonlicensed professionals in the human-services field investigate the issue and present their results in the form of a panel discussion. The discussion can focus on the advantages and disadvantages of the use of nonlicensed professionals, current trends, and other issues the panel deems important.

3. An issue you may well face in your practice is how to get through the resistance people have toward asking for psychological assistance. Ask yourself how you should respond to clients who have questions such as these: "What will people think if they find out that I am coming for professional help?" "Shouldn't I really be able to solve my problems on my own? Isn't it a sign of weakness that I need others to help me?" "Aren't most people who come to a community clinic really sick?" "Will I really be able to resolve my problems by consulting you?" After you have thought through your own responses, share them in dyads or in small groups.

4. How aware are you of the resources that exist in your community? Would you know where to refer clients for special help? How aware are you of the support systems that exist in your community? Individually or with other students, investigate a comprehensive community mental health center in your area. In doing so, find the answers to questions such as these:

- Where would you send a family who needed help?
- What facilities are available to treat drug and alcohol abuse?
- What kinds of crisis intervention are available? What are some common crises?
- Are health and medical services available at the center?
- What groups are offered?
- Is individual counseling available? for whom? at what fee? long-term? short-term?

- Where would you refer a couple seeking couples counseling?
- Are hot-line services available?
- What provisions are there for emergency situations?
- What do people have to do to qualify for help at the center?

5. Several students can interview a variety of professionals in the mental health field about the major problems they encounter in their institution. What barriers do they meet when they attempt to implement programs? How do they deal with obstacles or red tape? How does the system affect them? Divide this task up so that a wide range of licensed and nonlicensed professionals are interviewed, including some who have been in the same job for a number of years and others who are just beginning. Compare the responses of experienced and inexperienced personnel without revealing the identities of the persons interviewed.

6. In small groups develop a list of skills human-service professionals need to have to work effectively in the community. Then have each group give an example of how those skills can be applied in community work. Discuss ways that you can best acquire or refine these skills.

7. Once you recognize the need for change within an organization, you have taken an important step toward responding to an unacceptable situation. What other ways might you respond after recognizing that a problem exists within the organization for which you work? Identify skills you would need to have to make the desired changes. What are some ways that you can make changes in a system? How might you go about developing strategies for getting support from co-workers if you were interested in changing an agency?

8. Reflect on and discuss alternative roles human-service professionals might play when working in the community. Ask yourself which of the following roles you think you could assume as a community worker: (a) advocate, (b) change agent, (c) consultant, (d) adviser, (e) facilitator of indigenous support systems, or (f) facilitator of indigenous healing systems. In small groups discuss in which of these roles you would feel least comfortable functioning. How could you learn to carry out professional roles in the community different from those in which you were trained?

InfoTrac® College Edition Resources

For additional readings, explore InfoTrac College Edition, our online library. Go to *http://www.infotrac.college.com/wadsworth* and select these key word searches:

community W1 counseling
community W1 mental W1 health

mental W1 health paraprofessional*

Key words are listed in a form that enables the search engine to locate a wider range of articles in the online university library. Key words should be entered exactly as shown, including asterisks, "W1," "W2," "AND," and other search engine tools.

Abeles, N., & Barlev, A. (1999). End of life decisions and assisted suicide. *Professional Psychology: Research and Practice, 30*(3), 229–234.
Acuff, C., Bennett, B. E., Bricklin, P. M., Canter, M. B., Knapp, S. J., Moldawsky, S., & Phelps, R. (1999). Considerations for ethical practice of managed care. *Professional Psychology: Research and Practice, 30*(6), 563–575.
Adair, J. G., Dushenko, T. W., & Lindsay, R. C. L. (1985). Ethical regulations and their impact on research practice. *American Psychologist, 40*(1), 59–72.
*Ahia, C. E., & Martin, D. (1993). *The danger-to-self-or-others exception to confidentiality.* Alexandria, VA: American Counseling Association.
*Albright, D. E., & Hazler, R. J. (1995). A right to die? Ethical dilemmas of euthanasia. *Counseling and Values, 39*(3), 177–189.
American Association for Marriage and Family Therapy. (1994). *Membership requirements and applications.* Washington, DC: Author.
American Association for Marriage and Family Therapy. (1999). *Responsibilities and guidelines for AAMFT approved supervisors and supervisors-in-training.* Washington, DC: Author.
American Association for Marriage and Family Therapy. (2001). *AAMFT code of ethics.* Washington, DC: Author.
American Association of Pastoral Counselors. (1999). Supervision standards. *Certification committee operational manual* (p. 18). Fairfax, VA: Author.
American Counseling Association (1995). *Code of ethics and standards of practice.* Alexandria, VA: Author.
American Counseling Association (1999). *Ethical standards for Internet on-line counseling.* Alexandria, VA: Author.
American Psychiatric Association. (1994). *Diagnostic and statistical manual of mental disorders* (4th ed.). Washington, DC: Author.
American Psychiatric Association. (1998). *The principles of medical ethics with annotations especially applicable to psychiatry.* Washington, DC: Author.
American Psychological Association. (1985). *White paper on duty to protect.* Washington, DC: Author.
American Psychological Association. (1992). *Ethical principles of psychologists and code of conduct.* Washington, DC: Author.
American Psychological Association. (1993). Guidelines for providers of psychological services to ethnic, linguistic, and culturally diverse populations. *American Psychologist, 48*(1), 45–48.

* Books and articles marked with an asterisk are suggested for further study.

References and Suggested Readings

American Psychological Association, Division 44. (2000). Guidelines for psychotherapy with lesbian, gay, and bisexual clients. *American Psychologist, 55*(12), 1440–1451.

American Psychological Association. (2001). Ethical principles of psychologists and code of conduct [Draft for Comment]. *Monitor on Psychology, 32*(2), 77–90.

American School Counselor Association. (1998). *Ethical standards for school counselors.* Alexandria, VA: Author.

*Anderson, B. S. (1996). *The counselor and the law* (4th ed.). Alexandria, VA: American Counseling Association.

Anderson, S. K., & Kitchener, K. S. (1996). Nonromantic, nonsexual posttherapy relationships between psychologists and former clients: An exploratory study of critical incidents. *Professional Psychology: Research and Practice, 27*(1), 59–66.

*Anderson, S. K., & Kitchener, K. S. (1998). Nonsexual posttherapy relationships: A conceptual framework to assess ethical risks. *Professional Psychology: Research and Practice, 29*(1), 91–99.

*Aponte, H. J. (1994). How personal can training get? *Journal of Marital and Family Therapy, 20*(1), 3–15.

Arredondo, P. (1999). Multicultural counseling competencies as tools to address oppression and racism. *Journal of Counseling and Development, 77*(1), 102–108.

*Arredondo, P., Toporek, R., Brown, S., Jones, J., Locke, D., Sanchez, J., & Stadler, H. A. (1996). Operationalization of multicultural counseling competencies. *Journal of Multicultural Counseling and Development, 24*(1), 42–78.

*Arthur, G. L., & Swanson, C. D. (1993). *Confidentiality and privileged communication.* Alexandria, VA: American Counseling Association.

Association for Counselor Education and Supervision. (1993, Summer). Ethical guidelines for counseling supervisors. *ACES Spectrum, 53*(4), 3–8.

Association for Counselor Education and Supervision. (1995). Ethical guidelines for counseling supervisors. *Counselor Education and Supervision, 34*(3), 270–276.

Association for Specialists in Group Work. (1998). Best practice guidelines. *Journal for Specialists in Group Work, 23*(3), 237–244.

Association for Specialists in Group Work. (1999). Principles for diversity-competent group workers. *Journal for Specialists in Group Work, 24*(1), 7–14.

Association for Specialists in Group Work. (2000). Professional standards for the training of group workers. *The Group Worker, 29*(3), 1–10.

Atkinson, D. R., Morten, G., & Sue, D. W. (Eds.). (1998). *Counseling American minorities: A cross-cultural perspective* (5th ed.). Boston, MA: McGraw-Hill.

Atkinson, D. R., Thompson, C. E., & Grant, S. K. (1993). A three-dimensional model for counseling racial/ethnic minorities. *The Counseling Psychologist, 21*(2), 257–277.

Austad, C. S. (1996). *Is long-term psychotherapy unethical? Toward a social ethic in an era of managed care.* San Francisco, CA: Jossey-Bass.

Austin, K. M., Moline, M. M., & Williams, G. T. (1990). *Confronting malpractice: Legal and ethical dilemmas in psychotherapy.* Newbury Park, CA: Sage.

Axelson, J. A. (1999). *Counseling and development in a multicultural society* (3rd ed.). Pacific Grove, CA: Brooks/Cole.

Barnett, J. E., & Hillard, D. (2001). Psychological distress and impairment: The availability, nature, and use of colleague assistance programs for psychologists. *Professional Psychology: Research and Practice, 32*(2), 205–210.

Becvar, D. S. (1994). Can spiritual yearnings and therapeutic goals be melded? *Family Therapy News,* 13–14.

Bednar, R. L., Bednar, S. C., Lambert, M. J., & Waite, D. R. (1991). *Psychotherapy with high-risk clients: Legal and professional standards.* Pacific Grove, CA: Brooks/Cole.

*Benke, S. (1998). *The essentials of California mental health law: A straightforward guide for clinicians of all disciplines.* New York: W. W. Norton & Company.

Bennett, B. E., Bricklin, P. M., & VandeCreek, L. (1994). Response to Lazarus's "How certain boundaries and ethics diminish therapeutic effectiveness." *Ethics and Behavior, 4*(3), 263–266.

Bennett, B. E., Bryant, B. K., VandenBos, G. R., & Greenwood, A. (1990). *Professional liability and risk management.* Washington, DC: American Psychological Association.

Benningfield, A. B. (1994). The impaired therapist. In G. W. Brock (Ed.), *American Association for Marriage and Family Therapy ethics casebook* (pp. 131–139). Washington, DC: American Association for Marriage and Family Therapy.

Benson, H., with Stark, M. (1996). *Timeless healing: The power and biology of belief.* New York: Scribner.

Bergin, A. E. (1991). Values and religious issues in psychotherapy and mental health. *American Psychology, 46*(4), 393–403.

Bernard, J. L., & Jara, C. S. (1986). The failure of clinical psychology graduate students to apply understood ethical principles. *Professional Psychology: Research and Practice, 17*(4), 313–315.

Bernard, J. M. (1994). Multicultural supervision: A reaction to Leong and Wagner, Cook, Priest, and Fukuyama. *Counselor Education and Supervision, 34*(2), 159–171.

*Bernard, J. M., & Goodyear, R. K. (1998). *Fundamentals of clinical supervision* (2nd ed.). Needham Heights, MA: Allyn & Bacon.

Bersoff, D. N. (1994). Explicit ambiguity: The 1992 ethics code as an oxymoron. *Professional Psychology: Research and Practice, 25*(4), 382–387.

Bersoff, D. N. (1996). The virtue of principle ethics. *The Counseling Psychologist, 24*(1), 86–91.

*Bersoff, D. N. (1999). *Ethical conflicts in psychology* (2nd ed.). Washington, DC: American Psychological Association.

Biaggio, M., Paget, T. L., Chenoweth, M. S. (1997). A model for ethical management of faculty-student dual relationships. *Professional Psychology: Research and Practice, 28*(2), 184–189.

Birdsall, B., & Hubert, M. (2000, October). Ethical issues in school counseling. *Counseling Today,* pp. 30, 36.

Block, S., & Harari, E. (1996). Working with the family: The role of values. *American Journal of Psychotherapy, 50*(3), 274–284.

Bonger, B. (1991). *The suicidal patient: Clinical and legal standards of care.* Washington, DC: American Psychological Association.

Borders, L. D. (1991). A systematic approach to peer group supervision. *Journal of Counseling and Development, 69*(3), 248–252.

Borys, D. S. (1994). Maintaining therapeutic boundaries: The motive is therapeutic effectiveness, not defensive practice. *Ethics and Behavior, 4*(3), 267–273.

Borys, D. S., & Pope, K. S. (1989). Dual relationships between therapist and client: A national study of psychologists, psychiatrists, and social workers. *Professional Psychology: Research and Practice, 20*(5), 283–293.

Bouhoutsos, J., Holroyd, J., Lerman, H., Forer, B. R., & Greenberg, M. (1983). Sexual intimacy between psychotherapists and patients. *Professional Psychology: Research and Practice, 14*(2), 185–196.

Bowman, V. E., Hatley, L. D., & Bowman, R. (1995). Faculty-student relationships: The dual role controversy. *Counselor Education and Supervision, 24*(3), 232–242.

*Brabeck, M. M. (Ed.). (2000). *Practicing feminist ethics in psychology.* Washington, DC: American Psychological Association.

Brabeck, M. M., & Ting, K. (2000). Feminist ethics: Lenses for examining ethical psychological practice. In M. M. Brabeck (Ed.), *Practicing feminist ethics in psychology.* (pp. 17–35). Washington, DC: American Psychological Association.

Brace, K. (1997). Ethical considerations in the development of counseling goals. In *The Hatherleigh guide to ethics in therapy* (pp. 17–35). New York: Hatherleigh Press.

Bradley Center v. Wessner, 250 Ga. 199, 296 S.E. 2d 693 (1982).

*Bradley, L. J., Kottler, J. A., & Lehrman-Waterman, D. (2001). Ethical issues in supervision. In L. J. Bradley & N. Ladany, (Eds.), *Counselor supervision: Principles, process and practice* (3rd ed., pp. 342–360). Philadelphia, PA: Brunner-Routledge/Taylor & Francis Group.

*Bradley, L., & Ladany, N. (Eds.). (2001). *Counselor supervision: Principles, process and practice* (3rd ed.). Philadelphia, PA: Brunner-Routledge/Taylor & Francis Group.

*Brock, G. W. (Ed.). (1998). *Ethics casebook.* Washington, DC: American Association for Marriage and Family Therapy.

Brooks, D. K., & Gerstein, L. H. (1990). Counselor credentialing and interprofessional collaboration. *Journal of Counseling and Development, 68(5), 477–484.*

Broskowski, A. (1991). Current mental health care environments: Why managed care is necessary. *Professional Psychology: Research and Practice, 22*(1) 6–14.

Brown, C., & O'Brien, K. M. (1998). Understanding stress and burnout in shelter workers. *Professional Psychology: Research and Practice, 29*(4), 383–385.

Brown, D. (1993). Training consultants: A call to action. *Journal of Counseling and Development, 72*(2), 139–143.

Brown, L. S. (1990). Taking account of gender in the clinical assessment interview. *Professional Psychology: Research and Practice, 21*(1), 12–17.

Brown, L. S. (1994). Concrete boundaries and the problem of literal-mindedness: A response to Lazarus. *Ethics and Behavior, 4*(3), 275–281.

Burian, B. K., & O'Conner Slimp, A. (2000). Social dual-role relationships during internship: A decision-making model. *Professional Psychology: Research and Practice, 31*(3), 332–338.

Burke, M. T., Hackney, H., Hudson, P., Miranti, J., Watts, G. A., & Epp, L. (1999). Sprituality, religion, and CACREP curriculum standards. *Journal of Counseling and Development, 77*(3), 251–257.

Calfee, B. E. (1996). Legally defensive client record keeping. *Directions in Mental Health Counseling, 6,* 1–10.

Calfee, B. E. (1997). Lawsuit prevention techniques. In *The Hatherleigh guide to ethics in therapy* (pp. 109–125). New York: Hatherleigh Press.

Calhoun, K. S., Moras, K., Pilkonis, P. A., & Rehm, L. P. (1998). Empirically supported treatments: Implications for training. *Journal of Consulting and Clinical Psychology, 66,* 151–162.

California Association of Marriage and Family Therapists. (1996a, March/April). Disciplinary actions. *The California Therapist, 8*(2), 18.

California Association of Marriage and Family Therapists (1996b, May/June). Disciplinary actions. *The California Therapist, 8*(3), 25–26.

California Association of Marriage and Family Therapists. (1996c, July/August). Disciplinary actions. *The California Therapist, 8*(4), 34.

California Association of Marriage and Family Therapists. (2001, January/February). Disciplinary actions. *The California Therapist, 13*(1), 40.

California Department of Consumer Affairs. (undated). *Professional therapy never includes sex* (pamphlet). Sacramento: Author.

California Department of Consumer Affairs, Board of Psychology. (1999, May). Disciplinary actions. *Board of Psychology Update, 6,* 12–13.

California Department of Consumer Affairs, Board of Psychology. (2000, December). New regulations approved: Section 1387 of the California code of regulations—Supervised professional experience. *Board of Psychology Update, 8,* 1, 4–9.

*Campbell, J. M. (2000). *Becoming an effective supervisor: A workbook for counselors and psychotherapists.* Philadelphia, PA: Accelerated Development (Taylor & Francis).

*Canter, M. B., Bennett, B. E., Jones, S. E., & Nagy, T. F. (1994). *Ethics for psychologists: A commentary on the APA ethics code.* Washington, DC: American Psychological Association.

Carta-Falsa, J., & Anderson, L. (2001). A model of clinical/counseling supervision. *The California Therapist, 13*(2), 47–51.

Chauvin, J. C., & Remley, T. P. (1996). Responding to allegations of unethical conduct. *Journal of Counseling and Development, 74*(6), 563–568.

Chenneville, T. (2000). HIV, confidentiality, and duty to protect: A decision-making model. *Professional Psychology: Research and Practice, 31*(6), 661–670.

*Coale, H. W. (1998). *The vulnerable therapist: Practicing psychotherapy in an age of anxiety.* New York: Haworth Press.

Cobia, D. C., & Boes, S. R. (2000). Professional disclosure statements and formal plans for supervision: Two strategies for minimizing the risk of ethical conflicts in post-master's supervision. *Journal of Counseling and Development, 78*(3), 293–296.

Cohen, E. D. (1997). Ethical standards in counseling sexually active clients with HIV. In *The Hatherleigh guide to ethics in therapy* (pp. 211–233). New York: Hatherleigh Press.

*Cohen, E. D., & Cohen, G. S. (1999). *The virtuous therapist: Ethical practice of counseling and psychotherapy.* Pacific Grove, CA: Brooks/Cole.

*Cohen, R., & Cohen, J. (2000). *Chiseled in sand: Perspectives on change in human services organizations.* Pacific Grove, CA: Brooks/Cole.

Coleman, E., & Schaefer, S. (1986). Boundaries of sex and intimacy between client and counselor. *Journal of Counseling and Development, 64*(5), 341–344.

Committee on Professional Practice and Standards, Board of Professional Affairs. (1993). Record keeping guidelines. *American Psychologist, 48,* 984–986.

Committee on Women in Psychology, American Psychological Association. (1989). If sex enters into the psychotherapy relationship. *Professional Psychology: Research and Practice, 20*(2), 112–115.

*Constantine, M. G. (1997). Facilitating multicultural competency in counseling supervision: Operationalizing a practical framework. In D. B. Pope-Davis & H. L. K. Coleman, (Eds.), *Multicultural counseling competencies: Assessment, education and training, and supervision.* (pp. 310–324). Thousand Oaks, CA: Sage.

Conyne, R. K. (1996). The Association for Specialists in Group Work training standards: Some considerations and suggestions for training. *Journal for Specialists in Group Work, 21*(3), 155–162.

Cook, D. A. (1994). Racial identity in supervision. *Counselor Education and Supervision, 34*(2), 132–141.

Cooper, C. C., & Gottlieb, M. C. (2000). Ethical issues with managed care: Challenges facing counseling psychology. *The Counseling Psychologist, 28*(2), 179–236.

Corey, G. (2000). *Theory and practice of group counseling* (5th ed.) and *Manual.* Pacific Grove, CA: Brooks/Cole.

Corey, G. (2001a). *The art of integrative counseling.* Pacific Grove, CA: Brooks/Cole.

Corey, G. (2001b). *Case approach to counseling and psychotherapy* (5th ed.). Pacific Grove, CA: Brooks/Cole.

Corey, G. (2001c). *Theory and practice of counseling and psychotherapy* (5th ed.) and *Manual*. Pacific Grove, CA: Brooks/Cole.

Corey, G., & Corey, M. (2002). *I never knew I had a choice* (7th ed.). Pacific Grove, CA: Brooks/Cole.

Corey, G., Corey, M., Callanan, P., & Russell, J. M. (1992). *Group techniques* (2nd ed.). Pacific Grove, CA: Brooks/Cole.

Corey, G., & Herlihy, B. (1993). Dual relationships: Associated risks and potential benefits. *Ethical Issues in Professional Counseling, 1*(1), 3–11.

Corey, G., & Herlihy, B. (1996a). Client rights and informed consent. In B. Herlihy & G. Corey (Eds.), ACA *ethical standards casebook* (5th ed., pp. 181–183). Alexandria, VA: American Counseling Association.

Corey, G., & Herlihy, B. (1996b). Competence. In B. Herlihy & G. Corey (Eds.), *ACA ethical standards casebook* (5th ed., pp. 217–220). Alexandria, VA: American Counseling Association.

Corey, G., & Herlihy, B. (1996c). Counselor training and supervision. In B. Herlihy & G. Corey (Eds.), *ACA ethical standards casebook* (5th ed., pp. 275–278). Alexandria, VA: American Counseling Association.

Corey, G., & Herlihy, B. (1996d). Dual/multiple relationships: Toward a consensus of thinking. In *The Hatherleigh guide to ethics in therapy* (pp. 183–194). New York: Hatherleigh Press.

Corey, G., Williams, G. T., & Moline, M. E. (1995). Ethical and legal issues in group counseling. *Ethics and Behavior,* 5(2), 161–183.

Corey, M., & Corey, G. (1993). Difficult group members—difficult group leaders. *New York State Association for Counseling and Development, 8*(2), 9–24.

Corey, M., & Corey, G. (2002). *Groups: Process and practice* (6th ed.). Pacific Grove, CA: Brooks/Cole.

Corsini, R., & Wedding, D. (2000). *Current psychotherapies* (6th ed.). Itasca, IL: F. E. Peacock.

Costa, L., & Altekruse, M. (1994). Duty-to-warn guidelines for mental health counselors. *Journal of Counseling and Development, 72*(4), 346–350.

Coster, J. S., & Schwebel, M. (1997). Well-functioning in professional psychologists. *Professional Psychology: Research and Practice, 28*(1), 5–13.

Cottone, R. R. (2001). A social constructivism model of ethical decision making in counseling. *Journal of Counseling and Development, 79*(1), 39–45.

Cottone, R. R., & Claus, R. E. (2000). Ethical decision-making models: A review of the literature. *Journal of Counseling and Development, 78*(3), 275–283.

Cottone, R. R., & Tarvydas, V. M. (1998). *Ethical and professional issues in counseling*. Upper Saddle River, NJ: Merrill/Prentice-Hall.

Council for Accreditation of Counseling and Related Educational Programs. (CACREP) (1994). *CACREP accreditation standards and procedures manual.* Alexandria, VA: Author.

Crawford, I., McLeod, A., Zamboni, B. D., & Jordan, M. B. (1999). Psychologists' attitudes toward gay and lesbian parenting. *Professional Psychology: Research and Practice, 30*(4), 394–401.

Crawford, R. L. (1994). *Avoiding counselor malpractice.* Alexandria, VA: American Counseling Association.

Crawford, R. (1999). Law and ethics: Comparisons and contrasts. In P. Stevens (Ed.), *Ethical casebook for the practice of marriage and family counseling* (pp. 17–39). Alexandria, VA: American Counseling Association.

Crespi, T. D., Fischetti, B. A., & Butler, S. K. (2001, January). Clinical supervision in the schools. *Counseling Today,* pp. 7, 28, 34.

Cummings, N. A. (1990). The credentialing of professional psychologists and its implication for the other mental health disciplines. *Journal of Counseling and Development, 68*(5), 485–490.

Cummings, N. A. (1995). Impact of managed care on employment and training: A primer for survival. *Professional Psychology: Research and Practice, 26*(1), 10–15.

Custer, G. (1994, November) Can universities be liable for incompetent grads? *APA Monitor, 25*(11), 7.

D'Andrea, M., & Arredondo, P. (1996, December). ACES formally endorses multicultural counseling competencies. *Counseling Today*, p. 29.

Daniels, J. A. (2001). Managed care, ethics, and counseling. *Journal of Counseling and Development, 79*(1), 119–122.

Das, A. K. (1995). Rethinking multicultural counseling: Implications for counselor education. *Journal of Counseling and Development, 74*(1), 45–52.

Davis, J. W. (1981). Counselor licensure: Overskill? *Personnel and Guidance Journal, 60*(2), 83–85.

*Davis, S. R., & Meier, S. T. (2001). *The elements of managed care: A guide for helping professionals.* Pacific Grove, CA: Brooks/Cole.

DeBell, C., & Jones, R. D. (1997). Privileged communication at last? An overview of *Jaffee v. Redmond. Professional Psychology: Research and Practice, 28*(6), 559–566.

*DeLucia-Waack, J. L. (Ed.). (1996). *Multicultural counseling competencies: Implications for training and practice.* Alexandria, VA: Association for Counselor Education and Supervision.

DeMayo, R. A. (2000). Patients' sexual behavior and sexual harassment: A survey of clinical supervisors. *Professional Psychology: Research and Practice, 31*(6), 706–709.

Department of Consumer Affairs. (1990). *Professional therapy never includes sex.* Sacramento, CA: Author.

Deutsch, C. J. (1984). Self-reported sources of stress among psychotherapists. *Professional Psychology: Research and Practice, 15*(6), 833–845.

Diller, J. V. (1999). *Cultural diversity: A primer for the human services.* Pacific Grove, CA: Brooks/Cole•Wadsworth.

DiVerde-Nushawg, N., & Walls, G. B. (1998). The implications of pager use for the therapeutic relationship in independent practice. *Professional Psychology: Research and Practice, 29*(4), 368–372.

Donigian, J. (1991). Dual relationships: An ethical issue. *Together, 19*(2), 6–7.

Dougherty, A. M. (2000). *Psychological consultation and collaboration in schools and community settings* (3rd ed.). Pacific Grove, CA: Brooks/Cole.

Duncan, D. M., & Watts, R. E. (1999). Counseling and the Internet. In P. Stevens (Ed.), *Ethical casebook for the practice of marriage and family counseling* (pp. 159–170). Alexandria, VA: American Counseling Association.

Edwards, J. K., & Bess, J. M. (1998). Developing effectiveness in the therapeutic use of self. *Clinical Social Work Journal, 26*(1), 89–105.

Eisel v. Board of Education, 597 A.2d 447 (Md. 1991).

Elman, N., Forrest, L., Vacha-Haase, T., & Gizara, S. (1999). A systems perspective on trainee impairment: Continuing the dialogue. *The Counseling Psychologist, 27*(5), 712–721.

Emerson, S., & Markos, P. A. (1996). Signs and symptoms of the impaired counselor. *Journal of Humanistic Education and Development, 34*, 108–117.

Erickson, S. H. (1993). Ethics and confidentiality in AIDS counseling: A professional dilemma. *Journal of Mental Health Counseling, 15*(2), 118–131.

Evans, G. D., & Rey, J. (2001). In the echoes of gunfire: Practicing psychologists' responses to school violence. *Professional Psychology: Research and Practice, 32*(2), 157–164.

Everstine, L., Everstine, D. S., Heymann, G. M., True, R. H., Frey, D. H., Johnson, H. G., & Seiden, R. H. (1980). Privacy and confidentiality in psychotherapy. *American Psychologist, 35*(9), 828–840.

Ezell, M. (2001). *Advocacy in the human services.* Pacific Grove, CA: Brooks/Cole.

Faiver, C., Ingersoll, R. E., O'Brien, E., & McNally, C. (2001). *Explorations in counseling and spirituality: Philosophical, practical, and personal reflections.* Pacific Grove, CA: Brooks/Cole.

Faiver, C. M., Eisengart, S., & Colonna, R. (2000). *The counselor intern's handbook* (2nd ed.). Pacific Grove, CA: Brooks/Cole.

Faiver, C. M., & O'Brien, E. M. (1993). Assessment of religious beliefs form. *Counseling and Values, 37*(3), 176–178.

Faiver, C. M., O'Brien, E. M., & Ingersoll, R. E. (2000). Religion, guilt, and mental health. *Journal of Counseling and Development, 78*(2), 155–161.

*Falvey, J. (2002). *Managing clinical supervision: Ethical and legal risk management.* Pacific Grove, CA: Brooks/Cole.

Farber, B. A. (1983a). Psychotherapists' perceptions of stressful patient behavior. *Professional Psychology: Research and Practice, 14*(5), 697–705.

Farber, B. A. (1983b). *Stress and burnout in the human service professions.* New York: Pergamon Press.

Farberman, R. K. (1997). Terminal illness and hastened death requests: The important role of the mental health professional. *Professional Psychology: Research and Practice, 28*(6), 544–547.

Farrugia, D. (1993). Exploring the counselor's role in "right to die" decisions. *Counseling and Values, 37*(2), 61–70.

Feist, S. C. (1999). Practice and theory of professional supervision for mental health counselors. *Directions in Mental Health Counseling, 9*(9), 105–119.

Fenn, D. S., & Ganzini, L. (1999). Attitudes of Oregon psychologists toward physician-assisted suicide and the Oregon death with dignity act. *Professional Psychology: Research and Practice, 30*(3), 235–244.

Fogel, M. S. (1990, May/June). Supervisors should not dominate but doubt, reflect, innovate. *Family Therapy News,* pp. 5–6.

Forester-Miller, H. (1997). Rural communities: Can dual relationships be avoided? In B. Herlihy & G. Corey (Eds.), *Boundary issues in counseling: Multiple roles and responsibilities* (pp. 99–100). Alexandria, VA: American Counseling Association.

Forester-Miller, H., & Davis, T. E. (1995). *A practitioner's guide to ethical decision making.* Alexandria, VA: American Counseling Association.

*Forrest, L., Elman, N., Gizara, S., & Vacha-Haase, T. (1999). Trainee impairment: A review of identification, remediation, dismissal, and legal issues. *The Counseling Psychologist, 27*(5), 627–686.

Foster, R. P. (1998). The clinician's cultural countertransference: The psychodynamics of culturally competent practice. *Clinical Social Work Journal, 26*(3), 253–270.

Foster, S. (1996, January). The consequences of violating the "forbidden zone." *Counseling Today,* p. 24.

Foxhall, K. (2000). How will the rules on telehealth be written? *Monitor on Psychology, 31*(4), 38.

Frankel, A. S. (2000). Watch out for the third man death. *Board of Psychology Update, 8,* 2–3.

Freeman, S. J. (2000). *Ethics: An introduction to philosophy and practice.* Belmont, CA: Wadsworth/Thomson Learning.

Freeny, M. (2001). Better than being there. *Psychotherapy Networker, 25*(2), 30–70.

Fremon, C. (1991, January 27). Love and death. *Los Angeles Times Magazine,* pp. 17–35.

Fujimura, L. E., Weis, D. M., & Cochran, J. R. (1985). Suicide: Dynamics and implications for counseling. *Journal of Counseling and Development, 63*(10), 612–615.

Fukuyama, M. A. (1994). Critical incidents in multicultural counseling: A phenomenological approach to supervision research. *Counselor Education and Supervision, 34*(2), 142–151.

Fulero, S. M. (1988). *Tarasoff.* 10 years later. *Professional Psychology: Research and Practice, 19*(2), 184–190.

Gabbard, G. O. (1994). Teetering on the precipice: A commentary on Lazarus's "How certain boundaries and ethics diminish therapeutic effectiveness." *Ethics and Behavior, 4*(3), 283–286.

Gabbard, G. O. (1995, April). What are boundaries in psychotherapy? *The Menninger Letter, 3*(4), 1–2.

Gabbard, G. O. (1996). Lessons to be learned from the study of sexual boundary violations. *American Journal of Psychotherapy, 50*(3), 311–322.

Garcia, A. (1990). An examination of the social work profession's efforts to achieve legal regulation. *Journal of Counseling and Development, 68*(5), 491–497.

Gelso, C. J., & Carter, J. A. (1985). The relationship in counseling and psychotherapy: Components, consequences, and theoretical antecedents. *The Counseling Psychologist, 13*(2), 155–243.

Genia, V. (1994). Secular psychotherapists and religious clients: Professional considerations and recommendations. *Journal of Counseling and Development, 72*(4), 395–398.

Gerstein, L. H., & Brooks, D. K. (1990). Introduction for a special feature. The helping professions' challenge: Credentialing and interdisciplinary collaboration. *Journal of Counseling and Development, 68*(5), 475–476.

Getz, H. D. (1999). Assessment of clinical supervisor competencies. *Journal of Counseling and Development, 77*(4), 491–497.

Getz, J. G., & Protinsky, H. O. (1994). Training marriage and family counselors: A family-of-origin approach. *Counselor Education and Supervision, 33*(3), 183–200.

Gilliland, B. E., & James, R. K. (1997). *Crisis intervention strategies* (3rd ed.). Pacific Grove, CA: Brooks/Cole.

Gill-Wigal, J., & Heaton, J. A. (1996). Managing sexual attraction in the therapeutic relationship. *Directions in Mental Health Counseling, 6*(8), 4–15.

Glaberson, W. (2000, August 4). Judges dismiss civil suits in school killings. *The Times-Picayune*, p. A-4.

Gladding, S. T. (1997). *Community and agency counseling.* Upper Saddle River, NJ: Prentice-Hall.

Gladding, S. T., Remley, T. P., & Huber, C. H. (2001). *Ethical, legal, and professional issues in the practice of marriage and family therapy* (3rd ed.) Upper Saddle River, NJ: Merrill/Prentice-Hall.

Glosoff, H. L., Corey, G., & Herlihy, B. (1996). Dual relationships. In B. Herlihy & G. Corey, (Eds.), *ACA ethical standards casebook* (5th ed., pp. 251–257). Alexandria, VA: American Counseling Association.

*Glosoff, H. L., Garcia, J., Herlihy, B., & Remley, T. P. (1999). Managed care: Ethical considerations for counselors. *Counseling and Values, 44*(1), 8–16.

*Glosoff, H. L., Herlihy, S. B., Herlihy, B., & Spence, E. B. (1997). Privileged communication in the psychologist-client relationship. *Professional Psychology: Research and Practice, 28*(6), 573–581.

*Glosoff, H. L., Herlihy, B., & Spence, E. B. (2000). Privileged communication in the counselor-client relationship. *Journal of Counseling and Development, 78*(4), 454–462.

Goldblum, P. B., & Martin, D. J. (1999). Principles for the discussion of life and death options with terminally ill clients with HIV. *Professional Psychology: Research and Practice, 30*(2), 187–197.

Goldenberg, I., & Goldenberg, H. (2000). *Family therapy: An overview* (5th. ed.). Pacific Grove, CA: Brooks/Cole.

Goodyear, R. K., & Bernard, J. M. (1998). Clinical supervision: Lessons from the literature. *Counselor Education and Supervision, 38*(1), 6–22.

Gottlieb, M. C. (1990). Accusations of sexual misconduct: Assisting in the complaint process. *Professional Psychology: Research and Practice, 21*(6), 455–461.

Gottlieb, M. C. (1994). Ethical decision making, boundaries, and treatment effectiveness: A reprise. *Ethics and Behavior, 4*(3), 287–293.

Gray, L. A., & Harding, A. I. (1988). Confidentiality limits with clients who have the AIDS virus. *Journal of Counseling and Development, 66*(5), 219–223.

Greenhut, M. (1991, May/June). Professional networking: The downward spiral to "health." *The California Therapist*, pp. 47–48.

Greenspan, M. (1994). On professionalism. In C. Heyward, *When boundaries betray us* (pp. 193–205). San Francisco: HarperCollins.

Greenspan, M. (1995, July/August). Out of bounds. *Common Boundary*, pp. 51–54.

Grimm, D. W. (1994). Therapist spiritual and religious values in psychotherapy. *Counseling and Values, 38*(3), 154–164.
Guest, C. L., & Dooley, K. (1999). Supervisor malpractice: Liability to the supervisee in clinical supervision. *Counselor Education and Supervision, 38*(4), 269–279.
Gutheil, T G. (1989, November/December). Patient-therapist sexual relations. *The California Therapist*, pp. 29–31.
Gutheil, T. G. (1994). Discussion of Lazarus's "How certain boundaries and ethics diminish therapeutic effectiveness." *Ethics and Behavior, 4*(3), 295–298.
Gutheil, T. G., & Gabbard, G. O. (1993). The concept of boundaries in clinical practice: Theoretical and risk-management dimensions. *American Journal of Psychiatry, 150*(2), 188–196.
Guy, J. D. (1987). *The personal life of the psychotherapists.* New York: Wiley.
Guy, J. D. (2000). Holding the holding environment together: Self-psychology and psychotherapist care. *Professional Psychology: Research and Practice, 31*(3), 351–352.
Guy, J. D., & Liaboe, G. P. (1986a). The impact of conducting psychotherapy upon the interpersonal relationships of the psychotherapist. *Professional Psychology: Research and Practice, 17*(2), 111–114.
Guy, J. D., & Liaboe, G. P. (1986b). Personal therapy for the experienced psychotherapist: A discussion of its usefulness and utilization. *The Clinical Psychologist, 39*(l), 20–23.
Haas, L. J., & Cummings, N. A. (1991). Managed outpatient mental health plans: Clinical, ethical, and practical guidelines for participation. *Professional Psychology: Research and Practice, 22*(1), 45–51.
Hall, L. A. (1996). Bartering: A payment methodology whose time has come again or an unethical practice? *Family Therapy News, 27*(4), 7, 19.
Hamann, E. E. (1994). Clinicians and diagnosis: Ethical concerns and clinical competence. *Journal of Counseling and Development, 72*(3), 259–260.
Hamilton, J. C., & Spruill, J. (1999). Identifying and reducing risk factors related to trainee-client sexual misconduct. *Professional Psychology: Research and Practice, 30*(3), 318–327.
Hammel, G. A., Olkin, R., & Taube, D. O. (1996). Student-educator sex in clinical and counseling psychology doctoral training. *Professional Psychology: Research and Practice, 27*(1), 93–97.
Hanna, S. M., & Brown, J. H. (1999). *The practice of family therapy: Key elements across models* (2nd ed.). Pacific Grove, CA: Brooks/Cole.
Hansen, N. D., & Goldberg, S. G. (1999). Navigating the nuances: A matrix of considerations for ethical-legal dilemmas. *Professional Psychology: Research and Practice, 30*(5), 495–503.
Hansen, N. D., Pepitone-Arreola-Rockwell, E., & Greene A. F. (2000). Multicultural competence: Criteria and case example. *Professional Psychology: Research and Practice, 31*(6), 652–660.
Harrar, W. R., VandeCreek, L., & Knapp, S. (1990). Ethical and legal aspects of clinical supervision. *Professional Psychology: Research and Practice, 21*(1), 37–41.
Harris, S. M. (2001). Teaching family therapists about sexual attraction in therapy. *Journal of Marital and Family Therapy, 27*(1),123–128.
Harris, S. M., & Busby, D. M. (1998). Therapist physical attractiveness: An unexplored influence on client disclosure. *Journal of Marital and Family Therapy, 24*(2), 251–257.
Hatherleigh guide to ethics in therapy. (1997). New York: Hatherleigh Press.
Hedges, L. E. (1993, July/August). In praise of dual relationships. Part II: Essential dual relatedness in developmental psychotherapy. *The California Therapist*, pp. 42–46.
Hedlund v. Superior Court, 34 Cal. 3d 695, 669, P.2d 41 (1983).
Heiden, J. M. (1993). Preview-prevent: A training strategy to prevent counselor-client sexual relationships. *Counselor Education and Supervision, 33*(1), 53–60.
Heller, P. E., & Wood, B. (2000). The influence of religious and ethnic differences on marital intimacy: Intermarriage versus intramarriage. *Journal of Marital and Family Therapy, 26*(2), 241–252.

Hering, N. (2000). Managed care: Notes from the underground. *The California Therapist, 12*(4), 36–38.

Herlihy, B. (1996). When a colleague is impaired: The individual counselor's response. *Journal of Humanistic Education and Development, 34,* 118–127.

Herlihy, B., & Corey, G. (1994). Codes of ethics as catalysts for improving practice. *Ethical Issues in Professional Counseling, 2*(3), 2–12.

*Herlihy, B., & Corey, G. (Eds.). (1996a). *ACA Ethical standards casebook* (5th ed.). Alexandria, VA: American Counseling Association.

Herlihy, B., & Corey, G. (1996b). Confidentiality. In B. Herlihy & G. Corey (Eds.), *ACA ethical standards casebook* (5th ed., pp. 205–209). Alexandria, VA: American Counseling Association.

Herlihy, B., & Corey, G. (1996c). Working with multiple clients. In B. Herlihy & G. Corey (Eds.), *ACA ethical standards casebook* (5th ed., pp. 229–233). Alexandria, VA: American Counseling Association.

*Herlihy, B., & Corey, G. (1997). *Boundary issues in counseling: Multiple roles and responsibilities.* Alexandria, VA: American Counseling Association.

Herlihy, B., & Remley, T. P. (1995). Unified ethical standards: A challenge for professionalism. *Journal of Counseling and Development, 74*(2), 130–133.

Hermann, M. A. (2001). *Legal issues in counseling: Incidence, preparation, and consultation.* Doctoral dissertation, University of New Orleans.

Hermann, M. A., & Remley, T. P. (2000). Guns, violence, and schools: The results of school violence—litigation against educators and students shedding more constitutional rights at the school house gate. *Loyola Law Review, 46*(2), 389–439.

Herr, E. L. (1991). Challenges to mental health counselors in a dynamic society: Macrostrategies in the profession. *Journal of Mental Health Counseling, 13*(1), 6–20.

Hersch, L. (1995). Adapting to health care reform and managed care: Three strategies for survival and growth. *Professional Psychology: Research and Practice, 26*(1), 16–26.

*Hill, M., Glaser, K., & Harden, J. (1995). A feminist model for ethical decision making. In E. J. Rave & C. C. Larsen (Eds.), *Ethical decision making in therapy: Feminist perspectives* (pp. 18–37). New York: Guilford Press.

Hinnefeld, B., & Towers, K. D. (1996). Supreme Court ruling upholds psychotherapist-patient privilege. *Practitioner Focus, 9*(2), 4, 18.

Hoffman, M. A. (1991a). Counseling the HIV-infected client: A psychosocial model for assessment and intervention. *The Counseling Psychologist, 19*(4), 467–542.

Hoffman, M. A. (1991b). Training mental health counselors for the AIDS crisis. *Journal of Mental Health Counseling, 13*(2), 264–269.

Hogan-Garcia, M. (1999). *The four skills of cultural diversity competence: A process for understanding and practice.* Pacific Grove, CA: Brooks/Cole.

*Hogan-Garcia, M., & Scheinberg, C. (2000). Culturally competent practice principles for planned intervention in organizations and communities. *Practicing Anthropology, 22*(2), 27–29.

Holmes, J. (1996). Values in psychotherapy. *American Journal of Psychotherapy, 50*(3), 259–273.

Holroyd, J., & Bouhoutsos, J. C. (1985). Sources of bias in reporting effects of sexual contact with patients. *Professional Psychology: Research and Practice, 16*(5), 701–709.

Holub, E. A., & Lee, S. S. (1990). Therapists' use of nonerotic physical contact: Ethical concerns. *Professional Psychology: Research and Practice, 21*(2), 115–117.

Holzman, L. A., Searight, H. R., & Hughes, H. M. (1996). Clinical psychology graduate students and personal psychotherapy: Results of an exploratory study. *Professional Psychology: Research and Practice, 27*(1), 98–101.

*Homan, M. (1999a). *Promoting community change: Making it happen in the real world* (2nd ed.). Pacific Grove, CA: Brooks/Cole.

Homan, M. (1999b). *Rules of the game: Lessons from the field of community change.* Pacific Grove, CA: Brooks/Cole.

Hosie, T. W. (1995). Counseling specialties: A case of basic preparation rather than advanced specialization. *Journal of Counseling and Development, 74*(2), 177–180.

Hotelling, K. (1988). Ethical, legal, and administrative options to address sexual relationships between counselor and client. *Journal of Counseling and Development, 67*(4), 233–237.

Hotelling, K. (1991). Sexual harassment: A problem shielded by silence. *Journal of Counseling and Development, 69*(6), 497–501.

Housman, L. M., & Stake, J. E. (1999). The current state of sexual ethics training in clinical psychology: Issues of quantity, quality, and effectiveness. *Professional Psychology: Research and Practice, 30*(3), 302–311.

Howard, S. (1991). Organizational resources for addressing sexual harassment. *Journal of Counseling and Development, 69*(6), 507–511.

Huber, C. H. (1994). *Ethical, legal, and professional issues in the practice of marriage and family therapy* (2nd ed.). New York: Macmillan.

Humphreys, K., Winzelberg, A., & Klaw, E. (2000). Psychologists' ethical responsibilities in Internet-based groups: Issues, strategies, and a call for dialogue. *Professional Psychology: Research and Practice, 31*(5), 493–496.

*Hwang, P. O. (1995). *Other-esteem: A creative response to a society obsessed with promoting the self.* San Diego, CA: Black Forrest Press.

Ibrahim, E. A., & Arredondo, R M. (1990). Ethical issues in multicultural counseling. In B. Herlihy & L. B. Golden (Eds.), *AACD ethical standards casebook* (4th ed., pp. 137–145). Alexandria, VA: American Association for Counseling and Development.

Imber, S. D., Glanz, L. M., Elkin, I., Sotsky, S. M., Boyer, J. L., & Leber, W. R. (1986). Ethical issues in psychotherapy research: Problems in a collaborative clinical trials study. *American Psychologist, 41*(2), 137–146.

International Association for Marriage and Family Counselors. (2000). Ethical code for International Association for Marriage and Family Counselors. *The Family Journal, 1*, 73–77.

Isaacs, M. L. (1997). The duty to warn and protect: *Tarasoff* and the elementary school counselor. *Elementary School Guidance and Counseling, 31*, 326–342.

Itai, G., & McRae, C. (1994). Counseling older Japanese American clients: An overview and observations. *Journal of Counseling and Development, 72*(4), 373–377.

*Ivey, A. E., & Ivey, M. B. (1998). Reframing DSM-IV: Positive strategies from developmental counseling and therapy. *Journal of Counseling and Development, 76*(3), 334–350.

Ivey, A. E., & Ivey, M. B. (1999). Toward a developmental diagnostic and statistical manual: The vitality of a contextual framework. *Journal of Counseling and Development, 77*(4), 484–490.

Ivey, A. E., D'Andrea, M., Ivey, M. B., & Simek-Morgan, L. (2002). *Theories of counseling and psychotherapy: A multicultural perspective* (5th ed.). Boston: Allyn & Bacon.

*Ivey, A. E., Pedersen, P. B., & Ivey, M. B. (2001). *Intentional group counseling: A microskills approach.* Pacific Grove, CA: Brooks/Cole.

Ivey, A. E., & Rigazio-DiGilio, S. A. (1991). Toward a developmental practice of mental health counseling. Strategies for training, practice, and political unity. *Journal of Mental Health Counseling, 13*(1), 21–36.

Jablonski v. United States, 712 F.2d 391 (9th Cir. 1983).

Jackson, D. N., & Hayes, D. H. (1993). Multicultural issues in consultation. *Journal of Counseling and Development, 72*(2), 144–147.

Jackson, H., & Nuttall, R. L. (2001). A relationship between childhood sexual abuse and professional sexual misconduct. *Professional Psychology: Research and Practice, 32*(2), 200–204.

Jaffee v. Redmond, WL 315 841 (U.S. 1996).

Jeffords, J. M. (1999). Confidentiality of medical information: Protecting privacy in an electronic age. *Professional Psychology: Research and Practice, 30*(2), 115–116.

Jensen, J. P., & Bergin, A. E. (1988). Mental health values of professional therapists: A national interdisciplinary survey. *Professional Psychology: Research and Practice, 19*(3), 290–297.

Jones, C. L., & Higuchi, A. (1996). Landmark New Jersey lawsuit challenges "no cause" termination. *Practitioner Focus, 9*(2), 1, 13.

Jordan, A. E., & Meara, N. M. (1990). Ethics and the professional practice of psychologists: The role of virtues and principles. *Professional Psychology: Research and Practice, 21*(2), 107–114.

Jourard, S. (1968). *Disclosing man to himself.* Princeton, NJ: Van Nostrand.

Jourard, S. (1971). *The transparent self* (rev. ed.). New York: Van Nostrand.

*Kain, C. D. (1996). *Positive HIV affirmative counseling.* Alexandria, VA: American Counseling Association.

Kaiser, T. L. (1997). *Supervisory relationships: Exploring the human element.* Pacific Grove, CA: Brooks/Cole.

Kalichman, S. C., & Craig, M. E. (1991). Professional psychologists' decisions to report suspected child abuse: Clinician and situation influences. *Professional Psychology: Research and Practice, 22*(1), 84–89.

Kaplan, D. M. (2000). Using an informed consent brochure to help establish a solid therapeutic relationship. In R. E. Watts (Ed.), *Techniques in marriage and family counseling: Volume One* (pp. 3–10). Alexandria, VA: American Counseling Association.

Karon, B. P. (1995). Provision of psychotherapy under managed health care: A growing crisis and national nightmare. *Professional Psychology: Research and Practice, 26*(1), 5–9.

Keith-Spiegel, P., & Koocher, G. (1985). *Ethics in psychology: Professional standards and cases.* New York: Random House.

Kelly, E. W. (1995a). Counselor values: A national survey. *Journal of Counseling and Development, 73*(6), 648–653.

Kelly, E. W. (1995b). *Spirituality and religion in counseling and psychotherapy.* Alexandria, VA: American Counseling Association.

King, K. A., Price, J. H., Telljohann, S. K., & Wahl, J. (1999). How confident do high school counselors feel in recognizing students at risk for suicide? *American Journal of Health Behavior, 23,* 457–467.

King, K. A., Price, J. H., Telljohann, S. K., & Wahl, J. (2000). Preventing adolescent suicide: Do high school counselors know the risk factors? *Professional School Counseling, 3,* 255–263.

Kiser, J. D. (1996). Counselors and the legalization of physician-assisted suicide. *Counseling and Values, 40*(2), 127–131.

Kiser, J. D., & Korpi, K. N. (1996). The need for ethical reasoning regarding physician-assisted suicide. *Counseling Today,* p. 28.

Kitchener, K. S. (1984). Intuition, critical evaluation and ethical principles: The foundation for ethical decisions in counseling psychology. *The Counseling Psychologist, 12*(3), 43–55.

Kitchener, K. S., & Harding, S. S. (1990). Dual role relationships. In B. Herlihy & L. B. Golden (Eds.), *AACD ethical standards casebook* (4th ed., pp. 146–154). Alexandria, VA: American Association for Counseling and Development.

Knapp, S., & VandeCreek, L. (1982). *Tarasoff.* Five years later. *Professional Psychology, 13*(4), 511–516.

Knapp, S., & VandeCreek, L. (1990). Application of the duty to protect to HIV-positive patients. *Professional Psychology: Research and Practice, 21*(3), 161–166.

Knapp, S., & VandeCreek, L. (1997). *Jaffee v. Redmond:* The Supreme Court recognizes a psychotherapist-patient privilege in federal courts. *Professional Psychology: Research and Practice, 28*(6), 567–572.

Koocher, G. P., & Morray, E. (2000). Regulation of telepsychology: A survey of state attorneys general. *Professional Psychology: Research and Practice, 31*(5), 503–508.

Kramen-Kahn, B., & Hansen, N. D. (1998). Rafting the rapids: Occupational hazards, rewards, and coping strategies of psychotherapists. *Professional Psychology: Research and Practice, 29*(2), 130–134.

Kramer, S. A. (1990). *Positive endings in psychotherapy: Bringing meaningful closure to therapeutic relationships.* San Francisco: Jossey-Bass.

Kremer, T. G., & Gesten, E. L. (1998). Confidentiality limits of managed care and clients' willingness to self-disclose. *Professional Psychology: Research and Practice, 29*(6), 553–558.

*Ladany, N., Lehrman-Waterman, D., Molinaro, M., & Wolgast, B. (1999). Psychotherapy supervisor ethical practices: Adherence to guidelines, the supervisory working alliance, and supervisee satisfaction. *The Counseling Psychologist, 27*(3), 443–475.

Lamb, D. H., & Catanzaro, S. J. (1998). Sexual and nonsexual boundary violations involving psychologists, clients, supervisees, and students: Implications for professional practice. *Professional Psychology: Research and Practice, 29*(5), 498–503.

Lamb, D. H., Clark, C., Drumheller, P., Frizzell, K., & Surrey, L. (1989). Applying *Tarasoff* to AIDS-related psychotherapy issues. *Professional Psychology: Research and Practice, 20*(1), 37–43.

Lamb, D. H., Cochran, D. J., & Jackson, V. R. (1991). Training and organizational issues associated with identifying and responding to intern impairment. *Professional Psychology: Research and Practice, 22,* 291–296.

Lambert, M. J., & Cattani-Thompson, K. (1996). Current findings regarding the effectiveness of counseling: Implications for practice. *Journal of Counseling and Development, 74*(6), 601–608.

Lanning, W. (1997). Ethical codes and responsible decision-making. In J. A. Kottler (Ed.), *Finding your way as a counselor* (pp. 111–113). Alexandria, VA: American Counseling Association.

Laughran, W., & Bakken, G. M. (1984). The psychotherapist's responsibility toward third parties under current California law. *Western State University Law Review, 12*(1), 1–33.

Lawrence, G., & Kurpius, S. E. R. (2000). Legal and ethical issues involved when counseling minors in nonschool settings. *Journal of Counseling and Development, 78*(2), 130–136.

Lazarus, A. A. (1990). Can psychotherapists transcend the shackles of their training and superstitions? *Journal of Clinical Psychology, 4*(3), 351–358.

*Lazarus, A. A. (1994a). How certain boundaries and ethics diminish therapeutic effectiveness. *Ethics and Behavior, 4*(3), 255–261.

Lazarus, A. A. (1994b). The illusion of the therapist's power and the patient's fragility: My rejoinder. *Ethics and Behavior, 4*(3), 299–306.

Lazarus, A. A. (1998). How do you like these boundaries? *The Clinical Psychologist, 51*(1), 22–25.

Lazarus, A. A. (2000). Multimodal replenishment. *Professional Psychology: Research and Practice, 31*(1), 93–94.

Lazarus, A. A. (2001). Not all "dual relationships" are taboo: Some tend to enhance treatment outcomes. *The National Psychologist, 10*(1), 16.

Lee, C. C. (1997a). Cultural dynamics: Their importance in culturally responsive counseling. In C. C. Lee (Ed.), *Multicultural issues in counseling: New approaches to diversity* (pp. 15–30). Alexandria, VA: American Counseling Association.

Lee, C. C. (1997b). New approaches to diversity: Implications for professional counselor training and research. In C. C. Lee (Ed.), *Multicultural issues in counseling: New approaches to diversity* (pp. 353–360). Alexandria, VA: American Counseling Association.

Lee, C. C. (1997c). The promise and pitfalls of multicultural counseling. In C. C. Lee (Ed.), *Multicultural issues in counseling: New approachs to diversity* (pp. 3–13). Alexandria, VA: American Counseling Association.

Lee, C. C., & Kurilla, V. (1997). Ethics and multiculturalism: The challenge of diversity. In *The Hatherleigh guide to ethics in therapy* (pp. 235–248). New York: Hatherleigh Press.

Lee, W. M. L. (1999). *An introduction to multicultural counseling*. Philadelphia, PA: Accelerated Development (Taylor & Francis Group).

Lewis, G. J., Greenburg, S. L., & Hatch, D. B. (1988). Peer consultation groups for psychologists in private practice: A national survey. *Professional Psychology: Research and Practice, 19*(1), 81–86.

*Lewis, J. A., Lewis, M. D., Daniels, J. A., & D'Andrea, M. J. (1998). *Community counseling: Empowerment strategies for a diverse society* (2nd ed.). Pacific Grove, CA: Brooks/Cole.

Lindsey, R. I. (1984). Informed consent and deception in psychotherapy research: An ethical analysis. *The Counseling Psychologist, 12*(3), 79–86.

Locke, D. C. (1990). A not so provincial view of multicultural counseling. *Counselor Education and Supervision, 30*(1), 18–25.

Loewenberg, E., & Dolgoff, R. (1992). *Ethical decisions for social work practice* (4th ed.). Itasca, IL: F. E. Peacock.

Lum, D. (1999). *Culturally competent practice: A framework for growth and action.* Pacific Grove, CA: Brooks/Cole.

*Lum, D. (2000). *Social work practice and people of color. A process-stage approach* (4th ed.). Pacific Grove, CA: Brooks/Cole.

Lumadue, C. A., & Duffey, T. H. (1999). The role of graduate programs as gatekeepers: A model for evaluating student counselor competence. *Counselor Education and Supervision, 39*(2), 101–109.

*Lynch, V. J. (2000). *HIV/AIDS at year 2000: A sourcebook for social workers.* Boston, MA: Allyn & Bacon.

Mabe, A. R., & Rollin, S. A. (1986). The role of a code of ethical standards in counseling. *Journal of Counseling and Development, 64*(5), 294–297.

*MacCluskie, K. C., & Ingersoll, R. E. (2001). *Becoming a 21st century agency counselor: Personal and professional explorations.* Pacific Grove, CA: Brooks/Cole.

Maheu, M. M., & Gordon, B. L. (2000). Counseling and therapy on the Internet. *Professional Psychology: Research and Practice, 31*(5), 484–489.

Mahrer, A. R. (2000). How to use psychotherapy on, for and by oneself. *Professional Psychology: Research and Practice, 31*(2), 226–229.

Malley, P. B., & Reilly, E. P. (1999). *Legal and ethical dimensions for mental health professionals.* Philadelphia, PA: Accelerated Development (Taylor & Francis).

Mappes, D. C., Robb, G. P., & Engels, D. W. (1985). Conflicts between ethics and law in counseling and psychotherapy. *Journal of Counseling and Development, 64*(4), 246–252.

Margolin, G. (1982). Ethical and legal considerations in marital and family therapy. *American Psychologist, 37*(7), 788–801.

Markowitz, L. M. (1994). The cross-currents of multiculturalism. *The Family Therapy Networker, 18*(4), 18–69.

Martin, S. (1999). Revision of ethics code calls for stronger former client sex rule. *APA Monitor, 30*(7), 44.

*Maslach, C., & Leiter, M P. (1997). *The truth about burnout.* San Francisco: Jossey-Bass.

McCarthy, P., Sugden, S., Koker, M., Lamendola, F., Maurer, S., & Renninger, S. (1995). A practical guide to informed consent in clinical supervision. *Counselor Education and Supervision, 35*(2), 130–138.

McGrath, P., & Axelson, J. A. (1999). *Assessing awareness and developing knowledge: Foundations for skill in a multicultural society* (3rd ed.). Pacific Grove, CA: Brooks/Cole.

McGuire, J., Nieri, D., Abbott, D., Sheridan, K., & Fisher, R. (1995). Do *Tarasoff* principles apply in AIDS-related psychotherapy? Ethical decision making and the role of therapist homophobia and perceived client dangerousness. *Professional Psychology: Research and Practice, 26*(6), 608–611.

McMinn, M. R., Buchanan, T., Ellens, B. M., & Ryan, M. K. (1999). Technology, professional practice, and ethics: Survey findings and implications. *Professional Psychology: Research and Practice, 30*(2), 165–172.

McMinn, M. R., Chaddock, T. P., Edwards, L. C., Lim, B. R. K. B., & Campbell, C. D. (1998). Psychologists collaborating with the clergy. *Professional Psychology: Research and Practice, 29*(6), 564–570.

Meara, N. M., Schmidt, L. D., & Day, J. D. (1996). Principles and virtues: A foundation for ethical decisions, policies, and character. *The Counseling Psychologist, 24*(1), 4–77.

Melchert, T. P., & Patterson, M. M. (1999). Duty to warn and interventions with HIV-positive clients. *Professional Psychology: Research and Practice, 30*(2), 180–186.

Melton, G. B. (1988). Ethical and legal issues in AIDS-related practice. *American Psychologist, 43*(11), 941–947.

Miars, R. (2000, November 10). *The evolution of ethical responsibility and legal liability in clinical instruction and supervision.* Presentation given at Western Association for Counselor Education and Supervision, Los Gatos, California.

Miller, G. (1999). The development of the spiritual focus in counseling and counselor education. *Journal of Counseling and Development, 77*(4), 498–501.

Miller, G. M., & Larrabee, M. J. (1995). Sexual intimacy in counselor education and supervision: A national survey. *Counselor Education and Supervision, 34*(4), 332–343.

Miller, G. M., & Wooten, H. R. (1995). Sports counseling: A new counseling specialty area. *Journal of Counseling and Development, 74*(2), 172–173.

Miller, I. J. (1996a). Ethical and liability issues concerning invisible rationing. *Professional Psychology: Research and Practice, 27*(6), 583–587.

Miller, I. J. (1996b). Managed health care is harmful to outpatient mental health services: A call for accountability. *Professional Psychology: Research and Practice, 27*(4), 349–363.

Miller, I. J. (1996c). Time-limited brief therapy has gone too far: The result is invisible rationing. *Professional Psychology: Research and Practice, 27*(6), 567–576.

Miller, I. J. (1996d). Some "short-term therapy values" are a formula for invisible rationing. *Professional Psychology: Research and Practice, 27*(6), 577–582.

Miller, W. R. (Ed.). (1999). *Integrating spirituality into treatment: Resources for practitioners.* Washington, DC: American Psychological Association.

Miranti, J., & Burke, M. T. (1995). Spirituality: An integral component of the counseling process. In M. T. Burke & J. G. Miranti (Eds.), *Counseling: The spiritual dimension* (pp. 1–3). Alexandria, VA: American Counseling Association.

Moline, M. E., Williams, G. T., & Austin, K. M. (1998). *Documenting psychotherapy: Essentials for mental health practitioners.* Thousand Oaks, CA: Sage.

Monahan, J. (1993). Limiting therapist exposure to *Tarasoff* liability: Guidelines for risk containment. *American Psychologist, 48*(4), 242–250.

Morrison, C. F. (1989). AIDS: Ethical implications for psychological intervention. *Professional Psychology: Research and Practice, 20*(3), 166–171.

Morrissey, M. (1996). Supreme Court extends confidentiality privilege. *Counseling Today,* pp. 1, 6, 10.

Myers, J. E., Sweeney, T. J., & Witmer, J. M. (2000). The wheel of wellness counseling for wellness: A holistic model. *Journal of Counseling and Development, 78*(3), 251–266.

*Nagy, T. F. (2000). *Ethics in plain English: An illustrative casebook for psychologists.* Washington, DC: American Psychological Association.

National Association of Social Workers. (1994a). Client self-determination in end-of-life decisions. *Social Work Speaks: NASW Policy Statements* (3rd ed., pp. 58–61). Washington, DC: Author.

National Association of Social Workers. (1994b). *Guidelines for clinical social work supervision.* Washington, DC: Author.

National Association of Social Workers. (1999). *Code of ethics.* Washington, DC: Author.

National Board for Certified Counselors. (1997). Standards for the ethical practice of webcounseling. *NBCC NewNotes, 14*(2), 3–4.

National Board for Certified Counselors. (1999). *NBCC standards for the ethical practice of clinical supervision.* Greensboro, NC: Author.

National Organization for Human Service Education. (2000). *Ethical standards of the National Organization for Human Service Education.* Author.

Neimeyer, R. A. (2000). Suicide and hastened death: Toward a training agenda for counseling psychology. *The Counseling Psychologist, 28*(4), 551–560.

Nessman, A., & Herndon, P. (2000, December). New Jersey settlement offers strong protections for psychologists. *Monitor on Psychology, 31*(11), 20–21.

Neufeldt, S. A. (1999). *Supervision strategies for the first practicum* (2nd ed.). Alexandria, VA: American Counseling Association.

Newman, J. L. (1993). Ethical issues in consultation. *Journal of Counseling and Development, 72*(2), 148–156.

Newman, R. (1996). Supreme Court affirms privilege. *APA Monitor, 27*(8), 44.

Newman, R., & Bricklin, P. M. (1991). Parameters of managed mental health care: Legal, ethical, and professional guidelines. *Professional Psychology: Research and Practice, 22*(1), 26–35.

Nichols, M. P., & Schwartz, R. C. (1998). *Family therapy: Concepts and methods* (4th ed.). Boston: Allyn & Bacon.

Nicolai, K. M., & Scott, N. A. (1994). Provision of confidentiality information and its relation to child abuse reporting. *Professional Psychology: Research and Practice, 25*(2), 154–160.

Nuttall, E. V., Webber, J. J., & Sanchez, W. (1996). MCT theory and implications for training. In D. W. Sue, A. E. Ivey, & P. B. Pedersen (Eds.), *A theory of multicultural counseling and therapy.* Pacific Grove, CA: Brooks/Cole.

Okun, B. F., Fried, J., & Okun, M. L. (1999). *Understanding diversity: A learning-as-practice primer.* Pacific Grove, CA: Brooks/Cole.

Olarte, S. W. (1997). Sexual boundary violations. In *The Hatherleigh guide to ethics in therapy* (pp. 195–209). New York: Hatherleigh Press.

*O'Laughlin, M. J. (2001). Dr. Strangelove: Therapist-client dual relationship bans and freedom of association, or how I learned to stop worrying and love my clients. *University of Missouri-Kansas City School of Law Review, 69*(30), 697–731.

Orr, P. (1997). Psychology impaired? *Professional Psychology: Research and Practice, 28*(3), 293–296.

Overholser, J. C. (1991). The Socratic method as a technique in psychotherapy supervision. *Professional Psychology: Research and Practice, 22*(1), 68–74.

Paradise, L. V., & Siegelwaks, B. (1982). Ethical training for group leaders. *Journal for Specialists in Group Work, 7*(3), 162–166.

Patterson, C. H. (1985a). New light for counseling theory. *Journal of Counseling and Development, 63*(6), 349–350.

Patterson, C. H. (1985b). *The therapeutic relationship: Foundations for an eclectic psychotherapy.* Pacific Grove, CA: Brooks/Cole.

Patterson, C. H. (1996). Multicultural counseling: From diversity to universality. *Journal of Counseling and Development, 74*(3), 227–231.

Pedersen, P. (1991). Multiculturalism as a generic approach to counseling. *Journal of Counseling and Development, 70*(1), 6–12.

Pedersen, P. (1994). *A handbook for developing multicultural awareness* (2nd ed.). Alexandria, VA: American Counseling Association.

Pedersen, P. (1999). Training counselors to hear the self-talk of culturally different clients. *Directions in Mental Health Counseling, 9*(8), 91–102.

*Pedersen, P. (2000). *A handbook for developing multicultural awareness* (3rd ed.). Alexandria, VA: American Counseling Association.

Perlin, M. L. (1997). The "duty to protect" others from violence. In *The Hatherleigh guide to ethics in therapy* (pp. 127–146). New York: Hatherleigh Press.

Peruzzi, N., & Bongar, B. (1999). Assessing risk for completed suicide in patients with major depression: Psychologists' views of critical factors. *Professional Psychology: Research and Practice, 30*(6), 576–580.

Phillips, D. G. (1997). Legal and ethical issues in the era of managed care. In R. M. Alperin & D. G. Phillips (Eds.), *The impact of managed care on the practice of psychotherapy: Innovation, implementation, and controversy* (pp. 171–184). New York: Brunner/Mazel.

Plante, T. G. (1999). A collaborative relationship between professional psychology and the Roman Catholic church: A case example and suggested principles for success. *Professional Psychology: Research and Practice, 30*(6), 541–546.

Polanski, P. (2000). Training supervisors at the masters level: Developmental consideration. *ACES Spectrum Newsletter, 61*(2), 3–5.

Pope, K. S. (1985a, April). Dual relationships: A violation of ethical, legal, and clinical standards. *California State Psychologist, 20*(3), 3–5.

Pope, K. S. (1985b, July/August). The suicidal client: Guidelines for assessment and treatment. *California State Psychologist, 20*(5), 3–7.

Pope, K. S. (1987). Preventing therapist-patient sexual intimacy: Therapy for a therapist at risk. *Professional Psychology: Research and Practice, 18*(6), 624–628.

Pope, K. S. (1988). How clients are harmed by sexual contact with mental health professionals: The syndrome and its prevalence. *Journal of Counseling and Development, 67*(4), 222–226.

Pope, K. S., Keith-Spiegel, P., & Tabachnick, B. G. (1986). Sexual attraction to clients: The human therapist and the (sometimes) inhuman training system. *American Psychologist, 41*(2), 147–158.

*Pope, K. S., Sonne, J. L., & Holroyd, J. (1993). *Sexual feelings in psychotherapy: Explorations for therapists and therapists-in-training.* Washington, DC: American Psychological Association.

Pope, K. S., & Tabachnick, B. G. (1994). Therapists as patients: A national survey of psychologists' experiences, problems, and beliefs. *Professional Psychology: Research and Practice, 25*(3), 247–258.

*Pope, K. S., & Vasquez, M. J. T. (1998). *Ethics in psychotherapy and counseling: A practical guide for psychologists* (2nd ed.). San Francisco: Jossey-Bass.

*Porter, N., & Vasquez, M. (1997). Covision: Feminist supervision, process, and collaboration. In J. Worell & N. G. Johnson (Eds.), *Shaping the future of feminist psychology: Education, research, and practice* (pp. 155–171). Washington, DC: American Psychological Association.

Priest, R. (1994). Minority supervisor and majority supervisee: Another perspective of clinical reality. *Counselor Education and Supervision, 34*(2), 152–158.

Rabasca, L. (2000a). Self-help sites: A blessing or a bane? *Monitor on Psychology, 31*(4), 28–30.

Rabasca, L. (2000b). Taking telehealth to the next step. *Monitor on Psychology, 31*(4), 36–37.

Rabinowitz, E. E. (1991). The male-to-male-embrace: Breaking the touch taboo in a men's therapy group. *Journal of Counseling and Development, 69*(6), 574–576.

Radeke, J. T., & Mahoney, M. J. (2000). Comparing the personal lives of psychotherapists and research psychologists. *Professional Psychology: Research and Practice, 31*(1), 82–84.

Ray, D., & Altekruse, M. (2000). Effectiveness of group supervision versus combined group and individual supervision. *Counselor Education and Supervision, 40*(1), 19–30.

Remley, T. P. (1991). *Preparing for court appearances.* Alexandria, VA: American Association for Counseling and Development.

Remley, T. P. (1993). Consultation contracts. *Journal of Counseling and Development, 72*(2), 157–158.

Remley, T. P. (1995). A proposed alternative to the licensing of specialties in counseling. *Journal of Counseling and Development, 74*(2) 126–129.

Remley, T. P. (1996). The relationship between law and ethics. In B. Herlihy & G. Corey, (Eds.), *ACA ethical standards casebook* (5th ed., pp. 285–292). Alexandria, VA: American Counseling Association.

*Remley, T. P., & Herlihy, B. (2001). *Ethical, legal, and professional issues in counseling.* Upper Saddle River, NJ: Merrill/Prentice-Hall.

*Remley, T. P., Herlihy, B., & Herlihy, S. B. (1997). The U.S. Supreme Court decision in *Jaffee v. Redmond:* Implications for counselors. *Journal of Counseling and Development, 75*(3), 213–218.

Remley, T. P., & Hermann, M. A. (2000). Legal and ethical issues in school counseling. In J. Wittmer (Ed.), *Managing your school counseling program: K-12 developmental strategies* (pp. 314–329). Minneapolis, MN: Educational Media Corporation.

Remley, T. P., & Sparkman, L. B. (1993). Student suicides: The counselor's limited legal liability. *The School counselor, 40,* 164–169.

*Richards, P. S., & Bergin, A. E. (1997). *A spiritual strategy for counseling and psychotherapy.* Washington, DC: American Psychological Association.

*Richards, P. S., & Bergin, A. E. (Eds.). (2000). *Handbook of psychotherapy and religious diversity.* Washington, DC: American Psychological Association.

Richards, P. S., Rector, J. M., & Tjeltveit, A. C. (1999). Values, spirituality, and psychotherapy. In W. R. Miller (Ed.), *Integrating spirituality into treatment: Resources for practitioners* (pp. 133–160). Washington, DC: American Psychological Association.

Richardson, L. M., & Austad, C. S. (1991). Realities of mental health practice in managed-care settings. *Professional Psychology: Research and Practice, 22*(1), 52–59.

Richardson, T. Q., & Molinaro, K. L. (1996). White counselor self-awareness: A prerequisite for developing multicultural competence. *Journal of Counseling and Development, 74*(3), 238–242.

Ridley, C. R. (1989). Racism in counseling as an adversive behavioral process. In P. Pedersen, J. Draguns, W. Lormer, & J. Trimble (Eds.), *Counseling across cultures* (3rd ed., pp. 55–77). Honolulu: University of Hawaii Press.

Ridley, C. R. (1995). *Overcoming unintentional racism in counseling and therapy: A practitioner's guide to intentional intervention.* Thousand Oaks, CA: Sage.

Ridley, C. R., Mendoza, D. W., & Kanitz, B. E. (1994). Multicultural training: Reexamination, operationalization, and integration. *The Counseling Psychologist, 22*(2), 227–289.

Riemersma, M. (2000). What about record keeping? *The California Therapist, 12*(5), 22–24.

Riemersma, M., & Leslie, R. S. (1999). Therapy/counseling over the Internet: Innovation or unnecessary risk? *The California Therapist, 11*(6), 33–36.

Riger, S. (1991). Gender dilemmas in sexual harassment: Policies and procedures. *American Psychologist, 46*(5), 497–505.

Rivas-Vasquez, R. A., Blais, M. A., Rey, G. J., & Rivas-Vazquez, A. A. (2001). A brief reminder about documenting the psychological consultation. *Professional Psychology: Research and Practice, 32*(2), 194–199.

Rodolfa, E. R., Kitzrow, M., Vohra, S., & Wilson, B. (1990). Training interns to respond to sexual dilemmas. *Professional Psychology: Research and Practice, 21*(4), 313–315.

Rogers, C. (1961). *On becoming a person.* Boston: Houghton Mifflin.

Rogers, C. (1980). *A way of being.* Boston: Houghton Mifflin.

Rosenberg, J. I. (1999). Suicide prevention: An integrated training model using affective and action-based interventions. *Professional Psychology: Research and Practice, 30*(1), 83–87.

Rutter, P. (1989). *Sex in the forbidden zone.* Los Angeles: J. P. Tarcher.

Ryder, R., & Hepworth, J. (1990). AAMFT ethical code: "Dual relationships." *Journal of Marital and Family Therapy, 16*(2), 127–132.

Sales, B. D., & Folkman, S. (2000). *Ethics in research with human participants.* Washington, DC: American Psychological Association.

Salisbury, W. A., & Kinnier, R. T. (1996). Posttermination friendship between counselors and clients. *Journal of Counseling and Development, 74*(5), 495–500.

Sampson, J. P., Kolodinsky, R. W., & Greeno, B. P. (1997). Counseling on the information highway: Future possibilities and potential problems. *Journal of Counseling and Development, 75*(3), 203–212.

Samuel, S. E., & Gorton, G. E. (1998). National survey of psychology internship directors regarding education for prevention of psychologist-patient sexual exploitation. *Professional Psychology: Research and Practice, 29*(1), 86–90.

Sanders, J. R., & Keith-Spiegel, P. (1980). Formal and informal adjudication of ethics complaints against psychologists. *American Psychologist, 3*(12), 1096–1105.

Sapienza, B. G., & Bugental, J. F. T. (2000). Keeping our instruments finely tuned: An existential-humanistic perspective. *Professional Psychology: Research and Practice, 31*(4), 458–460.

Schaffer, S. J. (1997). Don't be aloof about record-keeping; it may be your best liability coverage. *The National Psychologist, 6*(1), 21.

Schank, J. A., & Skovholt, T. M. (1997). Dual-relationship dilemmas of rural and small-community psychologists. *Professional Psychology: Research and Practice, 28*(1), 44–49.

Seligman, L. (2001). *Systems, strategies, and skills of counseling and psychotherapy.* Upper Saddle River, NJ: Merrill/Prentice-Hall.

Seppa, N. (1996, August). Supreme Court protects patient-therapist privilege. *APA Monitor, 27*(8), 39.

Shapiro, D. E., & Schulman, C. E. (1996). Ethical and legal issues in e-mail therapy. *Ethics and Behavior, 6,* 107–124.

Sharf, R. S. (2000). *Theories of psychotherapy and counseling: Concepts and cases* (2nd ed.). Pacific Grove, CA: Brooks/Cole.

Sherry, R. (1991). Ethical issues in the conduct of supervision. *The Counseling Psychologist, 19*(4), 566–584.

Shore, K. (1996). Managed care: An alternative view. *Professional Psychology: Research and Practice, 27*(4), 323–324.

Shuman, D. W., & Foote, W. (1999). *Jaffee v. Redmond*'s impact: Life after the Supreme Court's recognition of a psychotherapist-patient privilege. *Professional Psychology: Research and Practice, 30*(5), 479–487.

Silverman, M. M. (2000). Rational suicide, hastened death, and self-destructive behaviors. *The Counseling Psychologist, 28*(4), 540–550.

Simon, R. I. (1997). Boundaries in psychotherapy: A safe place to heal. *Harvard Mental Health Letter, 13*(12), 4–5.

Simon, R. I. (1999). The suicide prevention contract: Clinical, legal, and risk management issues. *Journal of the American Academy of Psychiatry and the Law, 27*(3), 445–450.

Sinacore-Guinn, A. L. (1995). The diagnostic window: Culture- and gender-sensitive diagnosis and training. *Counselor Education and Supervision, 35*(1), 18–31.

Skorupa, J., & Agresti, A. A. (1993). Ethical beliefs about burnout and continued professional practice. *Professional Psychology: Research and Practice, 24*(3), 281–285.

*Skovholt, T. M. (2001). *The resilient practitioner: Burnout prevention and self-care strategies for counselors, therapists, teachers, and health professionals.* Boston: Allyn & Bacon.

Sleek, S. (1994, December). Ethical dilemmas plague rural practice. *APA Monitor,* pp. 26–27.

Sleek, S. (1996, April). Ensuring accuracy in clinical decisions. *APA Monitor, 26*(4), 30.

Smith, D., & Fitzpatrick, M. (1995). Patient-therapist boundary issues: An integrative review of theory and research. *Professional Psychology: Research and Practice, 26*(5), 499–506.

Smith, R. L. (1999). Client confidentiality in marriage and family counseling. In P. Stevens (Ed.), *Ethical casebook for the practice of marriage and family counseling* (pp. 83–92). Alexandria, VA: American Counseling Association.

Smith, R. L., Carlson, J., Stevens-Smith, P., & Dennison, M. (1995). Marriage and family counseling. *Journal of Counseling and Development, 74*(2), 154–157.

Smith, T. S., McGuire, J. M., Abbott, D. W, & Blau, B. I. (1991). Clinical ethical decision making: An investigation of the rationales used to justify doing less than one believes one should. *Professional Psychology: Research and Practice, 22*(3), 235–239.

Somberg, D. R., Stone, G. L., & Claiborn, C. D. (1993). Informed consent: Therapists' beliefs and practices. *Professional Psychology: Research and Practice, 24*(2), 153–159.

Sommers-Flanagan, J., & Sommers-Flanagan, R. (1995). Intake interviewing with suicidal patients: A systematic approach. *Professional Psychology: Research and Practice, 26*(1), 41–47.

Stadler, H. A. (1986a). Making hard choices: Clarifying controversial ethical issues. *Counseling and Human Development, 19*(1), 1–10.

Stadler, H. A. (1986b). To counsel or not to counsel: The ethical dilemma of dual relationships. *Journal of Counseling and Human Service Professions, 1*(1), 134–140.

Stake, J. E., & Oliver, J. (1991). Sexual contact and touching between therapist and client: A survey of psychologists' attitudes and behavior. *Professional Psychology: Research and Practice, 22*(4), 297–307.

Steenbarger, B. N., & Budman, S. H. (1996). Group psychotherapy and managed behavioral health care: Current trends and future challenges. *International Journal of Group Psychotherapy,* 46, 297–309.

Stevens, P. (Ed.). (1999). *Ethical casebook for the practice of marriage and family counseling.* Alexandria, VA: American Counseling Association.

St. Germaine, J. (1993). Dual relationships: What's wrong with them? *American Counselor, 2*(3), 25–30.

Storm, C. L. (1994). Defensive supervision: Balancing ethical responsibility with vulnerability. In G. W. Brock (Ed.), *American Association for Marriage and Family Therapy ethics casebook* (pp. 173–190). Washington, DC: American Association for Marriage and Family Therapy.

Strasburger, L. H., Jorgenson, L., & Sutherland, P. (1992). The prevention of psychotherapist sexual misconduct: Avoiding the slippery slope. *American Journal of Psychotherapy, 46,* 544–555.

Stromberg, C., & Dellinger, A. (1993, December). Malpractice and other professional liability. *The Psychologist's Legal Update.* Washington, DC: National Register of Health Service Providers in Psychology.

Stromberg, C., Schneider, J., & Joondeph, B. (1993, August). Dealing with potentially dangerous patients. *The Psychologist's Legal Update.* Washington, DC: National Register of Health Service Providers in Psychology.

Stromberg, C., and his colleagues in the Law Firm of Hogan & Hartson of Washington, DC. (1993, April). Privacy, confidentiality and privilege. *The Psychologist's Legal Update.* Washington, DC: National Register of Health Service Providers in Psychology.

Sue, D. W. (1996a). ACES endorsement of the multicultural counseling competencies: Do we have the courage? *ACES Spectrum Newsletter, 57*(1), 9–10.

Sue, D. W. (1996b). Ethical issues in multicultural counseling. In B. Herlihy & G. Corey (Eds.), *ACA ethical standards casebook* (5th ed., pp. 193–197). Alexandria, VA: American Counseling Association.

Sue, D. W. (1997a). Multicultural perspectives on multiple relationships. In B. Herlihy & G. Corey (Eds.), *Boundary issues in counseling: Multiple roles and responsibilities* (pp. 106–109). Alexandria, VA: American Counseling Association.

Sue, D. W. (1997b). Multiculturalism and discomfort: A response to Duane Brown. *ACES Spectrum Newsletter, 57*(3), 7–9.

Sue, D. W., Arredondo, P., & McDavis, R. J. (1992). Multicultural counseling competencies and standards: A call to the profession. *Journal of Counseling and Development, 70*(4), 477–486.

Sue, D. W., Bernier, J. E., Durran, A., Feinberg, L., Pedersen, P., Smith, E. J., & Nuttall, E. V. (1982). Position paper: Cross-cultural counseling competencies. *The Counseling Psychologist, 10*(2), 45–52.

*Sue, D. W., Carter, R. T., and colleagues. (1998). *Multicultural counseling competencies: Individual and organizational development.* Thousand Oaks, CA: Sage.

*Sue, D. W., Ivey, A. E., & Pedersen, P. B. (1996). *A theory of multicultural counseling and therapy.* Pacific Grove, CA: Brooks/Cole.

Sue, D. W., & Sue, D. (1985). Asian Americans and Pacific Islanders. In P. Pedersen (Ed.), *Handbook of cross-cultural counseling and therapy* (pp. 141–146). Westport, CT: Greenwood Press.

*Sue, D. W., & Sue, D. (1999). *Counseling the culturally different: Theory and practice* (3rd ed.). New York: Wiley.

Sumerel, M. B., & Borders, L. D. (1996). Addressing personal issues in supervision: Impact on counselors' experience level on various aspects of the supervisory relationship. *Counselor Education and Supervision, 35*(4), 268–286.

Summit on Spirituality. (1995, December). *Counseling Today,* p. 30.

Sweeney, T. J. (1995). Accreditation, credentialing, professionalization: The role of specialties. *Journal of Counseling and Development, 74*(2), 117–125.

Sweitzer, H. F., & King, M. A. (1999). *The successful internship: Transformation and empowerment.* Pacific Grove, CA: Brooks/Cole.

Swenson, L. C. (1997). *Psychology and law for the helping professions.* Pacific Grove, CA: Brooks/Cole.

Szasz, T. (1986). The case against suicide prevention. *American Psychologist, 41*(7), 806–812.

Tan, S. Y. (1997). The role of the psychologist in paraprofessional helping. *Professional Psychology: Research and Practice, 28*(4), 368–372.

Tarasoff v. Board of Regents of the University of California, 17 Cal. 3d 425, 551 (1976).

Thapar, v. Zezulka, 994 S. W. 2d 635 (Tex. 1999).

Tjeltveit, A. C. (2000). There is more to ethics than codes of professional ethics: Social ethics, theoretical ethics, and managed care. *The Counseling Psychologist, 28*(2), 242–252.

Tomm, K. (1993, January/February). The ethics of dual relationships. *The California Therapist,* pp. 7–19.

Totten, G., Lamb, D. H., & Reeder, G. D. (1990). *Tarasoff* and confidentiality in AIDS-related psychotherapy. *Professional Psychology: Research and Practice, 21*(3), 155–160.

Trull, T. J., & Phares, E. J. (2001). *Clinical psychology: Concepts, methods, and profession* (6th ed.). Belmont, CA: Wadsworth/Thomson Learning.

Truscott, D., Evans, J., & Mansell, S. (1995). Outpatient psychotherapy with dangerous clients: A model for clinical decision making. *Psychology: Research and Practice, 26*(5), 484–490.

Twemlow, S. W. (1997). Exploitation of patients: Themes in the psychopathology of their therapists. *American Journal of Psychotherapy, 51*(3), 357–375.

Tyler, J. M., & Tyler, C. L. (1997). Ethics in supervision: Managing supervisee rights and supervisor responsibilities. In *The Hatherleigh guide to ethics in therapy* (pp. 75–95). New York: Hatherleigh Press.

Tymchuk, A. J. (1981). Ethical decision making and psychological treatment. *Journal of Psychiatric Treatment and Evaluation, 3,* 507–513.

VandeCreek, L., & Knapp, S. (1994). Ethical and legal issues. In F. M. Dattilio & A. Freeman (Eds.), *Cognitive-behavioral strategies in crisis intervention* (pp. 362–373). New York: Guilford Press.

VandenBos, G. R., & Williams, S. (2000). The Internet versus the telephone: What is telehealth, anyway? *Professional Psychology: Research and Practice, 31*(5), 490–492.

Van Wormer, K., Wells, J., & Boes, M. (2000). *Social work with lesbians, gays and bisexuals: A strengths perspective.* Boston, MA: Allyn & Bacon.

Vasquez, M. J. T. (1988). Counselor-client sexual contact: Implications for ethics training. *Journal of Counseling and Development, 67*(4), 238–241.

Vasquez, M. J. T. (1992). Psychologist as clinical supervisor: Promoting ethical practice. *Professional Psychology: Research and Practice, 23*(3), 196–202.

*Vontress, C. E., Johnson, J. A., & Epp, L. R. (1999). *Cross-cultural counseling: A casebook.* Alexandria, VA: American Counseling Association.

*Walden, S. L. (1997). The counselor/client partnership in ethical practice. In B. Herlihy & G. Corey (Eds.), *Boundary issues in counseling: Multiple roles and responsibilities* (pp. 40–47). Alexandria, VA: American Counseling Association.

Waldo, S. L., & Malley, P. (1992). *Tarasoff* and its progeny: Implications for the school counselor. *The School Counselor, 40*, 46–54.

Wallace, W. A., & Hall, D. L. (1996). *Psychological consultation: Perspectives and applications.* Pacific Grove, CA: Brooks/Cole.

Watkins, C. E. (1985). Countertransference: Its impact on the counseling situation. *Journal of Counseling and Development, 63*(6), 356–359.

Weinrach, S. G., & Thomas, K. R. (1996). The counseling profession's commitment to diversity-sensitive counseling: A critical reassessment. *Journal of Counseling and Development, 74*(5), 472–477.

*Weinrach, S. G., & Thomas, K. R. (1998). Diversity-sensitive counseling today: A postmodern clash of values. *Journal of Counseling and Development, 76*(2), 115–122.

*Welfel, E. R. (2002). *Ethics in counseling and psychotherapy: Standards, research, and emerging issues* (2nd ed.). Pacific Grove, CA: Brooks/Cole.

Werth, J. L. (1996). *Rational suicide? Implications for mental health professionals.* Washington, DC: Taylor & Francis.

Werth, J. L., & Carney, J. (1994). Incorporating HIV-related issues into graduate student training. *Professional Psychology: Research and Practice, 25*(4), 458–465.

*Werth, J. L., & Holdwick, D. J. (2000). A primer on rational suicide and other forms of hastened death. *The Counseling Psychologist, 28*(4), 511–539.

Wheeler, N., & Bertram, B. (1994). Legal aspects of counseling: Avoiding lawsuits and legal problems. (Workshop material and video seminar). Alexandria, VA: American Counseling Association.

Whiston, S. C., & Emerson, S. (1989). Ethical implications for supervisors in counseling of trainees. *Counselor Education and Supervision, 28*(4), 318–325.

Wiederman, M. W., & Sansone, R. A. (1999). Sexuality training for professional psychologists: A national survey of training directors of doctoral programs and predoctoral internships. *Professional Psychology: Research and Practice, 30*(3), 312–317.

Williams, M. H. (2000). Victimized by "victims": A taxonomy of antecedents of false complaints against psychologists. *Professional Psychology: Research and Practice, 31*(1), 75–81.

Wineburgh, M. (1998). Ethics, managed care, and outpatient psychotherapy. *Clinical Social Work Journal, 26*(4), 433–443.

Wittmer, J., & Remley, T. P., Jr. (1994, Summer). A counselor-client contract, *NBCC News-Notes, 11*(1), 12.

Woodside, M., & McClam, T. (1998). *An introduction to human services.* Pacific Grove, CA: Brooks/Cole.

*Woody, R. H. (1998). Bartering for psychological services. *Professional Psychology: Research and Practice, 29*(2), 174–178.

Woody, R. H. (1999). Domestic violations of confidentiality. *Professional Psychology: Research and Practice, 30*(6), 607–610.

*Woody, R. H., & Woody, J. D. (2001). *Ethics in marriage and family therapy: Understanding the 2001 Ethics Code from the American Association for Marriage and Family Therapy.* Washington, DC: American Association for Marriage and Family Therapy.

Wrenn, C. G. (1962). The culturally encapsulated counselor. *Harvard Educational Review, 32*, 444–449.

Wrenn, C. G. (1985). Afterword: The culturally encapsulated counselor revisited. In P. Pedersen (Ed.), *Handbook of cross-cultural counseling and therapy* (pp. 323–329). Westport, CT: Greenwood Press.

Wright, J., Coley, S., & Corey, G. (1989, May). Challenges facing human services education today. *Journal of Counseling and Human Service Professions, 3*(2), 3–11.

Wubbolding, R. E. (1991). Professional issues: Consultation and ethics Part II. *Journal of Reality Therapy, 10*(2), 55–59.

Wubbolding, R. E. (1996). Working with suicidal clients. In B. Herlihy & G. Corey (Eds.), *ACA ethical standards casebook* (5th ed., pp. 267–274). Alexandria, VA: American Counseling Association.

Wyke v. Polk County School Board, 129 F. 3d 560 (11th Cir. 1997).

Wylie, M. S. (1995). Diagnosing for dollars? *The Family Therapy Networker, 19*(3), 22–69.

Yalom, I. (1995). *The theory and practice of group psychotherapy* (4th ed.). New York: Basic Books.

Yarhouse, M. A., & VanOrman, B. T. (1999). When psychologists work with religious clients: Applications of the general principles of ethical conduct. *Professional Psychology: Research and Practice, 30*(6), 557–562.

Young, M. E., & Long, L. (1998). *Counseling and therapy for couples.* Pacific Grove, CA: Brooks/Cole.

Younggren, J. N. (2000). Is managed care really just another, unethical Model T? *The Counseling Psychologist, 28*(2), 253–262.

Youngstrom, N. (1991a, July). Lesbians and gay men still find bias in therapy. *APA Monitor,* pp. 24–25.

Youngstrom, N. (1991b, July). Mandatory reporting deters sex treatment. *APA Monitor,* p. 35.

Zinnbauer, B. J., & Pargament, K. I. (2000). Working with the sacred: Four approaches to religious and spiritual issues in counseling. *Journal of Counseling and Development, 78*(2), 162–171.

Zur, O. (1999). The demonization of dual relationship: How prohibition on non-sexual dual relationships compromises effective therapy and keeps incompetent therapists in business. *Critical thinking about psychology series, monograph #2.* Oakland, CA: Independent Thinking Review.

Zur, O. (2000a). Going too far in the right direction: Reflections on the mythic ban of dual relationships. *The California Psychologist, 33*(4), 14–16.

Zur, O. (2000b). In celebration of dual relationships. *The Independent Practitioner, 20,* 97–100.

Name Index

Subject Index

TO THE OWNER OF THIS BOOK:

We hope that, as you read *Issues and Ethics in the Helping Professions,* 6th Edition, you found yourself challenged to clarify your positions on the issues we've raised. Only through your comments and the comments of others can we assess the impact of this book and improve it in the future.

School and address: ______________________________

Instructor's name: ______________________________

1. In what class did you use this book? ______________________________

2. What did you like *most* about this book? ______________________________

____

____

3. What did you like *least* about this book? ______________________________

____

____

4. How useful were the pre-chapter inventories and the other inventories within the chapters?

____

____

5. How useful were the cases and examples in helping you formulate and clarify your thoughts on the issues? ______________________________

____

6. Did you use *Ethics in Action* CD-ROM as a supplement to this book? If so, please write your comments. ______________________________

____

____

7. What topics do you think should be expanded or added to this book in future editions?

____

____

8. In the space below or in a separate letter, please write any other comments about the book you'd like to make. We welcome your suggestions! Thank you for taking the time to write to us.

Optional:

Your name: ____________________________ Date: ____________________________

May Brooks/Cole quote you, either in promotion for *Issues and Ethics in the Helping Professions,* Sixth Edition, or in future publishing ventures?

Yes: __________ No: _________

Sincerely,

Gerald Corey
Marianne Schneider Corey
Patrick Callanan

FOLD HERE

NO POSTAGE NECESSARY IF MAILED IN THE UNITED STATES

BUSINESS REPLY MAIL

FIRST CLASS PERMIT NO. 358 PACIFIC GROVE, CA

POSTAGE WILL BE PAID BY ADDRESSEE

ATT: *Corey/Corey/Callanan*

Brooks/Cole Publishing Company
511 Forest Lodge Road
Pacific Grove, California 93950-9968

FOLD HERE